Paying Out-of-Pocket for Drugs, Diagnostics and Medical Services

India Studies in Business and Economics

The Indian economy is considered to be one of the fastest growing economies of the world with India amongst the most important G-20 economies. Ever since the Indian economy made its presence felt on the global platform, the research community is now even more interested in studying and analyzing what India has to offer. This series aims to bring forth the latest studies and research about India from the areas of economics, business, and management science. The titles featured in this series will present rigorous empirical research, often accompanied by policy recommendations, evoke and evaluate various aspects of the economy and the business and management landscape in India, with a special focus on India's relationship with the world in terms of business and trade.

For further volumes:
http://www.springer.com/series/11234

Moneer Alam

Paying Out-of-Pocket for Drugs, Diagnostics and Medical Services

A Study of Households in Three Indian States

 Springer

Moneer Alam
Institute of Economic Growth
Delhi University
Delhi, India

ISBN 978-81-322-1280-5   ISBN 978-81-322-1281-2 (eBook)
DOI 10.1007/978-81-322-1281-2
Springer India Heidelberg New York Dordrecht London

Library of Congress Control Number: 2013940875

Printed on acid-free paper

Springer is part of Springer Science+Business Media (www.springer.com)

Affectionately dedicated to my wife,
Shahida Moneer

Acknowledgements

This study is the outcome of work conducted during 2008–2009 to examine the health-care expenses of low-income households in selected areas of UP, Rajasthan and Delhi. The study, financed by the SER Division of the Planning Commission Government of India, was designed particularly to investigate many significant health-related issues. These included the access to medical services for low-income people of the selected districts, how much they spend and to what effect, and the role of public sector health facilities in helping these highly vulnerable groups of population drawn from villages and smaller cities of the states concerned.

I am highly grateful to the Planning Commission officials of Govt. of India, in particular Dr. Syeda Hameed, member, Planning Commission (Health), for her keen interest and generous support. I am also very grateful to the Health Division of the Planning Commission, especially Mr. Ambrish Kumar, Adviser (Minority Division), for helping us all through, both academically and logistically. Mr. Kumar also took keen interest in developing the overall concerns of the study and shared with us many critical issues engaging the minds of planners and health mandarins of this apex body.

I am also grateful to my other professional friends, including Dr. A. B. Dey (Professor, Department of Medicine, All India Institute of Medical Sciences, New Delhi), Professor Nugroho Abikusno (WHO, SEARO, India), and my faculty colleagues at Institute of Economic Growth (IEG) for providing me with many useful inputs. M/S Fauzia Khan, a reputed data collection agency in New Delhi, provided excellent field support and arranged a team of well-trained investigators to visit the sample households in UP, Rajasthan and Delhi. I sincerely acknowledge their contributions to this study.

I also owe a debt of gratitude to my two colleagues, Mr. R. P. Tyagi and Mr. Anup Karan. Mr. Tyagi remained associated until the end of this study, helped to supervise field operations and worked on finalising the executive summary of the report. Though Mr. Anup Karan worked as a consultant to help in data analysis, his contribution was far more—he helped me write two critical chapters on catastrophic spending and on the share of drugs and medical services in households' out-of-pocket spending.

Back home, at the Institute of Economic Growth, my thanks are due to Professor Kanchan Chopra (Former Director, IEG) and Professor Manoj Panda (Director, IEG), for their unconditional support and encouragement. Members of the IEG staff, in particular those manning the finance, computer, library and project offices, were also extremely helpful and gave their best in making this study a success.

Special appreciation is extended to my project staff and younger colleagues, Mr. Sumit Gulati, Mr. S. Delka and Ms. Ayusmati Das, for their assistance in data management and analysis.

Finally, a big 'thank you' goes to my friend and manager of the editorial team at IEG, Mr. Surit Das, for all his excellent editorial support.

The entire Springer team, especially the Senior Editor Ms. Sagarika Ghosh and Senior Editorial Assistant Ms. Sahadi Sharma, has helped the book see the light of day. I owe a debt of gratitude to them.

The responsibility for any error or omissions, however, is mine and not of the individuals or institutions that have so generously supported us.

New Delhi, India   Moneer Alam

Contents

Abbreviations

APL	Above poverty line
ASHA	Accredited Social Health Activist
AYUSH	Ayurveda, Yoga and Naturopathy, Unani, Siddha and Homoeopathy
BoD	Burden of diseases
BE	Budget estimates
BPL	Below poverty line
CHC	Community health centre
CPI	Consumer price index
CSS	Circular systematic sampling
CV	Coefficient of variation
DALYs	Disability-adjusted loss of years
DPCO	Drug Price Control Order
HDI	Human Development Index
IMR	Infant mortality rate
IPL	Intellectual Property Law
MBP	Market-based pricing
MDGs	Millennium Development Goals
MMR	Maternal mortality rate
MoHFW	Ministry of Health and Family Welfare
MPO	Mean positive overshoot
NCMH	National Commission on Macroeconomics and Health
NFHS	National Family Health Survey
NHP	National Health Policy
NLEM	National List of Essential Medicines
NPPP	National Pharmaceutical Pricing Policy
NREGA	National Rural Employment Guarantee Act
NREGS	National Rural Employment Guarantee Scheme
NRHM	National Rural Health Mission
NSSO	National Sample Survey Organisation
OBC	Other backward caste
OOP	Out-of-pocket

ORS	Oral rehydration salt
PCMCE	Per capita monthly consumption expenditure
PG	Poverty gap
PHC	Primary health centre
PSU	Primary sampling unit
RBI	Reserve Bank of India
RE	Revised estimate
RKS	Rogi Kalyan Samiti
RSBY	Rashtriya Swasthya Bima Yojana
SC	Scheduled caste
ST	Scheduled tribe
SRS	Sample registration system
TRIPS	Trade-Related Aspects of Intellectual Property Rights
WPI	Wholesale Price Index
WHO	World Health Organization
WTO	World Trade Organization

List of Figures

List of Tables

List of Appendix Tables

About the Author

Moneer Alam has a Ph.D. in manpower planning and forecasting, is a professor of economics and the head of the Population Research Centre at the Institute of Economic Growth, Delhi. Professor Alam's research interests are the linkages between occupation and education, labour market issues, health financing and the economic and health issues of ageing in India and South Asia. He has published many books and a number of articles in peer-reviewed national and international journals. He consults with multilateral organisations (WHO, ILO, UNFPA) and serves on committees, boards and working groups (the Senior Citizens' Council, the Government of Delhi; the Committee on Social Security; the Committee on Health-Care Financing including Health Insurance; the Planning Commission; the Eleventh Five-Year Plan; and the Scientific Committee on Ageing in Developing Countries, IUSSP). He is a founder–member of the Asian Population Association and a life member of the Indian Econometric Society, the Indian Labour Economics Society and the Indian Association for the Study of Population.

Overview

Plagued by high morbidity and mortality, malnutrition, low standards of public health, short life expectancy and poor access to health-care services, the situation of an average person is dire. Despite a series of policy initiatives over the past decades and many attempts at various levels to build a healthy society on certain norms of equity and efficiency, health remains an issue of critical, increasing concern, with growing recognition that the country suffers because of an unacceptably high burden of diseases, premature deaths and public apathy. The Government of India constituted the National Commission on Macroeconomics and Health (NCMH) in March 2004; its report, made available in August 2005, highlighted this concern.[1]

---

[1] Addressing a joint parliamentary session on 4 June 2009, then President of India Pratibha Patil committed that the Ministry of Health, Government of India, will publish an Annual Report to the People on Health. So far, the Ministry has published two reports—one in September 2010 and the other in December 2011. These are two of the more recent attempts by the government to bring out the details of the health situation in the country. But neither report focuses largely on outcomes; instead, they underline various programmatic inputs and actions taken earlier by the government and presented details regarding (i) trends in health conditions of men, women and children; (ii) various health-care interventions by the government including National Rural Health Mission (NRHM); and (iii) a few of their achievements. The reports highlight improvements in several programmatic areas and health domains, including in key demographic parameters, and reduction in certain communicable and non-communicable diseases due to public intervention. The reports also detail the lack of various health-care infrastructure, especially the inadequacy of the financial resources provided to the health sector by governments and the shortage in medical and para-medical skills in the country. The discussion in this report on OOP health expenditure strongly backs our arguments, suggesting that drugs and medicines constitute the bulk of household expenditure on medical care. Similarly, a yearly Annual Health Survey (AHS) was also initiated since 2010–2011 on the recommendation of the National Commission on Population, Planning Commission and the Prime Minister Office to provide information on core vital and reproductive health indicators from nine demographically backward states including Uttarakhand, Rajasthan, Uttar Pradesh, Bihar, Assam, Jharkhand, Madhya Pradesh, Chhattisgarh and Orissa. The indicators covered in the survey are crude birth rate, crude death rate, infant mortality rate, neonatal mortality rate, under-five mortality rate, maternal mortality ratio, sex ratio at birth, sex ratio at 0–4 years and sex ratio at all ages.

The NCMH report drew upon inferences based on recent health surveys and is among the few public documents that agree that private out-of-pocket (OOP) health expenditure often pushes low-income households to face a catastrophe, forces many of them below the poverty line and often blocks intergenerational (young to old) flows, severely affecting family members including the co-residing old, especially women.

Health Situation

As poverty is still persistent in most rural areas and urban slums, reliance on private health providers is fraught with serious economic consequences, especially for low-income households engaged in the informal economy. There is now a realisation that the health situation in India is entrenched in widespread poverty, malnutrition and enormous disparities in almost every sphere of human life, particularly in rural areas where the per capita monthly consumption expenditure (PCMCE) is alarmingly low. Disease prevalence is in many cases large among low-income rural and urban households. The market plays an increasing role in delivering health and diagnostic services; consequently, health-care seekers incur very high OOP expenditure. Health services provided by the central, state and local governments face infrastructural bottlenecks that extend beyond physical or financial resources to cover all aspects of hospital administration, including large-scale deployment of doctors to non-clinical services, which forces public service users to avail private medical services and incur OOP expenses. All these issues are in direct contradiction of the tenets of the two most significant national policy documents—the National Population Policy (2000) and the National Health Policy (2002).

While recent studies have highlighted many physical, financial and manpower-related anomalies in Indian public health facilities, they have almost entirely neglected the effect on low-income households, particularly in backward districts of poor states, and the nature of households and the income level of those trapped in poverty or those who experience catastrophe as a result of losses suffered due to expenditure on various health-care services and components—especially drugs and medicines—in poverty-ridden rural and urban areas and sprawling slums.

The study that forms the basis of this book was conducted during March 2008 to June 2009 and used data from a uniformly designed household survey in selected districts of Uttar Pradesh (UP), Rajasthan and Delhi to highlight some of these neglected issues, and focuses largely on private expenditure on purchase of drugs and medicines for treatment of ailments both with and without hospitalisation.

In addition to very high coverage of sample units (census enumeration blocks in urban areas and villages in rural areas), another important feature of the survey is that it provides over time changes in core vital and reproductive health indicators.

None of these reports are however relevant for the analysis presented in this study.

Objectives

The study examined private household OOP expenditure after decomposition by various components of medical services, including drugs, diagnostics, consultations and other miscellaneous expenses. Attempts have also been made to assess the extent of household borrowings to finance medical expenditure and the effect on the basic food and nonfood requirements of their young and old.

The study focused on the following specific issues:

1. An analysis of the patterns of treatment of short (past 30 days) and long (past 365 days) duration morbidity under different socio-economic and ethnic settings. A part of the analysis was of the role of health expenditure in pushing households below the poverty line to face catastrophe—amounting to a significant decline in overall welfare of households and their nonfood consumption expenditure. There was also a concern with regard to the prevalence, intensity and causal risk factors associated with catastrophic health spending of households.
2. An assessment of the total and disaggregated expenditure incurred in the treatment of short- and long-duration ailments and the sources used to generate the requisite finances, including savings, asset liquidation, borrowing from money-lenders and assistance drawn from informal support networks.
3. A review of expenditure on the purchase of medical drugs (including life-saving drugs and general medicines) as a proportion of the total health budget for the treatment of short-duration ailments (without hospitalisation) and long-duration ailments (with hospitalisation). This analysis was conducted to derive a host of policy options required to reduce OOP health spending by households and its size. If drug expenses constitute the bulk of private (and often catastrophic) health spending, the government has to become more vigilant in terms of its drug pricing policy and TRIPS negotiations (including TRIPS Plus) by taking peoples' concern and implications of out-of-pocket expenditure on drugs into consideration. Overprescription of medicines and other malpractices may also need attention through advocacy or enforcement of law with tools necessary to eliminate such practices.
4. Resources mobilised by households to meet medical expenses, especially those on drugs, medicines and other services.
5. The contribution of the National Rural Health Mission 2005 (NRHM) in protecting poor households in rural areas from the adverse economic consequences of illness.

Study Area and Sample Design

This study was conducted in UP and Rajasthan, chosen because of their poverty and relatively weak demographic status. The capital city of Delhi was included to complete the regional configuration and examine the issues faced especially by slum households and due to its wider representation of population from different parts of the country. The districts were chosen on the basis of poverty measurements derived by the Ministry of Rural Development through its 2002 survey to identify below-poverty-line (BPL) households. The circular systematic sampling procedure was adopted.

A multistage sampling procedure was adopted to collect field data from a predetermined sample size of 2,010 households—1,250 rural and 400 urban households in UP and Rajasthan. In addition, a total of 360 households were surveyed in Delhi—102 from slums and the remaining 258 from non-slums. The households were the primary sampling unit (PSU) in the study.

Survey Questionnaire

A comprehensive, structured and multipart questionnaire was used. From beginning to end, the entire protocol was divided into 14 different parts and 5 major groups of information. These include:

- Socio-economic details of the households and their members, including their three broad social categorisations (scheduled caste (SC), scheduled tribe (ST) and upper castes), age–sex profiles, relationship with the head of the household (usually the basic point of consultation), educational attainment, work status, residential characteristics (rural–urban), housing conditions, access to public health facilities, road links with the primary health centres, possession of consumer durables and landholdings for agricultural purposes (both arable and fallow).
- Households' access to selected government-run health and non-health facilities. Some questions included in this part of the questionnaire explore households' experience of any improvement in service delivery since the inception of the NRHM.
- Household food and nonfood consumption expenditure was collected on the basis of dual reference periods—past 30 days and past 1 year—as is usually followed by the National Sample Survey Organisation (NSSO). Attempts have also been made to examine the debt incidence among sample households, type of moneylenders they borrowed from and the purpose of borrowing differentiated by events such as health, education, investment and major consumption requirements including marriage. All this information was used to examine the poverty status of households and the prevalence of health catastrophe suffered.
- Disease episodes, both with and without hospitalisation, utilisation of public/private health facilities, choice of health providers and other related details including itemised health-care expenditure and share of money spent on medicines and diagnostics.
- Last few sections of the survey protocol were devoted to understand the views of households on measures required to improve the delivery of health-care services in the country by public bodies. These households were also asked for their views on the introduction of a universal and low-premium health insurance system and their participation in such a scheme.

Socio-economic and Demographic Profile of Households

There are more men than women in many sample households in all four districts in UP and Rajasthan. The slum households of Delhi are the only exception—women constitute over 52 % of the sample. These results might seem somewhat arbitrary in a situation of growing male migration. Hindus dominate the overall distribution of the sample population, followed by Muslims; Sikhs are visible only in Delhi.

In terms of social groups, the sample represents the low and backward castes (SC and OBC) fairly well; the former is over a fifth (22.6 %) of the total sample, while the latter is nearly double that (38.7 %). Higher-caste representation is relatively small. As a whole, the higher castes constitute around a fourth of the total sample.

Often considered highly traditional, UP and Rajasthan are becoming dominantly nuclear; families comprise parents and dependent children. UP appears more nuclear than Rajasthan; the average size of sample households is between five and six, with the lowest relating to the non-slum urban households in Delhi. The share of female-headed households is also relatively higher in Delhi, though a large majority of them come from loner (one-person) households.

Socio-economic Characteristics of Sample Population

The age distribution of the sample population in all the districts reinforces the pattern observed in most of the country where a very high share of population is in the 15–59 years age group. This implies a growing pressure of jobseekers in coming years on the labour market and its clearance mechanism. The higher proportion of this age group in the population in all the four urban locations also indicates a considerable degree of migration of working age rural people to cities with a baggage of their past and may act to cause growing demand for health-care services in coming years.

The educational distribution of the sample population in all the four districts of UP and Rajasthan turns out to be poor. The same is true for the slum households in Delhi. It underscores the general perception that a large percentage of people in smaller towns and low-income residential areas of places like Delhi are still illiterate or semi-literate; their educational attainments are inadequate to prevent poor health and poverty. Around a third of the total sample population (30–36 %) in most of these places was illiterate; illiteracy was highest among slum residents in Delhi. Another 50 % of them had not studied until Class 10; a large fraction had studied up to the primary level or even less. Only about 5 % of the total respondents held a degree from higher educational institutions. A very small fraction of respondents had a professional degree or diploma. The gender gap in education is considerably high. The usual rural–urban divide in educational status is clearly visible in our sample.

A little less than a third of the sample population is economically active; the gender differential is considerable. The share of working women is under 13 % of their total reported population except in Dungarpur, Rajasthan, where almost a quarter of the women engage in some economic activity. Unlike gender, the place of residence does not apparently play a significant role in economic engagement. There are not many major differences in the activity status of rural and urban households from different districts/tehsils. Barring Dungarpur, where differentials in activity status between rural and urban areas are considerably large, there is no similar example in any other place covered in the study. In all other cases, the observed differentials remain marginal. This is true for the slums and non-slums in Delhi as well; the highest fraction of 'working' people belonged to the ST category over 35 % reported being economically active. The remaining three (in particular SC and OBC) were considerably behind, and the size of their working males and females was near 30–31 % of their respective populations.

About three-quarters (74.2 %) of working males have reported themselves as the main workers—implying they had paid employment for about 186 days or more during most of the preceding 12 months. The rest 25.8 % have however failed to meet this criterion and remained unemployed for a greater part of the year. They were, therefore, considered as marginal workers. Women, as usual, suffered from double jeopardy—only a fewer of them were economically active, and those active were largely in low-quality unskilled employment. A considerably large fraction of the unskilled employment created under the National Rural Employment Guarantee Act (NREGA, September 2005) to improve livelihood conditions of rural households has seemingly gone to women, especially in both the districts of Rajasthan—Dungarpur and Dausa. In addition to women, many of those engaged in lower-category employment invariably comprise persons from the lower echelons of the caste hierarchy including the scheduled caste (SC), scheduled tribe (ST) and other backward castes (OBC).

One of the most significant factors responsible for keeping a big majority of the younger population out of the workforce is their participation in educational activities. It turns out to be the case in all the districts including slums and non-slums. Also, this gap exists irrespective of the places under study and includes even households from the non-slum areas of Delhi. Another dominant reason for not being able to work is unemployment, especially among the people of Unnao in UP and the slums of Delhi. A significant proportion of people at both the places do not work for lack of employment. A more disturbing factor is the noticeable share of non-school-going children in almost every district and slum. While a large majority of those children (i.e. over three-quarters) were too young and under 4 years of age, almost a fifth of them were grown up and in higher ages as well. Those adding to the size of nonworking household population also include a fraction of persons comprising the mentally or physically challenged. A small number of persons have also reported to withdraw from active workforce because of post-sickness frailty or senescence. Males in most of these cases outnumber females, perhaps partly on account of reporting biases. Dausa in Rajasthan reports more such cases than UP or Delhi.

Quality of Life

The analysis brings out very clearly the poor economic background of most house-holds in the sample. It indicates that a large majority of the respondents lived in poor environment, most of them residing in non-bricked (*kutcha*) dwellings without access to many of the basic amenities like better (smoke-free) cooking fuels, drainage system, toilet facilities and scavenging. The situation is far worse among the rural residents where almost nine out of ten houses are non-bricked and their resi-dents survive without an in-house toilet or scavenging facility. These and most other facts clearly raise many big questions about the health prospects of rural people who are apparently torn between two basic issues—one being a more or less complete lack of preventive mechanism like drainage, regular scavenging, pit/flush toilets and smoke-free cooking fuels and the other arises from a lack of concern among health officials about the need for nonreproductive health-care services, leaving a big fraction of rural households in the clutches of private health-care providers. The former, i.e. lack of preventive mechanism, is also an issue that needs to be examined by keeping in mind the financial status of urban and rural bodies that are largely responsible for disease prevention services such as scavenging, waste disposal and creation of an all-weather drainage system. As most of the local governments/bodies are generally constrained because of poor governance and suffer from inadequate finances (partly because of their inelastic tax revenues), they usually remain non-functional in terms of services required to prevent many non-lifestyle-related diseases.

Urban areas, as expected, remain considerably better and are able to offer many of the basic facilities to a much bigger fraction of the sample population. And yet many respondents reported poor housing conditions and lack of civic services like chocked drainage and infrequent scavenging. There are inequalities in access to many of these facilities across socioreligious groups as well.

Barring to some extent in Delhi, house ownership in most places is either through inheritance or built and owned by the household head. Both the patterns jointly account for more than three-quarters of house ownerships in the sample. Inherited houses are found to be highest in UP (67.5 %), followed by Rajasthan (57.2 %). Delhi, in contrast, stands lowest on this criterion (merely 25.8 %). However, the percentage of houses owned by the family head is considerably large in Delhi. This is particularly true for slum dwellers (73.5 %). An inference that emerges—house ownership is decisive in holding the family reins—holds true for different social groups as well.

Distribution of sample households by size of landholding presents a worrisome picture. Even if we ignore Delhi, for obvious reasons, in the remaining two states that depend considerably on agriculture, almost half the rural households in both the states either are landless or own less than an acre of land. The fraction of households with a landholding size of over five acres is amazingly low in both the states—a little over 10 % in UP and over 4 % in Rajasthan.

While the slant in favour of relatively poor districts and households in our sample may have pulled some of our results down, these results may cause the concerned departments some alarm and perhaps generate greater realisation about the health risks of people in these districts and their necessary health delivery infrastructure. Simply, a programme with much of its focus remaining directed to reproductive and (certain domains of) child health may not suffice. The situation does not improve if we look at the land ownership status of the upper-caste households in the sample—about two-thirds are landless, which is even worse than the other lower-caste categories. They are nevertheless slightly better when it comes to bigger landholdings; a little over 5 % of the total upper-caste households owned more than 10 acres of land. Conforming to the general perception, Muslims are found way behind the Hindus—more of them are landless and their landholdings are also relatively smaller.

Fewer of the population own a telephone connection than a bank account—the two quality-of-life services. Considering the growing penetration of mobile phone services in most of the country, including UP and Rajasthan, our results may not be accepted at their face value. A possible explanation of this underestimation may be found in certain confusion among survey teams between landline and mobile telephone connections. Disregarding this, the bank account data seems interesting, as it indicates that a good number of people in most areas, particularly in Delhi and Rajasthan, own a bank account. Muslims and rural UP and ST households are exceptions. Non-slum Delhi, where 86 % of the total respondents own a bank account, is far ahead of many other areas.

Consumption Level, Poverty and Inequalities Among Sample Households

The analysis reveals a large-scale poverty situation in the two districts of UP (Unnao and Jhansi) with 50 % of their sample households reporting a total of Rs. 500 or less as their total PCMCE including food, nonfood and health care. Even allowing for some margin of error in data, the fact that a large number of people in the state survive at Rs. 17 a day or less is scary. Rajasthan (Dausa and Dungarpur), though in a slightly better situation with a lesser fraction of people at Rs. 500 (or Rs. 17 a day) consumption band, also suffers from an equally alarming poverty situation. Another interesting point to notice in both of these states is the fact that almost 90 % of their households belong to the first two PCMCE categories. Delhi turns out to be considerably better than both of them. The rest of the estimates are mostly along expected lines, with the share of households in the lowest per capita consumption category being highest both in slums and in rural areas. This is true for tribal and low-caste households as well, and Muslims trail behind Hindus, as expected.

Besides low PCMCE, many households also suffer from serious inequality issues. There are considerable disparities between the minimum and the maximum consumption levels of households or their mean consumption levels in all the three states under reference. The max–min differences are found highest in Delhi.

Analysis suggests UP and its two districts (Unnao and Jhansi) are in a more distressing situation, with larger shares of households falling below the poverty threshold level. This pattern is, however, true for rural UP alone. Urban UP and its districts have performed relatively better. They also perform better than Delhi slums. An interesting observation relates to a significant increase in the fraction of below-poverty households after netting out the health expenses. This is very clearly visible by comparing the two head count poverty levels—with and without expenses on medical care. The most visible effect of private spending on health may be found in rural and slum areas, where health services are scantier. While a certain marginal increase may be noticed in the fraction of poor after health-care expenses are deducted from the total PCMCE in most urban places, their magnitude is far less than those in villages and low-income slum areas. Even after so many years of NRHM, which had 7 years of life since its inception in 2005, rural health care is seen to hold a much significant place in cross movement of a big proportion of rural people from poverty to non-poverty and vice versa.

The measurements of poverty gap (PG) clearly reveal the negative impact of health spending on consumption standards of individuals and households. It also acts to drive low-income people deeper into poverty and may cause an added financial burden in lifting them above poverty level. Conforming to some of our earlier results, we observe rural parts of UP at a more disadvantageous position, though urban Rajasthan is no less problematic. Similarly, the tribal households are also in a difficult situation and health spending makes them suffer with greater PGs.

Health spending, which appears to constitute in many cases a much larger share of nonfood consumption expenditure, makes the situation worse. After dropping health spending from the consumption basket, a big fraction of households are left with deeper PGs. The situation compounds when the results are restricted to the poor households alone. Also, unlike the general perception, a slight modification in definition and composition of the consumption basket makes urban population—in particular its poor and tribal segments—look highly vulnerable. As a whole, two broad observations follow from most of the results. One, out-of-pocket (OOP) health spending remains a serious issue for a large number of people in both the states and also for the slum households in Delhi. Second, the poor remain highly vulnerable after they pay for their accessed health-care services themselves. What component (or components) of health spending brings greater vulnerability to the people is indeed a significant question.

A clear message emanating from the Lorenz curves and a series of Gini coefficients computed with or without OOP spending on health is that the consumption and health inequalities are severe at most places under study. All the Lorenz curves show steep gaps between the diagonal line of 45° and the area under the curve. At worst are the health inequalities, implying a group of households without any health-care expenditure. But there is perhaps nothing very surprising in these results. Based on the consumption expenditure survey for 2004–2005, almost a similar trend and loss of well-being was reported by the NSSO in its Report Number 508 (December 2006). If some of our results are a little different from that of the NSSO (2006), it may be largely because of certain minor technical differences or lack of conformity between the two samples.

Our results suggest fewer disparities in per capita consumption of nonfood items. However, there are disparities in mean expenditure on health care. Barring to a certain extent in Delhi, health inequalities are strikingly higher in most places, particularly in areas of UP. These results show that health care is accessed quite unevenly in most places, with almost no or negligible spending on health care by a group of people in both the states and slum dwellers of Delhi. It also works to generate a significant amount of inequalities in the total PCMCE.

Borrowings for Health Reasons: Prevalence and Sources

The analysis of data on the share of indebted households in our sample indicates that most rural households (52.4 %) are under cash debt in the villages of UP and Rajasthan. Urban households with cash debt obligations are, however, much lower in size, little over a quarter (26.7 %) of the total sample. Jhansi in UP and Dausa in Rajasthan in our sample are the most indebted areas—the latter shows the highest incidence of borrowings among the urban households, and the former counts highest in terms of rural indebtedness. Tribal households are the least indebted among the four social groups in rural areas for whatever reason. Of the remaining three, more than 50 % of each group has reported to be under debt at the time of the survey. Even the upper castes are no exception. Hindus and Muslims do conform closely to each other at least on this count.

Two broad reasons have been offered by the responding households to secure loans—medical and non-medical; the latter combines all categories of loans, including for consumption and for financing productive needs. With the exception of urban Dungarpur (Rajasthan), medical loans are quite prevalent in most areas under study. More than a quarter of indebted households in urban areas—and a little over 19 % in rural areas—have reportedly been driven to debt because of medical exigencies. Does it mean that public health-care facilities in urban areas are insufficient or that urban households can access loans more easily? While a categorical answer may not be possible based on the data available to us, these are indeed significant issues and need to be examined separately in all requisite detail.

Tribal and Muslim households are also ahead in loan borrowing in their respective categories. The role of private money lending appears to be especially large in rural areas where informal family sources appear to work less effectively, perhaps due to widespread poverty and cash flow constraints. A big majority of rural households had borrowed from private moneylenders. Interestingly, almost 52 % of urban households had to borrow from local moneylenders despite a growing emphasis in public pronouncements to improve medical care through involvement of remodelled watchdogs like Rogi Kalyan Samitis (RKSs).

The role of private moneylenders in medical borrowing is considerably high in most areas and population groups in question and indicates a very urgent need for an institutional mechanism to finance the health-care needs of low-income households. Apparently, antipoverty measures may not work to their real potential unless health services are scaled up to a considerable extent in every domain, disease occurrence is minimised, and the health-care system is brought to bear the needs of persons forced to borrow from private moneylenders.

The analysis of data about loan repayment status of households, under both medical and non-medical debt, indicates that the number of households deficient in capabilities to initiate loan repayment process is disturbingly large across all the categories of responding households. This has been particularly true for most rural households in both the districts of UP and among the slum dwellers in Delhi. Muslims and most social groups including upper-caste categories also fall in this category. Rural–urban differentials in loan repayment reveal that many among rural households and most other economically backward households may not be able to initiate the loan repayment process immediately—a moratorium may be required, which may not be possible. How far micro-credit institutions could lend support under these circumstances has to be considered. In addition, whether the micro-credit institutions can lend small amounts to meet medical contingencies also needs detailed examination.

Differentials in Health-Care Utilisation

There is a significantly large share of women utilising hospitalised treatment. It is true for nonhospitalised care as well. The reasons for an excess of health-care access by women over men in this analysis are however not very difficult to identify. Our sample is inclusive of women in child-bearing ages as well, and the overall hospitalisation cases are based on all forms of ailments including pre- or postnatal care, delivery and gynaecological–obstetric problems with most other normal health-related issues and injuries. The same explanation holds for nonhospitalised cases as well. This point is reiterated further by a perusal of the distribution of women accessing health care (both hospitalised and nonhospitalised) across five broad age categories: 0–4, 5–14, 15–39, 40–49 and 60 or above. We notice from this distribution that the share of women in the 15–39 age group—normally considered as prime years in the reproductive life span of women—is highest, followed by those in the 5–14 and 40–59 age groups.

The survey results reveal that the utilisation of health-care services by below-poverty-line (BPL) households—with or without hospitalisation—is considerably less than the above-poverty-line (APL) or nonpoor households. However, the correctness of these findings may be compromised because of limitation in self-reported morbidity by poor, illiterate and less informed households. It simply underscores the general observation of positive links between economic status and a better sense of suffering or ill health, leading to a better reporting of ailments and utilisation of in- or outpatient health-care services.

Gender-wise differences in hospitalisation are considerably large in both the districts of Rajasthan. The highest rate of women's hospitalisation may, however, be noticed in Delhi slums. The non-slum women too are in good numbers though they lagged behind their slum counterparts to a good extent. A possible inference may, therefore, be made that women at most of the places have begun to use institutional services for different reasons and their numbers may grow further with time, though such evidence is relatively weak in both the places of UP. Muslims and tribal women are also somewhat lagging.

A men–women comparison of health-care utilisation across comparable age brackets reconfirms the male bias, at least in early ages. The situation turns in favour of women in the 15–39 ages with higher child-bearing potential. Women in the 60+ age group are also prone to more hospitalisation than men. However, a generalisation of these results may need further evidence based on larger sample size from most other states of the country. Unfortunately, a study of this magnitude is apparently nonexistent.

The nonpoor utilise hospital care in greater proportions than the poor. But this is not decisively so in outpatient care; the poor outnumber the nonpoor in accessing physicians' care in certain areas. This may particularly be noticed in Rajasthan. In UP, however, the nonpoor appear to have greater access to nonhospitalised care as well and contribute to the general thinking that medical care and economic status go side by side.

As a whole, our results confirm the existing notion of gender bias in health-care utilisation, with females, in general, at a disadvantage. However, if disaggregated over different age spans, our results indicate that younger women in their prime child-bearing ages have accessed health care in higher percentages than their male counterparts. This is indeed interesting and needs to be re-examined with a bigger sample size and more focused survey instruments probing causes of health-care utilisation.

The issues relating to the access of health care by the poor and the nonpoor turned out to be more straightforward and on expected lines. It may be noticed from our results that the poor lag considerably behind the nonpoor in reported utilisation of health services—both in- and outpatient care. Similar results have been obtained in most of the literature on rich–poor differentials in consumption of health services, particularly in India and its neighbouring South Asian countries where public delivery of health care is both inadequate and inefficient.

Health-Care Utilisation and Disease Prevalence

Gender-wise differentials indicate a significantly large share of women in utilisation of hospitalised treatment. It happens almost across the board and is true, more or less, for nonhospitalised care as well. The reason for an excess of health care accessed by women is the fact that more women in child-bearing ages utilise health-care facilities for pre- or postnatal care, delivery and gynaecological/obstetric problems along with most other normal health-related issues and injuries. The same explanation holds for the nonhospitalised cases as well.

This point was further reiterated by a study of age distribution of women accessing health care (both hospitalised and nonhospitalised). We notice that the share of women in the 15–39 age group—normally considered prime years in the reproductive life span of women—is highest, followed by those in the 5–14 and 40–59 age groups. Gender-wise differences in hospitalisation are considerably large in both the districts of Rajasthan (2.8 for men and 3.2 for women in Dausa and 2.6 for men and 4.9 for women in Dungarpur). The highest rate of women hospitalisation may however be noticed in Delhi slums where it turns out to be 5.7 %. The non-slum women too are in good numbers, though they lag behind their slum counterparts. An inference is that women at most of the places have begun to use institutional services for different reasons and their number may grow further with time, though such an evidence is relatively weak in both the districts of UP.

Muslims and tribal women also somewhat lag behind. Health-care utilisation among males is comparatively higher in early ages. The situation turns in favour of women in the 15–39 age groups, who are of child-bearing age. Women in the 60+ age group are also prone to more hospitalisation than men. However, a generalisation of these results may need further evidence based on larger sample size. It may be noticed from the results that the fraction of BPL households reporting utilisation of health-care services—with or without hospitalisation—is considerably less than the nonpoor (APL).

Spending on Health Care

Examining the size of health-care expenditure by households in relation to their (i) total consumption budget comprising market goods and services and (ii) nonfood consumption expenditure, our results fail to compare with a few of the earlier studies suggesting an average of about 5 % of the total consumption budget (and 10 % of the nonfood consumption budget) on OOP health care in India. Our data indicate considerably higher OOP expenditure on medical bills in all the three states and their selected villages or towns. Also, this lack of comparison continues in relation to both the total and nonfood consumption budgets. This may partly be due to low-economic conditions of a large number of our sample households.

The mean OOP share of rural households is considerably large. Further, it exceeds the urban share as well. The mean OOP expenditure is, for example, 14–15 % of the total budget among rural households and 10.5–11 % in urban areas. People from slums have on average spent a much larger share of their consumption budget than those from the non-slums (14 % by the slum residents compared to only 9 % by those from non-slums). It strongly suggests a regressive nature of spending if we could assume that all the non-slum households are essentially more affluent. This also reflects a significant departure from the existing body of evidence that suggests that the poor pay less than the nonpoor.

We are nevertheless closer to the existing literature if we compare the mean OOP spending of households by consumption quintiles. While the magnitude of spending remains large, the OOP shares of the rich and the poor differ significantly with the highest quintile (or top 20 % of households according to their PCMCE) spending almost a quarter of their total consumption budget on health. In contrast, the same for the bottom 20 % is about 10–12 % in rural and urban areas. The progressivism, as argued in the literature, is therefore maintained.

OOP differentials among four social (SC, ST, OBC and upper castes) and two religious groups—Hindus and Muslims—reveal that lower-caste communities incur a much higher OOP payment than their upper-caste counterparts. In terms of religion, the differentials are marginal, i.e. less than a percentage point (i.e. 13.5 % of the total consumption expenditure by the Hindus, while 12.3 % for Muslims). The progressivism among five consumption quintiles has also been maintained.

A very high variation around the mean OOP has been observed. At almost every quintile level or socioreligious grouping, the coefficient of variation is more than 100 %, which tends to indicate extreme values at almost every level, quintile or social group. It also suggests that there are households in each category with negligible spending on health services—inpatient or ambulatory.

The differences between the two sets of results—our own and those in the literature cited above—raise an interesting question: Do studies based on macro-data, often regarded as more policy friendly, really provide the realities faced by impoverished households from poor districts or geographical locations? In all fairness, perhaps both have their own merits and ought to be supplemented by each other.

With the mean of OOP expenditure being very high in relation to the total consumption expenditure, the same relation can easily be guessed for nonfood consumption expenditure. It touches around 30 % of the total in rural areas and 20 % in urban areas. In other words, the mean of OOP in relation to nonfood expenditure is likely to be double the total consumption expenditure. The rest of the results follow exactly the pattern exhibited above and, therefore, bear a similar explanation.

Catastrophic Health Expenditure by Households

Using multiple threshold levels for both the catastrophes—the total consumption budget (catastrophe 1) and nonfood consumption budget (catastrophe 2)—the results clearly indicate that an overwhelming share of sample households have been facing a serious catastrophic situation because of high OOP expenses on health. At the lowest threshold level (i.e. health budget is over 5 % of the total consumption expenditure), over 67 % of rural households and 51 % of urban households exceed this limit. The same at the 10 % threshold level, which is generally considered catastrophic health spending by most analysts, turns out to be 49.5 % in rural areas and 32 % in urban areas. Furthermore, our results indicate that almost a fifth (18.5 %) of the rural households and over a tenth (11.6 %) of urban households spend more than a quarter of their total consumption budget on health care. It reflects the inadequacy of health-care services provided by the government in rural areas. Lower-caste people, particularly the SC communities, are also in a quandary for the same reason. Curiously, the share of Muslim households incurring catastrophic spending on health is marginally lower than the Hindus. How far does this happen? Is it because of their insensitivity towards poor health or because they lack access to health care? It could not, however, be judged on the basis of these results. Delhi slum residents are insulated to some extent because of better health-care infrastructure in and around the capital city, and, as a result, a lower fraction of them are found incurring catastrophic payments. Deviations around the mean are relatively smaller at the higher threshold levels and vice versa.

Catastrophe head count 2, computed on the basis of non-sustenance (nonfood) budgets of sample households, repeats the same grim reality and further reiterates that the rural households are worst affected due to inadequate government health-care infrastructure. The lower-caste SC households are at their worst. Very big percentages are shown to be incurring catastrophic payments, causing them to suffer from serious and highly disproportionate loss of well-being. Interestingly, the study areas chosen from both the major states (UP and Rajasthan) are mutually close to each other in terms of their population shares facing consumption catastrophe due to private health payments.

One of the more alarming observations stemming from the preceding results is that a considerably large fraction of households spend over 60 % of their nonfood budget on medical care. Can these households come out of this morass created by their OOP payments? It is indeed a serious issue and warrants contemplating immediate remedial action by policy institutions like the Planning Commission. It also requires enhancing existing health-care infrastructure, particularly in villages and low-income areas of UP and Rajasthan. Our results also indicate very high variation around the mean values.

Intensity of Catastrophic Payments: MPOs

Defined as the amount of excess payments (or overshoot) by which households exceed catastrophic threshold, the analysis suggests that those paying over 5 % of the total consumption expenditure on health care spent 20.6 % on an average (i.e. 5 % threshold level + 15.6 % overshoot). Similarly, those at threshold level of 15 % of nonfood budget actually spent 43 % (15 % + 28 %), which is indeed appalling. Interestingly, the mean overshoots turn out to be considerably large in most of the cases, irrespective of their residential pattern. This is true for households in non-slum areas of Delhi as well. While there are indications that the rural and slum households are exceeding their threshold limits considerably at a few specific values (e.g. at 15 and 25 % of nonfood budget shares and 25 % at the level of the total consumption expenditure), there is however no specific pattern to suggest a clear differential across households drawn from various states and socioreligious categories. Coefficients of variation indicate large intra-household variations. It also indicates a good number of households with no or a negligible amount of spending on health.

Drugs and Medical Services in OOP Health Spending: A Decomposition of Households' Medical Budget

The distribution of OOP spending on drugs and other health-care components shows the primacy of drugs in overall health-care budgets. This has been noticed across all the sample households—rural, urban, slum or non-slum—and irrespective of the districts or states they were located in. Our results confirm largely the earlier findings on the subject (Sakthivel 2005) suggesting that more than three-fourths of the money spent on health is invariably going to the allopathic drugs and medicines.

Almost a similar distribution pattern of health budgets is observed across all the study areas with around four-fifths of the total OOP expenditure going to drugs followed by another 5–10 % (depending upon rural–urban and in- or outpatient treatment) of the total expenses going to medical practitioners as their consultation fee. Expenditure on diagnostics remains in most cases between 5 and 7 % of the total budget, and almost an equal amount is devoted to meet other miscellaneous expenses including transportation.

Between the groups of households drawn from UP and Rajasthan, the share of money spent on consultation fee is much higher in the former, particularly in episodes requiring hospitalisation. Relatively, however, their expenses on drugs were much less. Both, however, followed almost a similar expenditure pattern in cases where hospitalisation was not required.

Moving to the OOP distribution for slum and non-slum households in Delhi, the former are almost at a competing edge with the latter in terms of their percentage expenditure on drugs and two major medical services, namely, consultation and diagnostics. Rather, their share of expenditure on consultation fee is relatively higher—2.7 % as against 0.5 % for the non-slum households. Also, they have shown to incur a larger share of expenditure on transportation than the non-slum households.

The results tend to portray certain degrees of equity between the slum and non-slum households in distribution of their health budgets. Two significant questions emerge from these results: (i) Does this equity represent certain peculiarities of Delhi alone or is it a wider phenomenon, and the poor in general encounter similar situation in other places as well, and (ii) is there a safeguard?

While a study comparing out-of-pocket expenditure on health by slum and non-slum populations is not available, a safeguard perhaps lies in pooling the risk and offering a certain form of health insurance mechanism—at least to the poor, if not to all. Another important safeguard derives from lowering inflation in the drug sector, raising the number of essential medicines and pro-poor negotiations in the World Trade Organization (WTO). Particularly, most generic medicines and formulations need protection from strict patenting and royalty laws. This is particularly essential because of a very large share of medicines in overall household health budgets.

Share of Drugs and Non-drugs in Health Expenditure: A Distribution by Consumption Quintiles

Analysis of data reveals that the poorest 20 % seeking outpatient treatment have spent a greater share of their health budget on medicines than any other quintile group. Further, it remains true for all the places covered in the study. The drug share of these households is 80–90 % of the total and remains particularly higher among slum and rural households. All other quintile groups spent a lesser share, although their differences in many cases remained marginal. The poorest groups in certain areas (slums and towns in UP and Rajasthan) spent a larger share of their health budget on medical consultation. The situation is however slightly reversed when it comes to hospitalised treatment. Nevertheless, the differentials are invariably small, and the richest appear to have drawn certain advantages over the lower-quintile groups.

A significant observation is that the poorer quintiles (poorest, next 20 % and middle) are not only spending heavily on drugs and medicines; they also spend a considerable part of their budget on consultation and diagnostics. It may be noticed even in cases of hospitalisation. A possible explanation may be that (i) people do not necessarily rely on public hospitals even if they require hospitalisation and (ii) many diagnostic services in public facilities are on payment basis. Also, doctors in public hospitals moonlight, especially in UP and Rajasthan.

Share of Drugs and Non-drugs in OOP Budget: Catastrophic Households

The results highlight drugs as the single expenditure item with the highest budget share (almost 80 % of the total and even more) followed by diagnostics and medical consultation. It is also interesting to note that in a few cases, the share of expenditure incurred by rural households on transportation is relatively higher than the shares on medical services. In other words, it is an indication of poor access to medical facilities closer to some villages.

Another interesting observation is that the poor and slum dwellers spend in many cases a much larger share of expenditure on drugs and other medical items than the nonpoor. And yet in no way do these results imply that the nonpoor do not spend on health. They largely follow a similar pattern with a maximum of their health budget going to drugs and diagnostics. How far they suffer in terms of their welfare losses due to these payments or to what extent their welfare losses differ with similar losses suffered by the poor may not be conjectured with the help of the data of the present study.

With all the differentials observed across households, a point of major policy concern that emerges from the underlying discussion is: How can the OOP health-care budget be reduced and poor households shielded from high costs of drugs and medical services? Besides risk pooling and universal health insurance coverage, two other solutions may follow. First is a strict drug control policy coupled with a judicious demand–supply management of pharmacy products and second, an improved health-care delivery mechanism in public hospitals and facilities. A well-designed strategy is required to deploy medical personnel at different medical units, places, hospitals and dispensaries. Currently, physicians and medical personnel are deployed for several non-clinical activities as well. They are in many cases governed by the district administration and pushed regularly to serve politicians or day-to-day political events. All this makes their availability to essential clinical activities or designated hospitals scarce and forces ailing people to rely on private practitioners.

Correlates of Catastrophic Health Spending: A Probit Regression Analysis

Drawing upon the results, which indicate a very high incidence of catastrophic health spending by households in most of our study areas, we tried an econometric exercise based on a probit analysis to examine some of the major risk factors likely to turn into perils of such eventualities. The exercise was designed to highlight the latent characteristic(s) of households that can turn into a catastrophe owing to a certain beyond-a-point spending—in our case, this spending relates to health. To ensure brevity, we have confined our estimations to only catastrophe 1, defined in relation to the total (food and nonfood) consumption expenditure of households. In addition, we have also restricted this exercise to only the lowest ($z=5$ %) and the highest ($z=25$ %) catastrophe thresholds. It may inter alia help us to examine if there are differences in factors related to the probabilities of having lower and higher catastrophic events.

The results indicate the effects of individual variables on the probability of having catastrophic spending by households in events of sickness episodes requiring in- or outpatient care. Among all the variables, the per capita household consumption expenditure, which is generally considered as representing the economic status of the households, turns out to be one of the most significant correlates of catastrophic spending. Although household size does not prove to be significant, the sign of the variable clearly indicates that the probability of making catastrophic payments increases with increase in household size. Households with brick-made *pucca* houses have greater probability of making catastrophic payment at only five per cent threshold level but have strong lower probability of such payments at higher thresholds such as 25 % or more. In general, better living conditions in terms of drinking water and sanitation facilities lead to reduced probability of making catastrophic payments by households.

The socio-economic and religious background of households reflects a mixed picture, with a strong indication that secondary level education leads to lowering the probability of catastrophic payments. Higher worker ratio in households (i.e. lower burden of economic dependency) leads to the lowering of the probability. It may as well be because of some sort of contributions from employers to health expenditure of households. However, unlike those who do not participate in the MGNREGS, employers of casual workers in social employment programmes such as the MGNREGS do not contribute to social security, and therefore, casual workers run higher risks of making catastrophic payments. Further, the results clearly indicate that households belonging to lower-caste and non-Hindu categories run a higher probability of catastrophic expenditure.

With an increase in the average age of family members, the probability of catastrophic payment increases at the 5 % threshold level but becomes insignificant at higher thresholds. Households with infants and children under 14 years have higher risk of making catastrophic payments at the 5 % threshold, while most of these demographic variables are insignificant at the higher threshold of 25 %. The locational factors such as state and region indicate a comparatively vulnerable situation of households living in the remote and poorer regions or areas. As compared to the non-slum areas of Delhi, households in all other places in our sample show a strong and positive association with probability of falling into catastrophic payments. The relationship becomes even stronger with the higher threshold of 25 %.

Utilisation of Public Health Facilities

The analysis shows a very high dependence of households on private facilities, despite the creation of a vast public-financed health-care infrastructure in most rural and urban areas. Alarmingly, this dependence holds for most rural and low-income areas covered in the study. Moreover, a considerable share of poor population from the lowest quintile also appears to have relied on private providers. Catastrophic households follow a similar pattern. Furthermore, even hospitalised treatment, where the public sector had an edge, is losing its earlier sheen.

The share of private providers is particularly high in UP, where almost three-quarters of both rural and urban health-care seekers have relied on private practitioners for their routine outpatient care. Interestingly, this share has turned out to be relatively smaller in the remaining states with the lowest in Rajasthan followed by Delhi. Nevertheless, nowhere the share of private practitioners in outpatient care drops below 50 %. It would be imperative for all stakeholders, in particular health administrators, to raise the level of health-care utilisation in the public sector.

Contrary to outpatient services, public facilities appear to have a greater role in providing hospital care at most places under reference. The utilisation of government hospitals is invariably higher among tribal, low-caste and low-income people, especially from slums and rural areas. Unfortunately, however, it does not prove to be conclusively so, as quite a large fraction of inpatient care accessed by the people from non-slum and urban areas of Delhi and UP has been delivered by private hospitals and nursing homes. This is true for upper-caste groups in the sample as well. These variations apart, public hospitals not only serve a big fraction of people from different stratums and residential areas; they also serve to regulate the overall functioning of the private providers in more ways than one including offering a tangible substitute to the private facilities.

Distribution by Quintile Groups

A majority of the outpatient care seekers, even from the bottom two consumption quintiles (i.e. comprising the lowest 40 %), largely rely on private providers. It may imply that no amount of economic hardship makes even the poorest to feel adamant to use the private facilities. The other observation, though reconfirms the primacy of public facilities when it comes to hospitalisation, underlies the fact that even the poorest may not be able to rely solely on government-run health-care facilities. The results clearly suggest that a good fraction of people from the two lowest consumption quintiles had to access care from private providers. Admittedly, while such fractions may not be used conclusively to vindicate certain line of arguments, they however make out a case to go into such instances further and deeper. These are also the issues to be taken up for consideration by the RKS or such other patient welfare bodies currently working at the district and subdistrict levels.

Distribution by Catastrophic Households

Interestingly, it emerges from the profile of recipients of medical care with or without hospitalisation that catastrophe is not entirely the outcome of private hospitals or private medical practitioners—it occurs to patients of public facilities as well. In nonhospitalisation cases, it results mainly because of private providers, from a little less than 67 % to over 73 % of the total cases. In addition, it holds alike for both the rural and urban areas. In contrast to this, it is also revealed that hospitalisation-driven catastrophe is also generally higher among patients treated in public hospitals. This is particularly true for the low-income households. Somewhat disappointing, but public medical facilities are shown to have pushed a good majority of rural and slum households to catastrophe. Besides, these results also indicate that a fraction of public hospital patients have also ended up with the most oppressive form of catastrophe ($z=25$ %) presumably because many of the services in public hospitals are now on payment basis. These are over and above the cost of drugs and medicines—some of them may not be essential.

While some of these results are constrained by a limited number of observations, they appear to be useful for drawing a few policy-level inferences. Two issues are apparently more significant on policy considerations and may need to be discussed at length. First, why could even those treated in public hospitals and other facilities not save themselves from catastrophe? Second, why do many low-income slum and rural people not go to public facilities and rely on private providers? In other words, what makes many of them wary of public facilities? These questions need to be probed further.

Factors for Non-utilisation of Public Health Facilities: Respondents' Views

Those who preferred not to access public hospital facilities found justification in four commonly known reasons: (i) public facilities are too far, (ii) public hospitals are inefficient, (iii) most drugs prescribed by the in-house doctors are either out of stock or for self-purchase, and (iv) public hospitals are invariably very crowded. While most of these factors are fairly known and oft repeated, it may be noted that medicines and efficiency in service delivery by public facilities are the two major expectations that need to be ensured by the government and its health apparatuses.

Another point to be noted in this context is that despite these perceptions, a very small fraction of respondents had complained against doctors' behaviour or growing burden of paid hospital services. Apparently, efficiency in service delivery and subsidised (if not free) drugs may bring substantial relief to a large number of low-income health seekers in public hospitals.

Similarly, patients needing non-ambulatory (or outdoor) care have also held three major constraining factors responsible for non-utilisation of consultation services provided by primary or secondary health centres or city hospitals. These are (i) misbehaviour by hospital staff, including doctors and paramedics; (ii) distant locations of public facilities; and (iii) overcrowding and non-availability of drugs. It implicitly suggests that the users of health-care facilities tend to substitute public health care in favour of private providers owing to some of these basic constraints. Particularly, non-availability of drugs and a drag on time are the two serious issues for many low-income health-care seekers. And yet it seems that the time factor remains diluted when it comes to hospitalisation. Yet another interesting observation relates to the affordability as a criterion to access private medical care. Many of those who decided not to utilise the public facilities were able to afford private consultation. In other words, there is a possible trade-off between the private and public health-care facilities—largely because of the latter's inefficient service delivery, non-availability of medicines and cost of transportation.

Role of the National Rural Health Mission (NRHM)

The survey revealed a low level of awareness about the NRHM as only smaller fractions of people from both the states, in particular from Rajasthan, knew about it or the priorities attached to improved child health and institutional delivery. Between the two states, residents of Unnao and its villages appear to be better informed about the NRHM. About a fifth of the total respondents in Unnao have reported their awareness about the mission. The same in Rajasthan was below 10 %. People from upper-caste categories and economically better-off respondents (e.g. above-poverty or higher-quintile households) have however shown greater awareness about this programme and a couple of its intended objectives, although even their shares do not exceed beyond a fifth or a quarter of their respective numbers. Interestingly, however, despite so much unawareness about the NRHM or its basic concerns, a much bigger fraction of respondents not only have reported satisfaction with the services provided by the primary health units but have also reported visible improvements in delivery of health services over the preceding 2 or 3 years. To be more specific, they further confirmed improvements in services covering reproductive and child health. On the flip side, these responses have remained considerably large across all the households distributed according to their socio-economic (social groups, quintile groups, etc.) characteristics. Even the two categories of catastrophic households, mild and severe, have also felt the same way. Some other interesting NRHM-related observations derived from the survey data include:

- Primary health-care centre (PHC) doctors visit regularly; it was reported by more than 80 % of the respondents.
- Accredited social health activists (ASHAs) already in place, confirmed by almost three-quarters of the sample households.
- Between 30 and 64 % of households from different socio-economic and religious categories have received help from the ASHAs. Interestingly, shares of low-income and catastrophic households among them were considerably large.
- As for vitamin tablets, oral rehydration therapy (ORT) or some other common medicines, respondents agreed to have received them from the health workers and their PHCs.
- Barring a sample of households from Dungarpur (Rajasthan), economically better-off and higher-caste households, very small fraction of respondents have used Ayurveda, Yoga and Naturopathy, Unani, Siddha and Homoeopathy (AYUSH) services. The share of AYUSH users remains invariably below 20 % of the respective samples. Muslims and residents of Unnao are the worst off on this count.

From the findings of the survey relating to NRHM, which may have partly suffered because of a limited time gap between its initiation and this study, two diametrical messages are emerging. On the one hand, a large share of responding households (even a majority in many cases) do not find it worthwhile to rely on facilities provided by the government, particularly for non-ambulatory or outpatient care. On the other, we notice that rural people did appreciate the services provided by the primary health units. They also report favourably about the PHC doctors, ASHA and certain qualitative improvements in rural health-care services since the NRHM. The question then is: Why are service users so apathetic towards much of public facilities and towards health-related catastrophe? Answers appear to lie at two levels: First, rural health care has largely been confined to a particular age segment. Second, it restricts to a particular health domain as well. A number of diseases falling beyond the reproductive health and its domains have remained poorly managed. As those diseases cause catastrophe to a very large extent, the government will have to consider ways to bring significant improvements in delivery of secondary and tertiary health-care services as well.

Conclusions of the Study and Policy Directions

Major Findings

Most of this analysis was broadly directed to focus on the following concerns: (i) OOP health payments and attendant issues of poverty and inequality, (ii) catastrophic health payments and some of its correlates, (iii) decomposition of health payments and share of drugs/medicines in the total health expenditure, (iv) share of public health services in hospitalisation and outpatient care, (v) public health-care utilisation and catastrophic payments, (vi) extent of untreated ailments mainly because of high health-care costs and (vii) attention generated by the NRHM among the rural households and their views on recent improvements in delivery of health services.

A number of observations have been drawn centred on the issues noted above. One of the more critical, perhaps, was the role played exclusively by OOP health payments in adding to the overall poverty level and bringing vulnerability to a significant fraction of rural and slum households. It was also noticed that health payments may easily push households below poverty level from above it. An analysis of household indebtedness in Chap. 3 shows that more than a quarter of indebted urban households had borrowed to meet medical exigencies. The same in rural areas turns out to be a little over 19 %. Chapter 3 also indicates a big share of private moneylenders in those borrowings. Does it mean to suggest that a significant percentage of households cannot afford health-care services in the country in their present form? While a categorical answer to this question may need further and more in-depth studies, this is indeed an issue that needs greater consideration, especially from health policy mandarins.

Moving to the issues of catastrophic health payments, this analysis indicates that catastrophe cut-off levels, as frequently used in the international literature, make no sense for the observed sample of households or very limited sense. This is to a greater extent true at the higher cut-off levels. With the share of nonfood consumption expenditure in many cases as low as observed in the present analysis, any fraction of OOP health expenditure may not only look catastrophic; it would rather overshoot the defined catastrophe limit. Yet another significant observation in this context was that even the users of public health-care facilities are not able to save themselves from catastrophic payments.

These results ultimately raise a very basic question: What component(s) of health spending drives the households to face a catastrophe? Intuitively, this question may have a role in pinning down a few policy interventions to minimise the catastrophic incidences. In response to this question, it was attempted to compute the shares of (i) consultation fees, (ii) expenditure on drugs and medicines, (iii) expenses on diagnostics and (iv) cost incurred on commutation and other related expenses in the total health expenditure of households under study. In a large number of cases, our computations reveal drugs as the biggest expenditure, and in some cases it turns out to be around 90 % of the total health budget. Even in normal situations, drugs and medicines account for over 75 % of the total OOP spending on health. This result is in consonance with some other studies recently conducted at the all India level. This raises many serious issues from the viewpoint of policy. Two factors need to be seriously considered. First, most public medical facilities do not provide medicines to their patients including the poor patients. Even in many cases, these facilities expect service users to provide sundry items like cotton or bandages. These are in addition to items such as registration fee, costs of various diagnostic tests and transportation. Besides being a push factor to catastrophe, it also dissuades even poor service users to use public facilities, especially in nonhospitalisation cases. The second relates to the drug pricing, and growing concerns have already been raised in many national and international literature regarding the WTO Agreement on Trade-Related Aspects of Intellectual Property Rights (TRIPS). These negotiations and agreements have clearly set minimum standards for the protection of intellectual property. It has also helped to generate considerable gains for pharmaceutical companies.

Where does the solution lie? This is a complex issue and requires deft TRIPS negotiations, along with a serious policy makeover on making medicines available to the patients at subsidised prices. Can the government find enough resources to provide medicines? While this analysis cannot answer this question clearly, OOP health expenditure, most attendant issues and drug pricing are interlinked, and none of them may be decided independently.

Somewhat alarming but a fairly known issue in the context of health delivery is the poor utilisation of public health-care facilities by health seekers—both ambulatory and non-ambulatory. Reasons remain oft repeated and primitive: long hours of wait, non-availability of drugs, poor outreach, lack of emergency services in local (village level) health centres and improper behaviour by the medical staff. And yet, a number of respondents have been disposed of fairly well and have started taking note of the NRHM and its services. There has especially been a positive response towards the role played by the ASHAs, availability of PHC doctors and distribution of certain medicines required by women during pregnancies and small children. How far the mission is able to cover the health-care needs of those in nonreproductive ages is not clear from this study and, therefore, an area worth of exploration in future research. The incidence of catastrophic health spending raises doubts about the versatility of the NRHM. Also, there appears to be very limited utilisation of consultation facilities provided by AYUSH practitioners in many health-care centres.

Respondents' Views on Critical Policy Issues

Survey respondents were asked to comment mostly on issues on which they were expected to have a better understanding. A few of those respondents, especially in rural areas, were also given certain background information, particularly on operational aspects of health insurance. Some of the more important questions included: (a) Do you feel that the health services have become costlier over the past 1 year? (b) Do you think doctors generally overprescribe medicines/diagnostic tests?

(c) In your opinion, would a low-premium health insurance be a workable solution?
(d) If required, would you be willing to subscribe to such an insurance scheme?
The last two questions were asked against the backdrop of a recent initiative by the government to launch a Rashtriya Swasthya Bima Yojana (RSBY) for the below-poverty households.

A large number of respondents, almost 8–9 out of 10, agreed that health services have become expensive by more than 50 % over the preceding 12 months. Those with better access to health care do not usually subscribe to the idea of buying an insurance product. We notice from the discussion in Chap. 8 that (i) the richest quintile, (ii) Delhi respondents and (iii) upper-caste persons have favoured such a scheme in much smaller fractions. Those who endorsed the health insurance idea were however in majority among other categories of respondents, including the rural and urban households of UP and Rajasthan. Almost a similar response has emerged from the last question: Would you be willing to join an insurance system on self-payment basis? Following from the earlier question, those with better access or affordability to health care largely showed disinterest. Others have, however, favoured it. But still it may be surmised that a self-paid health insurance is a strong possibility if the government is able to regulate the system well, particularly against the menaces of exclusions and cartelisation among medical professionals, service providers and major pharmaceutical companies.

Policy Directions

The results indicate that the supply-side management of the health market in India remains mired because of health-care seekers' growing dependence on private providers. In several cases, public sector facilities do not prove to be a close substitute to private providers. This is particularly true for outpatient services. Even in hospital services, a large segment of people depend on private providers. All these affect private medical services and their price determination system. This has aptly been summarised by respondents, when they report over 50 % escalation in their medical budget over the past 12 months—a brief period. A related point may be noticed from the perception that doctors overprescribe medicines. Does it reflect a certain laxity in administration of medical rules? Also, there is a serious problem with medical ethics. The medical profession is now largely guided by corporate practices, with the core objective being to maximise profit through increased occupancy rates or patients' consultation. An apprehension is that the RSBY may further aggravate the situation, particularly for uncovered families. Health policymakers may have to consider some of these factors to bring down the cases of catastrophe. Public facilities will have to become efficient, client responsive and a close substitute to private services. The recent initiative to appoint RKSs will have to be strengthened.

Patients of public hospitals facing catastrophe need to be examined. Drug pricing and availability of essential drugs to patients in public facilities warrant serious consideration. Deployment of manpower and management of public hospitals need considerable fine-tuning. Especially, there is a need to minimise non-clinical responsibilities of medical doctors in most public facilities. If at all viable, certain hours may be fixed in a week for every medical doctor to devote to their clinical responsibilities. Patient–doctor or patient–health worker relationship is a perennial issue and needs serious consideration. Medical ethics, particularly in allocation of scarce services like intensive care units or ventilators, prescription of medicines or diagnostic procedure, informed consent, confidentiality, etc., is another area requiring serious consideration.

Beyond all this, perhaps a most potent issue for consideration is to work on a comprehensive risk-pooling arrangement, covering both in- and outpatient treatments. While the RSBY is apparently a good initiative, it covers a very small segment of the poor population (roughly 12 million). In addition, it is directed only at the hospitalisation (including day care) cases. Given a very high prevalence of ailments requiring non-ambulatory care—around 15 % as against 2.5–3 % requiring hospitalisation—the noncoverage of outpatient care may leave most problems unresolved. Moreover, our study has highlighted that expenses on outpatient care have been equally catastrophic in nature, which is worth covering under schemes like the RSBY.

Intellectual patenting rights (IPRs), Trade-Related Intellectual Property Rights (TRIPS) and TRIPS Plus negotiations require understanding the health status of the country's population, which in turn needs a series of micro-level studies to know the health status of poor and low-income people, especially from economically low-performing districts and states.

Chapter 1
Introduction

For over past 60 years or even more, health has perhaps been among the few issues in India that has received unceasing attention from planners, policy makers, intellectuals and the political leadership. One of the earliest attempts in this direction was initiated years before the country gained independence from British rule in 1947. A committee—Health Survey and Development Committee—was constituted under the chairmanship of Sir Joseph Bhore[1] as far back as 1943 to suggest measures for improvements in delivery of health care to a vast populace in the country, especially in rural areas. The network of primary and community health centres that exists now in most of the rural areas draws its origin from the recommendations of the Bhore Committee (1943–1946).

The Bhore Committee was followed in subsequent years by a series of other high-power committees and commissions[2] and, more recently, by the two National Health Policies (NHPs)—the former was adopted by the government in 1983 with a focus on health for all by 2000, while the latter was legislated in 2002 with an explicit recognition of strong linkages between health and the overall growth objectives of the economy. Despite these concerns and a series of policy initiatives over the past decades, health remains a critical issue with growing concern in recent years about the high burden of diseases, premature deaths and functional incapacitations; all of these cost the nation dearly both socio-economically and in terms of its international rankings.

Some of these concerns have further been highlighted in a detailed report prepared by the National Commission on Macroeconomics and Health (NCMH), constituted by the Government of India under the chairmanship of Mr. P. Chidambaram and Dr. A. Ramadoss, then Union Ministers of Finance and Health, respectively. The Commission submitted its report in 2005 with a comprehensive review of major health issues and the contemporary situation in the country. The major issues raised by the report include

---

[1] For details of various other committees, see http://nihfw.org/NDC/DocumentationServices/Committe_and_commission.html.

[2] A few of these Committees include Mudaliar Committee (1959–1961), Chadha Committee (1963), Mukherjee Committee (1966), Kartar Singh Committee (1975) and subsequently the first National Health Policy adopted by the Parliament in 1983 with a focus on health for all by 2000.

M. Alam, *Paying Out-of-Pocket for Drugs, Diagnostics and Medical Services: A Study of Households in Three Indian States*, India Studies in Business and Economics, DOI 10.1007/978-81-322-1281-2_1, © Springer India 2013

inadequate health expenditure by the centre and state governments, inefficient delivery and poor utilisation of health services delivered by most public health-care services and demand–supply mismatch of medical professionals, especially paramedics and grass-root health workers. The other issues highlighted include rising drug prices which are expected to increase further under the new patent and Trade-Related Aspects of Intellectual Property Rights regime (TRIPS Plus), disproportionate burden of health cost on poorer households with far-reaching implications for their economic security and levels of consumption expenditure—both food and non-food. Drawing upon inferences based on recent health surveys, the Commission's report is among the few public documents which have clearly agreed that private OOP health expenditure often pushes low-income households to face catastrophe and forces many of them below the poverty line. In many situations, it may as well clog intergenerational (i.e. from young to old) flows with severe implications for the coresiding old, especially women.[3]

1.1   Existing Health Situation: A Few Stylised Facts

Of late and with the resurgence of the market forces in countries like India, health has increasingly been considered as one of the causal factors with a decisive role in fostering growth and development (Casanovas et al. 2005). This recognition has also promoted

---

[3]Ministry of Health and Family Welfare, Government of India, has been publishing since 2010 an 'Annual Report to the People on Health' with a view to provide:

1. Trends in core demographic parameters and recent developments in availability of various reproductive and child health services
2. Prevalence of selected communicable and non-communicable diseases
3. Public health-care interventions and achievements

In all, the Ministry has published two reports highlighting improvements in several programmatic areas and health domains including improvements in key demographic parameters. There has also been a brief discussion in the reports about the paucity of certain health-care infrastructure, especially inadequate financial resources provided to health sector by the governments and shortages of medical and paramedical skills in the country. Discussing out-of-pocket expenditure on health, these reports have mentioned drugs and medicines as a single component causing most of health-care expenditure by households.

The Ministry has started publishing this report annually on the advice of the President Mrs. Pratibha Patil at a joint session of parliament on 4 June 2009. As noted, the Ministry has so far published two reports, first in September 2010 and the second in December 2011. As usual, both the reports largely dealt with various programme inputs without going sufficiently into their outcomes.

Like the people's report by the Ministry of Health and Family Welfare, an Annual Health Survey (AHS) was also initiated by the Registrar General and Census Commissioner on the recommendation of the National Commission on Population, Planning Commission and the Prime Minister Office in 2010–2011 to provide information on core vital and reproductive health indicators from a group of demographically backward states including Uttarakhand, Rajasthan, Uttar Pradesh, Bihar, Assam, Jharkhand, Madhya Pradesh, Chhattisgarh and Orissa. The indicators covered in the survey are crude birth rate, crude death rate, infant mortality rate, neonatal mortality rate, under-five mortality rate, maternal mortality ratio, sex ratio at birth, sex ratio at 0–4 years old and sex ratio at all ages.

None of these reports are however relevant for the analysis presented in the underlying study.

a wider debate among health professionals and economists by linking health with individuals' overall economic well-being and, in particular, with their poverty status. As an offshoot, this debate has led to a question: Does poor health lead to poverty or is it a symptom?

Although the health–poverty nexus and its surrounding debate has never been without its takers in India (Dreze and Sen 1995; Fuchs 2004; Behrman and Deolalikar 1988; Osmani 1992), it came to greater visibility, especially at the policy level, only after the Cairo International Conference on Population and Development (ICPD, September 1994). This recognition was reiterated further in two subsequent policy documents of the Government of India—namely, the National Population Policy (2000) and the National Health Policy (2002).

From these accounts, it may not be very implausible to infer that human health has hardly ever lacked attention in India as a broader policy concern. And yet, a number of significant issues have either missed attention, especially at micro-level, or remained on the sidelines for one or the other reason. It may, for example, be noticed that a great deal of the health infrastructure in India, especially in most rural areas, has largely been directed to achieve fertility reduction, improve contraception level and make people aware about the needs of smaller families. More recently, a few additional, but interlinked, activities have also been added with an objective to fulfil a few of the Millennium Development Goals (MDGs) such as reduction in maternal, infant and child mortality and improvement in level of institutional deliveries. In the process, however, general or post-50 health care, required by a large percentage of poor in rural and urban areas, is left to market providers—a large fraction of them consists of quacks. As poverty is still persistent in most rural areas and urban slums, reliance on private health providers is fraught with serious economic consequences, especially for low-income households engaged in the informal economy.

Another significant issue, which dissuaded analysts to examine the health–poverty nexus, especially at the micro-level, relates to lack of adequate data and information. Admittedly, the NSSO does provide data on health spending at the household level as part of its (annual and quinquennial) consumption surveys; these are generally considered reliable at the state level. The same at the district or the subdistrict level may cause problems peculiar to studies suffering from a limited number of observations. More recently, there have been attempts by the Ministry of Health and Family Welfare (MoHFW) to supplement the data sources on major health issues, particularly on access to and utilisation of health services both in the public and private sectors—most of them, however, are once again confined to reproductive health.[4]

---

[4]More prominent among these data sources with a cross-country coverage and large sample size are the three different rounds of the National Family Health Survey (NFHS – 1, 1992–1993; NFHS – 2, 1998–1999; and NFHS – 3, 2005–2006), and the District Levels Health Surveys (generally known as the RCH surveys) designed to assess various population parameters including utilisation of health services required during the pre and postnatal phases along with the nutritional details and immunisations of children against certain early life diseases. Much of these information and data sources however concentrate on programme variables without making explicit concerns about the outcome variables.

Against this backdrop, there is now a realisation that the health situation in India is seriously entrenched in the following. First, despite its rising economy, India is still a country with widespread poverty, malnutrition and enormous disparities in almost every sphere of human life including health; women and the old suffer the most. This is particularly true for the rural areas where the per capita monthly consumption expenditure (PCMCE)—an important indicator of poverty—is alarmingly low (Alam 2008). Moreover, there is hardly any significant change in real per capita consumption level of rural households over the past decade (Alam 2008). Second, disease prevalence—both communicable and non-communicable—is invariably large among the low-income rural and urban households for poor socio-economic conditions and inadequate access to public health facilities. Third, the growing role of market in delivery of health and diagnostic services with a very high out-of-pocket (OOP) expenditure by seekers of health care, many of them, as has already been noted, at the lowest deciles of consumption levels. Fourth, the major contributory factor resulting into severity of health issues in India relates to various infrastructural bottlenecks suffered by health services provided by the centre, state or local governments. These bottlenecks go beyond the physical or financial resources and cover whole aspects of hospital administration including large-scale deployment of medical doctors to non-clinical services due to the interference of the local bureaucracy. Such deployments not only cause a considerable amount of dissatisfaction among users of public services but also force a shift to private medical services and incur OOP expenses.

Clearly, all these issues are not only detrimental to the economic well-being of a large number of poor households or their family members; they are also in direct contradiction to the National Population Policy (2000) and the National Health Policy (2002). In addition, these are in contradiction to the country's new economic regime as well.

1.2 Health Indicators and Underlying Issues

Three issues are often reported to have largely clouded the health indicators of the country and bring them directly in contradiction to the stated objectives of the country's population and health policies.[5] These are:

1. High prevalence of communicable and non-communicable diseases in the country causing premature deaths and loss of healthy life.
2. Inadequate public health expenditure, especially if judged by using the price-adjusted expenditure data.
3. Increasing role of private sector in health-care delivery causing very high OOP expenses on drugs (both common and life-saving) and other components, borne out disproportionately by the low-income households with grave risks of being

---

[5] See National Population Policy (2000) and National Health Policy (2002).

Table 1.1 Major health indicators: all India

Annual growth of GDP per capita: 2008–2012 (%)	5.4[a]
Annual growth of population: 2001–2011 (%)	1.64[b]
IMR per 1,000 live births, 2011	44[c]
Life expectancy: M/F (projected for 2006–2010)	65.8/68.1[d]
MMR per 100,000 live births, 2007–2009	212[e]
TFR: 2009	2.6[f]
Crude death rate per 1,000 population, 2009	7.3[g]
Average population served per government allopathic doctor, 2011	12,005[h]
Nurses per 1,000 population, 2011	1.6[h]
Pharmacists per 1,000 population, 2011	0.54[h]
Total hospital beds/population served per hospital bed (government sector), 2011	7,84,940/1512[h]
Non-institutional deliveries, 2005–2006	59.3[i]
Public expenditure on health as per cent of GDP: India, China and Sri Lanka, 2009	1.1[j] 1.9[j] 2.0[j]
Public expenditure as % of the total expenditure on health	20 %[j]
Anaemic children aged 6–35 months (%): NFHS-2/NFHS-3	74.2/78.9[i]
Pregnant anaemic women aged 15–49 (%): NFHS-2/NFHS-3	49.7/57.9[i]

Sources:
[a]World Bank National Accounts Data. World Development Indicator (2008) (Accessed January 2013: http://data.worldbank.org/indicator/NY.GDP.PCAP.KD.ZG/)
[b]Census of India, 2011
[c]SRS Bulletin, October 2012
[d]Report of the Technical on Population Projection, May 2006, MoH&FW
[e]SRS Bulletin, June 2011
[f]SRS Estimates, July 2011
[g]Family Welfare Statistics in India, 2011, MoH&FW
[h]National Health Profile, 2011
[i]NFHS-2 and NFHS-3 for the years 1998–1999 and 2005–2006
[j]International Human Development Indicators, World Development Indicators, World Bank, 2011

pushed to (i) serious welfare losses, (ii) catastrophic conditions and (iii) indebtedness. It also creates a divide between the health-care allocations by the government and the private needs.

We will deal briefly with some of these issues in the following discussion and provide a few corroborating evidences; a few of them have already been produced by the Commission on Macroeconomics and Health in its report.

1.2.1 Selected Health Indicators: All India

A perusal of Table 1.1 reveals that the annual population growth rate in the country is gradually declining over the preceding decades. It grew at the rate of 1.64 % per annum during the preceding two censuses—2001–2011. The infant mortality rate (IMR) at 44 per 1,000 live births is comparatively at a higher level and registered

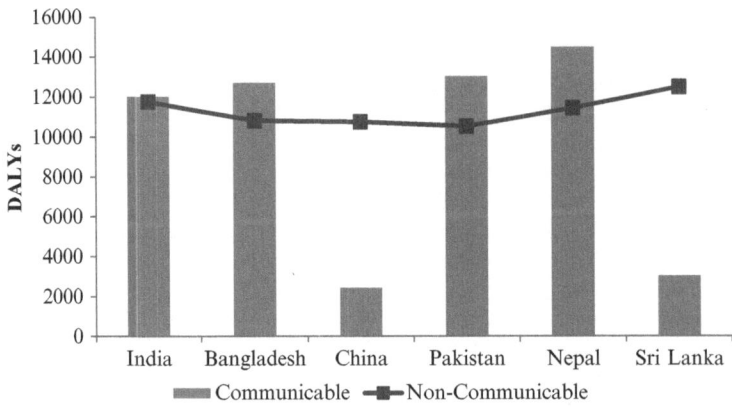

Fig. 1.1 Estimated DALYs (per 100,000 persons of all ages) by communicable and non-communicable diseases: India, China and neighbouring South Asian countries, 2004 (*Source*: WHO Department of Measurement and Health Information), December 2004, http://www.who.int/healthinfo/global_burden_disease/estimates_country/en/index.html (Accessed October 2012)

only a marginal decrease during the recent decade. The maternal mortality ratio (MMR) at 212 per hundred thousand live births is quite high in international comparison. The Millennium Development Goals (MDGs) that were officially adopted by India on the instance of United Nations in 2000 have included reduction in IMR and MMR on priority basis. The NRHM has also laid stress on increase in institutional deliveries for reduction of IMR and MMR, but still the percentage of domiciliary deliveries is quite high. Another cause of concern is the high level of anaemia among children and pregnant mothers; it was 78.9 % in case of children in the age group of 6–35 months and 57.9 % in case of women in the age group of 15–49 years as per the National Family Health Survey-3 (NFHS-3), 2005–2006. Some other major indicators of health in India may be noted from Table 1.1. Most of them appear least promising.

1.2.2   Disease Burden and Deaths: WHO Estimates (DALYs Rates and Death Rates)

A comparison of the World Health Organization (WHO) estimates of disability-adjusted loss of years (DALYs) in Fig. 1.1 reveals that the burden of communicable diseases in India is considerably higher than China or Sri Lanka, although it is lower than Pakistan, Nepal and Bangladesh. As regards the non-communicable diseases, it is equal to the level in Sri Lanka, but quite lower than in many other countries of South Asia and China.

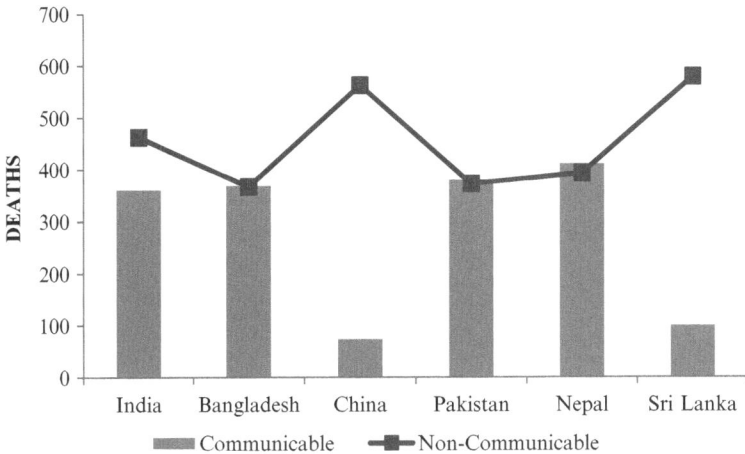

Fig. 1.2 Estimated deaths (per 100,000 persons of all ages) by communicable and non-communicable diseases: India, China and neighbouring South Asian countries, 2008 (*Source*: WHO, Department of Measurement and Health Information, (December 2008). http://www.who.int/healthinfo/global_burden_disease/estimates_country/en/index.html (Accessed October 2012))

The estimated deaths per hundred thousand by communicable diseases in India, China and a few other South Asian countries (Fig. 1.2) reveals that India is the second highest, the highest being Pakistan. India is more or less equal to Nepal. The other three countries including Bangladesh, Sri Lanka and China have lower estimated deaths in that order. The deaths by non-communicable diseases are the highest in Sri Lanka, followed by China, India, Nepal, Pakistan and Bangladesh. These statistics clearly suggest a high burden of diseases (BoD) and a high incidence of deaths by communicable diseases.

1.3   Health Financing by the Centre and States

Aggregate public expenditure on health (revenue and capital) as a percentage of GDP showed a rising trend; from merely 0.40 % in 1990–1991, it increased to a little over 0.60 % in 2000–2001. It again started declining and reached to its highest level of over 0.90 % in 2008–2009 (Fig. 1.3). It remained well below the trend line during the years starting from 2002 to 2003 to 2007–2008, i.e. the years during which Indian economy risen impressively. The capital expenditure has been at a very low level; it was virtually remained almost flat below 0.1 % up to 2002–2003 and increased to its highest level at little over 0.1 % in 2008–2009. The trend of revenue expenditure has matched the general trend as the share of revenue expenditure has been very high in the total expenditure (Fig. 1.3).

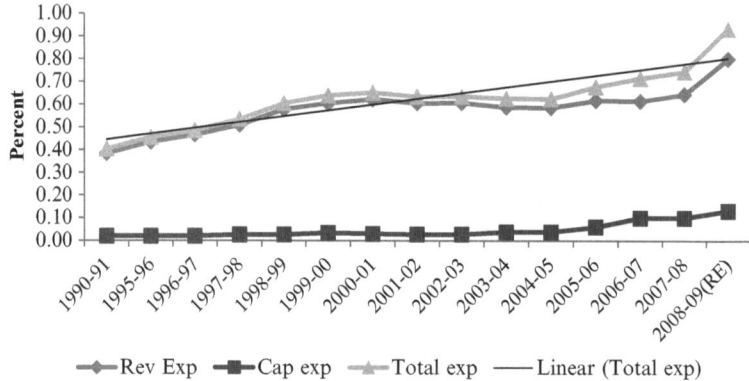

Fig. 1.3 Public expenditure on health as per cent of GDP: all India (*Source*: RBI's *Handbook of Statistics on State Government Finances*, 2004)

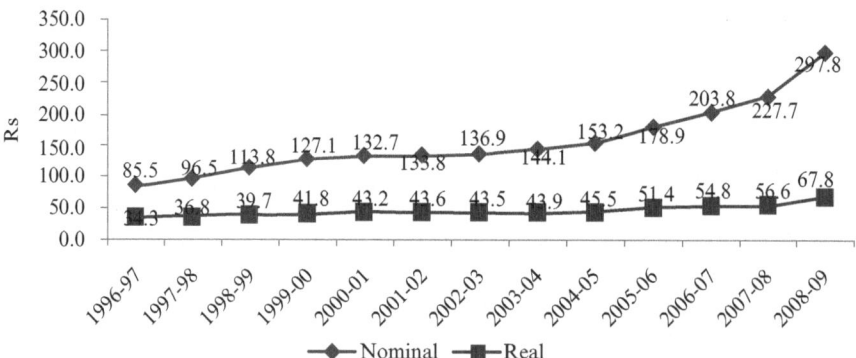

Fig. 1.4 Post-reform increase in per capita health expenditure: all India (nominal and real) (Base year: 1986–1987 = 100) (*Source*: RBI's *Handbook of Statistics on State Government Finances*, 2004. *Note*: Per capita health expenditure was adjusted by using consumer price index)

1.3.1 Per Capita Health Expenditure During Post-reform Period

The per capita aggregate health expenditure of the centre and state governments has risen continuously at nominal prices from 1996 to 1997 to 2008–2009. It rose from Rs. 85.5 in 1996–1997 to Rs. 297.8 in 2008–2009 (Fig. 1.4). At the real price level, however, the increase is not very substantial—i.e. only from Rs. 34.3 in 1996–1997 to Rs. 67.8 in 2008–2009. But the trend remains more or less the same.

Table 1.2 Percentage share of health in revenue budget of the centre and states: 1991–1992 to 2011–2012

	1991–1992	1995–1996	1999–2000	2003–2004	2007–2008	2011–2012 (RE)
AP	5.8	5.7	6.1	4.0	3.8	4.4
Assam	6.6	6.1	5.3	3.4	4.4	4.1
Bihar	5.7	7.8	6.3	3.7	4.2	3.7
Gujarat	5.4	5.3	5.2	3.5	3.3	3.8
Haryana	4.2	3.0	4.1	3.0	2.7	3.6
Karnataka	5.9	5.9	5.7	3.7	3.4	4.0
Kerala	6.9	6.8	6.0	4.6	4.4	5.3
Maharashtra	5.3	5.2	4.6	3.8	3.7	3.7
MP	5.7	5.1	5.2	3.6	3.8	4.0
Orissa	5.9	5.4	5.0	3.6	3.5	3.4
Punjab	4.3	4.6	5.3	3.5	3.0	4.1
Rajasthan	6.9	6.2	6.4	4.3	4.0	4.9
Tamil Nadu	4.8	6.4	5.5	4.0	3.4	4.1
UP	6.0	5.7	4.4	2.8	4.0	3.6
W. Bengal	7.3	7.2	6.3	4.6	4.0	4.2
All India	5.7	5.7	5.5	3.8	3.8	4.1

Source: RBI's *Handbook of Statistics on State Government Finances*, 2004 (State Finance Budgets)

1.3.2   Share of Health in Revenue Budget: Centre and States

The share of health expenditure in the revenue budget at the all-India level continuously declined from 5.7 % in 1991–1992 to little over 4 % in 2011–2012 (see Table 1.2). The states also represented more or less the all-India pattern. However, there were marginal variations in the case of Bihar, Punjab, Tamil Nadu, Kerala and West Bengal. The share of health in the revenue budget of Bihar increased to 7.8 % in 1995–1996 from 5.7 % in 1991–1992, but again came down to 6.3 % in 1999–2000 and further to 3.7 % in 2011–2012. In the case of Haryana, the share went down to as low as 3.0 % in 1995–1996 from 4.2 % in 1991–1992 and went up to 4.1 % in 1999–2000 and again to a low of 3.6 % in 2011–2012. In Tamil Nadu, the share of health went down drastically from 6.4 % in 1995–1996 to 3.4 % in 2007–2008 and slightly increased again in 2011–2012 (see Table 1.2). Figure 1.5 displays this trend very clearly. It is also clearly visible from the figure that the share allocated to health in revenue budget has fallen substantially in Gujarat, Haryana, Orissa and West Bengal over the years under reference. It may be interesting to note that the share of health has declined almost in every state during 2003 and 2008 and increased marginally thereafter. It may also be noticed that the share of health in revenue budget has remained depressed in recent years if compared to the 1990s when the country has started moving to economic liberalisation with pro-market reforms.

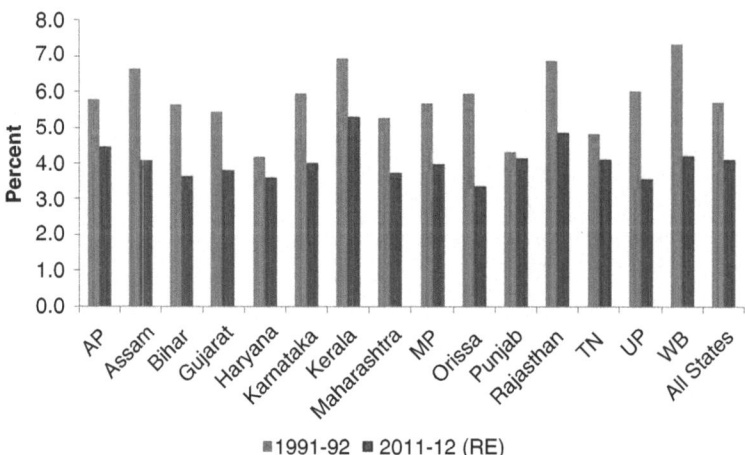

Fig. 1.5 Declining share of health in revenue budget of major states: 1991–1992 and 2011–2012
(*Source*: Table 1.2)

1.3.3   Utilisation of Public and Private Health Facilities

A perusal of Table 1.3 reveals that the countrywide share of the total cases treated
in private hospitals was 58.3 % in rural areas, while the same for the urban areas was
given as 61.7 %. State-level differentials reveal that rural Bihar had the highest
share of treatment in private hospitals; over 85.6 % of the total cases in rural areas
were treated in private facilities. This is followed by 79.4 % in Haryana, 72.7 % in
Andhra Pradesh and 71.3 % in Maharashtra. Contrary to this, Orissa, West Bengal
and Himachal Pradesh were at the other end with a greater share of the total cases
going to the public hospitals. Is it a reflection of better health-care delivery by public hospitals in these states? We refrain from commenting on that as it goes beyond
the scope of this book.

In the urban areas as well, the highest percentage of 78.5 % is in Bihar, followed by 73.9 in Gujarat and 73.6 in Punjab. On the other hand, the lowest percentage of the cases (10.5 %) was treated in private hospitals in Himachal
Pradesh, 13.5 % in Jammu and Kashmir and 26.9 % in Orissa. The lower utilisation of private hospitals in many cases and particularly in Orissa may be due to
widespread poverty.

The trend of the utilisation of public and private facilities in hospitalisation
cases can be seen in Fig. 1.6. In this figure, the share of public and private facilities in hospitalisation cases is given over three points of time from the National
Sample Surveys (NSS) conducted during 1986–1987 (42nd round), 1995–1996
(52nd round) and 2004 (60th round). A clear declining trend is visible, both for
urban and rural areas, as far as utilisation of public facilities is concerned. In rural
areas, the share of utilisation of public facilities has declined from 56.7 % in

Table 1.3 State-wise share of public and private hospitals in treated cases: 2004

States	Rural (%)		Urban (%)	
	Govt. hospital	Pvt. hospital	Govt. hospital	Pvt. hospital
AP	27.2	72.7	35.8	64.2
Assam	74.2	25.8	55.4	44.6
Bihar	14.4	85.6	21.5	78.5
Delhi	–	–	37.3	62.7
Gujarat	31.3	68.7	26.1	73.9
Haryana	20.6	79.4	29	71
HP	78.1	21.9	89.5	10.5
J & K	91.3	8.7	86.5	13.5
Karnataka	40	60	28.9	71.1
Kerala	35.6	64.4	34.6	65.4
MP	58.5	41.5	48.5	51.5
Maharashtra	28.7	71.3	28	72
Orissa	79.1	20.9	73.1	26.9
Punjab	29.4	70.6	26.4	73.6
Rajasthan	52.1	47.9	63.7	36.3
Tamil Nadu	40.8	59.2	37.2	62.8
UP	26.9	73	31.4	68.6
WB	78.6	21.3	65.4	34.6
India	41.7	58.3	38.2	61.8

Source: NSS 60th Round (January–June 2004), Statement 24.1

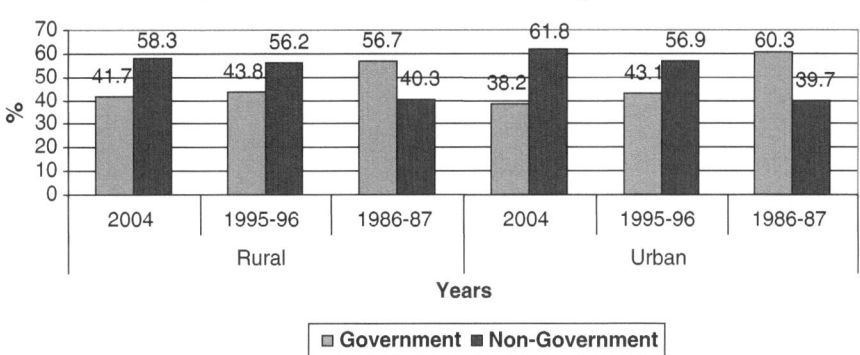

Fig. 1.6 Utilisation of public facilities in hospitalised care: rural–urban distribution (*Source*: NSS 60th Round (January–June 2004), Statement 24)

1986–1987 to 41.7 % in 2004, while in urban areas the share has declined from 60.3 % in 1986–1987 to 43.1 % in 1995–1996 to only 38.2 % in 2004. The declining utilisation of public facilities in hospitalisation cases has quite serious implications on OOP expenses on medical care.

Clearly, the preceding discussion underscores the argument that despite its persistent efforts and inputs received from a number of specially constituted bodies, India is critically lagging behind in terms of its long-standing commitments towards building a healthy society based on certain norms of equity and efficiency. The country, as may be noticed from the data presented above, is turning out to be much severely constrained due to high proportions of immature deaths as well as diminution in healthy life caused by a distressing combination of both communicable and non-communicable diseases. A more or less similar observation follows from the rest of the figures. The country has especially failed to enhance health sector finances in real terms. It has also failed to ensure health-care access for as many households—forcing many to shift eventually from the public to the private deliverers and face serious economic and financial consequences due to rising cost of privately delivered health services and out-of-pocket expenses.

While a great deal of these facts are now beginning to emerge from the studies conducted in recent years to highlight a range of physical, financial and manpower anomalies suffered by the public health facilities in India, how these anomalies have affected the low-income households, particularly in backward districts of high-poverty states, remains almost completely neglected. Many of these studies have also failed to examine the nature of households and their income level who are trapped into a poverty syndrome or experience catastrophe as a result of losses suffered due to expenditure on health-care services—especially drugs and medicines—in poverty-ridden rural and urban areas of the country. This study is basically designed to highlight some of these neglected issues using data from a uniformly designed household survey in selected districts of three states—namely, UP, Rajasthan and Delhi.

1.4   Out-of-Pocket Health Spending in India: A Brief About Some Existing Literature

Despite recognition of declining public sector share in overall health services and rising burden of private out-of-pocket expenditure on health in India, which in many cases result into severe financial issues to a large number of low-income households, there have been very few empirical studies that have investigated this issue or gone into some of their important correlates. To be more precise, there is perhaps no or very limited literature to show the implications of health-care expenditure on finances of low-income households in backward areas of economically less-performing states. The present book was written with this particular aspect at the centre stage. The book particularly emphasises the role of drugs and medicines (life-saving or otherwise) in escalating the overall health-care expenditure of a family or household.

Out-of-pocket health expenditure—defined by the WHO[6] as any exchange of cash or kind directly made by households to public or private health practitioners and suppliers of pharmaceuticals, therapeutic appliances or other goods and services—has often been viewed as a basis for examining two important, but mutually interconnected, issues in most of the developing world. One is essentially linked with health inequities due to lack of access to health services by many, and the second relates to rising inflation in health sector and its implications on low-income (or low consumption) households. Several developing countries including India have remained a victim to most of these issues and are now trying to implement a health insurance system financed by tax revenue for low-income households. In 2008, India has launched a public-funded Rashtriya Swasthya Bima Yojana (RSBY) to ensure access to hospitalisation facilities required by state-defined below-poverty households to protect them from health-related impoverishment. A few of the studies reviewing these insurance facilities,[7] which are currently moving towards gradual improvement in one way or the other, have recently appeared in prestigious journals like *Lancet*. Notably, a study by Lagomarsino, et al. (2012) and another by Kumar et al. (2011) may be cited for their comprehensive discussions on the health financing and insurance practices both in India and a group of nine other developing countries from Asia and Africa. The study by Kumar et al. (2011), based on public and private health spending obtained from India's National Health Accounts for 2001–2002 and 2004–2005, is exclusively devoted to describe limitations of health financing system in India. The study inter alia concludes that the health insurance in India is still premature and hardly covers a total of about 10 % population.

Driven by growing drug prices and escalations in other health-care expenses, out-of-pocket spending on medical treatment was also considered by many as a pathway to serious economic insecurities causing large-scale erosion in overall well-being of households. These spending may as well end up into a catastrophic poverty situation with considerable decline in size of basic consumption expenditure of low-income families. This line of approach was adopted in host of recent Indian studies based on household consumption expenditure surveys conducted by the National Sample Survey Organization (NSSO) at the all-India level. A few of these studies with considerable insight on poverty implications of OOP heath expenditure in India include Sakthivel and Karan (2009), Garg and Karan (2004, 2005, 2009) and Bonu et al. (2007). A similar study by O'Donnell et al. (2005) has tried to explain variations in the incidence of catastrophic

---

[6]For the most recent updates, see http://apps.who.int/nha/database.

[7]RSBY, a brainchild of the Ministry of Labour and Employment (MoL&E), Government of India, does not cover more than fivemembers of a household nor does it cover expenses requiring non-hospitalised treatments of an ailing member in a household. The size restriction often leaves older members of a family/household uncovered.

spending on health care across households of six Asian countries including India, Bangladesh, Sri Lanka, Thailand, Hong Kong and Vietnam. This study by O'Donnell and others (2005) inter alia indicates that the correlation of catastrophic payments with risk factors might vary with the development level of a country and nature of its health financing. The study also suggests a positive correlation between the total consumption of households and incidence of catastrophic payments. It further suggests that households make health payments either by using past savings or rely on borrowings. In certain conditions, they go for liquidation of assets as well.

The studies based on consumer expenditure surveys in India have in many cases tried to examine the factors raising possibilities of catastrophic health-care payments. These studies were generally conducted either at the all-India level or by states (Sakthivel and Karan 2009; Garg and Karan 2004, 2005, 2009; Bonu et al. 2007). As noted, there is no or very limited amount of literature available at the micro-level examining some of these issues faced by urban slum dwellers or those from rural areas of economically backward states or districts. The study presented by us in this book is perhaps one of the most comprehensive attempts to fill up this void and provide health spending of households by decomposing them into a well-identified drug and non-drug components and examine how even a small expenditure on those components leads households to a highly insecure or even catastrophic situation.

Despite a smaller geographical coverage of this study, there are some important commonalities between the results presented in this book and the studies cited earlier on the basis of the NSSO's consumption data. Both suggest socio-economic and demographic characteristics of households as important determinants of OOP health expenditure. They also suggest catastrophic threshold level of households in India as much lower than many other Asian countries.

On the question of the threshold limit of catastrophic expenditure, the available literature has no standard limit. It varies from OOP health expenditure above 10 % of the total household expenditure to 0 % in case of the below-poverty households. In our study, we have tried to follow a flexible threshold limit instead of relying on an arbitrary level of either 10 % or more or less.

1.5 Objectives of the Study and Spatial Coverage

As is evident, despite being a country with high economic potential and impressive GDP growth over the recent past, India remains seriously confronted with malfunctioning of its health system with serious implications for low-income rural and urban households, particularly in states and districts where the poverty situation is acute and the shares of population below the designated poverty line have been large. This is largely corroborated from a number of recent studies (Alam 2007; Chaudhury 2005; World Development Report 2004; Berman and

Khan 1993) and surveys with focus on delivery of services in various health domains (NFHS-3, 2005–2006; NSS 60th round, January–June 2004; NSS 52nd round, July 1995–June 1996). These studies also suggest a gradual decline in utilisation of public sector facilities, often on account of dissatisfaction with the service quality (Ager and Pepper 2005; Misra et al. 2003; Babu et al. 2000). This slippage, in other words, implies a growing dependence of households on private medical facilities resulting into disproportionately higher out-of-pocket expenses on diagnostics and other components of medical care. Studies reveal that the poorest 10 % of the country's population rely on sale of their assets or on borrowings to access and meet the cost of medical services (Dilip and Duggal 2002).

Besides generating a whole range of debate around the paucity of public health financing and market failure risks (see the edited volume by Preker and Guy 2004), this whole phenomenon has a number of other important social dimensions as well as significant implications for the well-being of individuals from low-income households. The entire issue becomes further complicated if other medical expenses, in particular the costs of drugs and medicines, are also accounted for.[8] There are apprehensions that the cost of medical drugs is likely to grow further with ongoing changes in drug pricing mechanism (alteration in list of essential drugs and changes in nature of disease mix) and also under the complex regime of patenting and TRIP rights.[9]

Two important documents—the 60th round of the National Sample Survey on Morbidity, Health Care and the Conditions of the Aged (January–June 2004) and the report of the NCMH (September 2005, Ministry of Health and Family Welfare, Government of India)—bring out some of these facts in considerable details. To illustrate, the 60th round of the National Sample Survey (electronic version) clearly reveals very poor utilisation of the health-care facilities provided by the government. Contrasted with earlier findings, these results indicate a significant decline even in utilisation of inpatient facilities offered by the state-run hospitals. The NCMH (September 2005) too has made more or less similar observations,[10] suggesting a disproportionately higher OOP spending on health services by the low-income rural and urban families.

Despite the reverberating nature of these apprehensions and their contributions towards the growing debate on the need for a greater and more effective role of public sector in delivery and financing of health services, the emerging literature has however largely failed to decompose the effects of health expenditure by some of its

---

[8]Reportedly, households in India spend 50 % of their total health expenditure on drugs.

[9]Many believe integration with the global pharmaceutical market will help in acquiring latest technology. It may however increase prices and hinder many from accessing a number of essential drugs, especially in a situation when over 75 % of the drugs in India are outside the price control regime.

[10]See, for example, the Financing and Delivery of Health Care Services in India, National Commission on Macroeconomics and Health, Ministry of Health and Family Welfare, Government of India (August 2005).

major components—diagnostics, medical consultations, drugs or medicine, etc.—on the coping up strategies of rural and urban households in general and those engaged in low-paid casual employment in particular. Several of these issues may be aggravated further if the households are located in high-poverty districts with inadequate income-generating opportunities.

This study was drawn on some of these considerations and designed to examine private household expenditure on treatment of ailing family members by its various components—drugs/medicines, diagnostics and other expenditure items including consultations. In addition, attempts were made to assess the extent of borrowings used to finance medical expenditures and their consequences for households' abilities to meet the basic food and non-food requirements of the family or household members. Opaquely, though, one of the important value additions of this study may also be noticed if judged from the viewpoint of an ever-growing debate in the public policy arena on drug pricing and enlisting of essential medicines commonly used by low-income rural and urban households in the country.

The study focuses more conclusively on the following specific issues:

1. An analysis of the patterns of treatment of short- (past 30 days) and long- (past 365 days) duration morbidity under different socio-economic and ethnic settings. A part of the analysis was also devoted to examine the role of health expenditure in pushing households to fall below the poverty line and face catastrophe— amounting to a significant decline in overall welfare and non-food consumption expenditure of households. There was also concern with regard to the prevalence, intensity and causal risk factors associated with catastrophic health spending of households.
2. An assessment of the total and disaggregated expenditure incurred in treatment of short- and long-duration ailments and the sources used to generate the requisite finances including past savings, asset liquidations, borrowings from moneylenders and assistance drawn from informal support networks.
3. A review of expenditure on the purchase of medical drugs (including life-saving drugs and general medicines) as a proportion of the total health budget for the treatment of short- (without hospitalisation) and long- (hospitalisation) duration ailments. This analysis was basically conducted to derive host of policy options required to reduce OOP health spending and its size. If drug expenses constitute the bulk of private health spending, leading many to face catastrophe, the government has to become more vigilant in terms of its drug pricing policy. Overprescription of medicines and other malpractices may also need attention.
4. Resources mobilised by households to meet medical expenses, especially those on drugs, medicines and other services.
5. If the NRHM has in any way helped in protecting poor households from the adverse economic consequences of illness episodes in rural areas.

The study specially attempted to identify policy interventions to help the low-income rural, urban and slum households during disease episodes and reduce the OOP expenses.

1.5.1   Spatial Coverage

Considering the inadequacy of secondary data sources to examine in depth the nature of health-care services accessed by households of smaller cities or villages at the time of disease incidence and what means do they adopt to meet the cost of these health services, this study was conducted with the help of a comprehensive survey conducted in selected districts of UP and Rajasthan. An attempt was also made to include Delhi as one of the study areas for its wider representation of population from different parts of the country. Further, coverage of Delhi was also considered to help in broadening the scope of this study by a brief review of the situation faced by slum dwellers in a city as significant as Delhi.

The choice of UP and Rajasthan as the states to examine some of the issues highlighted in the preceding section was made on two specific considerations: (i) their higher poverty levels (the real PCMCE in Rajasthan was Rs. 165 in 1995–1996 and grew to Rs. 177 in 2004; the same for UP turns out to be Rs. 143 and Rs. 163, respectively) and (ii) a relatively weaker demographic status (CBR, CDR and e^0 for Rajasthan: 29.0, 9.1 and 63 years in 2001, while for UP it was reported as 31.7, 10.9 and 60.4, respectively). The former has particularly been among the states with weak socio-demographic indicators and many of its districts with a very large fraction of people below the poverty level.

Yet another consideration in selection of these two states was their locational proximity, making data collection and associated logistics simpler. There was also no insurmountable language problem.

1.6   Collection of Primary Data: Survey Design and Selection of Households

This study was conducted largely through a survey in selected districts of UP and Rajasthan considering the inadequacy of town- or village-level data to examine in depth the nature of health-care services accessed at the time of disease incidence by households of different socio-economic denominations, what means they adopt to meet the cost of these health services and the economic ramifications. As was noted, both of these states have not only suffered from higher poverty ratios but they were also stymied because of their poor demographic performance. To complete the regional configuration and also to examine the issues faced especially by the slum households, it was subsequently decided to include the capital city of Delhi as well.

1.6.1   Selection of Study Areas and Sample Design

Confining somewhat narrowly in scope to only the country's northern belt (UP, Rajasthan and Delhi) and also to a predetermined sample size of 2010 rural and urban households, a multistage sampling procedure was adopted for the collection of field data. The PSU remains the household. To begin with, it was decided to select two districts each from both the major states. These districts were chosen on the basis of poverty measurements derived by the Ministry of Rural Development on the basis of its 2002 BPL Survey, using a set of about 13 critical attributes indicating level of deprivation and poverty at the unit level.[11] The same criterion and data source were used to select the districts in both the states.

Of the two districts, one was drawn from the high-poverty population, i.e. from the cluster of districts with more than 50 % population or families above the officially defined poverty norm. The reverse was followed to decide on the second district. To be more precise, the criteria adopted for selection of districts were as below:

District 1:	Selected from the group of districts with more than 50 % population (or families) below officially defined poverty level
	All the districts ranked in descending order and a median district chosen
District 2:	Selected from the group of districts with less than 50 % population (or families) below officially defined poverty level
	All the districts ranked in descending order and a median district chosen

Appendix Tables 1.A.1 and 1.A.2, respectively, provide a list of districts in each state and their corresponding below-poverty populations arranged in descending order. Based on this criterion, a total of four districts were selected from UP and Rajasthan:

UP	High-poverty district:	Unnao (59.5 % below-poverty population)
	Low-poverty district:	Jhansi (29.2 % below-poverty population)
Rajasthan	High-poverty district:	Dungarpur (57.1 % below-poverty families)
	Low-poverty district:	Dausa (17.6 % below-poverty families)

---

[11]Unlike the NSSO, the poverty estimates provided by the Ministry of Rural Development are based on total count data and therefore considered more reliable for application at district or sub-district levels. There are however questions about the adequacy of the deprivation indicators used to decide poverty. Further changes in the list of poverty indicators and methodology are currently in progress.

Fig. 1.7 Circular systematic
sampling procedure

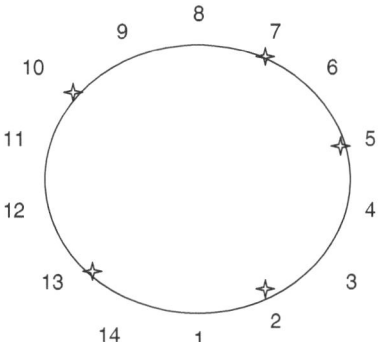

Second stage of the sampling was to select a tehsil (or town) from each of the four identified districts in both the states. These tehsils were later used for selection of villages and urban blocks from where the PSUs of households were drawn.[12] The tehsils were chosen purposively to ensure easier access to the PSUs as the survey was conducted during the peak summer months—April to June 2007—to avoid rains or busy agricultural season and also to minimise the risks of high seasonal diseases.

At the third stage, a set of villages and urban municipal wards was selected from every town by employing a circular systematic sampling (CSS).[13] A total of 5 urban wards and 15 villages from UP and 3 urban wards and 10 villages from Rajasthan were considered to derive the sample households (or PSUs). Finally, a sample of 50 households from each of these villages and urban ward were selected—again by using the CSS method. Figure 1.7 summarises this entire sampling procedure.

1.6.2   Selection of Sample Households: Delhi

Using district-wise shares of population in all the nine Census districts of Delhi, we have distributed a predetermined sample of 360 urban households across the city by covering a little over 28 % of them from the Census-identified slums. The remaining non-slum households combined a mix of all the income categories, social groups and residents from different localities.

---

[12]Towns and villages were drawn on the basis of 2001 Census records.

[13]The circular systematic sampling (CSS) method was suggested as part of the NSS instructions to field workers in 1952 and the NSSO has been using the CSS method since then. This method regards total (N) units of wards, villages or households as arranged around a circle, and consists in choosing a random start from 1 to N instead of from 1 to k, where k is the integral value nearest to N/n, where n is number of sample units. To illustrate, let $N=14$, $n=5$, and k (i.e. N/n) be taken as 3. If random start r ($1 \leq r \leq 14$) is 7, then the sample units with serial numbers 7, 10, 13, 2 and 5 are included. The CSS has two principle advantages: (1) It provides constant sample size; and (2) sample mean remains unbiased estimator of population mean (Murthy 1967). Diagrammatically, this method may be represented as below.

1.6.3   Distribution of the Total Sample

A final distribution of sample households across three different states and identified districts, towns, villages, slums and non-slums is given in Table 1.4 (also see Fig. 1.8). It may be noticed that the biggest share of the predetermined sample of households was assigned to UP because of its size followed by Rajasthan and Delhi. Rural households have received primacy as was expected because of the rural complexion of both the states. The reverse is true for Delhi.

In addition to our own unit-level data from high- and low-poverty districts of the selected states, several secondary data sources, in particular the 60th and 61st rounds of NSS and town and village directories of the Census 2001, were used for the analysis. The NSS reports and the household data obtained from them were used primarily to understand the broader picture and also to check for the accuracies of our own results. We nevertheless agree that the NSS data do not hold for making comparisons at the district or the subdistrict levels.

1.7   Research Questions and Profile of Study Areas

1.7.1   Survey Protocol and Its Issues

A comprehensive, structured and multi-part questionnaire was prepared to collect information from selected rural and urban households (PSUs) in UP, Rajasthan and Delhi. From beginning to end, the entire protocol was divided into 14 different parts, covering almost five major groups of information. These include:

- Socio-economic details of the households and their members including their age–sex profiles, relationship with the head of the household (usually the basic point of consultation), educational attainments, work status, residential characteristics (rural–urban), housing conditions, access to public health facilities, road links with the PHCs, possession of consumer durables and landholdings for agricultural purposes (both arable and fallow).
- Access of households to selected health and non-health facilities run by the government. Some of the questions included in this part of the questionnaire have also been directed to explore—although cursorily—any improvements in delivery of services experienced by households since the inception of the NRHM and the National Rural Employment Guarantee Scheme (NREGS).
- Food and non-food consumption expenditure of the households based on dual reference periods, namely, past 30 days and past 1 year as was usually followed by the NSSO. Attempts have also been made to examine the debt incidence among the sample households, type of moneylenders accessed by them and purpose of borrowings differentiated by taking into consideration events such as health, education, investment and major consumption requirements including

Table 1.4 Distribution of sample households: UP, Rajasthan and Delhi

UP: sample households—1,000		Rajasthan: sample households—650	
250 urban and 750 rural		150 urban and 500 rural	
Urban sample: Unnao	Urban sample: Jhansi	Urban sample: Dungarpur	Urban sample: Dausa
Unnao town (MB) Sample wards=3	Mauranipur town (MB) Sample wards=2	Sagwara town (MB) Sample wards=2	Bandikui town (MB) Sample wards=2
Municipal wards=25	Municipal wards=25	Municipal wards=20	Municipal wards=15
CSS $N/n=25/3$	CSS $N/n=25/2$	CSS $N/n=20/2$	CSS $N/n=15/1$
$K=8$	$K=13$	$K=10$	$K=15$
Sample HHDs=150	Sample HHDs=100	Sample HHDs=100	Sample HHDs=50
Rural sample: Unnao	Rural sample: Jhansi	Rural sample: Dungarpur	Rural sample: Dausa
Unnao tehsil Sample villages=9	Mauranipur tehsil Sample villages=6	Sagwara tehsil Sample villages=5	Baswa tehsil Sample villages=5
Total villages=288	Total villages=152	Total villages=203	Total villages=211
CSS $N/n=288/9$	CSS $N/n=152/6$	CSS $N/n=203/5$	CSS $N/n=211/5$
$K=32$	$K=25$	$K=41$	$K=42$
Sample HHDs=450	Sample HHDs=300	Sample HHDs=250	Sample HHDs=250

Delhi: no. of sample households by Census districts—total HHDs 360 (all urban)

Census districts	Pop. share (%)	No. of slum HHDs	Non-slum HHDs	District total
1. North-West District	18.6	15	52	67
2. North Delhi	5.5	6	14	20
3. North-East District	12.8	14	32	46
4. East Delhi	12.8	18	28	46
5. New Delhi	1.1	1	3	4
6. Central Delhi	4.7	5	12	17
7. West Delhi	15.0	17	37	54
8. South-West Delhi	9.4	1	33	34
9. South Delhi	20.0	25	47	72
Total	100.0	102	258	360

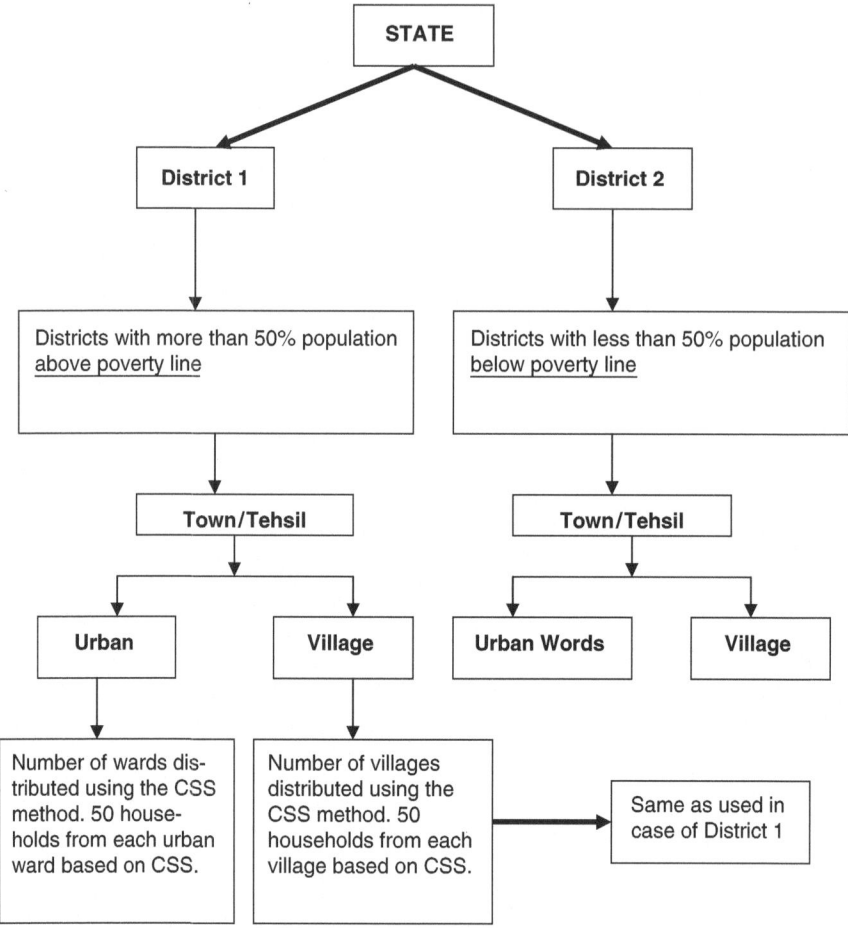

Fig. 1.8 Selection of PSUs in UP and Rajasthan

marriages. All the information was used to examine the poverty status of the households and health catastrophe suffered by them over the period of study. Some attempts have also been made to examine the household transfers to meet the health-care needs of the elderly (65 years or more) family members by sex.

- Disease episodes, both with and without hospitalisation, utilisation of public/ private health facilities, choice of health providers and other related details including itemised health-care expenditure and share of money spent on medicines, diagnostics and so on.
- Last few sections of the survey protocol were devoted to understand the views of the households on measures required to improve the health delivery mechanism in the country by public bodies. These households were also asked to give their views on introduction of a universal and low-premium health insurance system and their participation in such a scheme.

1.7.2   Districts' Profile

1.7.2.1   District Unnao

Situated between the two important cities—Lucknow, a cultural centre, and Kanpur, an industrial city—and flanked by rivers Ganga and Sai, Unnao is a part of central UP with a total population of 27,00,426 in 2001. The district is divided into five tehsils—Unnao, Hasanganj, Safipur, Purwa and Bighapur—and 16 development blocks including Ganj Moradabad, Bangarmau, Fatehpur Chaurasi, Safipur, Miyanganj, Auras, Hasanganj, Nawabganj, Purwa, Asoha, Hilauli, Bighapur, Sumerpur, Bichia, Sikandarpur Sirausi and Sikandarpur Karan. Primarily sustaining on agriculture, about 92 % of the district area is under cultivation.

The district is roughly a parallelogram in shape and lies between latitude 26°8′ N and 27°2′ N and longitude 80°3′ E and 81°3′ E. It is bound on the north by district Hardoi, on the east by district Lucknow, on the south by district Rae Bareli and in the west by the sacred river Ganga which separates it from districts Kanpur and Fatehpur.

1.7.2.2   District Jhansi

Jhansi is another historically significant district of UP and the gateway to economically backward and drought-prone region of Bundelkhand. The area grew in popularity during the reign of the Maratha rulers and its valiant queen Rani Lakshmibai who fought against the Britishers during the 1857 revolt.

Jhansi is the administrative seat of the entire Bundelkhand Division. The famous national highway project of the central government resulted in good economic progress and a reduction in the overall poverty level of the region and the Jhansi district by the end-1990s, but serious drought conditions and the slower pace of the highway project have restored poverty and severe economic strain to the entire region. It was decided to include this district in our analysis because of the rising concern expressed by planning bodies about its poor economic conditions and growing poverty levels.

1.7.2.3   Dausa District

A district of Jaipur Division in north-eastern Rajasthan, Dausa district has a total population of over 1.32 million according to the 2001 Census. Almost a third of this population is completely illiterate. Dausa is bound by several important districts including Alwar, Bharatpur, Karauli and Jaipur—most of them are among the famous tourist destinations of Rajasthan. The entire district is divided into five tehsils—Baswa, Dausa, Lalsot, Mahwa and Sikrai. The Sawa and Ban Ganga rivers run through the district.

Agriculture is the main occupation of the local people, and the main crops grown in the district are wheat, bajra, rapeseed, mustard and groundnuts.

1.7.2.4 Dungarpur District

Dungarpur is situated in the southernmost part of Rajasthan. On the eastern and northern sides of the district are Banswara and Udaipur, respectively. The southern and the western sides adjoin the state of Gujarat. Dungarpur is the smallest district of Rajasthan with a population size of about 1.11 million; more than half this population (i.e. 51.4 %) is illiterate. Most of the district is hilly with poor soil quality. The overall land productivity in the district is, therefore, rated very low with more than 50 % of the families living below the poverty level. The economic situation is slightly better in areas adjoining Gujarat state.

1.7.2.5 Delhi and Its District

The capital city of Delhi, which in many ways holds the status of a full state, is situated in the northern part of India and stands on the west bank of river Yamuna. The city is bound on one side by UP and on the north, west and southern sides by Haryana. Delhi is spread over an area of 1,483 km^2 and has an urban population of about 12.9 million as shown in 2001 Census. A very large proportion of this population is constituted by migrants from nearby states with a sizeable share of them engaged in low-income informal economic activities and residing in scattered slums all across the urban parts of the city.[14] Most of them are without adequate civic facilities, in particular water, power and sewage. Delhi is also the fifth most populated urban area in the world.

As was noted earlier, the entire state of Delhi has officially been divided into nine administrative districts.[15] These districts, further divided into 27 subdivisions, include North, Central, New Delhi, North-East, South, East, North-West, West and South-West; New Delhi (1.1 %) and South Delhi (20 %) are the smallest and the largest in terms of population size, respectively. The survey conducted for this study has attempted to cover all the nine districts and their slums; however, due to very small sample size for a few smaller districts, it was decided to combine them with neighbours to avoid null cells.

Delhi has the advantage of a mixed population originating not only from the neighbouring states but also from most of the country and its regions. The people from neighbouring states however outnumber the rest. This makes Delhi multi-ethnic, multicultural and multilinguistic.

---

[14] Around 16 % of the total population in urban Delhi was residing in slums as reported by the Census 2001 (Census of India 2001, Slum Population, Series – 1, Statement 1.1).

[15] More or less the same geographical distribution was followed for Census purposes as well.

Appendix

Table 1.A.1 Districts by size of BPL population: UP (rural), 2002 (%) used to decide study areas in UP

Districts by share of BPL population: descending order

BPL: 50 % and more		BPL: below 50 %					
1. Kaushambi	74.65	18. Kanpur (Nagar)	49.93	39. Gonda	36.95	60. Hathras	17.91
2. Hardoi	74.00	19. Pratapgarh	49.09	40. Kannauj	35.85	61. Etah	17.26
3. Bahraich	72.11	20. Lucknow	49.06	41. Balrampur	35.69	62. Mathura	16.24
4. Mirzapur	68.38	21. Ghazipur	48.50	42. Azamgarh	32.87	63. Aligarh	14.64
5. Sonbhadra	64.53	22. Jalaun (Orai)	48.34	43. Farukkhabad	32.64	64. Firozabad	13.61
6. Kanpur Dehat	60.87	23. Faizabad	48.22	44. Rampur	31.83	65. Budaun	12.24
7. Shravasti	60.53	24. Basti	47.64	45. Maharajganj	30.76	66. Muzaffarnagar	11.68
8. Unnao	**59.51**	25. Etawah	46.34	46. Lalitpur	30.47	67. Deoria	11.67
9. Ambedkar Nagar	59.15	26. Barabanki	46.15	**47. Jhansi**	**29.19**	68. Bulandshahar	10.34
10. Rae Bareli	57.78	27. S. K. Nagar	45.99	48. Gorakhpur	28.24	69. Meerut	8.38
11. Sitapur	57.46	28. Hamirpur	45.32	49. Allahabad	28.17	70. Ghaziabad	7.12
12. Chitrakoot	55.13	29. Pilibhit	45.23	50. Bareilly	27.50	71. Baghpat	6.66
13. Sultanpur	54.62	30. Jaunpur	43.65	51. Saharanpur	24.56		
14. Shahjahanpur	54.11	31. Mau	43.34	52. J.P. Nagar	24.45		
15. Ballia	51.55	32. Orraiya	43.23	53. Varanasi	24.24		
16. Lakhimpur Kheri	51.01	33. Chandauli	43.10	54. Bijnor	23.67		
		34. Fatehpur	42.77	55. S.R. Nagar	22.74		
		35. Siddharthnagar	42.74	56. Mahoba	21.33		
		36. Kushinagar	42.66	57. Moradabad	19.77		
		37. Mainpuri	42.52	58. Agra	19.43		
		38. Banda	40.85	59. G.B. Nagar	19.00		

Sources: Ministry of Rural Development, Government of India, BPL Survey (2002a); http://www.ansiss.org/doc/seminar2007July20-22/a_k_singh.doc

Table 1.A.2 Share of BPL families by districts: a criterion used to decide study areas in Rajasthan (rural–urban combined), 2002

S. No.	Districts	Percentage of BPL families
District with more than 50 % BPL families		
1	**Dungarpur**	**57.05**
Districts with less than 50 % BPL families		
1	Banswara	45.30
2	Barmer	36.45
3	Udaipur	36.27
4	Bikaner	32.56
5	Jalor	31.59
6	Karauli	27.17
7	Rajsamand	26.10
8	Jaisalmer	25.49
9	Baran	24.09
10	Ganganagar	21.01
11	Sawai Madhopur	18.93
12	Bundi	18.54
13	Hanumangarh	18.10
14	Dhaulpur	17.94
15	Bhilwara	17.92
16	**Dausa**	**17.59**
17	Churu	17.48
18	Jodhpur	17.22
19	Jhalawar	17.09
20	Chittaurgarh	15.73
21	Pali	13.55
22	Sirohi	13.52
23	Bharatpur	13.22
24	Nagaur	11.90
25	Tonk	10.89
26	Kota	10.22
27	Alwar	8.26
28	Jaipur	6.99
29	Sikar	6.31
30	Ajmer	6.03
31	Jhunjhunu	3.39

Source: Ministry of Rural Development, Government of India, BPL Family Survey (2002b)

Cut-off income to decide the BPL population

State	Rural	Urban
Delhi	410.38	612.91
UP	365.84	483.26
Rajasthan	374.57	559.63

References

Ager, A., & Pepper, K. (2005). Patterns of health service utilization and perceptions of needs and services in rural Orissa. *Health Policy and Planning, 20*(3), 176–184. http://heapol.oxford-journals.org/cgi/reprint/20/3/176

Alam, M. (2007, March 28–29). *Ageing, socio-economic disparities and health outcomes: Some evidence on quality of life of rural aged in India.* Paper presented at the 2nd Social Quality Conference hosted by National Taiwan University, Taipei (Taiwan).

Alam, M. (2008). *Ageing, socio-economic disparities and health outcomes: some evidence from rural India* (Institute of Economic Growth, Delhi Working Paper Series No. E/290/2008).

Babu, K. R., Swaminathan, S., Marten, S., Khanna, N., & Rinas, U. (2000). Production of interferon-alpha in high cell density cultures of recombinant *Escherichia coli* and its single step purification from refolded inclusion body proteins. *Applied Microbiology and Biotechnology, 53*, 655–660.

Behrman, J. R., & Deolalikar, A. B. (1988). Health and nutrition. In H. B. Chenery & T. N. Srinivasan (Eds.), *Handbook of development economics* (Ith ed.). Amsterdam: Elsevier Science Publishing Company.

Berman, P., & Khan, M. E. (Eds.). (1993). *Paying for India's health care.* New Delhi: Sage.

Bonu, S., Bhushan, I., & Peters, D. H. (2007, October). *Incidence, intensity and correlates of catastrophic out of pocket health payments in India* (ERD Working Paper No. 102). Asian Development Bank. Downloaded in January 2013. http://www2.adb.org/Documents/ERD/Working_Papers/WP102.pdf

Casanovas, G. L., Rivera, B., & Currais, L. (Eds.). (2005). *Health and economic growth: Findings and policy implications.* Cambridge, MA: The MIT Press.

Census of India. (2001). *Slum population, series – 1.* New Delhi: Office of the Registrar General and Census Commissioner, Ministry of Home Affairs, Government of India.

Chaudhury, S. (2005). *The WTO and India's pharmaceutical industry – Patent protection, TRIPS and developing countries.* New Delhi: Oxford University Press.

Dilip, T. R., & Duggal, R. (2002, December 9–11). *Incidence of non-fatal health outcomes and debt in urban India.* Paper prepared for Urban Research Symposium, Washington, DC, The World Bank.

Dreze, J., & Sen, A. (1995). *India: Economic development and social opportunity.* New Delhi: Oxford University Press.

Fuchs, V. R. (2004). Reflections on socio-economic correlates of health. *Journal of Health Economics, 23*(2004), 653–661.

Garg, C., & Karan, A. K. (2004). *Catastrophic and poverty impact of out-of-pocket expenditure in India: State wise analysis* (Working Paper No. 23). New Delhi: Institute for Human Development.

Garg, C., & Karan, A. K. (2005). Level and pattern of catastrophic health expenditure in India. In P. Sujata & C. Satyamala (Eds.), *Securing health for all: Dimensions and challenges.* New Delhi: Institute for Human Development.

Garg, C., & Karan, A. K. (2009). Reducing out-of-pocket expenditures to reduce poverty: A disaggregated analysis at rural–urban and state level in India. *Health Policy and Planning, 24*(2), 116–128.

GoI. (2000). *National population policy-2000.* New Delhi: Department of Family Welfare, Ministry of Health and Family Welfare, Government of India.

Hammer, L. B., Neal, M. B., Newsom, J., Brockwood, K. J., & Colton, C. (2005). A longitudinal study of the effects of dual-earner couples' utilization of family-friendly workplace supports on work and family outcomes. *Journal of Applied Psychology.*

Kumar, A. K. S., Chen, L.C., Choudhury, M., Ganju, S., Mahajan, V., Sinha, A., & Sen, A. (2011). India: Towards universal health coverage 6: Financing health care for all: Challenges and opportunities. *The Lancet*, www.thelancet.com. Published online January 12, 2011. doi:10.1016/S0140-6736(10)61884-3

Lagomarsino, G., et al. (2012, September 8). Moving towards universal health coverage: Health insurance reforms in nine developing countries in Africa and Asia. *The Lancet, 380*(9845), 933–943.

Ministry of Health and Family Welfare. (2002). *National health policy 2002 (India)*, New Delhi, India. http://www.mohfw.nic.in/NRHM/Documents/National_Health_policy_2002.pdf

Ministry of Health and Family Welfare (MoHFW), Government of India. (2011). *National health profile*. New Delhi: Central Bureau of Health Intelligence, Directorate General of Health Services. pp. 116 & 128.

Ministry of Rural Development, Government of India, BPL Survey. (2002a). http://www.ansiss.org/doc/seminar2007July20-22/a_k_singh.doc

Ministry of Rural Development, Government of India, Total BPL Families, BPL Family Survey. (2002b). http://tempweb225.nic.in/st_rep/st_scst.php?

Misra, R., Chatterjee, R., & Rao, S. (2003). *India health report*. New Delhi: Oxford University Press.

Murthy, M. N. (1967). *Sampling theory and methods*. Calcutta: Statistical Publishing Society.

National Commission on Macro Economics and Health, (2005, August). *Report of the National Commission on Macro Economics and Health*. New Delhi: MoHFW, Government of India.

NSSO. (2004, January–June). *NSS 60th round, morbidity, health care and the condition of the aged* (NSSO, Report No. 507), various statements. New Delhi: Government of India, Ministry of Statistics and Programme Implementation.

O'Donnell, O., van Doorslaer, E., Rannan-Eliya, R., Somanathan, A., Garg, C. C., Hanvoravongchai, P., Huq, M. N., Karan, A., Leung, G. M., Tin, K., & Vasavid, C. (2005). *Explaining the incidence of catastrophic expenditures on health care: Comparative evidence from Asia* (EQUITAP Working Paper #5). Rotterdam/Colombo: Erasmus University/IPS.

Office of Registrar General. (2011, June). *Special bulletin on maternal mortality in India (2007–2009)*. New Delhi: SRS, Office of Registrar General and Census Commissioner, Ministry of Home Affairs, Government of India.

Osmani, S. R. (1992). *Nutrition and poverty*. Oxford: Clarendon.

Preker, A. S., & Guy, C. (Eds.). (2004). *Health financing for poor people, resource mobilisation and risk sharing*. Washington, DC: The World Bank.

Reserve Bank of India (RBI). (2004). *Handbook of statistics on state government finances: 2004*. Mumbai: RBI Publications.

Sakthivel, S., & Karan, A. K. (2009, October). Deepening health insecurity in India: Evidence from national sample surveys since 1980s. *Economic and Political Weekly, XLIV*(40), 55–60.

The World Bank. (2011). *World development indicators*. Washington, DC: The World Bank.

WHO, Department of Measurement and Health Information. (2008, December). http://www.who.int/healthinfo/global_burden_disease/estimates_country/en/index.html. Accessed Oct 2012.

World Development Report. (2004). *Making services work for poor people*. Washington, DC: A co-publication of the World Bank and Oxford University Press.

WHO, Organisation Mondiale de la Sante. Department of Measurement and Health Information. (2004, December). http://www.who.int/healthinfo/statistics/bodgbddeathdalyestimates.xls. Accessed Oct 2012.

World Health Organization. (2008). *Commission on social determinants of health – Final report. Closing the gap in generation: Health equity through action on the social determinants of health*. Geneva: WHO.

Chapter 2
Population Size and Composition of Sample Households

Characteristically, perhaps there may not be too many commonalities to make the three underlying states—UP, Rajasthan and Delhi—mutually comparable. Among the few that make them to a certain extent comparable is that each of these states belongs mostly to the northern belt of the country and they largely remain monolingual with Hindi as the dominant language of daily usage. In most other cases, all the three states are mutually far apart with Delhi being the smallest in terms of population size and UP the largest. Compared to UP and Rajasthan, Delhi provides much better socio-economic opportunities to its residents and has a considerably higher per capita income with better access to medical and public health-care services. These interstate differences are expected to embody the socio-economic and health conditions of individuals and households described in the rest of this or in subsequent chapters.

2.1 Sample Households and Composition of Sample Population

Distribution of households in all the three states and their respective districts is given in Table 2.1. Three locational categories of households have been analysed in the rest of the analysis for their OOP spending on diseases with or without inpatient care. These are, as noted earlier, a total of 1,250 rural and 400 urban households from UP and Rajasthan and 360 households from Delhi. Delhi households were further broken into slums and non-slums with the latter numbering 258 and the remaining 102 were drawn from the identified slums. In all, rural households constituted over 62 % of the total sample while the rest came from slums and non-slums of the urban locations.

Population size, sex and religious composition of the households covered in the study are provided in Table 2.2. While all other distributions in this table are on expected lines, the share of women in the sample of all the four districts in UP and Rajasthan is smaller—implying more men in many of the sample households than

M. Alam, *Paying Out-of-Pocket for Drugs, Diagnostics and Medical Services: A Study of Households in Three Indian States*, India Studies in Business and Economics, DOI 10.1007/978-81-322-1281-2_2, © Springer India 2013

Table 2.1 Distribution of sample households by three reference states and districts

Sample districts and states	Rural		Urban		
	No. of villages	No. of HHDs	No. of urban wards	No. of HHDs	
Unnao	9	450	3	150	
Jhansi	6	300	2	100	
1. UP	15	750	5	250	
Dausa	5	250	1	50	
Dungarpur	5	250	2	100	
2. Rajasthan	10	500	3	150	
			Slums	Non-slums	Total HHDs
West Delhi	–	–	17	37	54
Central Delhi	–	–	5	12	17
South Delhi	–	–	25	47	72
East Delhi	–	–	18	28	46
New Delhi	–	–	1	3	4
North-West	–	–	15	52	67
North Delhi	–	–	6	14	20
South-West	–	–	1	33	34
North-East	–	–	14	32	46
3. Delhi	–	–	102	258	360

Table 2.2 Size and religious composition of sample households

States/ districts	No. of HHDs	Size and sex composition of sample population			Average HHD size	Religion-wise distribution of sample population (%)				
		Persons	Male	Female		Hindu	Muslim	Sikh	Christian	Others
Unnao	600	3,436	53.3	46.7	5.7	92.17	7.67	0.00	0.17	0.00
Rural	450	2,635	53.2	46.8	5.9	91.56	8.44	0.00	0.00	0.00
Urban	150	801	53.8	46.2	5.3	94.00	5.33	0.00	0.00	0.00
Jhansi	400	2,167	52.6	47.4	5.4	83.00	16.75	0.25	0.00	0.00
Rural	300	1,601	52.5	47.5	5.3	84.67	15.33	0.00	0.00	0.00
Urban	100	566	52.8	47.2	5.7	78.00	21.00	1.00	0.00	0.00
UP	1,000	5,603	53.0	47.0	5.6	88.5	11.3	0.10	0.10	0.00
Dausa	300	1,704	52.7	47.3	5.7	91.67	8.33	0.00	0.00	0.00
Rural	250	1,394	52.8	47.2	5.6	94.80	5.20	0.00	0.00	0.00
Urban	50	310	52.3	47.7	6.2	76.00	24.00	0.00	0.00	0.00
D. Pur	350	1,819	52.4	47.6	5.2	92.00	3.71	0.00	0.00	4.29
Rural	250	1,311	52.3	47.7	5.2	99.60	0.40	0.00	0.00	0.00
Urban	100	508	52.8	47.2	5.1	73.00	12.00	0.00	0.00	15.00
Rajasthan	650	3,523	52.6	47.4	5.4	92.00	3.71	0.00	0.00	4.29
Slum	102	569	47.5	52.5	5.6	74.50	24.50	0.00	1.00	0.00
Non-slum	258	1,368	52.3	47.7	5.3	89.53	4.65	3.49	1.94	0.39
Delhi	360	1,937	50.9	49.1	5.4	85.27	10.28	2.50	1.67	0.28

Table 2.3 Share of different social groups in sample population (%)

Districts/states	Social groups				
	SC	ST	OBC	Others	Total
UP	*23.90*	*2.60*	*51.70*	*21.80*	100
Unnao	23.00	0.17	55.50	21.33	100
Jhansi	25.25	6.25	46.00	22.50	100
Rajasthan	*20.46*	*33.08*	*29.23*	*17.23*	100
Dausa	29.67	30.00	34.67	5.67	100
Dungarpur	12.57	35.71	24.57	27.14	100
Delhi	*23.06*	*2.22*	*19.44*	*55.28*	100
Slums	35.29	3.92	21.57	39.22	100
Non-slum	18.22	1.55	18.6	61.63	100
Total sample	22.64	12.39	38.66	26.32	100

women. The slum households of Delhi are however the only exception where women constitute over 52 % of the sample. In a situation of growing male migration, these results may look somewhat arbitrary. They however match fairly closely with the Census figures for 2001.

Hindus dominate the overall distribution of the sample population followed by the Muslims. Sikhs are only visible in Delhi. No other religion seems to have any significant presence in study areas selected from UP and Rajasthan. In terms of social groups, the sample represents the low and the backward castes (SC and OBC) fairly well; the former, for example, turns out to be over a fifth (22.6 %) of the total sample while the latter is nearly double of that (38.7 %) (see Table 2.3). The share of upper castes in the sample is relatively much smaller in Dausa (Rajasthan) due to the primacy of the lower castes and STs in the region. As a whole, however, the upper castes constitute around a fourth of the total sample (Table 2.3).

2.2   Age–Sex Distribution of Sample Population, Average Household Size and Nuclearisation of Families: Rural and Urban Areas

Age distribution of the sample population in all the districts (Table 2.4, panel 1) reinforces the pattern observed for most of the country with very high share of working age populations in the 15–59 years age group, implying a large-scale pressure of jobseekers in the coming years on the clearance mechanism of the labour market. As the current economic regime in the country is either incapable of creating adequate employment opportunities for such a high proportion of a billion plus population or capable of creating new opportunities only in low-wage informal economy, the issues of poverty, working poor and income inequalities are likely to be more commonly

Table 2.4 Age distribution of sample population by districts and states (%)

Districts/state	0–4	5–14	15–24	25–39	40–59	60 and more	Total
Panel 1: age distribution by districts							
UP	9.46	23.93	20.92	21.22	17.15	7.32	100.0
Unnao	9.14	24.56	21.57	20.58	17.05	7.10	100.0
Jhansi	9.97	22.93	19.89	22.24	17.31	7.66	100.0
Chi2 (6)=6.615; Pr.=0.358							
Rajasthan	9.42	24.55	20.92	22.17	16.80	6.13	100.0
Dausa	8.57	25.35	22.59	20.25	17.14	6.10	100.0
Dungarpur	10.23	23.80	19.35	23.97	16.49	6.16	100.0
Chi2 (6)=14.240; Pr.=0.027							
Delhi	8.42	20.39	21.48	22.20	19.51	8.00	100.0
Non-slum	7.16	18.13	19.96	23.90	21.35	9.50	100.0
Slum	11.42	25.83	25.13	18.10	15.11	4.39	100.0
Chi2 (6)=52.577; Pr.=0.000							
Panel 2: age distribution of sample population by rural and urban							
Unnao (UP)							
Rural	9.94	26.41	21.25	19.77	15.94	6.68	100.0
Urban	6.49	18.48	22.6	23.22	20.72	8.49	100.0
Total	9.14	24.56	21.57	20.58	17.05	7.1	100.0
Chi2 (5)=38.904; Pr.=0.000							
Jhansi (UP)							
Rural	9.93	23.92	19.80	21.61	17.05	7.68	100.0
Urban	10.07	20.14	20.14	24.03	18.02	7.60	100.0
Total	9.97	22.93	19.89	22.24	17.31	7.66	100.0
Chi2 (5)=3.969; Pr.=0.554							
Dausa (Raj)							
Rural	8.25	25.47	22.96	19.44	17.50	6.38	100.0
Urban	10.00	24.84	20.97	23.87	15.48	4.84	100.0
Total	8.57	25.35	22.59	20.25	17.14	6.10	100.0
Chi2 (5)=5.445; Pr.=0.364							
Dungarpur (Raj)							
Rural	10.60	24.41	19.76	22.88	15.64	6.71	100.0
Urban	9.25	22.24	18.31	26.77	18.70	4.72	100.0
Total	10.23	23.80	19.35	23.97	16.49	6.16	100.0
Chi2 (5)=8.515; Pr.=0.130							
Social groups Panel 3: age distribution of sample population by social groups							
SC	9.56	24.85	22.09	20.23	16.59	6.67	100.0
ST	10.29	28.36	20.28	21.09	15.14	4.85	100.0
OBC	9.43	23.91	21.66	21.59	16.9	6.5	100.0
High caste	8.24	19.33	19.4	23.47	20.22	9.34	100.0
Total	9.27	23.51	21.02	21.69	17.45	7.06	100.0
Chi2 (15)=105.604; Pr.=0.000							

prevalent in many of the areas under study.[1] OOP expenses on health and inadequate health provisioning obviously are of a much serious concern under these settings. Some of these issues are examined in the next few chapters of this study.

---

[1] For interesting discussions on some of these issues, see Rodgers (2007), Chakravarty and Mitra (2009), Carr and Chen (2004), and RoyChowdhury (2007), etc.

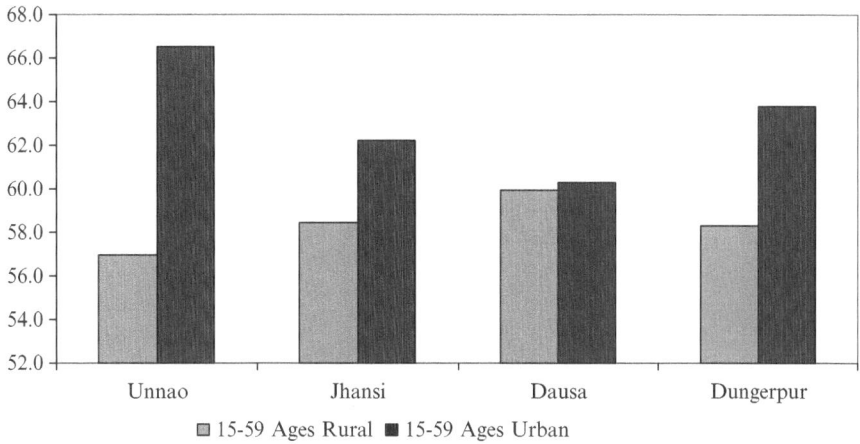

Fig. 2.1 Rural–urban differences in shares of working age population (*Source*: Table 2.4, panel 2)

Another notable observation stemming from panel 2 of Table 2.4 (see also Fig. 2.1) relates to the differentials in rural–urban age composition of populations. The higher proportions of 15–59 populations in all the four urban locations (Fig. 2.1) are indicative of the following: (i) There appears to be quite a high degree of migration to cities by working age rural people of the areas under review, and (ii) the pattern of age distribution given in Table 2.4 (panel 2) is indicative of the pattern of health-care services required in areas under study. A higher proportion of 15–59 population may, inter alia, bring greater demand for reproductive and childcare services. Similarly, a growing proportion of the older persons (considered in this analysis as those aged 60 or over) may press for geriatric services required for treatment of older persons. Significance of χ^2 in several cases indicates location (i.e. rural/urban) and caste (see panel 3 of Table 2.4) as influencing factors to bring differentials in age composition of populations.

From the viewpoint of living arrangement, India is fast moving towards becoming a nuclear household society, and this has emerged from various data sources including the National Family Health Survey (NFHS-3) conducted across the country in 2005–2006 (National Family Health Survey 2007). The NFHS-3 revealed that 60.5 % of the households at the all-India level were nuclear and only the remaining 40.5 % were either multigenerational or constituted by other forms of households. What was, however, to some extent surprising is that states like UP and Rajasthan, generally considered as traditional with older values still in practice, are also becoming dominantly nuclear with families comprising parents and dependent children. This may be noticed from Table 2.5 and its two graphs shown in Figs. 2.2 and b. UP appears to be more nuclear than Rajasthan, though a more definitive argument cannot be made based on this data. On hindsight, however, it appears that irrespective of location, families are changing their traditional roles and turning to participate more in income-generating

Table 2.5 Type of sample households (%)

Type of households	Unnao			Jhansi			Dausa			Dungarpur			Delhi		
	Rural	Urban	Total	Rural	Urban	Total	Rural	Urban	Total	Rural	Urban	Total	Slum	Non-slum	Total
Single member	2.2	3.3	2.5	1.0	0.0	0.8	2.4	0.0	2.0	4.0	1.0	3.1	2.3	1.0	1.9
Nuclear	70.4	59.3	67.7	64.7	75.0	67.3	62.4	52.0	60.7	61.6	66.0	62.9	59.7	81.4	65.8
Multigenerational	24.4	36.0	27.3	30.7	20.0	28.0	32.0	44.0	34.0	32.4	32.0	32.3	36.4	16.7	30.8
Multifamilies	2.9	1.3	2.5	3.7	5.0	4.0	3.2	4.0	3.3	2.0	1.0	1.7	1.6	1.0	1.4
Total	100	100	100	100	100	100	100	100	100	100	100	100	100	100	100
	Chi2(3)=9.193			Chi2(3)=5.572			Chi2(3)=3.788			Chi2(3)=2.686			Chi2(3)=15.336		
	Pr.=0.027			Pr.=0.134			Pr.=0.285			Pr.=0.443			Pr.=0.002		
Female-headed HHDs (%)	7.0	8.7	7.5	4.7	4.0	4.5	8.0	6.0	7.7	7.2	7.0	7.1	10.8	10.9	10.8

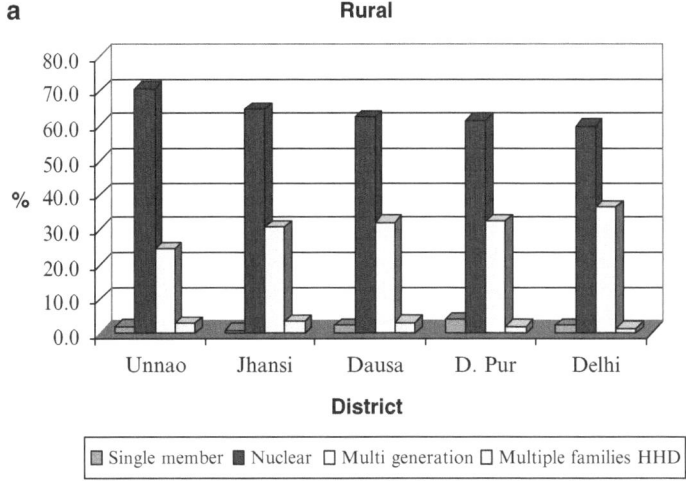

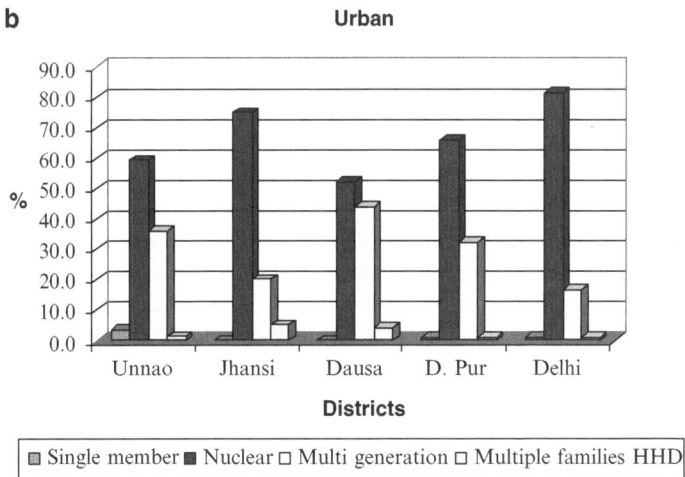

Fig. 2.2 (**a**) Type of households: rural (*Source*: Table 2.5). (**b**) Type of households: urban (*Source*: Table 2.5)

activities. This may however pose many serious questions including the one that arises from the growing need for elderly care or caring for the sick and disabled family members.

Average size of the sample households stood between five and six with the lowest (5.3) relating to the non-slum urban households in Delhi (Table 2.2). The share of female-headed households is also relatively higher in Delhi (Table 2.5), though a big majority of them come from the loner (or one person) households.

Appendix

Table 2.A.1 Distribution of sample populations in Delhi: slum and non-slum households

Districts	Sample population: non-slum			Sample population: slums		
	Male	Female	Total	Male	Female	Total
West Delhi	14.0	14.3	14.1	15.9	12.0	13.9
Central Delhi	4.9	4.4	4.7	5.9	3.0	4.4
South Delhi	18.0	17.6	17.8	24.8	24.4	24.6
East Delhi	11.3	11.3	11.3	17.0	18.7	17.9
New Delhi	1.0	1.2	1.1	1.1	1.3	1.2
North-West Delhi	20.5	21.0	20.8	13.3	14.0	13.7
North Delhi	6.3	5.5	5.9	7.0	9.4	8.3
South-West Delhi	10.1	11.3	10.7	1.1	0.7	0.9
North-East Delhi	14.0	13.2	13.6	13.7	16.4	15.1
Total Delhi (Nos.)	716	652	1,368	270	299	569

Source: Author's Survey on OOP Health Expenditure (2008)

References

Carr, M., & Chen, M. (2004). *Globalization, social exclusion and work: with special reference to informal employment.* World Commission on the Social Dimension of Globalization, Background Paper (Policy Integration Department Working Paper No. 20). Geneva: International Labour Organization (ILO).

Chakravarty, S., & Mitra, A. (2009). Is industry still the engine of growth? An econometric study of the organized sector employment in India. *Journal of Policy Modelling, 35*, 22–35.

National Family Health Survey (2005–2006). (2007, September). National Family Health Survey (NFHS-3) (Vol. 1, p. 23). International Institute for Population Sciences (Mumbai) and Macro International.

Rodgers, G. (2007). Decent work, social inclusion and development. *Indian Journal of Human Development, 1*, 21–32.

RoyChowdhury, S. (2007). Informality in globalized from of production. *The Indian Journal of Labour Economics, 50*(4), 765–774.

Chapter 3
Socio-economic Variations, Consumption Poverty and Health-Generated Inequalities in Sample Population

3.1 Socio-economic Characteristics of Sample Population

The preceding chapter has highlighted a few socio-demographic attributes of the sample households drawn from selected districts or subdistricts (also known as tehsils) in UP, Rajasthan and Delhi. It was noticed from the analysis of these attributes that the capital city of Delhi has certain advantages over the rest, although there appear to be some notable differences between its slum and non-slum households. The two, for example, differed largely in terms of sex distributions. To be more specific, of all the locations and districts covered in the study, a higher fraction of female population may only be noticed in the slum households in Delhi. In addition, the share of their youth population in the 15–24 age groups is also relatively higher, indicating certain differentials in their fertility behaviour with the rest of the sample.

All along these spatial differentials, there is another interesting phenomenon emanating from the same discussion, i.e. a large spread and abounding nuclearisation of families even in villages of UP and Rajasthan where many traditional values are still in vogue. This phenomenon of fast-growing changes in family norms and erosion of traditional forms of living may cause difficulties to many, especially while coping with serious family matters such as prolonged ailments or long-term care provisioning for the aged, diseased or functionally disabled. There may be added complexities if the households and its members are also goaded with poor literacy levels, lack of participation in remunerative economic activities and poor consumption levels and forced to rely on their own to meet expenses arising out of unexpected events like ailments and medications. We try to examine some of these issues focusing on sample of populations described in the preceding chapter. A great deal of this chapter is particularly devoted to discuss overall and health-driven poverty among the sample population.

M. Alam, *Paying Out-of-Pocket for Drugs, Diagnostics and Medical Services: A Study of Households in Three Indian States*, India Studies in Business and Economics, DOI 10.1007/978-81-322-1281-2_3, © Springer India 2013

3.1.1   Educational Status of Sample Population

The educational distribution of sample population in Table 3.1 does in no way contribute to the feelings of any marked improvement over past few decades in social status of populations in districts of both the major states under consideration. The same may as well be true for the slum households in Delhi.

Admittedly, while none of these samples are representative in character and may not therefore be used to make generalisations, there is indeed an indication that a very large percentage of people in smaller towns and low-income residential areas of places like Delhi are either illiterate or semi-literate with their educational attainments perhaps not adequate to prevent poor health and poverty. Table 3.1 brings out these facts very clearly. Broadly, about a third of the total sample population (i.e. between 30 and 36 %) in most of these places is shown as completely illiterate with the highest level of illiteracy being found among the slum residents in Delhi. Another 50 % of them are below matriculate with a large fraction being simply educated up to the primary level or even less. Only about a twentieth of the total respondents were holding a degree from higher educational institutions. There was also a very small fraction of respondents in all the three states with a degree or diploma in professional courses (Table 3.1).

Another significant but a long-drawn observation stemming from Table 3.1 relates to a considerably higher gender gap in levels of educational attainment. That the sex of an individual does have a role in educational attainment is clearly evident from the chi2 test as well (see χ^2 values in Table 3.1).

The usual rural–urban divide in terms of educational status of populations has remained clearly visible from our sample as well, with residents living in urban areas being better educated than their rural counterparts. These details are given in an Appendix Table both for the entire sample and for two major states under consideration. Like sex, individuals' place of residence is also an important source of differentials in educational status, and the χ^2 values in Appendix Table 3.A.1 reflect this significantly.

Indeed, while most of what has been described in the preceding discussion may not look different from many other studies or help to find an out-of-the-box solution to these long-drawn and well-recognised issues (see, e.g. Probe Team Report 1999; Shah and Rani 2003; Dreze and Murthi 2001), they may nevertheless prove as a marker to substantiate the argument that the country and its planning bodies may not be able to do much in terms of health as long as states like UP and Rajasthan—with a considerably high weightage in country's overall population—remain educationally weak. In addition, the current regime of the NRHM, believed to work wonders in improving the health status of rural people, may or may not go beyond a certain limit. A more holistic regime covering postprimary education and all other health domains beyond reproductive health may need to be developed.

Table 3.1 Literacy level of sample populations (%)

Educational level	Unnao			Jhansi		
	Male	Female	Total	Male	Female	Total
Panel 1: UP						
Illiterate	23.7	41.7	32.1	22.9	45.0	33.4
Lit. without formal education	2.1	2.0	2.0	2.4	1.0	1.7
Up to 5th standard (primary)	34.5	27.8	31.4	28.4	28.3	28.4
7th–8th standard (middle)	17.7	13.7	15.8	23.8	13.7	19.0
Matriculate	9.7	6.1	8.0	8.7	5.1	7.0
Higher secondary	5.7	4.9	5.3	6.5	3.7	5.2
Graduates and above	5.6	3.2	4.5	6.0	3.0	4.6
Diploma/certificate	0.6	0.2	0.4	1.1	0.2	0.7
Degree in technical/professional education	0.4	0.4	0.4	0.2	0.0	0.1
Total literacy level	76.3	58.3	67.9	77.1	55.0	66.6
Literate + illiterate	100.0	100.0	100.0	100.0	100.0	100.0
Chi-sq. (9)	Chi-sq. (9) = 136.421; Pr. = 0.000			Chi-sq. (9) = 153.224; Pr. = 0.000		

	Dausa			Dungarpur		
	Male	Female	Total	Male	Female	Total
Panel 2: Rajasthan						
Illiterate	21.2	49.4	34.5	22.9	38.8	30.5
Lit. without formal education	1.0	1.0	1.0	1.6	2.4	2.0
Up to 5th standard (primary)	28.6	28.6	28.5	30.3	28.2	29.3
7th–8th standard (middle)	27.3	15.4	21.7	19.3	14.7	17.1
Matriculate	11.8	4.5	8.3	10.1	7.9	9.0
Higher secondary	5.5	0.9	3.3	6.9	4.2	5.6
Graduates and above	4.5	0.3	2.5	6.6	3.0	4.9
Diploma/certificate	0.1	0.0	0.1	0.4	0.0	0.2
Degree in technical/professional education	0.2	0.1	0.2	2.0	0.8	1.4
Total literacy level	78.8	50.6	65.5	77.1	61.2	69.5
Literate + illiterate	100.0	100.0	100.0	100.0	100.0	100.0
Chi-sq. (9)	Chi-sq. (9) = 212.086; Pr. = 0.000			Chi-sq. (9) = 74.900; Pr. = 0.000		

	Non-slum			Slum		
	Male	Female	Total	Male	Female	Total
Panel 3: Delhi						
Illiterate	9.5	19.6	14.3	25.9	44.5	35.7
Lit. without formal education	0.4	1.4	0.9	1.5	1.3	1.4
Up to 5th standard (primary)	25.2	20.7	23.1	43.3	39.2	41.1
7th–8th standard (middle)	13.0	11.5	12.3	15.2	9.4	12.1
Matriculate	15.5	13.0	14.3	9.3	4.4	6.7
Higher secondary	11.9	12.0	11.9	3.3	1.0	2.1
Graduates and above	16.8	16.7	16.7	1.5	0.3	0.9
Diploma/certificate	1.0	1.5	1.2	0.0	0.0	0.0
Degree in technical/professional education	6.8	3.5	5.3	0.0	0.0	0.0
Total literacy level	90.5	80.4	85.7	74.1	55.5	64.3
Literate + illiterate	100.0	100.0	100.0	100.0	100.0	100.0
	Chi2 (9) = 41.068; Pr. = 0.000			Chi2 (7) = 38.386; Pr. = 0.000		

3.1.2 Work Status of Sample Population

Functional status of the sample population has been obtained by going into the following details. Initially, all the respondents were asked to provide their activity status, namely, working or nonworking. Those who reported working were again classified into 'main' and 'marginal' workers—with the former including men and women engaged physically or mentally in certain income generating activities for most of the year (those with a lesser duration of paid work were categorised as marginal workers). Finally, all the workers were regrouped into (i) regular workers, (ii) casual workers with uncertain length of employment, (iii) those working on their own or engaged in small family enterprises and (iv) persons employed under the centrally administered National Rural Employment Guarantee Scheme (NREGS).

Drawing upon the criteria noted above, functional status of the sample population is described in the rest of this discussion with two specific points to be highlighted clearly. First, the results of this analysis suggest a somewhat lower activity status of the population under reference; however, in several cases, it matches fairly closely with the Census figures obtained for corresponding districts in 2001 Census (see Appendix Table 3.A.2). And second, the female activity status in our case appears to be at a lower side and may therefore be an underestimate. Such issues however arise in surveys focusing on nonlabour issues.

It appears from the figures given in Table 3.2 that less than a third of the total sample population in majority of cases is economically active with considerable gender differentials. Barring Dungarpur in Rajasthan, nowhere the shares of working women exceed over 13 % of their reported total population. With almost a quarter of the total women engaged in one or the other economic activities, Dungarpur has indeed remained distinct from all other districts under the study (Table 3.2). The χ^2 values also indicate gender as an important distinguishing factor between men and women in their functional status.

Unlike gender, place of residence apparently plays hardly any significant role in pushing families and households to become economically more engaged. The figures given in Table 3.3 do not show too many major differences in activity status of rural and urban households recruited from different districts/tehsils. Barring Dungarpur where differentials in activity status between rural and urban areas are considerably large (see panel 1 of Table 3.3), there is no similar example from any other places covered in the study. In all other cases, the observed differentials remained marginal. This is true for the slums and non-slums in Delhi as well.

A distribution of sample population into four social groups—SC, ST, OBC and high castes—reveals that the highest fraction of 'working' people belonged to the ST category with more than 35 % of them having reported themselves as economically active (panel 3, Table 3.3). The rest three (in particular SC and OBC) were significantly behind, and the size of their working males and females was in the vicinity of 30–31 % of their respective populations.

Table 3.2 Activity status of sample population ($N = 11{,}063$) (%)

Activity status	UP (Unnao + Jhansi)			Unnao			Jhansi		
	Male	Female	Total	Male	Female	Total	Male	Female	Total
Working	49.1	7.7	29.6	48.3	7.0	29.1	50.2	8.9	30.6
Not working	50.9	92.3	70.4	51.7	93.0	71.0	49.8	91.2	69.4
Total	100.0	100.0	100.0	100.0	100.0	100.0	100.0	100.0	100.0
N (number)	2,972	2,631	5,603	1,833	1,603	3,436	1,139	1,028	2,167
Chi2	1.1E+03	Pr.	0.0E+00	709.444	Pr.	0.000	435.442	Pr.	0.000

Activity status	Rajasthan (Dausa + Dungarpur)			Dausa			Dungarpur		
	Male	Female	Total	Male	Female	Total	Male	Female	Total
Working	48.2	16.3	33.1	45.6	8.1	27.8	50.6	24.1	38.0
Not working	51.8	83.7	66.9	54.5	91.9	72.2	49.4	76.0	62.0
Total	100.0	100.0	100.0	100.0	100.0	100.0	100.0	100.0	100.0
N (number)	1,852	1,671	3,523	898	806	1,704	954	865	1,819
Chi2	402.014	Pr.	0.000	297.182	Pr.	0.000	136.084	Pr.	0.000

Activity status	Delhi (slum + non-slum)			Slum			Non-slum		
	Male	Female	Total	Male	Female	Total	Male	Female	Total
Working	48.4	11.7	30.4	49.3	10.0	28.7	48.0	12.4	31.1
Not working	51.6	88.3	69.6	50.7	90.0	71.4	52.0	87.6	68.9
Total	100.0	100.0	100.0	100.0	100.0	100.0	100.0	100.0	100.0
N (number)	986	951	1,937	270	299	569	716	652	1,368
Chi2	3.1E+02	Pr.	0.000	106.802	Pr.	0.000	202.194	Pr.	0.000

About three-quarters (74.2 %) of the working males have reported themselves as the main workers—implying they had paid employment for about 180 days or more during most of the preceding 12 months. The rest however failed to meet this criterion and reported being unemployed for a greater part of the year. They were therefore considered as marginal workers (Table 3.4, panel 1). Women, as usual, suffered from double jeopardy; only a fewer of them were working, and those working were mostly in low-quality unskilled employment (panel 2, Table 3.4).

A considerably large fraction of the unskilled employment created under the NREGA September 2005 to improve livelihood conditions of rural households has seemingly gone to women, especially in both districts of Rajasthan. In contrast, however, a bulk of employed women in UP is engaged in highly unsecure casual employment. In addition, they were also reportedly working in small home-based activities as self-employed or were own-account workers. Both underscore the earlier argument, suggesting women being a lower partner in economic well-being.

In addition to women, many of those engaged in lower category employment invariably comprise persons from the lower echelons of the caste hierarchy including the SC (29.7 % in regular employment and the rest as casuals, self-employed or NREGS-created activities), ST (16.6 % in regular employment) and OBC (23 % in regular employment) (Table 3.4, panel 3).

Table 3.3 Activity status of sample population by rural–urban and social groups

Analytical variables	Working (%)	Not working (%)	Row total (%)	N (number)	Chi2 Value	Pr.
Panel 1: rural–urban						
Unnao						
Rural	28.7	71.3	100.0	2,635	0.550	0.458
Urban	30.1	69.9	100.0	801		
Jhansi						
Rural	31.4	68.6	100.0	1,601	1.668	0.197
Urban	28.5	71.6	100.0	566		
UP total	29.6	70.4	100.0	5,603		
Dausa						
Rural	28.2	71.8	100.0	1,394	0.538	0.463
Urban	26.1	73.9	100.0	310		
Dungarpur						
Rural	40.6	59.4	100.0	1,311	13.386	0.000
Urban	31.3	68.7	100.0	508		
Rajasthan total	33.07	66.93	100.0	3,523		
Delhi slum	28.7	71.3	100.0	569	1.114	0.291
Delhi non-slum	31.1	68.9	100.0	1,368		
Delhi total	30.4	69.6	100.0	1,937		
Panel 2: total sample (UP, Rajasthan and Delhi) by sex and rural–urban						
Male	48.7	51.3	100.0	5,810	1.8e+03	0.000
Female	11.2	88.8	100.0	5,253	DF (1)	
Male–female combined	30.9	69.1	100.0	11,063		
Rural	31.5	68.5	100.0	6,941	3.202	0.074
Urban	29.8	70.2	100.0	2,185		
Rural–urban combined	30.9	69.1	100.0	11,063		
Panel 3: social groups						
Scheduled caste (SC)	30.2	69.8	100.0	2,531	17.687	0.001
Scheduled tribe (ST)	35.5	64.5	100.0	1,361	DF (3)	
Other backward (OBC)	29.6	70.4	100.0	4,367		
Upper caste (HC)	31.2	68.8	100.0	2,804		

DF degrees of freedom

3.1.3 Nonworking Population

Table 3.5 presents a few important underlying factors responsible for a big majority of the respondents to be out of the workforce. One of the most significant factors keeping a big majority of the younger population out of workforce is the participation in educational activities. It turns out to be the case in all the districts including slums and non-slums. It may however be interesting to note a big gender gap in reporting education as a reason for non-participation in labour force activities. Also, this gap exists irrespective of the places under study and includes even households from the non-slum areas of Delhi. Another dominant reason for not being able to

Table 3.4 Categorisation of workers and nature of activities: gender, rural–urban and social groups

	Type of workers			Nature of work			
Analytical variables	Total workers	Main workers	Marginal workers	Regular	Casual	Own account[a]	NREGS[b]
Panel 1: total sample							
Total sample	3,414	74.2	25.8	29.1	35.6	7.7	27.7
Male	2,827	80.4	19.6	29.5	38.3	30.3	1.9
Female	587	44.3	55.7	26.9	22.2	15.3	35.6
Rural	2,184	63.4	36.6	18.5	45.0	24.6	12.0
Urban	1,230	93.4	6.6	47.9	18.8	33.3	0.1
Panel 2: distribution by gender and place of residence							
Unnao							
Male	886	73.1	26.9	24.5	35.3	2.3	37.9
Female	112	49.1	50.9	29.5	42.0	0.0	28.6
Chi2	27.576	Pr.	0.000	Chi2 (3)	7.082	Pr.	0.069
Rural	757	64.9	35.1	17.8	40.4	39.1	2.6
Urban	241	88.0	12.0	47.7	22.4	29.9	0.0
Jhansi							
Male	572	75.9	24.1	12.2	56.3	30.4	1.1
Female	91	46.2	53.9	17.6	61.5	17.6	3.3
Chi2	34.246	Pr.	0.000	Chi2 (3)	9.544	Pr.	0.023
Rural	502	67.3	32.7	10.8	64.7	22.7	1.8
Urban	161	85.7	14.3	19.9	32.9	47.2	0.0
Dausa							
Male	409	74.8	25.2	20.8	56.5	22.3	0.5
Female	65	23.1	76.9	10.8	20.0	6.2	63.1
Chi2	68.685	Pr.	0.000	Chi2 (3)	266.832	Pr.	0.000
Rural	393	64.1	35.9	19.3	54.5	15.3	10.9
Urban	81	85.2	14.8	19.8	37.0	43.2	0.0
D. Pur							
Male	483	85.9	14.1	40.2	32.5	22.4	5.0
Female	208	18.3	81.7	12.0	3.4	5.3	79.3
Chi2	294.697	Pr.	0.000	Chi2 (3)	406.866	Pr.	0.000
Rural	532	56.9	43.1	25.9	25.9	12.6	35.5
Urban	159	94.3	5.7	50.9	16.4	32.7	0.0
Slum							
Male	133	96.2	3.8	45.9	27.8	25.6	0.8
Female	30	100.0	0.0	43.3	13.3	43.3	0.0
Total	163	96.9	3.1	45.4	25.2	28.8	0.6
Chi2 (1)	0.164	Pr.	0.281	Chi2 (3)	4.983	Pr.	0.173
Non-slum							
Male	344	99.4	0.6	60.2	7.0	32.9	0.0
Female	81	98.8	1.2	79.0	3.7	17.3	0.0
Total	425	99.3	0.7	63.8	6.4	29.9	0.0
Chi2 (1)	0.399	Pr.	0.528	Chi2 (3)	10.070	Pr.	0.007

(continued)

Table 3.4 (continued)

Analytical variables	Type of workers			Nature of work			
	Total workers	Main workers	Marginal workers	Regular	Casual	Own account[a]	NREGS[b]
Panel 3: distribution by social groups							
Social group							
SC	764	72.0	28.0	29.7	44.6	19.5	6.2
ST	483	53.2	46.8	16.6	49.1	9.1	25.3
OBC	1,292	73.3	26.7	23.0	38.2	33.8	5.0
UC	875	89.0	11.0	44.3	16.3	36.1	3.2
Total	3,414	74.2	25.8	29.1	35.6	27.7	7.7
Chi2 (3)	214.143	Pr.	0.000	Chi2 (9)	598.717	Pr.	0.000

[a]Including those working in family businesses
[b]Persons employed under the NREGS

Table 3.5 Distribution of nonworking population by states and districts (%)

	Unnao			Jhansi		
	Males	Females	Both	Males	Females	Both
Retired	4.5	1.9	2.9	1.6	0.1	0.7
Weak, frail, disabled, mentally weak	4.0	2.3	3.0	6.9	2.8	4.3
Students	57.1	30.9	41.1	58.1	27.4	39.0
Unemployed	11.9	8.5	9.8	8.5	4.9	6.3
Housewives	0.2	44.3	27.2	0.2	48.5	30.3
Non-school-going children	21.5	11.5	15.4	21.7	13.3	16.5
Others/voluntarily unemployed	0.6	0.6	0.6	3.0	3.0	3.0
N	947	1,491	2,438	566	937	1,503
Chi2 (8)	577.408, Pr. 0.000			406.016, Pr. 0.000		
	Dausa			**Dungarpur**		
Retired	1.6	0.4	0.9	3.0	0.2	1.3
Weak, frail, disabled, mentally weak	6.6	4.5	5.3	4.3	4.0	4.1
Students	66.6	30.9	45.1	59.7	35.2	45.4
Unemployed	5.1	6.9	6.2	5.9	4.0	4.8
Housewives	0.2	46.4	28.1	0.0	40.8	23.8
Non-school-going children	19.3	10.1	13.8	27.0	13.4	19.1
Others/voluntarily unemployed	0.6	0.8	0.7	0.2	2.6	1.6
N	488	741	1,229	471	657	1,128
Chi2 (8)	340.051, Pr. 0.000			284.681 Pr. 0.000		
	Delhi slum			**Delhi non-slum**		
Retired	1.5	0.4	0.7	8.6	2.1	4.67
Weak, frail, disabled, mentally weak	4.3	1.9	2.7	1.9	0.4	1.0
Students	54.4	28.6	37.4	64.8	30.1	43.8
Unemployed	15.9	9.7	11.8	5.1	4.0	4.5
Housewives	0.7	33.8	22.6	0.3	44.0	26.7
Non-school-going children	21.0	19.0	19.7	13.2	8.8	10.5
Others/voluntarily unemployed	2.2	6.7	5.2	6.2	10.7	8.9
N	138	269	407	372	571	943
Chi2 (8)	71.772, Pr. 0.000			259.581, Pr.0.000		

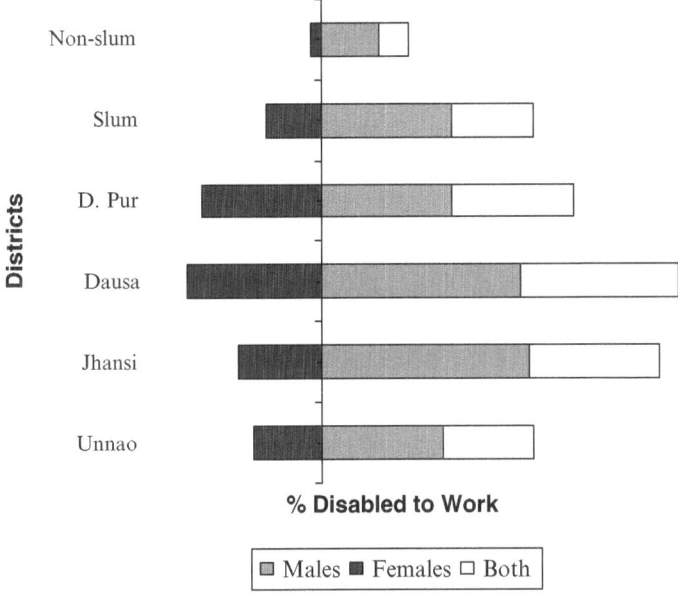

Fig. 3.1 Men and women with work disability: district-wise share

work is unemployment, especially among the people of Unnao in UP and slums of Delhi. A significant proportion of people at both the places do not work for lack of employment.

A more disturbing factor to notice from Table 3.5 is the share of non-school-going children in almost every district and slums. While a big majority of those children (i.e. over three-quarters) were too young and below 4 years of age, almost a fifth of them were grown up and in higher ages as well.[1] Their not attending schools, that too in most places, may look problematic. At stake in a situation like this may be the future of the demographic bonus India is expected to harness in coming years to add to its economic prospects.

Those adding to the size of nonworking household population also include a fraction of persons who are mentally or physically challenged. A small number of persons have also reported to withdraw from active workforce because of post-sickness frailty or senescence. Males in most of these cases outnumber females (Fig. 3.1), perhaps partly on account of the reporting biases. Dausa in Rajasthan reports such cases more than UP or Delhi.

---

[1] A further scrutiny of this data reveals that around 80 % of them were in the 0–4 age group. The rest were however between 5 and 14 years of age.

3.2   Quality of Life, Consumption Poverty and Inequalities Among the Sample Households

Three broader issues are subjected to a brief examination in the underlying discussion. First is the quality of life of households in terms of selected physical assets owned by groups of people under study and their access to various services relevant on health considerations including domestic power, cooking fuel, sources of water for drinking purposes, toilet system, nearby ponds/river/*nullah* causing dampness and mosquito breeding, scavenging, waste disposal, drainage facilities through public means, telephone communication and access to banking facilities. The other two issues to be examined in the underlying context include the levels and differentials in per capita consumption expenditure of the sample households, which are later used to draw inferences about existing inequalities, consumption poverty and health outcomes of households drawn specifically from high-poverty locations and states. To the extent possible, most of these issues are examined by allowing for differentials between the rural–urban and the slum–non-slum households. Interpretation of our results must however be within the constraints imposed by a small and purposive sampling procedure.

3.2.1   Quality of Life: Housing Conditions, Possessions and Access to Basic Services

Given the broader concerns of this study—which inter alia require examining the size and burden of self-paid health care accessed by households from low-income rural, urban and slum areas of three selected states—it may not be very unlikely to expect a slant in favour of households with poor or moderate living conditions. This comes out very clearly from the bivariate tables given in most of this section to highlight the quality of houses and the facilities availed by the sample population. Table 3.6 and its two sub-tables (Tables 3.6a and 3.6b) bring out very clearly the poor economic background of most households under consideration. Each of these three tables indicates a very modest living by a big majority of the respondents, most of them residing in non-bricked (*kutcha*) dwellings and without most of the facilities required for a healthy living.

The three preceding tables have clearly revealed that a very large number of families in rural and urban areas still reside in *kutcha* or semi-*kutcha* houses without many of the basic amenities like better (smoke-free) cooking fuel, drainage system, toilet facilities and scavenging to their access (see Tables 3.6a and 3.6b). The situation is far worse among the rural residents where almost nine out of ten houses are non-bricked and their residents survive without an in-house toilet or scavenging facilities. These and most other facts emanating from Table 3.6a clearly raise many big questions about the health prospects of rural people who are apparently torn between two basic issues. First is a more or less complete lack of preventive

Table 3.6 Quality of houses and access to daily life services and amenities: total households (%)

Variables	N	Kutcha and semi-kutch	Pucca house	Lighting arrangement		Cooking fuel		Toilet			Drainage (kutcha nali)	Safe drinking water	Scavenging		
				Electricity	Kerosene others	LPG	Coal, firewood, kerosene	Flush toilet	Pit toilet	Field and others			Weekly	Monthly	Rarely
Total sample	2010	60.3	39.7	53.6	46.4	30.9	69.1	14.6	25.9	59.5	12.8	96.3	46.9	5.8	47.3
UP	1,000	74.8	25.2	28.8	71.1	19.9	79.1	10.5	17.3	72.2	50.5	97.4	29.8	10.7	59.5
Unnao	600	70.3	29.7	28.8	71.0	24.7	74.3	17.5	12.7	69.8	51.3	96.7	22.7	13.1	64.1
Jhansi	400	81.5	18.5	28.8	71.3	12.8	86.3	0.0	24.3	75.8	49.3	98.5	43.8	6.0	50.3
Rajasthan	650	62.2	37.9	66.6	33.1	20.3	78.8	0.0	29.1	70.9	24.0	92.5	55.1	10.1	34.8
Dausa	300	65.7	34.3	60.7	39.0	10.7	88.7	0.0	21.7	78.3	20.0	96.3	61.3	8.1	30.7
Dungarpur	350	59.2	40.9	71.7	28.0	28.6	70.3	0.0	35.4	64.6	27.4	89.1	51.0	11.5	37.5
Delhi	360	16.7	83.3	99.2	0.8	80.3	8.9	40.3	44.2	15.6	48.6	100.0	73.4	8.3	18.3
Slums	102	46.1	53.9	97.1	2.9	46.1	22.6	0.0	64.7	35.3	76.5	100.0	50.0	7.3	42.7
Non-slum	258	5.0	95.0	100.0	0.0	93.8	3.5	54.3	36.1	9.7	37.6	100.0	80.9	8.6	10.6
Religion															
Hindu	1,789	61.1	38.9	52.8	47.0	29.7	67.5	12.3	24.2	63.5	39.1	95.9	47.0	10.4	42.6
Muslim	188	62.8	37.2	53.2	46.8	30.3	66.5	9.0	36.7	54.3	63.3	98.9	37.8	7.4	54.8
Social group															
SC	455	65.9	34.1	48.4	51.7	21.8	73.4	7.5	22.4	70.1	56.7	97.1	100.0	0.0	0.0
ST	249	85.1	14.9	37.8	61.9	6.4	92.0	1.2	6.8	92.0	4.8	85.9	0.0	0.0	100.0
OBC	777	69.0	31.0	45.1	54.7	23.9	74.4	6.7	24.5	68.9	49.2	97.2	38.9	5.6	55.6
Upper caste	529	31.0	69.0	78.3	21.7	60.3	36.7	30.4	40.1	29.5	42.7	99.1	33.3	11.9	54.8

Table 3.6a Quality of houses possessed by rural households and their access to daily services or amenities (%)

Instrumental variables	Sample households (N)	Kutcha and semi-kutcha house	Pucca house	Lighting arrangement		Safe[a] drinking water	Cooking fuel			Toilet			Drainage	Scavenging	
				Electricity	Kerosene and others		LPG	Firewood	Others	Flush toilet, inside	Pit toilet	Field and others	Kutcha nali	Frequently	Rarely
Total rural	1,250	81.4	18.6	28.8	71.2	94.2	6.2	93.0	0.8	3.6	9.7	86.7	30.1	4.4	95.6
UP	750	87.3	12.7	9.6	90.4	96.8	4.3	94.9	0.8	3.5	6.4	90.1	44.9	7.2	92.8
Unnao	450	85.8	14.2	8.2	91.8	95.6	6.7	92.7	0.7	5.8	3.8	90.4	52.4	8.5	91.5
Jhansi	300	89.7	10.3	11.7	88.3	98.7	0.7	98.3	1.0	0.0	10.3	89.7	33.7	4.0	96.0
Rajasthan	500	72.4	27.6	57.6	42.4	90.2	9.2	90.0	0.8	0.0	14.6	85.4	7.8	4.9	95.1
Dausa	250	69.6	30.4	54.0	46.0	95.6	5.6	94.0	0.4	0.0	12.4	87.6	7.2	10.0	90.0
Dungarpur	250	75.2	24.8	61.2	38.8	84.8	12.8	86.0	1.2	0.0	16.8	83.2	8.4	0.0	100.0
Religion															
Hindu	1,152	81.3	18.8	29.3	70.7	93.8	6.2	93.0	0.9	1.7	9.5	88.8	28.2	8.0	92.0
Muslim	98	82.7	17.4	22.5	77.6	99.0	7.1	92.9	0.0	6.1	12.2	81.6	52.0	0.0	100.0
Social group															
SC	291	82.8	17.2	23.0	77.0	96.2	3.1	95.9	1.0	0.3	8.3	91.4	35.1	2.8	97.2
ST	231	88.3	11.7	33.3	66.7	84.9	3.0	96.1	0.9	0.0	3.5	96.5	1.7	0.0	100.0
OBC	527	84.1	15.9	23.5	76.5	95.8	5.5	93.7	0.8	2.7	7.4	89.9	37.4	7.8	92.2
Upper caste	201	64.2	35.8	45.8	54.2	97.5	16.4	83.1	0.5	5.5	24.9	69.7	36.3	11.0	89.0

[a]Includes piped water and water from hand pumps and covered well

Table 3.6b Quality of houses possessed by urban households and their access to daily services and amenities (%)

Instrumental variables	Sample households (N)	Kutcha and semi-kutcha house	Pucca house	Lighting arrangement		Safe[a] drinking water	Cooking fuel			Toilet			Drainage	Scavenging	
				Electricity	Kerosene and others		LPG	Firewood	Others	Flush toilet, inside	Pit toilet	Field and others	Kutcha nali	Frequently	Rarely
Total urban	760	25.7	74.3	94.5	5.5	99.7	71.3	22.8	5.9	32.8	52.6	14.6	60.5	85.9	14.1
UP	250	37.2	62.8	86.4	13.6	99.2	66.8	31.6	1.6	31.6	50.0	16.4	67.2	94.0	6.1
Unnao	150	20.7	76.0	90.7	9.3	100.0	78.7	19.3	2.0	52.7	39.3	6.0	48.0	91.9	8.1
Jhansi	100	57.0	43.0	80.0	20.0	98.0	49.0	50.0	1.0	0.0	66.0	32.0	96.0	97.0	3.0
Rajasthan	150	28.0	72.0	96.7	3.3	100.0	57.3	41.3	1.3	0.0	77.3	22.7	78.0	87.2	12.8
Dausa	50	46.0	54.0	94.0	6.0	100.0	36.0	62.0	2.0	0.0	68.0	32.0	84.0	97.6	2.4
Dungarpur	100	19.0	81.0	98.0	2.0	100.0	68.0	31.0	1.0	0.0	82.0	18.0	75.0	81.3	18.7
Religion															
Hindu	637	24.7	75.4	95.3	4.7	99.8	72.4	21.5	6.1	31.4	50.9	17.7	58.7	89.1	10.9
Muslim	90	41.1	58.9	86.7	13.3	98.9	55.6	37.8	6.7	12.2	63.3	24.5	75.6	73.8	26.2
Social group															
SC	164	36.0	64.0	93.3	6.7	98.8	54.9	33.5	11.6	20.1	47.6	32.3	69.5	84.1	15.9
ST	18	44.4	55.6	94.4	5.6	100.0	50.0	38.9	11.1	16.7	50.0	33.3	44.4	91.7	8.3
OBC	250	37.2	62.8	90.4	9.6	100.0	62.8	33.6	3.6	15.2	60.4	24.4	74.0	86.5	13.5
Upper caste	328	10.7	89.3	98.2	1.8	100.0	87.2	8.2	4.6	45.7	49.4	4.9	46.7	89.0	11.0

[a]Includes piped water and water from hand pumps and covered well

Table 3.7 House ownership status of sample households by states

States/districts	House ownership: total sample			House ownership: rural			House ownership: urban		
	Ancestral house	HHD owned	Others	Ancestral house	HHD owned	Others	Ancestral house	HHD owned	Others
Total sample	56.7	35.1	8.2	70.5	27.2	2.3	34.1	48.0	17.9
UP	67.5	26.0	6.5	73.6	23.5	2.9	49.2	33.6	17.2
Unnao	58.7	32.2	9.1	67.1	28.4	4.4	33.3	43.3	23.4
Jhansi	80.7	16.8	2.5	83.3	16.0	0.7	73.0	19.0	8.0
Rajasthan	57.2	39.3	3.5	65.8	32.8	1.4	28.7	60.7	10.6
Dausa	68.3	30.3	1.4	72.0	27.2	0.8	50.0	46.0	4.0
Dungarpur	47.7	46.9	5.4	59.6	38.4	2.0	18.0	68.0	14.0
Delhi	25.8	52.8	21.4	–	–	–	–	–	–
Slums	13.7	73.5	12.8	–	–	–	–	–	–
Non-slum	30.6	44.6	24.8	–	–	–	–	–	–
Religion									
Hindu	57.3	34.9	7.8	70.1	27.9	2.0	34.1	47.7	18.2
Muslim	54.8	34.6	10.6	74.5	20.4	5.1	33.3	50.0	16.7

mechanism like drainage, regular scavenging, pit/flush toilets and smoke-free cooking fuels. The other significant issue arises due to lack of concern among health officials about the need for nonreproductive health-care services, leaving a big fraction of rural households in the clutches of private health-care providers. The former, which indicates a lack of preventive mechanism, is also an issue that needs to be examined by keeping in mind the financial status of urban and rural bodies which are largely responsible for disease preventive services like scavenging, waste disposal and creation of all weather drainage system. As most of the local governments/bodies are generally constrained because of poor governance and suffer from inadequate finances (partly because of their inelastic tax revenues), they usually remain non-functional in terms of services required to prevent many non-lifestyle diseases.

Urban areas, as expected, remained considerably better and have been able to offer many of the basic facilities to a much bigger fraction of the sample population. Yet, many of the respondents did report poor housing conditions and lack of civic services like chocked drainage and infrequent scavenging (Table 3.6b). Inequalities in access to many of these facilities may as well be noticed across socioreligious groups.

Barring to some extent in Delhi, house ownership in most places is either through inheritance or built and owned by the head of household. Both the patterns jointly account for more than three-quarters of house ownerships in the sample (Table 3.7). Inherited houses are found to be the maximum in UP (67.5 %) followed by Rajasthan (57.2 %). Delhi, in contrast, stands the lowest on this criterion (merely 25.8 %). However, the percentage of houses owned by the head of family is considerably large in Delhi. This is particularly true for the slum dwellers (73.5 %). An inference may therefore be made that the house ownership acts decisively in holding the rein of the family. It holds true for different social groups as well (Figs. 3.2 and 3.3).

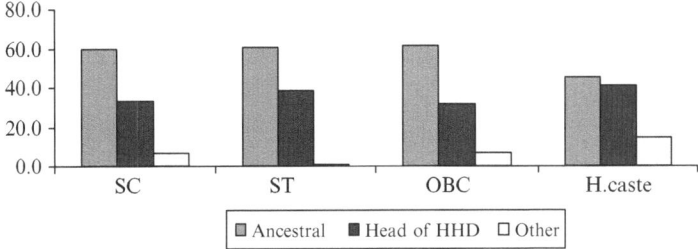

Fig. 3.2 House ownership status by social groups: total sample

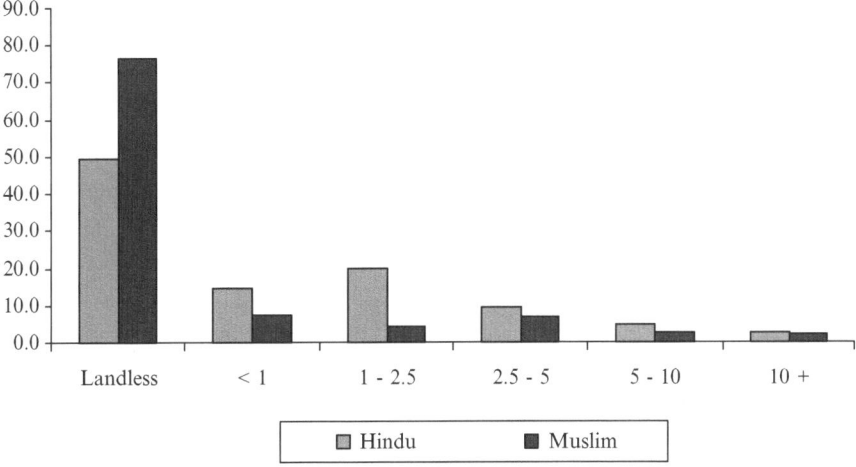

Fig. 3.3 Landholdings by Hindus and Muslims: total sample

Distribution of sample households by size of landholding is given in panels A, B and C of Table 3.8. A point to notice from this distribution is the size of landless households. Even if we ignore Delhi for obvious reasons, the remaining two states—with considerable dependence on agriculture—present a worrisome picture. Almost half of the rural households in both the states are either landless or own a small piece of land measured below an acre in size (Table 3.8, panels A and B). The fraction of households with landholding size over five acres is amazingly low in both the states, for example, little over 10 % in UP and over 4 % in Rajasthan. While it needs to be admitted that the slant in favour of relatively poor districts and households in our sample may have ended up in pulling some of our results down, it may as well be recognised that these results may help to cause some alarm among concerned departments with perhaps a greater realisation about the health risks of people in these districts and their necessary health delivery infrastructure. Simply, a programme with much of its focus being directed to reproductive and (certain domains of) child health may not suffice.

Table 3.8 Landholdings by sample households

Size of landholding (in acres)[a]	UP	Rajasthan	Delhi	Combined
Panel A: distribution by study areas				
Landless	42.6	42.8	98.1	52.6
<1	15.7	18.6	0.0	13.8
1–2.5	20.4	23.7	0.6	17.9
2.5–5	11.2	10.6	0.6	9.1
5–10	6.1	3.5	0.6	4.3
10 +	4.0	0.8	0.3	2.3
N	2,010	1,000	650	360

	UP		Rajasthan	
	Rural	Urban	Rural	Urban
Panel B: distribution by place of residence: rural–urban				
Landless	30.3	79.6	27.4	94.0
<1	19.5	4.4	23.6	2.0
1–2.5	24.8	7.2	30.4	1.3
2.5–5	13.7	3.6	13.2	2.0
5–10	6.8	4.0	4.4	0.7
10 +	4.9	1.2	1.0	0.0
N	750	250	500	150

	SC	ST	OBC	Upper caste
Panel C: distribution by social groups				
Landless	56.5	27.3	50.6	64.1
<1	14.5	21.3	16.6	5.7
1–2.5	19.1	35.3	15.4	12.3
2.5–5	6.8	12.9	9.9	8.1
5–10	3.1	2.8	5.3	4.5
10 +	0.0	0.4	2.2	5.3
N	455	249	777	529

Source: IEG Survey on OOP Expenditure on Health, April–June 2008

[a] 1 acre = 1.6 bigha

The situation does not improve either even if we look at the land ownership status of the upper-caste households in the sample. It may be observed from panel C of Table 3.8 that about two-thirds of them are landless, which is even worse than the other lower-caste categories. They are nevertheless slightly better off when it comes to bigger landholdings; more than 5 % of the total higher-caste households owned land above 10 acres in size.

Conforming to the general perception, Muslims are found way behind Hindus; more of them are landless and their landholdings are also relatively smaller.

Of the two other quality-of-life services—the telephone connection and a bank account—the former appears to be much less commonly possessed by the population under study than the latter (Fig. 3.4). Considering the growing penetration of mobile phone services in most of the country including UP and Rajasthan, our results may not be accepted at their face value. A possible explanation of this under-estimation may be found in certain confusion among survey teams between the

(Percentages)

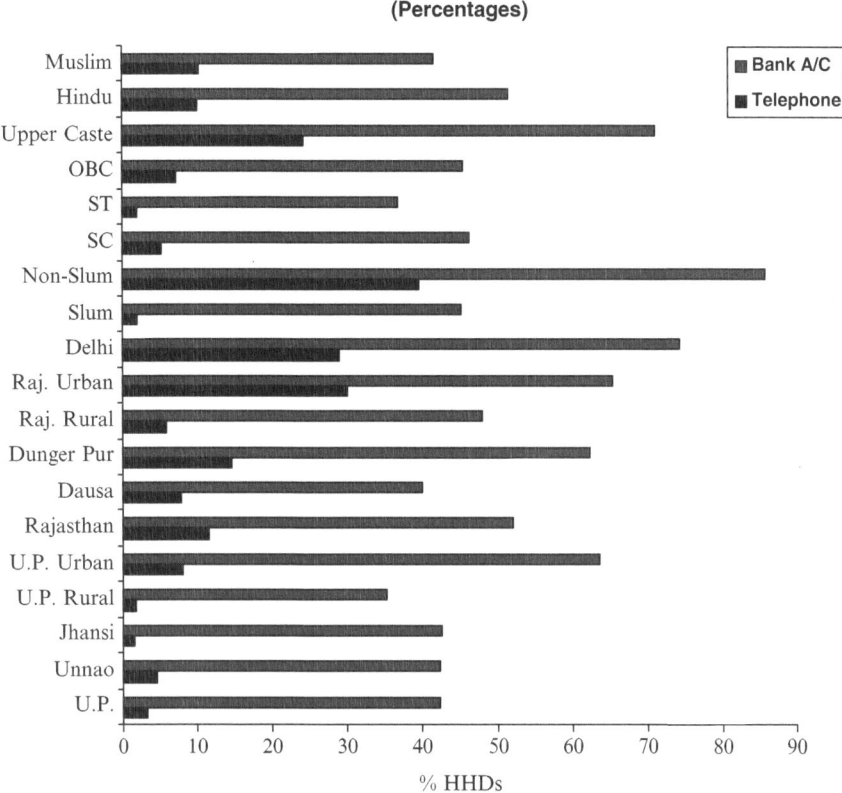

Fig. 3.4 Households with telephone and bank account (percentages) (*Source*: IEG Survey on OOP Expenditure on Health, April–June 2008)

landline and the mobile telephone connections. Disregarding this, the bank account data seems interesting as it indicates a good number of people in most areas, particularly in Delhi and Rajasthan, holding a bank account. Muslims and rural UP and ST households are the exceptions. With 86 % of the total respondents having a bank account, non-slum Delhi is obviously far ahead than many others.

3.3 Households' Consumption Level, Poverty and Inequality: Empirical Findings

This section brings two critical issues under investigation. First, it attempts to provide the socio-economic status of sample households determined on the basis of their food and nonfood consumption expenditure—with and without health care. This may inter alia help us to identify the share of those below an officially designated cut-off poverty level. A part of this discussion is also directed at examining certain forms of inequalities prevalent among the responding households in rural and urban areas under consideration. The other issue relates to the OOP health spending of households. This issue—one of the critical concerns of the study—is likely to shed some light on the question: How does the OOP spending on health affect the overall socio-economic status of households? In other words, how does this spending push many of the borderline nonpoor households in different states below the threshold level of poverty? There must however be a word of caution. The analysis bears two important data caveats:

1. Most of our data used to analyse poverty and other related issues are obtained on the basis of a compressed consumption schedule (see Appendix Table 3.A.3). This lends us to the risks of some underestimation in the overall consumption level of the respondents. It may in certain cases tend to inflate the poverty level.
2. Given the micro-level of our survey, that too with a tilt in favour of the poor households in relatively high-poverty districts of economically less developed states, our poverty estimates may not be comparable strictly with studies drawn on the basis of the National Sample Survey or other similar data sources. Also, the poverty lines in our analyses are not district specific and relate to the state as a whole.

A part of the analysis in this section is also devoted to making assessments about the households facing a catastrophic situation due to OOP spending on treatment of disease episode(s) in the family. A more decomposed analysis of OOP health-care spending is taken up in subsequent chapters.

In all, four interlinked issues are discussed below:

• First, we briefly present the share of households in each of the five (arbitrarily chosen) PCMCE categories, i.e. from the lowest category of Rs. 500 or below a month to the highest of Rs. 10,001 and above in each of the three states under discussion.
• This is followed by a discussion on sample households below or above the official cut-off levels of poverty (hereafter denoted by Z). Two alternative formulations are used to measure poverty levels among the sample households. Poverty type 1 was considered at the combined level after taking into consideration the overall consumption in the household including food, nonfood and all health-related OOP expenses (PCMCE – Z).[2] The other (poverty type 2) relates to the households' expenditure after deducting their OOP spending on health. The latter was inter alia computed with a view to make assessments as to how the OOP expenditure on health brings nonpoor households to a poverty situation or, in other words, pushes them into poverty from a non-poverty position.
• Thereafter, we move to the inequalities among the sample households both with and without spending on health care.

Households facing indebtedness because of health and non-health expenses are discussed at the end.

---

[2] All yearly nonfood data have been converted into monthly format before calculating the PCMCE.

3.3.1 Consumption Levels of Sample Households

A simple distribution of households into five broad levels of monthly per capita consumption expenditures is given in Table 3.9. This table reconfirms a large-scale poverty situation in the two districts of UP (Unnao and Jhansi) with 50 % of its sample households reporting a total of Rs. 500 or less as their total PCMCE including food, nonfood and health care. Even allowing for some overestimation due to data limitations, the fact that a large number of people in the state survive at Rs. 17 a day or less is a scary picture. Rajasthan (Dausa and Dungarpur) is however in a slightly better situation with a lesser fraction of people in Rs. 500 (or Rs. 17 a day) consumption band; its poverty situation is no way less alarming. Another interesting point to notice in both of these states is the fact that almost 90 % of their households belong to the first two PCMCE categories. Delhi turns out to be considerably better than both of them (Table 3.9). The rest of the estimates are mostly on the expected lines with the share of households in the lowest per capita consumption category being the highest both in slums and in rural areas. This is true for the tribal and low-caste households as well. Muslims trail behind the Hindus.

Apart from low PCMCE, a large number of households also suffer from serious inequality issues. While this issue will be considered independently in the next section, Fig. 3.5 clearly brings out considerable disparities between the minimum and the maximum consumption levels of households or their mean consumption levels. This is true for all the three states under reference. The max–min differences are found to be the highest in Delhi (see also Appendix Table 3.A.4).

3.3.2 Poverty Level and Its Measurements

3.3.2.1 Poverty Head Count Ratios

The discussion to follow in the next few sections uses two most commonly derived poverty measures to bring out the points in argument: (i) poverty head count and (ii) poverty gap (PG). Both the measures are applied differently. One is by taking the overall per capita monthly consumption expenditure (PCMCE) as it is and the second after netting out the health-care expenses from it. The latter, as was explained earlier, is expected to highlight the fraction of additional households slipping below the poverty level due to private expenses on health.[3] These measures may also help to judge differences in head count ratios of below-poverty households (H) in different states or by rural–urban and socioreligious groups. The fact that all of these measures are drawn at a micro-level adds to some of the value additions of this study and may also serve in drawing useful insights for making evidence-based policy interventions at the local level. A brief note on both the measures of poverty is in order.

---

[3] It ought to be pointed out that this study has nowhere tried to differentiate between emergency and nonemergency health-care items or expenditure.

Table 3.9 Distribution of households by PCMCE categories: UP, Rajasthan and Delhi

Household consumption items	Distribution of households by PCMCE levels (%)					
	<Rs. 500	Rs. 500–1,500	Rs. 1,501–5,000	Rs. 5,001–10,000	Rs. >10,000	N row-wise
a. Total consumption						
UP[a]	50.1	43.9	5.7	0.3	0.0	1,000
Rajasthan[a]	42.6	46.6	10.6	0.0	0.2	650
Delhi[b]	3.6	48.6	37.5	9.4	0.8	360
Combined states	39.4	45.6	13	1.8	0.2	2,010
b. Food exp.						
UP[a]	88.4	11.4	0.2	0.0	0.0	1,000
Rajasthan[a]	85.54	14.31	0.15	0.0	0.0	650
Delhi[b]	28.61	58.06	13.33	0.0	0.0	360
c. Nonfood exp.[e]						
UP[a]	83.1	14.2	2.6	0.1	0.0	1,000
Rajasthan[a]	75.7	19.4	4.8	0.0	0.2	650
Delhi[b]	40.3	30.3	25.6	3.6	0.3	360
d. Health exp.						
UP[a]	95.1	4.1	0.7	0.1	4.1	1,000
Rajasthan[a]	95.7	3.1	1.2	0.0	3.1	650
Delhi[b]	88.9	8.3	2.8	0.0	8.3	360
e. Place of residence						
Rural[c]	54.3	40.7	4.8	0.1	0.1	1,250
Urban[d]	14.7	53.7	26.5	4.7	0.4	760
Delhi slum	10.8	77.5	11.8	0.0	0.0	102
Delhi non-slum	0.8	37.2	47.7	13.2	1.2	258
f. Social groups (*total consumption*)						
SC	41.8	51.0	7.0	0.2	0.0	455
ST	65.1	29.7	4.4	0.4	0.4	249
OBC	45.6	45.7	8.5	0.3	0.0	777
Upper castes	16.1	48.4	28.7	6.2	0.6	529
f1. Social groups (*health exp.*)[f]						
SC	93.1	5.2	1.5	0.3	0.0	404
ST	97.3	2.7	0.0	0.0	0.0	221
OBC	94.5	4.1	1.3	0.0	0.0	677
Upper castes	89.9	7.9	2.2	0.0	0.0	456
g. Religion (*total consumption*)						
Hindu	39.5	45.7	12.7	2.0	0.2	1,789
Muslim	44.2	46.8	8.5	0.5	0.0	188

Notes:
[a]Rural–urban combined
[b]Combined slum and non-slum households
[c]Combined rural from UP and Rajasthan
[d]Including slums and non-slums
[e]Including health expenditure
[f]Excluding HHDs without any health expenditure during the reference period

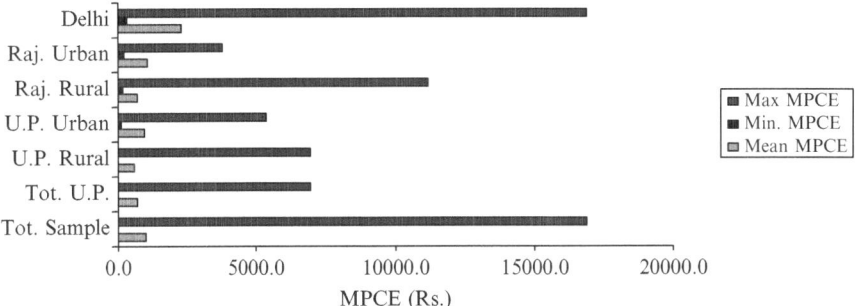

Fig. 3.5 Maximum, minimum and mean consumption level of sample population: UP, Rajasthan and Delhi

3.3.2.2   Poverty Head Count Index (*H*)

As was described before, this measure (hereafter referred to as *H*) provides the share of population below a defined poverty line (*Z*).[4] In other words, it provides the share of population or households below a defined income or consumption level (in our case, $H = Z - \text{PCMCE}$). Going by this definition of poverty, the head count index (*H*) is q/n where q is number of persons with $\text{PCMCE} < Z$ and n is the size of the total population (also see Box 3.1). Two measures of *H* are brought under discussion; one is with and the other is without OOP expenses on health.

3.3.2.3   Poverty Gap (PG)

PG, which is generally considered a measure representing the severity of poverty or poverty deficits, is the mean distance separating any population from the poverty line (*Z*). Also it assumes the nonpoor or above-poverty individuals (i.e. PCMCE > poverty line *Z*) at a zero poverty deficit. Like in the case of poverty head count ratios (*H*), here also we make two separate computations, i.e. with and without the households' spending on health. Algebraically, the PG may be expressed as

$$PG = 1/n \sum_{i=1}^{q} \left[\frac{Z - \text{PCMCE}_i}{z} \right]$$

---

[4]The defined poverty line for the three states were: UP, rural = 365.24 and urban = 483.26; Rajasthan: rural = 374.57 and urban = 559.63; and Delhi, urban = 612.91 (poverty estimates given by the Planning Commission for 2004–2005, released by Press Information Bureau, Government of India).

Box 3.1: Estimation of Poverty with and Without OOP Expenditure on Health

Consumption poverty head count = q/n

where q is the number of poor households defined as: PCMCE – poverty line Z

If PCMCE < Z, HHD is poor, and 'n' is the number of sample households.

Consumption poverty 1 = MPCE (monthly per capita household consumption expenditure) < Z.

Consumption poverty 2 = (MPCE – OOP health exp) < Z (Fig. 3.6).

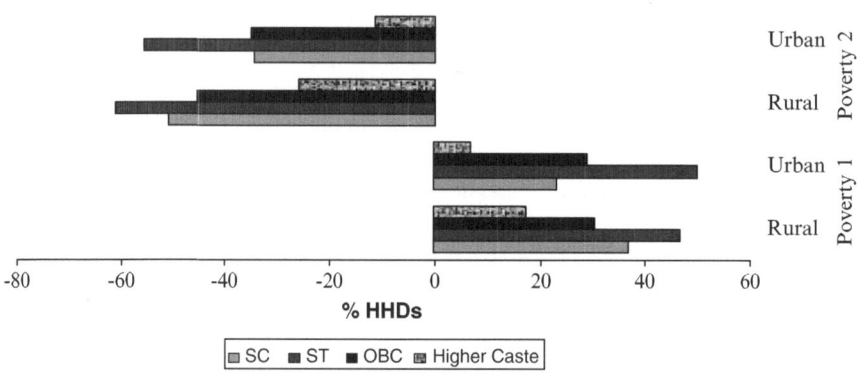

Fig. 3.6 Type 1 and type 2 poverty by social groups

where Z denotes the poverty line of individual states, q is below-poverty households (i.e. households with Z > PCMCE), and n is the number of persons in the sample.[5] At the policy level, PG serves to provide estimates of financial resources required to remove consumption (or income) poverty under a perfectly designed targeting framework. The PGs are calculated to represent both the total and the below-poverty populations.[6] While the former is termed as the *Average PG*, the latter is known as the *Mean Positive Gap*. These measures were bifurcated further by using (i) the total PCMCE and (ii) the PCMCE–OOP (also see Box 3.2).

---

[5]Poverty gaps are generally measured at the household level, but individual income or consumption can also be used as it is drawn as the mean household income or consumption and remains equal for the entire household.

[6]In one case, n includes poor and nonpoor both, and in another it simply comprises persons or households with Z > PCMCE.

Box 3.2: Estimation of PG with and Without OOP Expenditure on Health

PG: 1a	*PG: 1b*
$\sum (Z - \text{MPCE})/(\text{HHD}_{\text{Poor}} + \text{HHD}_{\text{Non-poor}})$ where, $\text{HHD}_{\text{Poor}} = $ No. of HHDs with MPCE $< Z$ $\text{HHD}_{\text{Non-poor}} = $ No. of HHDs with MPCE $> Z$ $Z = $ poverty line given by the Planning Commission	$\sum (Z - \text{MPCE})/\text{HHD}_{\text{Poor}}$ where, $\text{HHD}_{\text{Poor}} = $ No. of HHDs with MPCE $< Z$ $Z = $ poverty line given by the Planning Commission
PG: 2a	*PG: 2b*
$\sum [Z - (\text{MPCE} - \text{OOP})]/\sum \text{HHD}_{\text{Poor}}$ $\quad + \sum \text{HHD}_{\text{Non-poor}}$ where, Poor HHD $= (\text{MPCE} - \text{OOP}) < Z$ $\text{HHD}_{\text{Poor}} = $ No. of HHDs with MPCE $< Z$ $\text{HHD}_{\text{Non-poor}} = $ Number of non-poor $\quad$ HHDs (MPCE $> Z$) $Z = $ poverty line given by the Planning Commission	$\sum [Z - (\text{MPCE} - \text{OOP})]/\text{HHD}_{\text{Poor}}$ where, Poor HHD $= (\text{MPCE} - \text{OOP}) < Z$ $\text{HHD}_{\text{Poor}} = $ Number of poor HHDs $Z = $ poverty line given by the Planning Commission

3.3.2.4 Poverty Head Count and Poverty Gap: Estimation Results

Table 3.10 provides head count consumption poverty in all the three states and their districts including slum and non-slum households surveyed in the capital city of Delhi. It also gives poverty incidence by social and religious groups. Repeating broadly the pattern represented by the previous table, Table 3.10 also suggests UP and its two districts in a more distressing situation with larger shares of households falling below the poverty threshold level (Z). This pattern is however true for rural UP alone. Urban UP and its districts have performed relatively better. They also perform better than Delhi slums (see Table 3.10).

An interesting observation stemming from this and a few of the forthcoming exercises relates to a significant increase in the fraction of below-poverty households (and poverty deepening may also be noticed from subsequent tables) after netting out the health expenses. This is clearly visible by making a comparison between the two head count poverty levels, i.e. with and without expenses on medical care. 'Consumption poverty 1' and 'Consumption poverty 2' in Table 3.10 provide these details. A comparison between the two indicates that the latter increases the share of below-poverty households to a considerable extent in all the three states—though the magnitude of households falling below poverty level varies from one state to another. The most visible effect of private spending on health may be found in rural and slum areas where the health services are either missing

Table 3.10 Head count of consumption poverty with and without OOP expenditure on health: UP, Rajasthan and Delhi samples (percentage)

Households characteristics	Consumption poverty: 1 (with the total consumption expenditure)		Consumption poverty: 2 (without OOP expenditure on health)	
	Rural	Urban	Rural	Urban
a. UP total	36.0	25.6	49.60	29.60
Unnao	34.7	20.0	48.89	22.00
Jhansi	38.0	34.0	50.67	41.00
b. Rajasthan total	28.4	28.6	41.80	38.00
Dausa	21.6	38.0	34.00	56.00
Dungarpur	35.2	24.0	49.60	29.00
c. Delhi total	–	10.0	–	16.11
Delhi slums	–	26.5	–	41.18
Delhi non-slums	–	3.4	–	6.20
Social groups				
SC	37.1	23.2	50.9	34.2
ST	46.8	50.0	61.0	55.6
OBC	30.6	29.2	45.5	34.8
Upper caste	17.4	7.0	25.9	11.0
Religion				
Hindu	32.6	18.1	46.1	24.0
Muslim	37.8	30.0	51.0	38.9

Calculated on the basis of state-specific poverty line given by the Planning Commission, 2004–2005

or inefficient. This may as well be noticed from the poverty head count results for the urban and non-slum households in Table 3.10. While certain marginal increase may be noticed in the fraction of poor after health-care expenses are deducted from the total PCMCE in most of the urban places, their magnitude is far less than those in villages and low-income slum areas. Even after 3 years of the NRHM, rural health care is seen to hold a much significant place in cross movement of a big proportion of rural people from poverty to non-poverty statuses and vice versa.

PG or the poverty gap, as already described, helps to measure the depth or severity of poverty at different levels. It also provides an important and complementary measure to examine further poverty or its incidence among different population groups and also by taking into consideration alternative ways of defining the PG. The results presented in Table 3.11 are expected to work on some of those lines and help calculating changes in poverty depth by altering the overall (or per capita) consumption expenditure of households with or without OOP health spending—the former was described as PG 1 and the latter was given as poverty gap 2 in tables containing those results. In addition, our results also include calculations based on *Average PG* (total households in the sample including poor and nonpoor) as well as *mean positive poverty gap* (partial sample with only poor households) (see Box 3.2 for more details). Both the sets of calculations may help further in digging into the role of health spending or letting people sink deeper into poverty.

Table 3.11 gives PGs drawn on the basis of both the alternative definitions of consumption expenditure, i.e. with and without OOP spending. It clearly reveals the

Table 3.11 Poverty gap by states, districts, religion and social groups (in rupees)

States and districts	PG 1(including OOP health exp.)				PG 2 (excluding OOP health exp.)			
	PG: 1a		PG: 1b		PG: 2a		PG: 2b	
	(Average PG)		(Mean positive PG)		(Average PG)		(Mean positive PG)	
	Total HHDs		Below-poverty HHDs		Total HHDs		Below-poverty HHDs	
	Rural	Urban	Rural	Urban	Rural	Urban	Rural	Urban
UP	35.4	34.0	88.7	123.4	47.45	40.48	118.80	146.78
Unnao	37.1	21.3	93.3	108.5	48.75	24.67	122.68	125.88
Jhansi	32.7	52.1	81.1	134.1	45.32	62.85	112.50	161.70
Rajasthan	28.9	48.8	96.4	153.0	36.73	66.53	122.36	208.52
Dausa	19.9	48.6	87.2	124.5	26.44	74.84	115.90	191.74
Dungarpur	38.6	49.0	102.4	177.7	47.68	61.46	126.52	223.02
Delhi	–	12.2	–	103.3		16.95		143.97
Slums	–	31.7	–	103.7		44.17		144.43
Non-slums	–	4.0	–	102.3		5.63		142.49
Social group								
SC	35.9	27.6	87.5	117.5	47.8	38.3	116.5	163.1
ST	49.4	109.8	101.6	189.1	62.5	141.4	128.4	243.5
OBC	30.5	38.5	90.0	123.9	40.9	49.9	120.7	160.5
Upper caste	15.7	12.3	78.2	127.8	20.6	14.6	102.8	151.7
Religion								
Hindu	32.6	25.6	91.7	127.6	42.8	33.4	120.5	166.7
Muslim	36.3	40.2	86.3	124.4	48.3	50.8	114.6	156.9

Note: Calculated on the basis of poverty line (Z) for respective states, Planning Commission (2004–2005)

negative impact of health spending on consumption standards of individuals and households. It also acts to drive low-income people deeper into poverty and may cause an added financial burden to lift them above their fallen position of poverty. Conforming to some of our earlier results, we observe rural parts of UP to be at a more disadvantageous position, though Urban Rajasthan is no less problematic. Similarly, the tribals are also in a difficult situation and health spending makes them suffer with greater PGs (Table 3.11).

The more interesting observations however arise while making a comparison between PGs 1 and 2. The relevance of these results increases when the two PGs are again divided into *average poverty gap* and *mean positive poverty gap*; the latter essentially relies on non-health (i.e. only food and nonfood items) consumption expenditure and also relates to below-poverty households ($Z - PCMCE_{food+non-food-health\ exp.} > 0$). The former has no similar restrictions. Table 3.11a summarises these results with columns 4, 7 and 8 representing the differences between the PGs obtained by making alternative consumption baskets and with or without nonpoor. Without making too many assertions, it may easily be noticed from Table 3.11a that the health spending—which appears to constitute in many cases a much larger share of nonfood consumption expenditure—makes the situation worse. It may be noticed from this table (or even from the previous tables) that the results drawn after dropping the health spending from consumption basket leave a big fraction of households

Table 3.11a Differentials in PGs with and without health spending in PCMCE: total and below-poverty HHDs in sample areas of UP, Rajasthan and Delhi

States and districts	PG 1: total consumption expenditure			PG 2: excluding OOP expenditure on health			(1a–1b)/
	PG 1a	PG 1b	Diff.: 1a and 1b	PG 2a	PG 2b	Diff.: 2a and 2b	(2a–2b) (%)
Panel 1: rural							
(1)	(2)	(3)	(4)	(5)	(6)	(7)	(8)
UP	35.4	88.7	53.3	47.5	118.8	71.4	74.6
Unnao	37.1	93.3	56.2	48.8	122.7	73.9	76.0
Jhansi	32.7	81.1	48.4	45.3	112.5	67.2	72.0
Rajasthan	28.9	96.4	67.5	36.7	122.4	85.6	78.9
Dausa	19.9	87.2	67.3	26.4	115.9	89.5	75.2
Dungarpur	38.6	102.4	63.8	47.7	126.5	78.8	81.0
Delhi	–	–	–	–	–	–	–
Slums	–	–	–	–	–	–	–
Non-slum	–	–	–	–	–	–	–
SC	35.9	87.5	51.6	47.8	116.5	68.7	75.1
ST	49.4	101.6	52.2	62.5	128.4	65.9	79.2
OBC	30.5	90.0	59.5	40.9	120.7	79.8	74.6
Upper caste	15.7	78.2	62.5	20.6	102.8	82.2	76.0
Panel 2: urban							
UP	34.0	123.4	89.4	40.5	146.8	106.3	84.1
Unnao	21.3	108.5	87.2	24.7	125.9	101.2	86.2
Jhansi	52.1	134.1	82.0	62.9	161.7	98.9	82.9
Rajasthan	48.8	153.0	104.2	66.5	208.5	142.0	73.4
Dausa	48.6	124.5	75.9	74.8	191.7	116.9	64.9
Dungarpur	49.0	177.7	128.7	61.5	223.0	161.6	79.6
Delhi	12.2	103.3	91.1	17.0	144.0	127.0	71.7
Slums	31.7	103.7	72.0	44.2	144.4	100.3	71.8
Non-slum	4.0	102.3	98.3	5.6	142.5	136.9	71.8
SC	27.6	117.5	89.9	38.3	163.1	124.8	72.0
ST	109.8	189.1	79.3	141.4	243.5	102.1	77.7
OBC	38.5	123.9	85.4	49.9	160.5	110.6	77.2
Upper caste	12.3	127.8	115.5	14.6	151.7	137.1	84.2

with deeper PGs. The situation compounds when the results are restricted to the poor households alone. Also, unlike the general perceptions, a slight modification in definition and composition of consumption basket makes urban population—in particular its poor and tribal segments—look highly vulnerable (see columns 3 and 6 of Table 3.11a, panel 2).

As a whole, two broad observations follow from most of these results. One, OOP health spending still remains a serious issue for a large number of people in both the states and also for the slum households in Delhi. Second, the poor remain highly vulnerable after they pay for their accessed health-care services themselves. What component (or components) of health spending brings greater vulnerability to the people is indeed a significant question, and we will revert to this later.

3.4 Health Payments, Poverty and Inequality

3.4.1 Inequality Concept and Its Measurement

Inequality is generally considered as a much broader concept than the measures adopted to calculate head count poverty indices or a set of PGs using alternative definitions. An important distinction embedding the concept of inequality is that it relates to the entire population and not only to those below a certain predefined poverty level (Coudouel et al. 2002). In addition, generally inequality measures do not rely on mean of a distribution. Instead, they remain mostly concerned with the overall distribution of certain welfare augmenting factors and therefore considered as one of the most relevant issues in debates on distributional outcomes of various public policies or programmes initiated by governments (Atkinson 1983; Cowell 2000; Gwatkin 2000; Sen 1973, etc.). Presented below are a few preliminary (Lorenz curve and Gini Indices based) inequality exercises using the preceding sets of consumption data and making a few smaller changes in overall consumption basket as before, i.e. with and without OOP expenditure on health. The underpinnings behind these exercises are twofold. One is simply required to know about the level of inequalities suffered by the groups of people drawn from different states and also to check whether these inequalities broadly follow the pattern observed by the NSS 61st round (July 2004–June 2005). The second objective obviously is to know the additional inequalities generated by the OOP spending on health across different groups of households. To calculate the latter, it is proposed to follow the expenditure decomposition procedure used to compute poverty 1 and 2 in Table 3.11 (also see Box 3.2).

Methodologically, the Lorenz curve is a graphical representation of the 'cumulative distribution function of a probability distribution'. It is generally drawn to represent income or consumption distribution (in our case the latter) of a population, where the horizontal axis gives the cumulative share of population ranked by increasing share of per capita consumption expenditure. The vertical axis on the other hand provides the share of consumption enjoyed by the corresponding percentages of population. The Gini coefficient, in most cases, is measured as twice the surface between the Lorenz curves and a hypothetical line of perfect equality or a perfectly egalitarian distribution (i.e. 45° line).[7]

An attempt is made below to provide a set of Lorenz curves drawn by using a continuous cumulative distribution of PCMCE for the populations drawn from the rural and urban areas of all the three states under review. These curves are drawn

---

[7]In its simplest way, Gini is mathematically derived as the covariance between the consumption c of an individual (or household) and the F rank that the individual or household occupies in the distribution of consumption (this rank assumes 0 for the poorest to 100 for the richest). Denoting the per capita monthly consumption expenditure by $\bar{c}$, the standard Gini index is defined as $= 2$ cov $(y, F)/\bar{c}$. We have used STATA to obtain these results (Klugman 2002, Technical Note A.7, p. 415). Computationally, it matters whether or not the consumption (or income) is weighted by household size, since households with lower income or consumption may be larger in size. To avoid this problem, we have followed a weighted HHD system in the entire analysis.

Table 3.12 Gini coefficients based on decomposed monthly consumption expenditure

	PCMCE on:		
States	Gini 1: food, nonfood and health	Gini 2: food and nonfood	Gini 3: OOP health expenditure
UP and Rajasthan (rural)	0.367	0.350	0.706
UP and Rajasthan (urban)	0.374	0.358	0.775
UP districts (rural)	0.339 (0.287)	0.312	0.707
UP districts (urban)	0.379 (0.370)	0.343	0.806
Rajasthan districts (rural)	0.395 (0.248)	0.388	0.705
Rajasthan districts (urban)	0.357 (0.367)	0.366	0.704
Delhi (slums)	0.250	0.221	0.680
Delhi (non-slums)	0.417	0.430	0.696
Delhi (slum + non-slum)	0.386 (0.326)	0.375	0.698

Source: NSSO (2006a, Report No. 508, Statement 1)
Note: Figures in brackets show Gini coefficients computed on the basis of NSS 61st round (2004–2005) for the rural and urban areas of UP and Rajasthan and urban Delhi

only on the basis of the total consumption expenditure. A further extension of these exercises has also been attempted by decomposing the total household expenditure into (i) food and nonfood and (ii) OOP health spending. For the brevity of space, however, we refrain providing Lorenz curves based on the decomposed consumption data. Rather, a separate table (Table 3.12) has been added to give the Gini coefficients for all the three consumption baskets. Gini 1 relates to the total PCMCE, while Gini 2 and 3 relate to the decomposed distribution of PCMCEs, namely, $PCMCE_{food+non-food}$ and $PCMCE_{OOPexp}$.

A very clear message emanating from all the exercises—either Lorenz curves or a series of Gini coefficients obtained with or without OOP spending on health—goes to suggest that the consumption inequalities are severely higher at most of the places under the study. All the Lorenz curves show steep gaps between the diagonal line of 45° and the area under the curve (see Lorenz curves 3.1–3.7). But perhaps there is nothing very surprising in these results. Based on the consumption expenditure survey for 2004–2005, almost a similar trend and loss of well-being were reported by the NSSO in its Report Number 508 (December 2006). If some of our results are a little different from that of the NSSO (2006a), it may largely be on account of certain technical differences or lack of conformity between the two samples.

Table 3.12 clarifies some of these issues further. More specifically, it helps to make two points. One is the resemblance between the Gini coefficients drawn by our own data and the NSS 61st round. This is particularly true for the urban populations in UP and Rajasthan (NSSO 2006a). Undoubtedly, while such a comparison draws no or limited justification on theoretical reasoning, at least they are mutually close in terms of size (Table 3.12). Coefficient for urban Delhi is also not very far apart. The rural Gini however differs quite considerably, and this is true for both the states.

Our results suggest lesser disparities in per capita consumption of nonfood items. In most cases, the Gini 2 in Table 3.12 assumes smaller values. A point however to notice is the disparities shown in mean expenditure on health care (Gini 3 in

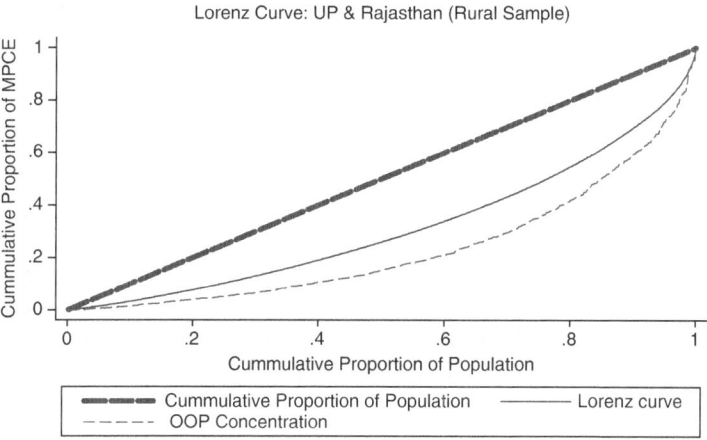

Fig. 3.7 Inequalities in PCMCE: sample HHDs of UP and Rajasthan (rural) (Gini 1 = 0.367; Gini 2 = 0.350; Gini 3 (OOP) = 0.706)

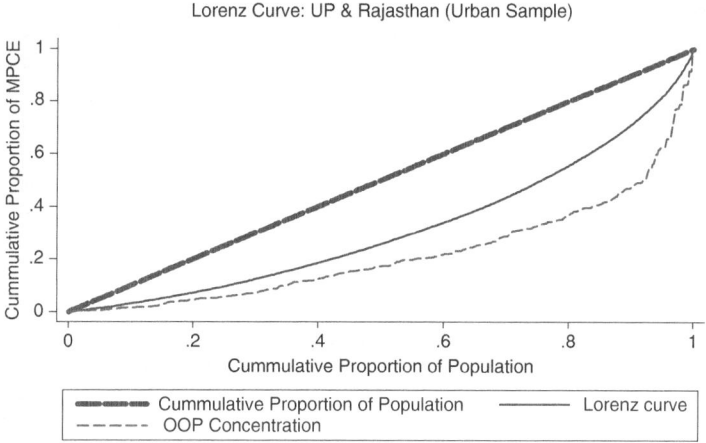

Fig. 3.8 Inequalities in PCMCE: sample HHDs of UP and Rajasthan (urban) (Gini 1 = 0.374; Gini 2 = 0.358; Gini 3 (OOP) = 0.775)

Table 3.12). Barring to a certain extent in Delhi, health inequalities are strikingly higher in most places, particularly in areas of UP. A tentative inference to draw from these results may be that health care is accessed quite unevenly in most of the places, with almost no or negligible amount of spending on health by a group of people and vice versa. It also works to generate a significant amount of inequalities in the total PCMCE (Figs. 3.7, 3.8, 3.9, 3.10, 3.11, 3.12, and 3.13).

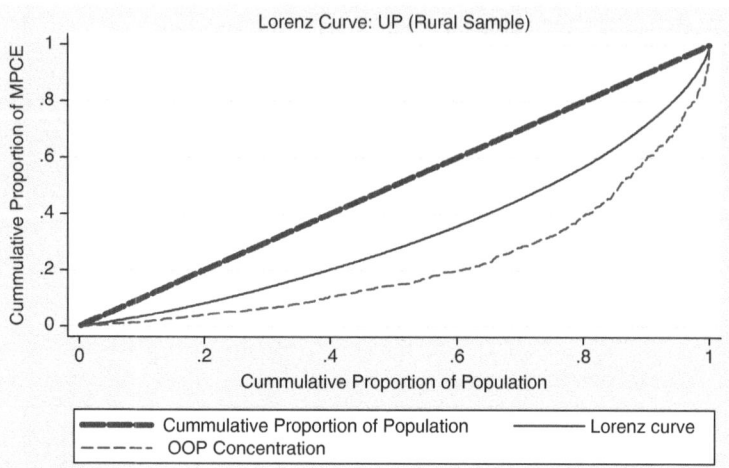

Fig. 3.9 Inequalities in PCMCE: sample HHDs of UP (rural) (Gini 1 = 0.339; Gini 2 = 312; Gini 3 (OOP) = 0.707)

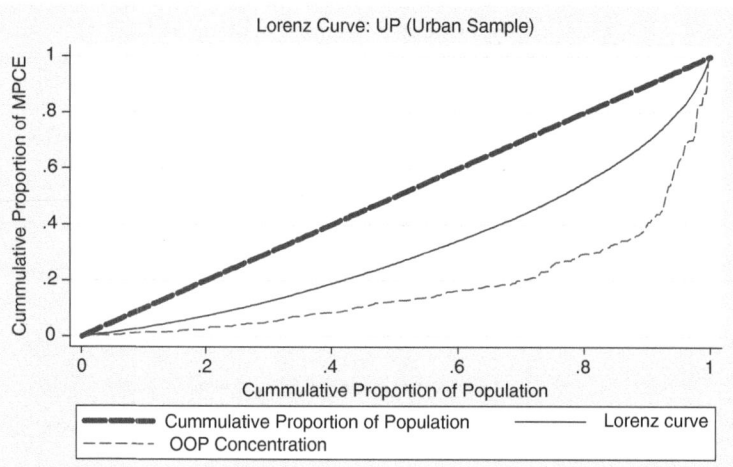

Fig. 3.10 Inequalities in PCMCE: sample HHDs of UP (urban) (Gini 1 = 0.379; Gini 2 = 343; Gini 3 (OOP) = 0.806)

3.5   Prevalence, Sources and Levels of Health-Related Loans and Borrowings

In addition to the total or per capita consumption level, another important criterion to judge the economic status or well-being of a household is to know about its financial obligations; one of them is the borrowings from external sources against certain interest payment. Borrowings are obviously for variety of reasons. Some are purely

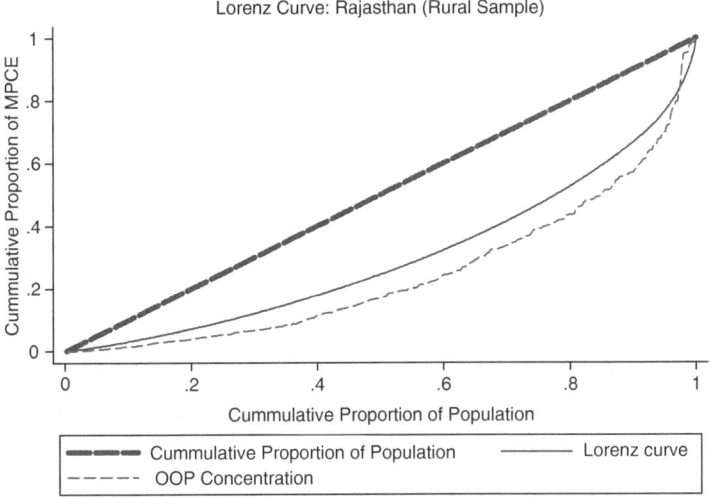

Fig. 3.11 Inequalities in PCMCE: sample HHDs of Rajasthan (rural) (Gini 1 = 0.395; Gini 2 = 388; Gini 3 (OOP) = 0.705)

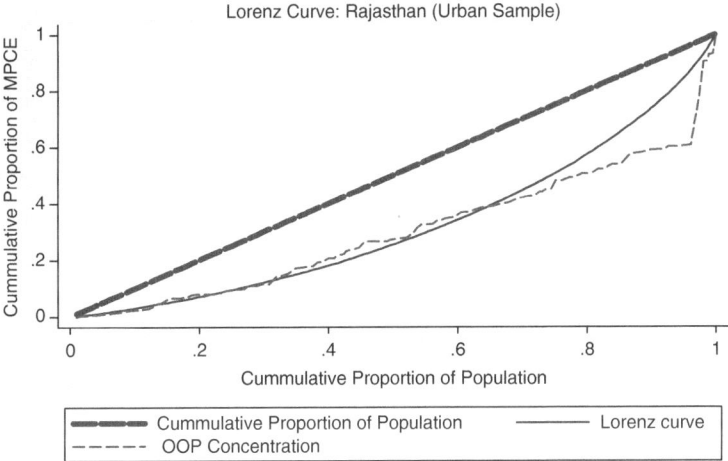

Fig. 3.12 Inequalities in PCMCE: sample HHDs of Rajasthan (urban) (Gini 1 = 0.357; Gini 2 = 366; Gini 3 (OOP) = 0.704)

for consumption purposes including OOP spending on treatment of a family member, and others arise due to financial needs of households to meet their socio-familial commitments, purchase of assets and consumer durables or even to repay their previous loans. But in many cases, an average household borrows out of duress to bridge the gap between income and expenditure. Our focus in this part of the analysis remains very limited and broadly confines to knowing the prevalence of cash

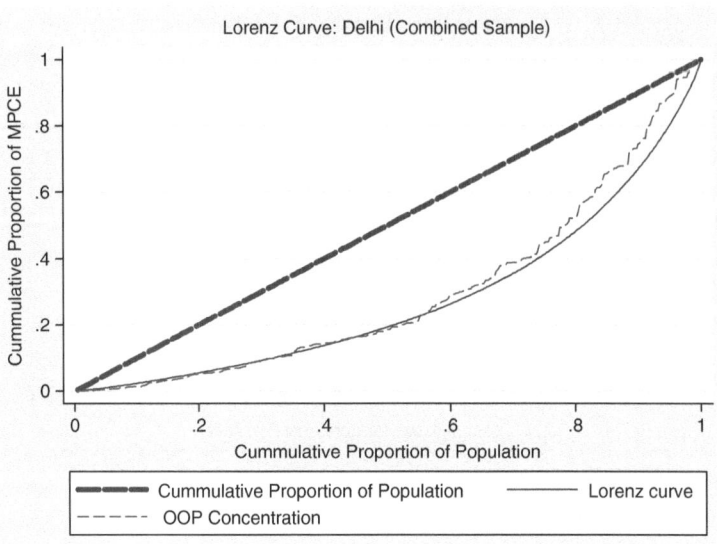

Fig. 3.13 Inequalities in PCMCE: sample HHDs of Delhi (Gini 1 = 0.86; Gini 2 = 0.375; Gini 3 (OOP) = 0.698)

borrowings for health purposes and its attendant details including the share of indebted households in the sample and how these households differ across places and so on. To be precise, three broader issues have been examined:

- Share of households with cash borrowings and purpose of loans: health or non-health? If for health, is it for treatment of an earning member, a child or an elderly person?
- Source of loans: relatives or nonrelatives, traditional lender or a banking institution?
- Source of loan repayment: sale of family asset, new loan, past savings or existing income sources?

We begin by examining the fraction of indebted households in the total sample, their rural–urban differentials and purpose of loans—in particular health-related cash loans.

3.5.1   Loans and Borrowings for Health and Non-Health Purposes

As mentioned, borrowings are made either to circumvent distress conditions due to unforeseen events in the family including ailments or to raise required finances by the households to meet their socio-investment goals. Therefore, an attempt was made to collect information from the households by asking them if they have any ongoing debt obligations at the time of the survey. The next set of questions included purpose

Table 3.13 Share of indebted households in the total sample

| | Indebted households: rural and urban samples | | | | | |
| | Rural | | Urban | | Total | |
Characteristics	N	Indebted HHDs (%)	N	Indebted HHDs (%)	N	Indebted HHDs (%)
Total sample	1,250	52.4	760	26.7	2,010	42.7
UP	750	56.3	250	26.0	1,000	48.7
Unnao	450	49.8	150	20.7	600	42.5
Jhansi	300	66.0	100	34.0	400	58.0
Rajasthan	500	46.6	150	31.33	650	43.1
Dausa	250	56.8	50	52.0	300	56.0
Dungarpur	250	36.4	100	21.0	350	32.0
Delhi	–	–	–	–	360	25.3
Delhi slums	102	37.3	–	–	–	–
Delhi non-slum	–	–	258	20.5	–	–
Social group						
SC	291	55.3	164	31.1	455	46.6
ST	231	41.1	18	27.8	249	40.2
OBC	527	55.4	250	29.2	777	47.0
Upper caste	201	53.2	328	22.6	529	34.2
Religion						
Hindu	1,152	52.3	637	26.5	1,789	43.1
Muslim	98	54.1	90	28.9	188	42.0

of loans, sources and other requisite details. The share of indebted households in our sample is given in Table 3.13. This table adds to the observation stemming from the All India Debt and Investment Survey of the NSSO (January–December 2003) suggesting a very large proportion of the total cash borrowings by the rural households. Table 3.13 indicates majority of rural households (52.4 %) under cash debt in combined villages of UP and Rajasthan. Urban households with cash debt obligations are however much lower in size, little over a quarter (26.7 %) of the total sample. Jhansi in UP and Dausa in Rajasthan in our sample are the most indebted areas—the latter shows the highest incidence of borrowings among the urban households, and the former counts the highest in terms of rural indebtedness. For whatever may be the reason, tribals are shown to be the least indebted among the four social groups in rural areas. Of the remaining three, more than 50 % of each group reported being in debt at the time of the survey. Even the high-caste population is no exception. Hindus and Muslims do conform closely to each other at least on this criterion.

Reasons given by responding households to secure loans are furnished in Table 3.14. Two broad reasons are presented: medical and non-medical. The latter combines all categories of loans including those for purely consumption purposes as also those required to finance productive needs of the families. With the exception of urban Dungarpur (Rajasthan), we notice from this table that medical loans are quite prevalent in most of the areas under study. More than a quarter of indebted households in urban areas (26.6 %) have reportedly been driven to take loan because of certain medical contingencies. The same in rural areas turns out to be little over

Table 3.14 Distribution of medical and non-medical loans (%)

Study groups and study areas	Number of indebted households (N)	Purpose of loans	
		Medical	Others (consumption and productive combined)
Total indebted HHDs	858	21.0	79.0
Total rural	655	19.2	80.8
Total urban	203	26.6	73.4
Unnao	255	25.1	74.9
Rural	224	22.3	77.7
Urban	31	45.2	54.8
Jhansi	232	18.5	81.5
Rural	198	18.7	81.3
Urban	34	17.6	82.4
UP	487	22.0	78.0
Rural	422	20.6	79.4
Urban	65	30.8	69.2
Dausa	168	18.4	81.6
Rural	142	16.9	83.1
Urban	26	26.9	73.1
Dungarpur	112	14.3	85.7
Rural	91	16.5	83.5
Urban	21	4.2	95.2
Rajasthan	280	16.8	83.2
Rural	233	16.7	83.3
Urban	47	17.0	83.0
Slums	38	47.4	52.6
Non-slums	53	15.1	84.9
Delhi combined	91	28.6	71.4
SC	212	26.4	73.6
ST	100	27.1	72.9
OBC	365	19.7	80.3
Upper caste	181	8.8	91.2
Hindu	771	19.6	80.4
Muslim	79	25.3	74.7

19 %. Does it mean that public health-care facilities in urban areas are insufficient or is it a reflection of easier loan accessibility to urban people through different sources? While a categorical answer to both of these questions may not be possible with the data available to us, these are indeed significant issues and need to be examined separately with necessary details. The following discussion may however give some idea about the intake of medical loans from private moneylenders.

Differentials in loan intake by various household categories are evident from Fig. 3.14 as well. This figure reconfirms a much bigger fraction of urban households under medical debt at different places (see, e.g. urban Unnao or Dausa). Perhaps the more disturbing evidence from this figure relates to the slum households in Delhi. They are the biggest borrowers of money for medical reasons. Tribals and Muslims are also ahead in their respective categories.

Medical loans

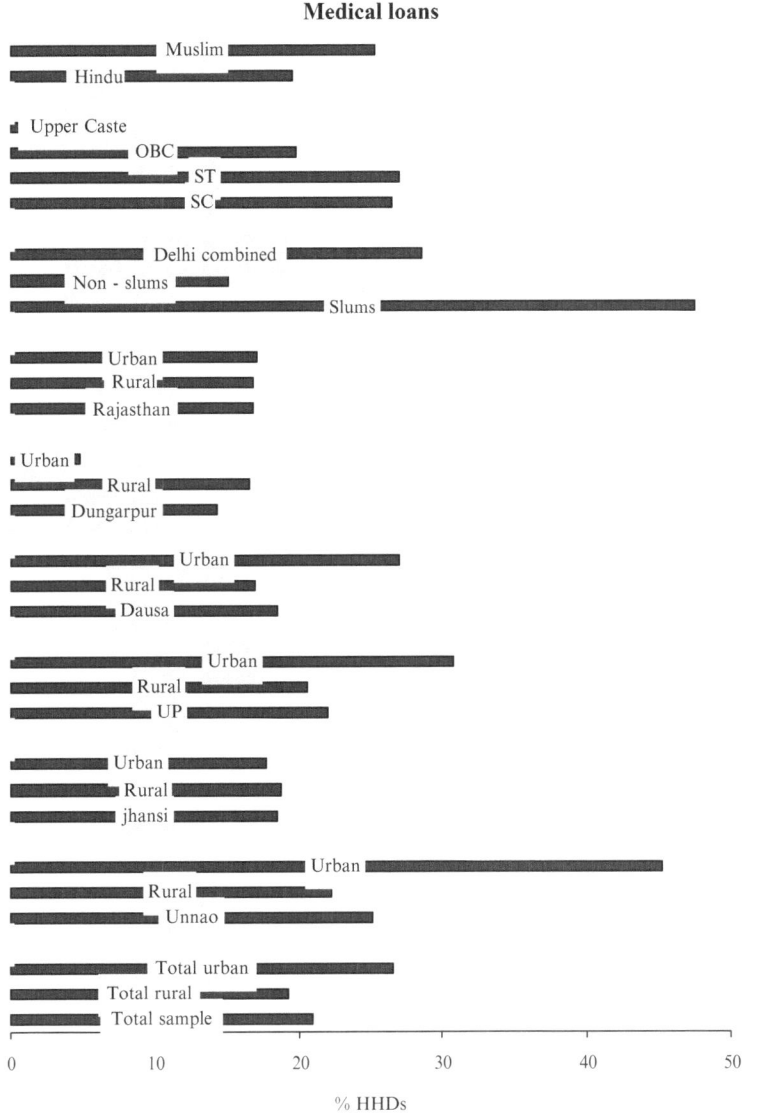

Fig. 3.14 Medical to the total loans by socioreligious groups and study areas

3.5.2 Sources of Loans and Borrowings

Seeking loans to meet contingencies may not be as much catastrophic. The worst perhaps lies with the source of borrowings. Unfortunately, due to no or limited access to modern banking facilities and complex lending rules even by public sector banks, most poor and low-income households may have no other option but to rely on private moneylenders with stringent repayment conditions including high interest rates. The details given in Table 3.15a clearly reveal private lending as the most commonly accessed method to meet medical expenses followed by a small percentage of households raising money from informal network of close family (mostly sons and daughters), friends or neighbours. The share of banks is obviously the lowest, rather minuscule, due to procedural difficulties.

The role of private lending appears to be especially large in rural areas where informal family sources appear to work less effectively—perhaps due to wider poverty and cash flow constraints. Table 3.15a indicates a big majority of rural households (about 71 % of those borrowed to access medical care) with borrowings from private moneylenders. Interestingly, urban households are not very far behind either. Almost 52 % of them had to borrow from local moneylenders despite growing emphasis in public pronouncements to improve medical care through involvement of remodelled watchdogs like RKSs.

Tables 3.15a and 3.15b are presented inter alia to compare the penetration of private moneylenders into medical and non-medical borrowing markets. As was expected, the presence of private moneylenders in medical borrowings is considerably big. Also, it turns out to be the case in most of the areas and population groups in question. Clearly, these figures indicate a very urgent need for an institutional mechanism to finance the health-care needs of low-income households in the country. Apparently, antipoverty measures may not work to its real potential unless health services are scaled up to a considerable extent in every domain, disease occurrences are minimised, and the health-care system is brought to bear to the needs of persons forced to borrow from private moneylenders.

3.5.3 Loan Repayment Status of Sample Households

Loan repayment status of households under both medical and non-medical debts is given in Table 3.16. Two straightforward observations may be made on the basis of this table. First, the size of households deficient in capabilities to initiate loan repayment process is disturbingly large across all the categories of responding households. This has been particularly true for most rural households in both the districts of UP and among the slum dwellers in Delhi. Muslims and most social groups including high-caste categories also fall in line. How or what happens to these households when they eventually start repaying their loans would indeed be an important issue to be examined with more detailed and focused data. Second observation relates to the rural–urban differentials in loan repayment as may be noticed from Fig. 3.15. It appears that rural and most other economically backward households may not be able to initiate the loan repayment process immediately. A cooling period may be required by many of them. This may or may not be possible depending upon the source of loan. How far the micro-credit institutions may lend support under these circumstances has to be considered. In addition, whether the micro-credit institutions can lend small amounts to meet medical contingencies also needs detailed examination.

Table 3.15a Sources of borrowings: households with medical loans (%)

	Total sample		UP		Rajasthan		Delhi		Social group				Religion	
	Rural	Urban	Rural	Urban	Rural	Urban	Slums	Non-slums	SC	ST	OBC	High caste	Hindu	Muslim
Banks[a]	9.5	9.3	11.5	20.0	5.1	0.0	5.6	0.0	7.8	7.4	9.3	14.8	10.2	0.0
Pvt. moneylenders	70.6	51.9	63.2	30.0	87.2	100.0	50.0	62.5	66.7	74.1	72.0	33.3	64.5	71.4
Relatives	19.8	38.9	25.3	50.0	7.7	0.0	44.4	37.5	25.5	18.5	18.7	51.9	25.3	28.6
Col. total	100.0	100.0	100.0	100.0	100.0	100.0	100.0	100.0	100.0	100.0	100.0	100.0	100.0	100.0

[a]Includes loans from cooperative and private banks

Table 3.15b Sources of borrowings: households with non-medical loans (%)

| | Total sample | | UP | | Rajasthan | | Delhi | | Social group | | | | Religion | |
	Rural	Urban	Rural	Urban	Rural	Urban	Slums	Non-slums	SC	ST	OBC	High caste	Hindu	Muslim
Banks[a]	43.9	32.9	53.4	28.9	27.3	43.6	0.0	42.2	35.4	28.8	42.4	52.0	43.0	24.6
Pvt. moneylenders	47.8	40.3	34.9	35.6	70.1	48.7	50.0	33.3	51.6	67.1	44.8	33.1	46.0	52.3
Relatives	8.3	26.9	11.6	35.6	2.6	7.7	50.0	24.4	13.0	4.1	12.8	14.9	11.1	23.1
Col. total	100.0	100.0	100.0	100.0	100.0	100.0	100.0	100.0	100.0	100.0	100.0	100.0	100.0	100.0

[a]Includes loans from cooperative and private banks

Table 3.16 Loan repayment status of sample households

	Rural HHDs		Urban HHDs	
	Payment	Non-payment	Payment	Non-payment
Unnao	35.3	64.7	64.5	35.5
Jhansi	32.8	67.2	50.0	50.0
UP	34.1	65.9	56.9	43.1
Dausa	66.2	33.8	88.5	11.5
Dungarpur	63.7	36.3	66.7	33.3
Rajasthan	65.2	34.8	78.7	21.3
Delhi	–	–	46.2	53.9
Slums	–	–	31.6	68.4
Non-slums	–	–	56.6	43.4
SC	43.5	56.5	45.1	54.9
ST	61.1	39.0	60.0	40.0
OBC	42.5	57.5	71.2	28.8
Upper caste	41.1	58.9	51.4	48.7
Hindu	45.4	54.7	58.0	42.0
Muslim	43.4	56.6	46.2	53.9

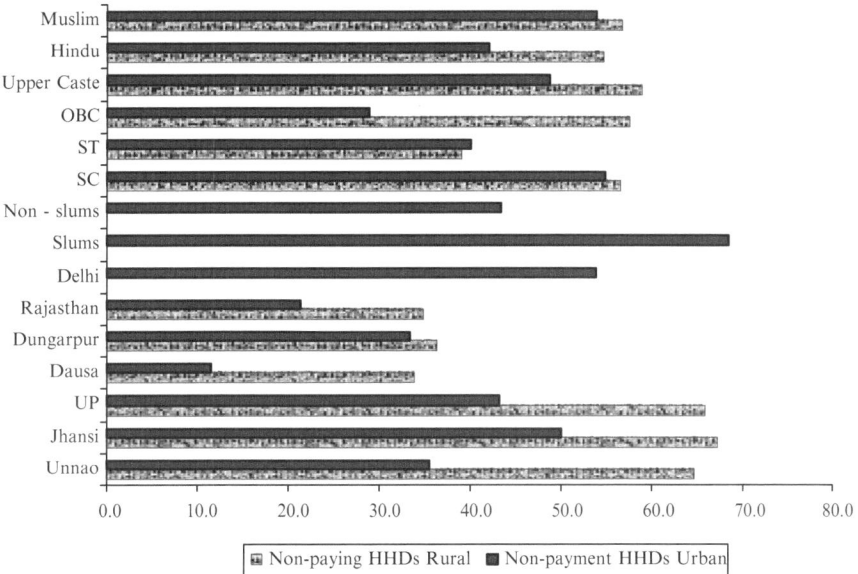

Fig. 3.15 Differentials in repayment of loans by rural and urban households

Appendix

Table 3.A.1 Distribution of sample population by education: rural and urban

Educational level	Combined sample			UP			Rajasthan		
	Rural[a]	Urban[b]	Total	Rural	Urban	Total	Rural	Urban	Total
Illiterate	36.1	20.9	30.4	36.7	20.0	32.6	35.3	22.9	32.4
Lit. without formal education	2.0	1.1	1.6	2.2	0.9	1.9	1.5	1.5	1.5
Up to 5th standard (primary)	30.7	27.3	29.5	31.9	25.1	30.2	29.0	28.7	28.9
7th–8th standard (middle)	18.0	15.1	16.9	17.1	17.0	17.1	19.5	18.6	19.3
Matriculate	6.7	12.1	8.7	6.0	12.7	7.6	7.9	11.3	8.7
Higher secondary	3.6	9.1	5.7	3.7	10.0	5.3	3.5	7.7	4.5
Graduates and above	2.3	11.2	5.6	2.1	12.0	4.5	2.6	7.6	3.7
Diploma/certificate	0.2	1.0	0.5	0.2	1.4	0.5	0.0	0.5	0.1
Degree in technical or professional education	0.3	2.3	1.1	0.1	0.9	0.3	0.7	1.3	0.8
Total literacy level	63.9	79.1	69.6	63.3	80.0	67.4	64.7	77.1	67.6
Literate + illiterate	100.0	100.0	100.0	100.0	100.0	100.0	100.0	100.0	100.0
	Chi2 (9) 959.970, Pr. 0.000			Chi2 (9) 522.245, Pr. 0.000			Chi2 (9) 118.430, Pr. 0.000		

Source: Author's Survey on OOP Health Expenditure (2008)
[a]Including slum population
[b]Including non-slum population

Table 3.A.2 Main and marginal workers by sample districts

	Total population (Nos.)	Main workers (%)	Marginal workers (%)	Total workers (%)
Unnao				
Person	2,700,324	25.4	8.9	34.3
Male	1,422,509	43.1	6.9	50.0
Female	1,277,815	5.6	11.1	16.8
Jhansi				
Person	1,744,931	26.8	10.3	37.02
Male	932,818	42.2	7.0	49.13
Female	812,113	9.1	14.0	23.12
Dausa				
Person	1,317,063	31.7	9.51	41.2
Male	693,438	41.3	4.47	45.8
Female	623,625	21.0	15.12	36.1
Dungarpur				
Person	1,107,643	24.6	23.4	48.0
Male	547,791	36.8	14.5	51.3
Female	559,852	12.6	32.1	44.7

Census of India. 2001. *District Census Handbook (for respective states)*, New Delhi: Ministry of Home Affairs, Government of India (http://www.censusindia.net/)

Table 3.A.3 Block 5: questions on households' food and nonfood consumption items

S. No.	Items	Past 1 year (Rs.)	Past 30 days (Rs.)	Past 7 days (Rs.)
1.1	Cereals and cereal products (flour, maida, suji, rice)			
1.2	Pulses/pulses products (dals, gram and products)			
1.3	Milk			
1.4	Milk products (baby food, ghee, butter, ice cream)			
1.5	All edible oils, vanaspati, refined oil			
1.6	Vegetables			
1.7	All kinds of fruits, nuts, dry fruits, etc.			
1.8	Eggs, meat, poultry, fish, sea food			
1.9	Sugar, gur, candy, misri, honey, khandsari			
1.10	Salt and spices (chilli powder, curry masala, seeds)			
1.11	Other food items (tea, coffee, biscuit, processed food, pickles, sauce, cooked meal, cake, chocolate)			
1.12	Any other food item			
2	Expenditure on bidi/cigarette/tobacco/gutka/pan			
3	Expenditure on liquor, wine			
4	Primary or secondary level education			
5.	Higher education (BA/B.Sc/B.Com and above)			
6.	Professional education: medical, Engg., IT, MBA			
7.	Expenditure on house: rent/tax/house loan			
8.	Expenditure on fuel and lighting			
9.	Clothing, bedding, shoes/footwear			
10	Social, religious expenditure or festival expenses			
11.	Health expenditure (self-medication/chemists)			
12	Health expenditure on doctor's advise (report only nonhospitalisation cases)			
13.	Health expenditure due to hospitalisation			
14.	Therapeutic appliances (eye glasses, hearing aids)			
15.	Jewellery, ornaments, other ladies' items			
16	Personal transport (car, motor bike, scooter, cycle)			
17.	Household electrical/other appliances, clock, TV			
18.	Crockery, utensils, furniture			
19.	Computer, mobile, wrist watch and misc. items			
20.	Any other including repair and maintenance			
21	*Total household expenditure*			

Interviewers: *Please ask these details for the entire household (including expenditure on pets)*

Table 3.A.4 Descriptive statistics: PCMCE of sample populations

	N	Mean MPCE	Std. dev	Min. MPCE	Max. MPCE
Total sample	**2,010**	**996.8**	**1264.2**	**79.1**	**16,885.4**
UP sample	1,000	663.2	594.6	79.1	6,958.3
UP rural	750	571.4	470.6	79.1	6,958.3
UP urban	250	938.6	806.7	120.0	5,356.5
Rajasthan sample	650	793.7	778.1	143.0	11,189.1

(continued)

Table 3.A.4 (continued)

	N	Mean MPCE	Std. dev	Min. MPCE	Max. MPCE
Rajasthan rural	500	715.6	774.5	143.0	11,189.1
Rajasthan urban	150	1,054.0	734.5	186.7	3,750.4
Delhi sample	360	2,290.2	2,191.6	328.2	16,885.4
Slums	102	903.8	455.7	328.2	2,869.3
Non-slum	258	2,838.3	2,358.6	339.1	16,885.4
Social groups					
SC	455	737.2	637.5	79.1	6,958.3
ST	249.0	644.2	986.1	143.0	11,189.1
OBC	777.0	731.0	653.3	117.4	6,987.5
Upper caste	529.0	1,776.5	1,954.0	147.3	16,885.4
Religion					
Hindu	1,789.0	994.3	1,263.9	79.1	16,885.4
Muslim	188.0	753.3	808.8	166.2	9,556.3

References

Atkinson, A. B. (1970). On the measurement of inequality. *Journal of Economic Theory, 2*, 244–263.

Atkinson, A. B. (1983). *The economics of inequality* (2nd ed.). Oxford: Clarendon.

Coudouel, A., Hentschel, J. S., & Wondon, Q. T. (2002). Poverty measurement and analysis (Chapter 1). In J. Klugman (Ed.), *A sourcebook of poverty reduction strategies* (Core techniques and cross-cutting issues, Vol. 1). Washington, DC: The World Bank.

Cowell, F. A. (2000). *Measurement of inequality*, Chapter 2. In A. B. Atkinson & F. Bourguignon (Eds.), *Handbook of income distribution* (Vol. 1, pp. 87–166). North Holland.

Dreze, J., & Murthi, M. (2001). Fertility, education and development in India. In K. Srinivasan & M. Vlassoff (Eds.), *Population development nexus in India – Challenges for the new millennium* (pp. 233–249). New Delhi: Tata McGraw Hill.

Gwatkin, D. R. (2000). Health inequalities and the health of the poor: What do we know? What can we do? *Bulletin of the WHO, 78*(1), 3–18.

Klugman, J. (Ed.). (2002). *A sourcebook of poverty reduction strategies* (Core techniques and cross-cutting issues, vol.1, Technical Note A.7). Washington, DC: The World Bank.

National Sample Survey Organization. (2006). *Morbidity, health care and conditions of the aged: sixtieth round (January–June 2004)*. New Delhi: National Sample Survey Organization.

NSSO. (2006a). *Level and Pattern of Consumer Expenditure*, 61st Round, 2004–2005 (61st Round) (Report No. 508). New Delhi: Government of India, Ministry of Statistics and Programme Implementation, December 2006.

NSSO. (2006b). *Press note on household borrowings and repayment in India during 2002–2003*, NSSO. New Delhi: Government of India, Press Information Bureau. Accessed 31 Jan 2006.

Planning Commission's. (2007, March 21). *Poverty estimates, 2004–2005*, released by the Press Information Bureau, Government of India.

Probe Team report in association with Centre for Development Economics. (1999). *Public report on basic education in India*. New Delhi: Oxford University Press.

Sen, A. K. (1973). *On economic inequality*. Oxford: Clarendon.

Shah, S., & Rani, M. (2003, April 1). *Worlds apart: Why are Kerala and UP so different in their human development outcomes?* (Background Paper for the World Development Report 2004: Making services work for the poor (mimeo)). World Bank/Oxford University Press.

Chapter 4
Self-Reported Ailments and Hospitalisation: Differentials in Utilisation of Health Care

This chapter brings two interesting issues into focus. And both of them have been treated with considerable interest in the contemporary literature on utilisation of health services (Rahman and Rao 2004; Kumar 2001; Fernandez et al. 1999; Ganatra and Hirve 1994; Koenig et al. 2001, etc.). First, the gender differentials in health-care access including hospitalisation and outpatient care. The second follows from the first and relates to similar differentials between the rich and the poor[1] or, as we have been terming in this analysis, above-poverty (APL) and below-poverty (BPL) populations.[2] In the remainder of this chapter, it is attempted to provide a few empirical details covering both of these issues, and once again our value addition lies in our focus on high-poverty areas of two major states and an exclusive, though small, sample of slum households in Delhi. Alongside, it may also be noted that self-reported data on health, morbidity and utilisation of health care require cautious interpretation because of variations in perceptions about one's own health, suffering and healing by individual respondents (Rahman and Barsky 2003; Sen 2002).

4.1 Interstate and Gender-Wise Differentials in Health Care

Despite years of hard work and long-drawn conviction to raise an inclusive society, India continues to remain a country with all forms of inequities and socio-economic divides. In health too, it is common to observe such divides. Preferential treatment given to males is particularly high in medical care, and there are studies by doctors to reveal that boys receive more prompt attention than girls in medical contingencies and cases of hospitalisation (Kumar 2001). It may however be interesting to

---

[1] With tremendous improvement in health status of populations all over the world, there are some who believe that this debate is losing its relevance. We however refrain from taking a position either way.

[2] The z values and the methodology used to derive below- and above-poverty populations remained as was in Box 3.1 (i.e. consumption poverty 1).

M. Alam, *Paying Out-of-Pocket for Drugs, Diagnostics and Medical Services: A Study of Households in Three Indian States*, India Studies in Business and Economics, DOI 10.1007/978-81-322-1281-2_4, © Springer India 2013

Table 4.1 Hospitalised and nonhospitalised care by gender and socioreligious groups (*N* = 11,063)

Operational variables	Sample population (*N*) (numbers)			Hospitalisation (%) (recall period: past 365 days)			Nonhospitalised treatments (%) (recall period: past 30 days)		
	Male	Female	Total	Male	Female	Total	Male	Female	Total
Tot. sample	5,810	5,253	11,063	2.2	3.8	3.0	14.6	16.9	15.7
UP	2,972	2,631	5,603	1.9	3.4	2.6	15.2	17.6	16.3
Unnao	1,833	1,603	3,436	2.1	3.4	2.7	15.1	17.2	16.1
Jhansi	1,139	1,028	2,167	1.5	3.4	2.4	15.3	18.2	16.7
Rajasthan	1,852	1,671	3,523	2.7	4.1	3.3	13.2	14.2	13.7
Dausa	898	806	1,704	2.8	3.2	3.0	14.6	16.5	15.5
Dungarpur	954	865	1,819	2.6	4.9	3.7	11.8	12.0	11.9
Delhi	986	951	1,937	2.3	4.6	3.5	15.5	19.8	17.6
Non-slum	716	652	1,368	2.0	4.1	3.0	15.6	20.4	17.9
Slum	270	299	569	3.3	5.7	4.6	15.2	18.4	16.9
SC	1,315	1,216	2,531	2.4	3.8	3.1	15.4	17.3	16.3
ST	705	656	1,361	2.6	2.9	2.7	15.2	15.2	15.2
OBC	2,314	2,053	4,367	2.2	3.9	3.0	13.3	15.9	14.5
Upper caste	1,476	1,328	2,804	1.9	4.2	3.0	15.7	18.8	17.2
Hindu	5,152	4,643	9,795	2.2	3.9	3.0	14.9	16.7	15.8
Muslim	578	534	1,112	2.1	3.6	2.8	12.5	17.4	14.8
BPL	1,705	1,665	3,370	0.6	1.9	1.2	13.0	13.9	13.4
APL	4,105	3,588	7,693	2.9	4.7	3.7	15.3	18.3	16.7

note that the results drawn in this study supplant a few of these arguments and portray a reverse picture. Table 4.1 indicates a significantly large share of women in utilisation of hospitalised treatment. In addition, it happens almost across the board. More or less the same is true for the nonhospitalised care as well. The reason why we draw an excess of health care by women over men in this analysis is however not very difficult to identify. Our sample is inclusive of women in child-bearing ages as well, and the overall hospitalisation cases are based on all forms of ailments including pre- or postnatal care, delivery and gynaecological problems along with most other normal health-related issues and injuries. The same explanation holds for the nonhospitalised cases as well. This point is reiterated further by Fig. 4.1 that gives a distribution of women accessing both hospitalised and nonhospitalised health care across five broad age categories, i.e. 0–4, 5–14, 15–39, 40–49 and 60 years or above. We notice from this figure that the share of women in the 15–39 age group—normally considered as the prime years in the reproductive lifespan of women—is the highest followed by those in the 5–14 and 40–59 age groups.

Gender-wise differences in hospitalisation are considerably large in both the districts of Rajasthan (2.8 % for men and 3.2 % for women in Dausa and 2.6 % for men and 4.9 % for women in Dungarpur). The highest rate of women hospitalisation may however be noticed from Delhi slums where it turns out to be 5.7 %. The non-slum women too are in good numbers although they lag behind their slum counterparts to a good extent. A possible inference may therefore be that women at most of the places

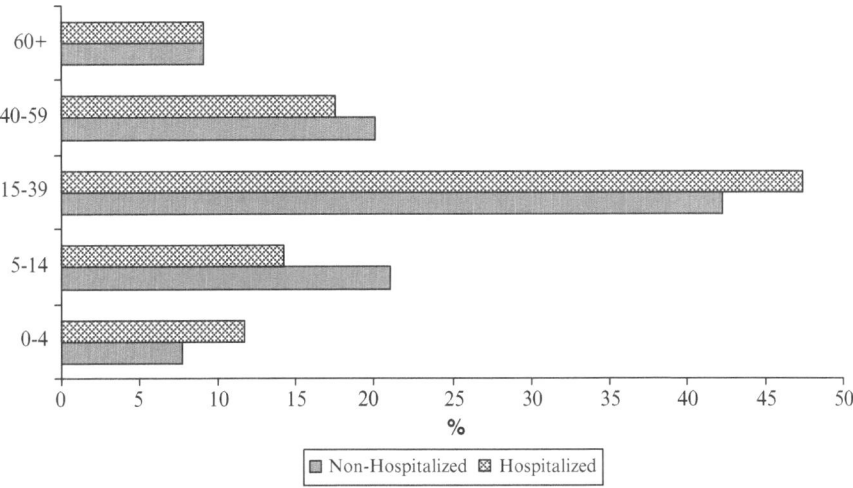

Fig. 4.1   Age distribution of women using hospital and nonhospital care (%)

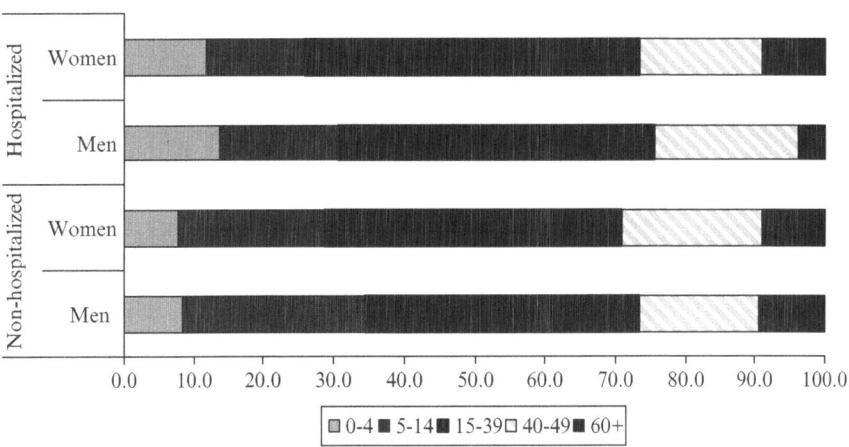

Fig. 4.2   Users of hospital and nonhospital care by age and sex (%)

have begun to use institutional services for different reasons and their number may grow further with time, though such an evidence is relatively weak in both the districts of UP. Muslims and tribal women are also somewhat lagging behind.

A men–women comparison of health-care utilisation across comparable age brackets in Fig. 4.2 reconfirms the male bias at least in early ages. The situation turns in favour of women in the 15–39 age group with higher child-bearing potential. Women in the 60+ age group are also prone to more hospitalisation than men (Fig. 4.2). However, a generalisation of these results may need further evidence based on larger sample size.

As a whole, our results do confirm the existing notion of gender biases in utilisation of health care with females, in general, at a disadvantageous position. However, if disaggregated over different age spans, our results indicate that younger women in their prime child-bearing ages have accessed health care in higher percentages than their male counterparts. This is indeed a somewhat interesting indication and needs to be re-examined with bigger sample size and more focused survey instruments detailing the causes of health-care utilisation.

4.2   Poor and Nonpoor Differentials in Utilisation of Health Care

There are positive links, as many analysts believe, between economic status and a better sense of suffering or ill health leading to a better reporting of ailments and utilisation of in or outpatient health-care services (Sen 2002). There are contrary views as well (Smith 2004; Crossley and Kennedy 2002). We have relied on the latter.

The poor and nonpoor in this analysis are defined as in Box 3.1 and configure with above-poverty and below-poverty populations. The details provided in Table 4.2 give a sex-wise distribution of health-care utilisation by poor and nonpoor in rural and urban areas of the states under consideration. This table lends support to the growing perception that the nonpoor utilise hospital care in greater proportions than the poor.

Table 4.2 Utilisation of health care by poor and nonpoor (%)

	Rural				Urban			
	Below poverty		Above poverty		Below poverty		Above poverty	
	Male	Female	Male	Female	Male	Female	Male	Female
Sample areas of UP								
Hospitalised	0.7	1.3	2.4	4.6	0.5	2.7	3.0	4.2
Nonhospitalised	13.5	15.3	18.1	20.0	6.8	8.1	13.4	19.3
N	867	825	1,375	1,169	192	185	538	452
Sample areas of Rajasthan								
Hospitalised	0.3	1.2	3.8	4.5	1.5	4.7	2.7	6.9
Nonhospitalised	14.0	13.8	13.4	14.6	13.5	10.9	11.1	15.0
N	406	406	1,016	877	133	128	297	260
	Slums and non-slums: Delhi							
	Slums				Non-slums			
	Below poverty		Above poverty		Below poverty		Above poverty	
	Male	Female	Male	Female	Male	Female	Male	Female
Hospitalised	1.2	3.2	4.2	6.8	0.0	3.6	2.0	4.2
Nonhospitalised	17.3	18.3	14.3	18.5	7.7	14.3	15.9	20.7
N	81	93	189	206	26	28	690	624

But this is not decisively so in outpatient care, and in certain areas, the poor outnumber the nonpoor in accessing physicians' care. This may particularly be noticed in Rajasthan. In UP, however, the nonpoor appear to have greater access to nonhospitalised care as well and contribute to the general thinking that medical care and economic status go side by side.

Notwithstanding these differences, it may be noticed from the results that a fraction of poor (BPL) households reporting utilisation of health-care services—with or without hospitalisation—is considerably less than the nonpoor (APL). However, it may not be easy to comment on the correctness of these findings because of limitations in self-reported morbidity by poor, illiterate and less informed households. There are some other issues also surrounding this entire debate that are delved later in this analysis.

References

Crossley, T. F., & Kennedy, S. (2002). The reliability of self-assessed health status. *Journal of Health Economics, 21*, 643–658.

Fernandez, E., et al. (1999). Gender inequalities in health and health care services use in Catalonia. *Journal of Epidemiology and Community Health, 53*(4), 218–222.

Ganatra, B., & Hirve, S. (1994). Male bias in health care utilisation for under fives in rural community in western India. *Bulletin of the WHO, 72*(1), 101–104.

Koenig, M. A., Bishai, D., & Khan, M. A. (2001). Health interventions and health equity: The example of measles vaccination in Bangladesh. *Population and Development Review, 27*(2), 283–302.

Kumar, A. K. S. (2001). Health and human security: Some consideration for priority setting. In S. M. Dev, P. Antony, V. Gayathri, & R. P. Mamgain (Eds.), *Social and economic security in India* (pp. 146–163). New Delhi: Institute of Human Development.

Rahman, M. O., & Barsky, A. J. (2003). Self-reported health among older Bangladeshis: How good a health indicator is it? *The Gerontologist, 43*, 856–863.

Rahman, L., & Rao, V. (2004). The determinants of gender equality in India: Examining Dyson and Mcore's thesis with new data. *Population and Development Review, 30*(2), 239–268.

Sen, A. (2002 April 13). Editorial: Health: Perception versus observation. *British Medical Journal, 324*(7342), 860–861.

Smith, J. P. (2004). Unraveling the SES-health connection. *Population and Development Review, 30*, 108–132.

Chapter 5
Catastrophic Spending on Health by Sample Households: Some Results

As was noted in Chap. 1, a good amount of literature at the all India or by states now already exists to suggest that health expenditure in India and some other low-income countries in Asia is considerably large (Bonu et al. 2007; Gottret and Schieber 2006; O'Donnell et al. 2008; Xu et al. 2003, etc.). A great deal of this expenditure—almost three-quarters or in some cases even more—is borne privately by households in many of these countries, in particular those with inadequate health-care systems. In a large number of cases, OOP spending on health causes serious implications for low-income households and affects their sustained living by affecting their normal expenditure pattern, particularly on a host of important nonfood items. A number of these issues have begun to receive much wider attention in India over the past few years, particularly after the seminal report by the NCMH (Ministry of Health and Family Welfare 2005). There has also been a growing concern over these years regarding major policy failures on the part of the centre and state governments in providing adequate resources—physical, financial and human—to meet health-care needs of the people, in particular the poor and the needy.[1] This Commission has also explicitly recognised in its report the prevalence of a very high OOP spending on health in several low-income states—in particular by the households in lowest income deciles—and its role in pushing a significant fraction of households to face poverty and debt trap (see Section 2 of the Commission's Report, 2005). More or less, a similar inference was drawn in Chap. 3 of this study indicating a large fraction of households sliding below poverty level after incurring OOP expenses on health. Many of them had to borrow from private money-lenders with high repayment liabilities leading to asset divestments.

Recently, India has received considerable attention from the world community for its potential to sustain high growth over the coming years. Alongside, however, there has also been a growing concern about serious disparities and unequal distribution of the nation's wealth (Asian Development Bank 2007). Health disparities and asymmetrically higher burden of health-care expenditure on poorer households have, in particular, remained a major concern in many of the recent studies with

---

[1] See reports cited in footnote 3, Chap. 1.

M. Alam, *Paying Out-of-Pocket for Drugs, Diagnostics and Medical Services: A Study of Households in Three Indian States*, India Studies in Business and Economics, DOI 10.1007/978-81-322-1281-2_5, © Springer India 2013

focus on issues relating to poverty and unequal sharing of welfare strategies initiated by the governments. The NCMH (2005) has clearly stated in its report that the 'inequity in the access to and distribution of public health services has been a concern because of the extent of impoverishment households face on account of ill-health and catastrophic illness in particular' (page 71).

As was highlighted in Chap. 1, over the past one decade or so, there have been several studies based on Indian data to examine catastrophic spending by poor and low-income households on health and some of its correlates (Bonu et al. 2007; Roy and Howard 2007; Ranson et al. 2006; Garg and Karan 2009; Peters et al. 2002). Most of these studies are, however, based on earlier rounds of the National Sample Surveys on household consumption or health expenditure. The study by Bonu et al. (2007) has however relied on most recent NSS (61st round conducted during the 12 months of July 2004 to June 2005) to investigate the incidence, intensity and important correlates of catastrophic health-care payments in India (NSSO 2006a, b). None of these studies have however tried to make use of data drawn from smaller towns and villages like the one collected by us with a particular focus on economically low-performing states and the slum community. An attempt is therefore made in the rest of this chapter to examine the catastrophic nature of spending made by a cross-section of households from the low-income districts of two major states and the capital city of Delhi. The focus of this chapter is largely directed towards three critical issues. These are:

- Size of health expenditure by households in relation to their (i) total consumption budget comprising goods and services purchased from market and (ii) nonfood consumption expenditure.
- Catastrophic health expenditure by households based on multiple cut-offs or threshold norms. Both total and nonfood consumption expenditures are used to define catastrophe.
- Correlates of catastrophic expenditure.

A limitation encountered by studies using head count of catastrophic spending on health ought not to be overlooked. In many cases, this otherwise very useful concept does not include the households unable to access health-care services due to extreme poverty or lack of understanding about certain ailments. There may also be households with a trade-off between OOP health-care spending and the risks of falling into impoverishment. A few may decide to bargain medical treatment against the risk of any further slippage into living standard or long-term consumption poverty. Catastrophe analyses unfortunately exclude all such factors.

5.1 Share of OOP Health-Care Spending in Total and Nonfood Consumption Budget

As noted, this section summarises the magnitude and distribution of OOP health-care spending by a sample of households drawn from selected rural and urban areas of UP (total 1,000 households—750 rural and 250 urban), Rajasthan (650—500 rural and 150 urban) and Delhi (360—102 from identified slums and 258 from non-slums).

Table 5.1a OOP health expenditure as a percentage of the total consumption expenditure: sample households (%)

OOP payments as % of HHDs' total PCMCE	Total sample		UP		Rajasthan		Delhi	
	Rural	Urban	Rural	Urban	Rural	Urban	Slums	Non-slum
Panel 1								
N	1,250	760	750	250	500	150	102	258
Mean	14.9	10.6	15.2	10.5	14.5	11.3	13.8	9.0
SD	0.1635	0.1446	0.1674	0.1552	0.1575	0.1449	0.1586	0.1251
CV	109.6	136.7	110.0	148.5	108.9	128.5	115.0	138.8
Panel 2								
Quintile means								
Poorest 20 %	9.4	7.9	9.7	6.3	8.9	12.2	5.9	7.3
2nd quintile	10.2	9.6	10.6	7.4	9.4	14.4	12.7	8.8
3rd quintile	13.8	9.6	13.2	9.4	14.7	9.4	12.2	9.3
4th quintile	17.5	12.6	18.3	19.0	16.4	6.4	13.0	11.8
Richest 20 %	23.7	13.1	27.2	29.9	20.0	19.8	25.6	8.0

There are two basic underpinnings that have helped to evolve this entire chapter. First, it tries to highlight further the cascading role played by the OOP payments in squeezing finances available to lower-quintile households and tamper with their budget allocations to different goods and services consumed by the family. Given the asymmetrical nature of intra-household (intra-family) distribution of resources, there are strong possibilities that the aged, women and other weaker members in the family with poor bargaining strength may get disproportionately affected (Agarwal 1990). The second objective obviously is to bring further evidence in support of an emerging consensus among analysts favouring added public resources to improve health care in order to cushion low-income households and bring down the risks of their falling below poverty threshold. Risk pooling measures a bigger proportion of population that must also be paid serious attention with measures to ensure a quicker implementation (Joglekar 2008). Yet another important issue relates to growing drug prices and cascading effect of patenting laws that make medicines simply unaffordable to people in many poor and low-income countries including India.

Tables 5.1a, 5.1b, 5.2a and 5.2b distribute households by the mean of their OOP health share in monthly consumption expenditure—both total and nonfood.[2] These

---

[2]The following steps were taken to derive the mean share of OOP in households' total (or per capita) consumption budget:

Step 1: $OOP_{share_i} = OOP_i / T_{c_i}$ where i = 1, 2, ..., N

OOP_i is the health payments of the ith HHD i = 1, 2, ..., N (where N is 2,010 for total sample).

T_{c_i} stands for total household consumption expenditure for the ith household.

As noted, N is the number of total households, by states, rural–urban or socioreligious characteristics.

Step 2: Mean $= \sum_{i=1}^{N} OOP_{share_i} / N$

A similar procedure was used to calculate OOP share in nonfood consumption expenditure.

Comparing shares of OOP spending separately on hospitalisation and outpatient care in total or nonfood consumption expenditures was not attempted because of certain data limitations and also to avoid the risks of recall lapses by households.

Table 5.1b OOP health expenditure as a percentage of the total consumption expenditure: socioreligious groups (%)

OOP payments as % of HHDs' total PCMCE	Social groups				Religions	
	SC	ST	OBC	Upper caste	Hindu	Muslim
Panel 1						
N	455	249	777	529	1,789	188
Mean	15.8	13.8	13.4	10.7	13.5	12.3
SD	0.1742	0.1355	0.1614	0.1440	0.1588	0.1559
CV	110.3	98.4	120.6	134.5	117.8	126.5
Panel 2						
Quintile means						
Poorest 20 %	9.3	9.2	9.0	8.9	9.3	7.6
2nd quintile	10.8	14.5	11.6	7.4	11.2	12.1
3rd quintile	17.6	20.1	13.7	10.2	14.9	10.3
4th quintile	18.4	19.6	16.1	11.1	15.8	14.6
Richest 20 %	26.9	14.5	20.2	11.7	16.4	19.0

Table 5.2a OOP health expenditure as a percentage of nonfood expenditure: sample households (%)

OOP payments as % of HHDs' nonfood exp.	Total sample		UP		Rajasthan		Delhi	
	Rural	Urban	Rural	Urban	Rural	Urban	Slums	Non-slums
N	1,250	760	750	250	500	150	102	258
Mean	31.2	19.8	32.6	20.0	29.1	21.2	27.9	15.5
SD	0.2540	0.2208	0.2615	0.2323	0.2411	0.2329	0.2461	0.1784
CV	81.4	111.7	80.2	116.3	82.9	109.9	88.1	115.2

Table 5.2b OOP health expenditure as a percentage of nonfood expenditure: socioreligious groups (%)

OOP payments as % of HHDs' nonfood exp.	Social groups				Religions	
	SC	ST	OBC	Upper caste	Hindu	Muslim
N	455	249	777	529	1,789	188
Mean	32.0	30.2	27.4	20.1	27.1	26.7
SD	0.2599	0.2324	0.2550	0.2193	0.2490	0.2490
CV	81.2	77.1	93.1	108.9	91.7	93.1

bivariate tables are further extended to highlight differentials across the observed socioreligious groups including SC, ST, OBC and upper castes as well as the two dominant religious categories in most survey areas, namely, Hindus and Muslims (see Tables 5.1b and 5.2b). As before, these results are presented without going into further desegregations to avoid small-sample biases and ensure sufficient number of observation within each response category.

Tables 5.1a and 5.1b provide the share of OOP health spending in total consumption budget—the latter furnishes similar information separately with a break-up by two religious and four social groups. Our results in many cases fail to compare with a few of the earlier studies, suggesting an average of about 5 % of the total consumption budget (and 10 % of the nonfood consumption budget) on OOP health care in India (van Doorslaer et al. 2007; Bonu et al. 2007). Our data indicate a considerably higher OOP mean spending on medical bills in all the three states and their selected villages or towns. Also, this lack of comparison continues in relation to both total and nonfood consumption budgets.

Table 5.1a (panel 1) gives the average share of OOP spending on health in total consumption of households located in rural and urban areas of both the states. Curiously, the mean OOP share of rural households is considerably large. Further, it exceeds the urban share as well. Among the rural households, for example, the mean OOP expenditure varies between 14 and 15 % of the total budget. The same in the urban areas is drawn between 10.5 and a little over 11 %. It may also be noticed from these results that the people from slums, on an average, spend a much larger share of their consumption budget than those from the non-slums (14 % by the slum residents compared to only 9 % by those from non-slums). It strongly suggests a regressive nature of spending if we could assume that all the non-slum households are essentially more affluent. This also reflects a significant departure on our part from the existing body of evidence that suggests that the poor pay less than the nonpoor.

We are nevertheless closer to the existing literature if we compare the mean OOP spending of households by consumption quintiles. While the magnitude of spending remained large, the OOP shares of the rich and poor differ significantly with highest quintile (or top 20 % of households according to their PCMCE) spending almost a quarter of their total consumption budget on health (Table 5.1a, panel 2). In contrast, the same for the bottom 20 % is about 10–12 % in rural and urban areas. The progressivism, as argued in the literature, is therefore maintained.

Table 5.1b provides OOP differentials among four social (SC, ST, OBC and upper castes) and two religious categories—Hindus and Muslims. Judged by social groupings, the lower-caste communities incur much higher OOP payments than their upper-caste counterparts. In terms of religion, though the two respective groups mutually differ, their differences at best remained marginal, i.e. less than a percentage point (Hindus 13.5 % of their total consumption expenditure, while for the Muslims it is given as 12.3 %). The progressivism among five consumption quintiles is also maintained.

Yet another important point to notice from Tables 5.1a and 5.1b is very high variations around the mean OOP. At almost every quintile level or socioreligious grouping, the coefficient of variation is more than 100 %, which tends to indicate extreme values at almost every level, quintile or social groups. It also amounts to suggest that there are households in each category with negligible spending on health services—inpatient or ambulatory.

The differences between the two sets of results—our own and those in the literature cited above—raise an interesting question: Do studies based on macro-data, often regarded as more policy friendly, really provide the realities faced by impoverished households from poor districts or geographical locations? In all fairness, perhaps both have their own merits and ought to be supplemented by each other.

With the mean of OOP payments as high in relation to total consumption expenditure as shown in Tables 5.1a and 5.1b, the same in relation to nonfood consumption expenditure can easily be guessed. It touches around 30 % of the total in rural areas and 20 % in urban areas (Tables 5.2a and 5.2b). In other words, mean of OOP in relation to nonfood expenditure is likely to stand double to that of the total consumption expenditure. The rest of the results follow exactly the same pattern exhibited above and therefore bear more or less similar explanation.

5.2   Catastrophic Health Spending: An Examination

With the mean of OOP health budget in total or nonfood consumption expenditure as high as was demonstrated in the preceding discussion, there is indeed every possibility that a large fraction of the low-income sample households must be facing a catastrophic situation, depending upon how the catastrophe is defined. Using the criterion employed in recent literature on catastrophic health spending—in particular by the WHO—this section is basically designed to examine a couple of these issues.[3] It also provides a head count of households faced with a catastrophic situation by both their place of residence and socioreligious characteristics. Intensity of catastrophic health spending, described in the literature as mean payment overshoot (MPO), is also discussed based on our sample data.

5.2.1   Computation of Catastrophic Health Spending: Methodology

Catastrophic health-care payments are defined by analysts as a fraction of total or nonfood consumption expenditure exceeding a certain threshold level. A higher health-care share often severely endangers the consumption level of the entire family and brings it to an economic quandary (Garg and Karan 2009; Bonu et al. 2007; Kawabata et al. 2002). Two levels of threshold OOP spending are generally used to define the catastrophe:

- Catastrophe 1: cut-off share of OOP health spending up to or beyond 10 % of the total family or household consumption budget.
- Catastrophe 2: OOP health share up to or beyond 40 % of the total family or household nonfood consumption budget.

To simplify the argument, we have slightly deviated from the general practice and used a set of multiple threshold levels (z) for both types of catastrophes—5, 10, 15 and 25 % of the total consumption budget for catastrophe 1 and 15, 25, 40 and 60 % of nonfood consumption budget for catastrophe 2. Algebraically, the following steps are taken to obtain the head count of households with health-care budget share exceeding z:

---

[3] See, for example, a comprehensive methodological note on catastrophic expenditures prepared by Xu (2004). It may also be noted that the OOP expenditure in this analysis does not include any form of reimbursement—insurance or noninsurance.

Step 1: $O_{hhd_i} = \left(O_{hhd_i} / hhd_i^{tot-con} \right) - \left(z \times hhd_i^{tot-con} \right)$

Step 2: $\bar{O}_{hhd} = \dfrac{1}{N} \sum\limits_{i=1}^{N} O_{hhd_i}$ (where $N = 1, 2, \ldots, 2{,}010$ for the total sample and z

(assigned with multiple values) denotes the threshold levels of both total and non-food consumption expenditure). Similarly, O_{hhd_i} stands for out-of-pocket health payment budget of ith household ($\bar{O}_{hhd_i}$ is the mean OOP budget), and $hhd_i^{tot-con}$ refers to total consumption expenditure of the same household. Barring changes in z values, an identical procedure was adopted to measure catastrophe based on non-food expenditure.

The entire calculations were made on the basis of the total and nonfood per capita monthly consumption expenditure (PCMCE).

5.2.2 Head Count of Catastrophic Spending: Some Results

Table 5.3 gives the socioreligious and state-wise distributions of households exceeding OOP thresholds in relation to their total consumption budget.[4] The results are indeed alarming at their face value and pose major challenges for the health planners and institutions engaged in delivery of health-care services. These results clearly indicate that an overwhelming share of households in study areas is facing a serious catastrophic situation because of high OOP expenses on health. To illustrate, at the lowest threshold level, i.e. at 5 % level of total consumption expenditure, there are more than 67 % of the rural and 51 % of the urban households exceeding this limit. The same at the 10 % threshold level—which is generally considered as a catastrophic health spending by most of the analysts—turns out to be 49.5 % in rural areas and 32 % in urban areas. Moreover, our results further indicate that almost a fifth (18.5 %) of the rural households and over a tenth (11.6 %) of the urban households spend more than a quarter of their total consumption budget on health care.

How far it would be plausible to a make a generalisation of these results is indeed an issue on which opinion may differ; it nevertheless vindicates the views commonly held that countries with higher incidence of OOP health-care financing are pregnable with a greater risk of catastrophe (van Doorslaer et al. 2007).

Yet another significant observation arising from Table 5.3 is the higher fractions of rural households in both the states with catastrophic health payments (also see Fig. 5.1). The same for the urban areas is turning out to be much less. In other words, it tends to supplement the point suggesting inadequate rural health-care services provided by the government. Low-caste people, particularly the SC communities, are also in the quandary for the same reason. Curiously enough, the share of Muslim households incurring catastrophic spending on health is marginally lower than of the Hindus. How far is this responsible due to their insensitivities towards poor health or how far does it indicate their lack of resources to access health care

---

[4]Note that the incidence of catastrophic payment declines with every successive increase in z values.

Table 5.3 Catastrophic payment 1: households incurring OOP spending exceeding chosen threshold of the total consumption budget

Catastrophe payments	Sample size (N)	Catastrophe 1: overall consumption thresholds Multiple z values				CV (sd/mean)* 100			
		z=5 %	z=10 %	z=15 %	z=25 %	z=5 %	z=10 %	z=15 %	z=25 %
Total sample	2,010	61.1	42.9	29.9	15.9	79.82	115.43	153.34	230.30
Rural	1,250	67.2	49.5	34.7	18.5	69.89	101.01	137.17	210.11
Urban	400	51.1	32.0	21.8	11.6	97.98	145.96	189.29	276.52
Slum	102	60.8	38.2	27.5	19.6	80.72	127.73	163.37	203.48
Non-slum	258	48.4	30.2	18.6	6.2	103.35	152.21	209.57	389.66
UP	1,000	62.2	44.6	32.2	17.6				
Rural	750	66.8	49.5	35.5	19.5	70.55	101.14	134.98	203.53
Urban	250	48.4	30.0	22.4	12.0	103.46	153.06	186.50	271.34
Rajasthan	650	64.5	46.0	31.1	16.5				
Rural	500	67.8	49.6	33.6	17.0	68.98	100.90	140.72	221.18
Urban	150	53.3	34.0	22.7	14.7	93.85	139.79	185.33	242.02
Delhi	360	51.9	32.5	21.1	10.0	96.32	144.32	193.58	300.42
Social groups									
SC	455	67.5	50.3	35.6	20.9	69.51	99.45	134.63	194.88
ST	249	69.9	50.6	34.1	16.1	65.79	99.00	139.18	229.04
OBC	777	60.1	42.6	30.1	16.0	81.53	116.15	152.43	229.63
Upper caste	529	52.9	33.3	22.5	11.3	94.39	141.76	185.79	279.85
Religious groups									
Hindu	1,789	62.0	43.7	30.5	16.3	78.23	113.51	150.92	226.49
Muslim	188	55.9	38.8	27.7	13.8	89.15	125.85	162.15	250.28

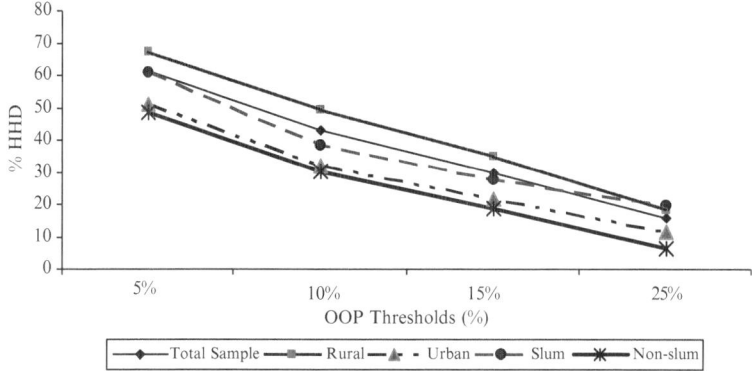

Fig. 5.1 Catastrophe head count: total consumption expenditure $N=2{,}010$ (total sample)

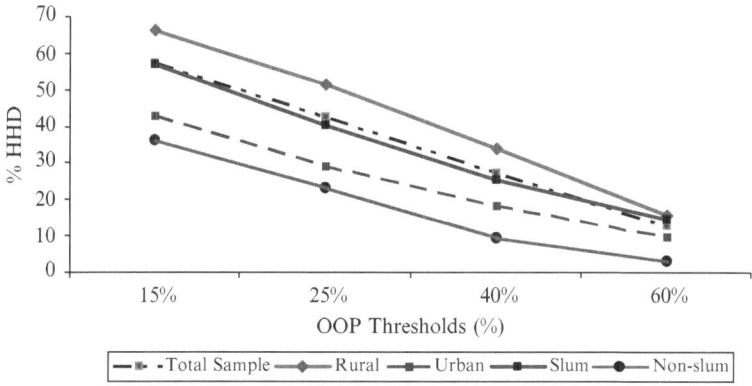

Fig. 5.2 Catastrophe head count: nonfood consumption expenditure $N=2{,}010$ (total sample)

may however not be judged on the basis of these results. Delhi slum residents are to some extent insulated because of better health-care infrastructure in and around the capital city, and as a result, a lesser proportion of them are found incurring catastrophic payments (Table 5.3). Deviations around the mean are relatively smaller at the higher threshold (z) levels and vice versa.

Catastrophe head count 2, computed on the basis of non-sustenance (nonfood) budgets of sample households, repeats the same grim reality and reiterates further that the rural households are worst affected due to inadequate health-care infrastructure of the government (see Fig. 5.2). The lower-caste SC households are at their worst. Their big percentages are shown to incur catastrophic payments, causing them to suffer from serious and highly disproportionate loss of well-being (Table 5.4). Interestingly, the study areas chosen from both the major states (UP and Rajasthan) are mutually close to each other in terms of their population shares facing consumption catastrophe due to private health payments.

Table 5.4 Catastrophic payment 2: households incurring OOP health spending exceeding chosen threshold of nonfood consumption budget

Catastrophe payments	Sample size (N)	Catastrophe 2: nonfood consumption thresholds Multiple z values				CV (sd/mean)* 100			
		z=15 %	z=25 %	z=40 %	z=60 %	z=15 %	z=25 %	z=40 %	z=60 %
Total sample	2,010	57.3	42.6	27.2	12.7	86.41	116.02	163.58	262.41
Rural	1,250	66.3	51.3	33.9	15.5	71.29	97.51	139.63	233.40
Urban	400	42.8	29.0	18.3	9.5	116.71	158.80	227.72	338.73
Slum	102	56.9	40.2	25.5	14.7	87.53	122.58	171.81	242.02
Non-slum	258	36.0	22.9	9.3	3.1	133.46	184.01	312.86	560.10
UP	1,000	61.6	47.4	31.5	15.5				
Rural	750	68.0	53.6	36.1	17.6	68.65	93.10	133.04	216.52
Urban	250	42.4	28.8	17.6	9.2	116.79	157.55	216.81	314.79
Rajasthan	650	59.1	43.5	28.0	11.8				
Rural	500	63.8	47.8	30.6	12.4	75.40	104.61	150.75	266.06
Urban	150	43.3	29.3	19.3	10.0	114.74	155.73	204.95	301.01
Delhi	360	41.9	27.8	13.9	6.4	117.81	161.47	249.34	383.31
Social groups									
SC	455	66.4	51.6	35.4	18.0	71.26	96.86	135.28	213.51
ST	249	68.7	51.0	32.9	12.4	67.67	98.21	143.00	265.72
OBC	777	56.6	43.2	27.5	13.5	87.57	114.64	162.30	253.15
Upper caste	529	45.0	30.1	17.0	7.0	110.68	152.69	221.07	365.00
Religious groups									
Hindu	1,789	58.0	43.3	27.8	13.0	85.18	114.42	161.28	258.49
Muslim	188	55.3	42.0	26.1	11.2	90.11	117.78	168.88	282.75

One of the more alarming observations stemming from the preceding results is a considerably large fraction of households paying more than 60 % of their nonfood budget on medical care. Further, barring certain number of non-slum households in Delhi, the MPO shares are considerably large in all other sample groups covered in the study (Fig. 5.2). In a situation like this, would it be possible for these households to come out of the morass created by their OOP payments? It is indeed a serious issue and warrants contemplating immediate remedial action by policy institutions like the Planning Commission. It also requires enhancing existing health-care infrastructure, particularly in villages and low-income areas of UP and Rajasthan. Our results also indicate very high variation around the mean values (see coefficients of variation (CVs)).

5.3 Intensity of Catastrophic Payments: Mean Positive Overshoot (MPO)

5.3.1 Computation of MPO

Besides catastrophic payments head count, another significant issue in the underlying context is the intensity of catastrophic payments, defined as the amount of excess payments (or overshoot) by which households exceeds catastrophic threshold z. The earlier set of results given in Tables 5.3 or 5.4 does not provide any idea about the amount paid in excess to z or intensity of overshoot occurring in our sample. A measure, known in the literature as catastrophic payment overshoot (C_{po}), has therefore been used to obtain the average degree by which health payments (as proportion of total or nonfood consumption budget) exceed the threshold z.

Algebraically:

$$C_{po}^{hhd_i} = E_i \left(\left(\frac{O_{hhd_{ii}}}{hhd_i^{tot\_con}} \right) - z \right)$$

where C_{po}^{hhd} is the catastrophic payment overshoot of ith household ($i = 1, 2, \ldots N$), E_i is the overshoot (or the amount exceeding z) paid by ith household, $O_{hhd_i} / hhd_i^{tot\_con}$ is the share of OOP payment in households' total consumption budget and z is the catastrophe threshold level with multiple values.

Average (or mean) positive overshoot is:

$$\overline{C}_{po}^{hhd} = \frac{1}{N} \left(\sum_{i=1}^{N} O_{hhd_i} \right)$$

where N is the number of persons whose health expenditure overshoots beyond the threshold level z.[5] By way of interpretation, this measure amounts to suggest that

---

[5]For an elaborate discussion on these concepts, see the WBI Learning Resources Series Analyzing Health Equity Using Household Survey Data: A Guide to Techniques and Their Implementation by O'Donnell et al. (2008).

those paying 5 % of their total consumption expenditure on health care (i.e. one of the values assigned to z) are actually spending 5 % of their consumption budget plus on an average another Rs. 15.6 as overshoot. This may be noticed from Table 5.5. Similarly, those at $z = 15$ % of their nonfood budget are actually paying 15 % plus Rs. 28 (see Table 5.6).

5.3.2 Discussion of the Results

The results providing excess payments by households over the z values (i.e. $z +$ the overshoot amount) are presented in Tables 5.5 and 5.6. The former table, as was explained earlier, relates to households' total consumption budget, and the latter was drawn on the basis of their nonfood consumption shares. Both the results are indeed disturbing and reveal a large amount of excess payments (overshoots) beyond the catastrophic threshold (z) limit. Interestingly, the mean overshoots are turning out to be considerably large in most of the cases, irrespective of their residential pattern. This is true for households in non-slum areas of Delhi as well. While there are indications that the rural and slum households are exceeding their threshold limits considerably at a few specific z values (e.g. $z = 15$ % and 25 % of nonfood budget shares and 25 % at the level of total consumption expenditure), there is how-ever no specific pattern to suggest any clear-cut differentials across households drawn from various states and socioreligious categories. Another notable observa-tion relates to the CV presented in the right-hand side of each table. These coeffi-cients remain considerably large in most of the tables, implying large intra-household variations in health payments. It also indicates a good number of households with no or negligible amount of spending on health.

5.4 Correlates of Catastrophic Health Spending: A Probit Regression Analysis

5.4.1 Formulation of the Model

Drawing upon the results presented in Sect. 5.3, which indicate a very high inci-dence of catastrophic health spending by households in most of our study areas, it is perhaps important to examine some of the major risk factors that are likely to build into perils of such eventualities. We therefore tried to carry out an econometric exercise based on a probit analysis, which follows a cumulative normal probability distribution of an S-type sigmoid curve (Maddala 2005). The exercise is basically designed to highlight the latent characteristic(s) of the households that may poten-tially be able to germinate into a catastrophe owing to certain *beyond-a-point* spend-ing; in our case, this spending relates to health. To estimate our model, we assume to have a regression of the following specification:

Table 5.5 Intensity of catastrophic health payments: mean positive overshoot in total consumption budget

Place of residence and sociorelig. attributes	Sample size (N)	MPO (excess over z thresholds)				CV (sd/mean)* 100			
		z=5 %	z=10 %	z=15 %	z=25 %	z=5 %	z=10 %	z=15 %	z=25 %
Total sample	2,010	15.6	16.2	17.3	18.5	105.62	102.80	96.28	84.23
Rural	1,250	16.3	16.3	17.2	18.3	101.54	102.13	96.38	84.80
Urban	400	14.0	16.1	17.5	18.9	115.26	104.73	96.29	83.20
Slum	102	16.1	19.2	20.6	16.9	103.85	84.77	71.85	74.52
Non-slum	258	11.6	12.5	14.0	23.1	123.64	123.46	119.21	72.56
UP	1,000	16.5	17.1	17.8	18.8	103.09	100.17	95.49	85.00
Rural	750	16.9	17.0	17.8	18.6	100.03	99.40	93.76	82.92
Urban	250	15.1	17.9	18.2	20.0	117.15	103.97	103.86	94.32
Rajasthan	650	15.2	15.4	16.7	17.6	104.59	104.71	96.86	86.83
Rural	500	15.4	15.2	16.3	17.9	103.78	106.47	100.95	88.60
Urban	150	14.5	16.4	18.7	16.3	108.73	97.52	79.20	79.29
Delhi	360	13.1	14.7	16.4	19.6	116.63	108.36	98.84	74.79
Social groups									
SC	455	17.5	17.6	19.0	19.2	100.84	100.25	90.80	83.17
ST	249	13.9	13.4	13.7	13.9	94.29	96.71	92.08	83.36
OBC	777	16.1	16.7	17.7	19.5	104.83	101.60	96.08	79.67
Upper caste	529	13.6	15.4	16.6	18.6	117.56	109.57	104.02	92.94
Religious groups									
Hindu	1,789	15.6	16.2	17.3	18.4	105.06	102.24	95.69	84.09
Muslim	188	15.5	16.3	16.8	19.2	108.19	105.44	104.22	89.63

Table 5.6 Intensity of catastrophic health payments: mean positive overshoot in nonfood consumption budget

	N	MPO (excess over z thresholds)				CV (sd/mean)* 100			
		z=5 %	z=10 %	z=15 %	z=25 %	z=5 %	z=10 %	z=15 %	z=25 %
Total sample	2,010	28.0	26.0	21.4	15.4	75.60	72.14	72.33	66.05
Rural	1,250	29.3	26.5	21.2	15.5	72.10	70.43	72.99	67.54
Urban	400	26.3	26.5	22.7	14.8	84.93	77.45	70.33	61.54
Slum	102	28.3	27.6	24.7	15.9	79.00	72.85	59.71	45.20
Non-slum	258	19.2	18.0	17.0	17.1	89.90	89.23	98.13	60.59
UP	1,000	29.7	27.3	22.2	15.7	73.26	70.46	71.45	67.88
Rural	750	30.5	27.5	22.1	15.7	71.07	69.74	71.04	66.96
Urban	250	25.9	26.0	22.4	15.6	84.51	75.08	74.68	74.61
Rajasthan	650	27.3	25.3	20.1	14.6	74.50	70.80	72.70	67.09
Rural	500	27.4	24.9	19.5	14.8	73.41	71.29	76.37	69.21
Urban	150	26.9	27.3	23.2	13.5	80.39	68.59	55.05	56.62
Delhi	360	22.7	21.9	21.0	16.3	87.24	83.70	76.28	50.34
Social groups									
SC	455	30.5	27.7	21.8	14.8	70.76	68.28	72.00	70.45
ST	249	26.6	24.1	18.1	11.1	71.06	66.88	68.88	82.68
OBC	777	29.3	26.8	22.7	16.6	74.34	72.50	69.80	58.64
Upper caste	529	23.6	23.2	20.3	17.1	87.00	80.50	79.83	64.05
Religious groups									
Hindu	1,789	28.1	25.9	21.3	15.3	75.37	72.32	72.75	66.30
Muslim	188	28.7	26.4	22.1	16.8	74.02	70.55	69.85	65.79

$$Y_i^* = \beta_0 + \sum_{i=1}^{n} \beta_i X_{ij} + u_i$$

where Y_i^* is not observed but remains latent. What is actually observed is a dichotomous (dummy) variable defined as $Y_i = 1$, if the ith household suffers from an OOP-driven catastrophic situation, otherwise 0. Similarly, the u_i follows a normal probability distribution,[6] and X_{ij} is a vector of socio-economic variables. Since the observed Y_i are just a realisation of a binomial process and vary from case to case depending on (X_{ij}), the log likelihood function of the probit may be written as

$$L = \prod_{y=1_i} P_i \prod_{y_i=1} \left(1 - P_i\right)$$

Since β follows a normal distribution, probit coefficients need to be interpreted in the Z (normal quintile) metric. The interpretation of a probit coefficient β may not be as straightforward and implies that one-unit increase in explanatory variable leads to increasing the probit score by β standard deviation. It indeed makes it difficult to interpret probit coefficients, and therefore, we mainly use our estimations to find (i) the direction of relationship between the explained (i.e. catastrophic payments) and the explanatory variables (i.e. sets of household or other characteristics) and (ii) significance of β—coefficients.

To ensure brevity, we have confined our estimations to only catastrophe 1, defined in relation to total (combined food and nonfood) consumption expenditure of households (see Sect. 5.3). In addition, we have also restricted this exercise to only the lowest (i.e. $z = 5 \%$) and the highest ($z = 25 \%$) catastrophe thresholds. It may inter alia help us to examine if there are differences in factors related to the probabilities of having lower and higher catastrophic events. Both the results are given in Table 5.7.

The correlates of catastrophic expenditures were examined by taking into consideration a set of socio-economic and demographic variables, grouped into five major categories.[7] These are:

- Households' size and per capita consumption expenditure
- Living condition of household members
- Socio-economic and religious background of the households
- Age–sex composition of household members
- Locational characteristics—e.g. rural, urban, slum and non-slum

Both non-slum residents and women in the age group 60 and above were the comparison groups. A detailed list of variables is given in Table 5.7.

---

[6]For a detailed discussion on distribution of ui and other related details of the probit model, see Maddla (2005, pp. 322–325).

[7]An exercise to estimate elasticities is currently in progress.

Table 5.7 Estimation of probit regression: list of variables

Variable names	Form of variables	Construction variables
A. HHD characteristics		
ln_mpce	Log of MPCE	Natural log
ln_size	Log of HHD size	Natural log
loghhdsize ~ q	(Log of HHD size)[2]	Natural log
Pucca/kutcha or a non-*pucca*	1 = pucca house, 0 otherwise	–
B. Living conditions		
Light	1 = electricity, 0 = no electricity	–
Water	1 = safe (tape/covered well), 0 = otherwise	–
Cooking fuel	1 = LPG, coal, electricity	–
	0 = all others (firewood, kerosene, etc.)	
Toilet	1 = flush or pit toilet	–
	0 = field and all others	
Drainage	0 = *kutcha nali*, 1 = *pucca nali*	–
Nala	1 = no open drain or *nala* near house	–
	0 = open drain near house (breeding mosquito)	
C. Socio-economic and religious		
Working	Share of working to nonworking members in a HHD	Number of workers/size of a HHD
Casual_NREGS	Share of persons in a household working as casual or NREGS worker*	Number of persons working as casual, NREGS/size of a HHD
Primary	Proportion of persons in a household educated above primary	Number of persons educated up to primary level/size of a HHD
Middle	Proportion of persons in a household educated above middle level	Number of persons educated up to middle level/size of a HHD
Secondary	Proportion of persons in a household educated up to secondary level	Number of persons educated up to secondary level/size of a HHD

Variable	Definition	
Religion	1=Hindu, 0=all others	–
Caste	1=SC,ST; 0=all others	–
OBC	1=other backward castes, 0=all others	–
D. Demographic profile		
mean_age	Average age of a household	Total age/size of HHD
sq_mean_age	Square of average age of a HHD	(Total age/size of HHD)^2
m0_4	Proportion of males aged 0–4 in a HHD	Males in 0–4 ages/size of HHD
m5_14	Proportion of males aged 5–14 in a HHD	Males in 5–14 ages/size of HHD
m15_40	Proportion of males aged 15–40 in a HHD	Males in 15–40 ages/size of HHD
m41_59	Proportion of males aged 41–59 in a HHD	Males in 41–59 ages/size of HHD
m60_above	Proportion of males aged 60 or more in a HHD	60+ males/size of HHD
f0_4	Proportion of females aged 0–4 in a HHD	Females in 0–4 ages/size of HHD
f5_14	Proportion of females aged 5–14 in a HHD	Females in 5–14 ages/size of HHD
f15_40	Proportion of females aged 15–40 in a HHD	Females in 15–40 ages/size of HHD
f41_59	Proportion of females aged 41–59 in a HHD	Females in 41–59 ages/size of HHD
f60_above	Proportion of females aged 60 or more in a HHD	60+ females/size of HHD
E. Residential character		
up_r	1=rural HHDs (UP), 0=others	–
up_u	1=urban HHDs (UP), 0=others	–
raj_r	1=rural HHDs (Rajasthan), 0=others	–
raj_u	1=urban HHDs (Rajasthan), 0=others	–
del_slum	1=slum HHDs (Delhi), 0=others	–

Explained variable=sample households with catastrophic payments ($z=5$ and 25 % of the total consumption expenditure)

5.4.2 Highlights of Probit Analysis

The results given in Table 5.8 indicate the effects of individual variables on the probability of having catastrophic spending by households in events of sickness episodes requiring inpatient or outpatient treatment. Among all the variables, it may be noticed from the results that the per capita household consumption expenditure, which is generally considered as representing the economic status of the households, turns out to be one of the most significant correlates of catastrophic spending with 'z' values as high as 6.1 at 5 % and 12.0 at 25 % thresholds, respectively. In both the scenarios, the variable is significant at 99 % confidence interval. The positive sign of the household expenditure is on expected lines implying that economically better-off households are running the greater risks of making catastrophic payments. A direct relationship between the per capita household consumption expenditure (mpce) and catastrophic payments should however be understood by keeping two perspectives into consideration: (i) the likely endogeneity between household expenditure and catastrophic payments and (ii) lower ability to pay (ATP) by the poor for health.

Although household size does not prove to be significant, the sign of the variable clearly indicates that the probability of making catastrophic payments increases with increase in household size. This essentially implies that economies of scale do not hold true for catastrophic payments. Larger households are in greater risk of making catastrophic payments. However, the probability of catastrophic payments *increases at a declining rate* with increase in the household size as indicated by the negative sign of the variable 'square of household size'. This may be because one or the other ailing members in large families may receive lesser attention for treatment.

Households with brick-made *pucca* houses have greater probability of making catastrophic payment at only 5 % threshold level but have strong lower probability of such payments at higher thresholds such as 25 % or more.

In general, better living conditions in terms of drinking water and sanitation facilities lead to reduced probability of making catastrophic payments by households. This is reflected by the negative signs linked with most of the variables used to characterise living conditions of sample households. It is important to note that among others, the availability of safe drinking water and improved cooking fuel turn out to be highly significant in reducing the probability of bigger catastrophes at the higher threshold of 25 %.

Socio-economic and religious background of households reflects a mixed picture, with a strong indication that secondary level education leads to the lowering of the probability of catastrophic payments. Even households with primary level education may find themselves protected to a certain extent. As compared to households with higher proportion of its members as illiterate, households with higher education are able to lower the risk of catastrophic payments. Similarly, higher worker ratio in households (i.e. lower burden of economic dependency) leads to the lowering of the probability. It may as well be because of some sort of contribution from employers to health expenditure of households. However, the households with

Table 5.8 Correlates of catastrophic health spending: probit analysis

Catastrophe threshold (z) = 5 %	Catastrophe threshold (z) = 25 %
No. of obs. 2,010	No. of obs. 2,010
Wald chi2(34) = 173.60	Wald chi2(34) = 203.33
Prob > chi2 = 0.000	Prob > chi2 = 0.000
Pseudo R^2 = 0.0751	Pseudo R^2 = 0.1761

Variables	Panel A—catastrophe 1: z = 5 % Coefficient	St. error	z	Panel B—catastrophe 1: z = 25 % Coefficient	St. error	z
A. HHD characteristics						
ln_mpce	0.399***	0.065	6.130	1.066***	0.089	12.000
ln_size	−7.737	67.621	−0.110	165.531*	101.356	1.630
loghhdsize ~ q	3.978	33.889	0.120	−82.739*	50.780	−1.630
B. Living conditions						
Pucca/kutcha or non-*pucca*	0.002	0.089	0.020	−0.237***	0.107	−2.210
Light	−0.180*	0.098	−1.840	−0.076	0.119	−0.640
Water	−0.094	0.166	−0.570	−0.453***	0.170	−2.670
Cooking fuel	−0.224**	0.108	−2.080	−0.423***	0.135	−3.140
Toilet	−0.158	0.104	−1.520	−0.071	0.123	−0.580
Drainage	0.121	0.119	1.020	0.014	0.178	0.080
Nala	−0.162*	0.091	−1.770	−0.130	0.106	−1.220
C. Socio-economic and religious characteristics						
Working	−0.365	0.226	−1.620	−0.831***	0.301	−2.760
Casual_NREGS	0.682***	0.216	3.160	0.924***	0.270	3.420
Primary	−0.118*	0.190	−0.620	0.149	0.238	0.630
Middle	0.291	0.201	1.450	−0.243	0.276	−0.880
Secondary	−0.915***	0.200	−4.570	−1.214***	0.284	−4.270
Religion	0.141	0.098	1.430	0.109	0.131	0.830
Caste	0.171*	0.092	1.870	0.230***	0.117	1.970
OBC	0.033	0.084	0.390	0.097	0.111	0.880
D. Demographic profile						
mean_age	0.063***	0.019	3.210	−0.004	0.024	−0.180
sq_mean_age	−0.001***	0.000	−2.490	0.000	0.000	0.650
m0_4	2.940***	0.835	3.520	0.845	1.018	0.830
m5_14	1.073	0.676	1.590	−0.518	0.843	−0.610
m15_40	0.261	0.587	0.440	−0.211	0.741	−0.290
m41_59	0.070	0.471	0.150	−0.321	0.673	−0.480
m60_above	0.018	0.443	0.040	−0.098	0.602	−0.160
f0_4	2.867***	0.853	3.360	1.083	1.038	1.040
f5_14	1.429*	0.689	2.080	0.108	0.844	0.130
f15_40	0.695	0.578	1.200	−0.244	0.725	−0.340
f41_59	0.711	0.452	1.570	0.153	0.570	0.270
E. Residential character						
up_r	0.292*	0.159	1.840	1.065***	0.239	4.470
up_u	0.201	0.133	1.510	1.064***	0.217	4.900
raj_r	0.312***	0.151	2.070	0.853***	0.231	3.700
raj_u	0.268*	0.155	1.720	1.036***	0.246	4.220
del_slum	0.338**	0.174	1.940	0.927***	0.256	3.630
Constant	−4.620	1.104	−4.180	−7.726	1.420	−5.440

Dependent variable = catastrophe threshold at 5 and 25 % of the total consumption budget

***$p < 0.001$; **$P < 0.05$; *$P < 0.10$

casual workers in social employment programmes such as NREGA, as compared to those who do not participate in the NREGA scheme, do not enjoy the facilities of employer's contribution and therefore run higher risks of making catastrophic payments. As far as social background of households is concerned, the results clearly indicate that households belonging to lower castes and non-Hindu run higher probability of catastrophic expenditure.

Age of the family members has important implications for catastrophic payments. With increase in the average age of family members, the probability of catastrophic payment increases at the 5 % threshold level but becomes insignificant at the higher thresholds. Further, households with infants and children below the age of 14 years have higher risk of making catastrophic payment at 5 % threshold, while most of these demographic variables are not significant at the higher threshold of 25 %.

Like the per capita consumption expenditure, the locational factors such as state and region also play an important role in the underlying context. It indicates a comparatively vulnerable situation of households living in the remote and poorer regions. As compared to non-slum areas of Delhi, households in all other areas in our sample show a strong and positive association with probability of catastrophic payments. The relationship becomes even stronger with the higher threshold of 25 %.

5.4.3 Concluding Observations

To cap a few of the critical observations arising from the preceding exercises, this whole chapter was mainly directed to examine three significant policy issues: (i) share of OOP health spending by households in their consumption budget, (ii) the extent to which these spending result in a catastrophe and force households to face serious vulnerabilities and (iii) a set of socio-economic, demographic and ethnic correlates liable to bring such catastrophic spending by households. The observations drawn from this entire analysis are rather worrisome as they reveal that in large number of cases, even a small share of consumption budget going to health care ended with catastrophe and loss of well-being. In particular, the head count of catastrophic payments in most of the study areas, particularly among rural and slum households, is turning out to be considerably large. The MPOs, computed to examine the intensity of OOP health spending exceeding a certain catastrophic threshold, also prove to be equally discouraging. Unfortunately, it happens without too many exceptions—geographical, place of residence or otherwise. Among the significant correlates of catastrophic spending are economic status of households surrogated by per capita consumption expenditure, their living conditions including access to sanitation and safe drinking water, nature of work, educational level, number of children in 0–4 age group and place of residence. Households living in remote and poorer regions are expected to face a much bigger risk of catastrophic spending. It vindicates the general perception that rural households seriously lack in terms of health-care facilities. Despite a few data limitations and caveats, these observations are expected to prove useful in framing appropriate policy responses.

Appendix

Table 5.A.1 Descriptive statistics: variables used in probit regression analysis

Variables	Obs.	Mean	Std. dev.	Min	Max
catcount5	2,010	0.611	0.488	0	1
ln_mpce	2,010	6.519	0.789	4.370	9.734
lnsize	2,010	1.619	0.440	0	2.773
loghhdsize~q	2,010	3.241	0.877	0.020	5.546
Pucca	2,010	0.397	0.489	0	1
Light	2,010	0.536	0.499	0	1
Water	2,010	0.963	0.190	0	1
Cooking	2,010	0.310	0.463	0	1
Toilet	2,010	0.405	0.491	0	1
Drainage	2,010	0.128	0.334	0	1
Nala	2,010	0.858	0.349	0	1
Working	2,010	0.333	0.182	0	1
Casual_NREGS	2,010	0.145	0.190	0	1
Primary	2,010	0.518	0.307	0	1
Middle	2,010	0.389	0.311	0	1
Secondary	2,010	0.129	0.228	0	1
Religion	2,010	0.890	0.313	0	1
Caste	2,010	0.350	0.477	0	1
OBC	2,010	0.387	0.487	0	1
Mean_age	2,010	27.653	10.936	11.200	84.500
sq_mean_age	2,010	884.257	819.541	125.440	7,140.250
m0_4	2,010	0.047	0.094	0	0.6
m5_14	2,010	0.119	0.144	0	0.667
m15_40	2,010	0.242	0.154	0	1
m41_59	2,010	0.080	0.117	0	1
m60_above	2,010	0.044	0.116	0	1
f0_4	2,010	0.038	0.087	0	0.600
f5_14	2,010	0.097	0.133	0	0.625
f15_40	2,010	0.220	0.135	0	1
f41_59	2,010	0.072	0.115	0	1
up_r	2,010	0.373	0.484	0	1
up_u	2,010	0.124	0.330	0	1
raj_r	2,010	0.249	0.432	0	1
raj_u	2,010	0.075	0.263	0	1
del_slum	2,010	0.051	0.220	0	1

References

Agarwal, B. (1990). Social security and the family: Coping with seasonality and calamity in rural India. *Journal of Peasant Studies, 17*(3), 314–412.

Asian Development Bank. (2007). *Key indicators 2007: Inequality in Asia*. Manila: Asian Development Bank.

Bonu, S., Indu, B., & Peters, D. H. (2007, October). *Incidence, intensity and correlates of catastrophic OOP health payment in India* (ERD Working Paper Series No. 102). Manila: Asian Development Bank.

Garg, C., & Karan, A. K. (2009). Reducing out-of-pocket expenditures to reduce poverty: A disaggregated analysis at rural-urban and state level in India. *Health Policy and Planning, 24*(2), 116–128.

Gottret, P., & Schieber, G. (2006). *Health financing revisited – A practitioner's guide*. Washington, DC: The World Bank.

Joglekar, R. (2008, September). *Can insurance reduce catastrophic OOP health expenditure*. Mumbai: Indira Gandhi Institute of Development Research, mimeo. Available at: http://www.igidr.ac.in/pdf/publication/WP-2008-016.pdf

Kawabata, K., Xu, K., & Carrin, G. (2002). Preventing impoverishment through protection against catastrophic health expenditure. *Bulletin of the WHO, 80*, 612.

Maddala, G. S. (2005). *Introduction to econometrics* (3rd ed.). Chichester: Wiley.

National Sample Survey Organisation. (2006a). *Level and pattern of consumer expenditure, 2004–2005: 61st round, July 2004–June 2005*. New Delhi: NSSO, Government of India, Ministry of Statistics and Programme Implementation.

National Sample Survey Organisation. (2006b). *Morbidity, health care and the condition of the aged: 60th round (January–June 2004)* (Report No. 507). New Delhi: NSSO. Available at: http://mospi.nic.in/rept%20_%20pubn/ftest.asp?rept_id=507&type=NSSO

NCMH, & MoHFW (Government of India). (2005, August). *Report of the National Commission on Macroeconomics and Health, Chapter 2 on India's health system: The financing and delivery of health care services* (pp. 15–81). New Delhi: NCMH, MoHFW (Government of India).

O'Donnell, O., van Doorslaer, E., Wagstaff, A., & Lindelow, M. (2008). *Analysing health equity using household survey data: A guide to techniques and their implementation*. Washington, DC: The World Bank.

Peters, D. H., Yazbeck, A. S., Sharma, R. R., Ramana, G. N. V., Pritchett, L. H., & Wafstaff, A. (2002). *Better health system for India's poor: Findings, analysis and options*. Washington, DC: The World Bank.

Ranson, M. K., Sinha, T., Chatterjee, M., Acharya, A., et al. (2006). Making health insurance work for the poor: Lessons from the Self-employed Women's Association's (SEWA) community-based health insurance scheme in India. *Social Science & Medicine, 62*, 707–720.

Roy, K., & Howard, D. H. (2007). Equity in OOP payments in hospital care: Evidence from India. *Health Policy, 80*(2), 297–307.

van Doorslaer, E., O'Donnell, O., Rannan-Eliya, R. P., et al. (2007, November). Catastrophic payments for health care in Asia. *Health Economics, 16*(11), 1159–1184.

Xu, K. (2004). *Distribution of health payments and catastrophic expenditure methodology* (Discussion Paper No. 2-2005 (EIP/HSF/DP.05.2)). Geneva: WHO. Available at: http://www.who.int/health_financing/documents/dp_e_05_2-distribution_of_health_payments.pdf

Xu, K., Evans, D. B., Kawabate, K., et al. (2003). Household catastrophic health expenditure: A multicountry analysis. *The Lancet, 362*(9378), 111–117.

Chapter 6
Decomposing Out-of-Pocket Health Spending: Share of Drugs, Medical Services and Other Components

The preceding discussion has perhaps clearly underscored the fact that ailments and poor health conditions contribute heavily in exposing households to serious economic issues, press them hard to make OOP expenses, push a number of them to slip below the threshold poverty level (see the last two columns in Appendix Table 6.A.1) and render many to meet with serious catastrophic situations—amounting to curtailments in their normal consumption pattern and forcing them in certain cases to borrow from private moneylenders. All these make analysts to ask an obvious question: Why is there so much of OOP health spending, and what and where public policy interventions could be directed to ameliorate the situation? In certain countries, the answer to these questions rests with demographically mediated age structure changes and rapid population ageing (Dormont and Huber 2006; Dormont et al. 2006; Getzen 1992). Given the fact that in many cases health-care expenses are determined by the progressing age of the older adults, the growing share of 60 or 65+ is expected to increase the size of health expenditure both in a society and in a household. With ageing in India yet to reach the level achieved by many developed countries, a great deal of health expenditure in this or similar other countries may not be simply considered as age-driven or caused by the ailing olds. Components of health care, in particular, high costs of medicinal drugs and diagnostics, may as well play a role and make families incur a much greater spending on health. This has also been argued by the studies conducted on the initiative of the government including NCMH (2005, Sec. II) or the Annual Report to the People on Health (Ministry of Health & Family Welfare, Government of India, December 2011, Chapter VII).

This chapter is therefore designed to decompose the expenses on health by households into four broader components: (i) fee paid to physician or medical consultant, (ii) cost of drugs and medicines (both prescription and self-medicated), (iii) expenses on diagnostic tests and (iv) money spent on transportation and stay. Most likely, the results of this analysis would help in identifying areas of major public concern and see if there are possible ways for the government to reduce the expenses incurred by households on items costing most to their health budget. Three interconnected exercises are presented. These include:

M. Alam, *Paying Out-of-Pocket for Drugs, Diagnostics and Medical Services: A Study of Households in Three Indian States*, India Studies in Business and Economics, DOI 10.1007/978-81-322-1281-2_6, © Springer India 2013

- A detailed distribution of OOP health-care expenditure by sample household into four broad categories listed above
- A similar distribution of households regrouped into five quintile groups, ranging from the poorest 20 % to the richest 20 %
- Decomposition of OOP expenses into four broad expenditure items incurred by households facing lowest ($z=5$ %) and highest ($z=25$ %) levels of catastrophe based on the total (i.e. food + nonfood) consumption criterion (refer to the discussion in Chap. 5 on z values)

All the results are presented separately for households drawn from rural and urban areas of both the districts in the two major states of UP and Rajasthan.[1] The same for Delhi was described by making a distinction between slum and non-slum households. The small-sample bias must nevertheless be kept in mind while interpreting the results.

6.1   Decomposition of Health-Care Expenditure: Share of Spending on Drugs, Diagnostics and Other Components

A great deal of literature on private financing of health care in India suggests drugs forming almost three-quarters or even more of the total private spending on health. This has particularly been noticed for the rural households (Sakthivel 2005).[2] Obviously, with such a huge share of drugs and medicines in the total OOP budget, any policy intervention to reduce the cost of health care may not be considered without capping the drug prices and reducing their weight in the overall health spending of rural or urban households. Despite a growing realisation of this fact (Rane 1999), it may not be easy to implement any significant price reduction in India or elsewhere due to changes in drug policy regime, adopted in compliance with a mix of external and internal forces including demand for liberalisation in drug control policies,[3] product patent regime, WTO patenting obligations and TRIPS.[4] Some recent studies have already raised concern about these changes followed by substantial increase

---

[1] These include Unnao and Jhansi in UP, and Dausa and Dungarpur in Rajasthan.

[2] Based on unit-level data from 55th round of the National Sample Survey (1999–2000), a study by Sakthivel (2005) has reported the share of drugs and medicine in total OOP expenditure of rural households as 77 %. The same for the households in urban areas has turned out to be 70 % of their total health budget.

[3] An example may be the demand for changes in Drugs Price Control Order (1995) under which a total of 74 bulk drugs and their formulations are controlled. The proposed modifications are however currently under legal scrutiny.

[4] After India joined the WTO and became a signatory to the agreement on Trade-Related Aspects of Intellectual Property Rights (TRIPS), it was obligatory on the part of Indian government to introduce patent protection for any invention including medicine and its manufacturing process. TRIPS agreement, effective from January 2005, makes it difficult for the Indian pharmaceutical industries to freely continue with the production of generics (*see next page*) of the new patented molecules without licence or payment of royalty to the innovator. Obviously, the negative impact

Table 6.1 Shares of drug and non-drug expenses in OOP expenditure on health: hospitalised and nonhospitalised care (%)

	Nonhospitalisation				Hospitalisation			
	UP	Rajasthan	Delhi	Total	UP	Rajasthan	Delhi	Total
Panel A: rural HHDs								
Doc. fee	6.3	7.0	–	6.5	6.8	4.8	–	5.8
Drugs	81.5	81.3	–	81.4	80.5	83.2	–	81.8
Transport	7.4	6.9	–	7.2	6.7	6.5	–	6.6
Diagnostics	4.9	4.8	–	4.9	6.1	5.5	–	5.8
Total	100.0	100.0	–	100.0	100.0	100.0	–	100.0
Panel B: urban HHDs								
Doc. fee	9.5	10.1	–	9.7	19.8	4.1	–	16.0
Drugs	77.7	77.3	–	77.5	67.4	87.5	–	72.2
Transport	5.7	6.8	–	6.0	3.7	5.0	–	4.0
Diagnostics	7.2	5.8	–	6.8	9.2	3.5	–	7.8
Total	100.0	100.0	–	100.0	100.0	100.0	–	100.0
Panel C: slums HHDs								
Doc. fee	–	–	1.7	1.7	–	–	2.7	2.7
Drugs	–	–	84.1	84.1	–	–	86.7	86.7
Transport	–	–	6.6	6.6	–	–	3.0	3.0
Diagnostics	–	–	7.7	7.7	–	–	7.6	7.6
Total	–	–	100.0	100.0	–	–	100.0	100.0
Panel D: non-slum HHDs								
Doc. fee	–	–	5.4	5.4	–	–	0.5	0.5
Drugs	–	–	83.1	83.1	–	–	88.8	88.8
Transport	–	–	4.5	4.5	–	–	1.3	1.3
Diagnostics	–	–	7.0	7.0	–	–	9.4	9.4
Total expenditure	–	–	100.0	100.0	–	–	100.0	100.0
Panel E: total HHDs								
Doc. fee	7.0	7.6	4.8	6.3	13.5	4.6	1.1	7.4
Drugs	80.6	80.6	83.3	81.6	73.7	84.3	88.2	80.9
Transport	7.0	6.8	4.8	6.2	5.1	6.1	1.7	4.3
Diagnostics	5.4	5.0	7.1	5.9	7.7	5.0	9.0	7.3
Total	100.0	100.0	100.0	100.0	100.0	100.0	100.0	100.0

in drug prices causing escalations in OOP expenses and erosion in health-care affordability (Kamiike and Sato 2011; Watal 2000; Srinivasan 1999).

Against this backdrop, we present in Table 6.1 the distribution of OOP spending on drugs and other health-care components to reiterate further the primacy of the former in overall health-care budgets. This has been noticed all across the sample of

---

of this law would not only affect India and make access to health care more expensive, it would also affect many other countries where Indian pharmaceutical products are exported to ensure availability of reasonably priced medicines. Globally, almost 60 developing countries do not have capacity to produce medicines and another 87 are only partially capable (Cullet 2005). Most of them rely on exports from India.

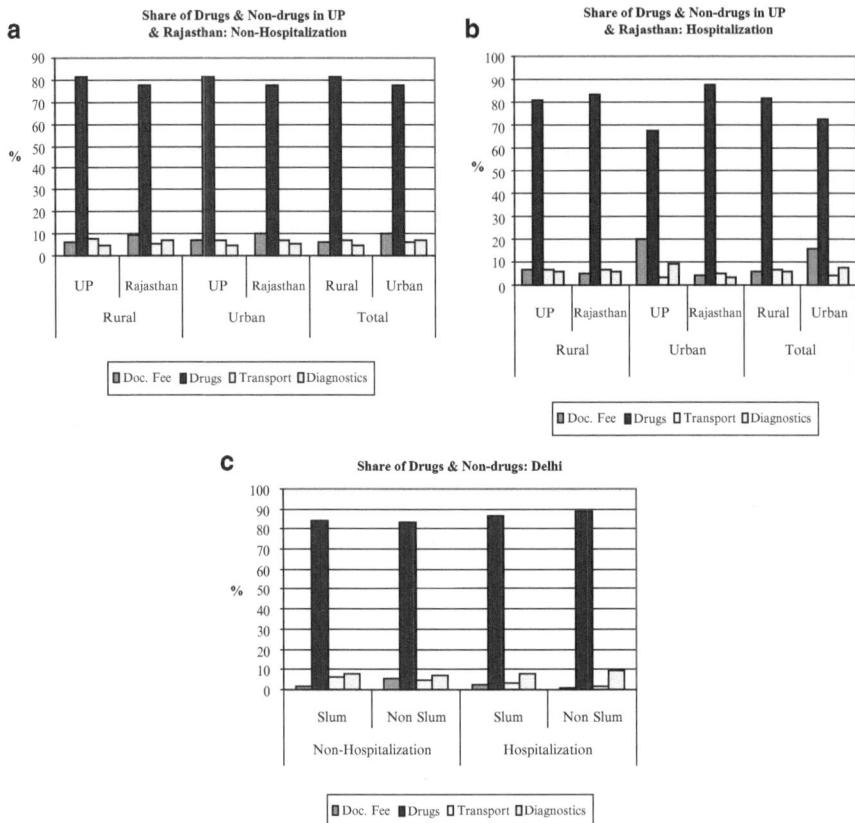

Fig. 6.1 Share of expenses on drugs, medical services and transportation in hospitalised and nonhospitalised care: rural–urban and slum–non-slum households (%) (*Source*: Table 6.1)

households—rural, urban, slum or non-slum and irrespective of the districts or states they were located in. Our results are also to a large extent in the vicinity of the earlier findings (Sakthivel 2005; Bonu et al. 2007), suggesting that more than three-fourths of the money spent on health care invariably goes to allopathic medicines. Share of other forms of treatment—and hence medicines—is minuscule as may be noticed from the discussion in the next chapter.

Without too much of variations, Table 6.1 indicates almost a similar distribution pattern of health budgets across all the study areas (see also Fig. 6.1) with around four-fifths of the total OOP expenditure going to drugs followed by another 5–10 % (depending upon rural–urban and inpatient or outpatient treatment) of the total expenses going to medical practitioners (both qualified and others) as their consultation fee. Expenditure on diagnostics remains in most cases between 5 and 7 % of the total budget, and almost an equal amount (between another 5 and 7 %) is devoted to meet a few sundry expenses, especially transportation (see Fig. 6.1a–c).

Between the two samples of households drawn from UP and Rajasthan, the share of expenditure gone to consultation fee is shown to be much higher in the former, particularly in sickness episodes requiring hospitalisation. Relatively, however, their expenses on drugs are much less. Both of them however follow almost a similar expenditure pattern in cases where hospitalisation was not required.

Moving to the OOP distribution for slum and non-slum households in Delhi, it is clear both from Table 6.1 (panels C and D) and Fig. 6.1c that the former are almost at a competing level with the latter in terms of their percentage expenditure on drugs and two other major medical services, namely, consultation and diagnostics. However, the share of expenditure on consultation fee is relatively higher for slum households, i.e. 2.7 % as against 0.5 % for the non-slum households (Table 6.1, panels C and D). Also, they are shown to incur a larger share of expenditure on transportation than the non-slum households.

From these results, which tend to portray certain degrees of equity between the slum and non-slum households in distribution of their health budgets, follow two significant questions: (i) Does this equity represent certain peculiarities of Delhi alone or is it a wider phenomenon and the poor in general encounter a similar situation in other places as well, and (ii) is there a safeguard to protect them?

Regarding the second question, safeguard perhaps lies in pooling the risk and offering certain form of health insurance mechanism—if not to all, at least to the poor.[5] Another important safeguard derives from lowering inflation in the drug sector and pro-poor negotiations in the WTO. Particularly, most generic medicines and formulations need protection from strict patenting and royalty laws. This is particularly essential because of a very large share of medicines in overall household budgets on health. Reverting to the first question, we extend this analysis, as was already noted in the beginning, by briefly describing the OOP budget distributions at two levels: (i) by five consumption quintile groups (poorest 20 %, next 20 %, middle, rich and the richest) and (ii) by two catastrophic groups ($z = 5$ and 25 %).

6.2   Share of Drugs and Non-drugs in OOP Budget: Households by Consumption Quintiles

Using unit-level consumption data, Table 6.2 distributes the health-care expenditure of sample households arranged in ascending order into five quintile groups—from the poorest 20 % to the richest 20 %. Expenditure items in all the calculations remain identical.

---

[5] Rashtriya Swathya Bima Yojna (i.e. National Health Insurance Programme) was launched by the Government of India in October 2007 to insure below-poverty-line (BPL) households against diseases requiring almost 700 inpatient medical procedures. Covering a total of 5 members—husband, wife and up to three children—the scheme mostly fails to cover elderly family members. The scheme enables eligible households to receive inpatient cover up to Rs. 30,000.

Table 6.2 Shares of drug and non-drug expenses in hospitalised and nonhospitalised care: households by consumption quintiles (%)

Consumption quintiles	OOP expenditure: nonhospitalised care					OOP expenditure: hospitalisation cases				
	Doc. fee	Drugs	Transport	Diagnostic	Total	Doc. fee	Drugs	Transport	Diagnostic	Total
Panel A: rural UP and Rajasthan										
Poorest 20 % households	4.9	85.1	8.1	1.9	100.0	3.1	77.6	18.8	0.5	100.0
Next	5.6	83.0	8.8	2.6	100.0	4.9	79.8	9.2	6.2	100.0
Middle	8.2	82.2	7.3	2.3	100.0	4.7	85.5	7.2	2.5	100.0
Rich	9.2	77.6	7.9	5.3	100.0	9.9	78.1	5.2	6.8	100.0
Richest 20 % households	5.3	81.9	6.5	6.3	100.0	4.4	82.9	6.8	5.9	100.0
Total sample	6.5	81.4	7.2	4.9	100.0	5.8	81.8	6.6	5.8	100.0
Panel B: urban UP and Rajasthan										
Poorest 20 % households	10.4	80.6	4.9	4.2	100.0	1.3	85.5	5.0	8.2	100.0
Next 20 %	11.8	74.6	8.2	5.4	100.0	8.1	85.0	4.9	2.0	100.0
Middle	11.0	80.2	3.6	5.2	100.0	9.3	80.9	2.9	6.9	100.0
Rich	7.8	79.6	6.1	6.5	100.0	1.1	86.8	4.0	8.1	100.0
Richest 20 % households	9.8	75.5	6.2	8.5	100.0	20.0	67.8	3.9	8.4	100.0
Total sample	9.7	77.7	5.9	6.8	100.0	16.0	72.2	4.0	7.8	100.0
Panel C: Delhi slum										
Poorest 20 % households	8.7	90.4	0.9	0.0	100.0	0.0	81.3	6.3	12.5	100.0
Next 20 %	2.6	80.7	8.7	8.0	100.0	3.4	84.0	5.3	7.3	100.0
Middle	1.1	87.2	9.5	2.2	100.0	0.0	77.9	1.1	21.0	100.0
Rich	4.3	77.3	2.6	15.8	100.0	5.6	90.9	2.7	0.8	100.0
Richest 20 % households	0.2	85.0	6.9	7.8	100.0	0.0	92.4	5.6	2.1	100.0
Total sample	1.7	84.1	6.6	7.7	100.0	2.7	86.7	3.0	7.6	100.0
Panel D: Delhi non-slum										
Poorest 20 % households	4.8	90.5	3.4	1.3	100.0	10.1	84.6	4.1	1.2	100.0
Next 20 %	5.0	87.2	6.7	1.2	100.0	0.0	89.5	1.6	8.9	100.0
Middle	4.3	84.7	2.7	8.2	100.0	0.6	81.8	2.7	14.9	100.0
Rich	5.7	81.4	4.6	8.3	100.0	0.0	89.7	0.9	9.4	100.0
Richest 20 % households	5.9	82.0	5.0	7.2	100.0	0.1	91.9	0.4	7.5	100.0
Total sample	5.4	83.1	4.5	7.0	100.0	0.5	88.8	1.3	9.4	100.0

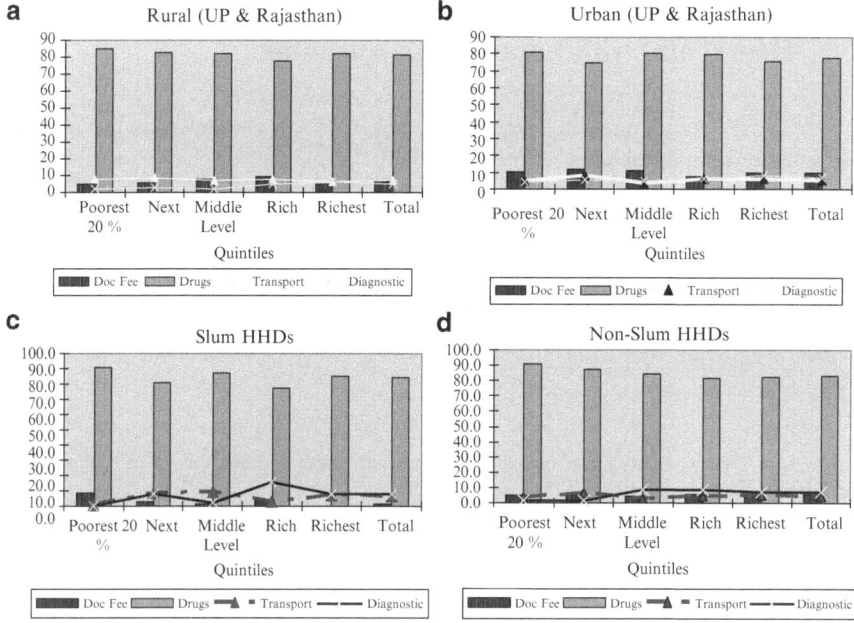

Fig. 6.2 Share of expenses on drugs, health services and transportation in OOP health budget: quintile groups (%) (*Source*: Table 6.2)

Replicating largely the pattern represented by Delhi, we notice from this table that the poorest 20 % seeking outpatient treatment have spent a greater share of their health budget on medicines than any other quintile group (see Fig. 6.2a–d). Further, the same remains true for all the places covered in the study. Drug share of these households varies between 80 and 90 % of the total and remained particularly higher among the slum and rural households (Table 6.2, panels A and C). All other quintile groups spent a lesser share, although their differences in many cases remained marginal. Poorest groups have also spent in certain areas (slums and towns in UP and Rajasthan) a larger share of their health budget on medical consultation. The situation is however slightly reversed when it comes to the hospitalised treatment. Nevertheless, the differentials are invariably small and the richest appear to have drawn certain advantages over the lower quintile groups.

A significant observation arising on the basis of Table 6.2 and its first three panels is that the poorer quintiles (poorest, next 20 % and middle) are not only spending heavily on drugs and medicines, they also spend their considerable budget shares on consultation and diagnostics. It may be noticed even in cases of hospitalisation (see the latter half of Table 6.2). A possible explanation may be drawn from two possibilities. First, people do not necessarily rely on public hospitals even if they require hospitalisation. Second, many diagnostic services in public facilities are on payment basis. Also, there are instances of doctors in public hospitals going for private practices, especially in UP and Rajasthan.

6.3 Share of Drugs and Non-drugs in OOP Budget: Households with Catastrophic Spending

Two exercises are reported in Tables 6.3a and 6.3b. Both are drawn on the basis of the total consumption budget of the households facing catastrophe due to spending on medical care, with or without hospitalisation. Two levels of catastrophe have been used: one, with a lower threshold of $z=5$ % or more and the other with a z value fixed at 25 % and beyond. The heads of medical expenditure remained as before.

Conforming closely to the patterns visible in the two preceding analyses, these results also highlight drugs as the single expenditure item with highest budget share (almost 80 % of the total and above) followed by diagnostics and medical consultation.

Table 6.3a Shares of drug and non-drug expenses in nonhospitalisation cases: catastrophic households (%)

	Nonhospitalisation cases: catastrophic HHDs ($z=5$ %)					Nonhospitalisation cases: catastrophic HHDs ($z=25$ %)				
	Rural	Urban	Slum	Non-slum	Total HHDs	Rural	Urban	Slum	Non-slum	Total HHDs
Panel A										
UP										
Doc. fee	6.3	8.8	–	–	6.9	6.9	7.0	–	–	6.9
Drugs	81.3	78.2	–	–	80.7	81.4	80.6	–	–	81.2
Transport	7.3	5.6	–	–	7.0	6.1	5.9	–	–	6.1
Diagnostic	5.0	7.3	–	–	5.5	5.6	6.5	–	–	5.8
Total	100.0	100.0	–	–	100.0	100.0	100.0	–	–	100.0
Panel B										
Rajasthan										
Doc. fee	6.7	9.4	–	–	7.2	4.9	6.6	–	–	5.2
Drugs	81.3	77.5	–	–	80.6	82.3	73.4	–	–	80.8
Transport	6.9	6.7	–	–	6.9	6.1	10.2	–	–	6.8
Diagnostic	5.0	6.5	–	–	5.3	6.7	9.8	–	–	7.2
Total	100.0	100.0	–	–	100.0	100.0	100.0	–	–	100.0
Panel C										
Delhi										
Doc. fee	–	–	1.4	4.9	4.2	–	–	0.0	2.5	1.8
Drugs	–	–	84.4	83.5	83.7	–	–	81.1	83.1	82.5
Transport	–	–	6.4	3.7	4.2	–	–	7.8	3.1	4.4
Diagnostic	–	–	7.8	8.0	7.9	–	–	11.1	11.3	11.3
Total	–	–	100.0	100.0	100.0	–	–	100.0	100.0	100.0
Panel D										
Total households										
Doc. fee	6.5	9.0	1.4	4.9	6.1	6.2	6.9	0.0	2.5	5.1
Drugs	81.3	78.0	84.4	83.5	81.7	81.7	78.2	81.1	83.1	81.5
Transport	7.2	5.9	6.4	3.7	6.0	6.1	7.3	7.8	3.1	5.8
Diagnostic	5.0	7.1	7.8	8.0	6.3	6.0	7.5	11.1	11.3	7.6
Total	100.0	100.0	100.0	100.0	100.0	100.0	100.0	100.0	100.0	100.0

Table 6.3b Shares of drug and non-drug expenses in hospitalisation cases: catastrophic households

	Hospitalisation cases: catastrophic HHDs ($z=5$ %)					Hospitalisation cases: catastrophic HHDs ($z=25$ %)				
	Rural	Urban	Slum	Non-slum	Total HHDs	Rural	Urban	Slum	Non-slum	Total HHDs
Panel A										
UP										
Doc. fee	6.9	19.9	–	–	13.7	6.9	22.8	–	–	15.5
Drugs	80.3	67.5	–	–	73.6	81.9	64.3	–	–	72.3
Transport	6.7	3.4	–	–	5.0	5.4	3.1	–	–	4.2
Diagnostic	6.2	9.2	–	–	7.8	5.8	9.8	–	–	8.0
Total	100.0	100.0	–	–	100.0	100.0	100.0	–	–	100.0
Panel B										
Rajasthan										
Doc. fee	4.5	4.1	–	–	4.4	4.6	2.7	–	–	4.2
Drugs	83.6	87.4	–	–	84.6	83.0	87.4	–	–	83.9
Transport	6.4	4.9	–	–	6.0	6.8	5.9	–	–	6.6
Diagnostic	5.6	3.6	–	–	5.1	5.7	4.1	–	–	5.3
Total	100.0	100.0	–	–	100.0	100.0	100.0	–	–	100.0
Panel C										
Delhi										
Doc. fee	–	–	2.8	0.4	1.0	–	–	0.0	0.0	0.0
Drugs	–	–	86.7	89.6	88.8	–	–	89.6	87.9	88.4
Transport	–	–	2.8	1.1	1.5	–	–	2.3	0.7	1.3
Diagnostic	–	–	7.7	9.0	8.6	–	–	8.1	11.4	10.3
Total	–	–	100.0	100.0	100.0	–	–	100.0	100.0	100.0
Panel D										
Total households										
Doc. fee	5.7	16.2	2.8	0.4	7.4	5.8	19.6	0.0	0.0	8.5
Drugs	81.9	72.2	86.7	89.6	81.1	82.4	67.9	89.6	87.9	79.5
Transport	6.5	3.7	2.8	1.1	4.2	6.1	3.5	2.3	0.7	4.0
Diagnostic	5.9	7.9	7.7	9.0	7.3	5.7	8.9	8.1	11.4	7.9
Total	100.0	100.0	100.0	100.0	100.0	100.0	100.0	100.0	100.0	100.0

It may also be interesting to note that in a few cases, the share of expenditure incurred by rural households on transportation is relatively higher than the shares on medical services (see Fig. 6.3a-1, a-3 and b-1, b-3). In other words, it is an indication of poor access to medical facilities closer to some villages.

Another interesting result to notice from these tables is the expenses borne by the slum households in Delhi. There is clear evidence that the poor and slum dwellers spend in many cases a much larger share of expenditure on drugs and other medical items than the nonpoor. Despite that, these results in no way imply that nonpoor do not spend on health. They largely follow a similar pattern with a maximum of their health budget going to drugs and diagnostics. How far they suffer in terms of their welfare losses due to these payments or to what extent their welfare losses differ with similar losses suffered by the poor may not be conjectured with the help of the results reported here.

With all those observed differentials across the households, a point of major policy concern stemming from the underlying discussion is how to reduce the size

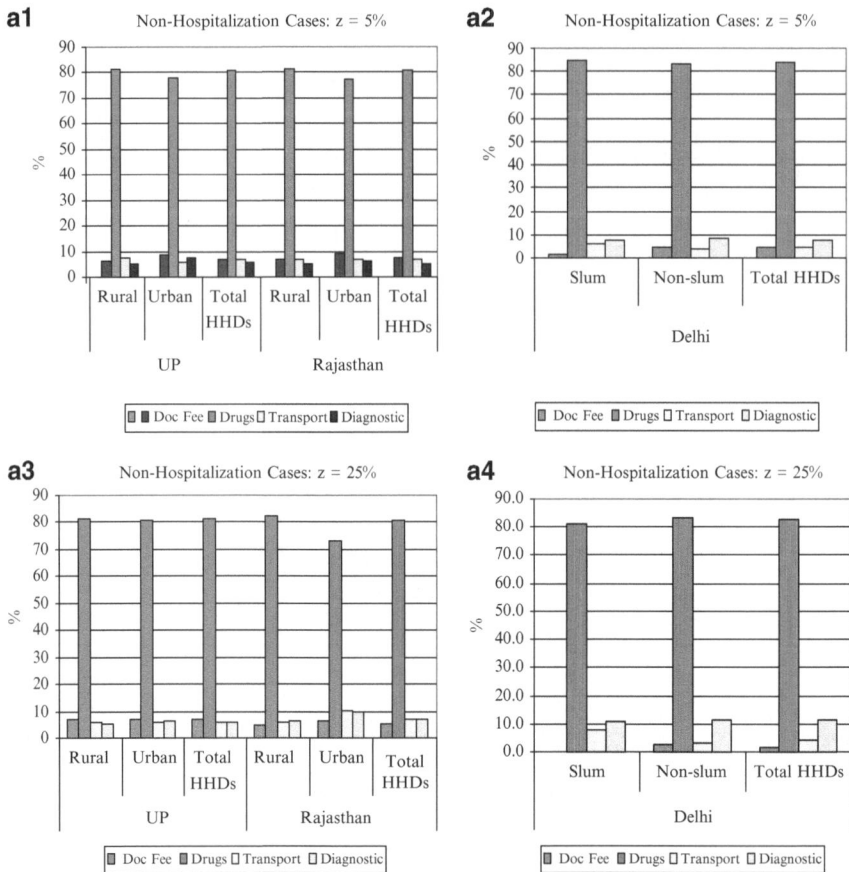

Fig. 6.3 (**a**) Share of expenses on drugs, health services and transportation in OOP health budget: catastrophic households ($z=5$ % of the total consumption) (*Source*: Table 6.3a). (**b**) Share of expenses on drugs, health services and transportation in OOP health budget: catastrophic households (Hospitalised episodes, $z=5$ and 25 % of the total consumption) (*Source*: Table 6.3b)

of the OOP health-care budget and shield poor household's from high costs of drugs and medical services. Besides the risk pooling and universal health insurance coverage, two other solutions may follow from the following: firstly, strict drug control policy coupled with a judicious demand–supply management of pharmaceutical products and, second, an improved health delivery mechanism in public hospitals and facilities. It requires a well-designed strategy to deploy medical personnel at different places, medical units, hospitals and dispensaries. Currently, physicians and medical personnel are deployed for several of non-clinical activities as well. They are in many cases governed by the district administration and pushed regularly to serve politicians or day-to-day political events. All this makes their availability to required clinical activities or designated hospitals scarce, thereby forcing ailing people to rely on private practitioners.

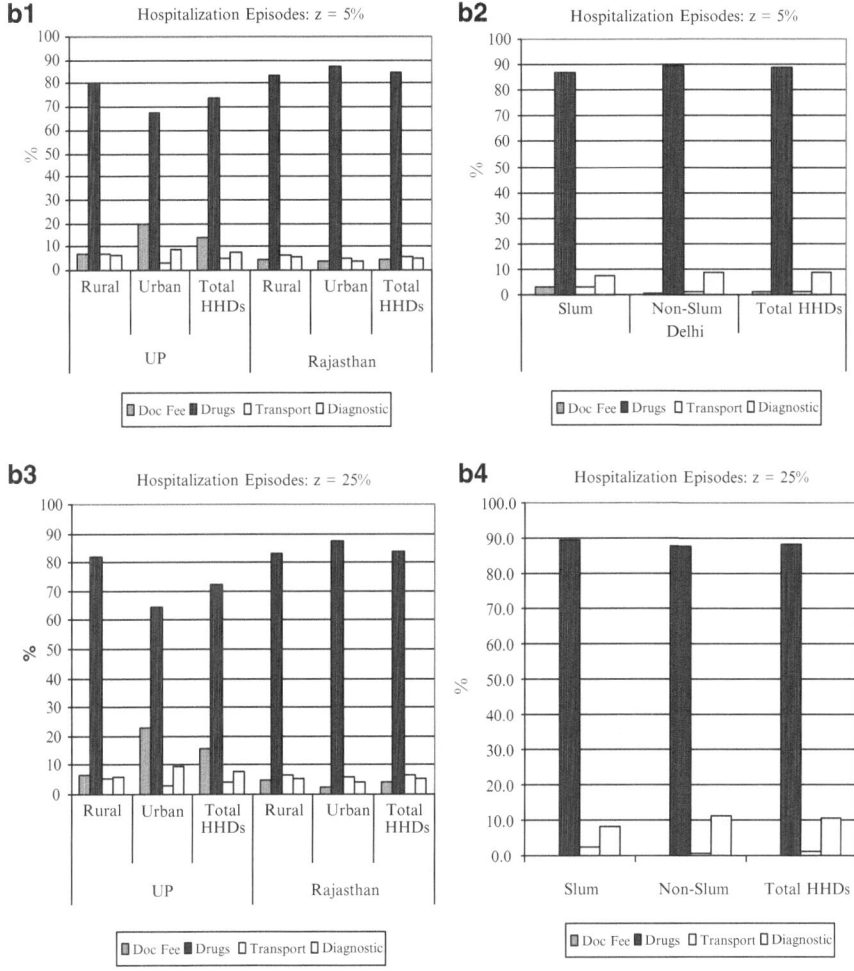

Fig. 6.3 (continued)

6.4   Government Policies Towards Drug Pricing: A Brief Overview

Of the many issues in availing health-care services in India, two are far more critical and mutually interconnected: the low level of public health expenditure, which has been hovering around 1 % of the country's GDP for the past few years, and high own-source spending by users of health services, particularly on purchase of drugs and medicines. With any increase in drug prices, the share of private out-of-pocket spending on health is bound to increase and worsen inequity and the inaccessibility of health services and might cause many more households economic hardship or push them below the poverty line.[6] All this happens although India ranks very high in the world in advanced life sciences and its pharmaceutical industry holds a top position in the international generics market (Narayan 2007).

6.4.1   Drug Pricing Policies in India

India has for long been producing pharmaceutical products to meet its domestic needs and has also been controlling the prices of selected non-innovative essential drugs for the past four decades and more. An effective drug price control regime came into existence in India in 1970 when the government issued a Drug Price Control Order (DPCO) under its Essential Commodities Act. The DPCO (1970) let the government control drug prices and complement these with the licencing system prevailing across the country, although at the expense of diluting intellectual property rights. There have, however, been several changes in subsequent years, and price control has been reduced successively—almost all drugs under price control in 1970 to a select list of 347 in 1979, to 142 bulk drugs in 1987 and to 76 in 1995, when India had to make major changes in its drug control regime as part of its economic liberalisation policies. After 1995, the government was willing to cut the number of essential drugs further to meet its WTO obligations but could not due to a pending Public Interest Litigation, initially in Karnataka High Court and later in the Supreme Court of India. It had to wait until 2005, when Trade-Related Intellectual Property Rights (TRIPS) rules and product payment for drugs became operational. During most of this period, India followed a cost-based pricing system.

6.4.2   Drug Price Policy: 2012

The evidence is growing of rising (non-essential) drug prices in recent years (Chaudhury 2005) that increase the very high financial burden on households with members with ailments. To alleviate this, and also because of certain relaxations— e.g. compulsory licencing—available under the TRIPS agreement,[7] the Government of India has rolled out a new National Pharmaceutical Pricing Policy (NPPP) on December 7, 2012 and increased the number of essential drugs from 74 (as determined by the 1995 Drug Price Control Order) to 348, almost the same given in the National List of Essential Medicines (NLEM) prepared in June 2011 by the Ministry of Health and Family, Government of India. These essential drugs, relying on a

---

[6] A recent study by Lalitha (2011) has cited the National Sample Survey on Consumer Expenditure (55th Round) to argue that OOP expenditure on health pushes more than 2 % of the people below-poverty line in 1 year. Our own results, presented in this book, show a similar result.

[7] India and some other developing countries have negotiated hard in WTO meetings to keep Intellectual Property Law (IPL) separate from the WTO. Finally, it was decided to follow Trade-Related Intellectual Property Rights (TRIPs) with certain relaxations like provisions of compulsory licences, although this right was pruned in effect.

Market-Based Ceiling Pricing (MBCP) system to determine final prices, are expected to cover almost 30 % of the total drugs sold in the country.[8]

Despite all these efforts and the purported objective of making drugs more accessible to low-income households, health analysts are sceptical (Selvaraj and Farooqui 2012) because (1) the NPPP excludes over three-quarters of medicines and (2) drug prices may not decline perceptibly because of the MBCP, designed to cover all 348 essential medicines. This may particularly be true for molecules (drugs) with high price variations. In such cases, mean prices will accompany high standard deviation and observed mean may exceed the prices of cheaper brands.[9]

Given these apprehensions and scepticism, would all these changes—e.g. enlarging the list of essential medicines or shifting from a cost-based pricing mechanism to a market-based system—help people to get affordable health care in India and avoid serious economic issues due to ailments? Answers to these questions need studies much deeper than the one conducted by us in this book. However, this analysis established an important point: Health care in India is a major cause of poverty among low-income rural and urban households and among the key policy areas for future governments, both central and state, given that health is a state subject and one of the biggest responsibilities of state governments.

Appendix

Table 6.A.1 Increase in poverty due to OOP health payments (%)

	Poverty 1[a]		Poverty 2[b]		Increase in below-poverty HHDs due to OOP	
	Rural	Urban	Rural	Urban	Rural	Urban
Total sample	33.0	18.8	46.5	24.9	13.5	6.1
UP	36.0	25.6	49.6	29.6	13.6	4.0
Unnao	34.7	20	48.89	22	14.2	2.0
Jhansi	38.0	34.0	50.7	41.0	12.7	7.0
Rajasthan	28.4	28.6	41.8	38.0	13.4	9.4
Dausa	21.6	38.0	34.0	56.0	12.4	18.0
Dungarpur	35.2	24	49.6	29.0	14.4	5.0
Delhi	–	10.0	–	16.1	–	6.1
Slum	–	26.5	–	41.2	–	14.7
Non-slum	–	3.4	–	6.2	–	2.8

[a]Poverty 1: Monthly per capita household consumption expenditure (MPCE) including OOP health care below defined poverty line (z), i.e. $MPCE < z$
[b]Poverty 2: MPCE excluding OOP health care below defined poverty line (z), i.e. $(MPCE - OOP) < (z)$

---

[8]Some projections suggest that the total market covered under this law would be around 18 %.

[9]The MBCP may be drawn by averaging the price of all the brands under a particular therapeutic (drug) area. Suppose a particular drug D has n number of brands and these brands are sold at price p such that $D_p 1$, $D_p 2$, …, $D_p n$. The market-based ceiling price under this formula would be the arithmetic mean computed on the basis of n numbers of brands and their p prices. If price variations across all these brands are high (i.e. a few p_s are very low and others are high), the ceiling price may not help and consumers may end up paying more.

References

Bonu, S., Indu, B., & Peters, David H. (2007, October). *Incidence, intensity and correlates of catastrophic OOP health payment in India* (ERD Working Paper No. 102). Malina: Asian Development Bank.

Chaudhury, S. (2005). *The WTO and India's pharmaceutical industry – Patent protection, TRIPS and developing countries*. New Delhi: Oxford University Press.

Cullet, P. (2005). *Intellectual property protection and sustainable development*. New Delhi: Lexis Nexis Butterworths.

Dormont, B., & Huber H. (2006, July–December). The predominance of changes in medical practices over population ageing. *Annales d' Économie et de Statis, 83/84*, Health, Insurance, Equity, 187–217. http://www.Jstor.org/stable/20079168. Accessed Apr 2009.

Dormont, B., Grignon, M., & Huber, H. (2006). Health expenditure growth: Reassessing the threat of ageing. *Health Economics, 15*, 947–967.

Getzen, T. E. (1992). Population ageing and the growth of health care expenditures. *Journal of Gerontology, 47*, S98–S104.

Kamiike, A., & Sato, T. (2011). *The TRIPs agreement and pharmaceutical industry: The Indian experience*. Paper presented in the conference on comparative aspects on culture and religion: India, Russia, China', SRC and CSCS, Bangalore. http://src-h.slav.hokudai.ac.jp/rp/group_06/activities/files/20110915_16/20110916_KamiikeSato.pdf Accessed in Feb.

Lalitha, N. (2011). Access to Indian generic drugs: Emerging issues. In K. C. Shadlen, S. Guennif, A. Guzman, & N. Lalitha (Eds.), *Intellectual property, pharmaceuticals and public health: Access to drugs in developing countries* (pp. 225–252). Cheltenham/Northampton: Edward Elgar.

Narayan, S. (2007, March 19). *Price control on pharmaceutical products in India* (ISAS Working Paper No. 20). Singapore: National University of Singapore: Institute of South Asian Studies (ISAS).

NCMH, MoHFW (Government of India). (2005, August). *Report of the National Commission on Macroeconomics and Health, Chapter 2 on India's health system: The financing and delivery of health care services* pp. 15–81.

Rane, W. (1999, June 30). Rise in drug prices since 1987 – An analysis. *Economic and Political Weekly*, 1375–1379.

Sakthivel, S. (2005, August). *Access to essential drugs and medicine*. Background paper prepared for the report "Financing and delivery of health care services in India" (pp. 185–212). National Commission on Macroeconomics and Health, Ministry of Health and Family Welfare, Government of India.

Selvaraj, S., & Farooqui, H. H. (2012, November 17). Draft drug price policy 2011: Legitimizing unaffordable medicine prices? *Economic and Political Weekly, 47*(46), 13–17.

Srinivasan, S. (1999). How many aspirins to the rupee: Runaway drug prices. *Economic and Political Weekly, 34*.

Watal, J. (2000). Pharmaceutical patents, prices and welfare losses: Policy options for India under the WTO rules agreement. *World Competition, Review of Law and Economics, 24*, 733–752.

Chapter 7
Utilisation of Public Health Facilities: A Situational Assessment

The preceding three chapters have lent considerable evidence to suggest that people in backward regions of UP and Rajasthan are severely pressured by OOP expenditure on health care. Almost a similar result was presented for the slum residents in Delhi as well. These results have also lent credence to the fact that a bulk of these households is marred by varying levels of catastrophe with possibilities of major curtailments in their living conditions. A probit regression analysis in Chap. 5 further indicates that the poor, economically less secured, lower caste, moderately educated, poor sanitation, lack of access to potable drinking water, low levels of living without proper lighting or cooking fuel and *kutcha* houses are among the factors making people susceptible to enhanced risks of health catastrophe. However, a question that needs to be examined in the context of these findings is: what happens to the public health facilities and despite high financial burden, why do people go to private practitioners? A related question may arise with regard to the utilisation of added services created in rural areas since the inception of the NRHM in April 2005. Do people even know about these facilities and their intended objectives to provide an added package of services including sanitation, potable drinking water, better childcare with timely vaccination and assistance to pregnant rural women with basic medicines and institutional deliveries? We will try to examine a few, if not all, of these issues in the rest of this chapter.

As was noted, two issues form the basic concern of this chapter. First is to examine the utilisation of public health-care facilities by households cross-classified according to: (i) rural–urban and slum–non-slum, (ii) consumption quintiles and (iii) catastrophe status. The second issue to be examined is as regards the reasons for non-utilisation or poor utilisation of the public facilities including primary health centres (PHC) or CHCs.[1] The focus of discussion in this part of analysis concerns the non-availability

---

[1] Primary health-care facilities created over the years by the government in rural areas have evolved on the basis of certain population norms. These include subcentres for every 3,000–5,000 population, primary health centres (PHCs) for a total of 20,000–30,000 population and community health centres (CHC) for 80,000–120,000 population. Lower population norms have been used for the tribal and hilly areas (Ministry of Health & Family Welfare, Government of India 2006). Most of these services have however been driven to a considerable extent by the family planning objectives of the government.

M. Alam, *Paying Out-of-Pocket for Drugs, Diagnostics and Medical Services: A Study of Households in Three Indian States*, India Studies in Business and Economics, DOI 10.1007/978-81-322-1281-2_7, © Springer India 2013

of doctors, particularly in rural areas, which may inter alia be an indication of (a) deficient manpower planning in government-run medical facilities and (b) poor management and/or deployment of available human resources by authorities and health-care planners. In between, we will also discuss about the NRHM and if people access the services provided under this scheme to a considerable extent.

7.1 Utilisation of Public Sector Facilities by Rural–Urban and Socioreligious Groups: Hospitalisation and Outpatient Care

Like the share of expenditure on drugs and medicines as observed in the preceding chapter, another significant issue in the context of health-driven poverty relates to a very high dependence of households on private facilities despite creation of a vast publicly financed health-care infrastructure in most rural and urban areas. Alarmingly, this dependence holds for most rural and low-income areas covered in the study. Moreover, a considerable share of poor population from the lowest quintile also appears to have relied on private providers. Catastrophic households follow a similar pattern. Furthermore, even in hospitalised treatment where it has an edge, the public sector is losing its earlier sheen. Tables 7.1a, 7.1b, 7.2a, 7.2b, 7.3a and 7.3b provide these details both for the hospitalised and outpatient treatments cross-classified by the sample areas and socioreligious groups. Major highlights of these tables are also represented graphically in figures drawn on the basis of the three tables mentioned above.

Tables 7.1a and 7.1b give the distribution of hospitalised (inpatient) and nonhospitalised (outpatient) cases treated in public or private facilities in rural and urban areas of the states under consideration. Two recall periods have been used—365 days for the former and 30 days for the latter (see also Fig. 7.1a, b). As has been noted, one of the most visible highlights of both the tables relates to the dominance of private facilities in the delivery of health services at all the places covered in the study. This pattern has been highlighted very sharply by Fig. 7.1b (and also Table 7.1b) with the help of a bivariate distribution of public–private shares in non-ambulatory (or outpatient) care across most of the survey areas and socioreligious groups. The share of private providers is particularly higher in UP where almost three-quarters of both rural and urban health-care seekers have relied on private practitioners for their routine outpatient care. Interestingly, this share has turned out to be relatively smaller in remaining states with the lowest in Rajasthan followed by Delhi (see the painted column in Table 7.1b). Nevertheless, at no place the share of private practitioners in outpatient care drops below 50 %. What does this lack of interest mean for the 11th Five-Year Plan (2007–2012) and its health objectives? The current Plan sets out to provide special attention to the health of marginalised groups like adolescent girls, women of all ages, children below the age of three, older persons, disabled and primitive tribal groups (Planning Commission 2008). However, a limited utilisation of health facilities, especially by the poor and

Table 7.1a Hospitalisation incidence and utilisation of public or private medical facilities: sample population (reference period: past 12 months)

States/socioreligious categories	Size of sample population (N)	Hospitalisation share (%)	Utilisation of facilities		Hospitalisation cases (number)
			Private (%)	Public[a] (%)	
UP	5,603	2.6	52.1	48.0	146
Rural	4,236	2.5	45.7	54.3	105
Urban	1,367	3.0	68.3	31.7	41
Rajasthan	3,523	3.4	40.2	59.8	117
Rural	2,705	3.1	37.8	62.2	82
Urban	818	4.2	45.7	54.3	35
Delhi	1,937	3.5	41.8	58.2	67
Slum	569	4.6	26.9	73.1	26
Non-slum	1,368	3.0	51.2	48.8	41
All social group	11,063	3.0	45.8	54.2	330
SC	2,531	3.1	46.2	53.9	78
ST	1,361	2.7	27.8	72.2	36
OBC	4,367	3.0	46.6	53.4	131
Upper caste	2,804	3.0	51.8	48.2	85
All religions	11,063	3.0	45.8	54.2	330
Hindu	9,795	3.0	45.6	54.4	294
Muslim	1,112	2.8	45.2	54.8	31
Total sample	11,063	3.0	45.8	54.2	330

[a]Includes city hospitals, CHCs and PHCs

Table 7.1b Outpatient treatment and utilisation of public or private medical facilities: sample population (reference period: past 30 days)

States/socioreligious categories	Number of persons	Nonhospitalised cases (%)	Type of medical doctor consulted:		Total outpatient cases (number)
			Private (%)	Public (%)	
UP	5,603	16.3	75.1	24.9	913
Rural	4,236	17.1	75.9	24.1	726
Urban	1,367	13.7	72.2	27.8	187
Rajasthan	3,523	13.7	58.4	41.6	481
Rural	2,705	13.9	57.6	42.4	377
Urban	818	12.7	61.5	38.5	104
Delhi	1,937	17.6	62.5	37.5	341
Slum	569	16.9	61.5	38.5	96
Non-slum	1,368	17.9	62.9	37.1	245
All social group	11,063	15.7	68.0	32.0	1,735
SC	2,531	16.3	70.6	29.4	412
ST	1,361	15.2	53.6	46.4	207
OBC	4,367	14.5	71.9	28.1	634
Upper caste	2,804	17.2	66.8	33.2	482
All religions	11,063	15.7	68.0	32.0	1,735
Hindu	9,795	15.8	67.8	32.2	1,544
Muslim	1,112	14.8	69.7	30.3	165
Total sample	11,063	15.7	68.0	32.0	1,735

Table 7.2a Utilisation of public and private hospitals: quintile groups

	Rural		Urban[a]		Slum		Non-slum		Total hospitalisation	
	Private	Public	Private	Public	Private	Public	Private	Public	Private	Public
Poorest 20 %	12.5	87.5	42.9	57.1	0.0	100.0	42.9	57.1	18.5	81.5
2	20.0	80.0	40.0	60.0	12.5	87.5	40.0	60.0	37.8	62.2
3	35.3	64.7	50.0	50.0	60.0	40.0	50.0	50.0	36.6	63.4
4	43.2	56.8	47.2	52.8	50.0	50.0	37.5	62.5	49.5	50.5
Richest 20 %	53.1	46.9	68.8	31.3	16.7	83.3	87.5	12.5	58.8	41.2
	42.3	57.8	50.4	49.7	26.9	73.1	51.2	48.8	45.8	54.2
Chi2(4)	Pr. = 0.021		Pr. 0.182		Pr. = 0.189		Pr. = 0.238		Pr. = 0.001	

Number of Hospitalisation Cases = 330
[a]Including households from slum and non-slum areas of Delhi

low-income households, may bring an element of contradiction between the ground realities and Plan objectives. It would therefore be imperative for all the stakeholders, in particular the health administrators, to raise the level of health-care utilisation in the public sector.

Contrary to the outpatient services, public facilities appear to have a greater role in providing hospital care at most of the places under reference. Table 7.1a summarises these details. This table shows that the utilisation of government hospitals is invariably higher among the tribal, low-caste and low-income people, especially from the slums and rural areas (see the coloured numbers in Table 7.1a; also see Fig. 7.1a). Unfortunately, however, it does not prove to be conclusively so as quite a bigger fraction of inpatient care accessed by the people from non-slum and urban areas of Delhi and UP has been delivered by the private hospitals and nursing homes. This is also true for those belonging to the upper-caste groups in the sample (see the coloured numbers in the table).

These variations apart, it needs to be admitted that the public hospitals not only serve a big fraction of people from different stratums and residential areas, they also serve to regulate the overall functioning of the private providers in more ways than one.

7.1.1 Distribution of Hospitalised and Nonhospitalised Care by Quintile Groups

Tables 7.2a and 7.2b distributes the users of public and private health-care services from different residential areas according to their consumption quintiles. Like before, this table has also been divided into two parts—7.2a and 7.2b—with the latter relating to the nonhospitalisation or outpatient cases with a reference period of

Table 7.2b Utilisation of public and private facilities: outpatient cases by quintile groups

	Rural		Urban[a]		Slum[b]		Non-slum[b]		Total cases	
	Private	Public	Private	Public	Private	Public	Private	Public	Private	Public
Poorest 20 %	62.1	37.9	49.5	50.5	59.1	40.9	59.1	40.9	61.1	38.9
2	69.0	31.0	65.9	34.2	52.6	47.4	72.1	27.9	65.5	34.5
3	62.3	37.7	66.4	33.6	61.5	38.5	60.4	39.6	67.6	32.4
4	75.0	25.0	76.1	23.9	52.4	47.6	61.1	38.9	71.8	28.3
Richest 20 %	79.3	20.8	63.8	36.2	81.0	19.1	62.8	37.3	73.6	26.4
Total	69.6	30.4	65.2	34.8	61.5	38.5	62.9	37.1	68.0	32.0
Chi2 (4)	Pr. = 0.000		Pr. = 0.001		Pr. = 0.311		Pr. = 0.727		Pr. = 0.003	

Number of cases = 1,735

[a]Including households from slum and non-slum areas of Delhi

[b]Very few observations

Table 7.3a   Utilisation of public–private hospitals by catastrophic households: $z=5$ and 25 %

Catastrophe	Place of residence									
levels	Rural		Urban[a]		Slum		Non-slum		Total hospitalisation	
	Private	Public	Private	Public	Private	Public	Private	Public	Private	Public
Catastrophe 1: 5 %	41.1	58.9	56.0	44.0	35.0	65.0	62.1	37.9	47.2	52.8
Chi2(1)	Pr. = 0.334		Pr. 0.005		Pr. = 0.090		Pr. = 0.031		Pr. = 0.197	
Catastrophe 2: 25 %	41.8	58.2	64.3	35.7	75.0	25.0	57.1	42.9	48.9	51.1
Chi2(1)	Pr. = 0.895		Pr. 0.032		Pr. = 0.000		Pr. = 0.731		Pr. = 0.351	

Number of Cases = 330
[a]Including households from slum and non-slum areas of Delhi

30 days, while the former provides a similar distribution for the hospitalisation episodes using a recall period of 12 months. Figure 7.2a and b give a graphical presentation of the two tables, respectively.

While both the tables, Tables 7.1a and 7.2b, broadly represent a similar pattern as was discussed before, the following two observations are expected to be of significance both for the present discussion as well as for the objectives of the 11th Five-Year Plan cited earlier. First, a big majority of the outpatient care seekers, even from the two poorest consumption quintiles (bottom 20 % and the next 20 %), largely rely on private providers. It may, in other words, imply that no amount of economic hardship makes even the poorest feel compelled to use private facilities. The other observation, though reconfirms to a large extent the primacy of public facilities when it comes to hospitalisation, underlies the fact that even the poorest may not be able to rely solely on public hospitals. Table 7.2a, for example, indicates that a good fraction of persons from the two lowest consumption quintiles received care from private providers (see coloured numbers in Table 7.2b). Admittedly, while such fractions may not be used conclusively to vindicate certain line of arguments, they however make out a case to go into such instances further and deeper. These are also the issues to be taken into consideration by the RKSs or such other patient welfare bodies currently working at the district and subdistrict levels.

7.1.2   Distribution by Catastrophic Households: Hospitalisation and Nonhospitalisation Care

As in the previous two sections, herein also we cite a distribution of public and private medical facilities utilised by two sets of households and their ailing family members, differentiated on grounds of mild and severe catastrophe. The former was characterised on the basis of health expenditure at 5 % of normal consumption budget ($z=5$ %), while the latter with an acute form of catastrophe was represented

Table 7.3b Utilisation of outpatient public and private facilities by catastrophic households: $z=5$ and 25 %

| | Place of residence | | | | | | | | | |
| | Rural | | Urban | | Slum | | Non-slum | | Total cases | |
Catastrophe levels	Private	Public	Private	Public	Private	Public	Private	Public	Private	Public
Catastrophe 1: 5 %	68.9	31.2	70.2	29.8	68.2	31.8	69.9	30.1	69.3	30.7
Chi2(1)	Pr. =0.216		Pr. =0.000		Pr. =0.045		Pr. =0.006		Pr. =0.045	
Catastrophe 2: 25 %	73.4	26.6	70.6	29.4	66.7	33.3	64.7	35.3	72.7	27.3
Chi2(1)	Pr. =0.136		Pr. =0.261		Pr. =0.579		Pr. =0.870		Pr. =0.038	

Number of cases=1,735

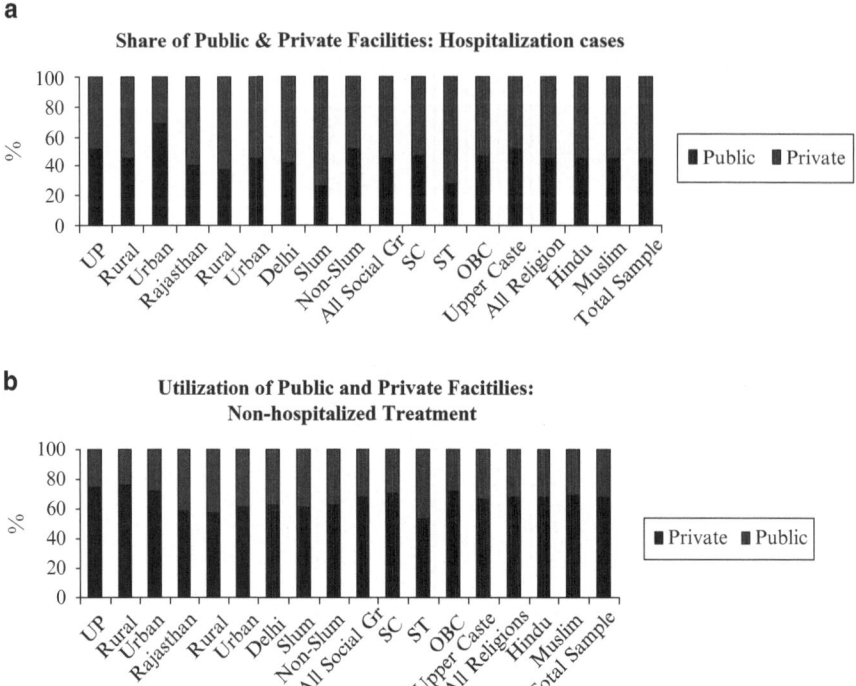

Fig. 7.1 Inpatient and outpatient treatment: utilisation of public and private medical facilities (*Source*: Table 7.1a, 7.1b)

with health budget exceeding almost a quarter of the total consumption expenditure ($z=25$ %). Tables 7.3a and 7.3b provide these details. For better illustration, these tables were also converted into Fig. 7.3a and b.

It may be interesting to note in both the tables, which profile recipients of medical care with or without hospitalisations, that catastrophe is not entirely the outcome of private hospitals or private medical practitioners. It occurs to patients of public facilities as well (Tables 7.3a and 7.3b; Fig. 7.3a, b). Although in nonhospitalisation cases, it mainly results because of private providers, i.e. from little less than two-thirds to over 73 % of the total cases (Table 7.3b). In addition, the case is the same for both rural and urban areas. Contrasting this, Table 7.3a indicates that hospitalisation-driven catastrophe is also generally higher among the patients treated in public hospitals. This is particularly true for the low-income households. While somewhat disappointing, public medical facilities are shown to have pushed a good majority of rural and slum households to face catastrophe (see coloured numbers in Table 7.3a). Besides, these results also indicate that a fraction of public hospital patients have also ended up with most of the oppressive forms of catastrophe ($z=25$ %),

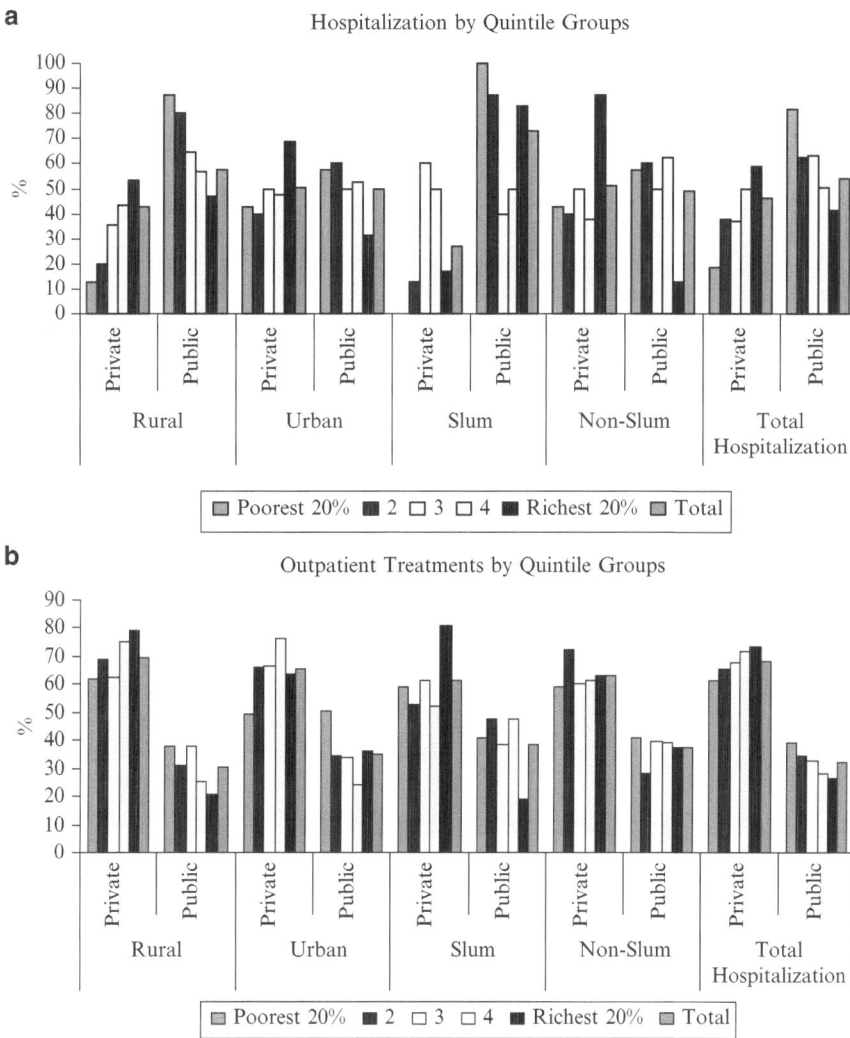

Fig. 7.2 (**a**) Types of health-care facilities utilised by sample inpatients (*Source*: Table 7.2a). (**b**) Types of health-care facilities utilised by sample outpatients (*Source*: Table 7.2b)

presumably because many of the services in public hospitals are now available on payment basis. These are over and above the cost of drugs and medicines; some of them may not be essential.

While some of these results are constrained by a limited number of observations, they appear to be still useful for drawing a few inferences at the policy level. Two issues are apparently more significant as regards policy considerations and

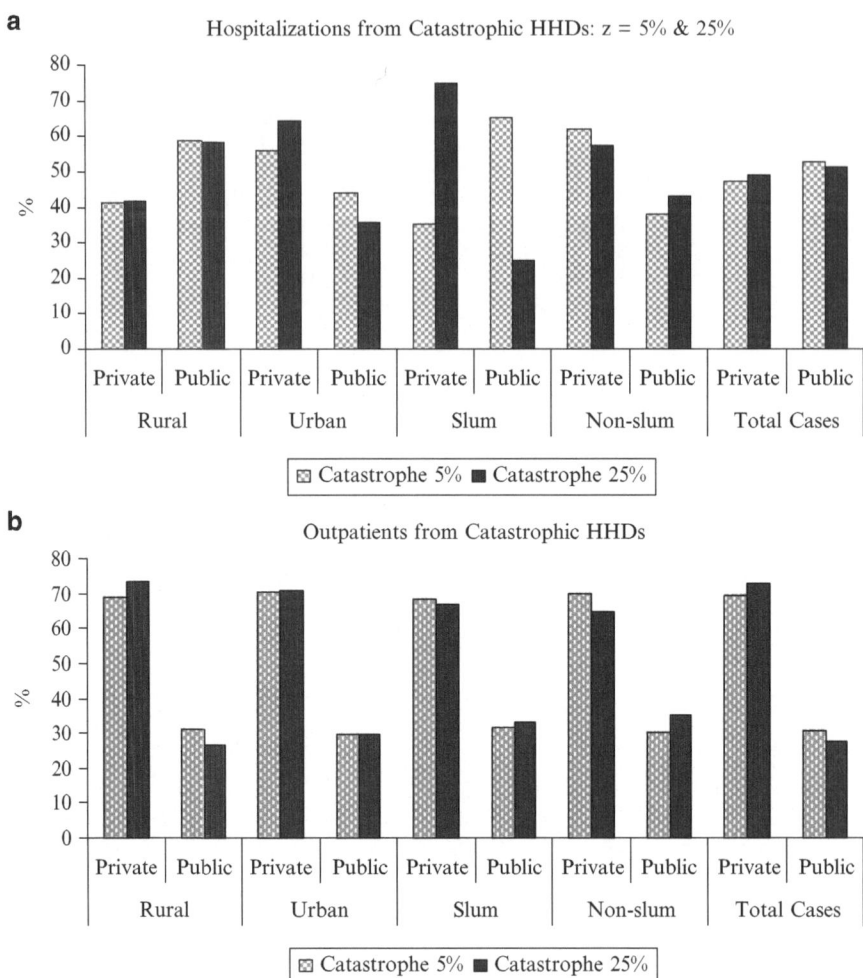

Fig. 7.3 (**a**) Inpatients treated in public and private facilities: catastrophic households (*Source*: Table 7.3a). (**b**) Outpatients treated in public and private facilities: catastrophic households (*Source*: Table 7.3b)

may need to be discussed at length. Firstly, why even those who were treated for ailments in public hospitals and other facilities could not save themselves from catastrophe? Secondly, why do not many low-income slum and rural people go to public facilities? In other words, what makes many of them wary of public facilities? A related question may as well be: Why is the NRHM, April 2005, which is believed to fill many of the voids in rural health-care system, unable to induce people to rely more on public facilities? The discussion to follow seeks to explore the last two issues more explicitly. Catastrophe–public facility linkages need a separate examination with additional data.

7.2   Factors in Non-utilisation of Public Health Facilities: Respondents' Views

One lead question and another two sets of eight questions each were asked at the time of the survey to identify factors responsible for the apathetic attitude of health-care users towards public medical facilities.[2] The lead question asked to the house-hold head was: Have you used public health-care services during ailments requiring hospitalisation as against outpatient care? Those who replied 'no' were asked to check for possible reasons from the relevant sets. A slightly different set of questions was used to probe the reasons linked with indoor (hospitalised) as against outdoor (nonhospitalised) treatment.

The options prompted to health seekers as possible reasons for not accessing public facilities—both outpatient and hospitalisation—included the following:

Reasons for: Non-utilisation of consultation facilities	Reasons for: Non-utilisation of hospital facilities
1. Financially comfortable, can afford private doctor	1. Govt. facilities too far and not easily accessible
2. Easy to access a private doctor at emergencies	2. Govt. hospitals charge for most services
3. PHC/CHC or government hospital refused to treat	3. PHC/CHC and government hospitals inefficient
4. PHC/CHC/government doctor not available	4. Doctors and staff in government hospitals rude
5. Govt. doctors and staff are generally rude	5. Govt. hospitals are mostly used by rich
6. Govt. doctors want patients to consult at home	6. Poor do not have easy access to govt. hospital
7. PHC/CHC or public hospital too far from home	7. No drugs or medicines in government hospital
8. Others (no medicines, non-available at odd hours)	8. Others (e.g. hospitals overcrowded)

A simple frequency distribution of responses drawn from both the categories of service users is presented in Tables 7.4a and 7.4b (also see the attached figures). It may be noted from both these tables that the factors that generally dissuade people to utilise public services remain more or less traditional. To illustrate, those who preferred not to access public hospital facilities found justification in four commonly known reasons: (1) public facilities too far, (3) public hospitals inefficient, (7) most drugs prescribed by the in-house doctors are either out of stock or for self-purchase and (8) public hospitals are invariably very crowded (see Fig. 7.4a). While most of these factors are fairly known and oft repeated, it may be noted that

---

[2]It ought to be mentioned that the debate on disassociating factors making people indifferent towards the public health facilities is decades old. There have been several studies directed to this issue in the past (see, e.g. Bose and Tyagi 1983: 104–122). What is however interesting is that the inferences drawn in those earlier studies match closely with our own. In other words, the public sector, despite major attempts, has not been able to shed many of its past limitations.

Table 7.4a Reasons for non-utilisations of public hospitals/facilities: respondents' views

States/Socio-religious categories	Non-utilisation of public hospitals: reasons								
	1	2	3	4	5	6	7	8	N*
UP (R+U)	9.2	1.4	31.6	5.3	0.0	3.9	36.8	11.8	76
Rural	8.3	0.0	35.4	4.2	0.0	6.3	33.3	12.5	48
Urban	10.7	3.6	25.0	7.1	0.0	0.0	42.9	10.7	28
Rajasthan (R+U)	0.0	2.1	44.7	0.0	2.1	0.0	27.7	23.4	47
Rural	0.0	3.2	45.2	0.0	3.2	0.0	35.5	12.9	31
Urban	0.0	0.0	43.8	0.0	0.0	0.0	12.5	43.7	16
Delhi (NS+S)	35.7	0.0	25.0	0.0	0.0	7.1	28.6	3.6	28
Non-slum	38.1	0.0	23.8	0.0	0.0	9.5	23.8	4.8	21
Slum	28.6	0.0	28.6	0.0	0.0	0.0	42.8	0.0	7
SC	19.4	0.0	33.3	0.0	2.8	0.0	22.2	22.3	36
ST	20.0	0.0	40.0	0.0	0.0	10.0	30.0	0.0	10
OBC	4.9	0.0	36.1	3.3	0.0	1.6	37.7	16.4	61
Upper caste	11.4	4.5	31.8	4.6	0.0	6.8	34.1	6.8	44
Hindus	11.9	1.5	33.6	1.5	0.7	3.7	32.8	14.2	134
Muslims	7.1	0.0	28.6	14.3	0.0	0.0	35.7	14.3	14

[a]N gives number of persons responding to a particular question from each study area and socio-religious groups. Small number of observations needs to be borne in mind while interpreting the results

Reasons for non-utilisation of Public Hospitals:

1. Public facilities too far. 2. Govt. Hospitals charge for most services. 3. Inefficient. 4. Doctors/Staff rude. 5. Govt. facilities used mostly by richer people. 6. Poor do not have easy access. 7. No drugs or medicine. 8. Others, which mostly include overcrowded facilities

medicines and efficiency in service delivery by public facilities are the two major expectations that need to be ensured by the government and its health apparatuses. Another point to be noted in the context of this discussion is that despite perceptions, a very small fraction of respondents had complained against doctors' behaviour or

Table 7.4b Reasons for non-consultation of public facilities/medical doctors: respondents' views

States/Socio-religious	Reasons for Non-consultation								
Categories	1	2	3	4	5	6	7	8	N*
UP (Total)	22.3	8.3	2.0	6.0	14.9	3.4	22.9	20.3	686
Rural	16.2	8.7	2.2	6.4	15.8	2.4	27.8	20.7	551
Urban	47.4	6.7	1.5	4.4	11.1	7.4	3.0	18.5	135
Rajasthan (Total)	21.0	8.2	2.8	3.6	1.8	1.1	17.1	44.5	281
Rural	17.1	9.2	1.8	3.7	1.8	1.4	22.1	42.9	217
Urban	34.4	4.7	6.3	3.1	1.6	0.0	0.0	50.0	64
Delhi (Total)	21.6	5.6	0.9	8.0	37.1	0.5	8.9	17.4	213
Non-Slum	24.7	3.2	1.3	9.7	36.4	0.6	5.8	18.2	154
Slum	13.6	11.9	0.0	3.4	39.0	0.0	16.9	15.3	59
SC	13.1	6.2	2.1	5.2	20.6	1.7	21.3	29.9	291
ST	11.7	9.9	1.8	0.0	3.6	0.9	34.2	37.8	111
OBC	24.1	9.0	2.6	6.6	12.1	2.4	19.3	23.9	456
Upper Caste	30.1	6.8	1.2	7.1	20.8	3.1	11.2	19.6	322
Hindu	21.4	8.0	1.9	5.3	15.5	2.6	19.3	26.1	1,047
Muslim	21.7	7.0	3.5	9.6	17.4	0.0	18.3	22.6	115

*N gives number of persons responding to a particular question from each study area and socio-religious groups. Small number of observations needs to be borne in mind while interpreting the results.

Reasons for non-utilisation of Public Hospitals:

1. Public facilities too far. 2. Govt. Hospitals charge for most services. 3. Inefficient. 4. Doctors/Staff rude. 5. Govt. facilities used mostly by richer people. 6. Poor do not have easy access. 7. No drugs or medicine. 8. Others, which mostly include overcrowded facilities

growing burden of paid hospital services. Apparently, efficiency in service delivery and subsidised drugs may help in bringing substantial relief to a large number of low-income health seekers of public hospitals.

Similarly, patients needing non-ambulatory (or outdoor) care have also held three major constraining factors responsible for non-utilisation of consultation services provided by primary or secondary health centres or city hospitals (Table 7.4b). These are: (5) misbehaviour by hospital staff including doctors and paramedics, (7) distant locations of public facilities and (8) others, which largely included overcrowding and non-availability of drugs. It implicitly suggests that the users of health-care facilities tend to substitute public health care in favour of the private providers owing to some of these basic constraints; non-availability of drugs and drag on time are the two particularly serious issues for many low-income health-care seekers. Yet it seems that

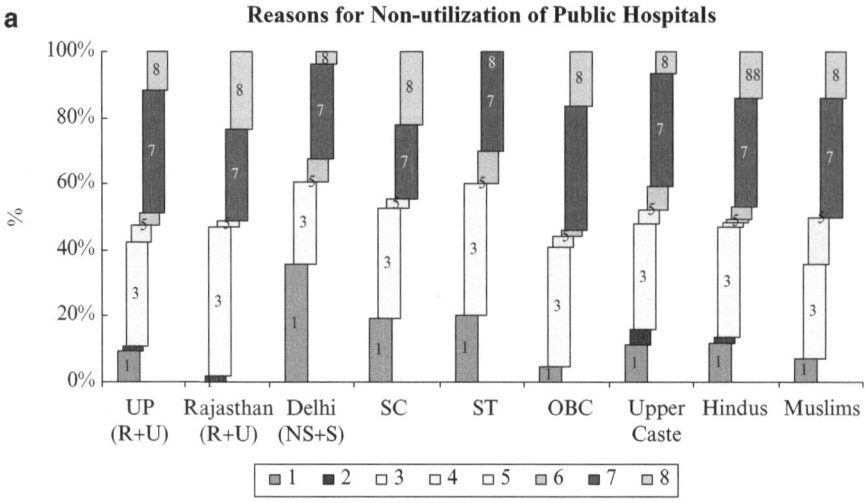

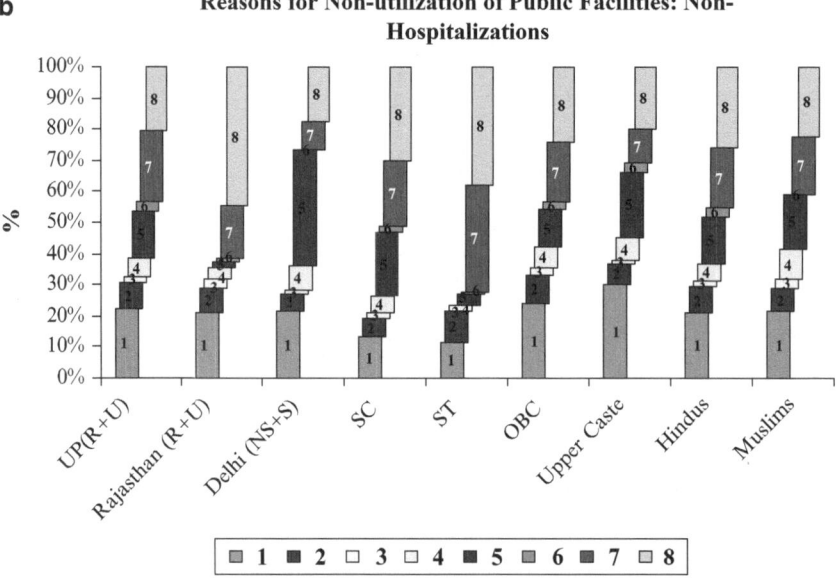

Fig. 7.4 (**a**) Reasons for non-utilisation of public hospitals/facilities (% respondents) (*Source*: Table 7.4a). (**b**) Reasons for non-utilisation of public outdoor facilities (% respondents) (*Source*: Table 7.4b)

the time factor remains diluted when it comes to hospitalisation. Another interesting observation relates to the affordability as a criterion to access private medical care. Many of those who decided not to utilise the public facilities were able to afford the cost of private consultation. In other words, there is a possible trade-off between the private and public health-care facilities—largely because of the latter's inefficient service delivery, non-availability of medicines and cost of transportation.

7.3 National Rural Health Mission: A Cursory Analysis

The Millennium Development Summit, which was perhaps among the most important meetings of world leaders convened by the United Nations, had adopted a Millennium Declaration on 8 September 2000 in committing all the member countries including India to achieve the following by the end of 2015:

- (i) Eradicate extreme poverty.
- (ii) Achieve universal primary education.
- (iii) Promote gender equality and empower women.
- (iv) Reduce child mortality.
- (v) Improve maternal mortality.
- (vi) Combat HIV/AIDS, malaria and other diseases.
- (vii) Ensure environmental sustainability.
- (viii) Develop a global partnership for development.

In pursuance of these MDGs, India has initiated in the preceding few years a number of programmes in the realms of education, employment and primary health care. The NRHM, April 2005, was essentially designed to achieve the specific objectives of improving child survival and reducing maternal mortality (i.e. objectives iv and v). Both the objectives are set to be fulfilled by the end of the current Plan period (2007–2012). Since its very inception, the NRHM has tried to differentiate itself from earlier programmes by working to integrate the key determinants of health outcomes including nutrition, drinking water, hygiene and sanitation facilities together with the components of rural health services; all of these were in a gender perspective with an emphasis on poor women and children. The NRHM has also tried to decentralise the health programmes by involving panchayats and other local bodies at district and subdistrict levels along with an easier access to financial resources.

Confining largely to its supply-side measures, a certain number of review articles have tried to bring out many of the key elements embodying this programme: provision for a completely new brand of health personnel like ASHA, greater role of practitioners trained in AYUSH, improved functioning of block level hospitals and ease in mobilisation of physical and financial resources (Sinha 2009; Kumar 2005). Contradicting to a large extent the views expressed by Sinha (2009) and Kumar (2005), Ashtekar (2008) tried to bring out several limitations—financial, skill-related and limited prospects of integrating sectors—that largely help to determine most health outcomes.

Unfortunately, a great deal of the ongoing debate on this programme—both in favour and against—has failed to make observations on the basis of certain outcome variables. We therefore try to present below a few simple facts with an objective to make inferences about the following:

1. The extent to which the NRHM has caught the attention of rural people from different socio-economic stratums including those suffering catastrophe due to disproportionate spending on health.

2. Post-NRHM improvements (if any) in availability of health-care services, PHC
   doctors and other health workers. Respondents' views on distribution of medi-
   cines/vitamins being given to women during pregnancies, utilisation of doctors
   trained in Indian systems of medicine (AYUSH) and ASHA.

Reponses collected from a total of 1,250 selected rural households from UP and
Rajasthan are summarised in Tables 7.5a and 7.5b. The two tables, as was mentioned, broadly reflect the awareness, utilisation and satisfaction with rural health-
care facilities post-NRHM. Unfortunately, however, to what extent these facilities
have been able to perform better from their pre-NRHM level (or have been able to
attain a better outcome) may not be discussed with the help of the data available to
us. In addition, the time gap involved between the launch of this programme and our
own study appears to be too limited to derive more conclusive observations.

Table 7.5a describes the availability of primary health services in the survey
areas. It also highlights the fraction of sample households aware about the NRHM
and its objectives such as the role of ASHAs or the services being provided by
primary health units to ensure institutional delivery. Respondents have also reacted
to certain qualitative questions like improvements in delivery of services during the
past few years (or since the introduction of NRHM). Nonetheless, risks of subjectivity
while interpreting those responses ought not to be ignored.[3]

On the awareness issue, Table 7.5a does not seem to be very encouraging as very
small fractions of people from both the states, in particular from Rajasthan, knew
about the NRHM or the level of priorities attached to improved child health and
institutional delivery. Between the two states, residents of Unnao and its villages
appear to be better informed about the NRHM. About a fifth of the total respondents
in Unnao have reported their awareness about the mission. The same in Rajasthan
was below 10 %. People from upper-caste categories and economically better-off
respondents (e.g. above poverty or higher quintile households) have however shown
a greater awareness about the rural health mission and a couple of its intended
objectives, although even their shares do not exceed far beyond a fifth or a quarter
of their respective numbers. Interestingly, however, despite so much of ignorance
about the NRHM or its basic concerns, a much bigger fraction of respondents have
not only reported satisfaction with the services provided by the primary health units
but have also reported visible improvements in the delivery of health services over
the preceding 2 or 3 years. To make it more specific, they further confirmed improvements in services covering reproductive and child health (Tables 7.5a and 7.5b).
Also there are reports that these services have improved further and ASHAs have
done well to enhance utilisation of maternal and child health services by taking
women to health centres for pre- and postnatal care.

On the flip side, these responses have remained considerably large across all the
households distributed according to their socio-economic (social groups, quintile

---

[3]In addition to subjectivity, it must also be confessed that the survey designed to undertake this study
and most of its questions were not framed with the NRHM as the central issue. Hence, a further
and more in-depth analysis of the issues raised here would require a separate study and database.

Table 7.5a Awareness about the NRHM and availability of primary health facilities: responses from rural households (%)

Percent

Households' Characteristics: States, Districts, Socio-religious, Consumption Quintile & Catastrophe Levels	Knowledge about NRHM	Village with a health centre in-cluding PHC/CHC	Developed PHC in the village	Satisfied with the delivery of services	Improvement in health ser-vices over past few years	Role of Panchayat/ Municipal Bodies in primary health ser-vices
	Share with Affirmative Responses					
A. District *Sample*						
Unnao	20.0	58.2	21.3	67.2	42.2	18.4
Jhansi	8.0	64.7	6.3	76.3	40.0	13.0
UP	15.2	60.8	15.3	71.1	41.3	16.3
Dausa	7.2	56.0	3.6	87.9	41.2	10.8
Dungarpur	8.4	74.8	4.8	90.4	66.4	10.8
Rajasthan	7.8	65.4	4.2	89.3	53.8	10.8
B. Economic Character-istics						
Below Poverty (BPL)	4.1	59.2	6.8	87.7	53.2	12.4
Above Poverty (APL)	16.2	64.3	12.9	74.6	43.0	14.9
Con. Quintiles						
Lowest 20%	2.4	62.4	5.6	89.1	56.0	11.6
2	7.6	58.8	8.8	83.7	47.6	14.0
3	9.6	67.7	11.6	73.5	44.2	15.1
4	14.9	59.0	11.2	73.5	41.8	13.3
Richest 20%	26.8	65.2	17.2	74.2	42.0	16.4

(continued)

Table 7.5a (continued)

Catastrophic HHDs						
Mild: z = 5%	12.3	63.7	11.3	77.9	47.0	13.3
Acute: z = 25%	13.4	59.7	9.5	73.9	38.1	13.4
C. Social Characteristics						
Social Groups						
SC	14.1	66.0	15.5	77.6	42.6	15.5
ST	2.6	57.6	0.9	87.2	45.9	9.1
OBC	12.7	58.1	11.8	77.5	45.5	12.9
Upper Caste	19.4	75.6	13.4	75.0	54.2	20.9
D. Religious Characteristics						
Religion						
Hindu	12.1	60.9	10.6	80.1	46.4	13.8
Muslim	14.3	82.7	14.3	66.7	44.9	17.3
E. Total Sample (N = 1250)	12.2	62.6	10.9	78.7	46.3	14.1

Table 7.5b Utilisation and perceived improvements in service delivery since NRHM: responses from rural households (%)

Households' characteristics: states, districts, socioreligious, consumption quintile and catastrophe levels	Improvement in reproductive and child health services over past 3 years	Regular visit by the PHC doctor(s)	ASHA in place	Recipients of ASHA service(s)	Distribution of certain medicines, vitamin tablets and ORT from PHCs	Users of traditional Indian system (AYUSH)
	Share with affirmative responses					
A. District sample						
Unnao	69.3	80.4	61.3	30.4	55.3	27.3
Jhansi	92.7	85.7	93.3	47.7	85.0	11.0
UP	78.7	82.5	74.1	37.3	67.2	20.8
Dausa	96.4	94.0	72.8	33.6	75.6	9.6
Dungarpur	98.8	91.6	88.8	43.6	68.8	53.2
Rajasthan	97.6	92.8	80.8	38.6	72.2	31.4

(continued)

Table 7.5b   (continued)

Households' characteristics: states, districts, socioreligious, consumption quintile and catastrophe levels	Improvement in reproductive and child health services over past 3 years	Regular visit by the PHC doctor(s)	ASHA in place	Recipients of ASHA service(s)	Distribution of certain medicines, vitamin tablets and ORT from PHCs	Users of traditional Indian system (AYUSH)
	Share with affirmative responses					
B. Economic characteristics						
Below poverty (BPL)	86.7	90.8	81.1	59.6	73.8	21.1
Above poverty (APL)	86.0	84.6	74.7	43.8	66.9	27.0
Consumption quintiles						
Lowest 20 %	86.4	89.6	82.0	63.9	75.6	20.8
2	87.6	89.6	78.8	54.8	72.0	21.2
3	87.6	90.4	77.7	43.6	68.9	26.7
4	85.1	82.7	73.5	45.9	65.5	21.7
Richest 20 %	84.4	80.8	72.0	36.1	64.0	34.8
Catastrophic HHDs						
Mild: $z=5$ %	86.1	84.9	76.3	53.5	66.9	26.5
Acute: $z=25$ %	82.7	86.1	71.0	43.3	57.1	22.9
C. Social characteristics						
Social groups						
SC	84.5	86.3	79.4	41.6	71.1	23.0
ST	97.0	91.3	84.9	42.4	68.4	26.0
OBC	82.5	85.6	68.9	33.4	67.9	21.1
Upper caste	86.1	84.6	84.6	38.8	70.6	37.3
D. Religious characteristics						
Religion						
Hindu	85.8	86.5	76.6	49.5	68.1	26.3
Muslim	91.8	87.8	78.6	46.8	81.6	10.2
E. Total sample (N=1,250)	86.2	86.6	76.8	37.8	69.2	25.0

groups, etc.) characteristics. Even the two categories of catastrophic households, mild ($z=5$ %) and severe ($z=25$ %), have also felt the same way. Some other interesting observations stemming from both the tables include:

- PHC doctors visit regularly. It was reported by more than 80 % of the respondents.
- ASHA already in place, confirmed by almost three-quarters of the sample people.
- Between 30 and 64 % of households from different socio-economic and religious categories has received help from the ASHA. Interestingly, shares of low-income and catastrophic households among them were considerably large (Table 7.5a).

- As for the vitamin tablets, ORT or some other common medicines, respondents admitted to have received them from the health workers and their PHCs.
- Barring sample of persons from Dungarpur (Rajasthan), economically better-off and upper-caste households, a very small fraction of respondents have used AYUSH services. The share of AYUSH users remains invariably below 20 % of the respective samples. Muslims and residents of Unnao are the worst off on this count.

Finally, to cap some of the discussions, it must be noted that the two diametrical messages are emerging from the analysis presented in this chapter. On the one hand, we observe that a large percentage of responding households (even a majority in many cases) do not find it worthwhile to rely on facilities provided by the government, particularly for non-ambulatory or outpatient care. On the other, we notice that the NRHM has caught recognition of a good number of rural people in a short span of 3 years (i.e. time gap between this study and the inception of NRHM in May 2005), and they did appreciate the services provided by the primary health units. They also report favourably about the PHC doctors, ASHA and certain qualitative improvements in rural health-care services since the NRHM. The question may therefore be: Why is there so much of health-related catastrophe or apathetic attitude among the service users towards public facilities? Answers appear to lie at two levels. First, rural health care has largely been confined to a particular age segment. In addition, it is restricted to a particular health domain as well. A large number of diseases falling beyond the reproductive health domains have remained poorly managed. As those diseases cause catastrophe to a very large extent, the government will have to consider ways to bring significant improvements in the delivery of secondary and tertiary health-care services as well.

References

Bose, A., & Tyagi, R. P. (1983). Rural health services: Present status. In A. Bose & P. B. Desai (Eds.), *Studies in social dynamics of primary health care* (pp. 104–122). Delhi: Hindustan Publishing Corporation (India).

Kumar, A. K. S. (2005, April 2). Budgeting for health: Some considerations. *Economic and Political Weekly*, 1391–1396.

MoHFW (Government of India). (2006). *Family welfare statistic in India – 2006* (p. 33).

Planning Commission, Government of India. (2008). *Eleventh Five Plan (2007–2012), social sector* (Vol. II, p. 58). New Delhi: Oxford University Press.

Shear, S. (2008, September 13). The national rural health mission – A stocktaking. *Economic and Political Weekly*, 23–26.

Sinha, A. (2009). In defence of the rural health mission. *Economic and Political Weekly*, 72–75.

Chapter 8
Broad Conclusions and Policy Directions

Drawing upon a set of comprehensive field-based data and an in-depth analysis of the OOP health payments by a cross-section of households from selected rural and urban areas of three different states—UP, Rajasthan and Delhi—there appear to be major challenges ahead for both the planners and administrators of health-care services. This can easily be noticed from the discussion so far. While this chapter however does not intend to replicate most of that discussion or its underlying messages in a conventional setting, it does attempt to cull out briefly a few of the major observations after piecing them together from different chapters as reference points.[1] As regards directions of policy, this chapter sets out to provide scores of considered opinion given by the respondents on issues of critical concerns, e.g. recent increase in health-care charges, overprescription of medicines and/or diagnostics by medical professionals and role of drugs in making health care expensive. This will be followed by another set of respondents' reactions covering issues in a policy framework such as health insurance and the extent respondents would be willing to go for such a product on a payment basis. Most of these questions and their responses are expected to help in deriving a host of policy recommendations based on considered judgments of those who really matter. It may nevertheless be noted that in no way these recommendations may be treated as out of the box.

Most of the analysis was broadly directed to focus on the following concerns:

1. OOP health payments and attendant issues of poverty and inequality
2. Catastrophic health payments and some of its correlates
3. Decomposition of health payments and share of drugs/medicines in the total health expenditure
4. Share of public health services in hospitalisation and outpatient care

---

[1] A summary of the major findings is already presented at the beginning of this study.

M. Alam, *Paying Out-of-Pocket for Drugs, Diagnostics and Medical Services: A Study of Households in Three Indian States*, India Studies in Business and Economics, DOI 10.1007/978-81-322-1281-2_8, © Springer India 2013

5. Public health-care utilisation and catastrophic payments
6. Extent of untreated ailments mainly because of high health-care costs
7. Attention generated by the NRHM among the rural households and their views
   on improvements in delivery of health services over the past few years, etc.

8.1 Highlights of Major Findings

As has already been pointed out, a number of observations have been cited in the
preceding chapters, and barring a few, most of them have not been repeated here to
ensure brevity. Among the notables, one of the more critical observations perhaps
relates to the role played exclusively by the OOP health payments in adding to the
overall poverty level. We have culled a table on the basis of certain earlier exercises
to show the role of health payments in poverty enhancements. Table 8.1 gives
poverty levels both before and after the OOP health expenditure. This table clearly
shows the vulnerability of a significant fraction of the rural and slum households to
health payments. In addition to deepening poverty of those who are already below
the poverty line, health payments, for instance, bring an additional 10–14 % of
households under the poverty net (see last two columns in Table 8.1). In addition,
there appears to be another significant policy message from this table—households
at the fringe of poverty level may easily experience a shift in their economic status
from above to below poverty level due to no or very limited affordability in terms
of health payments. It may further be construed that the declining poverty in many
situations remains deceptive as a good fraction of fringe level households, both
rural and urban, may remain vulnerable to situations like self or family ailments. An
analysis of household indebtedness in Chap. 3 (Sect. 3.3) has shown that more than
a quarter of indebted urban households had borrowed to meet medical exigencies.
The same in rural areas turns out to be little over 19 %. Chapter 3 also indicates a
big share of private moneylenders in those borrowings. Does it mean to suggest that
the health-care services in the country are not affordable in their present form for a
significant percentage of households? While a categorical answer to this question
may need further and more in-depth studies, this is indeed an issue that warrants a
greater consideration, especially from health policy mandarins.

   A related point in the underlying context that arose from the preceding discussion is that antipoverty measures in the country, and particularly in areas under
study, may not work to their real potential unless the health services are scaled up to
a considerable extent—that too in every health domain. It also requires taking into
account the needs of persons or households forced to borrow money from private
sources on coercive conditions at the time of ailments. Could there be a role for the
community-based micro-credit institutions to lend small amounts to the poor and
needy during certain health emergencies? This is indeed a significant issue and may
be considered from its different perspectives. A major stumbling block in raising
such institutions would be the intra-regional diversities requiring appropriate
changes in organisational matters. To be precise, perhaps a perfect replication of a

particular system or mode of organisational structure may not be possible across different places. Civil society institutions may have to be propped up to work on a system amenable with local conditions and environment.

An interesting point to note from most of our poverty analysis is the non-emergence of a well-specified target group that could become most eligible for health subsidies. In the context of poverty and inequality, for example, health expenses remain critical to most of the sample households—irrespective of their residential or socio-economic and religious characteristics. While these factors, particularly caste and place of residence, do matter in many ways, it cannot be argued conclusively that a particular segment or group of households must bear an overriding public concern over others. When it comes to health, a great deal of both rural and urban populations suffers from serious issues and faces inequalities. In many cases, a fraction of even higher-income people suffer from non-affordability (or lack of capacity to pay) problems. Despite that, our results do indicate the worsening state of the rural and slum households. A couple of Lorenz curves separately for the rural (UP and Rajasthan) and the urban (UP, Rajasthan and Delhi including the slums and non-slums) areas (Figs. 8.1 and 8.2 respectively) illustrate the points argued here. Health payments clearly bring inequality issues more sharply in urban areas, and logically the slum households bear most of the brunt. Certain higher-income categories also appear to pay for health care in excess of their affordable limit. In case of the rural sample, OOP inequality is seemingly less sharp (OOP Gini = 0.707), though the differences between the two are marginal. Two points may therefore be made. First, inequalities and critical nature of health issues remain more or less of

Table 8.1 Increase in poverty due to the OOP health expenditure: sample households (%)

	PCMCE 1		PCMCE 2 = PCMCE 1 − OOP		Increase in poverty due to OOP health payments	
	Poverty head count: 1^a		Poverty head count: 2^b			
	1(a): Rural	1(b): Urban	2(a): Rural	2(b): Urban	Rural: 2(a) − 1(a)	Urban: 2(b) − 1(b)
Total sample ($n = 2{,}010$)	33.0	18.8	46.5	24.9	13.5	6.1
UP ($n = 1{,}000$)	36.0	25.6	49.6	29.6	13.6	4.0
Unnao ($n = 600$)	34.7	20	48.89	22	14.2	2.0
Jhansi ($n = 400$)	38.0	34.0	50.7	41.0	12.7	7.0
Rajasthan ($n = 650$)	28.4	28.6	41.8	38.0	13.4	9.4
Dausa ($n = 300$)	21.6	38.0	34.0	56.0	12.4	18.0
Dungarpur ($n = 350$)	35.2	24	49.6	29.0	14.4	5.0
Delhi ($n = 360$)	–	10.0	–	16.1	–	6.1
Slums ($n = 102$)	–	26.5	–	41.2	–	14.7
Non-slum ($n = 258$)	–	3.4	–	6.2	–	2.8

[a]Poverty head count 1 = PCMCE of a household—state-wise poverty line (z) given by the Planning Commission (for details, see Chap. 3)
[b]Poverty head count two deducts the OOP health expenditure from the PCMCE before computing poverty

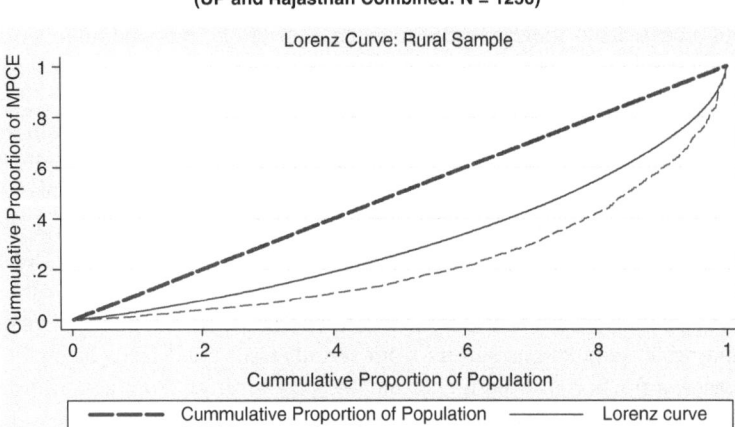

Fig. 8.1 Ability to pay and health inequalities: rural households (UP and Rajasthan combined: $N=1,250$) (Gini coefficient: ATP=0.367, OOP Gini: inequality in health payments=0.707)

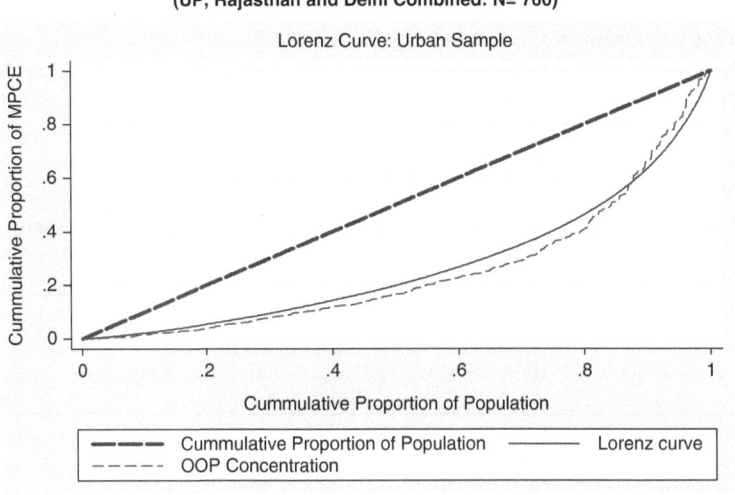

Fig. 8.2 Ability to pay and health inequalities: urban households (UP, Rajasthan and Delhi combined: $N=760$) (Gini coefficient (ATP)=0.473, OOP Gini: inequality in health payments=0.742)

equal importance for the households, irrespective of their place of residence. Second, inequalities in health payments are much larger than the consumption inequalities, implying inaccessibility of health services for a number of the poorest rural and urban households. A third point may be made that a segregation between the above- and the below-poverty households as claimants of public subsidies may not work as in many situations, both remain vulnerable to an equal measure.

Moving to the issues of catastrophic health payments, our results appear to indicate that the catastrophe cut-off levels, as frequently used in international literature, make no or a very limited sense for the observed sample of households. This is to a greater extent true at the higher cut-off levels. With the share of nonfood consumption expenditure as low as observed in the present analysis, any fraction of OOP health expenditure may not only look catastrophic, it would rather overshoot the defined catastrophe limit. There is thus no wonder that we are getting very high incidence of catastrophe (along with higher MPO values),[2] and its correlates mostly include the socio-economic and public health deficits. Stretching this argument little farther would imply that even a small amount of OOP spending on health may push a large number of households into some degree of consumption catastrophe. Also, it applies to both the rural and the urban households. Yet another notable observation in this context may be the fact that even the users of public health-care facilities are not able to save themselves from catastrophic payments. This is partly because of the systematic withdrawal of subsidies on drugs and diagnostics by the government.

All this boils down to a basic question: What component(s) of health spending drives households to face a catastrophe? Intuitively, this question may have a role in pinning down a few policy interventions to minimise the catastrophic incidences. In response to this question, we tried to compute the shares of: (i) consultation fee, (ii) expenditure on drugs and medicines, (iii) expenses on diagnostics and (iv) cost incurred on commutation and other related expenses in the total health expenditure of the sample households. In a large number of cases, our computations reveal drugs as the biggest expenditure and in some cases, it turns out to be around 90 % of the total health budget. Even in normal situations, drugs and medicines account for over three-fourths of the total OOP spending on health. This result is in consonance with some other studies recently conducted at the all-India level. This raises many serious issues from the policy viewpoint. Two of them bear serious considerations. First, most public medical facilities do not provide medicines to their patients including the poor patients. Even in many cases, these facilities expect service users to provide sundry items like cotton or bandages. These are in addition to items such as registration fee, costs of various diagnostic tests and commutations including attendant's stay. Besides being a push factor to catastrophe, it also dissuades even poor service users from using public facilities, especially in nonhospitalisation cases.

The second issue relates to drug pricing and there are growing concerns already in much national and international literature regarding the WTO's agreement on TRIPS.[3] These negotiations and agreements have clearly set minimum standards for the protection of intellectual property. It has also helped to generate considerable

---

[2] See Sect. 5.3.

[3] TRIPS agreement was drawn in January 1995 with a view to bring global minimum standards for the protection of intellectual property, including a minimum 20 years' patent protection on pharmaceuticals. The compliance of the agreement was however deferred until 2005 for the developing countries and 2016 for least developed countries (Smith et al. 2009a).

Table 8.2 Indian
pharmaceuticals and
health-care sector

	2006	2007
Generic market (US $ billions)	3.1	3.3
Generic market as % of total market	30	30
Market share: imports (%)	35	35
Market share: domestic output (%)	65	65
Health expenditure (US $ billions)	41.3	44.0
Hospital sector (US $ millions)	16,300	16,400

Source: Smith et al. (2009a, Table 3)

gains for the global pharma companies. Commenting on a study by Smith et al.
(2009b) in favour of TRIPS and its trade-related advantages, Stiglitz (2009) has
noted certain fundamental problems with the system as it restricts the use of knowledge, brings (temporary) monopoly power and gives rise to enormous economic
inefficiencies.

In India, despite the use of generic drugs, the share of non-generic market is as
high as 70 % of the total. In addition, the generic market has suffered a static growth
over the past few years. Table 8.2, cited in a study by Smith et al. (2009a), brings out the
significance of non-generic medicines in the context of the Indian health scenario
which is marred in many cases by the overprescription of drugs and diagnostics.
Two significant points follow from this table. As the non-generic products account
for 70 % of the domestic market, an inference may therefore be made that the drug
prices may not be completely in accord with the Indian poverty scenario. Market
forces would operate and influence the health budget with a disproportionate effect
on the poor and the deprived. The effects of increase in drug prices may also be felt
because of its share in the total health spending. Persons and households with
degenerating diseases, especially the aged, may suffer their worst. Growing roles of
TRIPS and patenting linked drug prices may also have a bearing on availability of
medicines in government facilities.

Where does the solution lie? This is perhaps a complex issue and requires a deft
handling of TRIPS negotiations along with a serious policy makeover with regard
to making medicines available at subsidised prices to patients. To be precise, would
it be possible for the government to find enough resources and to provide subsidy on
medicines? While a clear-cut answer to this question may not be found in this analysis, it may however be pointed out that all the three, i.e. the OOP health expenditure,
most of its attendant issues and drug pricing, are mutually interconnected. Therefore,
none of them may be decided independently.

Negotiations to make TRIPS less painful apparently involve a sustained and
evidence-based advocacy to sensitise the world community about the issues and the
catastrophic nature of health spending with the largest share of health budget being
allocated to buying medicines. Especially the TRIPS Plus may be far more difficult
and is expected to bring further complexities to the issues of poverty and OOP
health expenditure. Besides the evidence-based advocacy and policy dialogues,
health policy officials may also use the in-built flexibilities in patenting rights and
make use of the life-saving drugs clause to introduce compulsory licencing for a

maximum number of drugs. It may however require a deeper understanding about the disease profile and bulk drug requirements at regional and subregional levels along with the socio-economic background of those who suffer from these diseases. A small team of multidisciplinary experts may work in the MoHFW or in the Planning Commission exclusively on these issues by keeping the TRIPS Plus in perspective.

Somewhat alarming but a fairly known issue in the context of health delivery is the poor utilisation of public health-care facilities by health seekers—both ambulatory and non-ambulatory. Reasons remain primitive: long hours of wait, non-availability of drugs, poor outreach, lack of emergency services in local (village level) health centres and improper behaviour by the medical staff. Still a number of respondents have been disposed off fairly well and have started taking note of the NRHM and its services. There has especially been a positive response towards the role played by the ASHA, availability of PHC doctors and distribution of certain medicines required by women and children. How far the mission is able to cover the health-care needs of those in nonreproductive ages is not clear from this study and, therefore, an area worth of exploration in future research. The incidence of catastrophic health spending raises doubts about the versatility of the NRHM. Also, there appears to be very limited utilisation of consultation facilities provided by the AYUSH practitioners in many health-care centres. This is largely true for the low-income rural people. In contrast, while certain fractions of upper castes and economically better-off segments consult these doctors, their numbers remain small.

Given some of these major observations which only represent a part of the entire analysis, four issues appear to be critical at policy level:

1. Delivery of health services is of paramount importance if India is to succeed in its attempts to minimise poverty—although the current definition of poverty is oversimplistic.
2. Making drugs available at a subsidised price appears to be the most critical factor for any policy intervention as expenditure on drugs accounts for most of the health spending.
3. Prevalence of health catastrophe appears to be quite high and forces many households to face considerable loss of well-being.
4. Public health-care facilities do not insulate people from the risks of catastrophe.

The obvious question would then be: What interventions are likely to bring some respite? A number of earlier studies have already been grappled with this question with a plethora of suggestions. Many have, for instance, recommended improving the quality of health services, expanding the outreach of public facilities, bringing top-down planning approach, generating additional finances to introduce greater facilities, enhancing the role of community and charting community leaders as the watchdog, etc. Instead of making a remix of the earlier suggestions, we collected households' responses on certain key questions with considerable policy contents.

8.2   Respondents' Views on Critical Policy Issues

Survey respondents were basically asked to comment mostly on issues on which they were expected to have a better understanding. A few of those respondents, especially in rural areas, were also given certain background information, particularly on operational aspects of health insurance. Some of the more important questions included: (a) Do you feel that the health services have become costlier over the past 1 year? (b) Do you think doctors generally overprescribe medicines/diagnostic tests? (c) In your opinion, would a low-premium health insurance be a workable solution? (d) If required, would you be willing to subscribe to such an insurance scheme? The last two questions were asked against the backdrop of a recent initiative by the government to launch a RSBY for a segment of the below-poverty households.[4]

Table 8.3 summarises respondents' views on all the major questions. It may be noted that a very large number of respondents, almost 8–9 out of 10, have agreed that the health services have become expensive by more than 50 % over the preceding 12 months.

However, a smaller percentage of them have also agreed that their incomes grew almost in the same proportion simultaneously. Interestingly, however, such respondents were lowest in Delhi. Upper-caste respondents, Muslims and slum households have also largely disagreed to the 'proportional growth in income' idea. Another interesting observation arising from this table relates to the overprescription of medicines and diagnostic tests by medical doctors. Barring Delhi slum dwellers, most others felt the same way. Almost a similar response was drawn in case of the drug prices as well. Particularly, the catastrophic households (both mild and severe) and respondents from Rajasthan have agreed to the view that the drug prices play spoilsport and contribute to a significant extent in escalating the level of OOP expenditure on health.

When asked about health insurance, it may be interesting to note that those with better access to health care do not mostly subscribe to this suggestion. Table 8.3 shows that in the richest quintile, Delhi respondents as well as upper-caste people have favoured such a scheme in much smaller fractions. Those who endorsed the health insurance idea were however in majority among other categories of respondents including the rural and urban households of UP and Rajasthan. Almost a similar response has emerged from the last question, namely, would you be willing to join an insurance system on self-payment basis? Following from the earlier

---

[4]The government is currently in the process to launch three important insurance covers to fulfil some of its social security obligations: (i) the Aam Aadmi Bima Yojana to provide death and disability cover to the poor, (ii) the Janashree Bima Yojana with an objective to cover health and life risks and finally (iii) the Rashtriya Swasthya Bima Yojana (RSBY) in order to cover the medical risks. An interesting feature of the RSBY is that it proposes to remain without any exclusion clause. With an annual premium of Rs. 600, paid by the centre and states jointly on 75:25 basis, the below-poverty policyholders and their family will be authorised to avail hospitalisation benefits worth Rs. 30,000 a year.

Table 8.3 Respondents' views on critical policy issues

Household characteristics	Health services become costlier by more than 50 % during the past 1 year	Has income also grown almost at a similar pace?	Drugs have a maximum role in escalation of OOP expenditure on health	Doctors mostly overprescribe medicines	Doctors mostly overprescribe diagnostic tests	Low-premium health insurance may be a possible option for the poor	Would you be willing to join an insurance system on self-payment basis?
	Share of respondents in agreement (%)						
UP	79.2	45.2	46.8	63.6	52.8	55.7	51.6
Rural	80.0	48.0	48.5	64.5	52.7	54.7	51.7
Urban	76.8	36.8	41.6	60.8	53.2	58.8	51.2
Rajasthan	86.0	57.5	59.1	76.9	59.7	77.8	71.7
Rural	86.8	55.2	61.8	75.6	60.0	75.4	69.2
Urban	83.3	65.3	50.0	81.3	58.7	86.0	80.0
Delhi	92.5	21.9	28.1	38.6	48.9	30.6	28.3
Slum	90.2	16.7	29.4	35.3	31.4	38.2	36.3
Non-slum	93.4	24.0	27.5	39.9	55.8	27.5	25.2
Social groups							
SC	84.0	42.0	49.0	63.1	52.3	53.4	49.5
ST	82.3	51.0	55.8	66.7	50.6	69.9	65.5
OBC	81.2	45.3	48.4	66.5	55.5	63.1	58.3
Upper caste	88.1	44.4	40.6	57.7	56.1	50.3	45.9
Religious group							
Hindu	84.0	46.0	48.3	63.8	55.1	58.7	54.2
Muslim	81.4	34.6	44.7	60.6	48.9	57.4	53.2
Consumption quintiles							
Poorest 20 %	74.1	45.3	40.0	61.4	51.5	57.7	51.5
2	78.6	51.7	49.8	65.4	46.5	68.7	64.4
3	84.8	41.8	50.5	68.7	55.5	58.7	54.5

(continued)

Table 8.3 (continued)

Household characteristics	Health services become costlier by more than 50 % during the past 1 year	Has income also grown almost at a similar pace?	Drugs have a maximum role in escalation of OOP expenditure on health	Doctors mostly overprescribe medicines	Doctors mostly overprescribe diagnostic tests	Low-premium health insurance may be a possible option for the poor	Would you be willing to join an insurance system on self-payment basis?
	Share of respondents in agreement (%)						
4	87.8	45.0	54.5	68.4	58.5	61.2	57.2
Riches 20 %	93.5	41.3	42.3	53.2	59.7	45.5	42.0
Catastrophic HHDs							
Mild ($z=5$ %)	91.8	47.1	61.7	74.6	60.7	57.0	54.6
Acute ($z=25$ %)	94.7	45.1	83.7	82.1	66.8	58.3	57.7
Total sample	83.8	45.0	47.4	63.4	54.3	58.4	53.9

question, those with better access or affordability to health care largely showed disinterest. Others have however favoured. Still it may be surmised that a self-paid health insurance is a strong possibility if the government is able to regulate the system well, particularly against the menaces of exclusions and cartelisation among medical professionals, service providers and major pharma companies.

8.3 Broad Policy Directions

Now, where do we go from here? Perhaps the respondents' views underscore three significant points. Besides the couple of those which have already been discussed earlier, there is an indication that the supply-side management of the health market remains mired because of the growing dependence among health seekers on private providers. In several cases, public sector facilities do not prove a close substitute to private providers. This is particularly true for outpatient services. Even in hospital services, a large segment of people depend on private providers. All this affects the private medical services and their price determination system. This has aptly been summarised by the respondents when they report over 50 % escalation in their medical budget over a brief period of the past 12 months. A related point may be noticed from the perception that doctors overprescribe medicines. Does it reflect certain laxity in administration of medical rules? Also, there is a serious problem with the medical ethics in the country. Medical profession is now largely guided by corporate practices with core objective to maximise profit through increased occupancy rates or patients' consultation. An apprehension has also been made that the RSBY may further aggravate the situation, particularly for the uncovered families. Health policymakers may have to take some of these factors into consideration to bring down the cases of catastrophe. Public facilities will have to become efficient, client responsive and a close substitute to private services. The recent initiative to appoint RKSs will have to be strengthened.

Patients of public hospitals facing catastrophe need to be examined. Drug pricing and availability of essential drugs to patients in public facilities warrant serious consideration. Deployment of manpower and management of public hospitals need considerable fine-tuning. There is especially a need to minimise non-clinical responsibilities of medical doctors in most public facilities. If at all viable, certain hours may be fixed in a week for every medical doctor to devote to their clinical responsibilities. Poor patient–doctor or patient–health worker relationship is a perennial issue and needs serious consideration. Medical ethics is another area to minimise complaints such as overprescriptions.

Beyond all this, perhaps a most potent issue for consideration is to work on a comprehensive risk-pooling arrangement, covering both in- and outpatient treatments. While the RSBY is apparently a good initiative, it simply covers a very small segment of poor population (roughly 12 million). In addition, it is directed only at hospitalisation (including day care) cases. Given a very high prevalence of ailments requiring non-ambulatory care—i.e. around 15 % as against 2.5–3 % requiring hospitalisation—the noncoverage of outpatient care may leave most of the problems unresolved. Moreover, our study has highlighted that expenses on outpatient care have been equally catastrophic in nature and therefore worth covering under schemes like the RSBY.

Patenting rights and TRIPS negotiations require very serious understanding about the health status of the country's population. To achieve some of these objectives, there is a very strong need to undertake a series of micro-level studies to know about the health status of poor and low-income people, especially from economically low-performing districts and states.

References

Smith, R. D., Correa, C., & Oh, C. (2009a). Trade trips and pharmaceuticals. *The Lancet, 373*(9664), 684–691.

Smith, R. D., Lee, K., & Drager, N. (2009b). Trade and health: An agenda for action. *The Lancet, 373*(9665), 768–773. doi:10.1016/S0140-6736(08)61780-8. Published online 22 January 2009.

Stiglitz, J. E. (2009, January 31). Trade agreements and health in developing countries (Comment). *The Lancet, 373*(9661), 363–365.

Paulo Ventura Araújo

Differential Geometry

 Springer

Paulo Ventura Araújo
Department of Mathematics
Faculdade de Ciências da Universidade do Porto
Porto, Portugal

Translation from the Portuguese language edition: "Geometria Diferencial" by Paulo Ventura Araújo, © Paulo Ventura Araújo 1998. Published by IMPA. All Rights Reserved.

ISBN 978-3-031-62383-7   ISBN 978-3-031-62384-4 (eBook)
https://doi.org/10.1007/978-3-031-62384-4

Mathematics Subject Classification (2020): 53-XX, 51-XX

Cover illustration: Image created from two figured to place above the title.

This Springer imprint is published by the registered company Springer Nature Switzerland AG
The registered company address is: Gewerbestrasse 11, 6330 Cham, Switzerland

If disposing of this product, please recycle the paper.

Preface

This book is based on the lecture notes of the course Differential Geometry taught at the Faculty of Sciences of the University of Porto in the academic years 1992–93 and 1993–94. Students from different courses and with different mathematical backgrounds attended the course and, consequently, its prerequisites were reduced to Linear Algebra, Calculus (of one and several variables), and the study of curves up to the Frenet trihedron. Furthermore, we avoided the introduction of certain technical apparatus, such as Tensor Calculus, in order to insist instead on results with accessible geometric content whose proofs, although possibly long, used more elementary means.

That said, one understands why we have restricted ourselves to the study of curves and surfaces in Euclidean space. But, in our opinion, even for students pursuing a scientific career, this is the right approach for a first study of Differential Geometry, grounding intuition and motivating the problems that arise in higher dimensions.

Although the idea was to reproduce, in order and content, the course notes, the notes grew and included subjects not discussed in the lectures. There is a risk, when teaching Differential Geometry at an introductory level, that the harvest of interesting results will not compensate for the work spent in digesting definitions and assimilating techniques. The digressions in this text may lead the student to discover some of the richness of Differential Geometry which, by the imperative of bureaucratic "realism", is so often absent from the classroom.

The exercises included in the text are rarely routine, although few are really difficult, and were chosen on the assumption that a good exercise, with a medium level of difficulty, should reward the students' effort by teaching them something.

Among the books we consulted, Manfredo do Carmo's [6] deserves to be highlighted: some of the exercises and the structuring of some subjects come from there. But several exercises are original, and the selection of themes and the composition of the proofs reflect personal taste and work.

We now give some hints on how to use the book: Sections 1.1 – 1.3 cover subjects probably already known to the student, and may be omitted in well-prepared classes. Chapters 2–4 cover a basic course in Differential Geometry. Sections 3.3, 4.4 may be omitted if time is tight. If time permits, a choice of topics from Chapter 1 (sections

1.4 to 1.8) and Chapter 5 can be made; the interdependence between the various sections of these chapters is indicated at the beginning of each chapter.

Porto, July 1996
Paulo Ventura Araújo.

Contents

Chapter 1
Differentiable Curves

The first three sections of this chapter contain the basics on curves, and, because of their brevity, are rather a review of concepts and results, gathered in a form we will use later; in the last five sections we will deal with subjects whose inclusion in the course is optional. Section 1.5 should be read before 1.6 and 1.7, but otherwise, and except for a few exercises, sections 1.4 – 1.8 are independent of each other.

1.1 Velocity and Arc Length

In the space $\mathbb{R}^n$ we will denote vectors by the symbols $\mathbf{v}$, $\mathbf{w}$ and points by lowercase consonants p, q. This space is equipped with a canonical Euclidean structure in which the *inner product* of two vectors is the sum of the products of their components of equal index, i.e. $\langle \mathbf{v}, \mathbf{w} \rangle = v_1 w_1 + \cdots + v_n w_n$. The *norm* or *length* of a vector is given by $|\mathbf{v}| = \sqrt{\langle \mathbf{v}, \mathbf{v} \rangle}$, and the *angle* between the nonzero vectors $\mathbf{v}$ and $\mathbf{w}$ is the only number $\theta \in [0, \pi]$ such that

$$\cos \theta = \frac{\langle \mathbf{v}, \mathbf{w} \rangle}{|\mathbf{v}| \, |\mathbf{w}|}.$$

The *distance* between the points p and q is defined as the length of the vector $p - q$.

A *parametrized curve* is a continuous function $\alpha : I \to \mathbb{R}^n$ on an interval of $\mathbb{R}$ in Euclidean n-dimensional space, and its *trace* is the image of that function. Writing $\alpha(t) = (x_1(t), \ldots, x_n(t))$, the functions x_i are the *component functions* of α. We say that α is of *class* C^∞ if each of its component functions has continuous derivatives of all orders (if α is defined, for example, on a closed interval $[a, b]$, then we require the existence of all right-hand side derivatives at a and left-hand side derivatives at b).

The *velocity vector* of the curve is $\alpha'(t) = (x_1'(t), \ldots, x_n'(t))$ and, when nonzero, points in the direction tangent to the curve at time t. *Regular curves* are those whose velocity vector never vanishes and therefore have a well-defined tangent direction at each instant.

P. V. Araújo, *Differential Geometry*, https://doi.org/10.1007/978-3-031-62384-4_1

From now on, unless otherwise stated, by *curve* we mean a regular parametrized curve of class C^∞.

The simplest example of a curve is a straight line $p + t\mathbf{v}$, $t \in \mathbb{R}$, parametrized with nonzero constant velocity $\mathbf{v}$. Other examples are the circle $(\cos t, \sin t)$ and, shown in Fig. 1.1, the cloverleaf $(\cos 3t \ \cos t, \cos 3t \ \sin t)$ and the helix $(\cos t, \sin t, t)$.

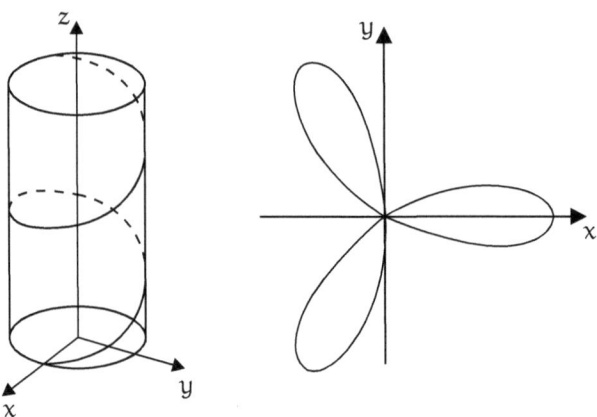

Figure 1.1

One of the first questions to ask about a curve is how to compute its length. Assume that the curve α is defined on a closed interval $[a, b]$. Take an arbitrary partition $a = t_0 < t_1 < \cdots < t_m = b$ of that interval. The sum

$$\sum_{i=1}^{m} |\alpha(t_i) - \alpha(t_{i-1})|$$

gives the length of the polygonal line obtained by replacing, for each $1 \le i \le m$, the trace of the curve in the interval $[t_{i-1}, t_i]$ by the line segment joining $\alpha(t_{i-1})$ with $\alpha(t_i)$ (see Fig. 1.2). The narrower and more numerous are the intervals of the partition, the better the sum should approximate the length of the curve. In Exercise 3 of this section we show that the limit of these sums, as the maximum of the differences $t_i - t_{i-1}$ tends to zero, is given by the integral $\int_a^b |\alpha'(t)| \, dt$, and this is how the *length* $l(\alpha)$ of the curve α is defined.

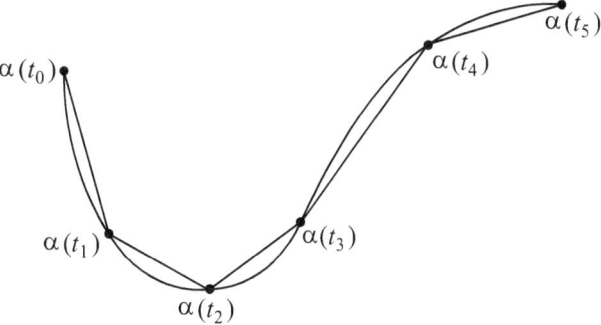

$\alpha(t_0)$ $\alpha(t_1)$ $\alpha(t_2)$ $\alpha(t_3)$ $\alpha(t_4)$ $\alpha(t_5)$

Figure 1.2

Our first result reassures us as to the correctness of the definition just given, by showing that the line is the shortest path between two points:

Proposition 1.1.1 *Let* $\alpha:[a,b] \to \mathbb{R}^n$ *be a curve. Then* $l(\alpha) \geq |\alpha(b) - \alpha(a)|$, *and equality holds if and only if the trace of* α *is a line segment.*

Proof We assume that $\alpha(b) \neq \alpha(a)$, otherwise there is nothing to be shown. We write $\alpha(b) - \alpha(a) = \int_a^b \alpha'(t)\,dt$, an equality in which the right-hand side is the vector whose coordinates are the integrals of the components of $\alpha'(t)$. Forming the inner product of both sides with the vector $\alpha(b) - \alpha(a)$, we obtain

$$|\alpha(b) - \alpha(a)|^2 = \int_a^b \langle \alpha'(t), \alpha(b) - \alpha(a) \rangle \, dt$$
$$\leq \int_a^b |\alpha'(t)||\alpha(b) - \alpha(a)| \, dt = l(\alpha)|\alpha(b) - \alpha(a)|,$$

from which, simplifying, we obtain the desired inequality. For equality to hold, the Cauchy-Schwarz inequality

$$\langle \alpha'(t), \alpha(b) - \alpha(a) \rangle \leq |\alpha'(t)||\alpha(b) - \alpha(a)|$$

will have to reduce to an equality for all $t \in [a, b]$, which happens if and only if $\alpha'(t)$ is a positive multiple of $\alpha(b) - \alpha(a)$ — i.e., if and only if the trace of α is the line segment joining $\alpha(a)$ to $\alpha(b)$.   □

The value $v(t) = |\alpha'(t)|$ is the *scalar velocity* of the curve α at time t, and

$$S(t) = \int_a^t v(r) \, dr$$

is the *arc length* function. When the scalar velocity is constant, the arc length is proportional to time. We recall that the curve $\tilde{\alpha}$ is a reparametrization of α if $\tilde{\alpha} = \alpha \circ h$, for some *increasing* diffeomorphism $h:J \to I$ between intervals of $\mathbb{R}$. (If h were decreasing, then we would obtain a curve with the same trace as α but with reversed orientation — that is, traversed in the opposite direction.) Let us now show, by defining a suitable function h, that it is *possible to reparameterize α so that $\alpha \circ h$ has constant scalar velocity, equal to* 1.

Since $S'(t) = v(t) > 0$, the function S is increasing and sends $[a, b]$ diffeomorphically onto the interval $[0, l(\alpha)]$. Defining h as the inverse of S, and putting $\tilde{\alpha}(s) = \alpha \circ h(s)$, we have

$$\tilde{\alpha}'(s) = h'(s)\alpha'(h(s)) = \frac{1}{v(t)}\alpha'(t),$$

where $t = h(s)$, and from this we see that $|\tilde{\alpha}'(s)| = 1$ for all s in $[0, l(a)]$.

We say that a curve is *parametrized by arc length* when it is traversed with constant scalar velocity equal to 1, regardless of whether the time at which the parameterization starts is zero.

Exercises

1. Let $\alpha : [a, b] \to \mathbb{R}^n$ and $\beta : [c, d] \to \mathbb{R}^n$ be two regular, injective curves with the same trace. Show that the function $\beta^{-1} \circ \alpha : [a, b] \to [c, d]$ is differentiable and its derivative never vanishes.

2. Let $\alpha(t) = (e^{bt}\cos t, e^{bt}\sin t)$, where b is a negative constant and $t \in \mathbb{R}$.
 (a) Sketch the trace of α.
 (b) Check that α has finite length on $[t_0, +\infty[$ and compute it.

3. Let $\alpha(t) = (x_1(t), \ldots, x_n(t))$, $t \in [a, b]$ be a curve of class C^1. Show that

(a) given $\varepsilon > 0$, there exists $\delta > 0$ such that for all $1 \le k \le n$,

$$|t - s| < \delta \Rightarrow \left| \frac{x_k(t) - x_k(s)}{t - s} - x_k'(t) \right| < \varepsilon;$$

(b) for the ε and δ just obtained, if $a = t_0 < t_1 < \cdots < t_m = b$ is a partition of $[a, b]$ such that $t_i - t_{i-1} < \delta$ for all $1 \le i \le m$, then

$$\left| \sum_{i=1}^{m} |\alpha(t_i) - \alpha(t_{i-1})| - \sum_{i=1}^{m} |\alpha'(t_i)|(t_i - t_{i-1}) \right| < \sqrt{n}(b-a)\varepsilon;$$

(c) the limit of sums

$$\sum_{i=1}^{m} |\alpha(t_i) - \alpha(t_{i-1})|, \quad \text{as} \ \max_{1 \le i \le m}(t_i - t_{i-1}) \to 0,$$

is $\int_a^b |\alpha'(t)| \, dt$.

4. A curve $\alpha : [a, b] \to \mathbb{R}^n$ is called *rectifiable* if the supremum of the sums

$$\sum_{i=1}^{m} |\alpha(t_i) - \alpha(t_{i-1})|,$$

where $t_0 < t_1 < \cdots < t_m$ is some partition of $[a, b]$, is finite. We call this supremum the length of α.

(a) Show that, for curves of class C^1, this new definition of length is equivalent to the previous one.

(b) Does a rectifiable curve necessarily have derivatives at all points?

(c) Is it true that the graph of any continuous and monotone function $[a, b] \to \mathbb{R}$ is a rectifiable curve?

(d) Consider the Weierstrass example of a continuous function $[0, 1] \to \mathbb{R}$ that is nowhere differentiable (see [24], chapter 23, Theorem 5), and find out whether the graph of this function is rectifiable.

1.2 Acceleration, Curvature and the Frenet Trihedron

In this section we only consider curves in three dimensional Euclidean space. In the previous section we learned how to compute the length of a curve with the help of its velocity or first derivative. This calculation does not exhaust the analysis of a curve, since it tells us nothing about the shape it can take, and does not distinguish a line from a circle. To proceed we will also have to take into account the second derivative.

Given a curve $\alpha: I \to \mathbb{R}^3$, the *tangent unit vector* to α is $\tau(t) = \frac{1}{v(t)}\alpha'(t)$. If $\tilde{\alpha}(r) = \alpha \circ h(r)$ is a reparametrization of α then the unit vector tangent to $\tilde{\alpha}$ is given by $\tilde{\tau} = \tau \circ h$. Hence, defining $\tilde{v}(r) = |\tilde{\alpha}'(r)|$, we have

$$\tilde{v}(r) = (v \circ h(r))h'(r),$$
$$|\tilde{\tau}'(r)| = |\tau'(h(r))||h'(r)|.$$

If we put

$$k(t) = \frac{1}{v(t)}|\tau'(t)|$$

and denote by $\tilde{k}$ the analogous function for $\tilde{\alpha}$, then we see that $\tilde{k} = k \circ h$. The quantity $k(t)$ is the *curvature* of α at the point $\alpha(t)$. The preceding calculations show that the curvature does not depend on the way the curve is traversed but only on the point at which it is computed, and does not change even when we reverse its orientation. We can thus assume, whenever convenient, that the parameter of the curve is the arc length. In this case we simply have $k(s) = |\alpha''(s)|$.

A line, for example, has zero constant curvature: in fact, when parametrized with constant scalar velocity, its second derivative vanishes. But the converse is also true, since the condition $k(s) \equiv 0$ implies that $\alpha''(s) \equiv 0$, which shows that there exist constants p and $\mathbf{v}$ such that $\alpha(s) \equiv p + s\mathbf{v}$.

Since $\tau(t)$ has constant norm, it is orthogonal to its derivative. In fact, by differentiating the equality $\langle \tau(t), \tau(t) \rangle = 1$, we obtain $2\langle \tau'(t), \tau(t) \rangle = 0$. Thus, when

$k(t) \neq 0$, the vector $\boldsymbol{\tau}'(t)$ points in a direction normal to the curve, the so-called *principal normal*. In these cases we can define the unit vector

$$\mathbf{n}(t) = \frac{1}{|\boldsymbol{\tau}'(t)|} \boldsymbol{\tau}'(t)$$

and the *center of curvature*, which is the point

$$\alpha(t) + \frac{1}{k(t)} \mathbf{n}(t).$$

The value $1/k(t)$ is the *curvature radius* at the point $\alpha(t)$. The *osculating plane* is the plane parallel to $\boldsymbol{\tau}(t)$ and $\mathbf{n}(t)$ that passes through $\alpha(t)$.

The curvature measures the variation of the direction of the curve, but it does not determine the form of the curve: both the circumference and the helix, for instance, have constant curvature, that of the former being equal to the inverse of the radius; and while the circumference is a planar curve, in the helix the osculating plane varies from point to point. What we lack then is to measure the variation of the osculating plane — or, to put it differently, how far a curve deviates from being planar.

Continuing to assume that $k(t) \neq 0$, the bi-normal vector $\mathbf{b}(t)$ is defined as the only vector such that $(\boldsymbol{\tau}(t), \mathbf{n}(t), \mathbf{b}(t))$ is a direct orthonormal trihedron — that is, an ordered triplet of unit vectors, orthogonal to each other, such that the 3×3-matrix whose columns are these vectors in the same order has positive determinant. Even simpler, we have $\mathbf{b}(t) = \boldsymbol{\tau}(t) \times \mathbf{n}(t)$, where $\times$ denotes the vector product on $\mathbb{R}^3$.

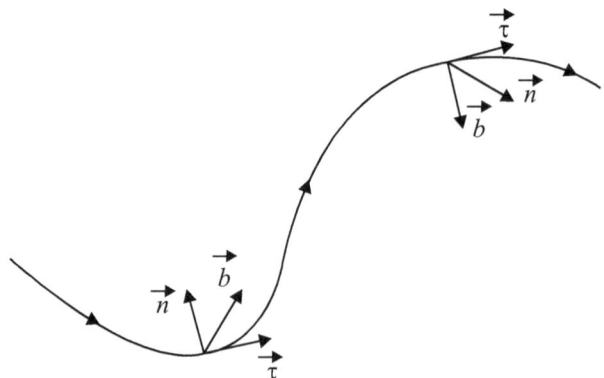

Figure 1.3

The trihedron $(\boldsymbol{\tau}(t), \mathbf{n}(t), \mathbf{b}(t))$ is the *Frenet trihedron*. Each of the vectors of the trihedron is orthogonal to its derivative, so that each derivative is expressible as a linear combination of the other two vectors. We will next study the coefficients of this linear combination. We have

$$\mathbf{b}'(t) = \frac{d}{dt}(\boldsymbol{\tau}(t) \times \mathbf{n}(t))$$
$$= \boldsymbol{\tau}'(t) \times \mathbf{n}(t) + \boldsymbol{\tau}(t) \times \mathbf{n}'(t)$$
$$= \boldsymbol{\tau}(t) \times \mathbf{n}'(t)$$

(because $\boldsymbol{\tau}'$ and $\mathbf{n}$ are collinear for each t). From this equality it follows that $\mathbf{b}'$, which we already knew to be orthogonal to $\mathbf{b}$, is also orthogonal to $\boldsymbol{\tau}$, and is therefore a multiple of $\mathbf{n}$. The *torsion* of α at the point $\alpha(t)$ is the value $v(t)$ defined by the equality

$$\frac{1}{v(t)}\mathbf{b}'(t) = v(t)\mathbf{n}(t);$$

the factor $1/v(t)$ again ensures that the torsion is independent of the parameterization. Note that torsion can assume negative values — although, like curvature, it does not depend on the orientation of the curve.

Differentiating the product $\mathbf{n}(t) = \mathbf{b}(t) \times \boldsymbol{\tau}(t)$, and using the formulas seen above for $\mathbf{b}'(t)$ and $\boldsymbol{\tau}'(t)$, we find that

$$\frac{1}{v(t)}\mathbf{n}'(t) = -k(t)\boldsymbol{\tau}(t) - v(t)\mathbf{b}(t).$$

We thus establish the equalities

$$\frac{1}{v}\boldsymbol{\tau}' = k\mathbf{n}$$
$$\frac{1}{v}\mathbf{n}' = -k\boldsymbol{\tau} - v\mathbf{b}$$
$$\frac{1}{v}\mathbf{b}' = v\mathbf{n},$$

which are known as *Frenet formulas*. When the curve is parametrized by arc length the factor $1/v$ (which is then equal to 1) is suppressed.

The next proposition gives us the geometric meaning of torsion being identically zero.

Proposition 1.2.1 *Assume that the curvature of α never vanishes. Then α is a planar curve if and only if it has zero constant torsion.*

Proof If α is all contained in the plane S, the vectors $\boldsymbol{\tau}(t)$ and $\mathbf{n}(t)$ are parallel to S and linearly independent, and the product $\mathbf{b}(t) = \boldsymbol{\tau}(t) \times \mathbf{n}(t)$ is a unit vector orthogonal to S; therefore $\mathbf{b}(t)$ can only take two distinct values and, since it varies continuously, it must be constant — from which it follows that $v \equiv 0$.

Conversely, if $v \equiv 0$ then $\mathbf{b}(t)$ is a nonzero constant vector $\mathbf{b}$ and for all t holds $\langle \mathbf{b}, \alpha'(t) \rangle = 0$. Therefore there exists a constant c such that $\langle \mathbf{b}, \alpha(t) \rangle \equiv c$, and this equality shows that the curve α is planar. □

Let us now consider a curve $\alpha(s)$, where the parameter $s \in [a, b]$ is the arc length, and whose curvature $k(s)$ never vanishes. We ask ourselves to what extent the functions $k(s)$ and $v(s)$ determine the curve α. They do not do so completely, since any rigid movement of $\mathbb{R}^3$ transforms α into another curve with the same curvature and torsion functions. (By *rigid movement* we mean the composition of a translation with a linear mapping that transforms the canonical basis of $\mathbb{R}^3$ into some direct orthonormal trihedron.) But this is the only freedom:

Theorem 1.2.2 *Let* $\alpha, \tilde{\alpha} : [a, b] \to \mathbb{R}^3$ *be curves parametrized by arc length and with nonzero curvature at all points. If we have* $k(s) = \tilde{k}(s)$ *and* $v(s) = \tilde{v}(s)$ *for all s on* $[a, b]$, *then there exists a rigid movement* $L : \mathbb{R}^3 \to \mathbb{R}^3$ *such that* $\alpha \equiv L \circ \tilde{\alpha}$.

Proof Let L_1 be the linear mapping that transforms the trihedron $(\tilde{\tau}(a), \tilde{\mathbf{n}}(a), \tilde{\mathbf{b}}(a))$ into the trihedron $(\tau(a), \mathbf{n}(a), \mathbf{b}(a))$, L_2 the translation that maps $L_1(\tilde{\alpha}(a))$ into $\alpha(a)$, and $L = L_2 \circ L_1$. Then the curve $\alpha_0 = L \circ \tilde{\alpha}$ has at the start time $s = a$ the same Frenet trihedron as α and satisfies $\alpha_0(a) = \alpha(a)$. Identifying by the subindex 0 the vectors and quantities concerning the curve α_0, we define the function

$$\delta(s) = \frac{1}{2} \left(|\tau(s) - \tau_0(s)|^2 + |\mathbf{n}(s) - \mathbf{n}_0(s)|^2 + |\mathbf{b}(s) - \mathbf{b}_0(s)|^2 \right).$$

We know that $\delta(a) = 0$; furthermore, we have

$$\delta' = \langle \tau' - \tau'_0, \tau - \tau_0 \rangle + \langle \mathbf{n}' - \mathbf{n}'_0, \mathbf{n} - \mathbf{n}_0 \rangle + \langle \mathbf{b}' - \mathbf{b}'_0, \mathbf{b} - \mathbf{b}_0 \rangle.$$

From this, using Frenet's formulas and the fact that $k_0 = k$ and $v_0 = v$, we easily obtain $\delta' \equiv 0$, therefore also $\delta \equiv 0$. In particular we have $\alpha'_0 = \alpha'$ — and, since $\alpha_0(a) = \alpha(a)$, we conclude that $\alpha_0 = \alpha$. $\square$

Note 1.2.3 To complement Theorem 1.2.2, we will now show the following result: *for any differentiable functions* $k, v : [a, b] \to \mathbb{R}$ *(with k strictly positive), there exists a curve* $\alpha(s)$, *parametrized by arc length, whose curvature and torsion functions are precisely* $k(s)$ *and* $v(s)$. We make use of the Theorem of Existence and uniqueness of solutions of differential equations that we will state in Section 3.3; it deserves mention that this approach provides another proof of Theorem 1.2.2. We keep the above proof though as it is more elementary.

Once functions $k(s)$ and $v(s)$ are fixed, Frénet's formulas can be viewed as a non-autonomous equation of the form $X = \mathbf{v}(s, X)$, where $X = (\tau, \mathbf{n}, \mathbf{b}) \in \mathbb{R}^9$ and where $\mathbf{v} : [a, b] \times \mathbb{R}^9 \to \mathbb{R}^9$ is differentiable. Take any direct orthonormal trihedron $(\tau(a), \mathbf{n}(a), \mathbf{b}(a))$. Then there exists $\varepsilon > 0$ such that the solution $X(s) = (\tau(s), \mathbf{n}(s), \mathbf{b}(s))$ with this initial condition is defined for $[a, a + \varepsilon]$. But since

$$\frac{d}{dt} \left\{ |\tau|^2 + |\mathbf{n}|^2 + |\mathbf{b}|^2 \right\} = 2 \left(\langle \tau, k\mathbf{n} \rangle + \langle \mathbf{n}, -k\tau - v\mathbf{b} \rangle + \langle \mathbf{b}, v\mathbf{n} \rangle \right) = 0,$$

we see that $X(s)$ stays in the compact set $\{X \in \mathbb{R}^9 : |X| = \sqrt{3}\}$, and is therefore defined on the entire interval $[a, b]$ (see Theorem 3 on p. 17 of [23]). By differentiating, we obtain the equalities

$$\langle \boldsymbol{\tau}, \mathbf{n} \rangle' = k|\mathbf{n}|^2 - k|\boldsymbol{\tau}|^2 - v\langle \boldsymbol{\tau}, \mathbf{b} \rangle$$
$$\langle \mathbf{n}, \mathbf{b} \rangle' = v|\mathbf{n}|^2 - v|\mathbf{b}|^2 - k\langle \boldsymbol{\tau}, \mathbf{b}|$$
$$\langle \boldsymbol{\tau}, \mathbf{b} \rangle' = k\langle \mathbf{n}, \mathbf{b} \rangle - v\langle \boldsymbol{\tau}, \mathbf{n} \rangle$$
$$(|\boldsymbol{\tau}|^2)' = 2k\langle \boldsymbol{\tau}, \mathbf{n} \rangle$$
$$(|\mathbf{n}|^2)' = -2k\langle \boldsymbol{\tau}, \mathbf{n} \rangle - 2v\langle \mathbf{n}, \mathbf{b} \rangle$$
$$(|\mathbf{b}|^2)' = 2v\langle \mathbf{n}, \mathbf{b} \rangle$$

– from which it follows that $\langle \boldsymbol{\tau}, \mathbf{n} \rangle$, $\langle \mathbf{n}, \mathbf{b} \rangle$, $\langle \boldsymbol{\tau}, \mathbf{b} \rangle$, $|\boldsymbol{\tau}|^2$, $|\mathbf{n}|^2$ and $|\mathbf{b}|^2$ are constant functions, equal to $0, 0, 0, 1, 1$ and 1 respectively, since, as it is easily seen, these constants constitute a solution, with the same initial condition, of the same differential equation defined in $\mathbb{R}^6$. This proves that $(\boldsymbol{\tau}(s), \mathbf{n}(s), \mathbf{b}(s))$ is an orthonormal, necessarily direct trihedron for all $s \in [a, b]$. To conclude we take for $\alpha(s)$ any primitive of $\boldsymbol{\tau}(s)$, e.g. $\alpha(s) = \int_a^s \boldsymbol{\tau}(t)\,dt$: we verify without difficulty that $(\boldsymbol{\tau}(s), \mathbf{n}(s), \mathbf{b}(s))$ is the Frenet trihedron of $\alpha(s)$, and that $k(s)$ and $v(s)$ are its curvature and torsion. □

Exercise

5. Show that if we permit curves whose curvature vanishes at some point then the conclusion of Theorem 1.2.2 holds — that is, there exists a pair of curves $\alpha, \tilde{\alpha}: [a, b] \to \mathbb{R}^3$ parametrized by arc length such that their curvature and torsion functions coincide whenever they are defined, but which cannot be transformed into each other by a rigid movement.
Hint: look for an example that also shows that in Proposition 1.2.1 the assumption that the curvature is positive is essential.

1.3 Planar Curves

We will deal in this section with planar curves, more specifically with curves in $\mathbb{R}^2$. To simplify the calculations, we only consider curves parametrized by arc length: the formulas we obtain are easily adapted to any other parameterizations.

Consider a curve $\alpha: I \to \mathbb{R}^2$. Then there exists, for each $s \in I$, a single vector $\mathbf{n}(s)$ such that the pair $(\boldsymbol{\tau}(s), \mathbf{n}(s))$ forms a direct orthonormal or positively oriented dihedron: if $\boldsymbol{\tau}(s) = (x'(s), y'(s))$ then $\mathbf{n}(s) = (-y'(s), x'(s))$. As before, we know that the vectors $\boldsymbol{\tau}'(s)$ and $\boldsymbol{\tau}(s)$ are orthogonal; but in this case we can conclude that $\boldsymbol{\tau}'(s)$ is a multiple of $\mathbf{n}(s)$. The *curvature* of α at the point $\alpha(s)$ is the number $K(s)$ such that $\boldsymbol{\tau}'(s) = k(s)\mathbf{n}(s)$.

This curvature can take negative values and is therefore sometimes called *signed curvature*; its absolute value is equal to the curvature defined in the previous section. Whenever we talk about the curvature of a curve in $\mathbb{R}^2$ we will be referring to the signed curvature.

Frenet's formulas in this case boil down to

$$\boldsymbol{\tau}' = k\mathbf{n}$$
$$\mathbf{n}' = -k\boldsymbol{\tau}.$$

Since $\boldsymbol{\tau}(s)$ is a unit vector, it describes the position vector of a point on $\mathbb{S}^1$ (circle with radius 1 centered at the origin). Denoting by $\varphi(s)$ the oriented angle that $\boldsymbol{\tau}(s)$ makes with the positive part of the x-axis, we have $\boldsymbol{\tau}(s) = (\cos\varphi(s), \sin\varphi(s))$ and $\mathbf{n}(s) = (-\sin\varphi(s), \cos\varphi(s))$. From this we obtain

$$\boldsymbol{\tau}'(s) = \varphi'(s)(-\sin\varphi(s), \cos\varphi(s)),$$
$$k(s) = \langle \boldsymbol{\tau}'(s), \mathbf{n}(s) \rangle = \varphi'(s). \tag{1.1}$$

This last formula gives a geometric interpretation of curvature, showing that it measures the variation of the angle φ that the tangent line to the curve makes with a fixed oriented line; and that the curvature is positive or negative according to whether the curve turns left or right (see Fig. 1.4).

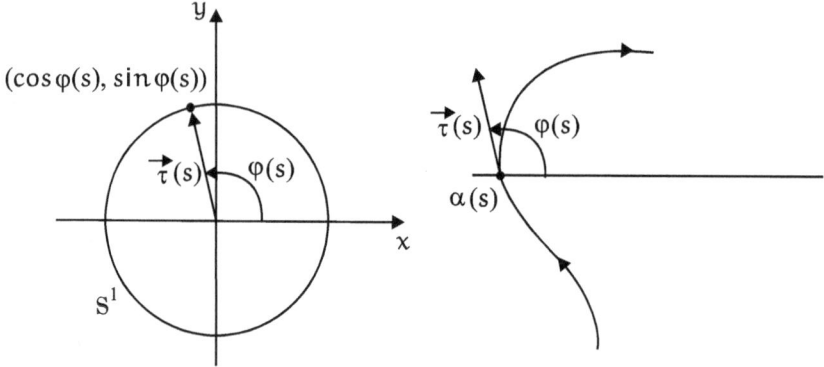

Figure 1.4

Note 1.3.1 We must make one caveat: the value $\varphi(s)$ of the angle is only determined up to an integer multiple of 2π, and it is not clear that we can make a choice for each s such that the resulting function is differentiable or even continuous. The way to solve this problem is to take advantage of the formula (1.1) to define $\varphi(s)$: fixing $s_0 \in I$ and a number φ_0 such that $\boldsymbol{\tau}(s_0) = (\cos\varphi_0, \sin\varphi_0)$, we put

$$\varphi(s) = \varphi_0 + \int_{s_0}^{s} k(t)\, dt.$$

The function φ is obviously differentiable and all that remains to be shown is that

$$\boldsymbol{\tau}(s) = (\cos\varphi(s), \sin\varphi(s))$$

– or, which is the same, that the function

$$\delta(s) = \frac{1}{2}|\tau(s) - (\cos\varphi(s), \sin\varphi(s))|^2$$

is identically zero. Let us put $\tau(s) = (x'(s), y'(s))$: by Frenet's formulas, we have
$x''(s) = -k(s)y'(s)$ and $y''(s) = k(s)x'(s)$. Therefore

$$\delta'(s) = \langle\tau'(s) - \varphi'(s)(-\sin\varphi(s), \cos\varphi(s)), \tau(s) - (\cos\varphi(s), \sin\varphi(s))\rangle$$
$$= (k(s) - \varphi'(s))(y'(s)\cos\varphi(s) - x'(s)\sin\varphi(s)) = 0,$$

since $\varphi'(s) = k(s)$. From this, and since $\delta(s_0) = 0$, we conclude that $\delta \equiv 0$.

We further stress that any other continuous choice of the angle between $\tau(s)$ and the x-axis is of the form $\varphi(s) + 2n\pi$, for some constant $n \in \mathbb{Z}$ (since the difference between two choices is continuous and only takes values in the discrete set $\{2n\pi : n \in \mathbb{Z}\}$).

We end this section with a result that is the version for planar curves of Theorem 1.2.2 and the note 1.2.3; its proof is kept as an exercise (it is possible to prove directly, without using the theorem on solutions of differential equations, the existence of α, and for uniqueness adapt the proof of Theorem 1.2.2)

Theorem 1.3.2 *Given a differentiable function $k: [a, b] \to \mathbb{R}$, there exists some curve $\alpha: [a, b] \to \mathbb{R}^2$ whose curvature at $\alpha(s)$ is $k(s)$. Any other curve with the same curvature function is the composite of α with some rigid plane movement.*

It follows in particular from Theorem 1.3.2 that the only planar curves with nonzero constant curvature are circles or arcs of circumference. A direct proof of this fact is certainly possible and is an exercise well worth to be done.

Exercises

6. (a) Consider a curve $\alpha(t) = (x(t), y(t))$ not necessarily parametrized by arc length, and put, as usual, $v(t) = |\alpha'(t)|$ and $\tau(t) = \frac{1}{v(t)}\alpha'(t)$. Prove each of the following formulas for the curvature of α:

$$k = \frac{1}{v}\langle\tau', \mathbf{n}\rangle = \frac{1}{v^2}\langle\alpha''\mathbf{n}\rangle = \frac{1}{v^3}\langle\alpha'', v\mathbf{n}\rangle$$
$$= \frac{x'y'' - x''y'}{((x')^2 + (y')^2)^{3/2}}.$$

(b) Show that the curvature of the ellipse given by the equation $\frac{x^2}{a^2} + \frac{y^2}{b^2} = 1$, parametrized by $\alpha(t) = (a\cos t, b\sin t)$, is given by

$$k(t) = \frac{ab}{(a^2\sin^2 t + b^2\cos^2 t)^{3/2}}.$$

7. Let $\mathbf{v}: [a, b] \to \mathbb{S}^1$ be a differentiable mapping. Show that there exists a differentiable function $\varphi: [a, b] \to \mathbb{R}$ such that $\mathbf{v}(t) = (\cos \varphi(t), \sin \varphi(t))$ for all t on $[a, b]$.

8. Let $\alpha:]a, b[\to \mathbb{R}^2$ be a regular curve parametrized by arc length. Given $s_0 \in]a, b[$ and $p \in \mathbb{R}^2 \setminus \{\alpha(s_0)\}$, let C be the circle with center p and radius $|\alpha(s_0) - p|$.

(a) Show that C is tangent to α at the point $\alpha(s_0)$ if and only if p is a point of the normal to α at $\alpha(s_0)$.

(b) Assume $p = \alpha(s_0) + \lambda \mathbf{n}(s_0)$ and consider the function $\rho(s) = |\alpha(s) - p|^2$. Show that if $\lambda k(s_0) > 1$ then s_0 is a strict local maximum of ρ and if $\lambda k(s_0) < 1$ then s_0 is a strict local minimum.

(c) Let $\mathcal{D} \subseteq \mathbb{R}^2$ be a circle with radius R such that $\alpha(]a, b[)$ is contained in the closed disk bounded by $\mathcal{D}$. Conclude that at the instants s_0 at which $\alpha(s_0) \in \mathcal{D}$, one has $|k(s_0)| \geq \frac{1}{R}$.

9. Let $\alpha: I \to \mathbb{R}^2$ be a regular curve of always nonzero curvature. The curve $\beta(t) = \alpha(t) + \frac{1}{k(t)} \mathbf{n}(t)$ $(t \in I)$ traversed by the center of curvature of α is called the *evolute* of α.

(a) Show that, if it is defined, the tangent line to its evolute at time t coincides with the normal to α at the same instant.

(b) Assume that the curve $\tilde{\beta}(t) = \alpha(t) + \lambda(t) \mathbf{n}(t)$ has the property described in (a). Show that $\lambda(t) = \frac{1}{k(t)}$.

(c) Consider the normals to α at two nearby points $\alpha(t_0)$ and $\alpha(t_0 + h)$. Show that as $h \to 0$, the point of intersection of the two normals tends to $\beta(t_0)$.

(d) Study the evolute of the ellipse $\frac{x^2}{a^2} + \frac{y^2}{b^2} = 1$.

1.4 Contact of Curves

We continue our study of curves by considering their Taylor polynomial expansions: given s_0 inside the interval I and $n \geq 1$, we can write

$$\alpha(s_0 + s) = \alpha(s_0) + s\alpha'(s_0) + \frac{1}{2}s^2 \alpha'(s_0) + \cdots + \frac{1}{n!}s^n \alpha^{(n)}(s_0) + o(s^n),$$

where the remainder $o(s^n)$ is a vector such that $\lim_{s \to 0} \frac{1}{s^n} |o(s^n)| = 0$. This expression of the curve can be used to detect its local properties: below we consider the contact theory of planar curves; in the exercises we obtain the geometric meaning of the osculating plane and the sign of torsion.

We now introduce a concept that measures the degree of closeness of two planar curves in the neighborhood of an intersection point. We say that the two curves α and $\tilde{\alpha}$ have *n*-order *contact* at the point $\alpha(s_0) = \tilde{\alpha}(s_0)$ if

$$\lim_{s \to 0} \frac{1}{s^n} |\tilde{\alpha}(s_0 + s) - \alpha(s_0 + s)| = 0.$$

Considering the Taylor polynomial expansion, it is easily seen that this condition is equivalent to the condition that the derivatives of α and $\tilde{\alpha}$ up to order n coincide at s_0. In particular, since $\alpha'(s_0) = \tau(s_0)$ and $\alpha''(s_0) = k(s_0)\mathbf{n}(s_0)$, we conclude that *two planar curves have second-order contact at a point p if and only if they are tangent to p and had equal curvature there* (of course when we speak of tangency here we require that the velocity vectors of the two curves are identical — i.e., point in the same direction); when the curvature is nonzero, this is equivalent to these two curves having the same center of curvature at p. From this we conclude that the *only circle which has second-order contact with α at a point of nonzero curvature is the one with center at the center of curvature of α at that point and radius equal to the radius of curvature* (of course there is no circle with second-order contact at a point of zero curvature).

The definition of n-order contact we have given is perhaps not the most natural nor the easiest to handle, since it depends on a special parameterization of the two curves. To improve the situation, we start by defining $\Delta(t)$ as the distance between the points $\alpha(s_0 + s)$ and $\tilde{\alpha}(s_0 + \tilde{s})$ given by the condition

$$\langle \alpha(s_0 + s) - \alpha(s_0), \tau(s_0) \rangle = t = \langle \tilde{\alpha}(s_0 + \tilde{s}) - \alpha(s_0), \tau(s_0) \rangle;$$

$\Delta(t)$ is thus the length of the line segment bounded by the intersections with α and $\tilde{\alpha}$ of the line orthogonal to $\tau(s_0)$ and the (oriented) distance t from $\alpha(s_0)$ (see Fig. 1.5).

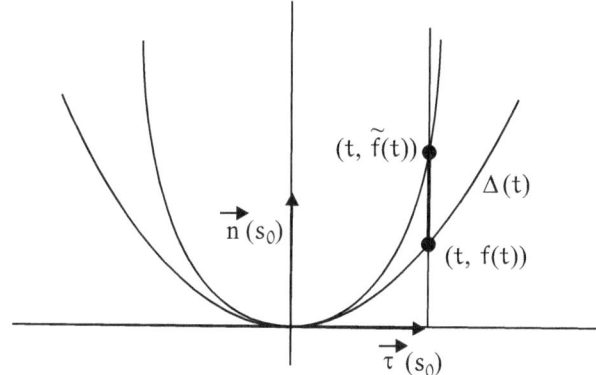

Figure 1.5

Proposition 1.4.1 *The curves α and $\tilde{\alpha}$ have n-order contact at the point $\alpha(s_0) = \tilde{\alpha}(s_0)$ if and only if $\lim\limits_{t \to 0} \frac{1}{t^n}\Delta(t) = 0$.*

Proof We first assume that α and $\tilde{\alpha}$ have n-order contact — i.e., that $\alpha(s_0) = \tilde{\alpha}(s_0)$ and $\alpha^{(i)}(s_0) = \tilde{\alpha}^{(i)}(s_0)$ for $1 \le i \le n$, — and we define functions g and $\tilde{g}$ by

$$g(s) = \langle \alpha(s_0 + s) - \alpha(s_0), \tau(s_0) \rangle$$
$$\tilde{g}(s) = \langle \tilde{\alpha}(s_0 + s) - \alpha(s_0), \tau(s_0) \rangle.$$

Note that $g(0) = \tilde{g}(0) = 0$ and $g^{(i)}(0) = \tilde{g}^{(i)}(0)$ for $1 \leq i \leq n$, and that, since the first derivative at 0 of these functions is nonzero, both have local inverses in a neighborhood of 0, which we will denote by g^{-1} and $\tilde{g}^{-1}$. Let us now put

$$F(s) = \langle \alpha(s_0 + s) - \alpha(s_0), \mathbf{n}(s_0) \rangle,$$
$$\tilde{F}(s) = \langle \tilde{\alpha}(s_0 + s) - \alpha(s_0), \mathbf{n}(s_0) \rangle,$$
$$f(t) = F \circ g^{-1}(t), \tilde{f}(t) = \tilde{F} \circ \tilde{g}^{-1}(t),$$

and note that, for t near 0, one has $\Delta(t) = |f(t) - \tilde{f}(t)|$ (see Fig. 1.5.). Moreover, the first n derivatives of f and $\tilde{f}$ at 0 coincide, since at this point also the first n derived from F are identical to those from $\tilde{F}$, and those from g^{-1} to those from $\tilde{g}^{-1}$. It follows, as desired, that $\lim_{t \to 0} \frac{1}{t^n} \Delta(t) = 0$.

We now prove the converse implication. To simplify the notation, we assume that $s_0 = 0$, take $\alpha(0) = \tilde{\alpha}(0)$ for the origin of the coordinates, and further assume that the tangent and normal vectors at this point are $(1,0)$ and $(0,1)$ respectively.

With the above notation, let $\beta(t) = \alpha \circ g^{-1}(t)$, $\tilde{\beta}(t) = \tilde{\alpha} \circ \tilde{g}^{-1}(t)$: we then have $\beta(t) = (t, f(t))$ and $\tilde{\beta}(t) = (t, \tilde{f}(t))$, and by hypothesis f and $\tilde{f}$ are functions whose derivatives up to the nth order coincide at 0. Since α and $\tilde{\alpha}$ are parametrized by arc length, we have

$$g^{-1}(t) = \int_0^t |\beta'(r)| \, dr = \int_0^t \sqrt{1 + [f'(r)]^2} \, dr,$$

$$\tilde{g}^{-1}(t) = \int_0^t |\tilde{\beta}'(r)| \, dr = \int_0^t \sqrt{1 + [\tilde{f}'(r)]^2} \, dr,$$

and these formulas show that the derivatives of g^{-1} and $\tilde{g}^{-1}$ at the point 0 coincide at least to the same order as the derivatives of f and $\tilde{f}$ at the same point — that is, to the order n. Since $\alpha = \beta \circ g$ and $\tilde{\alpha} = \tilde{\beta} \circ g$, we conclude that $\alpha^{(i)}(0) = \tilde{\alpha}^{(i)}(0)$ for $1 \leq i \leq n$, which means that α and $\tilde{\alpha}$ have n-order contact in $\alpha(0) = \tilde{\alpha}(0)$.

$\square$

Exercises

10. Assume that two planar curves α and $\tilde{\alpha}$, not necessarily parametrized by arc length, touch at the point $p = \alpha(0) = \tilde{\alpha}(0)$. Show that if $\lim_{t \to 0} \frac{1}{t^n} |\tilde{\alpha}(t) - \alpha(t)| = 0$, then the curves have n-order contact at p.

11. With the same terminology as in Proposition 1.4.1, but under the assumption that $s_0 = 0$ and $\varphi(s_0) = 0$, show that $f'(t) = tg\varphi(s)$ and $f''(t) = \frac{k(s)}{\cos^3 \varphi(s)}$, where $s = g^{-1}(t)$. Conclude that if $k(0) > 0$ then there exists $\varepsilon > 0$ such that, on an appropriate coordinate system, the trace of $\alpha|_{[-\varepsilon, \varepsilon]}$ is the graph of a convex function.

12. Let I be an open interval such that $o \in I$ and let $\alpha: I \to \mathbb{R}^3$ be a curve parametrized by arc length whose curvature at 0 is nonzero.

(a) Show that

$$\alpha(s) = \alpha(0) + \left(s - \frac{1}{6}k^2 s^3\right)\boldsymbol{\tau} + \left(\frac{1}{2}ks^2 + \frac{1}{6}k's^3\right)\mathbf{n} - \frac{1}{6}kvs^3 \mathbf{b} + o(s^3),$$

where the quantities k, v and the vectors $\boldsymbol{\tau}, \mathbf{n}, \mathbf{b}$ are computed at 0.

(b) Conclude that if $v(0) > 0$ then, when s reaches the instant 0, the curve crosses the osculating plane at $\alpha(0)$ from top to bottom (the "top part" is the one pointed to by $\mathbf{b}(0)$).

13. Using the notation and assumptions from Exercise 12, show that the plane that contains the points $\alpha(0), \alpha(h_0)$ and $\alpha(h_1)$, for $h_1 < 0 < h_0$, converges to the osculating plane at $\alpha(0)$ when $|h_0| + |h_1| \to 0$.
Hint: Using the Taylor expansion — just up to the second order — show that

$$\mathbf{v}(h_0, h_1) = \frac{(\alpha(h_0) - \alpha(0)) \times (\alpha(h_1) - \alpha(0))}{|(\alpha(h_0) - \alpha(0)) \times (\alpha(h_1) - \alpha(0))|}$$

has limit $\mathbf{b}(0)$ when $|h_0| + |h_1| \to 0$.

1.5 Convex Curves

Continuing with planar curves parametrized by arc length, let us talk about simple closed curves and characterize those that are convex. We say that a curve $\alpha: [a, b] \to \mathbb{R}^2$ is *closed* if $\alpha(a) = \alpha(b)$; if its periodic extension, defined by $\alpha(s + n(b - a)) = \alpha(s)$ for $s \in [a, b]$ and $n \in \mathbb{Z}$, is differentiable (i.e., C^∞), the curve is *closed regular*; and if the curve has no self-intersections — that is, if its restriction on $[a, b[$ is injective — we say it is *simple*.

In this section all closed curves are regular; and, where necessary, we consider them defined in $\mathbb{R}$ by periodic extension.

We recall from Section 1.3 that there is a continuous choice $\varphi(s)$ of the angle that the vector $\boldsymbol{\tau}(s)$ makes with the positive part of the x-axis. Since $\boldsymbol{\tau}(b) = \boldsymbol{\tau}(a)$, the difference $\varphi(b) - \varphi(a)$ is an integer multiple of 2π, which, by note 1.3.1, does not depend on the choice of $\varphi(s)$. We call *rotation index* of the closed curve α the integer $\mathfrak{R}(\alpha) = \frac{1}{2\pi}(\varphi(b) - \varphi(a))$; $\mathfrak{R}(\alpha)$ thus counts the number of turns that its tangent vector $\boldsymbol{\tau}(s)$ makes in the unit circle when the point $\alpha(s)$ completes one turn around the curve. Since $\varphi'(s) = k(s)$, the rotation index can be given in integral form

$$\mathfrak{R}(\alpha) = \frac{1}{2\pi} \int_a^b k(s)\, ds.$$

A closed curve $\alpha: [a, b] \to \mathbb{R}^2$ is called *convex* if, for every $s_0 \in [a, b]$, the curve is all on the same side of the tangent line to α at the point $\alpha(s_0)$ — that is, if the function

$h(s) = \langle \alpha(s) - \alpha(s_0), \mathbf{n}(s_0) \rangle$ does not change sign. Our next result characterizes these curves.

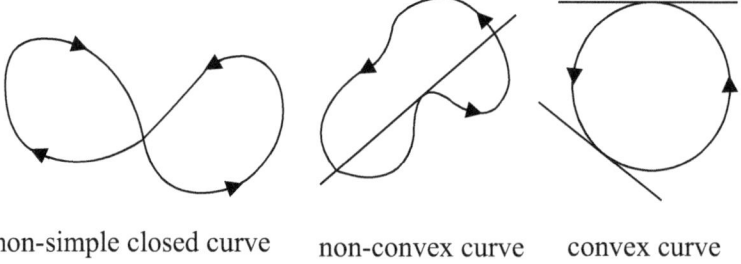

non-simple closed curve   non-convex curve   convex curve

Figure 1.6

Theorem 1.5.1 *A closed curve is convex if and only if its curvature does not change sign and its rotation index is* ± 1. *Any convex curve is simple.*

Proof (i) We begin by showing that any closed curve with non-negative curvature at all its points and rotation index 1 is convex. Let $\alpha \colon [a, b] \to \mathbb{R}^2$ be such a curve. Then the function $\varphi(s)$ is non-decreasing and $\varphi(b) = \varphi(a) + 2\pi$.

Given $s_0 \in [a, b]$, we want to prove that the function $h(s) = \langle \alpha(s) - \alpha(s_0), \mathbf{n}(s_0) \rangle$ does not change sign. Otherwise $h(s)$ reaches a positive maximum and a negative minimum at points $s_1, s_2 \in [a, b] \smallsetminus \{s_0\}$, and at each of these points the tangent line is parallel to the tangent line at $\alpha(s_0)$. Hence, there exist $i \neq j \in \{0, 1, 2\}$ such that $\varphi(s_i) = \varphi(s_j)$ and, φ being non-decreasing, this is only possible if φ is constant in the interval between s_i and s_j. This means that the curve contains the line segment from $\alpha(s_i)$ to $\alpha(s_j)$, and therefore the tangent lines at these points coincide — which is absurd given the way they were chosen. Therefore h does not change sign and α is convex.

(ii) We assume now and until the end of the proof that $\alpha \colon [a, b] \to \mathbb{R}^2$ is a convex curve. Let us first see that $k(s)$ does not change sign. Consider the function of two variables $(s, t) \in [a, b] \times [a, b]$ defined by

$$H(s, t) = \langle \alpha(s) - \alpha(t), \mathbf{n}(t) \rangle.$$

By hypothesis, for each $t \in [a, b]$ the function h_t given by $h_t(s) = H(s, t)$ has constant sign — that is, the restriction of H to each horizontal line segment $[a, b] \times \{t\}$ is either non-negative or non-positive. What we want for now is to prove that the function H itself does not change sign.

Assume, instead, that there exist $(s_0, t_0), (s_1, t_1) \in [a, b] \times [a, b]$ such that $H(s_0, t_0) < 0 < H(s_1, t_1)$; and let us agree that $t_0 < t_1$. Consider the set

$$A = \{\hat{t} \geq t_0 : H(s, t) \leq 0 \quad \forall (s, t) \in [a, b] \times [t_0, \hat{t}]\};$$

A is a non-empty interval (because $t_0 \in A$) and closed (because H is continuous). By continuity of H, there exists $\delta > 0$ such that $H(s_0, t) < 0$ whenever $t_0 \leq t \leq t_0 + \delta$, and therefore A contains the interval $[t_0, t_0 + \delta]$. Since $t_1 \notin A$, $t_2 = \sup(A)$ lies in $]t_0, t_1[$. Since $t_1 \in A$, we have $H(s, t_1) \leq 0$ for all $s \in [a, b]$. If for all s this inequality were strict, then the same argument as above would show that there exists $\delta > 0$ such that $[t_2, t_2 + \delta] \subset A$, which contradicts the definition of t_2. We then conclude that $H(s, t_2) = 0$ for all $s \in [a, b]$ — which is absurd because it means that the curve α is all contained in a straight line.

So we have proved that H does not change sign. That the curvature does not either is now immediate: when $k(t_0) > 0$, the function $h_{t_0}(s)$ has a strict local minimum for $s = t_0$ (since $h'_{t_0}(t_0) = 0$ and $h''_{t_0}(t_0) = k(t_0)$) and therefore $H(s, t_0) > 0$ for s near t_0; and, conversely, when $k(t_0) < 0$ one has $H(s, t_0) < 0$ for s near t_0.

(iii) Let us now prove that α is simple. Let us assume, to the contrary, that it has some self-intersection which, changing if necessary the initial point, we suppose to take place at $\alpha(a)$. Then there exists $x \in]a, b[$ such that $\alpha(c) = \alpha(a)$.

The function $H(s, t)$ vanishes for $(s, t) = (a, c)$ and, by (ii), reaches at that point a local extremum. Thus $\langle \tau(a), \mathbf{n}(c) \rangle = \left. \frac{\partial H}{\partial s} \right|_{(a,c)} = 0$, and therefore $\tau(a) = \pm \tau(c)$. If it were $\tau(a) = -\tau(c)$, we would have $H(s, a) = -H(s, c)$ for all $s \in [a, b]$, which is impossible by (ii). Therefore we have $\tau(a) = \tau(c)$.

To simplify the notation, we assume that $\alpha(a) = \alpha(c) = (0, 0)$. Let us put, (as in the proof of 1.4.1) for $s \geq 0$,

$$g(s) = \langle \alpha(a + s), \tau(a) \rangle, \qquad \tilde{g}(s) = \langle \alpha(c + s), \tau(a) \rangle,$$
$$F(s) = \langle \alpha(a + s), \mathbf{n}(a) \rangle, \qquad \tilde{F}(s) = \langle \alpha(c + s), \mathbf{n}(a) \rangle,$$
$$f(t) = F \circ g^{-1}(t), \qquad \tilde{f}(t) = \tilde{F} \circ \tilde{g}^{-1}(t)$$

– where the functions f and $\tilde{f}$ are defined on some interval $[0, \varepsilon]$, $\varepsilon > 0$. The graphs of f and $\tilde{f}$ are portions of the trace of α: in fact, putting $s = g^{-1}(t)$, $\tilde{s} = \tilde{g}^{-1}(t)$, we can write

$$\alpha(a + s) = t\tau(a) + f(t)\mathbf{n}(a),$$
$$\alpha(c + \tilde{s}) = t\tilde{\tau}(a) + \tilde{f}(t)\mathbf{n}(a).$$

From these formulas we obtain

$$H(a + s, c + \tilde{s}) = \{f(t) - \tilde{f}(t)\}\langle \mathbf{n}(a), \mathbf{n}(c + \tilde{s}) \rangle,$$
$$H(c + \tilde{s}, a + s) = \{\tilde{f}(t) - f(t)\}\langle \mathbf{n}(t), \mathbf{n}(a + s) \rangle.$$

In each of these products, and since $\mathbf{n}(a) = \mathbf{n}(c)$, the second factor is positive for s, $\tilde{s}$ sufficiently small; hence, if it were $f(t) \neq \tilde{f}(t)$ for some $t \in [0, \varepsilon]$, $H(a + s, c + \tilde{s})$ and $H(c + \tilde{s}, a + s)$ would have opposite signs, in contradiction to (ii). We thus have $f(t) = \tilde{f}(t)$ for all $t \in [0, \varepsilon]$ — and from this, since α is parametrized by arc length, we conclude that there exists $\delta > 0$ such that $\alpha(a + s) = \alpha(c + s)$ for all $s \in [0, \delta]$. A trivial argument now proves that for all $s \geq 0$ one has $\alpha(a + s) = \alpha(c + s)$, and this says that when the curve returns to the starting point, it repeats the same path from then on. The given hypothesis thus leads us to conclude that $\alpha\big|_{[a,b]}$ gives more than one turn to the same closed curve. Assuming this does not happen, such a $c \in \,]a,b[$ with $\alpha(c) = \alpha(a)$ does not exist and the curve is simple.

(iv) Let us now show that $\mathfrak{R}(\alpha) = \pm 1$. Assuming that α is positively oriented, and putting $\varphi(b) = \varphi(a) + 2n\pi$, we have $n = \mathfrak{R}(\alpha) \geq 1$, and we want to see that $n = 1$. We can assume, without loss of generality, that $k(a) > 0$. Take $c \in [a, b]$ such that $\varphi(c) = \varphi(a) + 2\pi$: then $H(a, c) = -H(c, a)$, and it follows by (ii) that $H(a, c) = 0$, which means that the tangent lines at $\alpha(a)$ and $\alpha(c)$ coincide. The function $\lambda(s) = H(c, a + s)$ reaches a minimum at 0, and so

$$0 = \lambda'(0) = -k(a)\langle \alpha(c) - \alpha(a), \tau(a)\rangle,$$

whence it follows, since $k(a) > 0$ and the points $\alpha(c)$ and $\alpha(a)$ lie on a straight line parallel to $\tau(a)$, that $\alpha(c) = \alpha(a)$. Since α is simple, we must have be $c = b$ and therefore $\mathfrak{R}(\alpha) = 1$.   □

It is important to note that any simple curve, whether convex or not, has rotation index ± 1: this is what the *rotation index theorem* says, the proof of which we give in the Appendix to Chap. 4, but of which a special case is given in Exercise 16 below. If we already had this result, the proof of 1.5.1 would be somewhat simplified; another simplification would be to suppress step (iii) if, as some authors do, we already required in the definition that a convex curve be simple.

One result we will not prove, but of which we will make important use, not always explicit, is the *Jordan curve theorem*. This theorem states that any simple closed curve divides the plane into two disjoint connected open subsets of which it is a common boundary. (For a proof of the theorem in the differentiable case, and its generalization to higher dimensions, see [15]; for the topological version we suggest [17], which also includes a proof of Schönflies' theorem: *the region bounded by a simple closed curve is homeomorphic to an open disc*).

To finish this section we mention that a convex curve of nonzero curvature at all its points is usually called *strictly convex*. In this case $\varphi(s)$ is strictly monotone and therefore every tangent line touches the curve at a single point.

Exercises

14. Show that if a line intersects a closed convex curve then one and only one of the following cases occurs: either the line is tangent to the curve, or it intersects the curve at exactly two points.

15. Let α be a closed, simple, regular curve, Ω be the open set bounded by α, and $\overline{\Omega} = \Omega \cup \alpha$ be the closure of α. Show that the following conditions are equivalent:

(i) $\overline{\Omega}$ is a convex set (i.e., $p, q \in \overline{\Omega} \Rightarrow$ the line segment $[p, q] \subseteq \overline{\Omega}$);

(ii) α is a convex curve.

(**Suggestion for (i)** $\Rightarrow$ **(ii):** Show that for each s_0, the image of the function s $(s \neq s_0) \mapsto (\alpha(s) - \alpha(s_0))/|\alpha(s) - \alpha(s_0)|$ is contained in a semicircle.)

16. (a) Let $\mathcal{H}:[0,1] \times [a,b] \to \mathbb{R}^2$ be a differentiable mapping such that every $\alpha_s = \mathcal{H}(s, \cdot)$ is a regular closed curve. Show that $\mathfrak{R}(\alpha_s)$ is constant. (Exercise 7 may be helpful.)

(b) Let $\alpha:[a,b] \to \mathbb{R}^2$ be a regular closed curve and $p \in \mathbb{R}^2 \setminus \alpha([a,b])$ such that each half-line with origin at p intersects α exactly once, and this intersection is transverse (i.e., the half-line is **not** tangent to α at the point of intersection). Prove that $\mathfrak{R}(\alpha) = \pm 1$.

(c) Now assume only that all intersections of α with half-lines r of origin p are transversal. Show that the cardinal of the set $T(r) = \{t \in [a,b[:\alpha(t) \in r\}$ is the same for all such half-lines.

1.6 Curves of Constant Width

In this section, we explore the varying width of a planar curve. The width of the curve in any given direction is the narrowest distance between two lines perpendicular to that direction that can contain the curve. This means that the width of a curve is not necessarily the same in all directions. Remarkably, besides the circle, there are other convex curves that have a constant width regardless of direction; and the perimeter of such curves is equal to that of the circle of the same width.

We will deal in this section with the width of a planar curve. The width of a curve in a given direction is the minimal width among the strips that contain the curve and are bounded by lines orthogonal to that direction.

Given a closed curve $\alpha:[a,b] \to \mathbb{R}^n$ we define, for $\mathbf{v} \in \mathbf{S}^1$, $h(\mathbf{v}) = \max\limits_{a \leq s \leq b} \langle \alpha(s), \mathbf{v}\rangle$. Since the maximum of $\langle \alpha(s), \mathbf{v}\rangle$ is only reached at points s such that $\langle \tau(s), \mathbf{v}\rangle = 0$, $h(\mathbf{v})$ is the maximum among the (oriented) distances from the origin to the tangent lines to α that are orthogonal to $\mathbf{v}$. The *width of α in the direction of* $\mathbf{v}$ is $\mathcal{L}(\mathbf{v}) = h(\mathbf{v}) + h(-\mathbf{v})$.

If α is a convex curve, then there are exactly two tangent lines to α that are orthogonal to $\mathbf{v}$ (although each of them may be tangent to α at more than one point), and $\mathcal{L}(\mathbf{v})$ is the distance between these lines (see Fig. 1.7). For example, the width of a circle is, in all directions, equal to its diameter.

Proposition 1.6.1 *In any closed curve the diameter and maximum width are equal.*

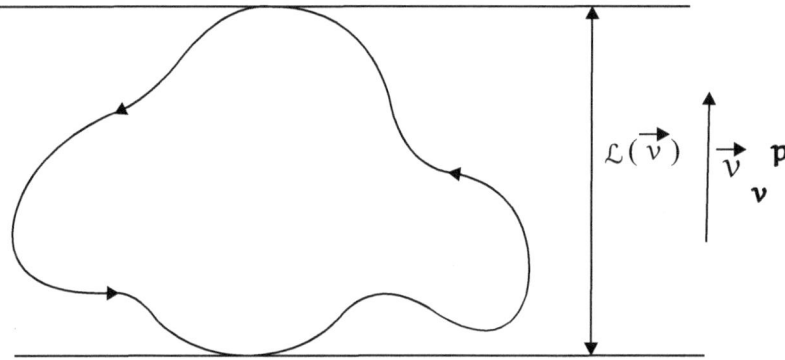

Figure 1.7

Proof We denote the diameter of α by $D = \max\{|\alpha(s) - \alpha(t)| : s,t \in [a,b]$, and by $\mathfrak{L} = \max\{\mathbf{L}(\mathbf{v}) : \mathbf{v} \in \mathbf{S}^1\}$ the maximum width of α.

Let us check that $D \leq \mathfrak{L}$. Consider the function $\mathcal{D}(s,t) = |\alpha(s) - \alpha(t)|$. This function reaches its maximum D on a pair of points (s_0, t_0) such that

$$\left.\frac{\partial\mathcal{D}}{\partial s}\right|_{(s_0,t_0)} = \left.\frac{\partial\mathcal{D}}{\partial t}\right|_{(s_0,t_0)} = 0,$$

conditions which are translated by the equalities

$$\langle\boldsymbol{\tau}(s_0), \alpha(s_0) - \alpha(t_0)\rangle = \langle\boldsymbol{\tau}(t_0), \alpha(s_0) - \alpha(t_0)\rangle = 0.$$

This shows that the tangent lines at $\alpha(s_0)$ and $\alpha(t_0)$ are parallel, both being orthogonal to the line segment joining $\alpha(s_0)$ to $\alpha(t_0)$. Moreover the curve is completely contained in the strip between these tangent lines, otherwise the maximum distance between distinct points of α would exceed D. Thus the width of the strip, which is D, is also equal to $\mathcal{L}(\mathbf{n}(s_0))$, and thus $D \leq \mathfrak{L}$.

Let us now deal with the opposite inequality. Given $\mathbf{v} \in \mathbf{S}^1$, let $s_0, t_0 \in [a,b]$ be such that $h(\mathbf{v}) = \langle\alpha(s_0), \mathbf{v}\rangle)$ and $h(-\mathbf{v}) = \langle\alpha(t_0), -\mathbf{v}\rangle$. Then

$$|\alpha(s_0) - \alpha(t_0)| \geq \langle\alpha(s_0) - \alpha(t_0), \mathbf{v}\rangle = \mathcal{L}(\mathbf{v}),$$

and therefore $D \geq \mathcal{L}(\mathbf{v})$. Since this inequality holds for all $\mathbf{v}$, it follows that $D \geq \mathfrak{L}$. $\square$

Let us now assume that the curve α is convex and has constant width $\mathfrak{L}$. By 1.6.1, also its diameter is equal to $\mathfrak{L}$. Let us now see that this diameter is realized by many pairs of points on the curve.

Fixing $s_0 \in [a,b]$, let $\alpha(s_1)$ be a point such that $\boldsymbol{\tau}(s_1) = -\boldsymbol{\tau}(s_0)$. We know from the analysis done in Section 1.5 that the curve is contained in the strip bounded by tangent lines at $\alpha(s_0)$ and $\alpha(s_1)$. Hence these tangent lines are at a distance $\mathfrak{L}$ from each other, and therefore $|\alpha(s_0) - \alpha(s_1)| \geq \mathfrak{L}$. Since the diameter of α is $\mathfrak{L}$, it must be $|\alpha(s_0) - \alpha(s_1)| = \mathfrak{L}$, an equality that is only possible if the line segment between

$\alpha(s_0)$ and $\alpha(x_1)$ is orthogonal to the tangent lines to α at these points. Furthermore, there is no other point $\alpha(\tilde{s}_1)$ such that $|\alpha(s_0) - \alpha(\tilde{s}_1)| = \mathfrak{L}$, for the proof of 1.6.1 shows that $\alpha(\tilde{s}_1)$ would also be on the normal to α at $\alpha(s_0)$.

We conclude that *for every point p of a convex curve of constant width $\mathfrak{L}$, there is a single point $\tilde{p}$ of the curve at the maximum distance $\mathfrak{L}$ from p, and $\tilde{p}$ is situated on the normal to α at p.* We call this point $\tilde{p}$ the *antipode* of p. Assuming that the curve is positively oriented (and therefore has non-negative curvature at all points), our conclusion translates into $\tilde{p} = p + \mathfrak{L}\mathbf{n}(p)$. We stress that "being antipodal to" is a reflexive relation, and that two tangent lines to α that are parallel and distinct meet α at points that are antipodes of each other.

Consider now the circle $\mathcal{C}$ with center $\tilde{p}$ and radius $\mathfrak{L}$. Such a circle is tangent to α at the point p; and all other points of α are contained in the interior of the disk bounded by $\mathcal{C}$. Exercise 8 then says that the absolute value of the curvature of α at p is greater than or equal to $1/\mathfrak{L}$. We thus conclude that *any convex curve of constant width is strictly convex.*

Example 1.6.2 At this point it is good to wonder about the existence of constant-width convex curves that are not circles. The above discussion suggests that such a curve is determined by knowing the arc between two antipodal points p and $\tilde{p}$: the remaining segment is found by marking, from each point of this arc, a distance of $\mathfrak{L}$ along the normal.

To construct an example where $\mathfrak{L} = 2$, we consider a curve $\alpha: [0, c] \to \mathbb{R}^2$ with the following properties:

(i) α is parametrized by arc length;
(ii) $\alpha(0) = (1, 0)$, $\alpha(c) = (-1, 0)$, and there exists $\varepsilon > 0$ such that $\alpha([0, \varepsilon] \cup [c - \varepsilon, c]) \subseteq \mathbf{S}_+^1 = \{(x, y) \in \mathbf{S}^1 : y \geq 0\}$;
(iii) the trace of α is not contained in $\mathbf{S}_+^1$;
(iv) the tangent vector $\tau(s)$, $s \in [0, c]$, describes a semicircle;
(v) $k(s) > \dfrac{1}{2}$ for all $s \in [0, c]$.

Such a curve can be obtained by considering $\mathbf{S}_+^1$ as the graph of a function $[-1, 1] \to \mathbb{R}$ and adding to that function a non-constant function of class C^∞ that is identically zero in the intervals $[-1, -1 + \delta]$ and $[1 - \delta, 1]$, for some $\delta > 0$. (See Exercise 17 for the existence of functions with these properties.) Reparameterizing such that the graph of the resulting function starts at $(1, 0)$, we obtain a curve α that verifies conditions (i)-(iv). If the added function and its first and second derivatives are close to zero then the curvature of α is close to that of $\mathbf{S}_+^1$, which guarantees (v).

We define $\beta: [0, 2c] \to \mathbb{R}^n$ by $\beta(t) = \alpha(t)$ for $0 \leq t \leq c$, and $\beta(t) = \alpha(t - c) + 2\mathbf{n}(t - c)$ for $c \leq t \leq 2c$. Condition (ii) guarantees that β is well-defined at $t = c$ and that $\beta(2c) = \beta(0)$. For $c \leq t \leq 2c$ we have $\beta'(t) = \{1 - 2k(t - c)\}\tau(t - c)$ and, by (v), this vector never vanishes. Furthermore conditions (ii) and (i) imply that, in neighborhoods of the "gluing points" $(1, 0)$ and $(-1, 0)$, the curve β runs through arcs of $\mathbf{S}^1$ and is parametrized by arc length. Therefore β is a regular closed curve.

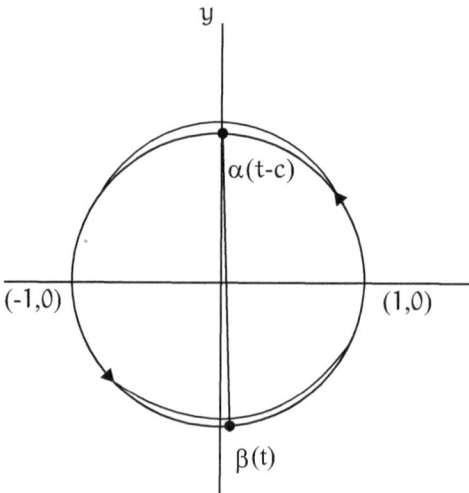

Figure 1.8

Noting that we have

$$k(t) = \frac{k(t-c)}{2k(t-c)-1},$$

for $c \le t \le 2c$, if $v(t) = 2k(t-c) - 1$ and $\tau(t) = -\tau(t-c)$ and this equality shows that the curvature of β is positive at all points. Finally, by (iv), the vector $\tau(t)$ turns exactly once around the circumference when t runs through $[0, 2c]$, and therefore $\mathfrak{R}(\beta) = 1$. By Theorem 1.5.1, β is convex. That β has constant width equal to 2 is now an immediate exercise. $\square$

We now state the most important result of this section, originally proved by E. Barbier in the 19th century using probabilistic methods (see [1]; Barbier's proof is also reproduced in [5], pp. 161-163).

Theorem 1.6.3 *The perimeter of any constant-width curve* $\mathfrak{L}$ *is equal to* $\pi\mathfrak{L}$.

Proof We fix a curve $\alpha\colon[0, L] \to \mathbb{R}^2$ that is convex and positively oriented and has constant width $\mathfrak{L}$. We assume that the parameter of the curve is given by arc length, so that its perimeter is L, and we consider α defined on $\mathbb{R}$ through its periodic extension. We further denote by $\varphi(s)$ a differentiable choice of the angle of $\tau(s)$ with the positive x-half-axis. The rotation index of α is 1, so $\varphi(s+L) = \varphi(s) + 2\pi$ for all $s \in \mathbb{R}$; and, since α is strictly convex, $\varphi\colon\mathbb{R} \to \mathbb{R}$ is strictly increasing and has differentiable inverse.

For each $s \in \mathbb{R}$, we denote the antipode of $\alpha(s)$ by $\tilde{\alpha}(s)$. This function $s \mapsto \tilde{\alpha}(s)$ is also periodic with period equal to L; and is differentiable, since we can write $\tilde{\alpha}(s) = \alpha(s) + \mathfrak{L}\mathbf{n}(s)$.

Lemma 1.6.4 *There exists a differentiable function* $f\colon\mathbb{R} \to \mathbb{R}$ *such that* $\tilde{\alpha}(s) = \alpha(f(s))$ *for all* $s \in \mathbb{R}$. *This function satisfies* $f(s+L) = f(s) + L$, *and its derivative is strictly positive at all points.*

Proof Assume that a certain function f satisfies the equation $\varphi \circ f(s) = \varphi(s) + \pi$. Then $\tau(f(s)) = (\cos(\varphi \circ f(s)), \sin((\varphi \circ f(s)))) = -\tau(s)$, and therefore the points $\alpha(s)$ and $\alpha(f(s))$ are antipodes of each other — that is, $\tilde{\alpha}(s) = \alpha(f(s))$ just as we intend.

This means that we just have to find f such that $\varphi \circ f(s) = \varphi(s) + \pi$. Such a function is given by $f(s) = \varphi^{-1}(\varphi(s) + \pi)$, which is differentiable and has positive derivative. Furthermore, we have $f(s+L) = \varphi^{-1}(\varphi(s+L) + \pi) = \varphi^{-1}(\{\varphi(s) + \pi\} + 2\pi) = f(s) + L$, as we want. $\qquad\square$

We now finish the proof of 1.6.3. Differentiating the equality $\alpha(s) + \mathfrak{L}\mathbf{n}(s) = \alpha(f(s))$, we obtain $\{1 - \mathfrak{L}k(s)\}\,\tau(s) = f'(s)\tau(f(s))$ — and from this, as $\tau(f(s)) = -\tau(s)$, yields $f'(s) = -1 + \mathfrak{L}k(s)$. Finally, using 1.6.4, and since the rotation index of α is 1, we have

$$L = f(L) - f(0) = \int_0^L f'(s)\,ds = -L + \mathfrak{L}\int_0^L k(s)\,ds = -L + 2\pi\mathfrak{L}.$$

Note 1.6.5 We cannot omit the simplest example of a non-circular curve of constant width: *Reuleaux's triangle*, which is formed by three arcs, each centered at one of the vertices of an equilateral triangle ABC and radius equal to the side of the triangle. Its perimeter L and width $\mathfrak{L}$ are also related by $L = \pi\mathfrak{L}$, but the proof of 1.6.3 does not cover this case: the antipode of each point of the arc $\overset{\frown}{BC}$ (resp. $\overset{\frown}{CA}$, $\overset{\frown}{AB}$) is the point A (resp. B, C).

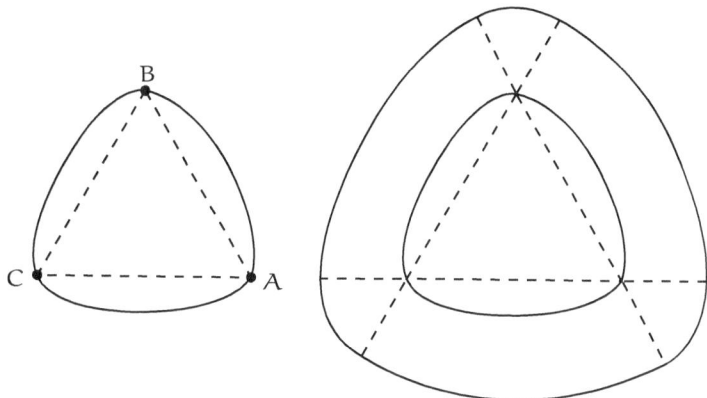

Figure 1.9

The Reuleaux triangle is a *piecewise regular* curve; we say that $\alpha:[a,b] \to \mathbb{R}^2$ is such a curve if there exists a partition $a = t_0 < t_1 \cdots < t_k = b$ of $[a,b]$ such that each restriction $\alpha|_{(t_{i-1}-t_i]}$ is regular. We now sketch how to extend 1.6.3 to piecewise regular convex closed curves, provided that each regular segment is at least of class C^2.

Given $d > 0$, let α_d be the curve which surrounds α at a constant distance from it equal to d. The curve α_d is called *parallel* to α, and if α has constant width $\mathfrak{L}$, α_d has constant width $\mathcal{L} + 2d$. In Fig. 1.9 we show a curve parallel to the Reuleaux triangle. Each "corner" of α is replaced by an arc of a circle at α_d. Therefore α_d already has a well-defined tangent vector $\tau_d(s)$ at each point; the angle $\varphi_d(s)$ that $\tau_d(s)$ makes with the x-axis is a continuous, strictly increasing function, which is piecewise C^1; and the antipode mapping is already a bijection of the curve onto itself. The proof of 1.6.3 can easily be adapted to show that the perimeter of α_d is

$$l(\alpha_d) = \pi(\mathcal{L} + 2d)$$

– and, letting $d \to 0$, we obtain $l(\alpha) = \pi\mathcal{L}$, as desired.   □

There are numerous results on constant width curves: [7] contains a careful discussion of the topic (and its generalization to higher dimensions) and an extensive bibliography. In Section 5.5 we give some results on constant width surfaces.

Exercises

17. (a) Check that the function $f(x) = e^{-1/x(1-x)}$ if $0 < x < 1$, $f(x) = 0$ otherwise it is C^∞, and that $F(x) = \int_0^x f(t)\,dt / \int_0^1 f(t)\,dt$ satisfies the conditions: $F(x) = 0$ for $x < 0$, F is strictly increasing on $[0, 1]$, $F(x) = 1$ for $x \geq 1$.

(b) Given $a < b$ and $y_1, y_2 \in \mathbb{R}$, show that there exists a nonconstant $g : \mathbb{R} \to \mathbb{R}$ of class C^∞ such that $g(x) = y_1 \ \forall x \in [-\infty, a]$, and $g(x) = y_2 \ \forall x \in [b, +\infty[$.

18. Let $\alpha : [a, b] \to \mathbb{R}^2$ be a closed curve and $\mathcal{L}(\mathbf{v})$ be the corresponding "width function". Show that:

(a) $\mathcal{L}$ is continuous and therefore there exists $\max_{v \in S} \mathcal{L}(\mathbf{v})$;

(b) if α is regular and strictly convex then $\mathcal{L}$ is differentiable (i.e., the function $\theta \to \mathcal{L}(\cos\theta, \sin\theta)$ is differentiable).

19. Show that the function of Lemma 1.6.4 is unique but for the addition of a constant.

20. Let α be a regular convex curve of constant width $\mathcal{L}$. Show that:

(a) $k(p) > 1/\mathcal{L}$ for any point p of α (assume that α has positive orientation);

(b) if p and $\tilde{p}$ are antipodal points then

$$\frac{1}{k(p)} + \frac{1}{k(\tilde{p})} = \mathcal{L};$$

(c) if each pair of antipodal points divide α into two arcs of equal length then α is a circle.

21. Convex curves of constant width $\mathcal{L}$ are characterized by the fact that all the rectangles that circumscribe them are squares of side $\mathcal{L}$. In this exercise we prove a generalization of Barbier's Theorem: *if α is a regular curve* **strictly** *convex such that all rectangles that surround it have perimeter $4\mathcal{L}$, then the perimeter of α is $\pi\mathcal{L}$.*

Using the same notation as in the proof of 1.6.3, denote by L the perimeter of the curve and by $\tilde{\alpha}(s)$ the only point of α at which the tangent vector is $-\tau(s)$. Show that:

(a) there exists a differentiable function $f:\mathbb{R} \to \mathbb{R}$ such that $\tilde{\alpha}(s) = \alpha(f(s))$ and $f(s+L) = f(s) + L$;

(b) there exist differentiable functions λ, η such that

$$\tilde{\alpha}(s) = \alpha(s) + \lambda(s)\tau(s) + \eta(s)\mathbf{n}(s);$$

(c) λ and η are periodic functions of period L;

(d) $f'(s) = -1 - \lambda'(s) + \eta(s)k(s)$;

(e) $2L = \displaystyle\int_0^L \eta(s)k(s)\,ds$.

Now make the change of variable $\theta = \varphi(s)$ to prove that

$$\int_0^L \eta(s)k(s)\,ds = \int_0^{2\pi} \eta(\theta)\,d\theta,$$

where $\eta(\theta)$ denotes $\eta(\varphi^{-1}(\theta))$. Note that $\eta(\theta)$ is periodic of period 2π and that the assumption about α translates to $\eta(\theta) + \eta\left(\theta + \dfrac{\pi}{2}\right) = 2\mathfrak{L}$. Finally, we can write

$$4L = \int_0^{2\pi} \eta(\theta)\,d\theta + \int_0^{2\pi} \eta\left(\theta + \frac{\pi}{2}\right)\,d\theta$$

$$= \int_0^{2\pi} \left\{\eta(\theta) + \eta\left(\theta + \frac{\pi}{2}\right)\right\}\,d\theta = 4\pi\mathfrak{L}.$$

22. Modify 1.6.2 to give examples of curves that satisfy the hypothesis of Exercise 21 but do not have constant width.

1.7 Theorem of the Four Vertices

We now give the four-vertex theorem, which states that the curvature of any closed convex curve has at least four critical points (this result is also valid for nonconvex closed planar curves, but we will not prove it in such generality). This result is best possible: a non-circular ellipse has exactly four vertices, which are its points of intersection with the axes (see Exercise 6).

Let $\alpha:[a,b] \to \mathbb{R}^2$ be a regular closed curve, and $k(s)$ its curvature function. A *vertex* of α is a point $\alpha(s_0)$ such that $k'(s_0) = 0$. This definition does not depend on the parameterization and so we assume that s is the arc length.

Theorem 1.7.1 *Any closed convex curve has at least four vertices.*

Proof We can assume that $k(s)$ has a finite number of critical points, because otherwise there is nothing to be shown. The function $k(s)$ attains some maximum and some minimum — which, changing the starting point if necessary, we suppose happen at the points $s = a$ and $s = s_0 \in\,]a, b[$. By applying a rotation or translation we can ensure that both points $\alpha(a)$ and $\alpha(s_0)$ are on the x-axis.

Let us check that there are no other points of α on the x-axis: for if there were another one — let it be p — then the tangent line to α at the one of the three points $\alpha(a)$, $\alpha(s_0)$ and p which lies between the other two is the x-axis; otherwise there would be points of α on opposite sides of this tangent line, in contradiction to the convexity of α. It follows that the tangent line at $\alpha(a)$ and $\alpha(s_0)$ is also the horizontal axis, and that (as in the proof of 1.5.1) the trace of $\alpha|_{[a,s_0]}$ is a line segment. This however contradicts our assumption that α has a finite number of vertices.

Putting $\alpha(s) = (x(s), y(s))$, we then have that $y(s)$ never vanishes on the intervals $]a, s_0[$ and $]s_0, b[$, taking on the second interval a sign opposite to the one it takes on the first; and the same is true of $k'(s)$ if we assume that α has at most two vertices. Under this assumption the function $k'(s)y(s)$ then has constant sign, vanishing only at a, x_0 and b, and so $\int_a^b k'(s)y(s)\, ds \neq 0$. But, writing $(x'(s), y'(s)) = (\cos\varphi(s), \sin\varphi(s))$, and using integration by parts and the equality $\varphi'(s) = k(s)$, we have

$$\int_a^b k'(s)y(s)\, ds = k(s)y(s)\Big|_a^b - \int_a^b k(s)y'(s)\, ds = -\int_a^b k(s)y'(s)\, ds$$

$$= -\int_a^b \varphi'(s)\sin\varphi(s)\, ds = \cos\varphi(s)\Big|_a^b = 0.$$

This contradiction shows that $k'(s)$ changes sign on some intervals $]a, s_0[$ and $]s_0, b[$. Since in each of them $k'(s)$ has the same sign near the endpoints, we conclude that $k'(s)$ changes sign at least twice in such an interval, which proves the theorem. □

The four-vertex theorem is still valid for non-convex curves. For a very elegant geometric proof that also covers this generalization, we suggest [21].

1.8 The Isoperimetric Inequality

The isoperimetric inequality states that, among all planar curves with a given perimeter, the circumference encompasses the largest area. The proof we give (by A. Hurwitz, 1902) makes essential use of the theory of Fourier series (see [11] for an introduction to this theory). An elementary proof appears in [18], and [9] contains a generalization of the isoperimetric inequality for convex bodies in dimensions greater than two.

Lemma 1.8.1 (Wirtinger) Let f be a function of class C^1, periodic of period 2π, such that $\int_0^{2\pi} f(t)\, dt = 0$. Then

$$\int_0^{2\pi} f'(t)^2\, dt \geq \int_0^{2\pi} f(t)^2\, dt,$$

and equality holds if and only if there exist a and b such that $f(t) = a \cos t + b \sin t$.

Proof Be

$$f(t) \sim \frac{a_0}{2} + \sum_{n=1}^{\infty} (a_n \cos nt + b_n \sin nt)$$

the Fourier series expansion of f. Since $f'(t)$ is continuous, its expansion is obtained from that of $f(t)$ by term-by-term differentiation, thus

$$f'(t) \sim \sum_{n=1}^{\infty} (n b_n \cos nt - n a_n \sin nt).$$

Since $\int_0^{2\pi} f(t)\, dt = \pi a_0$, our hypothesis yields $a_0 = 0$. Using Parseval's formula, we have

$$\frac{1}{\pi} \int_0^{2\pi} f(t)^2\, dt = \sum_{n=1}^{\infty} (a_n^2 + b_n^2),$$

$$\frac{1}{\pi} \int_0^{2\pi} f'(t)^2\, dt = \sum_{n=1}^{\infty} n^2 (a_n^2 + b_n^2).$$

It follows that

$$\int_0^{2\pi} f'(t)^2\, dt - \int_0^{2\pi} f(t)^2\, dt = \sum_{n=1}^{\infty} \pi(n^2 - 1)(a_n^2 + b_n^2) \geq 0,$$

and equality only holds if $a_n = b_n = 0$ for all $n > 1$. Since continuous functions are determined by their Fourier expansion, this is equivalent to $f(t) = a_1 \cos t + b_1 \sin t$. □

Theorem 1.8.2 (Isoperimetric inequality) Let α be a simple regular closed curve of perimeter L, bounding a region Ω of area A. Then

$$A \leq \frac{L^2}{4\pi},$$

and equality holds only when α is a circle.

We can rescale the figure using a homothety, so there is no loss of generality if we suppose that $L = 2\pi$, and therefore $\alpha(s) = (x(s), y(s))$, $s \in [0, 2\pi]$. With a translation, we can achieve $\int_0^{2\pi} x(s)\, ds = 0$. Furthermore, we assume that $\alpha(s)$ runs through the boundary of Ω in the counterclockwise direction. Applying Green's theorem

$$\left(\int_{\partial\Omega} P\, dx + Q\, dy = \iint_{\Omega} \left(\frac{\partial Q}{\partial x} - \frac{\partial P}{\partial y} \right) dx dy \right)$$

to the vector field $(P, Q) = (0, x)$, we obtain

$$A = \int_0^{2\pi} xy'\, ds,$$

and on the other hand

$$L = 2\pi = \int_0^{2\pi} (x'^2 + y'^2)\, ds.$$

We can then write

$$2(\pi - A) = \int_0^{2\pi} (x'^2 - x^2)\, ds + \int_0^{2\pi} (x - y')^2\, ds.$$

The second integral of this sum is non-negative and, by Wirtinger's lemma, so is the first. We thus conclude, as desired, that $A \le \pi$. To achieve equality both integrals have to be zero, so $y'(s) = x(s)$ and $x(s) = a \cos s + b \sin s$. We thus have

$$x(s) = a \cos s + b \sin x,$$
$$y(s) = a \sin s - b \cos s + c,$$

and α is therefore the unit circle with center at $(0, c)$.   □

Exercises

23. The coefficients of the Fourier series

$$f(t) \sim \frac{a_0}{2} + \sum_{n=1}^{\infty} (a_n \cos nt + b_n \sin nt)$$

of a periodic function of period 2π, integrable on $[0, 2\pi]$ (a class that includes bounded functions with a finite number of discontinuities), are defined by

$$a_0 = \frac{1}{\pi} \int_0^{2\pi} f(t)\, dt,$$

$$a_n = \frac{1}{\pi} \int_0^{2\pi} f(t) \cos nt\, dt,$$

$$b_n = \frac{1}{\pi} \int_0^{2\pi} f(t) \sin nt\, dt.$$

Show that:

(a) if f is of class C^1 and $(a'_n)_{n=0}^{+\infty}$ and $(b'_n)_{n=1}^{+\infty}$ are the Fourier coefficients of f', then $a'_0 = 0$ and $a'_n = n b_n$ and $b'_n = -n a_n$ for $n \ge 1$ (use integration by parts);

(b) the result of (a) is still true if f is only piecewise C^1;

(c) the isoperimetric inequality is valid for piecewise C^1 curves.

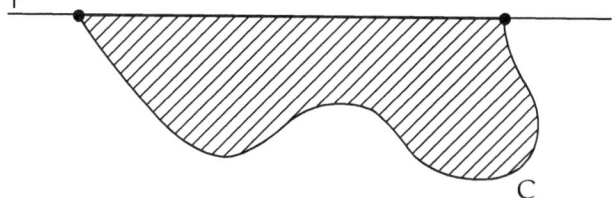

Figure 1.10

24. Consider a straight line r in the plane and a flexible string C of length L. By placing C in the plane so that its ends are on r, we obtain a figure bounded by r and by C and whose area depends on the shape we give the string (see figure above). Show that the figure of maximum area among all those so obtained is a semicircle based on r.

25. Given two points p and q in the plane and a flexible string C of length $L > |p - q|$, determine the figure of largest area among those bounded by C and by the line segment $\overline{pq}$.

26. Let α be a convex closed curve, piecewise C^1, of perimeter L, bounding a region Ω of area A. Let r_1 and r_2 be two parallel lines at a distance d from each other such that both touch α, and α is contained in the strip bounded by the them. Consider an orthonormal Cartesian coordinate system whose vertical axis is r_1 and whose origin is the midpoint of the line segment $r_1 \cap \alpha$ (a line segment which may contain a single point). There thus exist functions piecewise C^1 $f, g : [0, d] \to \mathbb{R}$ such that:

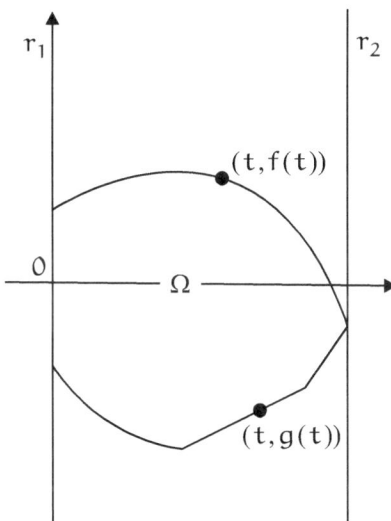

Figure 1.11

1. $f(t) \geq g(t)$ $\forall t \in [0,d]$, $f(0) = -g(0) \geq 0$;
2. the trace of α consists of the graphs of f and g and the vertical segments $\{0\} \times [g(0), f(0)]$ and $\{d\} \times [g(d), f(d)]$;
3. f is a concave function and g is a convex function.

(a) Define $h = \dfrac{1}{2}(f - g)$. Show that h is a concave function piecewise C^1, and conclude that the region $\widetilde{\Omega}$ bounded by r_1 and r_2 and by the graphs of the functions h and $-h$ is convex.

(b) Let $\widetilde{L}$ and $\widetilde{A}$ be the perimeter and area of $\widetilde{\Omega}$. Show that $\widetilde{A} = A$ and $\widetilde{L} \leq L$, and that the inequality is an equality only in the case where $f = -g$.

(c) Assume that α has minimal perimeter among all convex piecewise C^1 curves encompassing a fixed area A. Conclude, without using the isoperimetric inequality, that α is a circle.

Hint: α has an axis of symmetry in each direction. Show that all these axes pass through the same point.

27. Let α be a regular convex curve of constant width $\mathcal{L}$ that bounds a region of area A. Show that $A \leq \dfrac{\pi \mathcal{L}^2}{4}$, with equality only if α is a circle.

Chapter 2
Regular Surfaces

In this chapter we introduce regular surfaces, the object of all our further study, defining them as those subsets of $\mathbb{R}^3$ that can be described locally by two independent parameters. We introduce notions such as tangent space, differentiable function and diffeomorphism, and consider the problems of orientability and the measurement of quantities (areas, lengths ...) on surfaces.

2.1 Definition and Examples

We all have an intuitive notion of what a surface is, and any attempt to describe that notion would inevitably fall into redundancy. We accept, however, that the plane is the simplest surface of all, and that a good way to construct models of others is by gluing together various pieces of paper. Our definition of surface is the mathematical elaboration of this idea.

A subset S of $\mathbb{R}^3$ is called a *regular surface* if, for each $p \in S$, there exist an open neighborhood $V \subseteq \mathbb{R}^3$ of p, an open subset $U \subseteq \mathbb{R}^2$, and a bijection $\Phi: U \to V \cap S$ with the following properties:

- i. Φ is of class C^∞;
- ii. Φ is a homeomorphism (i.e., its inverse $\Phi^{-1}: V \cap S \to U$ is continuous);
- iii. for all $q \in U$ the Jacobian matrix $J\Phi(q)$ has rank two.

A mapping Φ with these three properties is named *parameterization* or *system of (local) coordinates* of S. We usually denote the points of U by (u, v), so that u and v are *local parameters* of S, and the partial derivatives of Φ are denoted by Φ_u and Φ_v. These vectors describe the velocities of the *coordinate curves*, which are the curves obtained by fixing one of the parameters and varying the other. Moreover the columns of the matrix $J\Phi(u, v)$ are precisely Φ_u and Φ_v, so that condition iii. above expresses that, for each $(u, v) \in U$, Φ_u and Φ_v are linearly independent.

© The Author(s), under exclusive license to Springer Nature Switzerland AG 2024
P. V. Araújo, *Differential Geometry*, https://doi.org/10.1007/978-3-031-62384-4_2

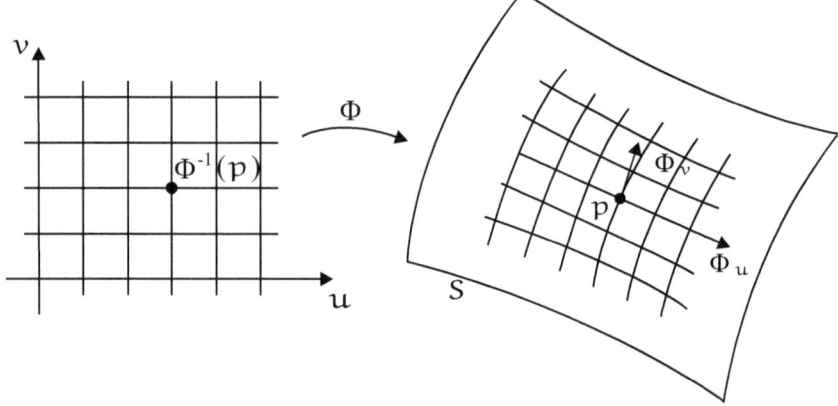

Figure 2.1

A subset of the surface S is called *open* if it is of the form $V \cap S$, where V is an open subset of $\mathbb{R}^3$. An important observation is that any point of S has an open neighborhood (in S) homeomorphic to a disk, and this neighborhood can be taken as small as we wish: indeed, if (U, Φ) is a parameterization in the neighborhood of p, there exists some open disk D (of arbitrarily small radius) containing $\Phi^{-1}(p)$ and contained in U, and $\Phi(D)$ is the sought neighborhood.

Examples 2.1.1 **A.** Any plane Π in $\mathbb{R}^3$ is a surface: in fact Π admits a description of the form $\phi(u, v) = p_0 + u\mathbf{w}_1 + v\mathbf{w}_2$, where $(u, v) \in \mathbb{R}^2$, $p_0 \in \Pi$ and $\mathbf{w}_1, \mathbf{w}_2$ are linearly independent vectors. The conditions i. and iii. are trivially verified, and ii. follows from the fact that the solution of the equations $\phi(u, v) = p$, for $p = (a, b, c) \in \Pi$, is a first degree function at a, b, c, hence continuous. This means that Π is all covered by a single (called *global*) parameterization.

B. If $f: U \to \mathbb{R}^2$ is a differentiable function defined on an open subset $\mathbb{R}^2$, its graph $\{(u, v, f(u, v)): (u, v) \in U\} \subseteq \mathbb{R}^3$ is a surface admitting the global parameterization $\Phi(u, v) = (u, v, f(u, v)), (u, v) \in U$.

C. The union $S = \Pi_1 \cup \Pi_2$ of two non-parallel planes is not a surface, since the points of $\Pi_1 \cap \Pi_2$ have on S no neighborhood homeomorphic to a disk.

D. A parameterization of the sphere $S^2 = \{(x, y, z) \in \mathbb{R}^3 : x^2 + y^2 + z^2 = 1\}$ covering the northern hemisphere is

$$\Phi(u, v) = \left(u, v, \sqrt{1 - (u^2 + v^2)}\right),$$

defined on the disk $\{(u, v): u^2 + v^2 < 1\}$. With a few more analogous parameterizations (how many are needed?) we can cover the whole sphere, which therefore is a surface.

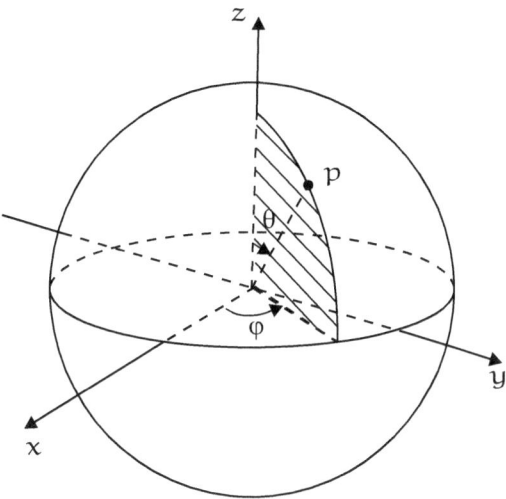

Figure 2.2

Another type of parameterization of $\mathbf{S}^2$, which excludes only one meridian, is given by the spherical coordinates, which are the colatitude $\theta \in]0, \pi[$ and the longitude $\varphi \in]-\pi, \pi[$ (Fig. 2.2), defining the point

$$\Psi(\varphi, \theta) = (\sin \theta \cos \varphi, \sin \theta \sin \varphi, \cos \theta).$$

The tangent vectors to the coordinate curves are

$$\Psi_\varphi(\varphi, \theta) = (-\sin \theta \sin \varphi, \sin \theta \cos \varphi, 0),$$
$$\Psi_\theta(\varphi, \theta) = (\cos \theta \cos \varphi, \cos \theta \sin \varphi, -\sin \theta),$$

whose vector product

$$\Psi_\varphi \times \Psi_\theta = -\sin \theta (\sin \theta \cos \varphi, \sin \theta \sin \varphi, \cos \theta)$$

has length $\sin \theta$, and so is nonzero: therefore Ψ_φ and Ψ_θ are linearly independent.

We mention that some authors use, in spherical coordinates, the latitude $\widetilde{\theta} = \frac{\pi}{2} - \theta$ $\left(\widetilde{\theta} \in \left]-\frac{\pi}{2}, \frac{\pi}{2}\right[\right)$ instead of the colatitude, thus obtaining

$$\widetilde{\Psi}(\varphi, \widetilde{\theta}) = (\cos \widetilde{\theta} \cos \varphi, \cos \widetilde{\theta} \sin \varphi, \sin \widetilde{\theta}).$$

E. The sphere is a special case of a surface of revolution, which is obtained by rotating a planar curve around an axis contained in the plane of the curve. Assuming that the curve $\alpha(v) = (\rho(v), 0, z(v))$ is defined on an open interval I, is a homeomorphism onto its image, and that $\rho(v) > 0$ for all $v \in I$, the mapping

$$\Phi(u, v) = (\rho(v) \cos u, \rho(v) \sin u, z(v)),$$

where $(u, v) \in \,]-\pi, \pi[\, \times I$, is a parameterization of the surface obtained by rotating α around the z-axis. To show that Φ^{-1} is continuous, we make use of the formula

$$\operatorname{tg} \frac{u}{2} = \frac{\sin u}{1 + \cos u}$$

and of the fact that $f(u) = \operatorname{tg} \dfrac{u}{2}$ is a diffeomorphism of $]-\pi, \pi[$ and $\mathbb{R}$. The equality $\Phi(u, v) = (x, y, z)$ is then equivalent to the combination of the two equalities

$$u = f^{-1}\left(\frac{y}{x + \sqrt{x^2 + y^2}}\right), \qquad v = \alpha^{-1}\left(\sqrt{x^2 + y^2}, 0, z\right),$$

which proves that Φ^{-1} is continuous.

F. By analogy with the definition of a parametrized curve, we define *parametrized surface* as a differentiable mapping Φ of a connected open subset of $\mathbb{R}^2$ into $\mathbb{R}^3$ whose Jacobian has rank two at all points. This definition does not require that Φ be injective, and so its image, being allowed to have self-intersections, is not necessarily a regular surface; but it may not be so even if Φ is injective, as the following example shows:

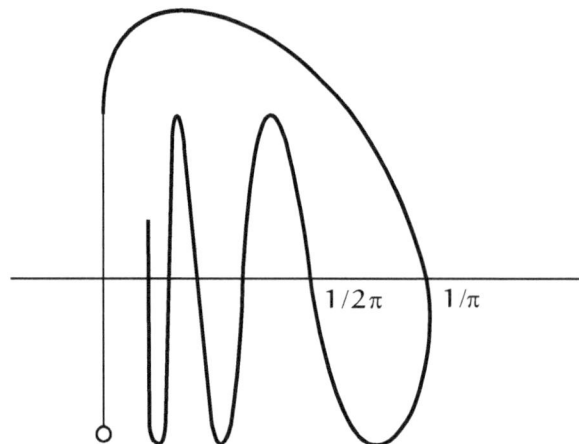

$1/2\pi$ $1/\pi$

Figure 2.3

Let $\alpha(u) = (x(u), y(u))$, $u>0$, be a simple regular curve of class C^∞ that includes the vertical line segment $\{0\} \times \,]1, 1]$ and the graph of the function $\sin \frac{1}{x}$, $x \in \,]0, \frac{1}{\pi}]$; this curve accumulates in the neighborhood of $\{0\} \times \,] -1, 1[$ (see Fig. 2.3). The trace S of the parametrized surface $\Phi(u, v) = (x(u), y(u), v)$ is **not** a surface: if it were, each $p \in S$ would have arbitrarily small neighborhoods V in $\mathbb{R}^3$ with $V \cap S$ homeomorphic to disks; but that does not happen if $p \in \{0\} \times \,] -1, 1[\, \times \mathbb{R}$, because $V \cap S$ has infinitely many connected components for all sufficiently small V.

This means that not all parametrized surfaces define regular surfaces. But it is also not easy, and in some cases not even possible, to describe regular surfaces as parametrized surfaces (i.e., as the image of **one single** function Φ). There is in general no reason to privilege a particular (even global) parameterization on a given surface.

In conclusion: surface for us means regular surface, and only in the exercises we will mention parametrized surfaces.

Exercises

28. For each $a \in \mathbb{R}$, the polar coordinates $\Phi(\rho, \varphi) = (\rho \cos \varphi, \rho \sin \varphi)$, with $\rho > 0$ and $\varphi \in]a - \pi, a + \pi[$, define a parameterization of $\mathbb{R}^2$ that excludes a half-line. (We consider $\mathbb{R}^2$ as a surface by identifying it with the plane $\mathbb{R}^2 \times \{0\} \subseteq \mathbb{R}^3$.)

29. Consider a helix parametrized by $(\cos t, \sin t, t)$ $(t \in \mathbb{R})$. The *helicoid* is the set formed by all (horizontal) lines connecting each point of the z-axis with the point of the helix at the same height (see Fig. 2.4). Show that the helicoid is a regular surface.

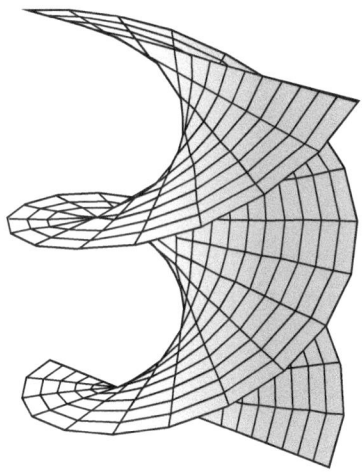

Figure 2.4

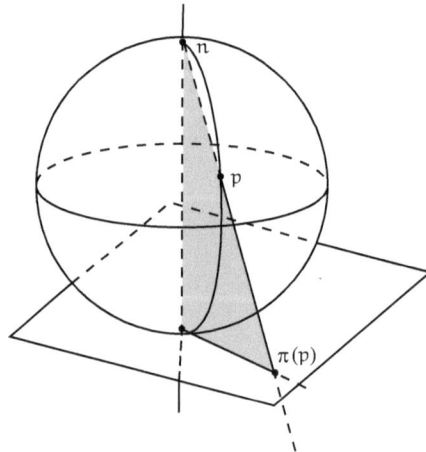

Figure 2.5

30. Consider the sphere $\mathbf{S}^2 = \{(x, y, z): x^2 + y^2 + z^2 = 1\}$. The *stereographic projection* is the mapping $\pi: \mathbf{S}^2 \backslash \{(0, 0, 1)\} \to \mathbb{R}^2$ defined as follows: $(\pi(p), -1)$ is the intersection point of the plane $z = -1$ with the line that contains the points $(0, 0, 1)$ and p (see Fig. 2.5).

(a) Obtain an explicit formula for π. Show that π is a bijection and that $(\mathbb{R}^2, \pi^{-1})$ is a parameterization of $\mathbf{S}^2$.

(b) Conclude that there are two parameterizations of $\mathbf{S}^2$ whose union covers the sphere.

(c) Is there any global parameterization of $\mathbf{S}^2$ (i.e., whose image is $\mathbf{S}^2$)?

31. Consider in $\mathbb{R}^2$ the circle $C = \{(x, y, z): (y - 2)^2 + z^2 = 1, x = 0\}$. Show that the set $\mathbb{T}^2$ which is obtained by rotating C around the z-axis is a regular surface (the *torus*) — a parameterization is given by $\Phi(u, v) = ((2 + \cos v) \cos u, (2 + \cos v) \sin u, \sin v)$, where $(u, v) \in]-\pi, \pi[\times]-\pi, \pi[$ (see Fig. 2.6).

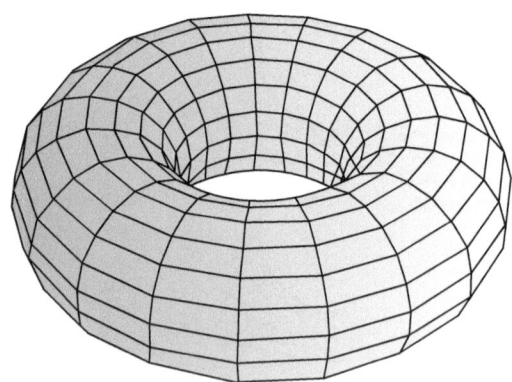

Figure 2.6

32. The *tractrix* is the planar curve obtained as follows: let us fix a line (let it be the z-axis); the distance from any point p on the curve to the point of intersection p' of the tangent line to the curve at p with the fixed line is constant, equal to $C > 0$. Parametrize the tractrix using the angle t in Fig. 2.7 as a parameter (note that $t \in]\frac{\pi}{2}, \pi[$). [The surface of revolution obtained from the tractrix around the z-axis is the *pseudosphere*].

2.2 Change of Parameters, Level Surfaces

In this section we gather a number of technical results, such as the change of parameters on a surface, level surfaces, and the fact that any surface is locally the graph of a function. We make systematic use of the inverse function theorem, and the proofs are largely routine — so it seems more instructive (and less monotonous) if, instead of reading all these proofs, the reader tries to reconstruct some of them by herself.

In our further study we will make use of local coordinates to express certain concepts, and our first caution is that such concepts should not depend on the coordinate system used, but only on the surface. Assume then that (U, Φ) and $(\tilde{U}, \Psi)$ are two parameterizations of the surface S, and that the open set $W = \Phi(U) \cap \Psi(\tilde{U})$ is non-empty. Under these assumptions (see Fig. 2.8) we have the following result.

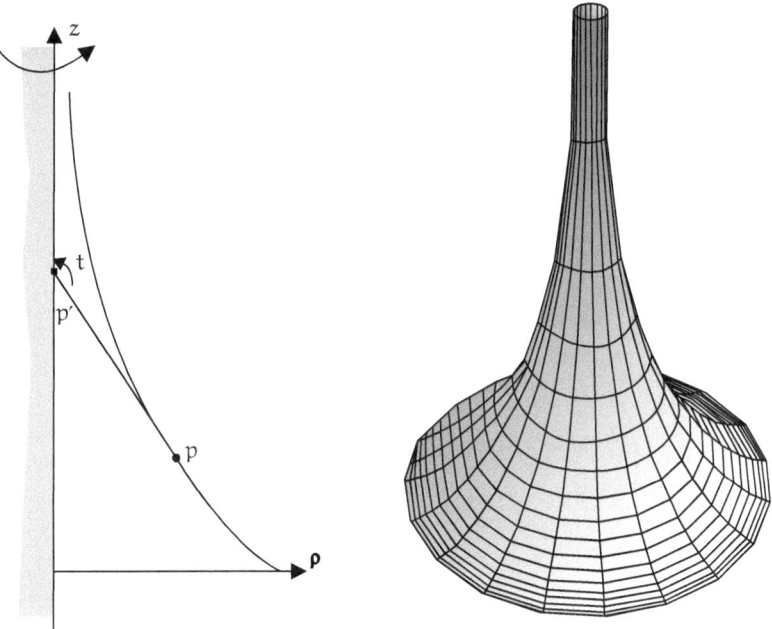

Figure 2.7

Proposition 2.2.1 *The coordinate change* $\Phi^{-1} \circ \Psi : \Phi^{-1}(W) \to \Psi^{-1}(W)$ *is a diffeomorphism.*

Proof It suffices to show that $\Phi^{-1} \circ \Psi$ is differentiable, because the same argument proves the differentiability of its inverse $\Psi^{-1} \circ \Phi$. We write

$$\Phi(u,v) = (x(u,v), y(u,v), z(u,v)),$$
$$\Psi(\widetilde{u}, \widetilde{v}) = (x(\widetilde{u}, \widetilde{v}), y(\widetilde{u}, \widetilde{v}), z(\widetilde{u}, \widetilde{v}));$$

and, given $(\widetilde{u}_0, \widetilde{v}_0) \in \Psi^{-1}(W)$, let us show that $\Phi^{-1} \circ \Psi$ is differentiable at $(\widetilde{u}_0, \widetilde{v}_0)$.

Putting $(u_0, v_0) = \Phi^{-1} \circ \Psi(\widetilde{u}_0, \widetilde{v}_0)$, some 2×2 submatrix of $J\Phi(u_0, v_0)$ has nonzero determinant, and we assume that it is the one formed by the first two rows (whose determinant is usually denoted by $\dfrac{\partial(x, y)}{\partial(u, v)}$). By the inverse mapping theorem, there exists some open neighborhood $D \subseteq \Phi^{-1}(W)$ of (u_0, v_0) such that the restriction of $f(u, v) = (x(u, v), y(u, v))$ to D is a diffeomorphism onto the image. It follows that $\Phi^{-1} \circ \Psi \big|_{\Psi^{-1} \circ \Phi(D)}$ is differentiable because it is a composition of differentiable mappings:

$$(\widetilde{u}, \widetilde{v}) \mapsto \Psi(\widetilde{u}, \widetilde{v}) = (x, y, z) \mapsto (x, y) \xrightarrow{f^{-1}} (u, v) = \Phi^{-1} \circ \Psi(\widetilde{u}, \widetilde{v}). \square$$

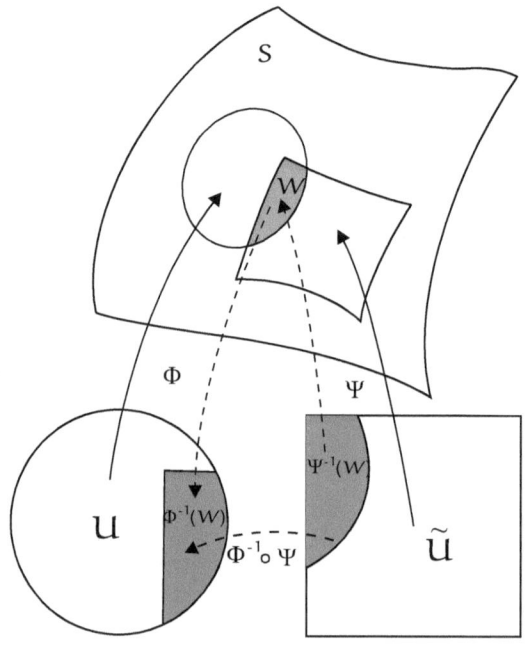

Figure 2.8

Let us point out that the foregoing proof establishes a more general fact than 2.2.1: *if α is a differentiable function defined on an open subset of $\mathbb{R}^n$ (a curve, for example)* *whose image is contained in a surface S, then, for any parameterization* Φ *of S,* $\Phi^{-1} \circ \alpha$ *is differentiable at all points where it is defined.*

In the previous section (example D) we noted that the graph of any differentiable function is a surface; the next proposition says that locally this example is as general as possible.

Proposition 2.2.2 *Any point p of a regular surface S has in S a neighborhood W of one of the following three forms:*

$$W = \{(x, y, h(x, y)): (x, y) \in R\},$$
$$W = \{(x, h(x, z), z): (x, z) \in R\},$$
$$W = \{(h(y, z), y, z): (y, z) \in R\}$$

— with, in all three cases, R is an open subset of $\mathbb{R}^2$ *and h is a differentiable function.*

Proof Let (U, Φ) be a parameterization in the neighborhood of p. One of the three determinants

$$\frac{\partial(x, y)}{\partial(u, v)}, \quad \frac{\partial(x, z)}{\partial(u, v)} \quad \text{and} \quad \frac{\partial(y, z)}{\partial(u, v)},$$

say the first one, is nonzero when computed at $\Phi^{-1}(p)$. The inverse mapping theorem then guarantees that there exists an open neighborhood $D \subseteq U$ of $\Phi^{-1}(p)$ restricted to which $f(u, v) = (x(u, v), y(u, v))$ is a diffeomorphism onto the image. Now $W = \Phi(D)$ is the sought neighborhood, since $R = f(D)$ is an open subset of $\mathbb{R}^2$, $h(x, y) = z \circ f^{-1}(x, y)$ is differentiable, and $W = \Phi \circ f^{-1}(R) = \{(x, y, h(x, y)): (x, y) \in R\}$. □

Example 2.2.3 Proposition 2.2.2 gives us a criterion to show that certain sets are not surfaces, which we illustrate with the cone

$$C = \{(x, y, z) \in \mathbb{R}^3 : z = \sqrt{x^2 + y^2}\}.$$

If C is a surface, there exists an open subset V of $\mathbb{R}^3$ containing the point $(0, 0, 0)$ such that $V \cap S$ is the graph of a differentiable function h. But h can only be a function of (x, y), because none of the projections of C on the other coordinate planes contains a neighborhood of $(0, 0)$. Thus $h(x, y) = \sqrt{x^2 + y^2}$ and this function is not differentiable at $(0, 0)$. Therefore, C is not a surface. [But the origin is the only problematic point: $C \backslash \{(0, 0, 0)\}$ is a surface]. □

A ready way to define a surface is by an equation of the form $f(x, y, z) = a$, where $f : V \subseteq \mathbb{R}^3 \to \mathbb{R}$ is a differentiable function. Not always, of course, does such an equation define a surface: we have to impose on f a certain degree of non-degeneracy, which we are going to describe.

A point $p \in V$ is called *regular* (for the function f) if the gradient vector

$$\nabla f = \left(\frac{\partial f}{\partial x}, \frac{\partial f}{\partial y}, \frac{\partial f}{\partial z} \right),$$

computed at p, is a nonzero vector; and $a \in \mathbb{R}$ is a *regular value* of f if $f^{-1}(\{a\})$ is non-empty and contains only regular points.

The condition $\dfrac{\partial f}{\partial z}(p) \neq 0$ guarantees that in a neighborhood U of $p \in f^{-1}(\{a\})$, f is strictly monotone along vertical segments, and therefore each of these segments intersects $f^{-1}(\{a\})$ at most one point. In fact, the proof of the next proposition consists *essentially* in showing that under these circumstances $f^{-1}(\{a\}) \cap U$ is the graph of a differentiable function of (x, y).

Proposition 2.2.4 *If a is a regular value of $f : V \to \mathbb{R}$ then $f^{-1}(\{a\})$ is a regular surface.*

Proof Assuming that $\dfrac{\partial f}{\partial z}(p) \neq 0$, we define

$$F(x, y, z) = (x, y, f(x, y, z)).$$

Since $\det JF(p) = \dfrac{\partial f}{\partial z}(p) \neq 0$, the function F is invertible in a neighborhood of p: so there exist open subsets $U, W \subseteq \mathbb{R}^3$ such that $p \in U \subseteq V$, and F sends U diffeomorphically onto W. Let us now note that the inverse $G : W \to U$ of $F|_U$ has the form $G(x, y, z) = (x, y, g(x, y, z))$ and that, for $(x, y, z) \in U$, all the following equalities are equivalent:

$$f(x, y, z) = a,$$
$$F(x, y, z) = (x, y, a),$$
$$(x, y, z) = G(x, y, a),$$
$$z = g(x, y, a).$$

The equivalence between the first and last subset of these equalities shows that $U \cap f^{-1}(\{a\})$ is the graph of the differentiable function $h(x, y) = g(x, y, a)$, whose domain is the open subset $R = \{(x, y) \in \mathbb{R}^2 : (x, y, a) \in W\}$ — and this concludes the proof that $f^{-1}(\{a\})$ is a surface. $\square$

The sets $f^{-1}(\{a\})$ are the *level sets* of f and, when a is a regular value, they are also called *level surfaces*. Taking for example

$$f(x, y, z) = \frac{x^2}{a^2} + \frac{y^2}{b^2} + \frac{z^2}{c^2},$$

we see that the ellipsoid

$$\frac{x^2}{a^2} + \frac{y^2}{b^2} + \frac{z^2}{c^2} = 1$$

is a regular surface, since $\nabla f(x, y, z)$ is nonzero for all $(x, y, z) \neq (0, 0, 0)$. In general, any non-degenerate quadric in $\mathbb{R}^3$ is a regular surface, since, for an appropriate orthonormal basis, it has equation $x + \varepsilon_2 y^2 + \varepsilon_3 z^2 = 0$ if it is a paraboloid, or $\varepsilon_1 x^2 + \varepsilon_2 y^2 + \varepsilon_3 z^2 = 1$, with $(\varepsilon_1, \varepsilon_2, \varepsilon_3) \neq (0, 0, 0)$, if it is a hyperboloid or an ellipsoid.

An important caveat is that *the condition that a be a regular value is by no means necessary for $f^{-1}(\{a\})$ to be a surface.* A simple example is given by $f(x,y,z) = x^2$: the set $f^{-1}(\{0\})$ is a surface, even though it consists only of singular points of f.

Note 2.2.5 A level surface is not necessarily connected, as shown by the two-leaf hyperboloid defined by the equation $z^2 - x^2 - y^2 = 1$. For the benefit of the reader unfamiliar with the concept, we give here the definition of connectedness and a brief discussion: a set $A \subseteq \mathbb{R}^n$ is called *connected* if it cannot be *split*, i.e., if **there are no** disjoint open subsets V and W of $\mathbb{R}^n$ such that $A \cap V \neq \varnothing \neq A \cap W$ and $A \subseteq V \cup W$. The hyperboloid above, for example, is not connected because it admits the splitting $V = \{(x,y,z) \in \mathbb{R}^3 : z > 0\}$ and $W = \{(x,y,z) \in \mathbb{R}^3 : z < 0\}$. The connected subsets of $\mathbb{R}$ are the intervals; the balls in $\mathbb{R}^n$ (disks in $\mathbb{R}^2$) are connected. Connectedness is a topological property, in the sense that the image of a connected set under a continuous function is still connected.

To put it suggestively, a surface is connected when it is made up of a single chunk. A useful connectivity criterion for surfaces (and for open subsets of $\mathbb{R}^n$) is the following: *S is connected if and only if, for every p and q on S, there exists a piecewise differentiable curve $\alpha : [a,b] \rightarrow S$ such that $\alpha(a) = p$ and $\alpha(b) = q$.* [**Proof:** if V and W split S, then there is no curve in S that joins $p \in S \cap V$ to $q \in S \cap W$, because the trace of a curve, being a continuous image of an interval, is connected. On the other hand, if S is connected and $p \in S$, consider the set $R = \{q \in S :$ there exists a curve in S from p to $q\}$. Given $q \in S$, let (D, Φ) be a parameterization in the neighborhood of q, where $D \subseteq \mathbb{R}^2$ is an open disk. Any $r \in \Phi(D)$ can be joined to q by a curve in S: the image under Φ of the line segment $[\Phi^{-1}(q), \Phi^{-1}(r)]$. Thus, if $q \in R$ (resp. $q \in S \backslash R$) then $\Phi(D) \subseteq R$ (resp. $\Phi(D) \subseteq S \backslash R$). Therefore R and $S \backslash R$ are open subsets of S and, since S is connected, one of them, necessarily $S \backslash R$, is empty. Therefore $S = R$, which proves what we wanted.] ☐

Now that we have a method for establishing that a set is a surface without using any parameterization, our next proposition states that if S is a surface, anything that appears to be a parameterization of S is indeed so.

Proposition 2.2.6 *Let S be a surface, U be an open subset of $\mathbb{R}^2$, and $\Phi : U \rightarrow S$ be a differentiable mapping. If Φ is injective and $J\Phi(u,v)$ has rank two for all (u,v) on U, then Φ is a parameterization of S.*

Proof One just has to check the continuity of the inverse $\Phi^{-1} : \Phi(U) \rightarrow U$. Given $(u_0, v_0) \in U$, the point $\Phi(u_0, v_0)$ has, by 2.2.2, an open neighborhood V in $\mathbb{R}^3$ such that $V \cap S$ is the graph of a function that we assume to depend on (x,y). Thus, $V \cap S = \{(x,y,h(x,y)) : (x,y) \in R\}$, where R is an open subset of $\mathbb{R}^2$; and, taking an open disk $D \subseteq U$ centered at (u_0, v_0) and such that $\Phi(D) \subseteq V$, the restriction of Φ to D can be written as $\Phi(u,v) = (x(u,v), y(u,v), h(x(u,v), y(u,v)))$. We then have

$$\Phi_u = \frac{\partial x}{\partial u}\left(1,0,\frac{\partial h}{\partial x}\right) + \frac{\partial y}{\partial u}\left(0,1,\frac{\partial h}{\partial y}\right),$$

$$\Phi_v = \frac{\partial x}{\partial v}\left(1,0,\frac{\partial h}{\partial x}\right) + \frac{\partial y}{\partial v}\left(0,1,\frac{\partial h}{\partial y}\right),$$

$$\Phi_u \times \Phi_v = \left\{\frac{\partial x}{\partial u}\frac{\partial y}{\partial v} - \frac{\partial x}{\partial v}\frac{\partial y}{\partial u}\right\}\left(1,0,\frac{\partial h}{\partial x}\right) \times \left(0,1,\frac{\partial h}{\partial y}\right)$$

$$= \frac{\partial(x,y)}{\partial(u,v)}\left(-\frac{\partial h}{\partial x},-\frac{\partial h}{\partial y},1\right)$$

– and from this, since $\Phi_u \times \Phi_v$ is nonzero, it follows that $\dfrac{\partial(x,y)}{\partial(u,v)} \neq 0$. We can therefore assume, shrinking D if necessary, that $\pi \circ \Phi\big|_D$ [where $\pi : \mathbb{R}^3 \to \mathbb{R}^2$ is the projection on the first two coordinates] is a diffeomorphism onto its image, which is then an open subset E of $\mathbb{R}^2$. Thus, $\Phi(D) = \{(x,y,h(x,y)) : (x,y) \in E\}$ is an open neighborhood of $\Phi(u_0,v_0)$ in S, and the restriction $\Phi^{-1}\big|_{\Phi(D)}$ is continuous, because it is given by the composite $\left(\pi \circ \Phi\big|_D\right)^{-1} \circ \pi$ of continuous functions. Thus Φ^{-1} is continuous on $\Phi(u_0,v_0)$. $\square$

Exercises

33. Show that any surface is locally a level surface. Given $p \in S$, there exist an open neighborhood V of p in $\mathbb{R}^3$ and a differentiable function $f : V \to \mathbb{R}$ such that $S \cap V = f^{-1}(\{0\})$ and 0 is a regular value of f.

34. Show that if two surfaces S_1 and S_2 intersect transversely at p then there exists an open neighborhood V of p (in $\mathbb{R}^3$) such that $S_1 \cap S_2 \cap V$ is the trace of a regular curve. (We say that S_1 and S_2 intersect transversely at p if $T_p S_1 \neq T_p S_2$.)

2.3 Differentiable Functions on Surfaces, Tangent Space

The results of the previous section prepared the setting to do Differential Calculus on surfaces; and we can now, in this section, explain what is a differentiable function in such a context. The derivatives of such functions are defined not on the surface but on its tangent spaces, a concept that we also introduce here.

Let S_1 and S_2 be two surfaces. A mapping $f : S_1 \to S_2$ is called *differentiable* if its expression in local coordinates is differentiable: more precisely, if there exist, for each $p \in S_1$, parameterizations (U,Φ) of S_1 and (V,Ψ) of S_2 in the neighborhoods of p and $f(p)$, respectively, such that $\Psi^{-1} \circ f \circ \Phi$ is differentiable. Similarly, a function $f : S_1 \to \mathbb{R}$ is called *differentiable* if every point of S_1 has a parametrized neighborhood (U,Φ) such that $f \circ \Phi$ is differentiable. A *diffeomorphism* is a differentiable bijection $f : S_1 \to S_2$ whose inverse is also differentiable.

Observations and Examples 2.3.1 **A.** Proposition 2.2.1 guarantees that if $f: S_1 \to S_2$ is differentiable, then, for all parameterizations Φ and Ψ, the mapping $\Psi^{-1} \circ f \circ \Phi$ is differentiable. This means that our definition does not depend on any choice of parameterization.

B. If $f: S_1 \to S_2$ is differentiable and (U, Φ) is a parameterization of S_1 then $f \circ \Phi: U \to \mathbb{R}^3$ is differentiable, because locally we can write $f \circ \Phi = \Psi \circ (\Psi^{-1} \circ f \circ \Phi)$, using appropriate local coordinates (V, Ψ) in S_2. But the converse is also true: if $f \circ \Phi$ is differentiable for any parameterization (U, Φ) of S_1 then $f: S_1 \to S_2$ is differentiable. This is a consequence of the observation we make following the proof of 2.2.1.

C. Let $f: \mathbb{R}^3 \to \mathbb{R}^3$ be a differentiable mapping such that $f(S_1) \subseteq S_2$. Then $f|_{S_1}: S_1 \to S_2$ is differentiable, and an analogous observation can be made for functions $g: \mathbb{R}^3 \to \mathbb{R}$. As examples, we have $g_1(p) = \langle p, \mathbf{v} \rangle$, where $\mathbf{v}$ is a unit vector of $\mathbb{R}^3$ [g_1 measures the "oriented height", in the direction of $\mathbf{v}$, of p relative to the origin $(0, 0, 0)$], and $g_2(p) = |p - p_0|^2$, which measures the square of the distance from p to a fixed point p_0. Both these functions, restricted to any surface S, are differentiable.

D. Let S be a surface of revolution around an axis r and let R_θ be the rotation of angle θ around r. The mapping $R_\theta|_S: S \to S$ is a diffeomorphism: its inverse is $R_{-\theta}|_S$. For a more interesting example, consider the torus of revolution $\mathbb{T}^2$ parametrized by $\Phi(u, v) = ((2 + \cos v) \cos u, (2 + \cos v) \sin u, \sin v)$. The restriction of Φ to any square of the form $]a - \pi, a + \pi[\times]b - \pi, b + \pi[$ is injective, and is therefore a parameterization of $\mathbb{T}^2$. Fixing $(u_0, v_0) \in \mathbb{R}^2$, we define a mapping $f: \mathbb{T}^2 \to \mathbb{T}^2$ by the condition:

- if $p = \Phi(u, v)$ then $f(p) = \Phi(u + u_0, v + v_0)$.

Let us show that f is differentiable: in fact, given $q \in \mathbb{T}$, $q = \Phi(u_1, v_1)$, the mappings

$$\widetilde{\Phi} = \Phi\big|_{]u_1 - \pi, u_1 + \pi[\times]v_1 - \pi, v_1 + \pi[}$$

$$\widetilde{\Psi} = \Phi\big|_{]u_1 + u_0 - \pi, u_1 + u_0 + \pi[\times]v_1 + v_0 - \pi, v_1 + v_0 + \pi[}$$

are parameterizations of $\mathbb{T}^2$ in the neighborhoods of q and $f(q)$, respectively; and $\widetilde{\Psi}^{-1} \circ f \circ \widetilde{\Phi}(u, v) = (u + u_0, v + v_0)$ is obviously differentiable, which proves that f is differentiable in a neighborhood of q. The same argument proves that the inverse is differentiable, and therefore f is a diffeomorphism. It follows in particular that, given any two points $p, q \in \mathbb{T}^2$, there exists some diffeomorphism $f: \mathbb{T}^2 \to \mathbb{T}^2$ such that $f(p) = q$. (See also Exercise 40 in this section.)   □

We now deal with the *tangent space* to a surface S at a point p, which we denote by $T_p S$. We define $T_p S$ to be the set of velocity vectors, at the point p, of the curves whose graph is in S:

$$T_p S = \{\alpha'(0) \mid \alpha:]-\varepsilon, \varepsilon[\to S \text{ is } C^\infty \text{ and } \alpha(0) = p\}.$$

Our next proposition shows that T_pS is a vector subspace of $\mathbb{R}^3$ of dimension two, which justifies calling $p + T_pS$ the *tangent plane* to S at p.

Proposition 2.3.2 *If* (U, Φ) *is a parameterization of* S *in the neighborhood of* p *then* $T_pS = D\Phi_{\Phi^{-1}(p)}(\mathbb{R}^2)$.

Proof Let us prove the inclusion $T_pS \subseteq D\Phi_{\Phi^{-1}(p)}(\mathbb{R}^2)$. Given $\alpha'(0) \in T_pS$, we can assume that $\alpha(]-\varepsilon, \varepsilon[) \subseteq \Phi(U)$. Then the curve $\beta = \Phi^{-1} \circ \alpha:]-\varepsilon, \varepsilon[\to U$ is differentiable; writing $\alpha = \Phi \circ \beta$, we obtain, by the chain rule, $\alpha'(0) = D\Phi_{\Phi^{-1}(p)}(\beta'(0))$.

Let us treat the opposite inclusion. Given a vector $\mathbf{w} \in \mathbb{R}^2$, let us take $\varepsilon > 0$ so that the line segment $\beta(t) = \Phi^{-1}(p) + t\mathbf{w}$, $|t| < \varepsilon$, is contained in U. Putting $\alpha = \Phi \circ \beta$, we have $D\Phi_{\Phi^{-1}(p)}(\mathbf{w}) = D\Phi_{\Phi^{-1}(p)}(\beta'(0)) = \alpha'(0) \in T_pS$. $\square$

In practice, what we did was to write the curve α in local coordinates: if $\alpha(t) = \Phi(u(t), v(t))$ then α is differentiable if and only if so are both functions $u(t)$ and $v(t)$; and the chain rule provides the equality $\alpha'(t) = u'(t)\Phi_u + v'(t)\Phi_v$, which shows that at each point of $\Phi(U)$ the tangent space is generated by the vectors Φ_u and Φ_v.

Example 2.3.3 The tangent space to the level surface $S_a = f^{-1}(\{a\})$ at point p is the orthogonal complement of the line generated by $\nabla f(p)$. In fact, if $\alpha:]-\varepsilon, \varepsilon[\to S_a$ satisfies $\alpha(0) = p$ then $f \circ \alpha(t) = a$ for all $t \in]-\varepsilon, \varepsilon[$, so that $\langle \nabla f(p), \alpha'(0) \rangle = (f \circ \alpha)'(0) = 0$ — which shows that $\nabla f(p)$ is orthogonal to T_pS_a. $\square$

Let $f: S_1 \to S_2$ be a differentiable mapping at $p \in S_1$. The *derivative* of f at p is the mapping $Df_p: T_pS_1 \to T_{f(p)}S_2$ defined as follows: if $\alpha'(0) \in T_pS_1$ then $Df_p(\alpha'(0)) = (f \circ \alpha)'(0)$. That is, Df_p sends the velocity vector at p of a given curve to the velocity vector at $f(p)$ of the transform of that curve by f. Of course, the same vector represents the velocity vector at p of many different curves, but we will see below that Df_p is well-defined. Let us take local coordinates $\Phi(u, v)$ and $\Psi(\widetilde{u}, \widetilde{v})$ at p and $f(p)$, and let us put $\widetilde{f} = \Psi^{-1} \circ f \circ \Phi$: with this notation we have the following result.

Proposition 2.3.4 $Df_p: T_pS_1 \to T_{f(p)}S_2$ *is a linear mapping whose matrix with respect to the bases* (Φ_u, Φ_v) *of* T_pS_1 *and* $(\Psi_{\widetilde{u}}, \Psi_{\widetilde{v}})$ *of* $T_{f(p)}S_2$ *is the Jacobian of* $\widetilde{f}$ *on* $\Phi^{-1}(p)$.

Proof Writing $\alpha(t) = \Phi(u(t), v(t))$, the curve $\beta = f \circ \alpha$ is given by $\beta(t) = \Psi(\widetilde{u}(t), \widetilde{v}(t))$, where $(\widetilde{u}(t), \widetilde{v}(t)) = \widetilde{f}(u(t), v(t))$. Differentiating the last equality, we obtain

$$\begin{pmatrix} \widetilde{u}'(0) \\ \widetilde{v}'(0) \end{pmatrix} = J\widetilde{f}_{(u(0), v(0))} \begin{pmatrix} u'(0) \\ v'(0) \end{pmatrix} = J\widetilde{f}_{\Phi^{-1}(p)} \begin{pmatrix} u'(0) \\ v'(0) \end{pmatrix} \qquad (*)$$

The equality $Df_p(\alpha'(0)) = (f \circ \alpha)'(0)$, which defines Df_p, can be rewritten as

$$Df_p(u'(0)\Phi_u + v'(0)\Phi_v) = \widetilde{u}'(0)\Psi_{\widetilde{u}} + \widetilde{v}'(0)\Psi_{\widetilde{v}}. \qquad (**)$$

From (*) and (**) it follows that $Df_p(\alpha'(0))$ is well-defined, not depending on α but only on $\alpha'(0)$; and that furthermore Df_p is linear and has matrix $J\widetilde{f}_{\Phi^{-1}(p)}$ with respect to the given bases. $\square$

We end this section with two results which are the transpositions of the inverse mapping theorem and the chain rule to the context of surfaces. The proof of the first one is left as an (easy) exercise.

Proposition 2.3.5 *Let $f:S_1 \to S_2$ be a differentiable mapping and $p \in S_1$ such that $Df_p:T_pS_1 \to T_{f(p)}S_2$ is a linear isomorphism. Then there exists an open neighborhood U of p in S_1 and an open subset V of S_2 such that $f|_U:U \to V$ is a diffeomorphism.*

Proposition 2.3.6 *If $f:S_1 \to S_2$ and $g:S_2 \to S_3$ are differentiable then $g \circ f$ is differentiable and, for all $p \in S_1$, we have $D(g \circ f)_p = Dg_{f(p)} \circ Df_p$.*

Proof The verification that $g \circ f$ is differentiable is left to the reader. As for the second statement, let us take $\mathbf{u} \in T_pS_1$ and a curve α such that $\alpha'(0) = \mathbf{u}$, and let us put $\beta = f \circ \alpha$, $\gamma = g \circ f \circ \alpha$, $\mathbf{v} = \beta'(0)$, $\mathbf{w} = \gamma'(0)$. We then have $Df_p(\mathbf{u}) = \mathbf{v}$ (because $\beta = f \circ \alpha$), $Dg_{f(p)}(\mathbf{v}) = \mathbf{w}$ (because $\gamma = g \circ \beta$), $D(g \circ f)_p(\mathbf{u}) = \mathbf{w}$ (because $\gamma = (g \circ f) \circ \alpha$), and therefore $D(g \circ f)_p(\mathbf{u}) = (Dg_{f(p)} \circ Df_p)(\mathbf{u})$. $\square$

Exercises

35. Consider the function $f:\mathbb{R}^3 \to \mathbb{R}$ given by $f(x, y, z) = 2x^2 - y^2 - z^2$. Determine the equations of the planes which are tangent to the surface $f^{-1}(\{1\})$ and parallel to the plane given by the equation $2\sqrt{2}x + y + z = 0$.

36. (a) Show that the paraboloid $z = x^2 + y^2$ is diffeomorphic to the plane.
(b) Show that the sphere S^2 and the ellipsoid

$$\frac{x^2}{a^2} + \frac{y^2}{b^2} + \frac{z^2}{c^2} = 1$$

are diffeomorphic.

37. Let V be a neighborhood of the origin in $\mathbb{R}^2$ and let $\Phi:V \to \mathbb{R}^3$ given by $\Phi(u, v) = f(u) + g(v)$ be a parameterization of a regular surface S. Show that the tangent planes to S along the curve $\Phi(u, 0)$ are all parallel to the same line.

38. A differentiable mapping $f:S_1 \to S_2$ is called a *local diffeomorphism* if each point $p \in S_1$ has a neighborhood W in S_1 such that $f|_W:W \to f(W)$ is a diffeomorphism. Show that if f is a local diffeomorphism then Df_p is a linear isomorphism for all $p \in S_1$.

39. Show that if all normal lines to a connected surface pass through the same point, then that surface is contained in a sphere.

40. (a) Given $0 < r_1 < r_2$ and φ_0, consider a function $g: \mathbb{R} \to \mathbb{R}$ that is C^∞, monotone and such that $g(x) = \varphi_0$ for $x \leq r_1$, and $g(x) = 0$ for $x \geq r_2$ (see ex. 17). Let $h: \mathbb{R}^2 \to \mathbb{R}^2$ be the mapping that sends the point with polar coordinates (ρ, φ) to the point with coordinates $(\rho, \varphi + g(\rho))$. Show that h is a C^∞ diffeomorphism. How does h behave in $\{p \in \mathbb{R}^2 : |p| \leq r_1\}$ and $\{p \in \mathbb{R}^2 : |p| \geq r_2\}$?

(b) Let (U, Φ) be a parameterization of S such that U contains the closed disk with radius r_2 centered at the origin. Show that $\Phi \circ h \circ \Phi^{-1} : \Phi(U) \to \Phi(U)$ extends to a diffeomorphism of S.

(c) Show that if S is connected then for any two points of S there exists a diffeomorphism of S that sends one of these points to the other one.

41. Define explicitly a differentiable mapping $\mathbb{T}^2 \to \mathbf{S}^2$ that is surjective.

42. Let $S = \{(x, y, z) \in \mathbb{R}^3 : x \neq 0, z = xf(y/x)\}$, where $f: \mathbb{R} \to \mathbb{R}$ is a C^∞ function. Show that S is a regular surface, and that all tangent planes to S pass through the origin.

43. Consider the mapping

$$\Phi(u, v) = \left(\frac{a(uv + 1)}{u + v}, \frac{b(u - v)}{u + v}, \frac{c(uv - 1)}{u + v} \right),$$

where $a, b, c \neq 0$ and $u + v \neq 0$. Find an equation that implicitly defines the image of Φ, and conclude that it is a surface. Compute the normal vector and the tangent plane at each point.

2.4 Orientability

A surface is orientable when it is possible to distinguish its top from the bottom, so that an observer placed on it can distinguish left from right. This approach works when the observer is three-dimensional and has an idea of the position of the surface in space; it is more intricate to explain how two-dimensional beings whose universe is the surface will know whether it is orientable or not.

Given two linearly independent vectors $\mathbf{v}$ and $\mathbf{w}$ in $\mathbb{R}^3$, the trihedron $(\mathbf{v}, \mathbf{w}, N)$, where

$$N = \frac{1}{|\mathbf{v} \times \mathbf{w}|} (\mathbf{v} \times \mathbf{w}),$$

forms a positively oriented basis of $\mathbb{R}^3$, meaning that the matrix whose columns are (in the same order) these vectors has positive determinant. The unit vector N is orthogonal to the plane Π generated by $\mathbf{v}$ and $\mathbf{w}$, introducing an orientation in Π as follows: a basis $(\mathbf{v}_1, \mathbf{w}_1)$ of Π is called *positively oriented* if the triplet $(\mathbf{v}_1, \mathbf{w}_1, N)$ is a positively oriented basis of $\mathbb{R}^3$; in other words, if

$$N = \frac{1}{|\mathbf{v}_1 \times \mathbf{w}_1|} (\mathbf{v}_1 \times \mathbf{w}_1).$$

We thus recognize that Π has exactly two orientations, one induced by N and the other one by $-N$.

We say that the surface S is *orientable* if it is possible to choose, for each $p \in S$, an orientation on T_pS that varies continuously with p — more precisely, if there exists a continuous function $N : S \to \mathbf{S}^2$ such that, for each p, $N(p)$ is orthogonal to T_pS. We call such a *field of normal vectors* N an *orientation* of S.

For example, *level surfaces are orientable*, because the vector field

$$N(p) = \frac{1}{|\nabla f(p)|} \nabla f(p)$$

is an orientation of $f^{-1}(\{a\})$ (see example 2.3.3).

Surfaces that admit a global parameterization $\Phi(u, v)$ are also orientable, because on them we can define

$$N(p) = \frac{1}{|\Phi_u \times \Phi_v|} \Phi_u \times \Phi_v \Big|_{\Phi^{-1}(p)} \, .$$

More generally, each parameterization (U, Φ) of S induces, by the preceding formula, an orientation in the open $\Phi(U) \subseteq S$; the problem is to "glue" together the various local orientations to obtain an orientation of the whole surface.

Proposition 2.4.1 *Any orientable connected surface has exactly two distinct orientations.*

Proof Given two orientations N and $\widetilde{N}$ of S, we have, for each p in S, $N(p) = \widetilde{N}(p)$ or $N(p)) = -\widetilde{N}(p)$, since these two unit vectors are orthogonal to the same plane T_pS. Thus, the function $\sigma : S \to \mathbb{R}$ defined by $\sigma(p) = \langle N(p), \widetilde{N}(p) \rangle$ is continuous and only takes the values 1 or -1. Since S is connected, its image $\sigma(S) \subseteq \{-1, 1\}$ is also connected, and is therefore reduced to only one element. Hence, we have $N(p) = \widetilde{N}(p)$ or $N(p) = -\widetilde{N}(p)$ for all $p \in S$. $\qquad\square$

Example 2.4.2 The Möbius strip $\mathbb{M}$ is the surface obtained by gluing the two ends of a paper strip so that their opposite vertices coincide. We will now see that this surface is non-orientable:

To obtain a parameterization of $\mathbb{M}$, we fix a circumference and consider a line segment that intersects, at its midpoint, orthogonally the circumference. We let the line segment travel around the whole circumference, letting it rotate around its midpoint and return to the starting point with reversed endpoints. We put

$$\Phi(\theta, t) = \left(\left(2 - t \sin \frac{\theta}{2}\right) \cos \theta, \left(2 - t \sin \frac{\theta}{2}\right) \sin \theta, t \cos \frac{\theta}{2} \right),$$

where $(\theta, t) \in \mathbb{R} \times\,]{-1}, 1[$. We note that every restriction of θ to some interval of length 2π yields a different parameterization of $\mathbb{M}$. The curves $\theta = c^{\underline{\text{te}}}$ represent the various positions of the generating line segment of $\mathbb{M}$ along the circumference $t = 0$. We also note that $\Phi(\theta + 2\pi, t) = \Phi(\theta, -t)$. To simplify the calculations, we introduce the moving orthonormal trihedron

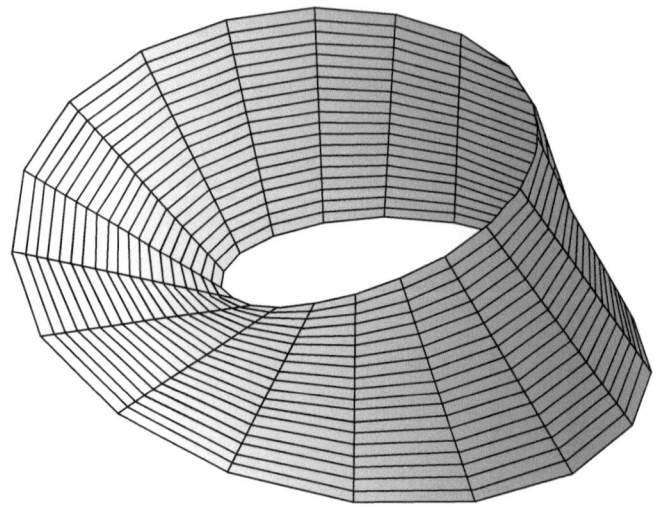

Figure 2.9

given by the three vectors

$$\mathbf{e_1}(\theta) = (\cos\theta, \sin\theta, 0)$$
$$\mathbf{e_2}(\theta) = (-\sin\theta, \cos\theta, 0)$$
$$\mathbf{e_3}(\theta) = (0, 0, 1),$$

which satisfies the relations $\mathbf{e_1}'(\theta) = \mathbf{e_2}(\theta)$, $\mathbf{e_2}'(\theta) = -\mathbf{e_1}(\theta)$, $\mathbf{e_1}(\theta) \times \mathbf{e_2}(\theta) = \mathbf{e_3}(\theta)$, $\mathbf{e_2}(\theta) \times \mathbf{e_3}(\theta) = \mathbf{e_1}(\theta)$, $\mathbf{e_3}(\theta) \times \mathbf{e_1}(\theta) = \mathbf{e_2}(\theta)$. Writing

$$\Phi(\theta, t) = \left(2 - t\sin\frac{\theta}{2}\right)\mathbf{e_1}(\theta) + t\cos\frac{\theta}{2}\,\mathbf{e_3}(\theta),$$

we easily conclude that

$$\Phi_\theta \times \Phi_t = \left(2 - t\sin\frac{\theta}{2}\right)\left[\cos\frac{\theta}{2}\,\mathbf{e_1}(\theta) + \sin\frac{\theta}{2}\,\mathbf{e_3}(\theta)\right] + \frac{t}{2}\,\mathbf{e_2}(\theta).$$

Let us now assume $\mathbb{M}$ orientable with orientation given by $N\colon\mathbb{M} \to \mathbf{S}^2$. The parameterization $\Phi|_{]0,2\pi[\times]-1,1[}$ induces the orientation $\widetilde{N} = \dfrac{1}{|\Phi_\theta \times \Phi_t|}\,\Phi_\theta \times \Phi_t$ on $W = \mathbb{M}\setminus\{(2, 0, t)\colon t \in\ ]-1, 1[\ \}$; and, by 2.4.1, we have $\widetilde{N} = N|_W$ or $\widetilde{N} = -N|_W$. We shall now see that $\widetilde{N}$ has no continuous extension to $\mathbb{M}$, which proves the non-existence of N.

In fact, if there was such an extension, then there would exist $\displaystyle\lim_{p \to (2,0,0)} \widetilde{N}(p)$, but

$$\lim_{\theta \to 0^+} \widetilde{N} \circ \Phi(\theta, 0) = \lim_{\theta \to 0^+} \left[\cos \frac{\theta}{2} \mathbf{e}_1(\theta) + \sin \frac{\theta}{2} \mathbf{e}_2(\theta) \right] = (1, 0, 0) \neq$$

$$\lim_{\theta \to 2\pi^-} \widetilde{N} \circ \Phi(\theta, 0) = \lim_{\theta \to 2\pi^-} \left[\cos \frac{\theta}{2} \mathbf{e}_1(\theta) + \sin \frac{\theta}{2} \mathbf{e}_2(\theta) \right] = (-1, 0, 0).$$

To sum up, what we have done shows that if a normal vector makes one complete turn around $\mathbb{M}$, then it returns to the starting position pointing in the opposite direction. It is thus possible to go "from up to down" by walking on the Möbius strip, which justifies the statement that it has only one side. $\square$

Our definition of orientability has the disadvantage of obscuring that this concept is invariant under diffeomorphisms. For example, we saw that a Möbius strip, corresponding to a certain $\mathbb{M}$ of $\mathbb{R}^3$, is non-orientable; but can we from this draw the same conclusion for all Möbius strips (i.e., for all surfaces that are diffeomorphic to $\mathbb{M}$)? There is another orientability criterion that allows one to more easily justify the (affirmative) answer to this question.

An *oriented atlas* of a surface S is a collection $(U_\alpha, \Phi_\alpha)_{\alpha \in \mathcal{I}}$ of parameterizations of S such that:

(i) the parameterizations cover S, i.e., $S = \bigcup_{\alpha \in \mathcal{I}} \Phi_\alpha(U_\alpha)$;

(ii) for all $\alpha, \beta \in \mathcal{I}$, the Jacobian of $\Phi_\beta^{-1} \circ \Phi_\alpha$ has positive determinant at all points where it is defined.

Before we move on, consider two parameterizations $\Phi(u, v)$ and $\Psi(\widetilde{u}, \widetilde{v})$ that intersect on an open W of S. We thus have

$$\Phi(u, v) = \Psi(\widetilde{u}, \widetilde{v}) \tag{*}$$

for $(u, v) \in \Phi^{-1}(W)$ and $(\widetilde{u}, \widetilde{v}) = \Psi^{-1} \circ \Phi(u, v)$. By differentiation of (*) we obtain the two equalities

$$\Phi_u = \frac{\partial \widetilde{u}}{\partial u} \Psi_{\widetilde{u}} + \frac{\partial \widetilde{v}}{\partial u} \Psi_{\widetilde{v}}, \qquad \Phi_v = \frac{\partial \widetilde{u}}{\partial v} \Psi_{\widetilde{u}} + \frac{\partial \widetilde{v}}{\partial v} \Psi_{\widetilde{v}},$$

from which

$$\Phi_u \times \Phi_v = \left(\frac{\partial \widetilde{u}}{\partial u} \frac{\partial \widetilde{v}}{\partial v} - \frac{\partial \widetilde{u}}{\partial v} \frac{\partial \widetilde{v}}{\partial u} \right) \Psi_{\widetilde{u}} \times \Psi_{\widetilde{v}} = (\det J(\Psi^{-1} \circ \Phi)_{(u,v)}) \Psi_{\widetilde{u}} \times \Psi_{\widetilde{v}}.$$

This latter formula allows us to conclude that the two conditions

a) $\dfrac{1}{|\Phi_u \times \Phi_v|} \Phi_u \times \Phi_v = \dfrac{1}{|\Psi_{\widetilde{u}} \times \Psi_{\widetilde{v}}|} \Psi_{\widetilde{u}} \times \Psi_{\widetilde{v}},$

b) $\det J(\Psi^{-1} \circ \Phi)_{(u,v)} > 0,$ $(**)$

are equivalent. We can now state the alternative orientability criterion.

Proposition 2.4.3 *S is orientable if and only if it has an orientable atlas.*

Proof Suppose that N is an orientation of S. Given $p_\alpha \in S$, let (U, Φ), with U connected, be a parameterization in the neighborhood of p_α. Then, by 2.4.1, we

have $\dfrac{1}{|\Phi_u \times \Phi_v|} \Phi_u \times \Phi_v = N\big|_{\Phi(U)}$ or $\dfrac{1}{|\Phi_u \times \Phi_v|} \Phi_u \times \Phi_v = -N\big|_{\Phi(U)}$. In the first
hypothesis, we take $(U_\alpha, \Phi_\alpha) = (U, \Phi)$; in the second one, we take $U_\alpha = \{(u, v) \in \mathbb{R}^2 : (u, -v) \in U\}$ and $\Phi_\alpha(u, v) = \Phi(u, -v)$; in each case Φ_α induces on $\Phi_\alpha(U_\alpha)$ the same orientation as N. The atlas $(U_\alpha, \Phi_\alpha)_{\alpha \in \mathcal{I}}$ obtained in this way covers S and, by the equivalence of conditions a) and b) above, is oriented.

Given now an oriented atlas $(U_\alpha, \Phi_\alpha)_{\alpha \in \mathcal{I}}$, we define an orientation $N : S \to \mathbf{S}^2$ by requiring that its restriction to each open subset $\Phi_\alpha(U_\alpha)$ is the orientation induced by Φ_α. By (**), there is no ambiguity in the definition of N; and, since $N\big|_{\Phi_\alpha(U_\alpha)}$ is continuous and $(\Phi_\alpha(U_\alpha))_{\alpha \in \mathcal{I}}$ is a covering of S by open sets, N is continuous. $\qquad \square$

It follows from this proof that any orientation $N : S \to \mathbf{S}^2$ is a differentiable mapping, because N is expressed as a differentiable function of the local parameters.

Let now $f : S_1 \to S_2$ be a diffeomorphism between surfaces. If S_1 is oriented then f induces an orientation on S_2 as follows: given an oriented atlas $(U_\alpha, \Phi_\alpha)_{\alpha \in \mathcal{I}}$ of S_1 (which is compatible with the orientation of S_1), then $\Psi_\alpha = f \circ \Phi_\alpha$, $(U_\alpha, \Psi_\alpha)_{\alpha \in \mathcal{I}}$ is an oriented atlas of S_2 — since, by $\Psi_\beta^{-1} \circ \Psi_\alpha = \Phi_\alpha^{-1} \circ \Phi_\alpha$, the coordinate changes in either atlas are precisely the same. We call the orientation defined by the atlas $(U_\alpha, \Psi_\alpha)_{\alpha \in \mathcal{I}}$ on S_2 the *orientation induced by the diffeomorphism f* (from the given orientation of S_1). In particular, *any two diffeomorphic surfaces are either both orientable or both non-orientable*.

In the case of a diffeomorphism $f : S \to S$ of an orientable *connected* surface onto itself, we say that f *preserves orientation* if the orientation induced by f on S from a given orientation of S is equal to the original one; if it is the opposite one, then we say that f *reverses orientation*.

Proposition 2.4.4 *Let $f : S \to S$ be a diffeomorphism of a connected orientable surface. Then:*

(i) Whether or not f preserves orientation only depends on f, not on the orientation of S.

(ii) For each oriented atlas $\mathcal{A}$ of $\mathbb{S}$, one and only one of the following statements holds:

$$\det J(\Psi^{-1} \circ f \circ \Phi) > 0 \quad \text{for any } (U, \Phi), (V, \psi) \in \mathcal{A};$$

or

$$\det J(\Psi^{-1} \circ f \circ \Phi) < 0 \quad \text{for any } (U, \Phi), (v, \psi) \in \mathcal{A}.$$

In the first case f preserves orientation, while in the second case it inverts it.

Proof Let N and $-N$ be the two orientations of S. We define two oriented atlases $\mathcal{A}_1$ and $\mathcal{A}_2$ of S as follows: $\mathcal{A}_1$ (resp. $\mathcal{A}_2$) includes all parameterizations (U, Φ) of S such that Φ induces in $\Phi(U)$ the orientation $N\big|_{\Phi(U)}$ (resp. $-N\big|_{\Phi(U)}$). Thus, any oriented atlas is included either in $\mathcal{A}_1$ or in $\mathcal{A}_2$, so that we can assume $\mathcal{A} = \mathcal{A}_1$. Furthermore, $\det J(\Psi^{-1} \circ \Phi) < 0$ whenever $(U, \Phi) \in \mathcal{A}_1$ and $(V, \Psi) \in \mathcal{A}_2$.

The set $f(\mathcal{A}_1)$ of the parameterizations $(U, f \circ \Phi)$ such that $(U, \Phi) \in \mathcal{A}_1$ is an oriented atlas of S, so that it defines on S one of the orientations N or

$-N$. In the first hypothesis, $f(\mathcal{A}_1) \subseteq \mathcal{A}_1$ and therefore $\det J(\Psi^{-1} \circ f \circ \Phi) > 0$ whenever $(U, \Phi), (V, \Psi) \in \mathcal{A}_1$; in the second hypothesis, $f(\mathcal{A}_1) \subseteq \mathcal{A}_2$ and thence $\det J(\Psi^{-1} \circ f \circ \Phi) < 0$ for $(U, \Phi), (V, \Psi) \in \mathcal{A}_1$. This proves (ii).

To prove (i), we take (U, Φ) in $\mathcal{A}_1$ and set $V = \{(u, v) \in \mathbb{R}^2 : (u, -v) \in U\}$, $\Psi(u, v) = \Phi(u, -v)$. Then (V, Ψ) belongs to $\mathcal{A}_2$, since the Jacobian of $\Psi^{-1} \circ \Phi(u, v) = (u, -v)$ is negative; and, for the same reason, the parameterizations $(U, f \circ \Phi)$ and $(V, f \circ \Psi)$ cannot belong both to $\mathcal{A}_1$ or both to $\mathcal{A}_2$. Therefore $f(\mathcal{A}_1)$ and $f(\mathcal{A}_2)$ define distinct orientations, which proves (i).   □

Example 2.4.5 Consider the diffeomorphism $f : \mathbf{S}^2 \to \mathbf{S}^2$ given by $f(x, y, z) = (-x, y, z)$. The parameterization

$$\Phi(u, v) = \left(u, v, \sqrt{1 - (u^2 + v^2)}\right)$$

belongs to some oriented atlas of $\mathbf{S}^2$, since its domain is connected; and, since the Jacobian of $\Phi^{-1} \circ f \circ \Phi(u, v) = (-u, v)$ is negative, we conclude that f reverses orientation.

Exercises

44. Find out whether the antipodal mapping $h : \mathbf{S}^2 \to \mathbf{S}^2$ given by $h(x, y, z) = (-x, -y, -z)$ preserves orientation or not.

45. Consider the Möbius strip $\mathbb{M}$ parametrized by $\Phi(\theta, t) = ((2 - t \sin \frac{\theta}{2}) \cos \theta, (2 - t \sin \frac{\theta}{2}) \sin \theta, t \cos \frac{\theta}{2})$. Show that if the circumference $t = 0$ is removed from $\mathbb{M}$, then the resulting surface is still connected but is then orientable.

46. Let $f : S_1 \to S_2$ be a local diffeomorphism. Check whether the following statements are true:

    (a) if S_2 is orientable then S_1 is orientable;

    (b) if S_1 is orientable and f is surjective then S_2 is orientable.

47. Let S be a connected orientable surface and let $f : S \to S$ be a diffeomorphism. Is it true that $f \circ f$ preserves orientation?

2.5 Areas, Lengths, and Angles: The First Fundamental Form

Any surface $S \subseteq \mathbb{R}^3$ inherits from the ambient space a notion of size that can be used to measure the area of regions and the length of curves in S. This metric structure, which we now introduce, enriches the concept of surface and enables a finer classification than that by diffeomorphisms.

The *first fundamental form* of S at $p \in S$ is the quadratic form $I_p : T_p S \to \mathbb{R}^+$ defined by $I_p(\mathbf{v}) = \langle \mathbf{v}, \mathbf{v} \rangle_p$, where $\langle \cdot, \cdot \rangle_p$ is the restriction to $T_p S$ of the usual inner product on $\mathbb{R}^3$.

If $\Phi(u, v)$ is a parameterization of S and $\alpha(t) = \Phi(u(t), v(t))$ is a differentiable curve, we have

$$I_{\alpha(t)}(\alpha'(t)) = \langle u'(t)\Phi_u + v'(t)\Phi_v, u'(t)\Phi_u + v'(t)\Phi_v \rangle_{\alpha(t)}$$

$$= I_{\alpha(t)}(\Phi_u)u'(t)^2 + 2\langle \Phi_u, \Phi_v \rangle_{\alpha(t)}u'(t)v'(t) + I_{\alpha(t)}(\Phi_v)v'(t)^2$$

$$= E\,u'(t)^2 + 2F\,u'(t)v'(t) + G\,v'(t)^2,$$

where E, F and G are the so-called *coefficients of the first fundamental form* for the parameterization $\Phi(u,v)$, defined by $E(u,v) = I_{\Phi(u,v)}(\Phi_u)$, $F(u,v) = \langle \Phi_u, \Phi_v \rangle_{\Phi(u,v)}$, $G(u,v) = I_{\Phi(u,v)}(\Phi_v)$. The above calculations show that the length of $\alpha(t)$, $t \in [a,b]$, is given by

$$l(\alpha) = \int_a^b \sqrt{E\,u'(t)^2 + 2F\,u'(t)v'(t) + G\,v'(t)^2}\,dt.$$

Therefore it is possible to compute the length of any curve in S knowing only the first fundamental form (and hence its coefficients in any parameterization) without further reference to the ambient space.

We point out that the matrix of the quadratic form $L_{\Phi(u,v)}$ relative to the basis (Φ_u, Φ_v) of $T_{\Phi(u,v)}S$ is $M = \begin{bmatrix} E & F \\ F & G \end{bmatrix}$: so if $\mathbf{v} = a\Phi_u + b\Phi_v$ and $\mathbf{w} = c\Phi_u + d\Phi_v$, the inner product of $\mathbf{v}$ and $\mathbf{w}$ is given by the matrix product $[a, b]\,M\begin{bmatrix} c \\ d \end{bmatrix} = E\,ac + F(ad + bc) + G\,bd$.

Examples 2.5.1 If $\mathbf{v}$ and $\mathbf{w}$ are orthonormal vectors and $p \in \mathbb{R}^3$ then the parameterization $\Psi(u,v) = p + u\mathbf{v} + v\mathbf{w}$ of the plane parallel to $\mathbf{v}$ and $\mathbf{w}$ which passes through p has coefficients $E = 1$, $F = 0$, $G = 1$. On the other hand, the coefficients of the parameterization $\Phi(u,v) = ((2+\cos v)\cos u, (2+\cos v)\sin u, \sin v)$ of $\mathbb{T}^2$ are $E = 1$, $F = 0$ and $G = (2 + \cos v)^2$. $\qquad \square$

The first fundamental form also allows one to compute the angle between two nonzero vectors $\mathbf{v}, \mathbf{w} \in T_p S$: this (non-oriented) angle is the only $\theta \in [0, \pi]$ such that

$$\cos\theta = \frac{1}{\sqrt{I_p(\mathbf{v})I_p(\mathbf{w})}}\langle \mathbf{v}, \mathbf{w} \rangle_p \,;$$

in local coordinates, writing $\mathbf{v} = a\Phi_u + b\Phi_v$ and $\mathbf{w} = c\Phi_u + d\Phi_v$, we have

$$\cos\theta = \frac{E\,ac + F(ad + bc) + G\,bd}{\sqrt{(E\,a^2 + 2F\,ab + G\,b^2)(E\,c^2 + 2F\,cd + G\,d^2)}}. \qquad (*)$$

If the surface S is oriented and $\Phi(u,v)$ is compatible with the orientation, we can assign a sign to the angles: the oriented angle $\angle(\mathbf{v}, \mathbf{w})$ (from $\mathbf{v}$ to $\mathbf{w}$) is the only $\theta \in\,]-\pi, \pi]$ such that equality $(*)$ is satisfied and such that it is negative when $ad - bc < 0$, non-negative when $ad - bc \geq 0$. [Since the oriented angles are defined up to integer multiples of 2π, the representatives of the angle $\angle(\mathbf{v}, \mathbf{w})$ are thus all numbers of the form $\theta + 2k\pi$, $k \in \mathbb{Z}$.]

The angle between two curves $\alpha(t)$ and $\beta(s)$ in S at an intersection point $\alpha(t_0) = \beta(s_0)$ is, by definition, the angle between the velocity vectors $\alpha'(t_0)$ and

$\beta'(s_0)$. For instance, it follows from the formulas deduced above that the angle between the coordinate curves of the parameterization $\Phi(u,v)$ is $\arccos\left(F/\sqrt{EG}\right) \in]0, \pi[$. When $F = 0$ the coordinate curves intersect each other orthogonally; in this case we say that $\Phi(u,v)$ is an *orthogonal parameterization*. The above examples 2.5.1 are orthogonal parameterizations; in fact, as we showed in Section 3.3, any surface admits orthogonal parameterizations.

We finally deal with the measurement of areas. If $\Delta \subseteq S$ is a region contained in a single coordinate system (U, Φ), its area is defined by the integral

$$\iint_{\Phi^{-1}(\Delta)} |\Phi_u \times \Phi_v|\, du\, dv$$

— if such an integral exists (and it certainly exists when Δ is open or closed and the closure of $\Phi^{-1}(\Delta)$ is a compact set contained in U). If Δ is not contained in a single parametrized neighborhood, we can write it as a disjoint, finite or countable union of regions Δ_n whose areas we can compute, and add up the results.

In Section 2.4 we deduced the formula $\Phi_u \times \Phi_v = (\det J(\psi^{-1} \circ \Phi)_{(u,v)})\Psi_{\widetilde{u}} \times \Psi_{\widetilde{v}}$. Therefore, if we have $\Delta \subseteq \Phi(U) \cap \Psi(U)$, the equality

$$\iint_{\Phi^{-1}(\Delta)} |\Phi_u \times \Phi_v|\, du\, dv = \iint_{\Psi^{-1}(\Delta)} |\Psi_{\widetilde{u}} \times \Psi_{\widetilde{v}}|\, d\widetilde{u}\, d\widetilde{v}$$

is a consequence of the change of variables theorem for multiple integrals, and it follows that the area is well-defined, being independent of any parameterizations used to compute it.

To motivate the formula

$$\iint_{\Phi^{-1}(\Lambda)} |\Phi_u \times \Phi_v|\, du\, dv$$

for the calculation of the area of Δ, let us cover $\Phi^{-1}(\Delta)$ with a fine lattice of horizontal and vertical lines, and let $R_{i,j} = [u_i, u_{i+1}] \times [v_j, v_{j+1}]$ be any rectangle of this lattice, whose intersection with $\Phi^{-1}(\Delta)$ be non-empty. Then the integral in question is the limit, as the maximum diameter of the $R_{i,j}$ tends to zero, of the sums

$$\sum_{i,j}(u_{i+1} - u_i)(v_{j+1} - v_j)|\Phi_u \times \Phi_v|\Big|_{(u_i, v_j)} =$$
$$= \sum_{i,j} |(u_{i+1} - u_i)\Phi_u \times (v_{j+1} - v_j)\Phi_v|$$

— where each summand gives the area of the parallelogram of sides $(u_{i+1} - u_i)\Phi_u$ and $(v_{j+1} - v_j)\Phi_v$. The sides of this parallelogram are tangent to $\Phi(u_i, v_j)$ and have lengths approximating the sides of the "rectangle" $\Phi(R_{i,j})$.

We now want to express the area using the coefficients E, F and G. From the identity

$$|\Phi_u \times \Phi_v|^2 + \langle \Phi_u, \Phi_v \rangle^2 = |\Phi_u|^2 |\Phi_v|^2,$$

we obtain

$$|\Phi_u \times \Phi_v| = \sqrt{EG - F^2},$$

and therefore the area of Δ is given by the integral

$$\iint_{\Phi^{-1}(\Delta)} \sqrt{EG - F^2} \, du \, dv.$$

We again point out that it follows from this formula that the notion of area depends only on the knowledge of the first fundamental form.

Example 2.5.2 The coefficients of the first fundamental form of the spherical coordinates (φ, θ) in $\mathbf{S}^2$ (example 2.1.1 **D**) are $E = \sin^2 \theta$, $F = 0$ and $G = 1$. The area of $\mathbf{S}^2$ is then given by the integral

$$\int_{-\pi}^{\pi} \left(\int_0^{\pi} \sin \theta \, d\theta \right) d\varphi = 4\pi.$$

It is also interesting to note that the area of the *spindle* between the meridians $\varphi = 0$ and $\varphi = \varphi_0$ is equal to $2\varphi_0$; more generally, any spindle of amplitude φ_0 (bounded by two **maximal semicircles** of $\mathbf{S}^2$ that intersect at an angle $\varphi_0 \in \,]0, \pi[$) has area $2\varphi_0$. This allows us to deduce *Girard's formula*, which gives the area of a spherical triangle (which is the figure inside $\mathbf{S}^2$ bounded by three maximal circular arcs) as a function of its interior angles.

Assume that such a triangle $\mathcal{T}$ has vertices A, B, C and interior angles φ_1, φ_2, φ_3 and denote by α, β, γ the maximal circles containing respectively the pairs of points B and C, A and C, A and B. The antipodes $\widetilde{A}$, $\widetilde{B}$, and $\widetilde{C}$ of the vertices of $\mathcal{T}$ form a triangle $\widetilde{C}$ bounded by arcs of the same maximal circles α, β and γ (see Fig. 2.10). Because they are antipodes of each other, $\mathcal{T}$ and $\widetilde{\mathcal{T}}$ have the same area (see Exercise 51 in this section).

The two maximal circles β and γ define two spindles of amplitude φ_1 in $\mathbf{S}^2$; one of them contains $\mathcal{T}$ and the other one $\widetilde{\mathcal{T}}$. We denote by Δ_1 the union of these two spindles, and define analogously (using the pairs α and γ, α and β) the regions Δ_2 and Δ_3. The union of the Δ_i covers $\mathbf{S}^2$, but each point of $T \cup \widetilde{\mathcal{T}}$ is counted three times, since, for $i \neq j$, we have $\Delta_i \cap \Delta_j = \mathcal{T} \cup \widetilde{\mathcal{T}}$. Thus,

$$\sum_{i=1}^{3} \text{area}(\Delta_i) = \text{area}(\mathcal{S}^2) + 2[\text{area}(\mathcal{T}) + \text{area}(\widetilde{\mathcal{T}})]$$

and therefore

$$\text{area}(\mathcal{T}) = \frac{1}{4} \left\{ \sum_{i=1}^{3} \text{area}(\Delta_i) - \text{area}(\mathbf{S}^2) \right\}$$

$$= \varphi_1 + \varphi_2 + \varphi_3 - \pi.$$

We can describe our conclusion by saying that the area of a spherical triangle is proportional to its *spherical excess* (with proportionality constant equal to the square of the radius). This formula is generalized by the remarkable Gauss-Bonnet theorem, which we discuss later.   □

We end this section by defining what is meant by the integral of a real function defined on a surface: given a function $f: S \to \mathbb{R}$, a parameterization (U, Φ) of S, and a region $\Delta \subseteq \Phi(U)$, the *integral of f along* Δ is

$$\int_{\Delta} f \, d\sigma = \iint_{\Phi^{-1}(\Delta)} f \circ \Phi(u, v) \sqrt{EG - F^2} \, du \, dv.$$

For regions not contained in a single parametrized neighborhood, we partition them, as before, into smaller regions and add up the results.

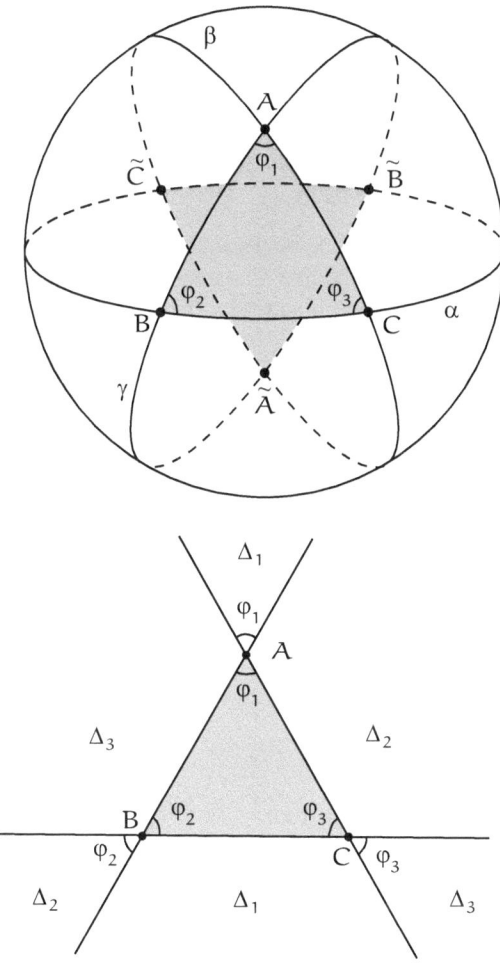

Figure 2.10

In particular, we have just defined what is meant by $\int_S f \, d\sigma$. Again it can be shown that these definitions do not depend on the parameterizations we use. The "quantity" $d\sigma$, which in local coordinates is written $\sqrt{EG - F^2} \, du \, dv$, is usually called *area element* of the surface.

Exercises

48. Obtain the coefficients of the first fundamental form for: (i) the helicoid (choose a parameterization); (ii) the sphere (parametrized by the inverse of the stereographic projection); (iii) a surface of revolution (parametrized as in example 2.1.1 **E**).

49. The coordinate curves of the parameterization $\Phi(u, v)$ constitute a Chebyshev net if the opposite sides of any quadrangle formed by them have the same lengths. Show that this happens if and only if $\dfrac{\partial E}{\partial v} \equiv \dfrac{\partial G}{\partial u} \equiv 0$.

50. Find all curves of the cylinder $\{(x, y, z) \in \mathbb{R}^3 : x^2 + y^2 = 1\}$ that intersect the generatrices (vertical lines) at a constant angle.

51. We say that a diffeomorphism of one surface onto another (or of an open subset of one surface onto an open subset of another surface) preserves area if the area of each open set is equal to that of its image.

(a) Let $\Psi : U \to S_1$ and $\Phi : U \to S_2$ be parameterizations of two surfaces, E, F, G and $\widetilde{E}, \widetilde{F}, \widetilde{G}$ the coefficients of the first fundamental form for Ψ and Φ, respectively. Show that $\Psi \circ \Phi^{-1}$ preserves areas if and only if the functions $EG - F^2$ and $\widetilde{E}\widetilde{G} - \widetilde{F}^2$ are identical.

(b) Show that the antipodal mapping $\mathbf{S}^2 \to \mathbf{S}^2$, $(x, y, z) \mapsto (-x, -y, -z)$, preserves areas.

(c) The *Archimedes projection* sends each point p of $\mathbf{S}^2$ (except the north and south poles) to the point of intersection of the circumscribing vertical cylinder with the half-line qp whose origin is the point q on the z-axis at the same height as p. Show that this mapping preserves areas.

(d) Find a mapping of an open subset of $\mathbb{T}^2$ into the plane that preserves areas.

52. Let U be a connected open subset of $\mathbb{R}^2$ and let $h : U \to \mathbb{R}$ be a differentiable function. Consider the surface $S = \{(x, y, z) \in \mathbb{R}^3 : (x, y) \in U, z = h(x, y)\}$. Show that:

(a) the mapping $\pi : S \to U$ given by $\pi(x, y, z) = (x, y)$ is a diffeomorphism;

(b) π decreases area (for any open subset $W \subseteq S$ the area of $\pi(W)$ is $\leq$ to the area of W);

(c) if π preserves areas then S is contained in a horizontal plane.

53. The *gnomonic projection* $\mathcal{P}_\Pi : \mathbf{S}^2 \setminus \gamma_\Pi \to \Pi$ sends each point on the sphere (except the points on a certain maximal circle γ_Π) into a tangent plane Π by projecting it from the center of the sphere. Show that:

(a) two points have the same image for $\mathcal{P}_\Pi$ if and only if they are antipodes, and the restriction $\mathcal{P}_\Pi$ to each of the hemispheres of $\mathbf{S}^2 \setminus \gamma_\Pi$ is a diffeomorphism;

(b) the maximal circles of $\mathbf{S}^2$ are transformed into the lines of Π;

(c) the two drawings of Fig. 2.10 are related by a gnomonic projection.

Chapter 3
The Geometry of the Gauss Map

In this chapter we deal with the extrinsic geometry of the surface, by defining quantities (curvatures) that express how the surface is embedded in its ambient space. The main tool for this study is the normal vector field to the surface; hence, we shall deal only with oriented surfaces.

3.1 The Gauss Map and its Derivative

Given an oriented surface S, the *Gauss map* is the field of normal vectors $N: S \to \mathbf{S}^2$ that defines the orientation of S. We noted in the previous chapter (following Proposition 2.4.3) that N is a differentiable mapping. By analogy with planar curves, it is to be expected that the study of the variation of N (i.e., of its derivative) will shed light on the local shape of S.

For $p \in S$ the tangent spaces T_pS and $T_{N(p)}\mathbf{S}^2$ are the same subspace of $\mathbb{R}^3$, since both are the orthogonal complement of the line generated by $N(p)$. This means that the derivative DN_p is an endomorphism $T_pS \to T_pS$. Let us now take a parameterization $\Phi(u,v)$ of S and put $N(u,v) = N \circ \Phi(u,v)$. By definition of the derivative, we have

$$N_u = DN_{\Phi(u,v)}(\Phi_u), \qquad N_v = DN_{\Phi(u,v)}(\Phi_v).$$

Differentiating the equalities $\langle \Phi_u, N \rangle = 0 = \langle \Phi_v, N \rangle$ with respect to v and u respectively, we obtain

$$\langle \Phi_{uv}, N \rangle + \langle \Phi_u, N_v \rangle = 0, \qquad \langle \Phi_{vu}, N \rangle + \langle \Phi_v, N_u \rangle = 0,$$

and from this, subtracting term by term, and given that $\Phi_{uv} = \Phi_{vu}$, we get $\langle \Phi_u, N_v \rangle = \langle \Phi_v, N_u \rangle$. The latter equality can be rewritten in the form $\langle \Phi_u, DN_{\Phi(u,v)}(\Phi_v) \rangle = \langle \Phi_v, DN_{\Phi(u,v)}(\Phi_u) \rangle$. It follows that for all vectors $\mathbf{w}_1, \mathbf{w}_2 \in T_{\Phi(u,v)}S$, we have

P. V. Araújo, *Differential Geometry*, https://doi.org/10.1007/978-3-031-62384-4_3

$$\langle \mathbf{w}_1, DN_{\Phi(u,v)}(\mathbf{w}_2) \rangle = \langle \mathbf{w}_2, DN_{\Phi(u,v)}(\mathbf{w}_1) \rangle, \tag{3.1}$$

To verify the equality it suffices to express $\mathbf{w}_1$ and $\mathbf{w}_2$ as linear combinations of Φ_u and Φ_v.

Equality (3.1) means that DN_p is a symmetric linear mapping of T_pS (with respect to the inner product $\langle \cdot, \cdot \rangle_p$ on T_pS). In general, a linear endomorphism $L: E \to E$ of a finite-dimensional real vector space equipped with an inner product $\langle\!\langle \cdot, \cdot \rangle\!\rangle$, is called *symmetric* (or *self-adjoint*) if, for all $\mathbf{w}_1, \mathbf{w}_2 \in E$, we have

$$\langle\!\langle \mathbf{w}_1, L(\mathbf{w}_2) \rangle\!\rangle = \langle\!\langle L(\mathbf{w}_1), \mathbf{w}_2 \rangle\!\rangle. \tag{3.2}$$

The next proposition, whose complete proof can be found in numerous Linear Algebra texts, gathers the essentials about symmetric endomorphisms.

Proposition 3.1.1 *Let E be a space with inner product $\langle\!\langle \cdot, \cdot \rangle\!\rangle$, $\mathcal{B} = (\mathbf{e}_1, \dots, \mathbf{e}_n)$ an orthonormal basis of E, and $L: E \to E$ an endomorphism. Then:*
(i) L is symmetric if and only if its matrix with respect to the basis $\mathcal{B}$ is symmetric;
(ii) if L is symmetric, E has an orthonormal basis formed by eigenvectors of L.

Proof (i) Since $\mathcal{B}$ is orthonormal, the matrix of L in this basis is $M = (a_{ij})_{1 \le i, j \le n}$ given by $a_{ij} = \langle\!\langle \mathbf{e}_i, L(\mathbf{e}_j) \rangle\!\rangle$. We thus observe that if L is symmetric then $a_{ij} = a_{ji}$ for all i, j, a condition, that expresses the symmetry of M. Conversely, if M is symmetric then $\langle\!\langle \mathbf{e}_i, L(\mathbf{e}_j) \rangle\!\rangle = \langle\!\langle L(\mathbf{e}_i), \mathbf{e}_j \rangle\!\rangle$ for all $1 \le i, j \le n$, and it follows that the symmetry condition (3.2) is verified for any two vectors that are linear combinations of the $\mathbf{e}_i$; but every vector of E is such a linear combination, and therefore L is symmetric.

(ii) We give the proof only in the case $n = 2$, the only one we will need. Let

$$M = \begin{bmatrix} a & c \\ c & b \end{bmatrix}$$

be the (symmetric) matrix of L with respect to the orthonormal basis $\mathcal{B} = (\mathbf{e}_1, \mathbf{e}_2)$. The eigenvalues of L are the roots of the characteristic polynomial $P(\lambda) = \lambda^2 - (a + b)\lambda + ab - c^2$, whose discriminant is $\Delta = (a - b)^2 + 4c^2 \ge 0$. If $\Delta = 0$ then $c = 0$ and $a = b$, which shows that L is a homothety, and so any orthonormal basis of E is formed by eigenvectors of L. If $\Delta > 0$, then L has two real eigenvalues $\lambda_1 < \lambda_2$, and we let $\mathbf{v}_1$ and $\mathbf{v}_2$ be the associated unit eigenvectors. These vectors constitute the promised basis, since

$$\lambda_1 \langle\!\langle \mathbf{v}_1, \mathbf{v}_2 \rangle\!\rangle = \langle\!\langle L(\mathbf{v}_1), \mathbf{v}_2 \rangle\!\rangle = \langle\!\langle \mathbf{v}_1, L(\mathbf{v}_2) \rangle\!\rangle = \lambda_2 \langle\!\langle \mathbf{v}_1, \mathbf{v}_2 \rangle\!\rangle,$$

and therefore $\langle\!\langle \mathbf{v}_1, \mathbf{v}_2 \rangle\!\rangle = 0$. $\qquad\square$

Corollary 3.1.2 *Let $\zeta: E \times E \to \mathbb{R}$ be a symmetric bilinear form on the Euclidean space E. Then there exists an orthonormal basis $\mathcal{C} = (\mathbf{v}_1, \dots, \mathbf{v}_n)$ of E such that $\zeta(\mathbf{v}_i, \mathbf{v}_j) = 0$ for all $1 \le i < j < n$.*

Proof Consider the matrix $M = (a_{ij})_{i \le i, j \le n}$ of the bilinear form ζ relative to an orthonormal basis $\mathcal{B} = (\mathbf{e}_1, \dots, \mathbf{e}_n)$ of E. This matrix, defined by $a_{ij} = \zeta(\mathbf{e}_i, \mathbf{e}_j)$, is symmetric because of the symmetry of ζ. Let L be the linear mapping whose matrix with respect to $\mathcal{B}$ is M: by 3.1.1 (i), L is symmetric. A simple calculation shows that $\zeta(\mathbf{v}, \mathbf{w}) = \langle\!\langle \mathbf{v}, L(\mathbf{w}) \rangle\!\rangle$. By 3.1.1 there exists an orthonormal basis $\mathcal{C}$ of E formed by eigenvectors of L, and $\mathcal{C}$ is the sought basis. $\qquad\square$

The eigenvalues $k_1(p) \le k_2(p)$ of the symmetric endomorphism $-DN_p$ (beware of the minus sign!) are called *principal curvatures* of S at the point p. If $k_1(p) < k_2(p)$, we call *principal directions* the two **orthogonal** directions defined in $T_p S$ by the eigenvectors of $-DN_p$.

To justify this terminology we introduce yet another definition. Let $\alpha:]a, b[\to S$ be a curve parametrized by arc length. The *normal curvature* of α at $\alpha(s)$ is the component of $\alpha''(s)$ in the direction of the normal to S at that point, and is given by $k_n(\alpha, s) = \langle \alpha''(s), N \circ \alpha(s)\rangle$. Note that this quantity does not depend on the orientation of the curve and that if the curve is not parametrized by arc length, the formula for computing the normal curvature is $k_n(\alpha, t) = \dfrac{1}{v(t)^2} \langle \alpha''(t), N \circ \alpha(t)\rangle$,

where $v(t) = |\alpha'(t)|$.

Proposition 3.1.3 *(i) The normal curvature $k_n(\alpha, s)$ at $\alpha(s)$ depends only on the tangent direction to the curve at instant s: more precisely, if α and β are curves in S tangent to each other at $\alpha(s_0) = \beta(t_0) = p_0$ then $k_n(\alpha, s_0) = k_n(\beta, t_0)$.*

(ii) The set of normal curvatures at p_0 is the interval $[k_1(p_0), k_2(p_0)]$. If $k_1(p_0) < k_2(p_0)$, then the minimum and maximum of these normal curvatures are the principal curvatures at p_0, which occur precisely in the principal directions associated with $k_1(p_0)$ and $k_2(p_0)$.

Proof Let us put $N(s) = N \circ \alpha(s)$. Differentiating the equality $\langle \alpha'(s), N(s)\rangle = 0$, we obtain $\langle \alpha''(s), N(s)\rangle + \langle \alpha'(s), N'(s)\rangle = 0$, and from this we get $k_n(\alpha, s) = \langle \alpha'(s), -N'(s)\rangle = \langle \alpha'(s), -DN_p(\alpha'(s))\rangle$, where we let $p = \alpha(s)$. This equality shows that $k_n(\alpha, s)$ only depends on $\alpha'(s) \in T_p S$ and proves statement (i).

Let us now fix $p_0 = \alpha(s_0)$ and let $(\mathbf{v}_1, \mathbf{v}_2)$ be an orthonormal basis of $T_{p_0} S$ consisting of eigenvectors of $-DN_{p_0}$. Putting $\alpha'(s_0) = a\,\mathbf{v}_1 + b\,\mathbf{v}_2$, we have $a^2 + b^2 = 1$; furthermore,

$$
\begin{aligned}
k_n(\alpha, s_0) &= \langle a\mathbf{v}_1 + b\mathbf{v}_2, -DN_{p_0}(a\mathbf{v}_1 + b\mathbf{v}_2)\rangle \\
&= a^2\langle \mathbf{v}_1, -DN_{p_0}(\mathbf{v}_1)\rangle + b^2\langle \mathbf{v}_2, -DN_{p_0}(\mathbf{v}_2)\rangle \\
&= k_1 a^2 + k_2 b^2.
\end{aligned}
$$

Thus we obtain the inequalities

$$
k_1 = k_1(a^2 + b^2) \le k_n(\alpha, s_0) \le k_2(a^2 + b^2) = k_2,
$$

From which it follows that the normal curvatures cover the entire interval $[k_1, k_2]$ and that if $k_1 < k_2$ then the minimum is only reached for $\alpha'(s_0) = \pm\mathbf{v}_1$ and the maximum for $\alpha'(s_0) = \pm\mathbf{v}_2$. $\qquad\square$

As we have said, the normal curvature $k_n(\alpha, s)$ gives the component of the curvature vector $\alpha''(s_0)$ of α in the direction of the normal $N \circ \alpha(s)$ to the surface. If these vectors are collinear, i.e., if the principal normal to the curve α at instant s points in the direction of the normal to the surface at $\alpha(s)$, then the absolute value of $k_n(\alpha, s)$ is equal to the curvature of α at that point.

Given an arbitrary direction $\mathbf{v} \in T_p S$ with $|\mathbf{v}| = 1$, there exists at least one curve that passes through p with velocity $\mathbf{v}$, and whose principal normal at p points in the direction of $N(p)$: the intersection of S with the plane that passes through p and is parallel to the vectors $N(p)$ and $\mathbf{v}$ (see Fig. 3.1 and Exercise 34 in Section 2.2). A curve obtained this way is called a *normal section* of S at p.

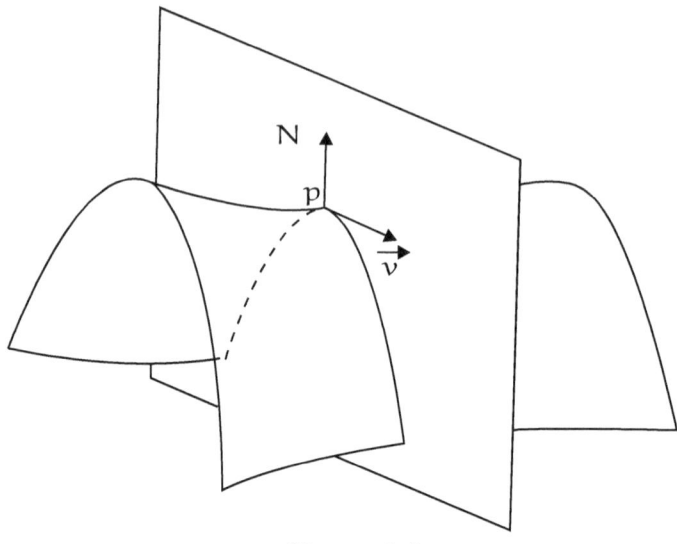

Figure 3.1

This means that to analyze the normal curvatures at $p \in S$ it suffices to study the curvatures of the normal sections. The sign of k_n will depend on whether the concavity at p of such a curve points in the direction of $N(p)$ or in the opposite direction.

The *Gaussian curvature* of S at p is defined by $K(p) = k_1(p)k_2(p)$, and the *mean curvature* is $H(p) = \frac{1}{2}(k_1(p) + k_2(p))$; equivalently, $K(p)$ and $H(p)$ are equal, respectively, to the determinant and the semi-trace of the linear mapping $-DN_p$. According to the value of these curvatures, a point $p \in S$ is called

- *elliptic* if $K(p) > 0$ (i.e., if $k_1(p)$ and $k_2(p)$ are both positive or both negative);
- *hyperbolic* if $K(p) < 0$ (the principal curvatures have opposite signs);
- *parabolic* if $K(p) = 0$ and $H(p) \neq 0$ (one of the principal curvatures is zero, the other one is nonzero);
- *planar* if $K(p) = 0 = H(p)$ (both principal curvatures are zero);
- *umbilical* if $k_1(p) = k_2(p)$ (this condition is equivalent to the equality $H(p)^2 - K(p) = 0$).

Note that any point on the surface belongs to one and only one of the first four classes, but that the umbilical points can be either elliptical or planar. We further note that although the sign of the principal curvatures depends on the orientation of S, the Gaussian curvature does not change when one changes the orientation and the classification of the points we gave above does not depend on the orientation chosen. Hence, since any surface is locally orientable (any parametrized neighborhood has an orientation induced by the parameterization), the classification given extends also to points on non-orientable surfaces.

In the next section we study the meaning of these definitions with the help of local coordinates. Now we give some examples.

Examples 3.1.4 **A.** All points in a plane are planar: in fact, the normal sections are straight lines, and therefore have zero curvature. This means that all normal curvatures (and hence both principal curvatures) of the plane are zero.

B. The normal sections of a sphere with radius r are maximal circles whose curvature is $1/r$. This means that at each point, the absolute values of all normal curvatures are equal to $1/r$, and therefore the two principal curvatures are equal (if they were $-1/r$ and $1/r$, some normal curvature would be zero, which is not the case) and have absolute value $1/r$. All points on the sphere are therefore umbilical, and their Gaussian curvature is constant and positive, equal to $1/r^2$.

Of course, the analysis of the signs of the normal curvatures could be replaced, in this example, by a simple calculation. But with this analysis we illustrate a useful principle: *at the point $p \in S$ there is some direction in which the normal curvature vanishes (called an asymptotic direction) if and only if $K(p) \le 0$.*

C. Consider the hyperbolic paraboloid $\{(x, y, z) : z = x^2 - y^2\}$ with the orientation induced by the parameterization $\Phi(u, v) = (u, v, u^2 - v^2)$, i.e.

$$N(u, v) = \frac{1}{\sqrt{1 + 4u^2 + 4v^2}} (-2u, 2v, 1).$$

At the point $O = \Phi(0, 0)$ we have

$$-N_u = (2, 0, 0) = 2\Phi_u,$$
$$-N_v = (0, -2, 0) = -2\Phi_v.$$

The principal curvatures at O are thus 2 and -2, the principal directions are those of the vectors $\Phi_u = (1, 0, 0)$ and $\Phi_v = (0, 1, 0)$, and the Gaussian curvature is negative, equal to -4.

D. Let E be the ellipsoid

$$\frac{x^2}{a^2} + \frac{y^2}{b^2} + \frac{z^2}{c^2} = 1,$$

where $a \ge b \ge c > 0$. We use the symmetric bilinear form $\zeta : \mathbb{R}^3 \times \mathbb{R}^3 \to \mathbb{R}$ given by

$$\zeta((x, y, z), (x', y', z')) = \frac{xx'}{a^2} + \frac{yy'}{b^2} + \frac{zz'}{c^2}$$

and we denote by Q the associated quadratic form:

$$Q(x, y, z) = \frac{x^2}{a^2} + \frac{y^2}{b^2} + \frac{z^2}{c^2}.$$

Given $p_0 \in \mathcal{E}$ and a plane Π passing through the origin $(0, 0, 0)$, let us study the intersection of $\mathcal{E}$ with the plane $\Pi_0 = p_0 + \Pi$.

Note that, for every vector $\mathbf{w} \in \mathbb{R}^3$, we have

$$\frac{1}{a^2} |\mathbf{w}|^2 \leq Q(\mathbf{w}) \leq \frac{1}{c^2} |\mathbf{w}|^2. \tag{3.3}$$

Given now $\mathbf{w} \in \Pi$ (so that $p_0 + \mathbf{w} \in \Pi_0$), we have

$$Q(p_0 + \mathbf{w}) = Q(\mathbf{w}) + 2\zeta(p_0, \mathbf{w}) + Q(p_0)$$
$$= Q(\mathbf{w}) + L(\mathbf{w}) + 1,$$

where $L: \Pi \to \mathbb{R}$ is a linear form. Thus, the intersection $\mathcal{F} = \mathcal{E} \cap \Pi_0$ is the set of sums $p_0 + \mathbf{w}$, where $\mathbf{w} \in \Pi$ satisfies $Q(\mathbf{w}) + L(\mathbf{w}) = 0$.

Consider the bilinear form $\widetilde{\zeta} = \zeta|_{\Pi \times \Pi}$ and the associated quadratic form $\widetilde{Q} = Q|_{\Pi}$. By corollary 3.1.2, there exists an orthonormal basis $(\mathbf{v}_1, \mathbf{v}_2)$ of Π such that $\widetilde{\zeta}(\mathbf{v}_1, \mathbf{v}_2) = 0$. By (3.3), $\widetilde{Q}(\mathbf{v}_1)$ and $\widetilde{Q}(\mathbf{v}_2)$ are positive, belonging to the interval $\left[\frac{1}{a^2}, \frac{1}{c^2}\right]$. We then have

$$\widetilde{Q}(\widetilde{x}\mathbf{v}_1 + \widetilde{y}\mathbf{v}_2) = \frac{\widetilde{x}^2}{\widetilde{a}^2} + \frac{\widetilde{y}^2}{\widetilde{b}^2},$$

where we can assume that $a \geq \widetilde{a} \geq \widetilde{b} \geq c$. Using coordinates $\widetilde{x}, \widetilde{y}$ the equation of $-p_0 + \mathcal{F}$ is written

$$\frac{\widetilde{x}^2}{\widetilde{a}^2} + \frac{\widetilde{y}^2}{\widetilde{b}^2} + \lambda \widetilde{x} + \mu \widetilde{y} = 0,$$

or, "completing squares",

$$\frac{(\widetilde{x} - \widetilde{x}_0)^2}{\widetilde{a}^2} + \frac{(\widetilde{y} - \widetilde{y}_0)^2}{\widetilde{b}^2} = r^2,$$

where λ, μ, $\widetilde{x}_0$, $\widetilde{y}_0$ and r are certain constants. Assuming that $r > 0$ (otherwise $\lambda = \mu = 0$ and $\Pi_0 \cap \mathcal{F} = \{p_0\}$), the last equation is equivalent to

$$\frac{(\widetilde{x} - \widetilde{x}_0)^2}{(\widetilde{a}r)^2} + \frac{(\widetilde{y} - \widetilde{y}_0)^2}{(\widetilde{b}r)^2} = 1,$$

which describes an ellipse of semi-major axis $\widetilde{a}r$ and semi-minor axis $\widetilde{b}r$. Thus, the maximum and minimum curvatures of $\mathcal{F}$ are, respectively,

$$\frac{\tilde{a}\,r}{\left(\tilde{b}\,r\right)^2} = \frac{\tilde{a}}{\tilde{b}^2 r} \quad \text{and} \quad \frac{\tilde{b}\,r}{\left(\tilde{a}\,r\right)^2} = \frac{\tilde{b}}{\tilde{a}^2 r}$$

(see Exercise 6, in Section 1.3). Since $\mathcal{F} \subseteq \mathcal{E}$ and the diameter of $\mathcal{E}$ is $2a$, we have $\tilde{a}\,r \leq a$. Hence, the curvature of $\mathcal{F}$ is, at all points, greater than or equal to

$$\frac{\tilde{b}}{\tilde{a}^2 r} \geq \frac{\tilde{b}}{a\,\tilde{a}} \geq \frac{c}{a^2} \,.$$

We thus prove that the normal curvatures of $\mathcal{E}$ are not less than $\dfrac{c}{a^2}$ in absolute value. Hence (see example **B**) *the Gaussian curvature of $\mathcal{E}$ is positive at all points, being bounded by c^2/a^4.*

We now want to obtain an upper bound for the principal curvatures of $\mathcal{E}$, and for this we need a lower bound for the diameter of its normal sections. The normal line to $\mathcal{E}$ at the point $(x_0, y_0, z_0) \in \mathcal{E}$, given by

$$t \mapsto (x_0, y_0, z_0) + t\left(\frac{x_0}{a^2}, \frac{y_0}{b^2}, \frac{z_0}{c^2}\right),$$

intersects $\mathcal{E}$ for $t = 0$ and for $t = t_0$, where

$$t_0 = \frac{-2\left(\frac{x_0^2}{a^4} + \frac{y_0^2}{b^4} + \frac{z_0^2}{c^4}\right)}{\frac{x_0^2}{a^6} + \frac{y_0^2}{b^6} + \frac{z_0^2}{c^6}} \,.$$

The length of the line segment between the two intersections is then

$$|t_0|\sqrt{\frac{x_0^2}{a^4} + \frac{y_0^2}{b^4} + \frac{z_0^2}{c^4}} = \frac{2\left(\frac{x_0^2}{a^4} + \frac{y_0^2}{b^4} + \frac{z_0^2}{c^4}\right)^{3/2}}{\frac{x_0^2}{a^6} + \frac{y_0^2}{b^6} + \frac{z_0^2}{c^6}}$$

$$\geq 2c^2 \sqrt{\frac{x_0^2}{a^4} + \frac{y_0^2}{b^4} + \frac{z_0^2}{c^4}}$$

$$\geq \frac{2c^2}{a}\sqrt{\frac{x_0^2}{a^2} + \frac{y_0^2}{b^2} + \frac{z_0^2}{c^2}} = \frac{2c^2}{a} \,.$$

Thus, under the assumption that $\mathcal{F} = \mathcal{E} \cap \Pi_0$ is a normal section of $\mathcal{E}$, we have $\tilde{a}\,r \geq \dfrac{c^2}{a}$, or $\dfrac{1}{r} \leq \dfrac{\tilde{a}\,a}{c^2}$. The curvature of $\mathcal{F}$ is then not greater than

$$\frac{\tilde{a}}{\tilde{b}^2 r} \leq \frac{\tilde{a}^2 a}{\tilde{b}^2 c^2} \leq \frac{a^3}{c^4},$$

and so the absolute values of the normal curvatures of $\mathcal{E}$ are also not greater than a^3/c^4. In conclusion: *at any point $p \in \mathcal{E}$ we have*

$$\frac{c^2}{a^4} \leq K(p) \leq \frac{a^6}{c^8} \,.$$

Note that when $\mathcal{E}$ is a sphere then $a = b = c$, and both these inequalities become the equality already seen in example B. It should however be made clear that it is possible, by more ingenious methods than ours, to obtain an explicit expression for the curvature of the points of $\mathcal{E}$. This example was intended to show that we can estimate (in this case obtain lower and upper bounds) the Gaussian curvature without computing it explicitly.   □

In examples 3.1.4 A, B we observed that all points on the plane and the sphere are umbilical; we end the section by showing that these are the only surfaces with such a property.

Proposition 3.1.5 *Let S be a connected surface whose points are all umbilical. Then S is contained in a sphere or in a plane.*

Proof Our hypothesis implies the existence of a function $\lambda: S \to \mathbb{R}$ such that, for every $p \in S$, DN_p is a homothety of ratio $\lambda(p)$. Let us take a parameterization (U, Φ) of S, with U connected, and put $N(u, v) = N \circ \Phi(u, v)$ and $\lambda(u, v) = \lambda \circ \Phi(u, v)$. We then have

$$N_u = \lambda(u, v)\Phi_u$$
$$N_v = \lambda(u, v)\Phi_v \tag{3.4}$$

and these equalities ensure that $\lambda(u, v)$ is differentiable, for we deduce from them that

$$\lambda(u, v) = \frac{\langle N_u, \Phi_u \rangle}{|\Phi_u|^2} = \frac{\langle N_v, \Phi_v \rangle}{|\Phi_v|^2} .$$

By differentiation of (3.4) we obtain

$$N_{uv} = \lambda_v \Phi_u + \lambda \Phi_{uv}$$
$$N_{vu} = \lambda_u \Phi_v + \lambda \Phi_{vu}$$

Whence, subtracting term by term,

$$\lambda_v \Phi_u - \lambda_u \Phi_v = 0,$$

an equality which is only possible when λ_v and λ_u are identically zero. Thus, the function $\lambda(u, v)$ is constant on U, and therefore $\lambda: S \to \mathbb{R}$ is locally constant, hence (since S is connected) constant, equal to $\lambda \in \mathbb{R}$.

If $\lambda = 0$ then by (3.4) the normal vector N is constant, and the function $p \mapsto \langle N, p \rangle$ is locally constant, hence constant, on S, which means that S is contained in a plane $\{p \in \mathbb{R}^3 : \langle N, p \rangle = a\}$, for some $a \in \mathbb{R}$.

If $\lambda \neq 0$ then, again by (3.4), the mapping $S \to \mathbb{R}^3$ given by $p \mapsto p - \frac{1}{\lambda}N(p)$ is locally constant, hence constant. Denoting by q_0 this constant, we have, for all p in S, $|p - q_0| = \left|\frac{1}{\lambda}N(p)\right| = \frac{1}{|\lambda|}$, and therefore S is contained in the sphere with center q_0 and radius $\frac{1}{|\lambda|}$.   □

Exercises

54. What is the region on the sphere covered by the image of the Gauss map of the surface given by the equation: (i) $z = x^2 + y^2$; (ii) $x^2 + y^2 - z^2 = 1$; (iii) $x^2 + y^2 = \cosh^2 z$.

55. (a) Compute the principal curvatures at $(0, 0, 0)$ of each of the following surfaces: (i) $z = x^2 + y^3$; (ii) $z = x^2 + y^4$; (iii) $z = x^3 - 3xy^2$. Sketch the surface (iii), indicating the region that lies above the plane $z = 0$.

(b) Conclude that when p_0 is a parabolic (or planar) point of S the following two cases are possible: (i) there exists a neighborhood of p_0 in S that lies entirely on the same side of the tangent plane to S at p_0; (ii) any neighborhood of p_0 in S contains points on both sides of the tangent plane.

56. (a) Show that at a point on a surface, the arithmetic mean of the normal curvatures in two orthogonal directions is equal to the mean curvature at that point.

(b) Show that the mean curvature at $p \in S$ is given by $\frac{1}{\pi} \int_0^\pi k_n(\theta)\, d\theta$, where $k_n(\theta)$ is the normal curvature at p in the direction that makes an angle θ with a fixed principal direction.

57. Let S be an oriented regular surface, and suppose that $p_0 \in S$ is a maximum of the function $f : S \to \mathbb{R}$, $f(p) = |p|^2$. Show that:

(a) the line segment $[O, p_0]$ is orthogonal to S at p_0;

(b) the Gaussian curvature of S at p_0 is greater than or equal to $1/f(p_0)$ (use Exercise 8, in Section 1.3);

(c) if S is compact, then S has some point with positive Gaussian curvature.

58. Show that if a surface is tangent to a plane along a regular curve then the points on that curve are parabolic or planar.

59. Let p be a hyperbolic point of S, and assume there exists a neighborhood U of p in S such that $(p + T_p S) \cap U$ is the union of two regular curves that intersect at p. Show that the tangent line at p to each of these curves defines an asymptotic direction in $T_p S$.

3.2 The Second Fundamental Form

Using local coordinates, we will in this section continue the study of Gaussian curvature, obtaining explicit formulas to compute it and a better understanding of its geometric meaning. The tool is again a quadratic form, now related to the Gaussian normal mapping.

We observed in Section 3.1 that $DN_p : T_p S \to T_p S$ is a symmetric linear mapping with respect to the inner product $\langle \cdot, \cdot \rangle_p$ on $T_p S$, which means that the bilinear form $(\mathbf{v}, \mathbf{w}) \mapsto \langle \mathbf{v}, -DN_p(\mathbf{w}) \rangle$ is symmetric. The *second fundamental form* at $p \in S$ is the quadratic form associated with this symmetric bilinear form, i.e. $\mathrm{II}_p(\mathbf{v}) = \langle \mathbf{v}, -DN_p(\mathbf{v}) \rangle$.

From the proof of 3.1.3 it follows that the normal curvature at p in the direction of $\mathbf{v}$ is precisely $\mathrm{II}_p(\mathbf{v})$ when $|\mathbf{v}| = 1$ [if $\mathbf{v} \neq 0$ is not a unit vector, then that normal curvature is given by $\mathrm{II}_p(\mathbf{v})/|\mathbf{v}|^2 = \mathrm{II}_p(\mathbf{v})/I_p(\mathbf{v})$] and that the principal curvatures are the maximum and minimum of the set $\{\Pi_p(\mathbf{v}): \mathbf{v} \in T_pS, |\mathbf{v}| = 1\}$. This means that at each point of the surface the second fundamental form gathers all information about normal curvatures, principal curvatures and Gaussian curvature.

Given a parameterization $\Phi(u,v)$, we want to determine the matrix $\begin{pmatrix} e & f \\ f & g \end{pmatrix}$ of $\Pi_{\Phi(u,v)}$ relative to the base (Φ_u, Φ_v) of $T_{\Phi(u,v)}S$. The entries e, f, g of this matrix, which are functions of (u,v), are called the *coefficients of the second fundamental form* in the coordinates (u,v), and are computed by the formulas

$$e = \langle \Phi_u, -DN_{\Phi(u,v)}(\Phi_u) \rangle = \langle \Phi_u, -N_u \rangle$$
$$= \langle \Phi_{uu}, N \rangle$$

$$f = \langle \Phi_u, -DN_{\Phi(u,v)}(\Phi_v) \rangle = \langle \Phi_v, -DN_{\Phi(u,v)}(\Phi_u) \rangle$$
$$= \langle \Phi_u, -N_v \rangle = \langle \Phi_v, -N_u \rangle$$
$$= \langle \Phi_{uv}, N \rangle)$$

$$g = \langle \Phi_v, -DN_{\Phi(u,v)}(\Phi_v) \rangle = \langle \Phi_v, -N_v \rangle$$
$$= \langle \Phi_{vv}, N \rangle.$$

For computational purposes, formulas that **do not involve** the derivatives of N are in general easier to handle. Once we have computed e, f, g it is easy to compute the normal curvature of a curve $\alpha(t) = \Phi(u(t), v(t))$ expressed in local coordinates: writing $\alpha'(t) = u'(t)\Phi_u + v'(t)\Phi_v$, we have

$$\Pi_{\alpha(t)}(\alpha'(t)) = \langle u'\Phi_u + v'\Phi_v, -DN_{\alpha(t)}(u'\Phi_u + v'\Phi_v) \rangle$$
$$= u'^2 \langle \Phi_u, -DN_{\alpha(t)}(\Phi_u) \rangle + u'v'(\langle \Phi_u, -DN_{\alpha(t)}(\Phi_v) \rangle +$$
$$+ \langle \Phi_v, -DN_{\alpha(t)}(\Phi_u) \rangle)) + v'^2 \langle \Phi_v, -DN_{\alpha(t)}(\Phi_v) \rangle$$
$$= eu'^2 + 2fu'v' + gv'^2,$$

where e, f, g are computed at $(u(t), v(t))$; the normal curvature is then

$$k_n(t) = \frac{eu'^2 + 2fu'v' + gv'^2}{|\alpha'(t)|^2}$$
$$= \frac{eu'^2 + 2fu'v' + gv'^2}{Eu'^2 + 2Fu'v' + Gv'^2}. \tag{3.5}$$

Let us now determine the matrix $\begin{bmatrix} a_{11} & a_{12} \\ a_{21} & a_{22} \end{bmatrix}$ of $-DN_{\Phi(u,v)}$ relative to the basis (Φ_u, Φ_v): the entries of the matrix are determined by the equalities

$$-N_u = a_{11}\Phi_u + a_{21}\Phi_v$$
$$-N_v = a_{12}\Phi_u + a_{22}\Phi_v .$$

Forming the inner product of each of these equalities with Φ_u and with Φ_v we obtain

$$e = a_{11}E + a_{21}F \qquad f = a_{11}F + a_{21}G$$
$$f = a_{12}E + a_{22}F \qquad g = a_{12}F + a_{22}G,$$

and these equalities can be written in matrix form as

$$\begin{bmatrix} e & f \\ f & g \end{bmatrix} = \begin{bmatrix} E & F \\ F & G \end{bmatrix} \begin{bmatrix} a_{11} & a_{12} \\ a_{21} & a_{22} \end{bmatrix},$$

i.e.

$$\begin{bmatrix} a_{11} & a_{12} \\ a_{21} & a_{22} \end{bmatrix} = \begin{bmatrix} E & F \\ F & G \end{bmatrix}^{-1} \begin{bmatrix} e & f \\ f & g \end{bmatrix}$$

$$= \frac{1}{EG - F^2} \begin{bmatrix} G & -F \\ -F & E \end{bmatrix} \begin{bmatrix} e & f \\ f & g \end{bmatrix}. \qquad (3.6)$$

From this we derive explicit formulas for the Gaussian curvature and mean curvature:

$$K \circ \Phi(u, v) = \det\left(-DN_{\Phi(u,v)} \right) = \frac{eg - f^2}{EG - F^2} \qquad (3.7)$$

$$H \circ \Phi(u, v) = \frac{1}{2} \operatorname{tr}\left(-DN_{\Phi(u,v)} \right) = \frac{1}{2}(a_{11} + a_{22})$$
$$= \frac{Ge - 2Ff + Eg}{2(EG - F^2)}; \qquad (3.8)$$

and also for the principal curvatures k_1 and k_2, which are the eigenvalues of the matrix $[a_{ij}]$:

$$k_1 = H - \sqrt{H^2 - K}, \qquad k_2 = H + \sqrt{H^2 - K}. \qquad (3.9)$$

Example 3.2.1 The surface of revolution

$$\Phi(u, v) = (\rho(v)\cos u, \rho(v)\sin u, z(v))$$

has coefficients

$$e \qquad = \frac{-z\rho}{\sqrt{\rho^2 + z^2}}, \qquad\qquad f = 0, \quad g = \frac{\rho z - \rho z}{\sqrt{\rho^2 + z^2}},$$

$$E = \rho^2, \qquad\qquad F = 0, \quad G = \rho^2 + z^2.$$

It then follows from (3.6) that the matrix $[a_{ij}]$ is diagonal. The principal directions at the non-umbilical points are thus those of Φ_u and Φ_v, the tangent lines to the meridians and the parallels. The principal curvatures are

$$\frac{e}{E} = \frac{-z}{\rho\sqrt{\rho^2 + z^2}} \quad \text{and} \quad \frac{g}{G} = \frac{\rho z - \rho z}{(\rho^2 + z^2)^{3/2}}$$

and the Gaussian curvature is

$$K = \frac{z(\rho z - \rho z)}{\rho(\rho^2 + z^2)^2} \, .$$

The expression of the curvature is simplified by assuming that the generating curve $\alpha(v) = (\rho(v), 0, z(v))$ is parametrized by arc length — that is, $\rho^2 + z^2 = 1$. Differentiating this equality we obtain $zz = -\rho\rho$, and replacing the left-hand side with the right-hand side in the expression of K yields

$$K = \frac{-\rho(\rho^2 + z^2)}{\rho(\rho^2 + z^2)^2} = \frac{-\rho}{\rho} \, .$$

Using this formula we will now determine the surfaces of revolution of constant curvature; to do this we simply solve the differential equation $\rho + K\rho = 0$, with K constant. Leaving the cases $K = 0$ and $K < 0$ as an exercise, let us deal with the case $K > 0$; to simplify the formulas we let $K = 1$.

The general solution of the equation $\rho + \rho = 0$ is of the form $\rho(v) = C\cos(v + B)$, where C and B are constants. We can choose $B = 0$, since the solutions we obtain with $B \neq 0$ correspond only to a translation of the domain; so we are reduced to the solutions $\rho_C(v) = C\cos v$. Since we want $\rho > 0$, we take $C > 0$ and restrict v to an interval of the form $] - v_0, v_0[$. Putting $z_C(0) = 0$ and integrating the equality $\rho_C^2 + z_C^2 = 1$, we obtain

$$z_C(v) = \int_0^v \sqrt{1 - C^2 \sin^2 t} \, dt$$

(the opposite solution gives another parameterization of the same surface).

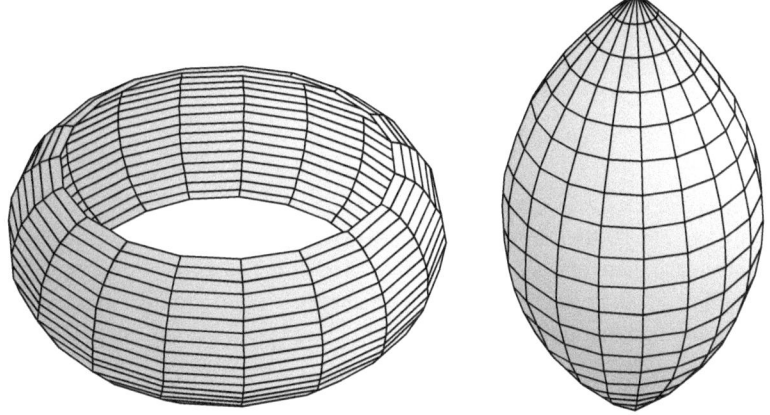

Figure 3.2

So necessarily $v_0 = \frac{\pi}{2}$ when $0 < C \leq 1$, and $v_0 = \arcsin(1/C) \in \left]0, \frac{\pi}{2}\right[$ when $C > 1$. The resulting surfaces S_C are symmetric with respect to the equator $z = 0$, whose radius is precisely C. When $C < 1$, then S_C has a cusp; when $C = 1$ it is the sphere with radius 1. When $C > 1$ it is a kind of bead of a rosary (flattened sphere pierced from one end to the other one). [See Figure 3.2].   □

We can now specify the meaning of the sign of the Gaussian curvature:

Proposition 3.2.2 *Let p_0 be a point on the surface S. Then:*
(i) if $K(p_0) > 0$ then there exists a neighborhood U of p_0 in S which is entirely on the same side of the plane tangent to S at p_0 ;
(ii) if $K(p_0) < 0$ then any neighborhood of p_0 in S contains points on either side of the plane tangent to S at p_0 .

Proof It suffices to analyze the sign of the function $\widetilde{h}\colon S \to \mathbb{R}$ given by $\widetilde{h}(p) = \langle N(p_0), p - p_0 \rangle$ at points p near p_0 . Let us consider a parameterization $\Phi(u, v)$ such that $\Phi(0, 0) = p_0$, and let $h = \widetilde{h} \circ \Phi$. The expansion of h into a Taylor polynomial at the point $(0, 0)$ gives

$$h(u, v) = h(0, 0) + \frac{\partial h}{\partial u} u + \frac{\partial h}{\partial v} v + \frac{1}{2}\left(\frac{\partial^2 h}{\partial u^2} u^2 + 2\frac{\partial^2 h}{\partial u \partial v} uv + \frac{\partial^2 h}{\partial v^2} v^2\right) + R(u, v),$$

where all partial derivatives are computed at $(0, 0)$ and

$$\lim_{(u,v)\to(00)} \frac{R(u, v)}{u^2 + v^2} = 0.$$

A quick calculation shows that $h(0, 0) = \dfrac{\partial h}{\partial u} = \dfrac{\partial h}{\partial v} = 0$ and that the second-order derivatives are nothing else but the coefficients at p_0 of the second fundamental form: i.e.,

$$\frac{\partial^2 h}{\partial u^2} = e, \qquad \frac{\partial^2 h}{\partial u \partial v} = f, \qquad \frac{\partial^2 h}{\partial v^2} = g.$$

This leaves us with

$$h(u,v) = \frac{1}{2}\left(eu^2 + 2fuv + gv^2\right) + R(u,v). \qquad (3.10)$$

Let us put $Q(u,v) = eu^2 + 2fuv + gv^2$. By (3.7), $K(p_0)$ and $eg - f^2$ have the same sign. If $eg - f^2 > 0$ then e, g are both positive or both negative: let us now show that in this case there exists $\delta > 0$ such that $h(u,v)$ is nonzero and has constant sign (positive if $e, g > 0$, negative otherwise) whenever $0 < |(u,v)| < \delta$.

Assuming then that $eg - f^2 > 0$ and that e, g are positive, we can write

$$Q(u,v) = e\left(u + \frac{f}{e}v\right)^2 + \frac{eg - f^2}{e}v^2 \geq \frac{eg - f^2}{e}v^2,$$

and analogously,

$$Q(u,v) \geq \frac{eg - f^2}{g}u^2.$$

From these inequalities we obtain $Q(u,v) \geq 2M(u^2 + v^2)$, where

$$M = \frac{eg - f^2}{4}\min\left\{\frac{1}{g}, \frac{1}{e}\right\} > 0.$$

Finally we have, by (3.10), that

$$\frac{h(u,v)}{u^2 + v^2} \geq M - \frac{R(u,v)}{u^2 + v^2} > 0$$

whenever $0 < |(u,v)| < \delta$, provided that $\delta > 0$ is chosen sufficiently small. The case where e, g are negative is treated analogously, and the first statement is thus proved.

If $eg - f^2 < 0$ then we can write $Q(u,v)$ as a product $\mathfrak{L}_1(u,v)\mathfrak{L}_2(u,v)$ of linearly independent linear forms $\mathfrak{L}_i : \mathbb{R}^2 \to \mathbb{R}$. The two lines $\mathfrak{L}_i(u,v) = 0$ divide the plane into four sectors: in two of these sectors $\mathfrak{L}_1$ and $\mathfrak{L}_2$ have equal signs, and in the other two they have opposite signs. There are therefore unit vectors $(u_0, v_0), (u_1, v_1) \in \mathbb{R}^2$ such that $a_0 = Q(u_0, v_0) < 0 < Q(u_1, v_1) = a_1$. Now observe that

$$\lim_{t \to 0} \frac{h(tu_i, tv_i)}{t^2} = \lim_{t \to 0}\left\{\frac{Q(tu_i, tv_i)}{2t^2} + \frac{R(tu_i, tv_i)}{|(tu_i, tv_i)|^2}\right\}$$

$$= \frac{a_i}{2} + \lim t \to 0 \frac{R(tu_i, tv_i)}{|(tu_i, tv_i)|^2} = \frac{a_i}{2}$$

for $i = 0.1$. This shows that $h(u,v)$ takes positive and negative values for (u,v) arbitrarily close to the origin and proves (ii).   □

Let us now study the contact between two surfaces. Assume that S_1 and S_2 are tangent at p_0, and denote $\pi : \mathbb{R}^2 \to p_0 + T_{p_0}S_1$ the orthogonal projection on the tangent plane to S at p_0: thus, the vector $\pi(p) - p_0$ belongs to $T_{p_0} S_1$, and $\pi(p) - p$ is orthogonal to the same plane. Note that the derivative at p_0 of the restriction of π to each of the surfaces is the identity. Hence, by 2.3.5, there exist open neighborhoods U_1 and U_2 of p_0 in S_1 and S_2, respectively, such that $\pi\big|_{U_2}$ and $\pi\big|_{U_2}$ are diffeomorphisms onto their image. Let us fix $\delta > 0$ such that

$$\{p \in p_0 + T_{p_0} S_1 : |p - p_0| < \delta\} \subseteq \pi(U_1) \cap \pi(U_2);$$

and, given an orthonormal basis $(\mathbf{w}_1, \mathbf{w}_2)$ of $T_{p_0} S_1$ and putting $N_0 = \mathbf{w}_1 \times \mathbf{w}_2$, define

$$\Phi(u, v) = \pi\big|_{U_1}^{-1} (p_0 + u\mathbf{w}_1 + v\mathbf{w}_2)$$
$$= p_0 + u\mathbf{w}_1 + v\mathbf{w}_2 + h_1(u, v)N_0,$$
$$\Psi(u, v) = \pi\big|_{U_2}^{-1} (p_0 + u\mathbf{w}_1 + v\mathbf{w}_2)$$
$$= p_0 + u\mathbf{w}_1 + v\mathbf{w}_2 + h_2(u, v)N_0,$$

whenever $u^2 + v^2 < \delta^2$. These parameterizations correspond to regarding S_1 and S_2 locally as the graphs of the functions h_1 and h_2 defined at $p_0 + T_{p_0} S_1$.

We say that S_1 and S_2 have *contact order* ≥ 2 at p_0 if

$$\lim_{(u,v) \to (0,0)} \frac{h_1(u, v) - h_2(u, v)}{u^2 + v^2} = 0.$$

Expanding the functions h_i into Taylor polynomials, we see that this happens if and only h_1 and h_2 and their partial derivatives up to second order are equal at $(0,0)$; but, since we have $h_i(0,0) = 0$ and

$$\frac{\partial h_i}{\partial u}\bigg|_{(0,0)} = \frac{\partial h_i}{\partial v}\bigg|_{(0,0)} = 0$$

for $i = 1, 2$, this condition boils down to

$$\frac{\partial^2 h_1}{\partial u^2}\bigg|_{(0,0)} = \frac{\partial^2 h_2}{\partial u^2}\bigg|_{(0,0)},$$
$$\frac{\partial^2 h_1}{\partial u \partial v}\bigg|_{(0,0)} = \frac{\partial^2 h_2}{\partial u \partial v}\bigg|_{(0,0)}, \qquad (3.11)$$
$$\frac{\partial^2 h_1}{\partial v^2}\bigg|_{(0,0)} = \frac{\partial^2 h_2}{\partial v^2}\bigg|_{0,0}.$$

Now if S_1 and S_2 are oriented such that their normal vectors both coincide with N_0 at the point p_0, then the second-order derivatives of h_1 and h_2 are the coefficients of the second fundamental form at p_0 of the parameterizations $\Phi(u, v)$ and $\Psi(u, v)$. Since $\Phi_u\big|_{p_0} = \Psi_u\big|_{p_0} = \mathbf{w}_1$ and $\Phi_v\big|_{p_0} = \Psi_v\big|_{p_0} = \mathbf{w}_2$, the equality of the coefficients implies that the second fundamental forms of the two surfaces coincide at the point p_0. We thus proved half of the following proposition.

Proposition 3.2.3 *Let S_1 and S_2 be two oriented surfaces tangent at p_0 whose normal vectors coincide at that point. Then the following two conditions are equivalent:*

(i) S_1 and S_2 have contact of order ≥ 2 at p_0;

(ii) the restrictions on $T_{p_0} S_1 = T_{p_0} S_2$ of the second fundamental forms of S_1 and S_2 coincide.

It is left to the reader to prove that (ii) $\Rightarrow$ (i).

Given a point p_0 on a surface S_1, the equalities 3.1.1, plus the fact that the function and its first derivatives vanish at $(0,0)$, completely determine a polynomial $h_2(u,v)$ of degree **at most two**, given by $h_2(u,v) = \dfrac{1}{2}\left(eu^2 + 2fuv + gv^2\right)$ — where e, f, g are the coefficients of the second fundamental form of $\Phi(u,v)$ at p_0. This means that *there is exactly one paraboloid which has contact of order ≥ 2 with S_1 on p_0*; it is called the *osculating paraboloid*. It is an elliptic paraboloid when p_0 is an elliptic point, hyperbolic when p_0 is hyperbolic; it is a plane when p_0 is planar, and when p_0 is parabolic it is a straight paraboloid (a figure generated by a line perpendicular to a plane when its base point runs through a parabola).

We end this section by considering two special types of curves on surfaces; the question of the existence of such curves will be dealt with in the next section.

We say that a regular curve $\alpha(t)$ in S is a *line of curvature* if, for every t, the vector $\alpha'(t)$ defines one of the principal directions in $\alpha(t)$ — that is, if $\alpha'(t)$ is an eigenvector of $DN_{\alpha(t)}$. Using this formulation, we recognize that α is a line of curvature if and only if there exists a function $\lambda(t)$ such that $(N \circ \alpha)'(t) = \lambda(t)\alpha'(t)$ and, if such a function exists, it is differentiable because it is defined by

$$\lambda(t) = \frac{\langle (N \circ \alpha)'(t), \alpha'(t)\rangle}{|\alpha'(t)|^2}.$$

An *asymptotic line* is a regular curve whose velocity vector defines at each point an asymptotic direction — that is, it is a curve whose normal curvature is constant and equal to zero. It follows from the argument in example 3.1.4 **B** that at all points on an asymptotic line the Gaussian curvature is nonpositive. In local coordinates, formula (3.5) implies that a regular curve $\Psi(u(t),v(t))$ is asymptotic if and only if $e(u')^2 + 2fu'v' + g(v')^2 \equiv 0$.

Exercises

60. Define orientations for $S_1 = \{(x,y,z): z = x^2 - y^2\}$ and $S_2 = \{(x,y,z): z = x^3 - 3xy^2\}$, and then determine for each of these surfaces:

(a) the Gaussian curvature and the mean curvature at each point;

(b) the points where the mean curvature vanishes.

(c) Do any of the answers to the above questions depend on the chosen orientations?

61. (a) Show that the Gaussian curvature of the Möbius strip $\mathbb{M}$ (with the parameterization given in 2.4.2) is given by

$$K(\theta, t) = -\left(\frac{1}{4}t^2 + \left(2 - t\sin\frac{\theta}{2}\right)^2\right)^{-2}.$$

(b) Show that if S is a surface of strictly positive curvature at all its points, then S is orientable. Show further that it is possible to choose this orientation such that all principal curvatures are positive. **Hint:** For every point p_0 of S, let U be the neighborhood given by 3.2.2 (i) and $N(p_0)$ the normal vector pointing to the side where U lies; then $N: S \to \mathbf{S}^2$ is an orientation of S.

62. Show that the pseudosphere (Exercise 32) has constant negative curvature.

63. (a) Show that the only surfaces of revolution with zero constant curvature are the cylinder, cone and plane.

(b) Show that any surface of revolution of constant curvature $K = -1$ is, up to reparametrization, of the form $\Phi(u, v) = (\rho(v)\cos u, \rho(v)\sin u, z(v))$, where the generating curve $v \mapsto (\rho(v), 0, z(v))$ is of one of the following three types:

(i) $\rho(v) = A\cosh v$, $z(v) = \int_0^v \sqrt{1 - A^2\sinh^2 t}\, dt$, $A > 0$;

(ii) $\rho(v) = Ae^{-v}$, $z(v) = \int_0^v \sqrt{1 - A^2 e^{-2t}}\, dt$, $A > 0$;

(iii) $\rho(v) = A\sinh v$, $z(v) = \int_0^v \sqrt{1 - A^2\cosh^2 t}\, dt$, $0 < A < 1$;

In each of the cases find the domain of v and sketch the generating curve.

(c) Show that the surface of type (ii) is the pseudosphere.

64. Let $p_0 \in S$ be such that $K(p_0) \neq 0$, and let (U, Φ) be a parametrized neighborhood of p_0 where K has constant sign. Show that:

(a) $N_u \times N_v = K(u, v)(\Phi_u \times \Phi_v)$;

(b) if $V \subseteq \Phi(U)$, then the area of $N(V) \subseteq \mathbf{S}^2$ is given by $\int_V |K|\, d\sigma$;

(c) $|K(p_0)|$ is the limit of the ratio $\frac{\text{area of} N(V)}{\text{area of} V}$ as the diameter of its neighborhood V tends to zero.

65. Complete the proof of Proposition 3.2.3.

66. Let p_0 be a point shared by the surfaces S_1 and S_2. Show that the following assertions are equivalent:

(i) S_1 and S_2 have contact of order ≥ 2 at p_0.

(ii) There exist parameterizations $\Phi(u, v)$ and $\Psi(u, v)$ of S_1 and S_2 such that $p_0 = \Phi(0, 0) = \psi(0, 0)$ and

$$\lim_{(u,v)\to(0,0)} \frac{|\Phi(u,v) - \Psi(u,v)|}{u^2 + v^2} = 0.$$

67. A regular surface S is a *ruled surface* if $S = \{\alpha(t) + \lambda\mathbf{v}(t) : t \in J, \lambda \in \mathbb{R}\}$, where J is an interval, $\alpha, \mathbf{v}: J \to \mathbb{R}^3$ are C^∞, and $\alpha'(t)$, $\mathbf{v}(t)$ are linearly independent vectors for all $t \in J$. Note that then $S = \bigcup_{t \in J} r_t$, where r_t is the line $\{\alpha(t) + \lambda\mathbf{v}(t) : \lambda \in \mathbb{R}\}$.

(a) Show that the hyperbolic paraboloid $z = x^2 - y^2$ and the hyperboloid $x^2 + y^2 - z^2 = 1$ are ruled surfaces, and find out whether the equation $e^x = z + y^2$ defines a ruled surface;

(b) Show that the tangent planes to the ruled surface S intersect S along a line, which is an asymptotic line; conclude that the curvature of S is ≤ 0 at all points.

68. With the notation of Exercise 67, let S be a ruled surface without planar points. Show that the following conditions are equivalent:

i. S has curvature 0 at all its points.

ii. The lines $\lambda \mapsto \alpha(t) + \lambda \mathbf{v}(t)$ are lines of curvature of S.

iii. For every $t \in I$, the vector $\mathbf{v}'(t)$ is a linear combination of $\mathbf{v}(t)$ and $\alpha'(t)$.

69. Given a point p on a compact surface $S \subseteq \mathbb{R}^3$, we define the diameter of S at p by $d(p) = \max \{|q - p| : q \in S\}$. Assume that S has constant diameter d — that is, that $d(p) = d$ for every point p of S. Show that:

(a) for every p in S there exists a single point $f(p)$ in S such that $|f(p) - p| = d$;

(b) f is an involutive diffeomorphism of S (i.e., $f \circ f = \mathrm{id}$);

(c) S has strictly positive curvature, and therefore [Exercise 61-b)] admits an orientation for which all principal curvatures are positive;

(d) if $k_2(p) \geq k_1(p)$ denote the principal curvatures of S then

$$\frac{1}{k_1(p)} + \frac{1}{k_2(f(p))} = d.$$

3.3 Vector Fields

A vector field assigns to each point in a surface a vector in the tangent space of the surface to that point. If this assignment is made in a sufficiently regular way, the vector field can be interpreted as a velocity field, and so it determines certain curves (*trajectories*) on the surface. With this approach we can establish in this section the existence of curves and parameterizations satisfying certain requirements (such as asymptotic lines, lines of curvature, and orthogonal parameterizations).

A *vector field* of class C^k ($k \geq 1$) in an open subset $V \subseteq \mathbb{R}^n$ is a mapping $\mathbf{v}: V \to \mathbb{R}^n$ of class C^k, and a *trajectory* (or *integral curve*) of $\mathbf{v}$ is a curve $\varphi: I \to V$ such that $\varphi'(t) = \mathbf{v}(\varphi(t))$. In other words, a trajectory is a curve whose velocity at each point is the vector $\mathbf{v}$ assigned to that point. The fundamental theorem of differential equations, which we now state, asserts the existence and uniqueness of the trajectory passing through each $p \in V$ at a given instant; for its proof we suggest [23].

Theorem 3.3.1 *Given a vector field* $\mathbf{v}: V \subseteq \mathbb{R}^n \to \mathbb{R}^n$ *of class* C^k ($k \geq 1$) *and* $p_0 \in V$, *there exist* $\varepsilon > 0$, *an open neighborhood* $U \subseteq V$ *of* p_0, *and a* C^k *mapping* $\varphi:]-\varepsilon, \varepsilon[\times U \to V$, *such that, for every* $p \in U$, *the curve* $t \mapsto \varphi(t, p)$ *is the only trajectory of* $\mathbf{v}$ *with initial condition* $\varphi(0, p) = p$ (*in the sense that any other trajectory with the same initial condition coincides with this one in the intersection of their domains*).

At a point p where the vector field $\mathbf{v}$ vanishes, one trajectory of $\mathbf{v}$ that passes through p is the constant curve $\varphi(t) = p$; the theorem guarantees that this is the only trajectory that passes through p. This means that the *singularities* of the vector field

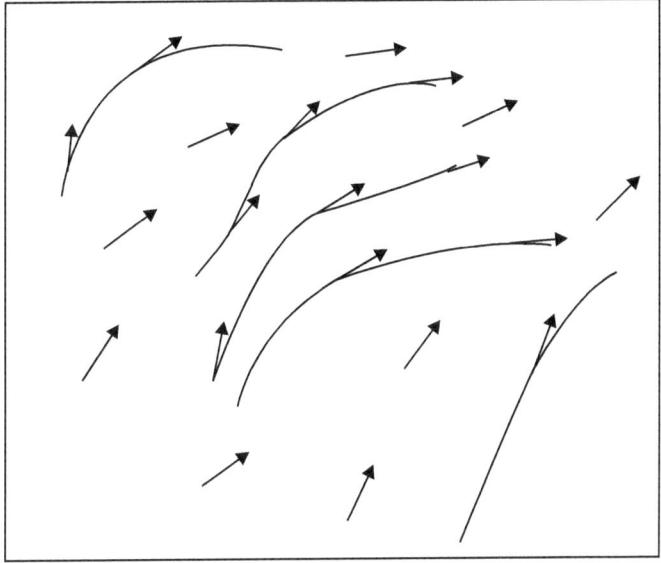

Figure 3.3

$\mathbf{v}$ correspond to the constant trajectories, and the trajectories of the other points are regular curves: for if the derivative of $\varphi(t)$ vanishes at t_0, then $\varphi(t_0)$ is a singularity of $\mathbf{v}$ and the only trajectory through $\varphi(t_0)$ is the constant one: so a non-constant trajectory cannot have points of zero velocity.

The mapping $\varphi(t, p)$ in 3.3.1 is called the *local flow* of the vector field $\mathbf{v}$. A frequent way to write the differential equation associated with a given field is in the form

$$X = \mathbf{v}(X)$$

where $X = (x_1, \ldots, x_n)$ is a point of V. A differential equation of this type is called *autonomous*. A *non-autonomous* equation is one where the right-hand side depends explicitly on the independent variable t, i.e. of the form

$$X = \mathbf{v}(t, X), \tag{3.12}$$

where $\mathbf{v}: I \times V \subseteq \mathbb{R} \times \mathbb{R}^n \to \mathbb{R}^n$ is of class C^k. A simple example is given by the equation $X = tX$: a curve $\alpha(t)$ in $\mathbb{R}^n$ is a solution of this equation if and only if $\alpha'(t) = t\alpha(t)$.

For non-autonomous equations there is also a theorem of existence, uniqueness and differentiable dependence on initial conditions. In this instance, given $(t_0, p_0) \in I \times V$, there exists a mapping $\varphi:]t_0 - \varepsilon, t_0 + \varepsilon[\times U \to V$ of class C^k (where U is an open neighborhood of p_0) such that, for every $p \in U$, the function $t \mapsto \varphi(t, p)$ is the only solution of 3.1.2 with $\varphi(t_0, p) = p$ defined in the interval $]t_0 - \varepsilon, t_0 + \varepsilon[$.

This result for non-autonomous equations, although seemingly more general than 3.3.1, can in fact be easily deduced from it. To this end we consider the autonomous equation

$$Y = \mathbf{w}(Y), \tag{3.13}$$

where we put $Y = (t, X) \in I \times V$, and where the vector field $\mathbf{w} : I \times V \subseteq \mathbb{R}^{n+1} \to \mathbb{R}^{n+1}$ is given by $\mathbf{w}(t, X) = (1, \mathbf{v}(t, X))$. If $\psi(s)$ is the solution of (3.13) with $\psi(0) = (t_0, p)$, then we have $\psi(s) = (t_0 + s, \widetilde{\varphi}(s))$, and therefore $t = t_0 + s$. Putting $\varphi(t) = \widetilde{\varphi}(t - t_0)$, we recognize that $\varphi(t)$ is the solution of (3.12) with initial condition $\varphi(t_0) = p$ if and only if $\psi(s) = (t_0 + s, \widetilde{\varphi}(s))$ is a solution of (3.13) with initial condition $\psi(0) = (t_0, p)$.

Returning to surfaces, a *vector field* in an open subset $V \subseteq S$ is a mapping $\mathbf{v}$ such that $\mathbf{v}(p) \in T_p S$ for every $p \in V$. Using local coordinates, we can write $\mathbf{v} \circ \Phi(u, v) = \alpha(u, v)\Phi_u + \beta(u, v)\Phi_v$ for certain functions α and β. We say that $\mathbf{v}$ is of class C^k if every point of V has a parametrized neighborhood $\Phi(u, v)$ in which the coordinate functions α and β of $\mathbf{v}$ are of class C^k (of course then the coordinate functions of $\mathbf{v}$ in any parameterization are of class C^k). Unless otherwise stated, our vector fields are C^∞.

The equation $X = \mathbf{v}(X)$, when X is contained in the image of $\Phi(u, v)$, is equivalent to the equation $(u, v) = (\alpha(u, v), \beta(u, v))$ defined in an open subset of $\mathbb{R}^2$: in fact, $\varphi(t)$ is a trajectory of the latter equation if and only if $\Phi \circ \varphi(t)$ is a trajectory of the former. Theorem 3.3.1 is then carried over without changes to surfaces, since it concerns local properties of trajectories.

Example 3.3.2 As an example of the application of these ideas, let us verify that through each **non-umbilical** point p pass exactly two lines of curvature, corresponding to the two principal directions at p: to prove this, it suffices to show that there are two differentiable vector fields $\mathbf{w}_1$ and $\mathbf{w}_2$, defined in a neighborhood of p, such that, for every q, the vectors $\mathbf{w}_1(q)$ and $\mathbf{w}_2(q)$ define the two principal directions in q: the two lines of curvature through p are then the integral curves of $\mathbf{w}_1$ and $\mathbf{w}_2$ that pass through p. (The precise choice of the $\mathbf{w}_i$ does not matter, since any other suitable vector fields would have the same trajectories up to reparametrization.)

Let us consider a parameterization $\Phi(u, v)$ in a neighborhood of the non-umbilical point $p = \Phi(0, 0)$. By the formulas (3.6)–(3.9), §2, the entries a_{ij} of the matrix of $-DN_{\Phi(u,v)}$ relative to the basis (Φ_u, Φ_v) are differentiable functions of (u, v), and so are the principal curvatures $k_1 < k_2$ in a neighborhood of $(0, 0)$. The eigenvectors of $-DN_{\Phi(u,v)}$ are $\alpha_i \Phi_u + \beta_i \Phi_v$, where

$$\begin{bmatrix} a_{11} - k_i & a_{12} \\ a_{21} & a_{22} - k_i \end{bmatrix} \begin{bmatrix} \alpha_i \\ \beta_i \end{bmatrix} = \begin{bmatrix} 0 \\ 0 \end{bmatrix}, \quad i = 1, 2. \tag{3.14}$$

If $a_{12}|_{(0,0)} \neq 0$, then nonzero solutions of (3.14) in a neighborhood of $(0, 0)$ are given by $(\alpha_i, \beta_i) = (-a_{12}, a_{11} - k_i)$ for $i = 1, 2$. If $a_{21}|_{(0,0)} \neq 0$, then we take $(\alpha_i, \beta_i) = (a_{22} - k_i, -a_{21})$. If $a_{12}|_{(0,0)} = a_{21}|_{(0,0)} = 0$, then the $k_i|_p$ will be precisely $a_{11}|_{(0,0)}$ and $a_{22}|_{(0,0)}$, and therefore $a_{11}|_{(0,0)} \neq a_{22}|_{(0,0)}$; assuming $k_1|_p = a_{11}|_{(0,0)}$ and $k_2|_p = a_{22}|_{(0,0)}$, we see that $(\alpha_1, \beta_1) = (a_{22} - k_1, -a_{21})$ and $(\alpha_2, \beta_2) = (-a_{12}, a_{11} - k_2)$ are nonzero solutions of (3.14) in some neighborhood of $(0,0)$.

In any case, we find non-trivial solutions of (3.14) that depend differentiably on (u, v), and the promised vector fields are given by $\mathbf{w}_i = \alpha_i \Phi_u + \beta_i \Phi_v$, $i = 1, 2$. The local character of this construction is unavoidable, because there may not exist differentiable vector fields, defined at all non-umbilical points in the surface, which always point to a principal direction.   □

What happens in the above example is that the principal directions do not define *vector* fields, but *direction* fields: a *direction field* is a mapping $\mathcal{D}$, defined in an open subset $U \subseteq S$, such that, for every $p \in U$, $\mathcal{D}(p)$ is a one-dimensional linear subspace of $T_p S$. The direction field $\mathcal{D}$ is called differentiable if every point of U has an open neighborhood V in which a differentiable vector field $\mathbf{v}$ is defined such that $\mathbf{v}(p)$ generates $\mathcal{D}(p)$ for all $p \in V$. All direction fields we consider are differentiable. An *integral curve* of the direction field is a curve whose velocity at each point has the same direction as the field at that point.

Locally, the study of direction fields amounts to that of vector fields, and so it readily follows that the integral curve of a direction field through a given point exists and is unique (up to reparametrization). But, by example of the "hay fork" in Fig. 3.4, we see that there are direction fields which globally do not arise from a vector field: it is impossible to choose a coherent (continuous) orientation for all the trajectories shown in the picture.

Figure 3.4

In local coordinates the direction fields are given by a linear relation $A(u, v)\alpha + B(u, v)\beta = 0$ between the coordinates α and β of a vector in the basis (Φ_u, Φ_v), so that the integral curves have the form $\Phi(u(t), v(t))$, where $A(u, v)u' + B(u, v)v' \equiv 0$.

For example, the asymptotic directions at a point of negative Gaussian curvature satisfy the equation $e\alpha^2 + 2f\alpha\beta + g\beta^2 = 0$. Since $eg - f^2 < 0$, the left-hand side of the equation is the product of two linear factors: so if $e \neq 0$ then $e\alpha^2 + 2f\alpha\beta + g\beta^2 = e(\alpha - \lambda_1\beta)(\alpha - \lambda_2\beta)$ with $\lambda_1 \neq \lambda_2$. Hence, the two asymptotic directions at each point are given by the relations $\alpha - \lambda_1\beta = 0$, $\alpha - \lambda_2\beta = 0$, which define two direction fields. The two families of asymptotic lines are the line integrals of these vector fields, having equations $u' - \lambda_1 v' = 0$, $u' - \lambda_2 v' = 0$.

Example 3.3.3 The hyperbolic paraboloid parametrized by $\Phi(u, v) = (u, v, u^2 - v^2)$ has coefficients

$$e = \frac{2}{\sqrt{1 + 4u^2 + 4v^2}}, \quad f = 0, \quad g = \frac{-2}{\sqrt{1 + 4u^2 + 4v^2}},$$

so that the equation of the asymptotic lines is

$$\frac{2}{\sqrt{1 + 4u^2 + 4v^2}} (u'^2 - v'^2) = 0$$

which is equivalent to

$$(u' - v')(u' + v') = 0.$$

Thus, the two families of asymptotic lines are $u - v = c$ and $u + v = c$ for $c \in \mathbb{R}$, and they can be parametrized by $t \mapsto (t + c, t, 2ct + c^2)$ and $t \mapsto (-t + c, t, -2ct + t^2)$. $\square$

We say that two direction fields $\mathcal{D}_1$ and $\mathcal{D}_2$, defined in the same open subset $U \subseteq S$, are *independent* if, for every $p \in U$, the linear subspaces $\mathcal{D}_1(p)$ and $\mathcal{D}_2(p)$ of T_pS are distinct. Our next result, the most important one in this section, establishes the existence of parameterizations in which tangent lines to coordinate curves have directions fixed beforehand.

Theorem 3.3.4 *Let $\mathcal{D}_1$ and $\mathcal{D}_2$ be two independent direction fields in $U \subseteq S$. Then each point of U is contained in a parametrized neighborhood whose coordinate curves are the integral curves of $\mathcal{D}_1$ and $\mathcal{D}_2$.*

Proof Given $p_0 \in U$, consider a parameterization $\Phi(u, v)$ with $\Phi(0, 0) = p_0$. One of the vectors $\Phi_u|_{(0,0)}$ and $\Phi_v|_{(0,0)}$ is not in $\mathcal{D}_2(p_0)$, and we assume that it is the first one. We can then find, in a neighborhood of p_0, a differentiable vector field of the form $\mathbf{w} = \alpha\Phi_u + \Phi_v$ that generates $\mathcal{D}_2$. We seek a parameterization of the form

$$\Psi(x, t) = \Phi(\varphi(t, x), t)$$

and such that the coordinate curves $x = $ constant are line integrals of $\mathcal{D}_2$; the curves $t = $ constant of such a parameterization coincide with the curves $v = $ constant of $\Phi(u, v)$. We then have

$$\Psi_x = \frac{\partial\varphi}{\partial x} \Phi_u,$$

$$\Psi_t = \frac{\partial\varphi}{\partial t} \Phi_u + \Phi_v,$$

We thus see that, in order to be $\Psi_t = \mathbf{w}$, φ has to satisfy the equation

$$\frac{\partial \varphi}{\partial t} = \alpha(\varphi(t,x),t). \tag{3.15}$$

Consider now the differential equation

$$y = \alpha(y,t). \tag{3.16}$$

By the version for non-autonomous equations of Theorem 3.3.1, there exists a differentiable mapping $\varphi:]-\varepsilon, \varepsilon[\times J \to \mathbb{R}$ (where $J \subseteq \mathbb{R}$ is an open interval containing 0) such that for $x \in J$ the curve $t \mapsto \varphi(t,x)$ is the solution of (3.16) with initial condition $\varphi(0,x) = x$. Of course, such a function φ satisfies (3.15); furthermore, we have $\frac{\partial \varphi}{\partial x}\big|_{(0,0)} = \frac{\partial \varphi}{\partial x}\big|_{(0,x)} = 1$, so that $\Psi_x\big|_{(0,0)}$ and $\Psi_t\big|_{(0,0)}$ are independent. Hence, the Jacobian of $\Psi(x,t)$ at $(0,0)$ has rank two and Ψ is a parameterization in a neighborhood of p_0.

In conclusion: keeping one of the families of coordinate curves, we modified the other one so that it now corresponds to the integral curves of the $\mathcal{D}_2$ field; applying this method again (fixing now the coordinate curves corresponding to $\mathcal{D}_2$), we obtain a parameterization whose coordinate curves are the integral curves of $\mathcal{D}_1$ and of $\mathcal{D}_2$.
□

The next two results are an immediate consequence of 3.3.4 and the preceding discussion.

Corollary 3.3.5 *Every point in a surface has a neighborhood covered by an orthogonal parameterization.*

Corollary 3.3.6 *In the neighborhood of any non-umbilical point (hyperbolic point) there exists a parameterization whose coordinate curves are lines of curvature (asymptotic lines).*

Exercises

70. Show that in a neighborhood of a non-umbilical point (hyperbolic point) the coordinate curves of $\Phi(u,v)$ are lines of curvature (asymptotic lines) if and only if the coefficients of this parameterization satisfy the condition $F \equiv 0 \equiv f$ $(e \equiv 0 \equiv g)$.

71. Consider $\mathbb{T}^2$ parametrized by

$$\Phi(u,v) = ((2 + \cos v) \cos u, (2 + \cos v) \sin u, \sin v).$$

(a) Show that the curvature of $\mathbb{T}^2$ in $\Phi(u,v)$ is $\frac{\cos v}{2+\cos v}$. What are the regions of $\mathbb{T}^2$ with positive, zero and negative curvature?

(b) Show that the curves $v = \frac{\pi}{2}$ and $v = \frac{3\pi}{2}$ are asymptotic lines, and that the other asymptotic lines admit the parameterization $\alpha(t) = \Phi(u(t), v(t))$, where

$$(u(t), v(t)) = \left(u_0 + \int_0^t \frac{dx}{\sqrt{\cos x(2 - \cos x)}} , \pi + t \right), \quad t \in \left] -\frac{\pi}{2}, \frac{\pi}{2} \right[$$

or

$$(u(t), v(t)) = \left(u_0 - \int_0^t \frac{dx}{\sqrt{\cos x(2 - \cos x)}} , \pi + t \right), \quad t \in \left] -\frac{\pi}{2}, \frac{\pi}{2} \right[.$$

(c) Show that $\lim\limits_{t \to -\frac{\pi}{2}} \alpha(t)$ and $\lim\limits_{t \to \frac{\pi}{2}} \alpha(t)$ exist and are points of the parallels $v = \frac{\pi}{2}$ and $v = \frac{3\pi}{2}$. Deduce that all asymptotic lines of $\mathbb{T}^2$ have finite length.

72. Let S be a surface of constant zero Gaussian curvature and let p be a **parabolic** point of S. Show that there exists a line segment through p which is entirely contained in S.

Chapter 4
The Intrinsic Geometry of Surfaces

By intrinsic geometry of a surface we mean those properties that depend exclusively on measurements made on the surface but not on how the surface is embedded in the ambient space. Hence, the length of a curve on a sheet of paper is an intrinsic property, because it doesn't change when we fold the sheet; but the distance in space between two points on that same sheet is not intrinsic. In this chapter we study the intrinsic properties of surfaces and the mappings that preserve such properties (isometries).

All sections of this chapter are basic and should be studied consecutively, except for 4.4, which can be omitted because it is only needed for sections 5.4 and 5.5; the Rotation Index Theorem, proved in the Appendix, is used in Section 4.5. (Sections 4.5 and 4.6 are independent of each other and, from a logical point of view, can be studied in any order; but the Gauss-Bonnet theorem should be included as early as possible.)

4.1 Conformal Mappings and Isometries

It is impossible to draw an entirely accurate map of the terrestrial globe on a plane: all known maps distort the relative size of regions — making those further away from the equator appear larger than they are in reality — and distort the shape of continents. Still, a map is an approximate depiction of the real world, the more accurate as the region so represented becomes smaller. In the terminology we now introduce, this means that there exist conformal mappings of spherical regions into planes, but there are no such mappings which are isometries.

A mapping $f : U \subseteq S_1 \to S_2$ (for an open subset U of S_1) is *conformal* if for every $p \in U$ the derivative $Df_p : T_p S_1 \to T_{f(p)} S_2$ at p is an isomorphism that preserves angles — i.e., if, for all $\mathbf{v}, \mathbf{w}$ in $T_p S_1$, the angles $\angle (Df_p(\mathbf{v}), Df_p(\mathbf{w}))$ and $\angle (\mathbf{v}, \mathbf{w})$ are equal. This means that two regular curves that intersect at p at a certain angle are

P. V. Araújo, *Differential Geometry*, https://doi.org/10.1007/978-3-031-62384-4_4

sent by the conformal mapping f into curves that intersect at $f(p)$ at the same angle. (Note that we are referring to *non-oriented* angles).

We now give a brief interlude of linear algebra showing several characterizations of linear maps which preserve angles.

Lemma 4.1.1 *Let* $(E_1, \langle \cdot, \cdot \rangle_1)$ *and* $(E_2, \langle \cdot, \cdot \rangle_2)$ *be spaces of the same dimension* n *equipped with an inner product and let* $L: E_1 \to E_2$ *be a linear isomorphism. Then the following conditions are equivalent:*

  i.   *L preserves angles;*
 ii.   *L is a similarity — that is, there exists $\lambda > 0$ such that $|L(\mathbf{v})|_2 = \lambda |\mathbf{v}|_1$ for all $\mathbf{v} \in E_1$;*
iii.   *there exists $\lambda > 0$ such that $\langle L(\mathbf{v}), L(\mathbf{w}) \rangle_2 = \lambda^2 \langle \mathbf{v}, \mathbf{w} \rangle_1$ for all $\mathbf{v}, \mathbf{w} \in E_1$;*
 iv.   *there exist $\lambda > 0$ and a basis $(\mathbf{v}_1, \ldots, \mathbf{v}_n)$ of E_1 such that $\langle L(\mathbf{v}_i), L(\mathbf{v}_j) \rangle_2 = \lambda^2 \langle \mathbf{v}_i, \mathbf{v}_j \rangle_1$ for all $1 \le i, j \le n$.*

Proof The equivalence between iii. and iv. is simple to verify, and ii. is included for informational purposes only; finally, to show that ii. ⇔ iii. may be left as an exercise.

i. ⇒ iii.   Let $(\mathbf{e}_1, \ldots, \mathbf{e}_n)$ be an orthonormal basis of E_1. The vectors $L(\mathbf{e}_1), \ldots, L(\mathbf{e}_n)$ are then pairwise orthogonal. Given $i \ne j$, the angle $\theta \in [0, \pi]$ between $\mathbf{e}_i$ and $\mathbf{e}_i + \mathbf{e}_j$ is given by

$$\cos \theta = \frac{\langle \mathbf{e}_i, \mathbf{e}_i + \mathbf{e}_j \rangle_1}{|\mathbf{e}_i|_1 |\mathbf{e}_i + \mathbf{e}_j|_1} = \frac{1}{\sqrt{2}}$$

so that $\theta = \frac{\pi}{4}$. Since L preserves angles, we also have

$$\frac{\langle L(\mathbf{e}_i), L(\mathbf{e}_i + \mathbf{e}_j) \rangle_2}{|L(\mathbf{e}_i)|_2 |L(\mathbf{e}_i + \mathbf{e}_j)|_2} = \frac{1}{\sqrt{2}},$$

and from this

$$|L(\mathbf{e}_i)|_2 = \frac{\langle L(\mathbf{e}_i), L(\mathbf{e}_i) \rangle_2}{|L(\mathbf{e}_i)|_2} = \frac{1}{\sqrt{2}} |L(\mathbf{e}_i + \mathbf{e}_j)|_2 .$$

Since the roles of $\mathbf{e}_i$ and $\mathbf{e}_j$ are interchangeable, we also have

$$|L(\mathbf{e}_j)|_2 = \frac{1}{\sqrt{2}} |L(\mathbf{e}_i + \mathbf{e}_j)|_2 ,$$

and so we deduce that $|L(\mathbf{e}_i)|_2 = |L(\mathbf{e}_j)|_2$ for all $1 \le i, j \le n$. We now easily conclude that iii. holds for $\lambda = |L(\mathbf{e}_i)|2$.

iii. ⇒. i.   Just note that if iii. holds then we have, for all vectors $\mathbf{v}, \mathbf{w} \in E_1$

$$\frac{\langle L(\mathbf{v}), L(\mathbf{w}) \rangle_2}{|L(\mathbf{v})|_2 |L(\mathbf{w})|_2} = \frac{\lambda^2 \langle \mathbf{v}, \mathbf{w} \rangle_1}{\lambda |\mathbf{v}|_1 \lambda |\mathbf{w}|_1} = \frac{\langle \mathbf{v}, \mathbf{w} \rangle_1}{|\mathbf{v}|_1 |\mathbf{w}|_1} . \quad \Box$$

From condition iii. of the lemma, it follows that $f: U \subseteq S_1 \to S_2$ is conformal if and only if there exists a function $\lambda: U \to \mathbb{R}^+$ such that, for all $p \in U$ and $\mathbf{v}, \mathbf{w} \in T_p S$,

$$\langle Df_p(\mathbf{v}), Df_p(\mathbf{w}) \rangle = \lambda(p)^2 \langle \mathbf{v}, \mathbf{w} \rangle. \tag{4.1}$$

By iv., condition (4.1) only needs to be checked for the vectors of a given basis of $T_p S$. This has the consequence that in local coordinates $\Phi(u, v)$ the condition that f is conformal is equivalent to the combination of the three equalities

$$\langle (f \circ \Phi)_u, (f \circ \Phi)_u \rangle = \lambda(u, v)^2 \langle \Phi_u, \Phi_u \rangle$$
$$\langle (f \circ \Phi)_u, (f \circ \Phi)_v \rangle = \lambda(u, v)^2 \langle \Phi_u, \Phi_v \rangle$$
$$\langle (f \circ \Phi)_v, (f \circ \Phi)_v \rangle = \lambda(u, v)^2 \langle \Phi_v, \Phi_v \rangle,$$

that express that the coefficients of the first fundamental form of the parameterization $\Phi(u, v)$ of S_1 are proportional to those of the parametrization $\Psi(u, v) = f \circ \Phi(u, v)$ of S_2. (There is a certain abuse of language here, since only locally can it be guaranteed that Ψ is a parameterization.) It further follows from these formulas that $\lambda: U \to \mathbb{R}^+$ is differentiable, because its expression $\lambda(u, v)$ in local coordinates is differentiable.

Example 4.1.2 Let us verify that the stereographic projection (Exercise 30, Section 2.1) $\pi: \mathbf{S}^1 \setminus \{(0, 0, 1)\} \to \mathbb{R}^2$ is conformal. We recall that

$$\pi(x, y, z) = \left(\frac{2x}{1 - z}, \frac{2y}{1 - z} \right);$$

so, using local coordinates

$$\Phi(u, v) = \left(\sqrt{1 - v^2} \cos u, \sqrt{1 - v^2} \sin u, v \right), \quad v \in \,]{-1}, 1[\, ,$$

in $\mathbf{S}^2$, the coordinates $\Psi = \pi \circ \Phi$ are given by

$$\Psi(u, v) = 2 \left(\sqrt{\frac{1 + v}{1 - v}} \cos u, \sqrt{\frac{1 + v}{1 - v}} \sin u \right).$$

The coefficients of $\Phi(u, v)$ are

$$E = 1 - v^2, \quad F = 0, \quad G = \frac{1}{1 - v^2},$$

and those of $\Psi(u, v)$ are

$$\overline{E} = \frac{4(1 + v)}{1 - v}, \quad \overline{F} = 0, \quad \overline{G} = \frac{4}{(1 - v)^3 (1 + v)}.$$

Noting that

$$\overline{E} = \lambda(u,v)^2 E, \quad \overline{F} = \lambda(u,v)^2 F, \quad \overline{G} = \lambda(u,v)^2 G,$$

where $\lambda(u,v) = \frac{2}{1-v}$, we conclude that the restriction of π to the image of $\Phi(u,v)$ is conformal. Such a parameterization excludes a meridian, but any point of $\mathbf{S}^2$, except the poles, can be covered by $\Phi(u,v)$ if we adjust the domain of u. We have thus shown that π is conformal at all points of $\mathbf{S}^2 \setminus \{(0,0,1),(0,0,-1)\}$. But since $\lim_{v \to -1} \lambda(u,v) = 1$, the function λ extends continuously to $\mathbf{S}^2 \setminus \{(0,0,1)\}$, and therefore π is conformal on its entire domain. $\qquad\qquad\qquad\qquad\qquad\qquad\qquad\qquad\qquad\qquad\qquad\qquad\qquad\qquad\square$

If $f: U \subseteq S_1 \to S_2$ is conformal, we have already observed that the function $\lambda: U \to \mathbb{R}^+$ given by (4.1) is differentiable, and hence continuous. This means that in a neighborhood of $p_0 \in U$, the mapping f is "approximately" a similarity of ratio $\lambda(p_0)$, which is the reason why cartographic mappings based on conformal mappings are more faithful to reality when representing small regions.

Given the importance of the concept, it is natural to ask whether between two arbitrary surfaces there exist conformal mappings, at least locally. Since the inverse and composite of conformal mappings are still conformal, the (affirmative) answer to this question is a consequence of the fact that any point on a surface has a neighborhood that can be parametrized by a conformal mapping. Such a parameterization is called *isothermal*.

The condition for $\Phi(u,v)$ to be isothermal is that its coefficients E, F, G are proportional to the coefficients of the parameterization $(u,v) \mapsto (u,v)$ of the plane, which are $1, 0, 1$ — that is, $E \equiv G$, $F \equiv 0$.

The existence of isothermal parameterizations for arbitrary surfaces is a deep result, and we therefore omit its proof (which you can find, in all generality, in [25], vol.IV, p. 455 ff.). Note that by 4.1.2 the inverse of the stereographic projection is an isothermal parameterization of the sphere; in the exercises we give other examples.

Let us now talk about isometries. We say that $f: U \subseteq S_1 \to S_2$ is a *local isometry* if for every $p \in U$ the derivative $Df_p: T_p S_1 \to T_{f(p)} S_2$ is a linear isometry — that is, if $\langle Df_p(\mathbf{v}), Df_p(\mathbf{w}) \rangle = \langle \mathbf{v}, \mathbf{w} \rangle$ for all $\mathbf{v}, \mathbf{w} \in T_p S_1$. An *isometry* is a **diffeomorphism** $f: S_1 \to S_2$ which is also a local isometry. Two surfaces are *isometric* if there exists an isometry between them. They are *locally isometric* if every point of each surface has an open neighborhood which is isometric to an open subset of the other surface.

A local isometry is thus a mapping that preserves the first fundamental form, and therefore preserves all the quantities that depend on it: the length of curves, the angle between two curves, and the area of small regions (i. e., such that the mapping, restricted to them, is injective). In local coordinates, f is a local isometry when the coefficients of the first fundamental form of the parameterizations $\Phi(u,v)$ and $\Psi(u,v) = f \circ \Phi(u,v)$ coincide.

Examples 4.1.3 **A.** The linear isometries of $\mathbb{R}^2$ are isometries in the sense just defined. The converse, which is more interesting, appears in the exercises of this section: any isometry of $\mathbb{R}^2$ is the composite of a linear isometry with a translation.

B. Let S be a surface of revolution with axis r and let $L: \mathbb{R}^3 \to \mathbb{R}^3$ be a rotation around r. Then $L|_S: S \to S$ is an isometry of S.

C. The plane and cylinder $C = \{(x, y, z) \in \mathbb{R}^3 : x^2 + y^2 = 1\}$ are locally isometric: a local isometry $\mathbb{R}^2 \to C$ is $f(u, v) = (\cos u, \sin u, v)$, and consists simply of wrapping the plane around the cylinder. By identifying $\mathbb{R}^2$ with $\mathbb{R}^2 \times \{0\} \subseteq \mathbb{R}^3$, this example shows that not all isometries or local isometries between surfaces are restrictions of isometries of $\mathbb{R}^3$.

D. The cone $\mathfrak{C}_k = \{(x, y, z) : z = k\sqrt{x^2 + y^2}, z \neq 0\}$, for all $k > 0$, is locally isometric to the plane: if we cut $\mathfrak{C}_k$ along a generatrix and unroll it, then we obtain a circular sector U bounded by two half-lines with origin O, in which the arcs of the circle with center O correspond to the parallels of $\mathfrak{C}_k$. If $\alpha \in]0, \frac{\pi}{2}[$ is the angle that the cone's generatrix makes with the z-axis, and $\beta \in]0, 2\pi[$ is the angle defined by U, then

$$\operatorname{tg} \alpha = \frac{1}{k}, \qquad \beta = 2\pi \sin \alpha,$$

and also $U = \{(\rho \cos \varphi, \rho \sin \varphi) \in \mathbb{R}^2 : \rho > 0, 0 < \varphi < \beta\}$. (See Fig. 4.1.)

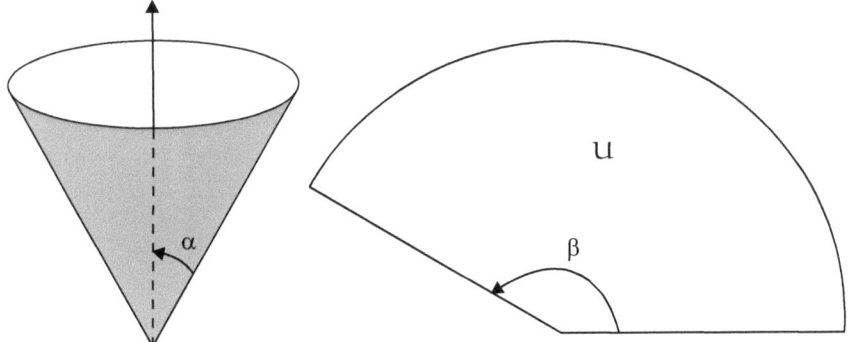

Figure 4.1

We define a mapping $f : U \to \mathfrak{C}_k$ by sending the point with polar coordinates (ρ, φ) to the point

$$\left(\frac{\rho\beta}{2\pi} \cos\left(\frac{2\pi\varphi}{\beta}\right), \frac{\rho\beta}{2\pi} \sin\left(\frac{2\pi\varphi}{\beta}\right), \rho \cos \alpha \right):$$

f is a local isometry because the parameterizations

$$\Phi(\rho, \varphi) = (\rho \cos \varphi, \rho \sin \varphi)$$

and

$$f \circ \Phi(\rho, \varphi) = \left(\frac{\rho\beta}{2\pi} \cos\left(\frac{2\pi\varphi}{\beta}\right), \frac{\rho\beta}{2\pi} \sin\left(\frac{2\pi\varphi}{\beta}\right), \rho \cos \alpha \right)$$

have the same coefficients: $E = 1$, $F = 0$, $G = \rho^2$. $\square$

Exercises

73. The *inversion* of the plane with respect to the circle with center O and radius r is the mapping that sends each point $p \neq O$ to the point p' of the half-line Op that verifies the condition $\overline{Op'}\,\overline{Op} = r^2$. Show that the inversion is a conformal mapping and that it reverses orientation of the plane.

74. Consider $\mathbf{S}^2$ parametrized by two angles: the longitude $\varphi \in]-\pi, \pi[$ and the latitude $\widetilde{\theta} \in]-\frac{\pi}{2}, \frac{\pi}{2}[$. The *Mercator projection* of the sphere into the plane (u, v) is defined by the following conditions: (i) the parallels $\widetilde{\theta} = $ constant are sent to the lines $v = $ constant, and the meridians $\varphi = $ constant to the lines $u = $ constant; (ii) it is a conformal mapping; (iii) the distances along the equator $\widetilde{\theta} = 0$ are converted into proportional distances; (iv) the point $\widetilde{\theta} = 0$, $\varphi = 0$ is sent to the origin.

Show that the point with coordinates $(\varphi, \widetilde{\theta})$ is sent to the point $u = \lambda\varphi$, $v = \lambda g(\widetilde{\theta})$, where λ is a constant and

$$ g'(\widetilde{\theta}) = \frac{1}{\cos\widetilde{\theta}} \left[\text{and therefore } g(\widetilde{\theta}) = \log \mathrm{tg}\left(\frac{\pi}{4} + \frac{\widetilde{\theta}}{2}\right) \right] $$

75. Find a conformal mapping of $\mathbb{T}^2$ into the plane.

76. The *catenoid* is the surface generated by the *catenary*

$$ v \mapsto (a\cosh v, 0, av) \quad (a > 0) $$

around the z-axis, and it can be parameterized by

$$ \Phi(u, v) = (a\cosh v \cos u, a\cosh v \sin u, av) $$

(see Figure 4.2). Consider also the helicoid parametrized by

$$ \Psi(\widetilde{u}, \widetilde{v}) = (\widetilde{v}\cos\widetilde{u}, \widetilde{v}\sin\cos u, a\widetilde{u}). $$

Using the change of coordinates $\widetilde{u} = u$, $\widetilde{v} = a\sinh v$, show that the helicoid is locally isometric to the catenoid. What are the images under this local isometry of the helices $\widetilde{v} = $ constant and the straight lines $\widetilde{u} = $ constant?

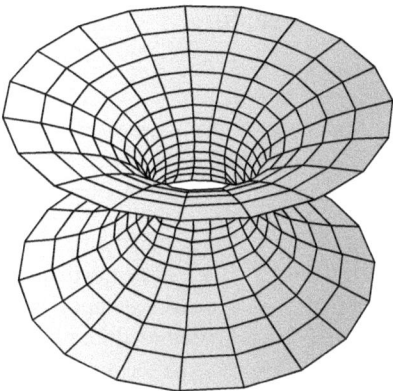

Figure 4.2

77. Let $f:\mathbb{R}^2 \to \mathbb{R}^2$ be an isometry such that $f(0,0) = (0,0)$.

(a) Show that $|f(p) - f(q)| \le |p - q|$ for all points p, q of $\mathbb{R}^2$. Conclude that f preserves the distance between points.

(b) Show that f is linear. **Hint:** (i) use the equality $\langle f(p), f(q) \rangle = \frac{1}{2}\{\|f(p)\|^2 + |f(q)|^2 - |f(p) - f(q)|^2\}$ to show that f preserves the inner product; (ii) computing $|f(p + q) - (f(p) + f(q))|^2$, show that $f(p + q) = f(p) + f(q)$.

(c) Deduce that any isometry of $\mathbb{R}^2$ is the composite of a linear isometry and a translation.

78. (a) Let $E(\tilde{v})$, $G(\tilde{v})$ be C^∞ functions defined on a compact interval I. Show that there exists a parameterization

$$\Psi(\tilde{u}, \tilde{v}) = (\rho(\tilde{v})\cos(a\tilde{u}), \rho(\tilde{v})\sin(a\tilde{u}), z(\tilde{v}))$$

of a surface of revolution whose coefficients of the first fundamental form are $E = E(\tilde{v})$, $F \equiv 0$, $G = G(\tilde{v})$.

(b) Consider the parametrized surface $\Phi(u, v) = (3u + 3uv^2 - u^3, -3v - 3u^2v + v^3, 3u^2 - 3v^2)$, where $(u, v) \neq (0, 0)$, and compute the coefficients E, F, G of this parameterization. Changing to the coordinates $\tilde{u}, \tilde{v}$ given by $u = \tilde{v}\cos\tilde{u}$, $v = \tilde{v}\sin\tilde{u}$, conclude that the given surface is locally isometric to a surface of revolution.

79. Construct an isometry between the surface defined by the equation $z = y^2$ and the plane $z = 0$ which sends the parabolas $z = y^2$, $x = x_0$ to the lines $z = 0$, $x = x_0$.

80. Show that if $f: S_1 \to S_2$ is a diffeomorphism that preserves lengths of curves then f is an isometry.

4.2 Gauss's Theorema Egregium

In this section we give a necessary condition for two surfaces to be locally isometric, from which it will follow, for example, the non-existence of a local isometry between the plane and the sphere. In the proof we make use of Christoffel symbols, which are functions of local parameters that are invariant under isometries.

Given a parameterization $\Phi(u, v)$ of an oriented surface S, we consider at each point the trihedron (Φ_u, Φ_v, N), where $N(u, v)$ is the normal field to S compatible with the orientation. [It suffices that N be a **local** orientation, since all the considerations we make are local in character — and therefore all the results in this section hold for non-orientable surfaces.] We can express the second-order derivatives of Φ in terms of this trihedron:

$$\Phi_{uu} = \Gamma_{11}^1 \Phi_u + \Gamma_{11}^2 \Phi_v + \lambda_1 N,$$

$$\Phi_{uv} = \Gamma_{12}^1 \Phi_u + \Gamma_{12}^2 \Phi_v + \lambda_2 N,$$

$$\Phi_{vu} = \Gamma_{21}^1 \Phi_u + \Gamma_{21}^2 \Phi_v + \lambda_3 N,$$ \hfill (4.2)

$$\Phi_{vv} = \Gamma_{22}^1 \Phi_u + \Gamma_{22}^2 \Phi_v + \lambda_4 N.$$

The λ_i in (4.2) are just the coefficients of the second fundamental form: indeed, by the formulas in Section 3.2, we have $\lambda_1 = \langle \Phi_{uu}, N \rangle = e$, $\lambda_2 = \lambda_3 = \langle \Phi_{uv}, N \rangle = f$, $\lambda_4 = \langle \Phi_v, N \rangle = g$. The coefficients Γ_{ij}^k are the *Christoffel symbols* of the parameterization $\Phi(u, v)$, and it follows from the definition that they are symmetric with respect to the lower indices: thus, $\Gamma_{ij}^k = \Gamma_{ji}^k$. To compute them, we form the inner product of the equalities (4.2) with Φ_u and Φ_v, obtaining

$$\begin{cases} \Gamma_{11}^1 E + \Gamma_{11}^2 F = \langle \Phi_{uu}, \Phi_u \rangle = \tfrac{1}{2} E_u \\ \Gamma_{11}^1 F + \Gamma_{11}^2 G = \langle \Phi_{uu}, \Phi_v \rangle = F_u - \tfrac{1}{2} E_v \end{cases}$$

$$\begin{cases} \Gamma_{12}^1 E + \Gamma_{12}^2 F = \langle \Phi_{uv}, \Phi_u \rangle = \tfrac{1}{2} E_v \\ \Gamma_{12}^1 F + \Gamma_{12}^2 G = \langle \Phi_{uv}, \Phi_v \rangle = \tfrac{1}{2} G_u \end{cases}$$ \hfill (4.3)

$$\begin{cases} \Gamma_{22}^1 E + \Gamma_{22}^2 F = \langle \Phi_{vv}, \Phi_u \rangle = F_v - \tfrac{1}{2} G_u \\ \Gamma_{22}^1 F + \Gamma_{22}^2 G = \langle \Phi_v, \Phi_v \rangle = \tfrac{1}{2} G_v . \end{cases}$$

Each of the equation systems in (4.3) has determinant $EG - F^2 > 0$, which shows that they suffice for computing the Christoffel symbols, and that these are functions of the coefficients E, F, G and their derivatives. In particular, and since local isometries preserve E, F, G, *they also preserve the coefficients* Γ_{ij}^k — more precisely, *if f is a local* *isometry then the Christoffel symbols of the parameterization* $\Psi(u,v) = f \circ \Phi(u,v)$ *coincide with the Christoffel symbols of* $\Phi(u,v)$.

It is more sensible to solve the systems of equations (4.3) in each case instead of determining general expressions for the Γ_{ij}^k. However, we observe that when we deal with orthogonal parameterizations ($F \equiv 0$), the calculation of the Christoffel symbols is greatly simplified. For example, the symbols of the parameterization $(\rho(v)\cos u, \rho(v)\sin u, z(v))$ of a surface of revolution, where $E = \rho^2$, $F = 0$, $G = \rho^2 + z^2$, are

$$\Gamma_{11}^1 = 0, \quad \Gamma_{11}^2 = \frac{-\rho\rho}{\rho^2 + z^2}, \quad \Gamma_{12}^1 = \frac{\rho}{\rho},$$

$$\Gamma_{12}^2 = 0, \quad \Gamma_{22}^1 = 0, \quad \Gamma_{22}^2 = \frac{\rho\rho + zz}{\rho^2 + z^2} \tag{4.4}$$

We now look for relations between the Christoffel symbols, starting from the identity

$$(\Phi_{uu})_v = (\Phi_{uv})_u. \tag{4.5}$$

Differentiating the first and second equalities of (4.2) with respect to v and to u, respectively, we obtain

$$(\Phi_{uu})_v = (\Gamma_{11}^1)_v \Phi_u + (\Gamma_{11}^2)_v \Phi_v + \Gamma_{11}^1 \Phi_{uv} + \Gamma_{11}^2 \Phi_{vv} + e_v N + e N_v,$$

$$(\Phi_{uv})_u = (\Gamma_{12}^1)_u \Phi_u + (\Gamma_{12}^2)_u \Phi_v + \Gamma_{12}^1 \Phi_{uu} + \Gamma_{12}^2 \Phi_{uv} + f_u N + f N_u.$$

Using again (4.2) and expressing N_v and N_u in terms of Φ_u and Φ_v, we can write each of the terms of (4.5) as a linear combination of the vectors Φ_u, Φ_v, N. Equating the coefficients of Φ_v in the two linear combinations, we obtain

$$(\Gamma_{11}^2)_v + \Gamma_{11}^1 \Gamma_{12}^2 + \Gamma_{11}^2 \Gamma_{22}^2 - e a_{22} = (\Gamma_{12}^1)_u + \Gamma_{12}^1 \Gamma_{11}^2 + \Gamma_{12}^2 \Gamma_{12}^2 - f a_{21}. \tag{4.6}$$

By the formulas (3.6) and (3.7) in Section 3.2, we have

$$ea_{22} - fa_{21} = \frac{e(-Ff + Eg)}{EG - F^2} - \frac{f(-Fe + Ef)}{EG - F^2}$$

$$= E \frac{eg - f^2}{EG - F^2} = EK. \tag{4.7}$$

Combining (4.6) and (4.7), we obtain the following expression for the Gaussian curvature:

$$K = \frac{1}{E}\left((\Gamma_{11}^2)_v - (\Gamma_{12}^2)_u + \Gamma_{12}^1(\Gamma_{11}^1 - \Gamma_{12}^2) + \Gamma_{11}^1(\Gamma_{22}^2 - \Gamma_{12}^1)\right). \tag{4.8}$$

Although its utility is questionable, formula (4.8) has this consequence: *it is possible to compute the Gaussian curvature knowing only the coefficients of the first fundamental form and their derivatives.* In the calculation of the principal curvatures k_1 and k_2, the Gauss map and its derivative (i.e., the second fundamental form) are crucial ingredients. It is remarkable that their product $K = k_1 k_2$ is after all an intrinsic concept, for it depends only on the first fundamental form.

As a consequence of this discussion we have the following theorem, which the author himself has called "egregious".

Theorem 4.2.1 (Gauss). *The Gaussian curvature is invariant under local isometries. More precisely, if $f:U \subseteq S_1 \to S_2$ is a local isometry then, for all p in U, the curvature of S_1 at p is equal to the curvature of S_2 at $f(p)$.*

This theorem already shows, in many cases, that two given surfaces — such as the sphere (which has curvature > 0) and the plane (curvature 0) — are not locally isometric.

The deduction of formula (4.8) seems like magic: how did we pull such a rabbit out of such a hat? Later on we will deduce, by more transparent means, other formulas that also establish the invariance of the curvature by local isometries.

Exercises

81. Let $S_1 = \{(x,y,z):z = 0\}$ and $S_2 = \{(x,y,z):x^2 + y^2 = z\}$.
   (a) Check that $f:S_1 \to S_2$ given by $f(x,y,0) = (x,y,x^2 + y^2)$ is not an isometry.
   (b) Show that S_1 and S_2 are not locally isometric.

82. Consider the surfaces S_1 and S_2 given by

$$\Phi(u,v) = (u\cos v, u\sin v, \log u), \quad (u \in \mathbb{R}^+, 0 < v < 2\pi)$$

and

$$\Psi(u,v) = (u\cos v, u\sin v, v) \quad (u,v \in \mathbb{R}).$$

Show that $\Psi \circ \Phi^{-1}: S_1 \to S_2$ is not a local isometry, although the curvature of S_2 at $\Psi(u,v)$ is equal to that of S_1 at $\Phi(u,v)$.

83. Consider $\mathbb{T}^2$ with the usual parameterization. Show that any isometry of $\mathbb{T}^2$ sends the equator $v = 0$ to itself (use Exercise 71-a) in Section 3.3).

84. Show that a conformal mapping that preserves areas (see Exercise 71, in Section 2.5) is necessarily a local isometry (and therefore all maps of the Earth's surface have to choose one of two defects: either they distort areas, or they distort shapes).

4.3 Covariant Derivative, Parallel Transport, Geodesic Curvature

All the concepts we define in this section belong to intrinsic geometry, in the sense that they are invariant under local isometries. The method, used here repeatedly, to establish the intrinsic character of a certain concept consists of showing that it is a function solely of the coefficients E, F, G and their derivatives — which is the case whenever we can express it by means of these quantities and the Christoffel symbols only.

Let $\mathbf{v}$ be a vector field defined on an open subset $U \subseteq S$. Given a regular curve $\alpha: I \rightarrow U$, the *covariant derivative of* $\mathbf{v}$ along α is the orthogonal projection of $(\mathbf{v} \circ \alpha)'(t)$ on the tangent plane $T_{\alpha(t)}S$, denoted by $\dfrac{D\mathbf{v}}{dt}(t)$. So, to compute $\dfrac{D\mathbf{v}}{dt}(t)$, we just have to subtract from $(\mathbf{v} \circ \alpha)'(t)$ its component with respect to the normal $N \circ \alpha(t)$ to the surface.

Example 4.3.1 Consider a unit vector field $\mathbf{v}$ in $\mathbf{S}^2 \setminus \{(0,0,1),(0,0,-1)\}$ having constant angle $\frac{\pi}{4}$ with the parallels of the sphere. In spherical coordinates

$$\Phi(\varphi, \theta) = (\sin\theta \cos\varphi, \sin\theta \sin\varphi, \cos\theta),$$

we put

$$\mathbf{v}(\varphi,\theta) = \frac{1}{\sqrt{2}}\left(-\Phi_\theta + \frac{1}{\sin\theta}\Phi_\varphi\right)$$

$$= \frac{1}{\sqrt{2}}(-\cos\theta\cos\varphi - \sin\varphi, -\sin\theta\sin\varphi + \cos\varphi, \sin\theta).$$

Let us compute the covariant derivative of $\mathbf{v}$ along the parallel $\theta = \theta_0$, parametrized by $\alpha_{\theta_0}(t) = \Phi(t, \theta_0)$. We now have

$$\mathbf{v}'(t) = \frac{1}{\sqrt{2}}(\cos\theta_0 \sin t - \cos t, -\sin\theta_0 \cos t - \sin t, 0),$$

and we obtain $\dfrac{D\mathbf{v}}{dt}(t)$ by subtracting from $\mathbf{v}'(t)$ its normal component:

$$\frac{D\mathbf{v}}{dt}(t) = \mathbf{v}'(t) - \langle \mathbf{v}'(t), N(t,\theta_0)\rangle N(t,\theta_0)$$

$$= \frac{1}{\sqrt{2}}(\cos\theta_0 \sin t - \cos t, -\sin\theta_0 \cos t - \sin t, 0)+$$

$$+ \frac{1}{\sqrt{2}}\sin\theta_0(\sin\theta_0 \cos t, \sin\theta_0 \sin t, \cos\theta_0)$$

$$= \frac{-\cos\theta_0}{\sqrt{2}}\left(\frac{1}{\sin\theta_0}\Phi_\varphi\big|_{(t,\theta_0)} + \Phi_\theta\big|_{(t,\theta_0)}\right). \qquad \Box$$

It is worthy to note that the covariant derivative of $\mathbf{v}$ along α depends on the parameterization of α, but not on the orientation of the surface. Let us now establish its intrinsic character. In local coordinates, if we write $\mathbf{v}(u,v) = a(u,v)\Phi_u + b(u,v)\Phi_v$, $\alpha(t) = \Phi(u(t), v(t))$, $a(t) = a(u(t), v(t))$ and $b(t) = b(u(t), v(t))$, we have

$$\mathbf{v}(t) = a(t)\Phi_u + b(t)\Phi_v,$$

$$\mathbf{v}'(t) = a'\Phi_u + a(u'\Phi_{uu} + v'\Phi_{uv}) + b'\Phi_v + b(u'\Phi_{uv} + v'\Phi_{vv})$$

$$= (a' + au'\Gamma^1_{11} + av'\Gamma^1_{12} + bu'\Gamma^1_{12} + bv'\Gamma^1_{22})\Phi_u \qquad (4.9)$$

$$+ (b' + au'\Gamma^2_{11} + av'\Gamma^2_{12} + bu'\Gamma^2_{12} + bv'\Gamma^2_{22})\Phi_v$$

$$+ (au'e + av'f + bu'f + bv'g)N.$$

Ignoring the normal component, the components of $\mathbf{v}'(t)$ with respect to Φ_u and Φ_v give the expression of the covariant derivative $\dfrac{D\mathbf{v}}{dt}(t)$ in local coordinates. If we look at the coefficients of Φ_u and Φ_v, we see that they have "intrinsic character" and are therefore preserved by isometries. To formalize this observation, let us take a mapping $f: U \to S_2$ that is a diffeomorphism onto the image, and consider the vector field $\mathbf{u} = Df(\mathbf{v})$ which is the transfer of $\mathbf{v}$ by f, defined on $f(U)$ by $\mathbf{u}(f(p)) = Df_p(\mathbf{v}(p))$. Let us denote by $\dfrac{D\mathbf{u}}{dt}$ the covariant derivative of $\mathbf{u}$ along the curve $\beta(t) = f \circ \alpha(t)$. We claim that if f is an isometry, then

$$\frac{D\mathbf{u}}{dt} = Df_{\alpha(t)}\left(\frac{D\mathbf{v}}{dt}\right). \tag{4.10}$$

In fact, using coordinates $\Phi(u, v)$ on S and $\Psi(u, v) = f \circ \Phi(u, v)$ on S_2, we see by (4.9) that the expressions of $\dfrac{D\mathbf{u}}{dt}$ with respect to the basis (Ψ_u, Ψ_v) and of $\dfrac{D\mathbf{v}}{dt}$ with respect to the basis (Φ_u, Φ_v) have the same coefficients, which proves (4.10).

Another property of the covariant derivative $\dfrac{D\mathbf{v}}{dt}$ of $\mathbf{v}$ along α is that at each instant it only depends on the velocity vector of the curve at that instant.

Proposition 4.3.2 $\dfrac{D\mathbf{v}}{dt}(t)$ *only depends on* $\alpha'(t) = u'(t)\Phi_u + v'(t)\Phi_v$ *and not on the curve* α.

Proof In fact, noting that

$$a'(t) = \frac{\partial a}{\partial u}u'(t) + \frac{\partial a}{\partial v}v'(t),$$

$$b'(t) = \frac{\partial b}{\partial u}u'(t) + \frac{\partial b}{\partial v}v'(t),$$

we recognize that the functions $u(t)$, $v(t)$ only enter in (4.9) through the value they and their first derivatives u' and v' take at time t. $\qquad\square$

We further observe that the expression of $\dfrac{D\mathbf{v}}{dt}$ is linear in u', v'. Thanks to Proposition 4.3.2, for every $p \in U$, a linear mapping $D\mathbf{v}_p: T_pS \to T_pS$ is defined as follows: given $\mathbf{w} \in T_pS$, let $\alpha(t)$ be a curve in U such that $\alpha(t_0) = p$ and $\alpha'(t_0) = \mathbf{w}$; then $D\mathbf{v}_p(\mathbf{w})$ is the covariant derivative of $\mathbf{v}$ along α computed at t_0. Intuitively, $D\mathbf{v}_p(\mathbf{w})$ is a kind of directional derivative of $\mathbf{v}$ in the direction of $\mathbf{w}$.

Given a field $\mathbf{v}$ in $U \subseteq S$, the *divergence* of $\mathbf{v}$ is the mapping $\operatorname{Div}\mathbf{v}: U \subseteq S \to \mathbb{R}$ such that, at every $p \in U$, its value $\operatorname{Div}\mathbf{v}(p)$ is the trace of the linear mapping $D\mathbf{v}_p$.

Example 4.3.3 If $\mathbf{v}(u, v) = (f_1(u, v), f_2(u, v))$ is a vector field on an open subset $U \subseteq \mathbb{R}^2$, its covariant derivative along a curve $\alpha: I \to U$ is the usual derivative $(\mathbf{v} \circ \alpha)'(t)$, and therefore the linear mapping $d\mathbf{v}_p$ is just the derivative of $\mathbf{v}$ as the mapping $U \rightarrow \mathbb{R}^2$. The matrix of Dv_p with respect to the canonical basis of $\mathbb{R}^2$ is the Jacobian

$$\begin{bmatrix} \dfrac{\partial f_1}{\partial u} & \dfrac{\partial f_1}{\partial v} \\[2ex] \dfrac{\partial f_2}{\partial u} & \dfrac{\partial f_2}{\partial v} \end{bmatrix}_p$$

and its trace $\dfrac{\partial f_1}{\partial u}\Big|_p + \dfrac{\partial f_2}{\partial v}\Big|_p$ is the divergence of $\mathbf{v}$ computed at p. $\qquad\square$

Proposition 4.3.4 *Divergence is invariant under isometries: if $f: U \subseteq S \rightarrow S_2$ is an isometry into its image and $\mathbf{v}$ is a vector field on U, then $\mathrm{Div}(Df\mathbf{v})(f(p)) = \mathrm{Div}\, \mathbf{v}(p)$.*

Proof We put $\mathbf{u} = Df\mathbf{v}$, and start by rewriting formula (4.10) using the linear mappings

$$D\mathbf{u}_{f(p)}: T_{f(p)}S_2 \rightarrow T_{f(p)}S_2 \quad \text{and} \quad D\mathbf{v}_p: T_pS \rightarrow T_pS.$$

Let us fix a curve $\alpha(t)$ such that $\alpha(0) = p$, and let us put $\beta(t) = f \circ \alpha(t)$, $\mathbf{w}_1 = \alpha'(0)$ and $\mathbf{w}_2 = \beta'(0)$. Then we have $\dfrac{D\mathbf{u}}{dt}(0) = D\mathbf{u}_{f(p)}(\mathbf{w}_2)$ and $\dfrac{D\mathbf{v}}{dt}(0) = D\mathbf{v}_p(\mathbf{w}_1) = D\mathbf{v}_p(Df_p^{-1}(\mathbf{w}_2))$. By (4.10) we can write

$$D\mathbf{u}_{f(p)}(\mathbf{w}_2) = Df_p \circ D\mathbf{v}_p \circ Df_p^{-1}(\mathbf{w}_2) \text{ for every } \mathbf{w}_2 \in T_{f(p)}S_2,$$

i.e.

$$D\mathbf{u}_{f(p)} = Df_p \circ D\mathbf{v}_p \circ Df_p^{-1}, \tag{4.11}$$

which means that $D\mathbf{u}_{f(p)}$ and $D\mathbf{v}_p$ are conjugate linear mappings, and therefore have the same trace. $\qquad\square$

We will revisit the notion of divergence in the next section, where we prove a theorem that adapts the divergence theorem known from vector calculus to surfaces. For now, we return to the covariant derivative.

The reader must have noticed that in the computation of the covariant derivative of $\mathbf{v}$ along α, only the way $\mathbf{v}$ is defined on the trace of the curve plays a role, and so it is not necessary that the field be defined on other points. We thus define a *vector field along a regular curve* $\alpha(t)$ as a function $\mathbf{v}(t)$ such that, for every t, the vector $\mathbf{v}(t)$ belongs to $T_{\alpha(t)}S$; if $\mathbf{v}$ is differentiable (i.e., if, by writing $\mathbf{v}(t) = a(t)\Phi_u + b(t)\Phi_v$, the functions $a(t)$ and $b(t)$ are differentiable), we can as before compute the covariant derivative of $\mathbf{v}$ along α.

Lemma 4.3.5 *If $\mathbf{v}(t)$, $\mathbf{w}(t)$ are two vector fields along the curve $\alpha(t)$ then*

$$\frac{d}{dt}\langle \mathbf{v}, \mathbf{w}\rangle = \left\langle \frac{D\mathbf{v}}{dt}, \mathbf{w}\right\rangle + \left\langle \mathbf{v}, \frac{D\mathbf{w}}{dt}\right\rangle.$$

Proof Denoting by the superscript n the normal component of a vector, we have

$$\frac{d}{dt}\langle \mathbf{v}, \mathbf{w} \rangle = \langle \mathbf{v}', \mathbf{w} \rangle + \langle \mathbf{v}, \mathbf{w}' \rangle$$

$$= \left\langle \frac{D\mathbf{v}}{dt} + (\mathbf{v}')^n, \mathbf{w} \right\rangle + \left\langle \mathbf{v}, \frac{D\mathbf{w}}{dt} + (\mathbf{w}')^n \right\rangle$$

$$= \left\langle \frac{D\mathbf{v}}{dt}, \mathbf{w} \right\rangle + \left\langle \mathbf{v}, \frac{D\mathbf{w}}{dt} \right\rangle. \qquad\qquad \square$$

We now introduce the concept of *geodesic curvature*. Given a regular curve $\alpha: I \to S$ on an oriented surface, we can consider the unit tangent vector field along α, given by $\tau_1(t) = \frac{1}{|\alpha'(t)|} \alpha'(t)$, and also the vector field $\tau_2 = N \times \tau_1$. This means that at each instant t, the pair $(\tau_1(t), \tau_2(t))$ is an orthonormal and positively oriented basis of $T_{\alpha(t)}S$. By 4.3.5 we have

$$\left\langle \tau_1(t), \frac{D\tau_1}{dt}(t) \right\rangle = \frac{d}{dt}\left(\frac{1}{2}|\tau_1|^2 \right) = 0,$$

and so the vectors $\dfrac{D\tau_1}{dt}(t)$ and $\tau_2(t)$ are collinear. The *geodesic curvature* $k_g(t)$ of α at the point $\alpha(t)$ is defined by the equality

$$\frac{D\tau_1}{dt}(t) = |\alpha'(t)| \, k_g(t)\tau_2(t). \qquad\qquad (4.12)$$

So the geodesic curvature gives us the tangential component of the curvature of α, and is also the generalization, for curves on oriented surfaces, of the signed curvature for planar curves (1.3). Like the signed curvature, the geodesic curvature depends only (up to sign) on the point of the curve at which it is computed and not on the parameterization. In fact, if $\alpha(t)$ and $\alpha(s)$ are two parameterizations of the same curve and $\mathbf{v}$ a vector field along α, then

$$\frac{D\mathbf{v}}{dt} = \frac{ds}{dt}\frac{D\mathbf{v}}{ds}, \qquad\qquad (4.13)$$

$$|\alpha'(t)| = \left| \frac{ds}{dt} \right| |\alpha'(s)|. \qquad\qquad (4.14)$$

Assuming that $\alpha(t)$ and $\alpha(s)$ have the same orientation (so that $\dfrac{ds}{dt} > 0$), we apply (4.13) to the vector field τ_1 and use (4.12) and (4.14), obtaining $k_g(t) = k_g(s)$, which proves our claim. For purposes of computation, we note that from (4.12) it follows that

$$k_g = \frac{1}{|\alpha'|}\left\langle \frac{D\tau_1}{dt}, \tau_2 \right\rangle = \frac{1}{|\alpha'|}\langle \tau_1', N \times \tau_1 \rangle$$

$$= \frac{1}{|\alpha'|^3}\langle \alpha'', N \times \alpha' \rangle, \qquad\qquad (4.15)$$

and formula (4.15) further simplifies to $k_g = \langle \alpha'', N \times \alpha' \rangle$ when α is parametrized by arc length.

From formula (4.15) it follows that the sign of the geodesic curvature is changed when we reverse orientation of the curve or change the orientation of the surface. In our next proposition we gather some simple properties of the geodesic curvature.

Proposition 4.3.6 *(i) The geodesic curvature is invariant under local isometries that preserve orientation — that is, if $f: U \subseteq S_1 \to S_2$ is such a mapping and $\alpha: I \to U$ is a regular curve, then the geodesic curvatures of α in S_1 (computed at $\alpha(t)$) and of $f \circ \alpha$ in S_2 (computed at $f \circ \alpha(t)$) are equal.*
(ii) If $\alpha(t)$ is a regular curve in S, then

$$k(t)^2 = k_g(t)^2 + k_n(t)^2,$$

where k, k_n, k_g are respectively the curvature, the normal curvature and the geodesic curvature of α.

Proof The derivative Df transforms the "moving" orthonormal frame $(\tau_1(t), \tau_2(t))$ that appears in the calculation (4.12) of the geodesic curvature of α into another "moving" orthonormal frame $\tau_1(t)$, $\tau_2(t)$. Furthermore, τ_1 is the unit tangent vector field along the curve $f \circ \alpha$ and, if f preserves orientation, this second frame is also positively oriented. Statement (i) is then an immediate consequence of (4.10).

To prove (ii), it suffices to note that from the decomposition

$$\tau_1' = \frac{D\tau_1}{dt} + (\tau_1')^n$$

into the tangential and normal components, it follows that

$$|\tau_1'|^2 = \left|\frac{D\tau_1}{dt}\right|^2 + |(\tau_1')^n|^2,$$

i.e.

$$|\alpha'(t)|^2 k(t)^2 = |\alpha'(t)|^2 (k_g(t)^2 + k_n(t)^2). \qquad \square$$

Now let $\mathbf{v}$ be any vector field along α. We say that $\mathbf{v}$ is *parallel along α* if its covariant derivative along α is constantly zero. Assume that α is defined on $[a, b]$, that $\mathbf{w}_1 \in T_{\alpha(a)}S$, and let $\mathbf{v}$ be a parallel vector field along α such that $\mathbf{v}(a) = \mathbf{w}_1$. Then the vector $\mathbf{w}_2 = \mathbf{v}(b)$ in $T_{\alpha(b)}S$ is called the *parallel transport* of $\mathbf{w}_1$ along α from $\alpha(a)$ to $\alpha(b)$. To justify the use of the definite article **the**, we have to show that there is only one parallel vector field along α with initial position $\mathbf{w}_1$; this is done in the next proposition. However, we note first that by formula (4.13) the fact that $\mathbf{v}$ is parallel along α does not depend on the parameterization of the curve. Therefore the notion of parallel transport is also independent of the parameterization.

Proposition 4.3.7 *Let $\alpha: [a, b] \to S$ be a regular curve in S. Then:*
(i) if $\mathbf{v}$ and $\mathbf{w}$ are parallel vector fields along α, the norms $|\mathbf{v}(t)|$, $|\mathbf{w}(t)|$ and the angle between $\mathbf{v}(t)$ and $\mathbf{w}(t)$ are constant;
(ii) given $\mathbf{w}_1 \in T_{\alpha(a)}S$, there exists one and only one parallel vector field $\mathbf{v}(t)$ along α such that $\mathbf{v}(a) = \mathbf{w}_1$.

Proof (i) If $\mathbf{v}$ is a parallel vector field then by 4.3.5 we have

$$\frac{d}{dt}|\mathbf{v}|^2 = 2\left(\frac{D\mathbf{v}}{dt}, \mathbf{v}\right) = 0,$$

and so $|\mathbf{v}|$ is constant, and the same holds for $|\mathbf{w}|$ and for the inner product $\langle \mathbf{v}, \mathbf{w} \rangle$. Therefore each of these vector fields is either always or never zero. Assuming they are both nonzero, the angle $\theta(t) = \angle(\mathbf{v}(t), \mathbf{w}(t))$ is constant, since $\cos\theta(t) = \dfrac{\langle \mathbf{v}, \mathbf{w} \rangle}{|\mathbf{v}||\mathbf{w}|}$.

(ii) It follows from (i) that two parallel vector fields $\mathbf{v}$ and $\mathbf{u}$ such that $\mathbf{v}(a) = \mathbf{u}(a)$ must be identical, since they both have constant norm equal to $|\mathbf{v}(a)|$, and the angle between them is always zero. Thus there exists at most one parallel vector field $\mathbf{v}(t)$ such that $\mathbf{v}(a) = \mathbf{w}_1$.

Assuming that $\mathbf{w}_1 \neq 0$, it remains to prove the existence of $\mathbf{v}$. For this, consider the vector fields $\boldsymbol{\tau}_1(t) = \frac{1}{|\alpha'(t)|}\alpha'(t)$ and $\boldsymbol{\tau}_2 = N \times \boldsymbol{\tau}_1$. We write $\mathbf{v}(t)$ in the form

$$\mathbf{v}(t) = a(t)\boldsymbol{\tau}_1(t) + b(t)\boldsymbol{\tau}_2(t).$$

Since $\mathbf{v}$ is parallel, $\mathbf{v}$ has constant norm $r = |\mathbf{w}_1|$. We can thus try to find $\varphi(t)$ such that $a(t) = r\cos\varphi(t)$ and $b(t) = r\sin\varphi(t)$. Note that

$$\left(\frac{D\boldsymbol{\tau}_2}{dt}, \boldsymbol{\tau}_1\right) = -\left(\frac{D\boldsymbol{\tau}_1}{dt}, \boldsymbol{\tau}_2\right) = -k_g|\alpha'|$$

and therefore $\dfrac{D\boldsymbol{\tau}_2}{dt} = -k_g|\alpha'|\boldsymbol{\tau}_1$. Noting that the covariant derivative obeys the usual rules of differentiation, we then have

$$\frac{1}{r}\frac{D\mathbf{v}}{dt} = -\varphi\sin\varphi\,\boldsymbol{\tau}_1 + \cos\varphi\,\frac{D\boldsymbol{\tau}_1}{dt} + \varphi\cos\varphi\,\boldsymbol{\tau}_2 + \sin\varphi\,\frac{D\boldsymbol{\tau}_2}{dt}$$
$$= (\varphi + k_g|\alpha'|)(-\sin\varphi\,\boldsymbol{\tau}_1 + \cos\varphi\,\boldsymbol{\tau}_2),$$

so that $\mathbf{v}$ is a parallel vector field along α if and only if $\varphi'(t) = -k_g(t)|\alpha'(t)|$. To finish, it is therefore sufficient to define $\varphi(t) = \varphi_0 - \int_a^t k_g(s)|\alpha'(s)|\,ds$, where φ_0 satisfies $\mathbf{w}_1 = r\cos\varphi_0\,\boldsymbol{\tau}_1(a) + r\sin\varphi_0\,\boldsymbol{\tau}_2(a)$. □

Observations and Examples 4.3.8 **A.** Every local isometry f sends a parallel vector field along α to a parallel vector field along $f \circ \alpha$. This is a consequence of formula (4.10).

B. In the plane a vector field is parallel along a certain curve if and only if it is constant along that curve, which shows that in this case the parallel transport only depends on the initial and final points of the curve, not on the path covered. This property is shared (locally) by those surfaces which are locally isometric to the plane, such as the cylinder and the cone: thus, each point of these surfaces has an open neighborhood U such that the parallel transport along any curve **contained in** U depends only on the initial and final points of the curve. Later on we will conclude that it is only on surfaces of zero curvature that this holds true.

C. If the surfaces S_1 and S_2 are tangent along the regular curve $\gamma(t)$, the covariant derivative of a vector field $\mathbf{v}$ along γ is the same computed with respect to S_1 or S_2 (since the normal component we subtract from $\mathbf{v}'(t)$ is the same in both cases), and therefore also the parallel transport along γ is the same on the two surfaces. Using this observation, let us determine the parallel transport on the sphere $\mathbf{S}^2$ along the parallel of colatitude θ_0, which we denote by γ.

Consider the cone of revolution $\mathfrak{C}$ tangent to the sphere along γ. The angle that the generatrices of $\mathfrak{C}$ make with the axis is $\frac{\pi}{2} - \theta_0$, and therefore (see example 4.1.3 D) $\mathfrak{C}$ is isometric to a planar region U that defines an angle $\beta = 2\pi \cos \theta_0$ (see Figure 4.3). By such an isometry, the parallel transport along γ corresponds to the parallel transport in U along the arc with center O and radius equal to $\mathrm{tg}\,\theta_0$. However, in U parallel transport is simply translation; but a vector $\mathbf{w}_1$ which is tangent to the generatrix of the cone is translated to a vector $\mathbf{w}_2$ which makes an angle of β with that same generatrix (the generatrices of $\mathfrak{C}$ correspond in U to the half-lines of origin O, and the two half-lines bounding U are identified with the same generatrix).

In conclusion: parallel transport in $\mathbf{S}^2$ along one complete turn of the parallel $\theta = \theta_0$ makes each vector rotate through an angle of $2\pi \cos \theta_0$ at the end of a complete turn. □

We end this section by defining one of the most important concepts of Differential Geometry: a *geodesic* of the surface S is a regular curve $\alpha(t)$ on S whose geodesic curvature is constantly zero. By

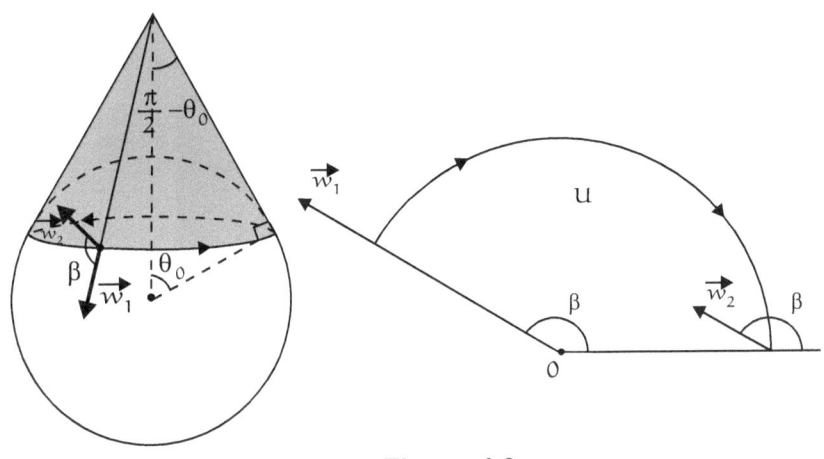

Figure 4.3

(4.12), this is equivalent to the unit vector field $\tau_1 = \frac{1}{|\alpha'|}\alpha'$ tangent to α being parallel. This simply means that at points where the curvature of α is nonzero, the principal normal to the curve is also normal to the surface.

We leave the in-depth study of geodesics to a later section; to finish this one, we give some simple examples.

Examples 4.3.9 Geodesics on the plane are simply straight lines, since in the plane geodesic curvature is the same as signed curvature. On the sphere any maximal circle is a geodesic, because the principal normal to a maximal circle passes through the center of the sphere, and therefore coincides with the normal to the sphere itself (later on we will see that there are no other geodesics on the sphere). More generally, the meridians of any surface of revolution are geodesics. □

Exercises

85. Consider on the sphere S^2 the meridian $\varphi = 0$, which we denote by γ, and the points $\mathcal{N} = (0, 0, 1)$ and $S = (0, 0, -1)$. We define a mapping $L_\gamma: T_\mathcal{N}S^2 \to T_S S^2$ as follows: $L_\gamma(\mathbf{v})$ is the parallel transport of the vector $\mathbf{v}$ from N to S along γ.
   (a) Compute $L_\gamma(1, 0, 0)$ and $L_\gamma(0, 1, 0)$.
   (b) Show that L_γ is linear.
   (c) Does L_γ depend on the choice of meridian?

86. (a) Describe all the geodesics of the cylinder $x^2 + y^2 = 1$.
   (b) Compare the geodesic curvatures of the same helix in the cylinder and in the helicoid.

87. (a) Let $S = \{\alpha(t) + \lambda \mathbf{v}(t) : T \in I, \lambda \in \mathbb{R}\}$ be a ruled surface. Show that the lines $r_t(\lambda) = \alpha(t) + \lambda \mathbf{v}(t)$ are all geodesics, and find out whether the curves $c_\lambda(t) = \alpha(t) + \lambda \mathbf{v}(t)$ are geodesics.

   (b) Show that on any surface an asymptotic line that is also a geodesic is necessarily a (segment of) straight line.

88. Show that on the surface of revolution

$$\Phi(u, v) = (\rho(v) \cos u, \rho(v) \sin u, z(v)),$$

the parallel $v = v_0$ is a geodesic if and only if the tangent line to the generating curve at v_0 is parallel to the axis of revolution.

89. (a) Check that in the cone $C_k = \{(x, y, z): z \neq 0, z = k\sqrt{x^2 + y^2}\}$ there is always some geodesic connecting each pair of points.

   (b) The generatrices $t \mapsto t(x_0, y_0, k\sqrt{x_0^2 + y_0^2})$ are geodesics of C_k that are not defined for $t \leq 0$. Show that any other geodesic of C_k parametrized with constant scalar velocity extends to all values of the parameter.

90. Let $\mathcal{E}$ be the intersection of the cylinder $x^2 + y^2 = 1$ with a plane which passes through the x-axis and makes an angle θ with the xy plane. Show that $\mathcal{E}$ is an ellipse, and compute the absolute value of the geodesic curvature of $\mathcal{E}$ (relative to the cylinder) at the points where $\mathcal{E}$ intersects its axes.

91. Show that the geodesic curvature of the curve α at $p \in S$ is equal to the curvature at p of the curve obtained by projecting α orthogonally on $p + T_p S$.

4.4 The Divergence Theorem. First Variation of Area

In this section we give a simple expression for the divergence of a vector field and prove the divergence theorem. We also prove a formula for the variation of the area of a surface when it undergoes a perturbation induced by a vector field (and mention how this is related to minimal surfaces). These results are used in Section 5.4 in the proof of the Minkowski integral formulas (which in turn we use to establish the rigidity of the sphere and in the proof of Theorem 5.5.3) and otherwise are not used in the remainder of this book. This being said, we must acknowledge that some subjects treated here do not pertain to intrinsic geometry, but we could find no better place to fit them in.

Let $\mathbf{v}$ be a vector field on an open subset U of an oriented surface S. In the previous section we defined the linear mapping $D\mathbf{v}_p$ as follows: given $\mathbf{w} \in T_pS$, $D\mathbf{v}_p(\mathbf{w})$ is the covariant derivative of $\mathbf{v}$, computed at p, along any curve in S that passes through p with velocity $\mathbf{w}$. Using coordinates $\Phi(u,v)$, the vectors $D\mathbf{v}_{\Phi(u,v)}(\Phi_u)$ and $D\mathbf{v}_{\Phi(u,v)}(\Phi_v)$ are then the tangential components of $\dfrac{\partial \mathbf{v}}{\partial u}$ and $\dfrac{\partial \mathbf{v}}{\partial v}$ respectively — that is, if we write

$$\frac{\partial \mathbf{v}}{\partial u} = b_{11}\Phi_u + b_{21}\Phi_v + \lambda_1 N$$
$$\frac{\partial \mathbf{v}}{\partial v} = b_{12}\Phi_u + b_{22}\Phi_v + \lambda_2 N, \tag{4.16}$$

then the matrix of $D\mathbf{v}_{\Phi(u,v)}$ relative to the basis (Φ_u, Φ_v) of $T_{\Phi(u,v)}S$ is

$$B = \begin{bmatrix} b_{11} & b_{12} \\ b_{21} & b_{22} \end{bmatrix}.$$

Divergence is the trace of this matrix. That is,

$$\text{Div } \mathbf{v}(\Phi(u,v)) = \text{tr } B = b_{11} + b_{22}.$$

Our goal is to obtain an explicit formula for divergence. Using (4.16), we have

$$\frac{\partial \mathbf{v}}{\partial u} \times \Phi_v + \Phi_u \times \frac{\partial \mathbf{v}}{\partial v} = (b_{11} + b_{22})(\Phi_u \times \Phi_v) + \lambda_1(N \times \Phi_v) + \lambda_2(\Phi_u \times N),$$

and therefore

$$\left\langle \frac{\partial \mathbf{v}}{\partial u} \times \Phi_v + \Phi_u \times \frac{\partial \mathbf{v}}{\partial v}, N \right\rangle = (b_{11} + b_{22})\langle \Phi_u \times \Phi_v, N \rangle \tag{4.17}$$
$$= (\text{Div } \mathbf{v})\sqrt{EG - F^2},$$

provided that $\Phi(u,v)$ is compatible with the orientation of S.

The expression (4.17) for Div $\mathbf{v}$ can still be simplified. It is convenient, for the calculations below, to work with a vector field $\mathbf{v}$ which is **not necessarily** tangent to S. By letting $\mathbf{v} = \alpha\Phi_u + \beta\Phi_v + \gamma N$, and using the matrix

$$\begin{bmatrix} a_{11} & a_{12} \\ a_{21} & a_{22} \end{bmatrix}$$

of $-DN_{\Phi(u,v)}$ relative to the basis (Φ_u, Φ_v) to express the vectors N_u and N_v (see (3.6) in Section 3.2), we have

$$
\begin{aligned}
\Phi_v \times N_u + N_v \times \Phi_u &= -\Phi_v \times (a_{11}\Phi_u + a_{21}\Phi_v) - (a_{12}\Phi_u + a_{22}\Phi_v) \times \Phi_u \\
&= (a_{11} + a_{22})(\Phi_u \times \Phi_v) \\
&= 2H\sqrt{EG - F^2}N
\end{aligned}
\tag{4.18}
$$

$$
\begin{aligned}
\langle \mathbf{v}, \Phi_v \times N \rangle &= \langle \alpha\Phi_u + \beta\Phi_v + \gamma N, \Phi_v \times N \rangle \\
&= \langle \alpha\Phi_u, \Phi_v \times N \rangle = \alpha\langle \Phi_u \times \Phi_v, N \rangle \\
&= \alpha\sqrt{EG - F^2}
\end{aligned}
\tag{4.19}
$$

$$
\langle \mathbf{v}, N \times \Phi_u \rangle = \beta\sqrt{EG - F^2}
\tag{4.20}
$$

Pursuing our calculations, we further have

$$
\begin{aligned}
\left\langle \frac{\partial \mathbf{v}}{\partial u} \times \Phi_v + \Phi_u \times \frac{\partial \mathbf{v}}{\partial v}, N \right\rangle &= \left\langle \frac{\partial \mathbf{v}}{\partial u}, \Phi_v \times N \right\rangle + \left\langle \frac{\partial \mathbf{v}}{\partial v}, N \times \Phi_u \right\rangle \\
&= \left\langle -\mathbf{v}, \frac{\partial}{\partial u}(\Phi_v \times N) + \frac{\partial}{\partial v}(N \times \Phi_u) \right\rangle + \\
&\quad + \frac{\partial}{\partial u}\langle \mathbf{v}, \Phi_v \times N \rangle + \frac{\partial}{\partial v}\langle \mathbf{v}, N \times \Phi_u \rangle \\
&= -\langle \mathbf{v}, \Phi_v \times N_u + N_v \times \Phi_u \rangle + \\
&\quad + \frac{\partial}{\partial u}\langle \mathbf{v}, \Phi_v \times N \rangle + \frac{\partial}{\partial v}\langle \mathbf{v}, N \times \Phi_u \rangle \\
&= -\sqrt{EG - F^2}\langle \mathbf{v}, 2HN \rangle + \\
&\quad + \frac{\partial}{\partial u}\left(\alpha\sqrt{EG - F^2}\right) + \frac{\partial}{\partial v}\left(\beta\sqrt{EG - F^2}\right),
\end{aligned}
$$

where we apply (4.18), (4.19), and (4.20). Of course, when the vector field $\mathbf{v}$ is tangent to S, the first summand of the last expression vanishes. Combining this formula with (4.17), we obtain the desired formula for divergence:

Proposition 4.4.1 *Let $\mathbf{v}$ be a (not necessarily tangent) vector field on an open subset U covered by a parameterization $\Phi(u, v)$ compatible with the orientation of S. Then:*

(i) if we denote by $\mathbf{v}^\top$ the tangential component of $\mathbf{v}$, then we have

$$
\frac{1}{\sqrt{EG - F^2}}\left\langle \frac{\partial \mathbf{v}}{\partial u} \times \Phi_v + \Phi_u \times \frac{\partial \mathbf{v}}{\partial v}, N \right\rangle = -\langle \mathbf{v}, 2HN \rangle + \mathrm{Div}(\mathbf{v}^\top);
$$

(ii) if **v** *is a tangent field to S and we write* $\mathbf{v} = \alpha\Phi_u + \beta\Phi_v$, *then we have*

$$\text{Div } \mathbf{v} = \frac{1}{\sqrt{EG - F^2}} \left\{ \frac{\partial}{\partial u}\left(\alpha\sqrt{EG - F^2}\right) + \frac{\partial}{\partial v}\left(\beta\sqrt{EG - F^2}\right) \right\}.$$

The divergence theorem reduces the calculation of a certain surface integral on a simple region to a line integral along its boundary. By *simple region* (or *Jordan region*) $\Omega \subseteq S$ we mean a connected region whose boundary is a simple closed curve and whose closure (in S) is homeomorphic to a closed disk (in the plane); if the boundary of Ω is piecewise regular, then Ω is also called a *polygonal region*. We now state the most important result in this section.

Divergence Theorem 4.4.2 *Let* **v** *be a field of tangent vectors on S, and let* $\Omega \subseteq S$ *be a polygonal region. Then*

$$\int_\Omega \text{Div } \mathbf{v} \, d\sigma = \int_\gamma \langle \mathbf{v}, -\boldsymbol{\tau}_2 \rangle \, ds, \tag{4.21}$$

where $\gamma(s)$ *is the boundary of* Ω *and* $\boldsymbol{\tau}_2(s) \in T_{\gamma(s)}S$ *is the unit vector orthogonal to* $\gamma'(s)$ *that points to the interior of* Ω.

Proof We assume that $\gamma(s)$ is parametrized by arc length and runs in the positive direction — i.e., in such a way that Ω is always to the left of γ (in other words, we have $\boldsymbol{\tau}_2(s) = N(s) \times \gamma'(s)$) (see Fig. 4.4). Of course, $\boldsymbol{\tau}_2$ is not defined at the vertices of γ, but this happens only for a finite number of values of s, which do not affect the integration.

It is sufficient to prove the theorem under the hypothesis that the closure of Ω is contained in some parametrized neighborhood. For if this is not the case, we can decompose Ω into a finite number of sufficiently small polygonal regions $(\Omega_i)_{i=1}^k$. Supposing that (4.21) holds for the Ω_i, and

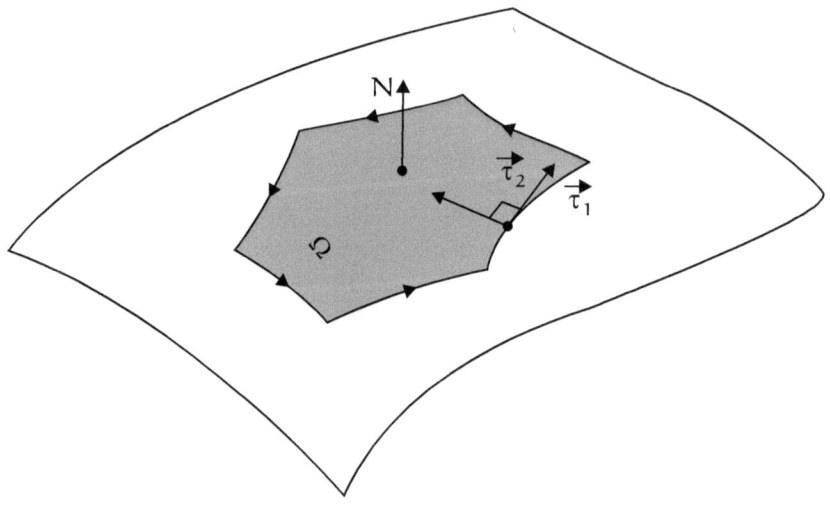

Figure 4.4

denoting by γ_i the boundary of Ω_i moving in the positive direction and by $\tau_2{}^i$ the associated unit vector, we obtain

$$\int_\Omega \text{Div } \mathbf{v}\, d\sigma = \sum_{i=1}^k \int_{\Omega_i} \text{Div } \mathbf{v}\, d\sigma =$$

$$= \sum_{i=1}^k \int_{\gamma_i} \langle \mathbf{v}, -\tau_2{}^i \rangle\, ds = \int_\gamma \langle \mathbf{v}, -\tau_2 \rangle\, ds$$

– since any "edge" (segment of some γ_i) inside Ω is run through twice, with the integrand function $\langle \mathbf{v}, -\tau_2{}^i \rangle$ taking up opposite signs in both instances, and therefore we are left with only the integrals relative to the edges that are part of γ.

We can thus assume that Ω is covered by the parameterization $\Phi(u, v)$, and we put $\gamma(s) = \Phi(u(s), v(s))$ for every $s \in [0, L]$. Furthermore, we require that $\Phi(u, v)$ be compatible with the orientation of S. We thus have, with the notation of 4.4.1 and using Green's theorem

$$\int_\Omega \text{Div } \mathbf{v}\, d\sigma = \iint_{\Phi^{-1}(\Omega)} \left\{ \frac{\partial}{\partial u} \left(\alpha \sqrt{EG - F^2} \right) + \frac{\partial}{\partial v} \left(\beta \sqrt{EG - F^2} \right) \right\} du dv$$

$$= \int_0^L \sqrt{EG - F^2}\, (\alpha(s)v'(s) - \beta(s)u'(s))\, ds.$$

(Note that, since Φ is compatible with the orientation of S, the curve $(u(s), v(s))$ moves along the boundary of $\Phi^{-1}(\Omega)$ in the positive direction, and we have used this fact when we applied Green's theorem.) To simplify the latter integral, we form the vector product of the two equalities

$$\mathbf{v}(s) = \alpha(s)\Phi_u + \beta(s)\Phi_v, \qquad \gamma'(s) = u'(s)\Phi_u + v'(s)\Phi_v,$$

obtaining

$$\mathbf{v}(s) \times \gamma'(s) = (\alpha(s)v'(s) - \beta(s)u'(s))(\Phi_u \times \Phi_v)$$
$$= \sqrt{EG - F^2}\,(\alpha(s)v'(s) - \beta(s)u'(s))N.$$

The above integral can then be rewritten as

$$\int_0^L \langle \mathbf{v}(s) \times \gamma'(s), N \rangle\, ds = \int_0^L \langle \mathbf{v}(s), \gamma'(s) \times N \rangle\, ds$$
$$= \int_0^L \langle \mathbf{v}(s), -\tau_2(s) \rangle\, ds = \int_\gamma \langle \mathbf{v}, -\tau_2 \rangle\, ds. \qquad \square$$

The divergence theorem can be generalized to regions bounded by more than one closed curve, making the sum of all integrals relative to each curve constituting the boundary of Ω appear in the right-hand side of (4.21). However, it is more interesting, in the case of a compact surface S, to consider the integral of Div $\mathbf{v}$ over the whole surface. Choosing a "polygonal decomposition" $(\Omega_i)_{i=1}^k$ of S, and applying 4.4.2 to each of the Ω_i, what happens, when adding up the results, is that all the terms vanish, because now none of the edges is run through only once. Thus we have just proved (i) of the corollary below.

Corollary 4.4.3 *Let $\mathbf{v}$ be a vector field on a compact surface S. Then:*

(i) $\int_S \mathrm{Div}\, \mathbf{v}\, d\sigma = 0$;

(ii) there exists $p \in S$ such that Div $\mathbf{v}(p) = 0$.

To prove (ii) we can assume that S is connected, because in any case its connected components are compact. Hence, if Div $\mathbf{v}$ has no zeros, then it has constant sign and therefore $\int_S \mathrm{Div}\, \mathbf{v}\, d\sigma \neq 0$, in contradiction to (i). Therefore Div $\mathbf{v}$ has some zero, which proves (ii).

Given a differentiable vector field $\mathbf{v}$, not necessarily tangent, on a **compact** surface S, let $S_t = \{p + t\mathbf{v}(p) : p \in S\}$. The family $(S_t)_t$ is called a *variation* of S (when $\mathbf{v}$ is a normal field to S, not necessarily unitary, $(S_t)_t$ is called a *normal variation* of S); see Fig. 4.5. Denoting by $A(t)$ the area of S_t, our goal is to prove a formula for $A'(0)$ as an integral over S. First, however, we must guarantee that S_t is a surface for sufficiently small t, which we do in the proposition below.

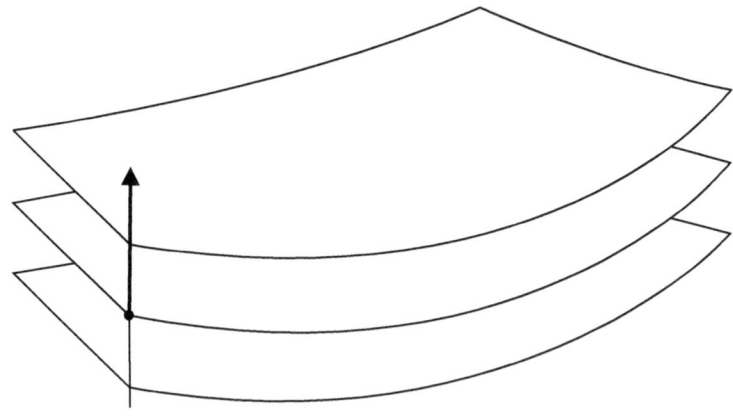

Figure 4.5

Proposition 4.4.4 *There exists $\eta > 0$ such that, for all $t \in \;]-\eta, \eta[$, S_t is a compact surface.*

Proof We define the mapping $L_t: S \to \mathbb{R}^3$ by $L_t(p) = p + t\mathbf{v}(p)$, and so S_t is the image of S under L_t. Using this notation, let us start by proving two auxiliary claims:

Claim 1. *For every point p of S, there exist a parametrized neighborhood $\Phi(u, v)$ of p and $\varepsilon > 0$ such that, for all $t \in \;]-\varepsilon, \varepsilon[$, the mapping*

$$L_t \circ \Phi(u, v) = \Phi(u, v) + t\mathbf{v}(u, v)$$

is injective and its Jacobian matrix has rank two.

Taking a parameterization $\Phi(u, v) = (x(u, v), y(u, v), z(u, v))$ with $\Phi(0, 0) = p$, we can assume that

$$\frac{\partial(x, y)}{\partial(u, v)}\Big|_{(0,0)} \neq 0.$$

Denoting by x_t, y_t, z_t the component functions of $L_t \circ \Phi$, we define

$$F(u, v, t) = (x_t(u, v), y_t(u, v), t) = (G_t(u, v), t).$$

It is easily seen that $\det(JF_{(u,v,t)}) = \det(F(G_t)_{(u,v)})$. In particular, we have

$$\det(JF_{(0,0,0)}) = \det(J(G_0)_{(0,0)}) = \frac{\partial(x, y)}{\partial(u, v)}\Big|_{(0,0)} \neq 0.$$

Hence, by the inverse mapping theorem, there exists an open neighborhood $U \times \;]-\varepsilon, \varepsilon[$ of $(0, 0, 0)$ such that the restriction of F to this neighborhood is a diffeomorphism onto its image. The local inverse of F has the form $F^{-1}(x, y, t) = ((G_t)^{-1}(x, y), t)$, and so, for every $t \in \;]-\varepsilon, \varepsilon[$, the mapping $G_t|_U$ has a differentiable inverse, which guarantees that it is injective and its Jacobian matrix has rank two. Since $L_t \circ \Phi(u, v) =$

$(G_t(u, v), z_t(u, v))$, the same holds for $L_t \circ \Phi\big|_{U'}$. The parameterization (U, Φ) thus satisfies the conditions of Claim 1.

Claim 2. *For $|t|$ sufficiently small, L_t is injective.*

By compactness of S, we can find $\varepsilon > 0$ and parameterizations (U_i, Φ^i), with $i = 1, \ldots, k$, which cover S and such that each of them satisfies Claim 1 for the given ε. Next, we take $\delta > 0$ such that, for every $p \in S$, the ball $B_\delta(p, S) = \{q \in S : |q - p| < \delta\}$ is contained in one of the open subsets $\Phi^i(U_i)$, and we put $M = \max_{p \in S} |\mathbf{v}(p)|$ and $\eta = \min\{\frac{\delta}{4M}, \varepsilon\}\}$. We claim that L_t is injective for $|t| < \eta$. In fact, if $|q - p| < \delta$ it is clear that $L_t(p) \ne L_t(q)$, since in this case p and q both belong to some $\Phi^i(U_i)$ and, by Claim 1, the restriction of L_t to $\Phi^i(U_i)$ is injective. If $|q - p| \ge \delta$ then

$$|L_t(p) - L_t(q)| = |(p - q) - t(\mathbf{v}(p) - \mathbf{v}(q))|$$
$$\ge |p - q| - |t|(|\mathbf{v}(p)| + |\mathbf{v}(q)|)$$
$$\ge \delta - 2\eta M \ge \frac{\delta}{2},$$

which concludes the proof of Claim 2.

Finally we show that S_t is a surface when $|t| < \eta$. Since L_t is continuous and injective and S is compact, L_t is a homeomorphism $S \to S_t$ (in particular, S_t is also compact). Now, since the images of the mappings $L_t \circ \Phi^i$, $i = 1, \ldots, k$, cover S_t, it suffices to show that each of them is a parameterization. By Claim 1, the Jacobian of $L_t \circ \Phi^i$ has rank two; furthermore, $(L_t \circ \Phi^i)^{-1}$ is continuous since it is given by the composite $(\Phi^i)^{-1} \circ L_t^{-1}$ of continuous functions. This shows that $L_t \circ \Phi^i$ is a parameterization and concludes the proof of the proposition. □

It deserves mention that the mapping L_t is a diffeomorphism $S \to S_t$. In fact, and as we have seen, it is a homeomorphism. Its expression in local coordinates (U_i, Φ^i) on S and $(U_i, L_t \circ \Phi^i)$ on S_t is clearly a diffeomorphism, since it is just the identity $U_i \to U_i$. This means that all surfaces of the variation $(S_t)_{-\eta < t < \eta}$ are diffeomorphic to S.

Recalling that $A(t)$ denotes the area of the surface S_t, let us now present the formula for $A'(0)$.

Theorem 4.4.5 (*First variation of area*). $A'(0) = - \int_S \langle \mathbf{v}, 2HN \rangle \, d\sigma$.

Proof We can consider a polygonal decomposition $(\Omega_j)_{1 \le j \le r}$ of S such that the closure of each Ω_j is contained in the image of one of the parameterizations (U_i, Φ^i) defined in the proof of 4.4.4. Thus, for $|t| < \eta$, the sets $\Omega'_j = L_t(\Omega_j)$ form a decomposition of S_t and each of them is covered by some parameterization

$$L_t \circ \Phi^i(u, v) = \Phi^i(u, v) + t\mathbf{v}(u, v).$$

We fix j and the corresponding i, and we let $W_j = (\Phi^i)^{-1}(\Omega_j)$. The area of Ω'_j is given by

$$A_j(t) = \iint_{W_j} |(L_t \circ \Phi^i)_u \times (L_t \circ \phi^i)_v| \, du \, dv$$

and therefore

$$A'_j(0) = \iint_{W_j} \frac{\partial}{\partial t} |(L_t \circ \Phi^i)_u \times (L_t \circ \phi^i)_v|\Big|_{t=0} \, du dv.$$

Now we have

$$|(L_t \circ \Phi^i)_u \times (L_t \circ \Phi^i)_v| = \left|(\Phi^i_u \times \Phi^i_v) + t\left(\frac{\partial \mathbf{v}}{\partial u} \times \Phi^i_v + \Phi^i_u \times \frac{\partial \mathbf{v}}{\partial v}\right) + t^2\left(\frac{\partial \mathbf{v}}{\partial u} \times \frac{\partial \mathbf{v}}{\partial v}\right)\right|.$$

Therefore, using 4.4.1 (i), we have

$$\frac{\partial}{\partial t}|(L_t \circ \Phi^i)_u \times (L_t \circ \Phi^i)_v|\Big|_{t=0} = \frac{\langle \frac{\partial}{\partial t}((L_t \circ \phi^i)_u \times (L_t \circ \Phi^i)_v)|_{t=0}, \Phi^i_u \times \Phi^i_v \rangle}{|\Phi^i_u \times \Phi^i_v|}$$

$$= \left\langle \frac{\partial \mathbf{v}}{\partial u} \times \Phi^i_v + \Phi^i_u \times \frac{\partial \mathbf{v}}{\partial v}, N \right\rangle$$

$$= \left\{ -\langle \mathbf{v}, 2HN \rangle + \mathrm{Div}(\mathbf{v}^\top) \right\} |\Phi^i_u \times \Phi^i_v|,$$

where $\mathbf{v}^\top$ denotes the tangential component of $\mathbf{v}$. We thus conclude that

$$A'_j(0) = \int_{\Omega_i} \left\{ -\langle \mathbf{v}, 2HN \rangle + \mathrm{Div}(\mathbf{v}^\top) \right\} d\sigma$$

– and, using 4.4.3 (i), we finally obtain

$$A'(0) = \sum_{j=1}^r A'_j(0) = \int_S \left\{ -\langle \mathbf{v}, 2HN \rangle + \mathrm{Div}(\mathbf{v}^\top) \right\} d\sigma$$

$$= -\int_S \langle \mathbf{v}, 2HN \rangle \, d\sigma. \qquad \qquad \Box \, .$$

Observation 4.4.6 If S is not compact but the vector field $\mathbf{v}$ has compact support (the *support* of $\mathbf{v}$ is the closure in S of the set $\{p \in S : \mathbf{v}(p) \neq 0\}$), then the sets S_t are still surfaces for $|t|$ small and, suitably interpreted, formula 4.4.5 remains valid. We choose a compact region $\Omega \subseteq S$ whose boundary is made up of a finite number of piecewise regular closed curves and whose closure contains the support of $\mathbf{v}$, and we take a polygonal decomposition $(\Omega_j)_{1 \leq j \leq r}$ of Ω. We denote by $A(t)$ the area of $L_t(\Omega) \subseteq S_t$. Proceeding as in 4.4.5, and using the divergence theorem, we obtain

$$A'(0) = -\int_\Omega \langle \mathbf{v}, 2HN \rangle \, d\sigma + \int_{\partial\Omega} \langle \mathbf{v}^\top, -\tau_2 \rangle \, ds$$

$$= -\int_S \langle \mathbf{v}, 2HN \rangle \, d\sigma,$$

where $\partial\Omega$ indicates the boundary of Ω (restricted to which $\mathbf{v}^\top$ vanishes).

In particular, if $H \equiv 0$ then $A'(0) = 0$. A *minimal surface* is a surface whose mean curvature H is constantly zero (by Exercise 57 in Section 3.1, no such surface can be compact). This name arose as follows: assume that S has the property that, for every region $\Omega \subseteq S$ as above, the area of Ω is less than or equal to that of any other portion $\widetilde{\Omega}$ of the surface such that $\partial\widetilde{\Omega} = \partial\Omega$. Then S is a minimal surface: indeed, denoting by $A(t)$ the area of $L_t(\Omega)$ (for a variation with support contained in Ω), $A(t)$ has a minimum at 0 and therefore $A'(0) = 0$. This implies that for every vector field $\mathbf{v}$ with compact support we have $-\int_S \langle \mathbf{v}, 2HN\rangle \, d\sigma = 0$ — which is only possible with $H \equiv 0$.

Not all minimal surfaces minimize area in the sense just stated, but the name has stuck. Besides the plane, the reader can verify (using formula (3.8) in the Section 3.2) that the helicoid and the catenoid are minimal surfaces (Exercise 76). In the exercises of this section we prove that besides the plane the catenoid is the only minimal surface of revolution.

For more examples and an in-depth study of minimal surfaces we recommend Osserman's book [19].

Exercises

92. (a) Compute the divergence of the vector field $\mathbf{v}(\varphi, \theta)$ in $\mathbf{S}^2$ of example 4.3.1. For that example, directly compute $\int_{\mathbf{S}^2} \mathrm{Div}\, \mathbf{v}\, d\sigma$. Could you use corollary 4.4.3?

(b) Let S be a compact surface, let $F \subseteq S$ be a **finite** set, and let $\mathbf{v}$ be a field of tangent vectors defined on $S \setminus F$ such that the set sup $\{|\mathbf{v}(p)|: p \in S \setminus F\}$ is bounded. Show that $\int_S \mathrm{Div}\, \mathbf{v}\, d\sigma = 0$.

93. If $\mathbf{v}$ is a tangent field to S and $f: S \to \mathbb{R}$ a differentiable function, then

$$\mathrm{Div}(f\mathbf{v})(p) = Df_p(\mathbf{v}) + f(p)\,\mathrm{Div}\,\mathbf{v}(p).$$

94. Given a differentiable function $f: S \to \mathbb{R}$, the *gradient* of f is the tangent vector field ∇f defined on S as follows: for each $p \in S$ and all $\mathbf{v} \in T_p S$, we have $Df_p(\mathbf{v}) = \langle \nabla f(p), \mathbf{v}\rangle$. Equivalently, ∇f is the gradient of f if we have $\alpha: I \to S$ for every differentiable curve $(f \circ \alpha)'(t) = \langle \nabla f(\alpha(t)), \alpha'(t)\rangle$.

(a) Show that in local coordinates $\Phi(u, v)$ we have

$$\nabla f = \frac{1}{\sqrt{EG - F^2}} N \times \left(\frac{\partial f}{\partial v}\Phi_u - \frac{\partial f}{\partial u}\Phi_v\right)$$

$$= \frac{1}{EG - F^2}\left\{\left(-\frac{\partial f}{\partial v}F + \frac{\partial f}{\partial u}G\right)\Phi_u + \left(-\frac{\partial f}{\partial v}E - \frac{\partial f}{\partial u}F\right)\Phi_v\right\}.$$

(b) Conclude that the vector field $\mathbf{w} = N \times \nabla f$ has zero divergence. Conversely, show that if $\mathrm{Div}\, \mathbf{w} \equiv 0$ then $\mathbf{v} = \mathbf{w} \times N$ is locally a gradient field (i.e., each point of S has a neighborhood U such that $\mathbf{v}|_U$ is the gradient of some function $U \to \mathbb{R}$).

(c) Show that a vector field $\mathbf{v}$ on S is a gradient field if and only if, for every curve piecewise differentiable $\alpha: [a, b] \to S$, the line integral $\int_a^b \langle \mathbf{v} \circ \alpha(t), \alpha'(t)\rangle \, dt$ depends only on the initial and final points of α.

95. Let $\Phi(u, s) = (\rho(s) \cos u, \rho(s) \sin u, z(s))$ be a parameterization of a surface of revolution S, where s is the arc length of the generating curve (i.e., $\rho'^2 + z'^2 \equiv 1$) and $\rho(s) > 0$. Assume that S is not a plane (so that z is not constantly zero). Show that:

(a) S is a minimal surface if and only if

$$\frac{z'}{\rho} = \rho' z'' - \rho'' z' \quad (\text{apply } 3.2.1)$$

(b) assuming that $z'(s_0) \neq 0$, there exists $\varepsilon > 0$ such that, for $s \in]s_0 - \varepsilon, s_0 + \varepsilon[$, the above equation is equivalent to

$$\rho \rho'' + \rho'^2 = 1 \Leftrightarrow \frac{d^2}{ds^2} \left(\frac{1}{2} \rho^2 \right) = 1$$

$$\Leftrightarrow \exists\, A, B \in \mathbb{R} : \rho(s) = \sqrt{s^2 + As + B};$$

(c) by shifting the domain of s, we can guarantee that there exist $a > 0$ and a non-empty open interval I such that $\rho(s) = \sqrt{s^2 + a^2}$ for all $s \in I$;

(d) $\rho(s) = \sqrt{s^2 + a^2}$ for all $s \in \mathbb{R}$;

(e) assuming that $z(0) = 0$ (if not, apply a vertical translation to S) and that $z > 0$,

$$z(s) = \int_0^s \frac{a}{\sqrt{t^2 + a^2}}\, dt = a \sinh^{-1} \left(\frac{s}{a} \right);$$

(f) by letting $v = \dfrac{z}{a} = \sinh^{-1} \left(\dfrac{s}{a} \right)$, we have $\rho(v) = a \cosh v$, and therefore S is the catenoid.

4.5 The Gauss-Bonnet Theorem

The Gauss-Bonnet Theorem is one of the deepest results in the Differential Geometry of surfaces establishing an unexpected connection between the Euler characteristic of a compact surface (a purely topological concept) and its Gaussian curvature. Moreover, it provides a general context for a seemingly rather particular result as Girard's formula for spherical triangles (example 2.5.2).

We work with an oriented surface S. Let Ω be a polygonal region (as defined in Section 4.4) and $\alpha(s)$, $s \in [0, L]$, a parameterization of $\partial\Omega$ by arc length with positive orientation. Let $0 = s_0 < s_1 < \cdots < s_k = L$ be the k vertices of α; $\gamma_i \in [-\pi, \pi]$, for $i = 1, \ldots, k - 1$, the oriented angle of $\alpha'(s_i^-)$ and $\alpha'(s_i^+)$; and $\gamma_k \in [-\pi, \pi]$ the angle between $\alpha'(s_k^-)$ and $\alpha'(s_0^+)$. These angles γ_i are called the *exterior angles* of Ω.

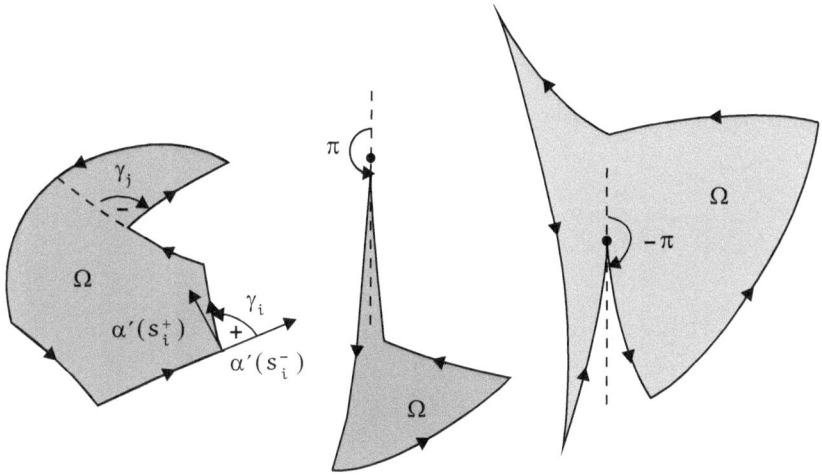

Figure 4.6

(Note: if $\alpha'(s_i^+) = -\alpha'(s_i^-)$, we have to decide which of the values π or $-\pi$ we choose for γ_i. We take $\gamma_i = \pi$ when, for $s \to s_i^-$, the trace of $\alpha|_{[s_i, s_i+\varepsilon]}$ (for small $\varepsilon > 0$) stays, like Ω, to the left of the curve; otherwise, we take $\gamma_i = -\pi$. We can make this criterion rigorous with the help of local coordinates, but Fig. 4.6 is more illuminating).

Let us state the first version of our theorem:

Gauss-Bonnet Theorem 4.5.1 (**Local version**). *Let $\Omega \subseteq S$ be a polygonal region whose closure is covered by some parameterization. Let γ_i $(i = 1, \ldots, k)$ be the exterior angles of Ω. Then*

$$\int_\Omega K \, d\sigma + \int_{\partial\Omega} k_g(s) \, ds + \sum_{i=1}^k \gamma_i = 2\pi.$$

Let $\Phi(u, v)$ be a parameterization compatible with the orientation of S containing the closure of Ω. Consider the unit tangent field $\mathbf{v}_1 = \frac{1}{\sqrt{E}} \Phi_u$ and define, for each interval $[s_{i-1}, s_i]$, a continuous choice $\theta_i(s)$ of the oriented angle between $\mathbf{v}_1$ and $\alpha'(s)$. (See the Appendix to this chapter for the existence of such continuous choices.) The *Rotation Index theorem* (Theorem A.4 of the Appendix) states that

$$\sum_{i=1}^k \{\theta_i(s_i) - \theta_i(s_{i-1})\} + \sum_{i=1}^k \gamma_i = 2\pi. \tag{4.22}$$

Let $\mathbf{w}(s)$, $s \in [0, L]$, be a **unit** vector field along α: the vector field $\mathbf{w}$ is therefore continuous, and is parallel along each regular arc $\alpha([s_{i-1}, s_i])$. Let $\varphi_i(s)$ ($s \in [s_{i-1}, s_i]$) be a continuous choice of the angle between $\alpha'(s)$ and $\mathbf{w}(s)$. The proof of Proposition 4.3.7 (ii) shows that

$$\varphi_i'(s) = -k_g(s). \tag{4.23}$$

Further, let $\psi(s)$, $s \in [0, L]$, be a choice of the angle between $\mathbf{v}_1$ and $\mathbf{w}(s)$. By the equality between oriented angles

$$\angle(\mathbf{v}_1, \alpha'(s)) = \angle(\mathbf{v}_1, \mathbf{w}(s)) + \angle(\mathbf{w}(s), \alpha'(s))$$
$$= \angle(\mathbf{v}_1, \mathbf{w}(s)) - \angle(\alpha'(s), \mathbf{w}(s)),$$

we see that we can assume, for $i = 1, \ldots, k$, that

$$\theta_i(s) = \psi(s) - \varphi_i(s) \quad \text{for} \quad s \in [s_{i-1}, s_i]. \tag{4.24}$$

In view of (4.24), equality (4.22) can then be rewritten as

$$\psi(L) - \psi(0) - \sum_{i=1}^{k} \{\varphi_i(s_i) - \varphi_i(s_{i-1})\} + \sum_{i=1}^{k} \gamma_i = 2\pi,$$

or, using (4.23),

$$\psi(L) - \psi(0) + \int_0^L k_g(s) \, ds + \sum_{i=1}^{k} \gamma_i = 2\pi.$$

In view of this formula, the next lemma concludes the proof of the Gauss-Bonnet theorem.

Lemma 4.5.2
$$\psi(L) - \psi(0) = \int_\Omega K \, d\sigma. \tag{4.25}$$

Proof Let $\mathbf{v}_2 = N \times \mathbf{v}_1$, so that the pair $(\mathbf{v}_1, \mathbf{v}_2)$ forms at each point a direct orthonormal frame. Since $\mathbf{v}_1$ is a unit vector field, $\dfrac{D\mathbf{v}_1}{ds}$ is orthogonal to $\mathbf{v}_1$, and is therefore collinear with $\mathbf{v}_2$. We thus have $\dfrac{D\mathbf{v}_1}{ds} = a(s)\mathbf{v}_2$, where $a(s) = \left\langle \dfrac{D\mathbf{v}_1}{ds}, \mathbf{v}_2 \right\rangle = \langle \mathbf{v}_1', \mathbf{v}_2 \rangle - \langle \mathbf{v}_1, \mathbf{v}_2' \rangle$, from which we conclude that

$$\frac{D\mathbf{v}_1}{ds} = \langle \mathbf{v}_1', \mathbf{v}_2 \rangle \mathbf{v}_2, \qquad \frac{D\mathbf{v}_2}{ds} = -\langle \mathbf{v}_1', \mathbf{v}_2 \rangle \mathbf{v}_1. \tag{4.26}$$

From the equality
$$\mathbf{w}(s) = \cos \psi(s) \mathbf{v}_1 + \sin \psi(s) \mathbf{v}_2$$

we obtain, by taking the covariant derivative of both sides and using (4.26),

$$\frac{D\mathbf{w}}{ds} = (\psi'(s) + \langle \mathbf{v}_1' \mathbf{v}_2 \rangle)(-\sin \psi(s) \mathbf{v}_1 + \cos \psi(s) \mathbf{v}_2).$$

But since $\mathbf{w}$ is parallel, we have $\dfrac{D\mathbf{w}}{ds} \equiv 0$ and therefore

$$\psi'(s) = -\langle \mathbf{v}_1'(s), \mathbf{v}_2(s) \rangle.$$

Hence

$$\psi(L) - \psi(0) = -\int_0^L \langle \mathbf{v_1}'(s), \mathbf{v_2}(s) \rangle \, ds$$

$$= -\int_0^L \left(\left\langle \frac{\partial \mathbf{v_1}}{\partial u}, \mathbf{v_2} \right\rangle u'(s) + \left\langle \frac{\partial \mathbf{v_1}}{\partial v}, \mathbf{v_2} \right\rangle v'(s) \right) ds$$

$$= -\iint_{\Phi^{-1}(\Omega)} \left\{ \frac{\partial}{\partial u} \left\langle \frac{\partial \mathbf{v_1}}{\partial v}, \mathbf{v_2} \right\rangle - \frac{\partial}{\partial v} \left\langle \frac{\partial \mathbf{v_1}}{\partial u}, \mathbf{v_2} \right\rangle \right\} du \, dv$$

(by Green's theorem)

$$= \iint_{\Phi^{-1}(\Omega)} \left\{ \left\langle \frac{\partial \mathbf{v_1}}{\partial u}, \frac{\partial \mathbf{v_2}}{\partial v} \right\rangle - \left\langle \frac{\partial \mathbf{v_1}}{\partial v}, \frac{\partial \mathbf{v_2}}{\partial u} \right\rangle \right\} du \, dv.$$

To complete the proof of the lemma, it is now sufficient to show that

$$\left\langle \frac{\partial \mathbf{v_1}}{\partial u}, \frac{\partial \mathbf{v_2}}{\partial v} \right\rangle - \left\langle \frac{\partial \mathbf{v_1}}{\partial v}, \frac{\partial \mathbf{v_2}}{\partial u} \right\rangle = K\sqrt{EG - F^2}. \tag{4.27}$$

We begin by observing that from the equalities

$$N_u = \langle N_u, \mathbf{v_1} \rangle \mathbf{v_1} + \langle N_u, \mathbf{v_2} \rangle \mathbf{v_2} = -\left\langle N, \frac{\partial \mathbf{v_1}}{\partial u} \right\rangle \mathbf{v_1} - \left\langle N, \frac{\partial \mathbf{v_2}}{\partial u} \right\rangle \mathbf{v_2},$$

$$N_v = -\left\langle N, \frac{\partial \mathbf{v_1}}{\partial v} \right\rangle \mathbf{v_1} - \left\langle N, \frac{\partial \mathbf{v_2}}{\partial v} \right\rangle \mathbf{v_2},$$

it ensures, taking into account the identity $\mathbf{v_1} \times \mathbf{v_2} = N$, that

$$N_u \times N_v = \left\{ \left\langle N, \frac{\partial \mathbf{v_1}}{\partial u} \right\rangle \left\langle N, \frac{\partial \mathbf{v_2}}{\partial v} \right\rangle - \left\langle N, \frac{\partial \mathbf{v_1}}{\partial v} \right\rangle \left\langle N, \frac{\partial \mathbf{v_2}}{\partial u} \right\rangle \right\} N. \tag{4.28}$$

If we write

$$\frac{\partial \mathbf{v_1}}{\partial u} = a\mathbf{v_2} + \left\langle N, \frac{\partial \mathbf{v_1}}{\partial u} \right\rangle N, \qquad \frac{\partial \mathbf{v_2}}{\partial v} = b\mathbf{v_1} + \left\langle N, \frac{\partial \mathbf{v_2}}{\partial v} \right\rangle N,$$

and form the scalar product, then we obtain

$$\left\langle \frac{\partial \mathbf{v_1}}{\partial u}, \frac{\partial \mathbf{v_2}}{\partial v} \right\rangle = \left\langle N, \frac{\partial \mathbf{v_1}}{\partial u} \right\rangle \left\langle N, \frac{\partial \mathbf{v_2}}{\partial v} \right\rangle,$$

and analogously

$$\left\langle \frac{\partial \mathbf{v_1}}{\partial v}, \frac{\partial \mathbf{v_2}}{\partial u} \right\rangle = \left\langle N, \frac{\partial \mathbf{v_1}}{\partial v} \right\rangle \left\langle N, \frac{\partial \mathbf{v_2}}{\partial u} \right\rangle.$$

Together with (4.28), the last two equalities give

$$N_u \times N_v = \left\{ \left(\frac{\partial \mathbf{v}_1}{\partial u}, \frac{\partial \mathbf{v}_2}{\partial v} \right) - \left(\frac{\partial \mathbf{v}_1}{\partial v}, \frac{\partial \mathbf{v}_2}{\partial u} \right) \right\} N,$$

and therefore

$$\left(\frac{\partial \mathbf{v}_1}{\partial u}, \frac{\partial \mathbf{v}_2}{\partial v} \right) - \left(\frac{\partial \mathbf{v}_1}{\partial v}, \frac{\partial \mathbf{v}_2}{\partial u} \right) = \langle N_u \times N_v, N \rangle$$

$$= K \langle \Phi_u \times \Phi_v, N \rangle = K \sqrt{EG - F^2}.$$

This concludes the proof of (4.27) and hence that of the lemma.   □

Observations 4.5.3 **A.** The difference $\psi(L) - \psi(0)$ in Lemma 4.5.2 is the angle between the initial and final positions of a vector that is carried in parallel along a closed curve. If K has constant (nonzero) sign on Ω, Lemma 4.5.2 shows that this angle is nonzero and becomes smaller as the region bounded by the curve becomes smaller. It follows that a surface has constant zero curvature if parallel transport along any curve on the surface depends only on the starting and ending points of the curve (and not on the path t covered). The reader is invited to elaborate the argument in the exercises in this section.

B. The formula (4.27) can be rewritten in the form

$$K = \frac{1}{\sqrt{EG - F^2}} \left\{ \frac{\partial}{\partial u} \left(\mathbf{v}_1, \frac{\partial \mathbf{v}_2}{\partial v} \right) - \frac{\partial}{\partial v} \left(\mathbf{v}_1, \frac{\partial \mathbf{v}_2}{\partial u} \right) \right\} \tag{4.29}$$

$$= \frac{1}{\sqrt{EG - F^2}} \left\{ \frac{\partial}{\partial u} \left(\mathbf{v}_1, \frac{D\mathbf{v}_2}{\partial v} \right) - \frac{\partial}{\partial v} \left(\mathbf{v}_1, \frac{D\mathbf{v}_2}{\partial u} \right) \right\}, \tag{4.30}$$

and formula (4.30) gives another proof of Gauss's Theorema Egregium, for it expresses K via intrinsic quantities: in fact, any isometry transforms $(\mathbf{v}_1, \mathbf{v}_2)$ into another orthonormal dihedron and, by (4.10) in Section 4.3, preserves the covariant derivative. We can further apply (4.29) to express K as a function of the coefficients E, F and G. For simplicity, we assume that $\Phi(u, v)$ is an orthogonal parameterization ($F \equiv 0$), so $\mathbf{v}_1 = \frac{1}{\sqrt{E}} \Phi_u$ and $\mathbf{v}_2 = \frac{1}{\sqrt{G}} \Phi_v$. We then have

$$\frac{\partial \mathbf{v}_2}{\partial v} = \frac{\partial}{\partial v} \left(\frac{1}{\sqrt{G}} \right) \Phi_v + \frac{1}{\sqrt{G}} \Phi_v, \qquad \frac{\partial \mathbf{v}_2}{\partial u} = \frac{\partial}{\partial u} \left(\frac{1}{\sqrt{G}} \right) \Phi_v + \frac{1}{\sqrt{G}} \Phi_{vu},$$

so that

$$\left(\mathbf{v}_1, \frac{\partial \mathbf{v}_2}{\partial v} \right) = \frac{1}{\sqrt{EG}} \langle \Phi_u, \Phi_{vv} \rangle = \frac{-1}{\sqrt{EG}} \langle \Phi_{uv}, \Phi_v \rangle = \frac{-G_u}{2\sqrt{EG}},$$

$$\left(\mathbf{v}_1, \frac{\partial \mathbf{v}_2}{\partial u} \right) = \frac{1}{\sqrt{EG}} \langle \Phi_u, \Phi_{uv} \rangle = \frac{E_v}{2\sqrt{EG}}.$$

Finally, by (4.29), we have

$$K = \frac{-1}{2\sqrt{EG}} \left\{ \frac{\partial}{\partial u} \left(\frac{G_u}{\sqrt{EG}} \right) + \frac{\partial}{\partial v} \left(\frac{E_v}{\sqrt{EG}} \right) \right\}, \qquad (4.31)$$

which is the promised formula.   □

The condition, in Theorem 4.5.1, that Ω is contained in a parametrized neighborhood, is dispensable, since it holds for every polygonal region. To prove this, we consider a *triangulation* $(\Delta_j)_{1 \le i \le r}$ of Ω such that each Δ_j is a **closed** polygonal region that is contained in some parametrized neighborhood (so that we can apply Theorem 4.5.1 to it). Moreover:

(i) the closure of Ω is equal to the union of the Δ_j;

(ii) for each j the simple closed curve $\partial\Delta_j$ has three *vertices*; the portions of $\partial\Delta_j$ between each pair of consecutive vertices are regular curves called *edges*. The sets Δ_j are called the *faces*;

(iii) the intersection of two distinct faces is either empty, or reduces to a vertex, or is an edge common to both.

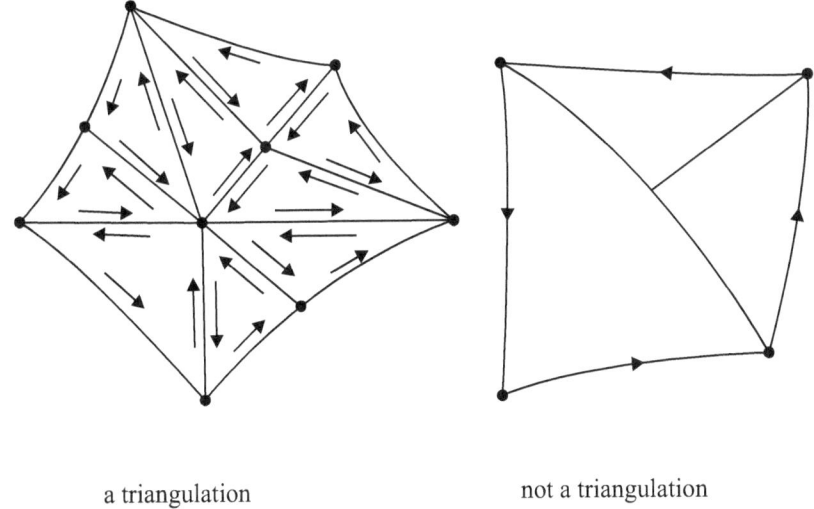

a triangulation   not a triangulation

Figure 4.7

We denote by $\mathcal{V}$ the set of vertices of the triangulation, and by V, A, F the numbers of vertices, edges and faces, respectively. Denoting by γ_j^l ($l = 1, 2, 3$) the exterior angles of Δ_j, Theorem 4.5.1 gives, for each $1 \le j \le F$,

$$\int_{\Delta_j} K \, d\sigma + \int_{\partial\Delta_j} k_g(s) \, ds + \sum_{l=1}^{3} \gamma_j^l = 2\pi.$$

Each interior edge of Ω is run through twice in opposite directions (the geodesic curvature showing up with opposed sign), and by summing the above formulas for $j = 1, \ldots, F$ only the edges that make up $\partial\Omega$ are left. We thus obtain

$$\int_\Omega K\, d\sigma + \int_{\partial\Omega} K_g(s)\, ds + \sum_{j=1}^{F}\sum_{l=1}^{3} \gamma_j^l = 2\pi F. \tag{4.32}$$

For each vertex $v \in V$, let:

$$\mathcal{I}_v = \{(j,l): \gamma_j^l \text{ is adjacent to } v\};$$
$$S(v) = \sum_{(j,l)\in\mathcal{I}_v} \gamma_j^l;$$

$A(v)$ = number of edges starting from v.

We break V into three subsets V_1, V_2, V_3 defined as follows: V_1 is the set of vertices inside Ω; V_2 contains the vertices that belong to $\partial\Omega$ but are not vertices of Ω; V_3 contains the vertices of Ω. Denoting by $\eta_j^l = \pi - \gamma_j^l$ the interior angles of Δ_j, we have:

- if $v \in V_1$ then

$$S(v) = \sum_{(j,l)\in\mathcal{I}_v} (\pi - \eta_j^l) = \pi\#\mathcal{I}_v - \sum_{(j,l)\in\mathcal{I}_v} \eta_j^l = \pi A(v) - 2\pi,$$

- if $v \in V_2$ then

$$S(v) = \pi\mathcal{I}_v - \sum_{(j,l)\in\mathcal{I}_v} \eta_j^l = \pi(A(v) - 1) - \pi = \pi A(v) - 2\pi,$$

- if $v \in V_3$ then v is one of the k vertices of Ω and, if γ_i is the corresponding exterior angle, we have

$$S(v) = \pi\#\mathcal{I}_v - \sum_{(j,l)\in\mathcal{I}_v} \eta_j^l = \pi(A(v) - 1) - (\pi - \gamma_i) = \pi A(v) - 2\pi + \gamma_i.$$

Adding up all these formulas, we obtain

$$\sum_{j=1}^{F}\sum_{l=1}^{3} \gamma_j^l = \sum_{v\in V} S(v) = \pi \sum_{v\in V} A(v) - 2\pi V + \sum_{i=1}^{k} \gamma_i$$

$$= 2\pi(A - V) + \sum_{i=1}^{k} \gamma_i$$

— because each edge is counted twice (once for each one of its endpoints). Replacing in (4.32) and using Lemma 4.5.4 below, we obtain

$$\int_\Omega K\, d\sigma + \int_{\partial\Omega} k_g(s)\, ds + \sum_{i=1}^{k} \gamma_i = 2\pi(V - A + F) = 2\pi,$$

which establishes the Gauss-Bonnet formula for any polygonal region $\Omega \subseteq S$.

Lemma 4.5.4 (Euler's formula). $V - A + F = 1$.

Proof We have to show that for every triangulation of a polygonal region we have $V - A + F = 1$. We proceed by induction on the number of faces F. If $F = 1$, then there are three vertices and three edges and the formula is true. If $F > 1$, then let Δ_j be a face where at least one of the edges is part of $\partial\Omega$, and such that $\widetilde{\Omega} = \Omega \setminus \Delta_j$ is a polygonal region. Consider in $\widetilde{\Omega}$ the triangulation induced by the triangulation of Ω. Denoting by $\widetilde{V}$, $\widetilde{A}$ and $\widetilde{F}$ the numbers of vertices, edges and faces of the triangulation of $\widetilde{\Omega}$, we have:

- if $\partial\Omega$ contains a single edge of Δ_j, then $\widetilde{V} = V$, $\widetilde{A} = A-1$, $\widetilde{F} = F-1$;
- if $\partial\Omega$ contains two edges of Δ_j, then $\widetilde{V} = V-1$, $\widetilde{A} = A-2$, $\widetilde{F} = F-1$.

In both cases, $V - A + F = \widetilde{V} - \widetilde{A} + \widetilde{F}$ and the proof by induction is complete. $\square$

There is a special case of the Gauss-Bonnet formula that is worthy to note: if the boundary of Ω consists of geodesic arcs $(k_g \equiv 0)$, we are left with

$$\int_\Omega K \, d\sigma + \sum_{i=1}^{k} \gamma_i = 2\pi,$$

or, denoting by $\eta_i = \pi - \gamma_i$ the interior angles of Ω,

$$\sum_{i=1}^{k} \eta_i - (k - 2)\pi = \int_\Omega K \, d\sigma.$$

When $k = 3$, Ω is called a *geodesic triangle*, and we have just obtained the promised generalization of Girard's formula:

Corollary 4.5.5 *The difference between the sum of the interior angles of a geodesic triangle Δ and π is given by the integral, extended to Δ, of the Gaussian curvature:*

$$(\eta_1 + \eta_2 + \eta_3) - \pi = \int_\Delta K \, d\sigma.$$

If in particular the curvature of the surface is constant, then this difference is proportional to the area of the triangle, equal to $(\eta_1 + \eta_2 + \eta_3) - \pi = K \cdot area\,(\Delta)$.

Let us now assume that S is a compact surface, and consider a triangulation $\mathcal{T} = (\Delta_i)_{1 \leq i \leq r}$ of S: conditions (i) – (iii) are satisfied, but it is not required that each Δ_j is contained in a parametrized neighborhood. (The existence of triangulations for arbitrary surfaces is a deep result, and a proof is given in [17]; for regular compact surfaces — the case we are concerned with — we will give a proof in Exercise 115.) The *Euler characteristic* of S is $\chi(S) = V - A + F$, where V, A and F are the numbers of vertices, edges and faces of $\mathcal{T}$.

Gauss-Bonnet Theorem 4.5.6 *(Global Version)*. *If S is a compact surface then*

$$\int_S K \, d\sigma = 2\pi\chi(S).$$

Proof Writing down the Gauss-Bonnet formula for each of the faces of a triangulation $\mathcal{T}$ and summing them up, the integrals of the geodesic curvatures all cancel, because each edge is run through twice in opposite directions. Furthermore, the vertices of $\mathcal{T}$ are all inside S (of type $\mathcal{V}_1$) and the sum of the interior angles adjacent to each of them is 2π. By the above calculations, we are left with

$$\int_S K \, d\sigma = 2\pi(V - A + F),$$

which is the desired formula. $\square$

The integral $\int_S K \, d\sigma$ is called the *total curvature* of S. The equation now obtained shows that $\chi(S)$ is welldefined, independent of the triangulation of S chosen to compute it. Furthermore, $\chi(S)$ is invariant under diffeomorphisms (because a diffeomorphism $f: S \to S_2$ maps any triangulation $\mathcal{T}$ of S to another triangulation $f(\mathcal{T})$ of S_2 with the same number of vertices, edges and faces). We thus obtain the following result.

Corollary 4.5.7 *Any two diffeomorphic compact surfaces have the same total curvature.*

For example, any surface S diffeomorphic to the sphere has total curvature 4π. This is not surprising if the curvature of S is positive at all points (as in the ellipsoid), because in this situation we will see later on that $N: S \to \mathbf{S}^2$ is a diffeomorphism, and $\int_S K \, d\sigma$ is nothing but the area of the image of S under N (cf. Exercise 64 in Section 3.2), which in this case is $\mathbf{S}^2$. But if we call to mind that S can also have regions of negative curvature we more readily appreciate the strength of the result.

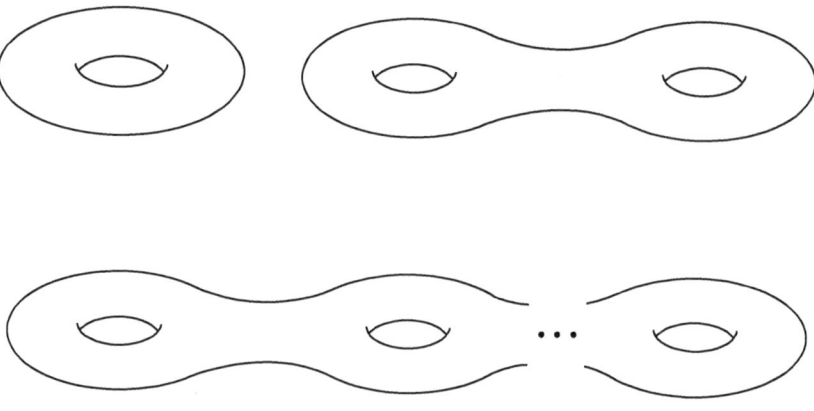

Figure 4.8

The Euler characteristic (and hence the total curvature) of the torus is zero; that of the double torus is -2. That of the n-torus ($n \geq 1$) is $2 - 2n$. Together with the sphere, and up to diffeomorphisms, this list exhausts all orientable compact surfaces (see Fig. 4.8); this is a classical result whose proof you can find, for example, in [17]. In particular, among the compact surfaces, only those which are diffeomorphic to the sphere have non-negative total curvature.

Example 4.5.8 A non-compact surface may have finite total curvature. Consider, on a surface of revolution S given by $\rho = \rho(z)$, $z \in \mathbb{R}$, the region $\Omega(z_0, z_1)$ bounded by the two parallels $z = z_0$ and $z = z_1$ ($z_0 < z_1$). We can break $\Omega(z_0, z_1)$ into two "four-sided polygons" by two meridians and add up the two resulting Gauss-Bonnet formulas. Since there are four vertices and the sum of the two exterior angles adjacent to each vertex is π, we obtain

$$\int_{\Omega(z_0, z_1)} K \, d\sigma + \int_{\partial\Omega(z_0, z_1)} k_g \, ds + 4\pi = 4\pi,$$

i.e.,

$$\int_{\Omega(z_0, z_1)} K \, d\sigma = \int_{\partial\Omega(z_0, z_1)} -k_g \, ds.$$

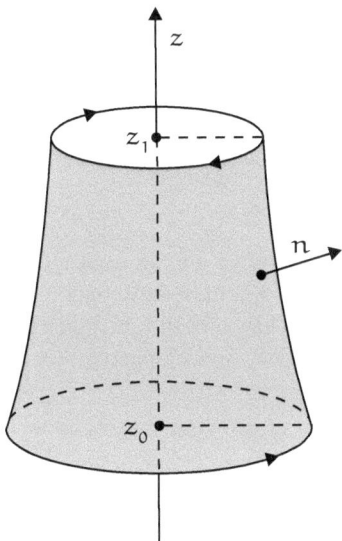

Figure 4.9

Taking in S the orientation given by

$$N(\varphi, z) = \frac{1}{\sqrt{1 + \rho^2}} (\cos \varphi, \sin \varphi, -\rho),$$

the parallel $z = z_0$ is run through counterclockwise, and $z = z_1$ clockwise. A quick calculation then shows that their geodesic curvatures are

$$k_g(z_0) = \frac{-\rho(z_0)}{\rho(z_0)\sqrt{1 + \rho(z_0)}^2}, \quad k_g(z_1) = \frac{\rho(z_1)}{\rho(z_1)\sqrt{1 + \rho(z_1)}^2},$$

and therefore

$$\int_{\Omega(z_0,z_1)} K \, d\sigma = -2\pi \left(\frac{\rho(z_1)}{\sqrt{1+\rho(z_1)^2}} - \frac{\rho(z_0)}{\sqrt{1+\rho(z_0)^2}} \right).$$

This formula guarantees that in many cases the limit

$$\int_S K \, d\sigma = \lim_{\substack{z_1 \to +\infty \\ z_0 \to -\infty}} \int_{\Omega(z_0,z_1)} K \, d\sigma$$

exists and is finite; we will call it the *total curvature* of S.

For example, the total curvature of the hyperboloid $x^2 + y^2 = 1 + z^2$ is $-2\sqrt{2}\pi$, since $\rho(z) = \sqrt{1+z^2}$ and $\lim_{z \to \pm\infty} \rho(z) = \pm 1$.

It would not be difficult to compute directly $\int_{\Omega(z_0,z_1)} K \, d\sigma$ (see example 3.2.1) — but, besides illustrating a use of the Gauss-Bonnet Theorem, this method is applicable to surfaces other than surfaces of revolution (e.g., to those non-compact surfaces S for which $S \setminus \mathfrak{C}$ is a surface of revolution for some compact $\mathfrak{C} \subseteq S$).   □

Exercises

96. Assume that S has non-positive curvature at all its points. Show that if two geodesics start from the same point in S, they cannot meet again in such a way that their traces constitute the boundary of a simple region of S (in particular, no closed geodesic of S can be the boundary of a simple region).

97. Show that if γ is a regular closed simple curve in $\mathbf{S}^2$ then $\left| \int_\gamma k_g \, ds \right| < 2\pi$.

98. Let $p \in S$ be such that $K(p) > 0$, and let (U, Φ) be a parameterization such that $p \in \Phi(U)$ and $K \circ \Phi(u,v) > 0$ for all $(u,v) \in U$. Consider a family of circles $(C_r)_{0<r<\delta}$ such that:

i. each C_r has radius r;

ii. for every r, $\Phi^{-1}(p) \in C_r$ and the closed disk bounded by C_r is contained in U;

iii. if $r < \tilde{r}$ then C_r is inside $C_{\tilde{r}}$.

Further denote by $\psi_r \in [-\pi, \pi]$ the oriented angle between the initial and final positions of a vector carried parallel from p to p along the closed curve $\Phi(C_r)$ in S.

(a) Show that there exists $\varepsilon \in]0, \delta[$ such that

$$0 < r < \tilde{r} < \varepsilon \implies 0 < |\psi_r| < |\psi_{\tilde{r}}| < \pi.$$

(b) Conclude that any surface on which parallel transport depends only on the initial and final points of the curve has constant zero curvature:

Give an example of a surface with constant zero curvature that does not have this property.

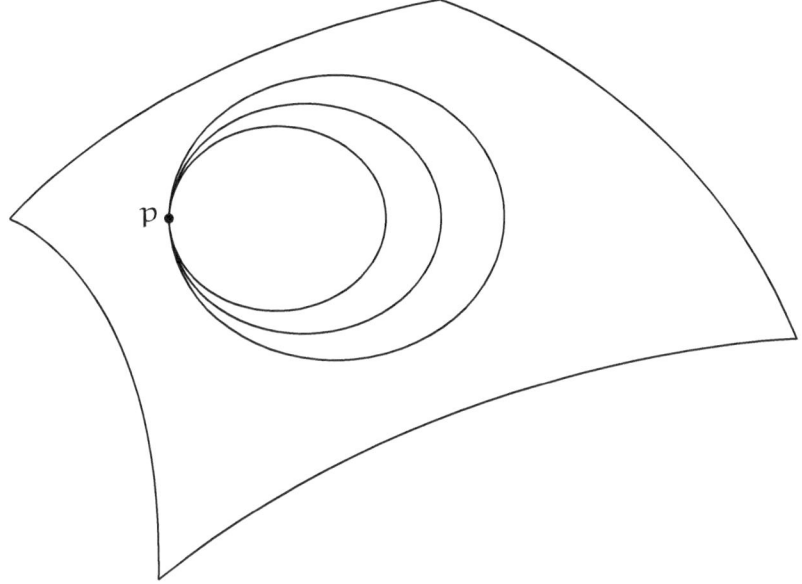

Figure 4.10

99. Is it true that two non-compact diffeomorphic surfaces necessarily have the same total curvature?

4.6 Minimizing Properties of Geodesics

We begin this section by establishing the local existence of geodesics on arbitrary surfaces: to this end we will observe that, in local coordinates, geodesics are characterized by second-order differential equations. We then introduce polar geodesic coordinates that allow us to show that the shortest path *on the surface* between any two points is, *when it exists*, given by a geodesic.

Recall that a curve α of S is a geodesic if the unit vector field tangent to the curve $\tau_1 = \frac{1}{|\alpha'|}\alpha'$ is a parallel vector field. Taking coordinates (U, Φ) and assuming that $\alpha(t) = \Phi(u(t), v(t))$ is parametrized with constant scalar velocity $m > 0$, we have

$$\tau_1 = \frac{1}{m}\alpha' = \frac{1}{m}\left(u'\Phi_u + v'\Phi_v\right).$$

From formula (4.9), we obtain

$$\frac{D\tau_1}{dt} = \frac{1}{m} \{ (u'' + u'^2\Gamma_{11}^1 + 2u'v'\Gamma_{12}^1 + v'^2\Gamma_{22}^1)\Phi_u$$

$$+ (v'' + u'^2\Gamma_{11}^2 + 2u'v'\Gamma_{12}^2 + v'^2\Gamma_{22}^2)\Phi_v \}$$

— and, if α is a geodesic, then $\dfrac{D\tau_1}{dt} \equiv 0$, so that

$$\begin{cases} u'' + u'^2\Gamma_{11}^1 + 2u'v'\Gamma_{12}^1 + v'^2\Gamma_{22}^1 = 0, \\ v'' + u'^2\Gamma_{11}^2 + 2u'v'\Gamma_{12}^2 + v'^2\Gamma_{22}^2 = 0. \end{cases} \tag{4.33}$$

Conversely, if $(u(t), v(t))$ is a non-constant solution of (4.33) then $\alpha(t) = \Phi(u(t), v(t))$ is a regular curve and its scalar velocity is constant, since in this case the covariant derivative of the vector field α' is zero and $\dfrac{d}{dt}|\alpha'|^2 = 2\left(\alpha', \dfrac{D\alpha'}{dt}\right) = 0.$
It follows that $\tau_1 = \dfrac{1}{m}\alpha'$ is a parallel vector field and therefore α is a geodesic.

We define *parametrized geodesics* to be either a parameterization $\alpha(t)$ of a geodesic with constant scalar velocity $|\alpha'(t)|$, or a constant curve. This means that the solutions of the system give us, locally, all parametrized geodesics of the surface: we therefore call the equations in (4.33) the *differential equations of the geodesics*.

The system of equations (4.33) can be restated in the form

$$\begin{cases} u'' = H_1(u, v, u', v'), \\ v'' = H_2(u, v, u', v'), \end{cases} \tag{4.34}$$

or otherwise

$$\begin{cases} u' = a, \\ v' = b, \\ a' = H_1(u, v, a, b), \\ b' = H_2(u, v, a, b) \end{cases} \tag{4.35}$$

— where H_1, H_2 are differentiable functions defined on $U \times \mathbb{R}^2 \subseteq \mathbb{R}^4$ where U is the domain of the parameterization Φ. Theorem 3.3.1 guarantees that every $(u_0, v_0, a_0, b_0) \in U \times \mathbb{R}^2$ has an open neighborhood W such that there exist $\varepsilon > 0$ and a differentiable mapping

$$]-\varepsilon, \varepsilon[\times W \to U \times \mathbb{R}^2, \ (t; u, v, a, b) \mapsto \tilde{\varphi}(t; u, v, a, b)$$

enjoying the following conditions: for every $(u, v, a, b) \in W$, the curve

$$t \mapsto \tilde{\varphi}(t; u, v, a, b)$$

is the only solution of the system (4.35) with initial condition $\tilde{\varphi}(0; u, v, a, b) = (u, v, a, b)$.

Writing $\tilde{\varphi} = (\varphi_1, \varphi_2, \varphi_3, \varphi_4)$, it is clear that φ_3 and φ_4 are redundant, since $\varphi_3 = \dfrac{\partial \varphi_1}{\partial t}$ and $\varphi_4 = \dfrac{\partial \varphi_2}{\partial t}$. Letting $\varphi = (\varphi_1, \varphi_2)$, the conclusion we obtain for the system (4.34), and hence for (4.33), is as follows. The mapping $\varphi:]-\varepsilon, \varepsilon[\times W \to U$, where W is a neighborhood of (u_0, v_0, a_0, b_0), is such that, for $(u, v, a, b) \in W$, the curve $t \mapsto \varphi(t; u, v, a, b)$ is the only solution of (4.34) with initial conditions

$$\varphi(0; u, v, a, b) = (u, v), \qquad \frac{d}{dt} \varphi(t; u, v, a, b)\Big|_{t=0} = (a, b).$$

In summary, determining $(u(0), v(0))$ and $(u'(0), v'(0))$ completely determines a solution $(u(t), v(t))$ of (4.33). The solutions depend differentiably on these initial conditions. Let us now define

$$D\Phi: U \times \mathbb{R}^2 \to \bigcup_{p \in \Phi(U)} (\{p\} \times T_p S)$$

$$(u, v, a, b) \mapsto (\Phi(u, v), (a\Phi_u + b\Phi_v)\big|_{(u,v)})$$

(4.36)

and note that $D\Phi$ is a continuous bijection. Given $p_0 = \Phi(u_0, v_0) \in \Phi(U)$, consider the corresponding neighborhood W associated with $(u_0, v_0, 0, 0)$ (which we can assume to be of the form $W = W_1 \times W_2$), $\varepsilon > 0$ and the mapping φ. Let us take $V \subseteq S$, an open neighborhood of p_0 whose closure is compact and contained in $\Phi(W_1)$, and choose $\delta > 0$ such that the set

$$B_\delta(V) = \{(p, \mathbf{v}): p \in V, \mathbf{v} \in T_p S, |\mathbf{v}| < \delta\}$$

is contained in $D\Phi(W)$ (that such a choice of δ is possible is an easy exercise). We then define the mapping

$$\gamma:]-\varepsilon, \varepsilon[\times B_\delta(V) \to S, \quad \gamma(t; p, \mathbf{v}) = \Phi \circ \varphi(t; (D\Phi)^{-1}(p, \mathbf{v})),$$

and it follows from our analysis that for every $(p, \mathbf{v}) \in B_\delta(V)$, the curve $t \mapsto \gamma(t; p, \mathbf{v})$ is the only parametrized geodesic that at time 0 passes through p with velocity $\mathbf{v}$; the constant parametrized geodesics are those of the form $\gamma(t; p, 0)$. Furthermore, for $\lambda \in \mathbb{R}$ we have

$$\gamma(\lambda t; p, \mathbf{v}) = \gamma(t; p, \lambda \mathbf{v}), \qquad (4.37)$$

because the two terms of (4.37) are parametrized geodesics satisfying the same initial conditions: at time 0, they both pass through p with velocity $\lambda \mathbf{v}$. It follows that, up to reparametrization, *there is exactly one geodesic whose tangent line at a given point has a given direction.*

Observation 4.6.1 At this point we can already state that there are no geodesics on the sphere other than the maximal circles (see example 4.3.9), since through each point passes a maximal circle tangent to each given direction. The sphere thus has the particularity that all its geodesics are closed. (A non-constant parametrized geodesic $\gamma(t)$ is called *closed* if it is periodic — that is, if there exists $T > 0$ such that $\gamma(t + T) = \gamma(t)$ for all $t \in \mathbb{R}$. A necessary and sufficient condition for γ to be closed is that there exist $t_1 < t_2$ such that $\gamma(t_1) = \gamma(t_2)$ and $\gamma'(t_1) = \gamma'(t_2)$ — i.e., γ is closed if and only if it passes again through the same point with the same velocity vector.) Surprisingly, there are other surfaces with the same property, as shown in [4]. □

Let us now apply (4.37) to show that, choosing $|\mathbf{v}|$ sufficiently small, $\gamma(t; p, \mathbf{v})$ is defined for $|t| < 2$. In fact, since $\gamma(t; p, \mathbf{v}) = \gamma\left(\frac{\varepsilon}{2} t; p, \frac{2}{\varepsilon} \mathbf{v}\right)$, we can state that, for $\left|\frac{2}{\varepsilon} \mathbf{v}\right| < \delta$ (i.e., for $|\mathbf{v}| < \frac{\varepsilon \delta}{2}$), $\gamma(t; p, \mathbf{v})$ is defined whenever $\left|\frac{\varepsilon}{2} t\right| < \varepsilon$ — i.e., whenever $|t| < 2$. In summary:

For every $p_0 \in S$ there exist $\eta > 0$ and a neighborhood V of p_0 such that whenever $p \in V$ and $\mathbf{v} \in B_\eta(p) = \{\mathbf{v} \in T_p S : |\mathbf{v}| < \eta\}$ the geodesic $t \mapsto \gamma(t; p, \mathbf{v})$ is defined for $t \in \,]-2, 2[$.

Given $p \in S$, the *exponential mapping* $\exp_p$ is defined by $\exp_p(\mathbf{v}) = \gamma(1; p, \mathbf{v})$. By the above reasoning, there exists some $\eta > 0$ such that $\exp_p$ is defined on $B_\eta(p)$; one can choose such an η suitable for all points in a neighborhood of p.

The geodesic $t \mapsto \gamma(t; p, \mathbf{v})$ has constant scalar velocity $|\mathbf{v}|$, and therefore its arc length in the interval $[0, 1]$ is also $|\mathbf{v}|$. The geometric meaning of the exponential mapping is therefore as follows: $\exp_p(\mathbf{v})$ is the point that travels a distance of $|\mathbf{v}|$ on the geodesic that begins at p and whose direction and orientation is given by $\mathbf{v}$. Note that, by (4.37), we have $\exp_p(t\mathbf{v}) = \gamma(1; p, t\mathbf{v}) = \gamma(t; p, \mathbf{v})$ — which means that the geodesics starting from p are the image of the lines (or line segments) in $T_p S$ that **pass through the origin** under $\exp_p$.

To make full use of the exponential mapping, we need the next proposition:

Proposition 4.6.2 *Given $p_0 \in S$, there exist $\delta > 0$ and an open neighborhood $W \subseteq S$ of p_0 such that, for all $p \in W$, $\exp_p\big|_{B_\delta(p)}$ is a diffeomorphism onto the image.*

Proof We know that there exist $\eta > 0$ and an open neighborhood $V \subseteq S$ of p_0 such that, for all p on V, the exponential mapping $\exp_p$ is defined on $B_\eta(p)$. We can thus consider the differentiable mapping

$$F: B_\eta(V) \longrightarrow S \times S$$
$$(p, \mathbf{v}) \longmapsto (p, \exp_p(\mathbf{v})).$$

(A caveat: both $B_{\eta(V)}$ and $S \times S$ are spaces of dimension four, since $S \times S$ is the product of two spaces of dimension two and $B_\eta(V)$ can be identified, via $D\Phi$ as defined in (4.36), with an open subset of $\mathbb{R}^4$. Our proof can be made rigorous by applying the inverse mapping theorem to $(\Phi \times \Phi)^{-1} \circ F \circ D\Phi$, which is the expression of F in "local coordinates".)

The tangent spaces to $B_{\eta(V)}$ at $(p_0, 0)$ and to $S \times S$ at $(p_0, p_0) = F(p_0, 0)$ coincide: both are $T_{p_0} S \times T_{p_0} S$. Given $\mathbf{v} \in T_{p_0} S$, let α be a curve in V such that $\alpha(0) = p_0$ and $\alpha'(0) = \mathbf{v}$. Then $t \mapsto (\alpha(t), 0)$ is a curve in $B_\eta(V)$ that passes through $(p_0, 0)$ with velocity $(\mathbf{v}, 0)$. Thus

$$DF_{(p_0,0)}(\mathbf{v}, 0) = \frac{d}{dt} F(\alpha(t), 0)\Big|_{t=0} = \frac{d}{dt} (\alpha(t), \alpha(t))\Big|_{t=0} = (\mathbf{v}, \mathbf{v}).$$

On the other hand, if $\mathbf{w} \in T_{p_0}S \setminus \{0\}$ then the curve $t \mapsto (p_0, t\mathbf{w})$, $|t| < \dfrac{\eta}{|\mathbf{w}|}$, is contained in $B_\eta(V)$ and passes through $(p_0, 0)$ with velocity $(0, \mathbf{w})$, and therefore

$$DF_{(p_0,0)}(0, \mathbf{w}) = \frac{d}{dt} F(p_0, t\mathbf{w})\Big|_{t=0} = \left(0, \frac{d}{dt}\exp_{p_0}(t\mathbf{w})\big|_{t=0}\right) = (0, \mathbf{w}).$$

We thus conclude that

$$DF_{(p_0,0)}(\mathbf{v}, \mathbf{w}) = (\mathbf{v}, \mathbf{v} + \mathbf{w}) \text{ for every } (\mathbf{v}, \mathbf{w}) \in T_{p_0}S \times T_{p_0}S$$

– which shows that $DF_{(p_0,0)}$ is a linear isomorphism. The inverse mapping theorem then guarantees that the restriction of F to some neighborhood of $(p_0, 0)$ in $B_\eta(V)$ is a diffeomorphism onto the image, and we can choose such a neighborhood of the form $B_\delta(W)$, where W is an open subset of S and $\delta > 0$; it is easily verified that these choices of W and δ satisfy the desired condition. $\square$

Given $p \in S$, a neighborhood $V \subseteq S$ of p is called a *normal neighborhood of p* if there exists $\delta > 0$ such that $\exp_p\big|_{B_\delta(p)}$ is a diffeomorphism onto the image and $V \subseteq \exp_p(B_\delta(p))$. For such a δ, we write $D_\delta(p) = \exp_p(B_\delta(p))$: hence, $D_\delta(p)$ is the neighborhood of p covered by the geodesic rays of length δ starting from p, but note that for now we only define $D_\delta(p)$ for sufficiently small δ.

Let $(\mathbf{v}_1, \mathbf{v}_2)$ be an orthonormal basis of T_pS. $\exp_p$ gives rise to several coordinate systems in $D_\delta(p)$:

$$\Phi(u, v) = \exp_p(u\mathbf{v}_1 + v\mathbf{v}_2) \text{ (set on disk } u^2 + v^2 < \delta^2);$$
$$\Psi(\rho, \varphi) = \exp_p(\rho \cos \varphi\, \mathbf{v}_1 + \rho \sin \varphi\, \mathbf{v}_2) \ (0 < \rho < \delta, \varphi \in \,]\varphi_0 - \pi, \varphi_0 + \pi[\,).$$

The coordinates $\Psi(\rho, \varphi)$ are known as *geodesic polar coordinates*, and we call $\Phi(u, v)$ *geodesic Cartesian coordinates*. Of course, these coordinates depend on the choice of the basis $(\mathbf{v}_1, \mathbf{v}_2)$. If we want them to respect the orientation of S, it suffices that $(\mathbf{v}_1, \mathbf{v}_2)$ are positively oriented. In the case of geodesic polar coordinates, we obtain different parameterizations by restricting φ to intervals of length 2π, and each of these parameterizations excludes a *radial geodesic* $(\varphi = \text{constant})$. However, since the excluded radial geodesic is arbitrary, the conclusions we draw with one of these parameterizations are valid throughout the "punctured disc" $D_\delta(p) \setminus \{p\}$.

The next lemma says, among other things, that $\Psi(\rho, \varphi)$ is an orthogonal parameterization. Geometrically, this means that the radial geodesics $(\varphi = \text{constant})$ starting from p and the *circumference geodesics* $(\rho = \text{constant})$ with center p intersect orthogonally (see Fig. 4.11.).

Lemma 4.6.3 *The coefficients E, F, G of the geodesic polar coordinates satisfy*

$$E \equiv 1, \quad F \equiv 0, \quad \lim_{\rho \to 0} \sqrt{G} = 0, \quad \lim_{\rho \to 0} (\sqrt{G})_\rho = 1.$$

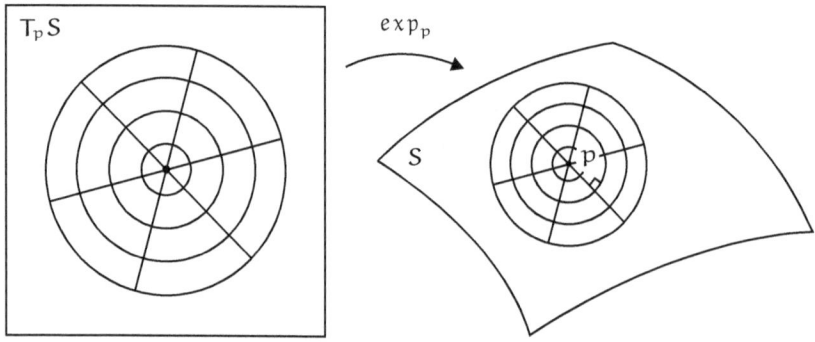

Figure 4.11

Proof To shorten the notation, we write $\mathbf{v}_\varphi = \cos\varphi\,\mathbf{v}_1 + \sin\varphi\,\mathbf{v}_2$ and $\mathbf{w}_\varphi = -\sin\varphi\,\mathbf{v}_1 + \cos\varphi\,\mathbf{v}_2$. We have

$$E = |\Psi_\rho|^2 = \left|\frac{\partial}{\partial\rho}\exp_p(\rho\mathbf{v}_\varphi)\right|^2 = |\mathbf{v}_\varphi|^2 = 1,$$

since $\rho \mapsto \exp_p(\rho\mathbf{v}_\varphi)$ is a parametrized geodesic, and so has constant scalar velocity. Furthermore, denoting by $\dfrac{D\Psi_\rho}{\partial\rho}$ the derivative covariant of Ψ_ρ along $\rho \mapsto \Psi(\rho,\varphi)$ — which is zero because Ψ_ρ is the velocity field of a parametrized geodesic — we have

$$F_\rho = \frac{\partial}{\partial\rho}\langle\Psi_\rho,\Psi\varphi\rangle = \left\langle\frac{D\Psi_\rho}{\partial\rho},\Psi_\varphi\right\rangle + \langle\Psi_\rho,\Psi_{\varphi\rho}\rangle$$

$$= \frac{\partial}{\partial\varphi}\left(\frac{1}{2}|\Psi_\rho|^2\right) = 0 \qquad \text{(because } E \equiv 1\text{)}.$$

We thus conclude that F does not depend on ρ. Since

$$F = \langle D(\exp_p)_{\rho\mathbf{v}_\varphi}(\mathbf{v}_\varphi), D(\exp_p)_{\rho\mathbf{v}_\varphi}(\rho\mathbf{w}_\varphi)\rangle$$

$$= \rho\langle D(\exp_p)_{\rho\mathbf{v}_\varphi}(\mathbf{v}_\varphi), D(\exp_p)_{\rho\mathbf{v}_\varphi}(\mathbf{w}_\varphi)\rangle,$$

we have

$$|F| \le \rho\,|D(\exp_p)_{\rho\mathbf{v}_\varphi}(\mathbf{v}_\varphi)|\,|D(\exp_p)_{\rho\mathbf{v}_\varphi}(\mathbf{w}_\varphi)|,$$

which, together with the facts that $D(\exp_p)_O$ is the identity (as we saw in the proof of Proposition 4.6.2) and $\mathbf{v}_\varphi$ and $\mathbf{w}_\varphi$ are unit vectors, implies $\lim_{\rho\to 0} F = 0$ and therefore $F \equiv 0$.

It remains to prove the last two equalities. For this let us consider the geodesic Cartesian coordinates $\Phi(u,v)$, whose coefficients we denote by $\overline{E}, \overline{F}, \overline{G}$. Noting that for $(u,v) \ne (0,0)$, we have $u = \rho\cos\varphi$, $v = \rho\sin\varphi$ and that at $(0,0)$ the coefficients $\overline{E}, \overline{F}, \overline{G}$ are equal to 1, 0, 1 (because $\Phi_u|(0,0) = \mathbf{v}_1$ and $\Phi_v|_{(0,0)} = \mathbf{v}_2$), we have

$$\sqrt{G} = \sqrt{EG - F^2} = \left|\frac{\partial(u,v)}{\partial(\rho,\varphi)}\right| \sqrt{\overline{E}\,\overline{G} - \overline{F}^2} = \rho\sqrt{\overline{E}\,\overline{G} - \overline{F}^2}$$

and therefore $\lim_{\rho \to 0} \sqrt{G} = 0$. Finally, differentiating the last equality, we obtain

$$(\sqrt{G})_\rho = \sqrt{\overline{E}\,\overline{G} - \overline{F}^2} + \rho\, \frac{\partial}{\partial\rho}\left(\sqrt{\overline{E}\,\overline{G} - \overline{F}^2}\right)$$

$$= \sqrt{\overline{E}\,\overline{G} - \overline{F}^2} + \rho\left\{\frac{\partial}{\partial u}\left(\sqrt{\overline{E}\,\overline{G} - \overline{F}^2}\right)\cos\varphi + \frac{\partial}{\partial v}\left(\sqrt{\overline{E}\,\overline{G} - \overline{F}^2}\right)\sin\varphi\right\},$$

and thus

$$\lim_{\rho \to 0} (\sqrt{G})_\rho = \lim_{(u,v)\to(0,0)} \sqrt{\overline{E}\,\overline{G} - \overline{F}^2} = 1. \qquad\qquad \square$$

Example 4.6.4 Let us make explicit a geodesic coordinate system in $\mathbf{S}^2$ with origin at the North Pole $\mathcal{N} = (0,0,1)$. Fixing the orthonormal basis $\mathbf{v}_1 = (1,0,0)$, $\mathbf{v}_2 = (0,1,0)$, the geodesic $\varphi = $ constant is the meridian that forms angle φ with the plane $y = 0$; its parameterization by arc length is s $(0 \le s < \pi) \mapsto$ $(\sin s \cos\varphi, \sin s \sin\varphi, \cos s)$, and we find the point $\Psi(\rho,\varphi)$ at distance ρ from $\mathcal{N}$. Thus $\Psi(\rho,\varphi) = (\sin\rho\cos\varphi, \sin\rho\sin\varphi, \cos\rho)$ — which shows that these geodesic coordinates are just the spherical coordinates. Let us also point out that $\mathbf{S}^2 \smallsetminus \{(0,0,-1)\} = D_\pi(\mathcal{N})$ is a normal neighborhood of $\mathcal{N}$, because it is the diffeomorphic image of the disk $B_\pi(\mathcal{N})$ under $\exp_\mathcal{N}$. $\square$

We can now almost specify under what conditions a geodesic describes a shortest path on the surface. But first, let us define the *intrinsic distance* on the surface, which is the distance "experienced" by those who move on it. For a **connected** surface S and $p,q \in S$, we define $d(p,q)$ to be the least of the lengths of the curves in S that connect p to q:

$$d(p,q) = \inf\{l(\alpha) \mid \alpha\colon [a,b] \to S \text{ is piecewise regular,}$$
$$\alpha(a) = p \text{ and } \alpha(b) = q\}.$$

The intrinsic distance d is a true distance, since it enjoys the following three properties:

(i) $d(p,q) \ge 0$ and $d(p,q) = 0$ if and only if $p = q$ (*positivity*);

(ii) $d(p,q) = d(q,p)$ (*symmetry*);

(iii) $d(p,q) \le d(p,r) + d(r,q)$ (*triangular inequality*).

These properties are easily verified; we prove property (iii) via an example. If $\alpha_1\colon [a,b] \to S$ is a curve from p to r, and $\alpha_2\colon [c,d] \to S$ another from r to q, then their juxtaposition $\alpha_1 * \alpha_2$, defined on $[a, b+d-c]$ by

$$(\alpha_1 * \alpha_2)(t) = \begin{cases} \alpha_1(t) & \text{if } a \le t \le b \\ \alpha_2(t+c-b) & \text{if } b \le t \le b+d-c, \end{cases}$$

is a piecewise regular curve from p to q, and $l(\alpha_1 * \alpha_2) = l(\alpha_1) + l(\alpha_2)$. We then have

$$d(p,q) \leq \inf_{\alpha_1,\alpha_2} l(\alpha_1 * \alpha_2) = \inf_{\alpha_1,\alpha_2} \{l(\alpha_1) + l(\alpha_2)\}$$
$$= \inf_{\alpha_1} l(\alpha_1) + \inf_{\alpha_2} l(\alpha_2) = d(p,r) + d(r,q)$$

— which proves (iii).

We say that the curve α in S from p to q, which is piecewise regular, *minimizes distance* (or is *minimizing*) if $l(\alpha) = d(p,q)$ (indeed, by Proposition 4.6.8 below, any minimizing curve is a geodesic and is therefore regular).

Example 4.6.5 There do not always exist minimizing curves in S. It is sufficient to take for S a punctured plane (i.e., a plane from which a point O has been removed) and consider for S two points p, q such that $O \in [p,q]$: the intrinsic distance in S between p and q is $|p-q|$, but there is in S no curve from p to q with length $|p-q|$. □

Proposition 4.6.6 *Geodesics locally minimize distance. More exactly, if $D_\delta(p)$ is a normal neighborhood of p, and $q \in D_\delta(p)$, then the radial geodesic from p to q is the only minimizing curve between p and q.*

Proof Take geodesic polar coordinates $\Psi(\rho, \varphi)$ centered at p, and let (ρ_0, φ_0) be such that $\Psi(\rho_0, \varphi_0) = q$. Given a curve $\alpha : [a,b] \to S$, piecewise regular, such that $\alpha(a) = p, \alpha(b) = q$, our goal is to show that $l(\alpha) > \rho_0$, unless α is a reparametrization of the radial geodesic ρ $(0 \leq \rho \leq \rho_0) \mapsto \Psi(\rho, \varphi_0)$.

We first deal with the case where $\alpha([a,b]) \subseteq D_\delta(p)$. We may assume, truncating the curve if necessary, that $\alpha(t) \neq p$ for all $t \in]a,b]$. Under this hypothesis, there exist functions $\rho(t)$ and $\varphi(t)$, piecewise differentiable, such that $\varphi(b) = \varphi_0$ and $\alpha(t) = \Psi(\rho(t), \varphi(t))$ for $t \in]a,b]$. Using Lemma 4.6.3, we then have

$$l(\alpha) = \int_a^b \sqrt{E\rho^2 + 2F\rho\varphi + G\varphi^2}\, dt$$
$$= \int_a^b \sqrt{\rho^2 + G\varphi^2}\, dt \geq \int_a^b \sqrt{\rho^2}\, dt \geq \int_a^b \rho\, dt = \rho_0,$$

and equality holds only if $\varphi \equiv 0$ (i.e., if φ is constant) and $\rho \geq 0$, which implies that α is the radial geodesic from p to q.

If $\alpha([a,b])$ is not contained in $D_\delta(p)$ then, given $0 < r < \delta$, let t_r be the first point such that $\alpha(t_r)$ belongs to the geodesic circumference $\rho = r$. By the above conclusion, we have $l(\alpha) \geq l(\alpha|_{[a,t_r]}) \geq r$. This inequality, valid for all $r < \delta$, implies that $l(\alpha) \geq \delta > \rho_0$.   □

Observations 4.6.7 **A.** From the proof of Proposition 4.6.6 it also follows that, for every point $q \in S \smallsetminus D_\delta(p)$, we have $d(p,q) \geq \delta$. In short, if we put, for arbitrary $\delta > 0$, $D_\delta(p) = \{q \in S : d(p,q) < \delta\}$, this agrees with our previous definition when $D_\delta(p)$ is a normal neighborhood of p.

B. We should stress that we can only guarantee locally that geodesics are minimizing. On the cylinder $x^2 + y^2 = 1$, for example, the geodesic $\alpha(t) = (\cos t, \sin t, t)$ does not minimize the distance between $\alpha(0) = (1, 0, 0)$ and $\alpha(2\pi) = (1, 0, 2\pi)$: the line segment $\{(1, 0)\} \times [0, 2\pi]$ is shorter.   □

Proposition 4.6.8 *Every minimizing curve is a geodesic.*

Proof Let $\alpha : [0, L] \to S$ be a minimizing curve, piecewise regular, parametrized by arc length. It suffices to see that, given any point $p_0 = \alpha(s_0)$ on the curve, there exists $\varepsilon > 0$ such that the restriction from α to $[s_0 - \varepsilon, s_0 + \varepsilon]$ ($[0, \varepsilon]$ or $[L - \varepsilon, L]$, if $s_0 = 0$ or $s_0 = L$) is a geodesic. We take $\delta > 0$ and the neighborhood W of p_0 given in Proposition 4.6.2, and we choose $\varepsilon > 0$ so that $\varepsilon < \frac{\delta}{2}$ and the points $p = \alpha(s_0 - \varepsilon)$ and $q = \alpha(s_0 + \varepsilon)$ are both in W. Since $\alpha\big|_{[s_0 - \varepsilon, s_0 + \varepsilon]}$ is minimizing, we have $d(p, q) = 2\varepsilon$ and, by note 4.6.7, **A**, q belongs to the normal neighborhood $D_\delta(p)$ of p. It follows then from Proposition 4.6.6 that $\alpha\big|_{[s_0 - \varepsilon, s_0 + \varepsilon]}$ is a geodesic.   □

Note that in the above proof, $V = W \cap D_{\delta/2}(p_0)$ is a normal neighborhood of all its points, therefore enjoying the following property: any two points of V are joined by a single minimizing curve, which is a geodesic of length δ.

In note 4.5.3 **B** we gave a formula (4.31) for the curvature K as a function of the coefficients of an orthogonal parameterization. This formula simplifies substantially for geodesic polar coordinates $\Psi(\rho, \varphi)$, where $E \equiv 1$:

$$K = \frac{-1}{2\sqrt{G}} \frac{\partial}{\partial \rho} \left(\frac{G_\rho}{\sqrt{G}} \right) = \frac{-(\sqrt{G})_{\rho\rho}}{\sqrt{G}}. \tag{4.38}$$

The formula (4.38) becomes even more interesting when K is constant. We now need an elementary result of Calculus:

Lemma 4.6.9 *Let $f : [a, b[\to \mathbb{R}$ be a continuous function, differentiable on $]a, b[$, and such that $\lim\limits_{x \to a^+} f'(x)$ exists and is finite. Then f is differentiable at a and $f'(a) = \lim\limits_{x \to a^+} f'(x)$.*

Fixing φ, Lemmas 4.6.3 and 4.6.9 say that the continuous extension of ρ ($0 < \rho < \delta) \mapsto \sqrt{G}(\rho, \varphi)$ defined by $\sqrt{G}(0, \varphi) = 0$ is differentiable and its derivative at 0 has value 1. Another application of Lemma 4.6.9 (together with the equality $(\sqrt{G})_{\rho\rho} + K\sqrt{G} = 0$) further ensures that it is twice differentiable at 0. We thus have ρ ($\rho \geq 0) \mapsto \sqrt{G}(\rho, \varphi)$ as solution of the differential equation

$$x(\rho) + K x(\rho) = 0 \tag{4.39}$$

with initial conditions $x(0) = 0$ and $x(0) = 1$. There are three cases to consider:

i. if $K < 0$ then $\sqrt{G} = \dfrac{1}{\sqrt{-K}} \sinh(\sqrt{-K}\rho)$, and therefore $G = -\dfrac{1}{K} \sinh^2(\sqrt{-K}\rho)$;

ii. if $K = 0$ then $\sqrt{G} = \rho$, $G = \rho^2$;

iii. if $K > 0$ then $\sqrt{G} = \dfrac{1}{\sqrt{K}} \sin(\sqrt{K}\rho)$, $G = \dfrac{1}{K} \sin^2(\sqrt{K}\rho)$.

We thus conclude that if K is constant then the coefficients E, F, G of the coordinates $\Psi(\rho, \varphi)$ only depend on K. As a consequence we have the following result.

Theorem 4.6.10 *Any two surfaces of equal constant Gaussian curvature are locally isometric.*

Proof Assume that S_1 and S_2 have the same constant curvature. Given $p \in S_1$ and $q \in S_2$, let $\delta > 0$ be such that $D_\delta(p)$ and $D_\delta(q)$ are normal neighborhoods of p and q. Fixing orthonormal bases $(\mathbf{v}_1, \mathbf{v}_2)$ on $T_p S_1$ and $(\mathbf{w}_1, \mathbf{w}_2)$ on $T_q S_2$, let $L : T_p S_1 \to T_q S_2$ be the linear isometry such that $L(\mathbf{v}_i) = \mathbf{w}_i$ $(i = 1, 2)$. We shall see that $f = \exp_q \circ L \circ \exp_p^{-1}\big|_{B_\delta(p)}$ is an isometry of $D_\delta(p)$ onto $D_\delta(q)$: in fact, f is clearly a diffeomorphism. Furthermore, the geodesic coordinates $\Psi(\rho, \varphi)$ in $D_\delta(p)$ associated with $(\mathbf{v}_1, \mathbf{v}_2)$ are sent by f to the geodesic coordinates $\widetilde{\Psi}(\rho, \varphi)$ in $D_\delta(q)$ associated with $(\mathbf{w}_1, \mathbf{w}_2)$. From what we have seen above, Ψ and $\widetilde{\Psi}$ have the same coefficients, and therefore $f\big|_{D_\delta(p) \setminus \{p\}} = \widetilde{\Psi} \circ \Psi^{-1}$ is an isometry. Thus, and since $Df_q = L$, we see that Df_r is a linear isometry for all $r \in D_\delta(p)$, which completes the proof.   □

Every surface of constant Gaussian curvature is thus locally isometric to the pseudosphere $(K < 0)$, to the plane $(K = 0)$, or to the sphere $(K > 0)$, but these three examples do not exhaust all surfaces of constant curvature (see, in Section 3.2, example 3.2.1 and Exercise 63). Later on, however, we will see that any **compact** surface in $\mathbb{R}^3$ of constant Gaussian curvature is a sphere.

Exercises

100. (a) Check that the differential equations of the geodesics of a surface of revolution parametrized by

$$\Phi(u, v) = (\rho(v) \cos u, \rho(v) \sin u, z(v))$$

are

$$\begin{cases} u'' + \dfrac{2\rho}{\rho} u'v' = 0, \\[2mm] v'' - \dfrac{\rho\rho}{\rho^2 + z^2} u'^2 + \dfrac{\rho\rho + zz}{\rho^2 + z^2} v'^2 = 0 \end{cases}$$

— where ρ, z, etc. denote the derivatives with respect to v, and u', v', etc. the derivatives with respect to the curve parameter.

(b) Use these equations to conclude again that any meridian $u = $ constant is a geodesic, and that the parallel $v = v_0$ is a geodesic if and only if the tangent line to the generating curve at v_0 is parallel to the z-axis.

(c) Show that if $\gamma(s) = \Phi(u(s), v(s))$ is a geodesic parametrized by arc length then $(\rho(s))^2 u'(s)$ is constant. Check that $(\rho(s))^2 u'(s) = \rho(s) \cos \theta(s)$, where

$\rho(s) = \rho \circ v(s)$ is the radius of the parallel where γ lies at time s and $\theta(s)$ is the angle of intersection of the curve with that parallel. (The equality $\rho \cos \theta = $ constant is the *Clairaut Equation*, and plays a fundamental role in the study of geodesics on surfaces of revolution.)

101. (In this exercise use the Clairaut Equation from Exercise 100.) Consider the geodesic γ that starts from a point p on the upper half $(z > 0)$ of the hyperboloid of revolution $x^2 + y^2 - z^2 = 1$ and makes angle θ given by $\cos \theta = \frac{1}{\rho}$ with the parallel (with radius ρ) passing through p. Put $\gamma(s) = (\rho(s) \cos \varphi(s), \rho(s) \sin \varphi(s), z(s))$, $\gamma(0) = p$. Show that:
  (a) while $\gamma(s)$ stays in the upper half $z > 0$, however $z'(s) \neq 0$;
  (b) if $z'(0) < 0$ then

$$z(s) > 0 \ \forall \ s \in \mathbb{R}, \quad \lim_{s \to +\infty} z(s) = 0, \quad \lim_{s \to +\infty} z'(s) = 0, \quad \lim_{s \to +\infty} \varphi'(s) = 1.$$

102. Consider, on the paraboloid of revolution $z = x^2 + y^2$, the geodesic $\alpha(t) = (0, t, t^2)$, $t \in \mathbb{R}$.
  (a) Show that there exists $\varepsilon > 0$ such that for all $0 < t_0 \leq \varepsilon$, $\alpha|_{[-t_0, t_0]}$ minimizes the intrinsic distance between $\alpha(-t_0)$ and $\alpha(t_0)$.
  (b) Show that, for t_0 sufficiently large, $\alpha|_{[-t_0, t_0]}$ no longer minimizes the distance between $\alpha(-t_0)$ and $\alpha(t_0)$.

103. Let S be a connected surface on which the sum of the interior angles of any geodesic triangle is equal to π. Show that S is locally isometric to a plane.

104. Show that if all geodesics of a connected surface are planar curves then that surface is contained in a sphere or in a plane.

105. Let S be a surface of constant curvature, and let Δ_1, Δ_2 be geodesic triangles of S. Assuming that Δ_1, Δ_2 are "sufficiently small", show that:
  (a) if two of the sides of Δ_1 are equal then the angles opposite to those sides are also equal;
  (b) if Δ_1 and Δ_2 have pairwise equal sides then there exist open subsets $W_1 \supseteq \Delta_1$, $W_2 \supseteq \Delta_2$ and an isometry $f : W_1 \to W_2$ for which $f(\Delta_1) = \Delta_2$. **Hint:** consider first the case where the Δ_i have the same angle and sides adjacent to that angle.

106. Show that on the surface of revolution $(\rho(z) \cos \varphi, \rho(z) \sin \varphi, z)$ (where $\rho(z) > 0$ for all $z \in \mathbb{R}$), the only minimizing geodesic between two points on the same meridian $\varphi = $ constant is precisely that meridian.

107. Let S be a connected surface, p a point on S, and let $\alpha: \,]a, b[\to S$ be a regular curve that does not pass through p. Consider the intrinsic distance on S.
  Show that if $\alpha(t_0)$ is a point of α at the minimizing distance from p and γ a minimizing geodesic starting from p to $\alpha(t_0)$ then γ intersects α orthogonally.

108. Let S_C $(C \neq 1)$ be the surface of revolution of constant curvature 1 given in example 3.2.1 and $\gamma \subseteq S_C$ the meridian $u = \pi$.

(a) Explicitly define a local isometry $f: S_C \setminus \gamma \to S^2$. **Hint:** send the equator of S_C to the equator of S^2 and use spherical coordinates.

(b) The equator $v = 0$ is a closed (i.e., periodic) geodesic of S_C. Show that S_C has other closed geodesics if and only if C is rational.

109. Consider a geodesic polar coordinate system (ρ, φ) centered at a point $p_0 \in S$ with curvature $K(p_0)$. Prove that:

(a) $\sqrt{G} = \rho - \dfrac{K(p_0)}{6} \rho^3 + o(\rho^3)$, where $\lim\limits_{\rho \to 0} \dfrac{o(\rho^3)}{\rho^3} = 0$ uniformly on φ.

Hint: Lemma 4.6.9 and formula (4.38) should show that, given φ, the function $\rho \mapsto \sqrt{G}(\rho, \varphi)$ admits a Taylor polynomial expansion around 0 as above — the problem lies in proving that the said limit is uniform on φ.

(b) by denoting by $l(\rho)$ the perimeter of the geodesic circle with radius ρ centered at p_0 at $K(p_0) = \lim\limits_{\rho \to 0} \dfrac{6\pi\rho - 3l(\rho)}{\pi\rho^3}$.

110. (a) Show that in geodesic polar coordinates (ρ, φ) the geodesic curvature of the geodesic circumferences ρ = constant is given by $\dfrac{G_\rho}{2G}$.

(b) Conclude that these circles all have constant geodesic curvature if and only if there exist differentiable and strictly positive functions $\beta(\rho)$ and $\lambda(\varphi)$ such that

$$G(\rho, \varphi) = \beta(\rho)\lambda(\varphi). \tag{4.40}$$

(c) Show that if G is of the form (4.40) then the Gaussian curvature along each geodesic circumference ρ = constant is constant.

(d) Conclude that the only oriented connected surfaces on which any geodesic circumference has constant geodesic curvature are surfaces of constant Gaussian curvature.

111. Show that a conformal mapping $f: S_1 \to S_2$ that sends geodesics of S_1 to geodesics of S_2 is necessarily a similarity — i.e., there exists $\lambda > 0$ such that $|Df_p(\mathbf{v})| = \lambda|\mathbf{v}|$ for all $p \in S_1$ and $\mathbf{v} \in T_p S_1$.

112. Let p be a point of S and $\alpha(u)$, $|u| < \varepsilon$, a regular curve in S such that $\alpha(0) = p$. Choose along α a unit vector field $\mathbf{w}(u)$ of tangent vectors orthogonal to $\alpha'(u)$ and write $\Phi(u, v) = \gamma(v - v_0; \alpha(u), \mathbf{w}(u))$ (i.e., $\Phi(u, \cdot)$ is the geodesic that at time v_0 passes through $\alpha(u)$ with velocity $\mathbf{w}(u)$). Show that:

(a) $\Phi(u, v)$ is a parameterization in a neighborhood of p (the coordinates $\Phi(u, v)$ obtained this way are called *semi-geodesic*);

(b) $\Phi(u, v)$ is an orthogonal parameterization;

(c) geodesic polar coordinates are an example of semi-geodesic coordinates.

113. Let S be a connected oriented surface and let $f: S \to S$ be a local isometry. Show that:

(a) if there exists $p \in S$ such that $f(p) = p$ and $Df_p = \mathrm{id}\big|_{T_p S}$ then f is the identity (**Hint:** what are the geodesics that start from p mapped to?);

(b) if f is not the identity and if there exists a regular curve $\alpha: I \to S$ such that $f \circ \alpha = \alpha$ then f reverses orientation of S;

(c) the curve α in b) is a geodesic.

114. Let S_1, S_2 be connected surfaces, $f: S_1 \to S_2$ be a diffeomorphism, and d_1, d_2 be the intrinsic distances on S_1 and S_2. Show that the following conditions are equivalent:

(1) f is an isometry;

(2) $d_1(p,q) = d_2(f(p), f(q))$ for all $p, q \in S_1$.

(**Hint for** (2) $\Rightarrow$ (1); a) show that f transforms geodesics of S_1 into geodesics of S_2, preserving scalar velocity; b) use the equivalence between (ii) and (iii) for $\lambda = 1$ in Lemma 4.1.1, §1.)

115. In this exercise we show that any compact surface has a triangulation (a fact used when establishing the global version of the Gauss-Bonnet theorem). Fix $\delta > 0$ so that, for all $p \in S$, $D_\delta(p)$ is a normal neighborhood of p, and consider a family $(\mathcal{R}_k)_{1 \le j \le k}$ of geodesic triangles such that:

- the interiors of $\mathcal{R}_j$ $(j = 1, \ldots, k)$ cover S;
- the diameter of each $\mathcal{R}_j$ is δ (i.e., if $p, q \in \mathcal{R}_j$ then $d(p,q) < \delta$).

(a) Show that any two edges of two distinct $\mathcal{R}_j$ are either disjoint, or intersect at a single point, or intersect along an arc common to both. Hence, the intersections of the $\mathbb{R}_j$ form a finite number of regions Ω_l.

(b) By properly triangulating each region Ω_l, obtain a triangulation of S.

Appendix: Rotation Index

In this appendix we prove the Rotation Index theorem that we used in the proof of the Gauss-Bonnet theorem. First however let us explain what we mean by *continuous choice of the angle between two vector fields*, an expression used repeatedly in Section 4.5. Let us take two unit vector fields $\mathbf{v_1}(s)$ and $\mathbf{w}(s)$ along a certain curve $\alpha(s)$, for $s \in [a, b]$, and consider an auxiliary vector field $\mathbf{v_2}(s)$ so that $(\mathbf{v_1}, \mathbf{v_2})$ is, for every s, an orthonormal and positively oriented basis of $T_{\alpha(s)}S$. We can then write $\mathbf{w}(s) = \lambda_1(s)\mathbf{v_1}(s) + \lambda_2(s)\mathbf{v_2}(s)$, where

$$[\lambda_1(s)]^2 + [\lambda_2(s)]^2 = |\mathbf{w}(s)|^2 = 1.$$

This shows that $s \mapsto (\lambda_1(s), \lambda_2(s))$ is a mapping of $[a, b]$ into the unit circle $\mathbf{S}^1$. If the vector fields considered are differentiable, then also this mapping is differentiable, and therefore (see note 1.3.1 and Exercise 7 in Section 1.3) there exists a differentiable mapping $\varphi(s)$ such that $(\lambda_1(s), \lambda_2(s)) = (\cos \varphi(s), \sin \varphi(s))$ — that is, such that

$$\mathbf{w}(s) = \cos \varphi(s)\mathbf{v_1}(s) + \sin \varphi(s)\mathbf{v_2}(s).$$

It is this function $\varphi(s)$ that we call the continuous choice of the oriented angle between $\mathbf{v}_1(s)$ and $\mathbf{w}(s)$. As we noted in note 1.3.1, any other choice of the same angle is the sum of $\varphi(s)$ with an integer multiple of 2π.

For later use, it is convenient to obtain a description like the one we saw above for functions $[a, b] \to \mathbf{S}^1$ that are not necessarily differentiable:

A.1 Lemma. *Let $F: [a, b] \to \mathbf{S}^1$ be a continuous function. Then there is a lift of F, that is, a continuous function $\varphi: [a, b] \to \mathbb{R}$ such that $F(s) = (\cos \varphi(s), \sin \varphi(s))$ for all s on $[a, b]$. Every other lift of F is the sum of φ with a constant integer multiple of 2π.*

Proof Consider the mapping $\Pi(t) = (\cos t, \sin t)$ which wraps the line $\mathbb{R}$ into $\mathbf{S}^1$. Note that the restriction of Π to any interval $[t_1, t_2]$ with $t_2 - t_1 < 2\pi$ is a homeomorphism onto its image, since $[t_1, t_2]$ is compact and $\Pi|_{[t_1, t_2]}$ is continuous and injective. What we are looking for is a continuous function φ such that $F = \Pi \circ \varphi$. The idea is to restrict F to small intervals where we can apply a local inverse of Π to both sides of this equality.

By uniform continuity of F, there exists $\delta > 0$ such that for $|s - t| < \delta$, the points $F(s)$ and $F(t)$ are never diametrically opposite in $\mathbf{S}^1$. If we take a partition $s_0 < s_1 < \cdots < s_k$ of $[a, b]$ with $s_i - s_{i-1} < \delta$, then, for every $1 \le i \le k$, the image $F([s_{i-1}, s_i])$ is contained in a semi-circle. Let us now define φ recursively, starting at the interval $[s_0, s_1]$. By construction, there exists an interval J_1, of amplitude π, such that the arc $\Pi(J_1)$ contains $F([s_0, s_1])$: thus, for $s \in [s_0, s_1]$, we define $\varphi(s) = \Pi|_{J_1}^{-1} \circ F(s)$. Assuming we have defined $\varphi(s)$ for all $s \in [s_0, s_{i-1}]$, we take J_i, of amplitude π, such that $\varphi(s_{i-1}) \in J_i$ and $F([s_{i-1}, s_i]) \subseteq \Pi(J_i)$, for $s \in [s_{i-1}, s_i]$, we define $\varphi(s) = \Pi|_{J_i}^{-1} \circ F(s)$. This ends the construction of φ. It is clear that $F = \Pi \circ \varphi$. Since φ is continuous (because it is continuous on every interval $[s_{i-1}, s_i]$), φ is a lift of F.

Regarding uniqueness of φ (minus a constant), the proof is given in note 1.3.1. □

In general, a *lift(ing)* of a continuous function $F: \Omega \to \mathbf{S}^1$, where Ω is a domain of $\mathbb{R}^n$, is a continuous function $\varphi: \Omega \to \mathbb{R}$ such that $F = \Pi \circ \varphi$. If we do not impose conditions on Ω, it is not true that all such functions F have a lifting. But we can guarantee the existence of a lifting if, for example, Ω is a rectangle (i.e., the Cartesian product of compact intervals): the next lemma proves this in the two-dimensional case, the only one we need besides the case $n = 1$ treated in A.1.

A.2. Lemma. *Let $F(s, t)$ be a continuous function $[a, b] \times [c, d] \to \mathbf{S}^1$. Then F has a lifting — that is, there exists $\varphi(s, t)$ continuous such that $F(s, t) = (\cos \varphi(s, t), \sin \varphi(s, t))$.*

Proof Let $\theta(t)$ be a lifting of the mapping $t \mapsto F(0, t)$, whose existence is guaranteed by A.1. Again, using A.1, let us next take, for every $t \in [c, d]$, a lifting $s \mapsto \varphi(s, t)$ of $s \mapsto F(s, t)$ that satisfies $\varphi(0, t) = \theta(t)$. The function φ obtained this way satisfies the equality $F = \Pi \circ \varphi$, and it remains to show that φ is continuous. By construction, its restriction to each of the horizontal segments $[a, b] \times \{t\}$, and to the vertical line segment $\{0\} \times [c, d]$, is continuous.

Given $\varepsilon > 0$ with $\varepsilon < \frac{\pi}{2}$, the uniform continuity of F gives us $\delta > 0$ such that the angle between $F(s, t)$ and $F(\widetilde{s}, \widetilde{t})$ has amplitude ε whenever $|(s, t) - (\widetilde{s}, \widetilde{t})| < \delta$. Thus, given (s_0, t_0), and under the assumption that $|(s, t) - (s_0, t_0)| < \delta$, we can write

$$\varphi(s, t) - \varphi(s_0, t_0) = \varepsilon(s, t) + 2\pi k(s, t),$$

where $k(s, t)$ is an integer and $|\varepsilon(s, t)| < \varepsilon$. If we show that $k(s, t) = 0$, the continuity of φ on (s_0, t_0) follows. Now, since $\varphi|_{\{0\} \times [c, d]}$ is continuous, we have $|\varphi(0, t) - \varphi(0, t_0)| < \varepsilon < \frac{\pi}{2}$. Furthermore, since the difference $\varphi(\cdot, t) - \varphi(\cdot, t_0)$ is continuous and takes neither of the values $\pm \frac{\pi}{2}$, it takes values in the interval $\left]-\frac{\pi}{2}, \frac{\pi}{2}\right[$; we conclude that $|\varphi(s, t) - \varphi(s, t_0)| < \frac{\pi}{2}$. But as also $|\varphi(s, t_0) - \varphi(s_0, t_0)| < \frac{\pi}{2}$, it follows that

$$\pi > |\varphi(s, t) - \varphi(s_0, t_0)| = |\varepsilon(s, t) + 2\pi k(s, t)| \geq 2\pi |k(s, t)| - |\varepsilon(s, t)|,$$

and therefore $k(s, t) = 0$. This concludes the proof of the continuity of φ. □

Here, in a simplified version, is the Rotation Index theorem:

A.3. Rotation Index theorem (first version). *If $\alpha: [a, b] \to \mathbb{R}^2$ is a closed, regular, simple curve, then $\Re(\alpha) = \pm 1$, where the sign depends on the orientation of the curve.*

Proof We suppose, as usual, that α is parametrized by arc length, and define a continuous function $F: [a, b] \times [a, b] \to \mathbf{S}^1$ as follows: if $0 < |s - t| < b - a$, we put

$$F(s, t) = \frac{\alpha(s) - \alpha(t)}{|\alpha(s) - \alpha(t)|};$$

in the other cases, we put $F(s, s) = \alpha'(s)$ and $F(a, b) = -F(b, a) = \alpha'(a)$. Denoting by $\varphi(s, t)$ a lifting of $F(s, t)$, the restriction of φ to the diagonal $\{(s, s) : to \leq s \leq b\}$ is a lifting of $s \mapsto \alpha'(s)$, and therefore the rotation index is

$$\Re(\alpha) = \frac{1}{2\pi} \left(\varphi(b, b) - \varphi(a, a)\right).$$

Suppose that the initial point $\alpha(a)$ is chosen so that the curve α is all on the same side of its tangent line at that point (such a choice is always possible: see for example Section 1.6). Then the image of $F(s, a)$, for $s \in [a, b]$, is contained in a semi-circle, and therefore its lift $\varphi(s, a)$ covers at most an interval of amplitude π. But since $F(a, a) = -F(b, a)$, we have

$$\varphi(b, a) - \varphi(a, a) = \varepsilon\pi,$$

where $\varepsilon = 1$ if α is positively oriented, and $\varepsilon = -1$ otherwise. Since $F(b, t), t \in [a, b]$, runs exactly along the curve at $\mathbf{S}^1$ diametrically opposite to $F(s, a)$, we also have

$$\varphi(b,b) - \varphi(b,a) = \varepsilon\pi.$$

Adding these two equalities, we obtain $\Re(\alpha) = \varepsilon$, which concludes the proof. $\quad\square$

Before we move to a generalization of Theorem A.3, we note that the above proof works under the assumption that α is only of class C^1.

We will now show that A.3 remains valid for curves on surfaces, provided such curves are contained in parametrized neighborhoods. Let $\alpha(s)$, for $s \in [a,b]$, be a closed, simple, regular curve of class C^1, contained in the image of the parameterization $\Phi(u,v)$ that we assume to be compatible with the orientation of the surface. Let $\mathbf{v_1} = \dfrac{1}{\sqrt{E}}\Phi_u$, and let $\theta(s)$ be a continuous choice of the oriented angle between $\mathbf{v_1}$ and $\alpha'(s)$. We claim that *if α is positively oriented, then $\theta(b) - \theta(a) = 2\pi$.*

The idea, of course, is to apply Theorem A.3 to the planar curve $\beta = \Phi^{-1} \circ \alpha$. If Φ were an isothermal parameterization, our statement would be an immediate consequence of A.3, but it is unnecessary to invoke such a strong result as the existence of isothermal parameterizations. Let $\varphi(s)$ be a continuous choice of the angle between $(1,0)$ and $\tau(s) = \dfrac{\beta'(s)}{|\beta'(s)|}$. For every instant s, and since Φ preserves orientation and $D\Phi_{\beta(s)}$ sends $(1,0)$ and $\tau(s)$ to vectors that are positive multiples of $\mathbf{v_1}$ and $\alpha'(s)$, the dihedra $\big((1,0),\tau(s)\big)$ and $\big(\mathbf{v_1},\alpha'(s)\big)$ are both positively oriented or both negatively oriented. Hence, $\varphi(s) - \theta(s) \neq \pm\pi$ for all s; choosing $\theta(a)$ and $\varphi(a)$ with $|\varphi(a) - \theta(a)| < \pi$, we also have $|\varphi(b) - \theta(b)| < \pi$. It follows that

$$\left|\{\varphi(b) - \varphi(a)\} - \{\theta(b) - \theta(a)\}\right| < 2\pi$$

or, using A.3,

$$\left|2\pi - (\theta(b) - \theta(a))\right| < 2\pi,$$

and therefore, since $\theta(b) - \theta(a)$ is an integer multiple of 2π,

$$\theta(b) - \theta(a) = 2\pi,$$

which proves our assertion.

Let us now state the more general version of Theorem A.3. used in the proof of the Gauss-Bonnet theorem. Consider a curve $\alpha(s)$, for $s \in [a,b]$, closed, simple, piecewise regular, which is the boundary of a polygonal region Ω contained in a neighborhood parametrized by $\Phi(u,v)$. Let $a = s_0 < s_1 < \cdots < s_k = b$ be the $k+1$ vertices of α.

A.4. Rotation Index theorem (second version). *Let γ_i, for $i = 1,\ldots,k$, be the exterior angles of Ω and $\theta_i(s)$, for $s \in [s_{i-1}, s_i]$, a continuous choice of the angle between $\mathbf{v_1} = \dfrac{1}{\sqrt{E}}\Phi_u$ and $\alpha'(s)$. Then, if α runs through $\partial\Omega$ with positive orientation, we have*

$$\sum_{i=1}^{k}\{\theta_i(s_i) - \theta_i(s_{i-1})\} + \sum_{i=1}^{k}\gamma_i = 2\pi.$$

For the proof, we approximate α by curves α_ε of class C^1, obtained by rounding each of the vertices of α. For sufficiently small $\varepsilon > 0$, $\alpha_\varepsilon:[0, L_\varepsilon] \to S$ is thus a closed, simple, regular curve, parametrized by arc length, for which there exist disjoint and consecutive intervals $[a_i^\varepsilon, b_i^\varepsilon] \subseteq [0, L_\varepsilon]$ $(i = 1, \ldots, k)$ such that each arc $\alpha_\varepsilon([a_i^\varepsilon, b_i^\varepsilon])$ is a segment of the regular arc $\alpha([s_{i-1}, s_i])$, traversed with the same orientation. Furthermore, the total length of the arcs of α and α_ε that are not common to both curves, i.e., in the complement of

$$\bigcup_{i=1}^k \alpha_\varepsilon([a_i^\varepsilon, b_i^\varepsilon]),$$

is ε.

Let us denote by $\theta_\varepsilon(s)$ a continuous choice of the angle between $\mathbf{v_1}$ and $\alpha'_\varepsilon(s)$. It is clear then that each of the differences

$$\theta_\varepsilon(b_i^\varepsilon) - \theta_\varepsilon(a_i^\varepsilon)$$

comes arbitrarily close to $\theta_i(s_i) - \theta_i(s_{i-1})$, taking ε sufficiently small, and in this way also

$$\theta_\varepsilon(a_{i+1}^\varepsilon) - \theta_\varepsilon(b_i^\varepsilon), \quad \text{for } i = 1, \ldots, k - 1,$$

$$\text{and } \theta_\varepsilon(a_1^\varepsilon) - \theta_\varepsilon(0) + \theta_\varepsilon(L_\varepsilon) - \theta_\varepsilon(b_k^\varepsilon), \quad \text{for } i = k,$$

lie close to γ_i for $i = 1, \ldots, k$. We thus conclude that

$$2\pi = \theta_\varepsilon(L_\varepsilon) - \theta_\varepsilon(0)$$

$$= \left\{\theta_\varepsilon(L_\varepsilon) - \theta_\varepsilon(b_k^\varepsilon)\right\} + \sum_{i=1}^k \left\{\theta_\varepsilon(b_i^\varepsilon) - \theta_\varepsilon(a_i^\varepsilon)\right\} +$$

$$+ \sum_{i=1}^{k-1} \left\{\theta_\varepsilon(a_{i+1}^\varepsilon) - \theta_\varepsilon(b_i^\varepsilon)\right\} + \left\{\theta_\varepsilon(a_1^\varepsilon) - \theta_\varepsilon(0)\right\}$$

is arbitrarily close to

$$\sum_{i=1}^k \left\{\theta_i(s_i) - \theta_i(s_{i-1})\right\} + \sum_{i=1}^k \gamma_i,$$

which proves the theorem.

Exercises

116. Lemma A.2 applies not only to rectangles, but also, obviously, to any regions that are homeomorphic to rectangles. For example, any continuous function $F:\mathbb{D}^2 \to \mathbf{S}^1$, where $\mathbb{D}^2$ is the closed disk $\{p \in \mathbb{R}^2 : |p| \leq 1\}$, has a lifting. Using this fact, we next give a proof of Brouwer's fixed point theorem: *any continuous function* $f:\mathbb{D}^2 \to \mathbb{D}^2$ *has some fixed point* (i.e., a point p such that $f(p) = p$).

Assuming that f has no fixed points, we define $F: \mathbb{D}^2 \to \mathbf{S}^1$ by

$$F(p) = \frac{f(p) - p}{|f(p) - p|},$$

and consider a lifting $\varphi: \mathbb{D}^2 \to \mathbb{R}$ of F.

(a) Write $\gamma(t) = F(\cos t, \sin t)$, for $t \in [0, 2\pi]$, and let $\theta(t)$ be a lifting of γ such that $\theta(0) \in \left] \frac{\pi}{2}, \frac{3\pi}{2} \right[$. Show that $\theta(t) \in \left] t + \frac{\pi}{2}, t + \frac{3\pi}{2} \right[$ for all t, and conclude that $\theta(2\pi) - \theta(0) = 2\pi$.

(b) Note that $\tilde{\theta}(t) = \varphi(\cos t, \sin t)$ is also a lift of $\gamma(t)$, but that $\tilde{\theta}(2\pi) = \tilde{\theta}(0)$. What follows?

117. Let $\Omega \subseteq \mathbb{R}^2$ be an open disk and let $\mathbf{w}: \Omega \to \mathbb{R}^2$ be a differentiable field of unit vectors. Given a regular closed curve $\alpha: [a, b] \to \Omega$, show that the rotation index of α is also equal to

$$\frac{1}{2\pi} (\theta(b) - \theta(a)),$$

where θ is a continuous choice of the (oriented) angle of $\mathbf{w}(\alpha(t))$ and $\alpha'(t)$.

118. Consider, in $\mathbf{T}^2$ with the parameterization of Exercise 31, the vector field $\mathbf{w}(u, v) = (-\sin v \cos u, -\sin v \sin u, \cos v)$. Let the *rotation index* of a regular closed curve $\alpha: [a, b] \to \mathbf{T}^2$ be the integer

$$\Delta(\alpha) = \frac{1}{2\pi} (\theta(b) - \theta(a)),$$

where θ is a continuous choice of the oriented angle of $\mathbf{w}$ and $\alpha'(t)$.

(a) Compute $\Delta(\alpha)$ for the curve $t \mapsto \Phi(t, nt)$, where $n \in \mathbb{Z}$ is a constant and $t \in [0, 2\pi]$.

(b) Does the result of (a) depend on the vector field $\mathbf{w}$?

Chapter 5
The Global Geometry of Surfaces

Global geometry deals with those results that concern the surface as a whole. In Chapter 4 we have already seen examples of global theorems, such as the divergence theorem (Corollary 4.4.3.i) and the Gauss-Bonnet theorem (Theorem 4.5.6). Another example is the sphere theorem that we will present in this chapter: any compact surface of constant curvature in $\mathbb{R}^3$ is a sphere. As we already observed, the assumption that the curvature is constant is insufficient, and a global condition (in this case, the compactness of the surface) is needed to draw such a conclusion.

Compact surfaces are inextensible, in the following sense: if S_1 and S_2 are connected surfaces such that S_1 is compact and $S_1 \subseteq S_2$ then $S_1 = S_2$. The global results must naturally deal with inextensible surfaces. In Section 5.1 we will define the notion of a complete surface, which is a sufficient but not necessary condition for a surface to be inextensible.

This chapter includes a mixed bag of topics unusual in introductory texts of Differential Geometry: for instance, a Blaschke formula for surfaces of constant width (Theorem 5.5.3) and the description of all complete surfaces of constant non-negative curvature (Theorems 5.7.7 and 5.7.10). To help the readers in their choice of topics, we mention that Sections 5.1 and 5.2 form the main body of the chapter, from which two independent branches emerge, one consisting of 5.4 and 5.5 and the other one of 5.3, 5.6 and 5.7.

All surfaces in this chapter are connected.

5.1 Complete Surfaces

In Chapter 4 we gave an example (4.6.5) of a surface on which no minimizing geodesic exists between given two points. Even though this example seems disingenuous (the surface in question is a plane from which a point has been removed "unduly"), it points out a possible problem: although there is a geodesic γ that starts from p in the direction of q, γ is not defined for some value of the parameter and therefore does not reach q.

© The Author(s), under exclusive license to Springer Nature Switzerland AG 2024
P. V. Araújo, *Differential Geometry*, https://doi.org/10.1007/978-3-031-62384-4_5

We say that a surface S is *complete* if any parametrized geodesic $\gamma(t; p, \mathbf{v})$ of S is defined for all $t \in \mathbb{R}$. Equivalently, S is complete if $\exp_p$ is defined on the entire tangent space T_pS for all $p \in S$. The next result gives us many examples of complete surfaces.

Proposition 5.1.1 *If a surface $S \subseteq \mathbb{R}^3$ is closed in $\mathbb{R}^3$ then S is complete.*

Proof Given $p \in S$ and $\mathbf{v} \in T_pS$ with $|\mathbf{v}| = 1$, we verify that the geodesic $\gamma(s) = \gamma(s; p, \mathbf{v})$ is defined for every $s \in [0, +\infty[$ (replacing $\mathbf{v}$ by $-\mathbf{v}$, it follows that $\gamma(s)$ is also defined on the entire interval $]-\infty, 0]$). For this, it suffices to check that if γ is defined on $[0, s_0[$ then it is defined on some interval $[0, s_0 + \delta[$ for $\delta > 0$ as well.

Take a monotone sequence $(s_n)_{n \geq 1}$ on $[0, s_0[$ that converges to s_0. Since

$$|\gamma(s_n) - \gamma(s_m)| \leq d(\gamma(s_n), \gamma(s_m)) \leq |s_n - s_m|,$$

it follows that $(\gamma(s_n))_{n \geq 1}$ is a Cauchy sequence in $\mathbb{R}^3$. Since S is closed, the limit p of this sequence is a point of S. We can then choose $\eta > 0$ and a neighborhood U of p in S such that, for all $q \in U$, the radial geodesics starting from q have length at least η. We fix n so that $s_n > s_0 - \frac{\eta}{2}$ and $\gamma(s_n) \in U$, and let $q = \gamma(s_n)$, $\mathbf{w} = \gamma'(s_n)$. The geodesic $\widetilde{\gamma}(t) = \gamma(t; q, \mathbf{w})$ is defined for $t \in]-\eta, \eta[$, and $\gamma(s) = \widetilde{\gamma}(s - s_n)$. Thus $\gamma(s)$ is extensible to the interval $[0, s_n + \eta[\supseteq [0, s_0 + \frac{\eta}{2}[$.   □

In particular, it follows from the above proposition that all compact surfaces are complete. However, we observe that there are complete surfaces other than those closed in $\mathbb{R}^3$:

Example 5.1.2 Let S be the surface given by

$$\Phi(u, v) = ((1 + e^{-u}) \cos u, (1 + e^{-u}) \sin u, v),$$

$u, v \in \mathbb{R}$. S is complete because it is isometric to the plane, which is a complete surface. However, S is not a closed subset of $\mathbb{R}^3$: a point of the cylinder $x^2 + y^2 = 1$ lies outside of S, and is moreover the limit of a sequence of points in S (see Fig. 5.1).

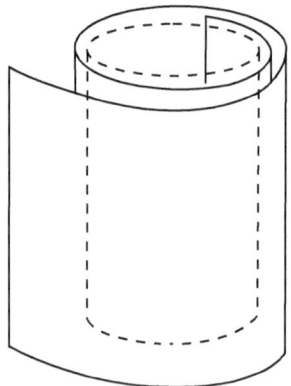

Figure 5.1

The intrinsic distance d in S and the distance $|\ |$ in $\mathbb{R}^3$ are *equivalent*, in the sense that a sequence (p_n) in S converges to $p \in S$ for one of these distances if and only if it converges for the other one. However, this example shows that they do not have to be *uniformly equivalent*: there can be a sequence of points on S that is Cauchy for $|\ |$ but is not so for d. $\hfill\square$

The major advantage of complete surfaces is that there exist minimizing geodesics between any two points on them. Before we prove this, we note that it follows from the triangle inequality (see Section 4.6) that, for every $p \in S$, the mapping $q \mapsto d(p,q)$ is continuous (since $|d(p,q) - d(p,r)| \le d(q,r) \quad \forall\, q,r \in S$) — and therefore its restriction to any compact S attains a maximum and a minimum.

Theorem 5.1.3 *Let p, q be two points of a complete surface S. Then there is on S some minimizing geodesic from p to q.*

Proof Let $D_\delta(p)$ be a normal neighborhood of p. If $q \in D_\delta(p)$, there is nothing to show. Otherwise, letting $l = d(p,q)$, we have $l \ge \delta$. Consider now the geodesic circumference $\mathbf{S}^1\!\left(p, \frac{\delta}{2}\right)$ with center p and radius $\frac{\delta}{2}$, and let r be a point of $\mathbf{S}^1\!\left(p, \frac{\delta}{2}\right)$ at the shortest possible distance from q. By the triangle inequality, we have

$$d(r,q) \ge d(p,q) - d(p,r) = l - \frac{\delta}{2}. \tag{5.1}$$

Let $\alpha(t)$, for $t \in [a,b]$, be any piecewise regular curve from p to q, and let t_0 be the first instant at which $\alpha(t_0) \in \mathbf{S}^1\!\left(p, \frac{\delta}{2}\right)$. Then

$$l(\alpha) = l\!\left(\alpha\big|_{[a,t_0]}\right) + l\!\left(\alpha\big|_{[t_0,b]}\right) \ge d(p,\alpha(t_0)) + d(\alpha(t_0),q) \ge \frac{\delta}{2} + d(r,q),$$

which implies $l \ge \frac{\delta}{2} + d(r,q)$. Together with (5.1), this gives $d(r,q) = l - \frac{\delta}{2}$. Let $\gamma(s)$ be the radial geodesic, parametrized by arc length, such that $\gamma(0) = p$ and $\gamma\!\left(\frac{\delta}{2}\right) = r$. Note that for $s \ge 0$ we have $d(\gamma(s),q) \ge d(p,q) - d(p,\gamma(s)) \ge l - s$. Defining

$$I = \{s \in [0,l] : d(\gamma(s),q) = l - s\},$$

the preceding inequality shows that $s \in I$ if and only if $s \ge 0$ and $d(\gamma(s),q) \le l - s$. It follows that I is a (necessarily closed) interval: in fact, if $s \in I$, and $0 \le t < s$, then $d(\gamma(t),q) \le d(\gamma(t),\gamma(s)) + d(\gamma(s),q) \le (s-t) + (l-s) = l - t$, and therefore $t \in I$. We have already seen that $\left[0, \frac{\delta}{2}\right] \subseteq I$; let us now show that $I = [0,l]$. To this end, it suffices to show that if $s_0 \in\ ]0,l[$ is in I then also $s_0 + \eta \in I$ for some $\eta > 0$ — because then necessarily $\sup I = l$. Let us fix a normal neighborhood $D_{2\eta}(\gamma(s_0))$ of $\gamma(s_0)$ so that $d(\gamma(s_0),q) > \eta$, and let $\widetilde{r}$ be a point of $\mathbf{S}^1(\gamma(s_0),\eta)$ at the shortest possible distance from q: the above argument shows that

$$d(\widetilde{r},q) = d(\gamma(s_0),q) - \eta = l - (s_0 + \eta) \quad \text{(because } s_0 \in I\text{)}, \tag{5.2}$$

and therefore

$$d(\gamma(s_0 - \eta), \widetilde{r}) \geq d(\gamma(s_0 - \eta), q) - d(\widetilde{r}, q) = 2\eta. \tag{5.3}$$

The restriction $\gamma\big|_{[s_0-\eta,s_0]}$, followed by the radial geodesic from $\gamma(s_0)$ to $\widetilde{r}$, is a piecewise regular curve from $\gamma(s_0 - \eta)$ to $\widetilde{r}$ whose length is exactly 2η. By (5.3) the curve is minimizing and therefore a geodesic

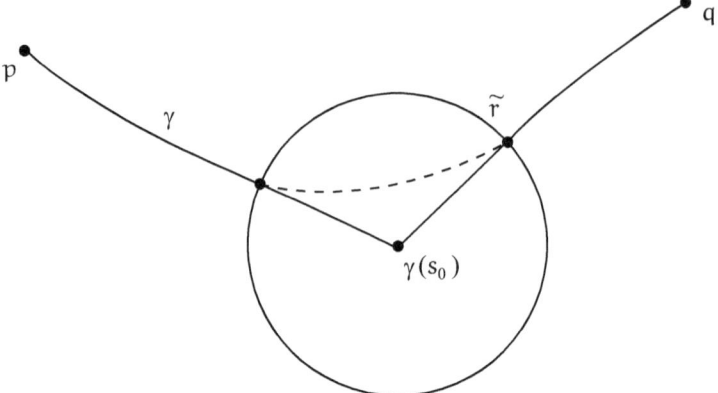

Figure 5.2

(Proposition 4.6.8), so that it coincides with $\gamma\big|_{[s_0-\eta,s_0+\eta]}$. It follows that $\gamma(s_0 + \eta) = \widetilde{r}$ and, by (5.2), $s_0 + \eta \in I$. We then have $I = [0, l]$; in particular, $d(\gamma(l), q) = 0$ and therefore $\gamma(l) = q$. Thus, and since $d(p, q) = l$ as well, $\gamma\big|_{[0,l]}$ is a minimizing geodesic from p to q. ☐

If we read the above proof carefully, we obtain: if $p \in S$ *is such that all geodesics starting from* p *extend to all values of the parameter then, for every point* q *of S, there is some minimizing geodesic from* p *to* q. This observation lets us easily assert that any complete surface S is *inextensible*: if S is contained in another surface S_1 then $S_1 = S$. In fact, S is necessarily open in S_1, and therefore the geodesics of S are also geodesics of S_1. Let us fix $p \in S$: the geodesics of S_1 that start from p, because they are geodesics of S, are defined for all values of the parameter. This means that, given $q \in S_1$, there exists some minimizing geodesic γ from p to q. But $\gamma \subseteq S$ and therefore $q \in S$ — which shows that $S_1 \subseteq S$.

Example 5.1.4 Besides the punctured plane, also the cone C given by the equation $z = \sqrt{x^2 + y^2}$ ($z > 0$) is a non-complete surface, since the generating lines are geodesics that are not defined for all parameter values. Nevertheless, between every pair of points of C there exists a minimizing geodesic (Exercise 89 of Section 4.3) — and C is inextensible. To prove the latter statement let us suppose, to the contrary, that there exists a connected surface S such that $C \subseteq S$ but $C \neq S$. Let p be a point on the boundary of C in S: p does not belong to C because C is open in S. Let $(p_n)_{n\geq 1}$ be a sequence of points of C that converges to p.

Lemma *Given* $\varepsilon > 0$, *there exists* n_0 *such that* p_n *is* **below** *the plane* $z = \varepsilon$ *for all* $n \geq n_0$.

If the lemma is false, then some infinite subsequence of $(p_n)_{n \geq 1}$ is contained in $C \cap \{z \geq \varepsilon\}$ — which is a closed subset of $\mathbb{R}^3$ and therefore contains all the accumulation points of the mentioned subsequence; then $p \in C \cap \{z \geq \varepsilon\} \subseteq C$, which is absurd. We have thus proved the lemma.

It immediately follows that $\lim\limits_{n \to +\infty} p_n = (0,0,0)$. Thus the boundary of C on S consists only of the point $(0,0,0)$, which implies $S = C \cup \{(0,0,0)\}$, otherwise $S \setminus \{(0,0,0)\}$ would not be connected. But $C \cup \{(0,0,0)\}$ is not a surface, which proves the non-existence of S.   □

Exercises

119. (a) Show that S is a complete surface if and only if (S,d) (where d is the intrinsic distance on S) is a complete metric space. (*Complete* means that any Cauchy sequence converges. Try to prove the stronger statement that any bounded sequence has a convergent subsequence.)

(b) Show that if there exists $p \in S$ such that any geodesic passing through p is defined in $\mathbb{R}$, then S is complete.

120. If S is a non-compact, complete surface, and p a point of S, then there exists a geodesic $\gamma(s)$ of S such that $\gamma(0) = p$ and that minimizes the distance between p and $\gamma(s)$ for all $s \in \mathbb{R}$.

121. Let S be a complete surface, p a point of S, and $\mathbf{v} \in T_p S$ a unit vector. Write $\gamma(s) = \exp_p(s\mathbf{v})$, and suppose that there exists $s > 0$ such that $\gamma|_{[0,s]}$ does not minimize the distance between p and $\gamma(s)$. Consider the set $I = \{s \geq 0 : d(p, \gamma(s)) = s\}$. Show that:

(a) I is a closed interval $[0, s_0]$;

(b) for $s > s_0$ there exists a geodesic $\tilde{\gamma}$ of length s connecting p to $\gamma(s)$;

(c) for $0 < s < s_0$, $\gamma|_{[0,s]}$ is the only minimizing geodesic connecting p with $\gamma(s)$;

(d) for $s = s_0$ two cases could apply:

• there is another minimizing geodesic connecting p with $\gamma(s_0)$;

• $s_0 \mathbf{v}$ is not a regular point of $\exp_p$.

122. Consider in $\mathbb{T}^2$, parametrized by

$$\Phi(u, v) = ((2 + \cos v) \cos u, (2 + \cos v) \sin u, \sin v),$$

the points $p = \Phi(0,0)$, $q = \Phi(u_0, v_0)$ and $r = \Phi(u_0, \pi)$, where $0 < u_0 < \pi$, for $0 < v_0 < \pi$. Let $\gamma(s) = \Phi(u(s), v(s))$, for $s \in [0, a]$, be a minimizing geodesic from p to q with $u(0) = v(0) = 0$. Show that:

(a) $0 \leq u(s) \leq u_0$, $0 \leq v(s) < \pi$ for all $s \in [0, a]$;

(b) there are two and only two minimizing geodesics from p to r (use the Clairaut Equation, Exercise 100, to conclude that there is only one such geodesic in the region $0 \leq u \leq u_0$, $0 \leq v \leq \pi$);

(c) if $\tilde{\gamma}(s)$ is a geodesic such that $\tilde{\gamma}(0) = p$ and $\tilde{\gamma}(b) = r$, then $\tilde{\gamma}(2b) = \Phi(2u_0, 0)$;

(d) if $\frac{\pi}{u_0}$ is rational then the geodesic $\tilde{\gamma}$ is periodic, otherwise it is dense in $\mathbb{T}^2$;

(e) all geodesics (except the parallel $v = \pi$) intersect the parallel $v = 0$;

(f) there exist in $\mathbb{T}^2$ geodesics that are neither periodic nor dense.

123. Consider in $\mathbb{T}^2$ the parameterization $\Phi(u,v)$ from Exercise 122. Let Δ be the geodesic triangle of vertices $p = \Phi(0,0)$, $q = \Phi\left(\frac{\pi}{2},0\right)$, $r = \Phi\left(\frac{\pi}{2},v_0\right)$, where $0 < v_0 < \pi$, and where $\widehat{pq} = \left\{\Phi(u,0):0 \le u \le \frac{\pi}{2}\right\}$, $\widehat{qr} = \left\{\Phi\left(\frac{\pi}{2},v\right):0 \le v \le v_0\right\}$, and $\widehat{pr}$ is a minimizing geodesic from p to r.

Use the Clairaut Equation to show that the sum of the interior angles of Δ is greater than π. Can you draw the same conclusion from the Gauss-Bonnet theorem?

124. Let S be a connected surface such that for every p on S, there exists an isometry $\xi_p : S \to S$ with $\xi_p(p) = p$ and $D(\xi_p)_p = -\,\mathrm{id}$. Show that:

(a) the sphere satisfies that condition;

(b) such a surface is complete and has constant curvature.

125. Let C be the cone $z = \sqrt{x^2 + y^2}$, $z > 0$. Show that there is no mapping $f: C \to S$ such that S is a complete surface and f an isometry onto the image (i.e., there is no isometric *embedding* of C into a complete surface).

5.2 Coverings

The notion of a covering is one of the most fruitful in topology — but, to save time, we will restrict ourselves to coverings of surfaces, though they prove useful in more general topological spaces. The theory developed here will allow us to show that a good number of surfaces are (globally) images of local diffeomorphisms of standard surfaces like the plane or the sphere.

A mapping $f: S_1 \to S_2$ between two surfaces is called a *covering (map)* of S_2 if each $q \in S_2$ has an open neighborhood U with the following property: $f^{-1}(U)$ is a collection of disjoint open subsets $(U_i)_i$ such that, for every i, the restriction $f|_{U_i}$ is a diffeomorphism of U_i on U. Such an open subset U is called an *evenly covered neighborhood* of q — or simply an *evenly covered open subset*; see Fig. 5.3.

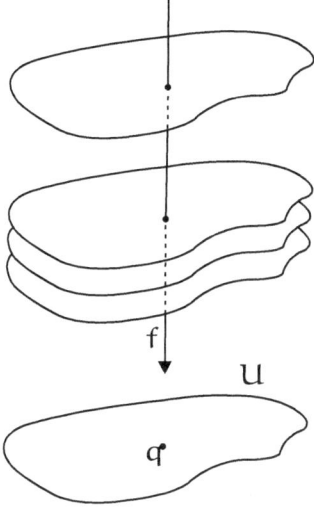

Figure 5.3

Example 5.2.1 The mapping $\mathbb{R}^2 \to \{x^2 + y^2 = 1\}$ given by $(u, v) \to (\cos u, \sin u, v)$ is a covering; as is the usual mapping $\mathbb{R}^2 \to \mathbb{T}^2$ given by

$$\Phi(u, v) = ((2 + \cos v) \cos u, (2 + \cos v) \sin u, \sin v).$$

It follows from the definition that any covering is a locally surjective diffeomorphism, but it is worthy to note that not all locally surjective diffeomorphisms are coverings. An example is the restriction of Φ to the square $]-2\pi, 2\pi[\times]-2\pi, 2\pi[$: in Figure 5.4, the preimage of the marked open subset U joins nine disjoint open subsets, but only one of them is surjectively sent onto U under Φ. □

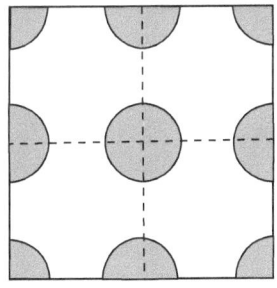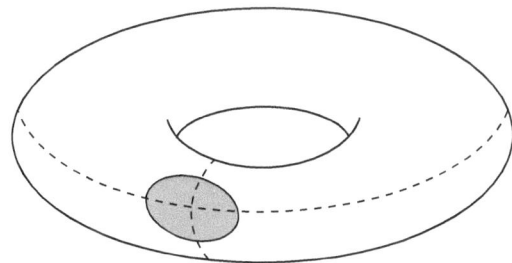

Figure 5.4

There is however an additional condition under which a local diffeomorphism is guaranteed to be a covering:

Proposition 5.2.2 *If S_1 is compact and $f: S_1 \to S_2$ a local diffeomorphism then f is a covering.*

Proof Let us first show that f is surjective. Since f is a local diffeomorphism, its image $f(S_1)$ is open in S_2. Given a sequence $(f(p_n))_{n \geq 1}$ on $f(S_1)$ that converges to $q \in S_2$, if $p \in S_1$ is an accumulation point of $(p_n)_{n \geq 1}$ (which exists because S_1 is compact), then $f(p) = q$. Thus $f(S_1)$ is also closed in S_2 and, since S_2 is connected, necessarily $f(S_1) = S_2$.

We now observe that each point q of S_2 has a finite number of preimages, otherwise they would accumulate in the neighborhood of some point of S_1, in contradiction to f being a local diffeomorphism. Let $p_1, \ldots, p_k$ be the preimages of q, and let us choose open neighborhoods V_i of p_i such that each $f|_{V_i}$ is a diffeomorphism onto the image and $V_i \cap V_j$ is empty if $i \neq j$.

Claim: *There is $\varepsilon > 0$ such that $f^{-1}(\{r \in S_2 : |r - q| < \varepsilon\}) \subseteq \bigcup\limits_{i=1}^{k} V_i$.*

In fact, the negation of this statement implies the existence of a sequence $(\widetilde{r}_n)_{n \geq 1}$ in $S_1 \setminus \left(\bigcup\limits_{i=1}^{k} V_i \right)$ such that $\lim\limits_{n \to +\infty} f(\widetilde{r}_n) = q$, and any accumulation point of $(\widetilde{r}_n)_{n \geq 1}$ is a preimage of q distinct from $p_1, \ldots, p_k$. Finally, for the ε given by the claim, the open subset $\{r \in S_2 : |p - q| < \varepsilon\} \cap \left(\bigcap\limits_{i=1}^{k} f(V_i) \right)$ is an evenly covered neighborhood of q. $\qquad\square$

We say that a differentiable mapping $f: S_1 \to S_2$ *lifts curves* if, for every curve $\alpha: [a, b] \to S_2$ and $p \in S_1$ such that $f(p) = \alpha(a)$, there exists a single curve $\widetilde{\alpha}: [a, b] \to S_1$ such that $\widetilde{\alpha}(a) = p$ and $f \circ \widetilde{\alpha}(t) = \alpha(t)$ for all $t \in [a, b]$. That is, for every preimage p of the final point $\alpha(a)$ of α, there exists a single curve in S_1 that starts from p and whose image under f is α. Note that any mapping that lifts curves is necessarily surjective.

Proposition 5.2.3 *Every covering lifts curves.*

Proof Let $f: S_1 \to S_2$ be a covering, $\alpha: [a, b] \to S_2$ a curve, and $p \in S_1$ a preimage of $\alpha(a)$. By compactness of $[a, b]$ there exists a partition

$$a = t_0 < t_1 < \cdots < t_k = b$$

such that each $\alpha([t_{i-1}, t_i])$ is contained in an evenly covered open subset W_i. We construct $\widetilde{\alpha}$ step by step, starting with the interval $[t_0, t_1]$: denoting by $\widetilde{W}_1$ the component of $f^{-1}(W_1)$ that contains p, we define $\widetilde{\alpha}|_{[t_0, t_1]} = f|_{\widetilde{W}_1}^{-1} \circ \alpha|_{[t_0, t_1]}$: $\widetilde{\alpha}$ is continuous and obviously satisfies $\widetilde{\alpha}(t_0) = p$ and $f \circ \widetilde{\alpha} = \alpha$.

Assuming that we constructed $\widetilde{\alpha}\big|_{[t_0,t_{j-1}]}$ and defined $\widetilde{W}_i$ for $i = 0,\ldots, j-1$, we denote by $\widetilde{W}_j$ the component of $f^{-1}(W_j)$ that contains $\widetilde{\alpha}(t_{j-1})$ and we put $\widetilde{\alpha}\big|_{[t_{j-1},t_j]} = f\big|_{\widetilde{W}_j}^{-1} \circ \alpha\big|_{[t_{j-1},t_j]}$. Repeating this until $j = k$, we complete the construction of $\widetilde{\alpha}$.

Regarding uniqueness of $\widetilde{\alpha}$, it follows from the following general observation: if $f: S_1 \to S_2$ is a *local diffeomorphism and* $\widehat{\alpha}, \widetilde{\alpha}: [a,b] \to S_1$ *are curves such that* $\widehat{\alpha}(a) = \widetilde{\alpha}(a)$ *and* $f \circ \widehat{\alpha} = f \circ \widetilde{\alpha}$, *then* $\widehat{\alpha} = \widetilde{\alpha}$.

To see this, we observe that $I = \{t \in [a,b] : \widehat{\alpha}(t) = \widetilde{\alpha}(t)\}$ is open and closed on $[a,b]$, by which $I = [a,b]$ (I is closed because $\widehat{\alpha}$ and $\widetilde{\alpha}$ are continuous, and is open because f is a local diffeomorphism). □

A remarkable property of coverings $f: S_1 \to S_2$ is that *all points of S_2 have the same number of preimages*, which is a simple consequence of Proposition 5.2.3. Indeed, given p and q in S_2, consider a curve α in S_2 from p to q. For each preimage p_i of p, let α_i be the lifting of α that starts from p_i. The endpoint q_i of α_i is a preimage of q. By Proposition 5.2.3, if $i \neq j$ then $q_i \neq q_j$ — since, obviously, there is a unique lifting for a given endpoint. Thus $\#f^{-1}(\{p\}) \leq \#f^{-1}(\{q\})$, and swapping the roles of p and q we obtain the opposite inequality.

The number of preimages of each point of S_2 is usually called the *number of sheets* of the covering.

By Proposition 5.2.3, we see that any covering $f: S_1 \to S_2$ enjoys the following properties:

(i) f is a local diffeomorphism,

(ii) f lifts curves,

— and the converse is also true:

Proposition 5.2.4 *If $f: S_1 \to S_2$ has properties (i) and (ii) then f is a covering.*

Note: In topological spaces other than surfaces — where, instead of diffeomorphisms, we would speak of local homeomorphisms — (i) and (ii) no longer guarantee that a mapping is a covering.

We say that two curves $\alpha_0, \alpha_1: [a,b] \to S_2$ with $\alpha_0(a) = \alpha_1(a) = q_0$ and $\alpha_0(b) = \alpha_1(b) = q_1$ are *homotopic with fixed endpoints* if there exists a continuous function

$$H: [0,1] \times [a,b] \to S_2$$

such that $H(0,t) = \alpha_0(t)$, $H(1,t) = \alpha_1(t)$ for all $t \in [a,b]$, and $H(s,a) = q_0$, $H(s,b) = q_1$ for all $s \in [0,1]$. Letting $\alpha_s = H(s,\cdot)$, the family of curves $(\alpha_s)_{0 \leq s \leq 1}$ is called a *continuous deformation of α_0 with fixed endpoints*. Note that if α_0 is closed then all α_s curves are also closed.

Lemma 5.2.5 *With the above notation, let $\widetilde{\alpha}_s$, for $0 \leq s \leq 1$, be a lifting of α_s in S_1. If all the curves $\widetilde{\alpha}_s$ have the same initial point p_0, then they also all have the same endpoint.*

Proof It suffices to show that, given $s_0 \in [0,1]$, there exists $\delta > 0$ such that if $|s - s_0| < \delta$, for all $s \in [0,1]$ then $\tilde{\alpha}_s(b) = \tilde{\alpha}_{s_0}(b)$. Let $a = t_0 < t_1 < \cdots < t_l = b$ be a partition of $[a,b]$ such that $\tilde{\alpha}_{s_0}([t_{i-1}, t_i]) \subseteq \tilde{D}_i$, where for each i:

- $\tilde{D}_i$ is an open subset diffeomorphic to a disk of the plane;
- if $i < k$ then there exists an open subset including the closure of $\tilde{D}_i \cup \tilde{D}_{i+1}$ such that the restriction of f to it is a diffeomorphism onto the image.

Every $D_i = f(\tilde{D}_i)$ is an open subset of S_2 diffeomorphic to a disk. By (uniform) continuity of $H(s,t) = \alpha_s(t)$, there exists $\delta > 0$ such that if $|s - s_0| < \delta$, for all $s \in [0,1]$, then $\alpha_s(t) \in D_i$ for all $t \in [t_{i-1}, t_i]$ and $i = 1, \ldots, k$.

Fixing $s \in [0,1] \cap]s_0 - \delta, s_0 + \delta[$, let us show that $\tilde{\alpha}_s([t_{i-1}, t_i]) \subseteq \tilde{D}_i$ for $i = 1, \ldots, k$. For $i = 1$, we have $\tilde{\alpha}_s(t_0) = p_0 \in \tilde{D}_i$; if not $\tilde{\alpha}_s([t_0, t_i]) \subseteq \tilde{D}_1$, there is $t \in]t_0, t_1]$ such that $\tilde{\alpha}_s(t)$ is on the boundary of $\tilde{D}_1$. For this t, the point $\alpha_s(t)$ is on the boundary of D_1, which contradicts the choice of s. We then have $\tilde{\alpha}_s([t_0, t_1]) \subseteq \tilde{D}_1$. Assuming now that $\tilde{\alpha}_s([t_{i-1}, t_i]) \subseteq \tilde{D}_i$ $(i < k)$, we observe that $\alpha_s(t_i) = f(\tilde{\alpha}_s(t_i))$ is in $D_i \cap D_{i+1}$. Since, by the second condition above, the restriction of f to $\tilde{D}_i \cup \tilde{D}_{i+1}$ is a bijection onto $D_i \cup D_{i+1}$, we have $f|_{\tilde{D}_i \cup \tilde{D}_{i+1}}^{-1}(D_i \cap D_{i+1}) = \tilde{D}_i \cap \tilde{D}_{i+1}$ and therefore $\tilde{\alpha}_s(t_i) \in \tilde{D}_{i+1}$. From this, as above, we conclude that $\tilde{\alpha}_s([t_i, t_{i+1}]) \subseteq \tilde{D}_{i+1}$ — and the proof by induction is finished. Finally, from the fact that $\tilde{\alpha}_s(b) \in \tilde{D}_k$ and $f(\tilde{\alpha}_s(b)) = q_1 = f(\tilde{\alpha}_{s_0}(b))$, it follows, just as desired, that $\tilde{\alpha}_s(b) = \tilde{\alpha}_{s_0}(b)$. $\qquad\square$

We now prove Proposition 5.2.4. Let us fix $q_0 \in S_2$ and an open neighborhood V of it that is diffeomorphic to a disk. We say that two points of $f^{-1}(V)$ are in the same *connected component* if there exists a curve in $f^{-1}(V)$ that connects them, and we write

$$f^{-1}(V) = \bigcup_j V_j,$$

where the V_j are the connected components. Each V_j is open: in fact, if $p \in V_j$ and $W \subseteq f^{-1}(V)$ is a neighborhood of p diffeomorphic to a disk, then $W \subseteq V_j$.

Let us now verify that $f|_{V_j} : V_j \to V$ is bijective. Take $p \in V_j$ and let $q = f(p)$. Given $r \in V$, let $\alpha : [a,b] \to V$ be a curve with $\alpha(a) = q$ and $\alpha(b) = r$, and let $\tilde{\alpha}$ be the lifting of α that starts from p. By definition, $\tilde{\alpha}(b)$ is in the same component V_j as p and $f(\tilde{\alpha}(b)) = r$. Therefore $f|_{V_j}$ is surjective. Regarding injectivity, assume that $\tilde{p}, \hat{p} \in V_j$ have the same image q, and $\tilde{\alpha}_0 : [a,b] \to V_j$ is a curve from $\tilde{p}$ to $\hat{p}$, and $\alpha_0 = f \circ \tilde{\alpha}_0$. This curve α_0 is then closed. Since V is diffeomorphic to a disk, there exists a continuous deformation $(\alpha_s)_{0 \le s \le 1}$ of α_0 with fixed endpoints such that the trace of each α_s is in V and α_1 is the constant curve equal to q. Denoting by $\tilde{\alpha}_s$ the lifting of α_s that starts from $\tilde{p}$, Lemma 5.2.5 guarantees that the curves $\tilde{\alpha}_s$ all have the same endpoints $\tilde{p}$ and $\hat{p}$. But $\tilde{\alpha}_1$ is constant, and therefore $\tilde{p} = \tilde{\alpha}_1(a) = \tilde{\alpha}_1(b) = \hat{p}$. Thus $f|_{V_j}$ is injective.

In conclusion: each component V_j is diffeomorphically sent into V, and therefore V is an evenly covered neighborhood of q_0. This shows that f is a covering and concludes the proof of Proposition 5.2.4.

In this proof we used that, for every open subset U diffeomorphic to a disk, every closed curve in U is homotopic (with fixed endpoints) to a constant curve by a homotopy that only takes values in U. A set U with such a property is called *simply connected*. Examples of simply connected surfaces are the plane and the sphere (recall that S^2 minus one point is diffeomorphic to the plane via stereographic projection). If S_2 is simply connected and $f: S_1 \to S_2$ a covering then $f^{-1}(S_2)$ has only one connected component, which is all of S_1 — and, by the proof of Proposition 5.2.4, f is injective, hence a diffeomorphism. This proves our next result.

Proposition 5.2.6 *Every covering of a simply connected surface is a diffeomorphism.*

We now have gathered all necessary tools about coverings and it is good to start at once to make interesting use of it.

Theorem 5.2.7 (Hadamard)

Let $S \subseteq \mathbb{R}^3$ be a compact surface with positive curvature at all points. Then S is diffeomorphic to the sphere.

In fact, such a surface is orientable (e.g. Example 61-b in Section 3.2), and the hypothesis implies that the normal mapping $N: S \to S^2$ is a local diffeomorphism, hence (by Proposition 5.2.2 and the compactness of S) a covering, hence (by Proposition 5.2.6 and S^2 being simply connected) a diffeomorphism.

In Section 5.4 we will discuss in more depth the compact surfaces of positive curvature in $\mathbb{R}^3$ (called *ovals*) and show that ovals are convex (in the sense that they bound convex regions of $\mathbb{R}^3$).

Exercises

126. Show that in Lemma 5.2.5 the function defined by $\widetilde{H}(s,t) = \widetilde{\alpha}_s(t)$ is continuous.

127. Let S_1 and S_2 be two connected surfaces and $f: S_1 \to S_2$ a covering. Further, let $\Im(f)$ be the set of diffeomorphisms $g: S_1 \to S_1$ such that $f \circ g = g$. Show that:
    (a) $\Im(f)$ is a group with respect to composition of functions;
    (b) if S_1 is simply connected, then for every pair of points p_0, p_1 in S_1 such that $f(p_0) = f(p_1)$, there exists a unique $g \in \Im(f)$ such that $g(p_0) = p_1$;
    (c) if S_1 is not simply connected, then the property in (b) may fail.

5.3 Complete Surfaces of Non-Positive Curvature

In this section, S is a complete surface of non-positive curvature. For every $p \in S$, the exponential mapping $\exp_p$ is then defined on the entire tangent space $T_p S$. We shall show the assumption that the curvature of S is non-positive implies that $\exp_p$ is a covering.

Fixing $p \in S$ and an orthonormal basis $(\mathbf{v}_1, \mathbf{v}_2)$ of $T_p S$, we note that the coefficients of the geodesic polar coordinates $\Psi(\rho, \varphi)$ centered at p have a well-defined meaning for all (ρ, φ) with $\rho > 0$, even if globally $\Psi(\rho, \varphi)$ is not a parameterization. For example,

$$G(\rho, \varphi) = |D(\exp_p)_{\rho \mathbf{v}_\varphi}(\rho \mathbf{w}_\varphi)|^2, \tag{5.4}$$

where $\mathbf{v}_\varphi = \cos\varphi \mathbf{v}_1 + \sin\varphi \mathbf{v}_2$, $\mathbf{w}_\varphi = -\sin\varphi \mathbf{v}_1 + \cos\varphi \mathbf{v}_2$. Furthermore, the equalities $E \equiv 1$, $F \equiv 0$ are valid for all (ρ, φ) without having to change anything in the proof of Lemma 4.6.3.

Ψ is a true parameterization in the neighborhood of any point (ρ, φ) such that $G(\rho, \varphi) \neq 0$, and hence formula (4.38) is valid. That is,

$$\left(\sqrt{G}\right)_{\rho\rho} + K\sqrt{G} = 0 \tag{5.5}$$

whenever $G \neq 0$. We know that with φ fixed the function $\rho \mapsto \sqrt{G}(\rho, \varphi)$ extends continuously to $\rho = 0$, and such an extension is twice differentiable at 0 (see Lemma 4.6.9) — with $\sqrt{G}(0, \varphi) = 0$ and $\left(\sqrt{G}\right)_\rho(0, \varphi) = 1$. Assuming that $K \leq 0$ on S, we obtain from (5.5) that $\left(\sqrt{G}\right)_{\rho\rho} \geq 0$; thus

$$\begin{aligned} \left(\sqrt{G}\right)_\rho(\rho, \varphi) &\geq \left(\sqrt{G}\right)_\rho(0, \varphi) = 1 \\ \Rightarrow \quad \sqrt{G}(\rho, \varphi) &\geq \sqrt{G}(0, \varphi) + \rho = \rho. \end{aligned} \tag{5.6}$$

Both these inequalities hold, as does (5.5), up to the first $\rho_0 > 0$ where $G(\rho_0, \varphi) = 0$. But (5.6) ensures that such a ρ_0 does not exist, and therefore the inequalities hold for all $\rho \geq 0$. Since $G(\rho, \varphi)$ is nonzero for all $\rho > 0$, it follows that $\exp_p$ is a local diffeomorphism. This proves one part of the following theorem:

Theorem 5.3.1 *Let S be a complete surface of non-positive curvature at all points. Then, for every $p \in S$, the local diffeomorphism $\exp_p : T_p S \to S$ is a covering.*

In view of Proposition 5.2.4, to complete the proof of Theorem 5.3.1, it is only left to show that $\exp_p$ lifts curves. The next result says that $\exp_p$ increases the length of curves:

Lemma 5.3.2 *If $\beta : [a, b] \to T_p S$ is a differentiable curve then $l(\beta) \leq l(\exp_p \circ \beta)$.*

Proof It suffices to show that for every $r \in T_p S$, and vector $\mathbf{v}$, we have $|D(\exp_p)_r(\mathbf{v})| \geq |\mathbf{v}|$, since then

$$l(\beta) = \int_a^b |\beta'(t)| \, dt \leq \int_a^b |D(\exp_p)_{\beta(t)}(\beta'(t))| \, dt = l(\exp_p \circ \beta).$$

Since $D(\exp_p)_O$ is the identity, we can assume that $r = \rho \mathbf{v}_\varphi$ with $\rho > 0$. The vectors $\mathbf{v}_\varphi$ and $\mathbf{w}_\varphi$ form an orthonormal basis of $T_p S$, and the vectors $D(\exp_p)_r(\mathbf{v}_\varphi)$ and $D(\exp_p)_r(\mathbf{w}_\varphi)$ are also orthogonal ($F \equiv 0$). Moreover,

$$|D(\exp_p)_r(\mathbf{v}_\varphi)| = 1 = |\mathbf{v}_\varphi|,$$

$$|D(\exp_p)_r(\mathbf{w}_\varphi)| = \frac{\sqrt{G}}{\rho} \geq 1 = |\mathbf{w}_\varphi| \quad \text{[by (5.4) and (5.6)]}$$

– and therefore

$$|D(\exp_p)_r(\lambda\mathbf{v}_\varphi + \mu\mathbf{w}_\varphi)|^2 = \lambda^2|D(\exp_p)_r(\mathbf{v}_\varphi)|^2 + \mu^2|D(\exp_p)_r(\mathbf{w}_\varphi)|^2$$
$$\geq \lambda^2 + \mu^2 = |\lambda\mathbf{v}_\varphi + \mu\mathbf{w}_\varphi|^2. \square$$

Returning to the proof of Theorem 5.3.1, consider a differentiable curve $\alpha:[a,b] \to S$, and let r be a point of T_pS such that $\exp_p(r) = \alpha(a)$. Taking a neighborhood of r that is diffeomorphically sent onto the image, we see that there exists $c \in {]a,b]}$ such that the lifting $\tilde{\alpha}$ of α starting at r is defined on $[a,c]$ (in the proof of Proposition 5.2.3 we saw that for a local diffeomorphism $S_1 \to S_2$ the lifting in S_1 of a curve in S_2 for a given fixed initial point is unique, whenever it exists). Let $\tilde{t}$ be the supremum of the set

$$I = \{t \in [a,b] : \tilde{\alpha} \text{ is defined on } [a,t]\} :$$

$\tilde{\alpha}$ is therefore defined on $[a,\tilde{t}[$. If $a \leq s < t < \tilde{t}$ then, using Lemma 5.3.2,

$$|\tilde{\alpha}(t) - \tilde{\alpha}(s)| \leq l(\tilde{\alpha}|_{[s,t]}) \leq l(\alpha|_{[s,t]})$$

— and therefore

$$\lim_{s,t \to \tilde{t}^-} |\tilde{\alpha}(t) - \tilde{\alpha}(s)| = 0,$$

which implies the existence of $\lim_{t \to \tilde{t}^-} \tilde{\alpha}(t)$. We thus conclude that $\tilde{t} \in I$, and it follows that $\tilde{t} = b$, otherwise the fact that $\exp_p$ is a local diffeomorphism would allow $\tilde{\alpha}$ to be extended beyond $\tilde{t}$. Hence $\exp_p$ lifts curves, which concludes the proof of Theorem 5.3.1.

Combining Theorem 5.3.1 with Proposition 5.2.6 we obtain the following corollary.

Theorem 5.3.3 (Hadamard)

If S is a complete, simply connected surface of curvature $K \leq 0$, then, for every $p \in S$, the local diffeomorphism $\exp_p: T_pS \to S$ is a diffeomorphism.

We saw in Chapter 4 how to construct local isometries between two surfaces of equal **constant** curvature K (Theorem 4.6.10): given $p \in S_1$, $q \in S_2$, and a linear isometry $L:T_pS_1 \to T_qS_2$, the mapping $\exp_q \circ L \circ \exp_p^{-1}$ is defined in a neighborhood of p and is an isometry onto the image. Let us now assume that $K \leq 0$, that both S_1 and S_2 are complete, and that S_1 is simply connected. Then $f = \exp_q \circ L \circ \exp_p^{-1}$ is defined on the entire surface S_1 (by Theorem 5.3.3), is a local isometry, and is still a covering (by Theorem 5.3.1). In case S_2 is also simply connected, f is a (global) isometry between S_1 and S_2. To summarize, we proved the following theorem:

Theorem 5.3.4 *Let S_1 be a complete, simply connected surface of constant curvature $K \leq 0$, and let S_2 be another complete surface with the same curvature K. Then:*

i. there exists a covering $f: S_1 \to S_2$ which is a local isometry;
ii. if S_2 is simply connected, the covering f is an isometry.

For every $K \leq 0$, there is therefore, up to isometry, only one complete surface, simply connected, of constant curvature K, and all other complete surfaces of equal curvature are images of this one under some *isometric covering*. The cylinder $x^2 + y^2 = 1$, for example, is (as we already knew) the image of the plane under an isometric covering: the function that wraps the plane around the cylinder.

We now face a problem: we do not yet know any **complete** surface on $\mathbb{R}^3$, simply connected or not, with negative constant curvature. Indeed, a famous theorem by Hilbert (of which a proof is found in [6]) states that such a surface does not exist. Do we have to conclude that Theorem 5.3.4 is void when $K < 0$? The solution is to consider, as we will do in Section 5.6, abstract surfaces whose metric structure is not induced by any ambient space.

Theorem 5.3.4 also holds for $K > 0$, with a slightly different proof; but in this case, for surfaces in $\mathbb{R}^3$, Theorem 5.3.4 is a triviality, since S_1 and S_2 have to be compact (see Exercise 129), and therefore are spheres of equal radius (Section 5.4). Again we have to consider abstract surfaces for the result to be interesting.

Exercises

128. Let S be a complete surface, of non-positive curvature, and p a point of S.
  (a) Show that the equations of geodesics in geodesic polar coordinates are

$$\rho - \frac{1}{2} G_\rho \varphi^2 = 0, \qquad \varphi + \frac{G_\rho}{G} \rho\varphi + \frac{G_\varphi}{2G} \varphi^2 = 0.$$

  (b) Let $\gamma(s)$ be a geodesic of S that does not pass through p, and denote by $\tilde{\gamma}: \mathbb{R} \to T_p S$ a lifting of γ. Show that the function $\rho(s) = |\tilde{\gamma}(s)|$ is convex (i.e., $\rho \geq 0$) and has at most one local minimum.
  (c) Assume now that S is simply connected. Show that the trace of any geodesic of S is a closed set on S and that, given a geodesic $\gamma(s)$ that does not pass through p, there exists a single point of γ at the minimal distance from p.
  (d) Compare the result of (c) with the case of the sphere. Give an example of a complete surface of non-positive curvature where not all geodesics are closed sets.

129. Let S be a complete surface of constant curvature $K > 0$. Using polar geodesic coordinates, show that any minimizing geodesic of S has length $\leq \dfrac{\pi}{\sqrt{K}}$. Conclude that S is compact.

5.4 Ovals (First Part): The Rigidity of the Sphere

The *oval surfaces* (or simply *ovals*) are the compact surfaces in $\mathbb{R}^3$ with positive curvature at all points. Such surfaces are, as we saw in Section 5.2 (Theorem 5.2.7), diffeomorphic to the sphere, the field of normal vectors $N\colon S \to \mathbf{S}^2$ being a diffeomorphism.

A surface S is *strictly convex* if, for every $p \in S$, the intersection of S with the tangent plane $\{p\} + T_pS$ with S reduces to the point p; equivalently, if $S \smallsetminus \{p\}$ is entirely in one of the two half-spaces into which $\{p\} + T_pS$ divides $\mathbb{R}^3$.

Proposition 5.4.1 *Every oval S is strictly convex.*

Proof Fixing $p \in S$, we must check that the mapping $S \to \mathbb{R}$ given by $h_p(q) = \langle N(p), q - p \rangle$ has constant sign, vanishing only at p. Otherwise h_p reaches a minimum and a maximum at points $q_0, q_1 \in S \smallsetminus \{p\}$. Each of the tangent spaces $T_{q_i}S$ $(i = 0, 1)$ is then orthogonal to $N(p)$, which implies that two of the vectors $N(p)$, $N(q_0)$ and $N(q_1)$ are equal — in contradiction to N being a diffeomorphism.

Now suppose that $p_0 \in S$ satisfies $\langle N(p_0), q - p_0 \rangle > 0$ for all $q \in S \smallsetminus \{p_0\}$. Let us verify that one also has $\langle N(p), q - p \rangle > 0$ for all distinct points $p, q \in S$. Since h_p has constant sign, we can assume $q \ne p_0$ and consider a curve $\alpha\colon [a, b] \to S$ such that $\alpha(a) = p_0$, $\alpha(b) = p$, and $\alpha(t) \ne q$ for all $t \in [a, b]$. The function $t \mapsto \langle N(\alpha(t)), q - \alpha(t) \rangle$ never vanishes, and therefore takes the same sign for $t = a$ and $t = b$, which proves that $\langle N(p), q - p \rangle > 0$. $\square$

From now on we fix an orientation N of S such that $\langle N(p), q - p \rangle > 0$ for all $p \ne q \in S$. With this orientation the principal curvatures (and the mean curvature) at each point are positive.

Our goal now is to show that the region Ω of $\mathbb{R}^3$ bounded by S is convex in the usual sense: the line segment joining each pair of points in Ω is also contained in Ω. Let us consider the sets

$$\mathcal{C} = \{q \in \mathbb{R}^3 \colon \langle N(p), q - p \rangle > 0 \ \forall \, p \in S\},$$
$$\mathcal{D} = \{q \in \mathbb{R}^3 \colon \exists \, p \in S \text{ such that } \langle N(p), q - p \rangle < 0\}.$$

Proposition 5.4.2 *The sets $\mathcal{C}$ and $\mathcal{D}$ are connected open, $\mathcal{C}$ is convex and bounded, S is the boundary of both sets $\mathcal{C}$ and $\mathcal{D}$, and $\mathbb{R}^3 \smallsetminus S = \mathcal{C} \cup \mathcal{D}$.*

Proof Each of the sets $\mathcal{D}_p = \{q \in \mathbb{R}^3 \colon \langle N(p), q - p \rangle < 0\}$, for $p \in S$, is open, and $\mathcal{D}$ is the union of them all. Therefore $\mathcal{D}$ is open, and it is easily seen to be connected. The set $\mathcal{C}$ is the intersection of the convex sets $\mathcal{C}_p = \{q \in \mathbb{R}^3 \colon \langle N(p), q - p \rangle > 0\}$ $(p \in S)$, and is therefore convex; and any convex set is connected.

Given $q \in \mathcal{C}$, let us consider $\delta = \min_{p \in S} \langle N(p), q - p \rangle > 0$. If $|r - q| < \delta$ then we have, for every $p \in S$,

$$\langle N(p), r - p \rangle = \langle N(p), q - p \rangle - \langle N(p), q - r \rangle \ge \delta - |q - r| > 0,$$

so that $r \in \mathcal{C}$ — which proves that $\mathcal{C}$ is open.

We shall show that $S \subseteq \partial\mathcal{C} \cap \partial\mathcal{D}$. Let us fix $p_0 \in S$ and a **unit** vector $\mathbf{v}$ such that $\langle N(p_0), \mathbf{v} \rangle > 0$, and let $p_t = p_0 + t\mathbf{v}$. When $t < 0$, we have $\langle N(p_0), p_t - p_0 \rangle = t\langle N(p_0), \mathbf{v} \rangle < 0$ and therefore $p_t \in \mathcal{D}$. This shows that $p_0 \in \partial\mathcal{D}$, and we thus conclude that $S \subseteq \partial\mathcal{D}$.

Now let $U \subseteq S$ be an open neighborhood of p_0 such that $\langle N(p), \mathbf{v} \rangle > 0$ whenever $p \in U$, and let us put $\varepsilon = \min_{p \in S \setminus U} \langle N(p), p_0 - p \rangle$. It follows immediately that if $p \in U$ and $t > 0$ then $\langle N(p), p_t - p \rangle > 0$. On the other hand, if $p \in S \setminus U$ and $0 < t < \varepsilon$ then

$$\langle N(p), p_t - p \rangle = \langle N(p), p_0 - p \rangle + t \langle N(p), \mathbf{v} \rangle \ge \varepsilon - t |N(p)| \, |\mathbf{v}| > 0$$

— which shows that $p_t \in C$ for $t \in]0, \varepsilon[$. Thus $p_0 \in \partial C$, and therefore $S \subseteq \partial C$.

We now show that $\mathbb{R}^3 \setminus (C \cup \mathcal{D}) \subseteq S$. Indeed, if $q \in \mathbb{R}^3 \setminus (C \cup \mathcal{D})$ then there exists some $p_0 \in S$ such that $\langle N(p_0), q - p_0 \rangle = 0$. If $q \ne p_0$ then we can consider a curve $\alpha :]-\eta, \eta[\to S$ such that $\alpha(0) = p_0$ and $\alpha'(0) = DN_{p_0}^{-1}(q - p_0)$, where

$$\frac{d}{dt} \langle N \circ \alpha(t), q - \alpha(t) \rangle \Big|_{t=0} = \langle DN_{p_0}(\alpha'(0)), q - p_0 \rangle = |q - p_0|^2 > 0.$$

This implies that $\langle N \circ \alpha(t), q - \alpha(t) \rangle < 0$ for $t < 0$ near 0, and therefore $q \in \mathcal{D}$, in contradiction to our hypothesis. We thus conclude that $p = p_0 \in S$ and $\mathbb{R}^3 \setminus (C \cup \mathcal{D}) \subseteq S$ — which, together with what we have shown above, also proves $\partial C = \partial \mathcal{D} = S$.

Finally, let us take $\lambda > 0$ such that $S \subseteq D_\lambda = \{q \in \mathbb{R}^3 : |q| \le \lambda\}$. The complement of D_λ, being connected and disjoint to S, is contained in either of the sets C or $\mathcal{D}$; but as $\mathcal{D}$ is not bounded, $\mathcal{D} \cap (\mathbb{R}^3 \setminus D_\lambda)$ is non-empty and therefore $\mathbb{R}^3 \setminus D_\lambda \subseteq \mathcal{D}$. Thus $C \subseteq D_\lambda$ and C is bounded.   □

The next result is used immediately afterwards in the proof of the rigidity of the sphere, and in the proof of a Blaschke formula in the next section (Theorem 5.5.3).

Theorem 5.4.3 (Minkowski integral formulas)

Let S be an oval and $p_0 \in \mathbb{R}^3$. Then, denoting by A the area of S, we have

$$A = -\int_S H(p) \langle p - p_0, N(p) \rangle \, d\sigma, \tag{5.7}$$

$$\int_S H(p) \, d\sigma = -\int_S K(p) \langle p - p_0, N(p) \rangle \, d\sigma. \tag{5.8}$$

Both formulas (5.7) and (5.8) are valid for every compact surface $S \subseteq \mathbb{R}^3$, and indeed we prove (5.7) [but not (5.8)] in this generality. We will make use of the results of Section 4.4, in particular of Theorem 4.4.5 (first variation of area).

Let us consider the vector field on S given by $\mathbf{v}(p) = p - p_0$, and let S_t be the variation of S induced by $\mathbf{v}$. Since S_t is the image of S under the homothety with center p_0 and ratio $1 + t$, its area is $A(t) = (1+t)^2 A$, which implies $A'(0) = 2A$. Comparing with Theorem 4.4.5, we obtain

$$2A = -\int_S \langle \mathbf{v}(p), 2H(p)N(p) \rangle \, d\sigma = -2 \int_S H(p) \langle p - p_0, N(p) \rangle \, d\sigma,$$

which proves (5.7).

The proof of (5.8) follows the steps of the previous one. We denote by $M = \int_S H(p) \, d\sigma$ the *total mean curvature* of S, and we denote by $M(t)$ the analogous quantity for S_t. Note that the parameterization $\Phi(u, v)$ of S is transformed, when composed with the homothety just mentioned, into the parameterization $(1+t)\Phi(u, v) - t p_0$ of S_t; the coefficients of the first fundamental form are multiplied by $(1+t)^2$ and the coefficients of the second by $1+t$. Hence the area element is multiplied by $(1+t)^2$ and, by formula (3.8) in Section 3.2, H is divided by $1+t$. We hence have $M(t) = (1+t)M$ and therefore $M'(0) = M$; (5.8) is an immediate consequence of the lemma below:

Lemma 5.4.4 *Let S be an oval and let S_t be the variation of S induced by a vector field* **v**. *Then, if $M(t)$ denotes the total mean curvature of S_t, we have*

$$M'(0) = - \int_S K(p)\langle \mathbf{v}(p), N(p)\rangle \, d\sigma.$$

Proof Given a parameterization (U, Φ) of S, compatible with the orientation, let

$$\Phi^t(u, v) = \Phi(u, v) + t\mathbf{v}(u, v);$$

(U, Φ^t) is a parameterization of S_t for sufficiently small $|t|$. Let us denote by $N^t(u, v)$ the field of normal vectors in $\Phi^t(U)$. By formula (4.18) of Section 4.4 we have

$$H^t|\Phi_u^t \times \Phi_v^t| = -\frac{1}{2}\langle \Phi_u^t \times N_v^t + N_u^t \times \Phi_v^t, N^t\rangle. \tag{5.9}$$

We now look at the derivative of the second term in (5.9). We have

$$\frac{d}{dt}\langle \Phi_u^t \times N_v^t + N_u^t \times \Phi_v^t, N^t\rangle\big|_{t=0}$$

$$= \left\langle \Phi_u \times N_v + N_u \times \Phi_v, \frac{d}{dt}N^t\big|_{t=0}\right\rangle + \left\langle \frac{d}{dt}\{\Phi_u^t \times N_v^t + N_u^t \times \Phi_v^t\}\big|_{t=0}, N\right\rangle$$

$$= \left\langle \frac{\partial \mathbf{v}}{\partial u} \times N_v + N_u \times \frac{\partial \mathbf{v}}{\partial v}, N\right\rangle + \left\langle \Phi_u \times \left(\frac{d}{dt}N_v^t\big|_{t=0}\right) + \left(\frac{d}{dt}N_u^t\big|_{t=0}\right) \times \Phi_v, N\right\rangle \tag{5.10}$$

(because $\frac{d}{dt}N^t\big|_{t=0}$ is orthogonal to N, and $\phi_u \times N_v + N_u \times \Phi_v$ is collinear with N).

If we consider the field of tangent vectors $\mathbf{w} = \frac{d}{dt}N^t\big|_{t=0}$ and use Proposition 4.4.1, the right-hand side of (5.10) becomes

$$\left\langle \Phi_u \times \frac{\partial \mathbf{w}}{\partial v} + \frac{\partial \mathbf{w}}{\partial u} \times \Phi_v, N\right\rangle = (\mathrm{Div}\,\mathbf{w})|\Phi_u \times \Phi_v|. \tag{5.11}$$

Regarding the left-hand side in (5.9), we note that $N: S \to \mathbf{S}^2$ induces in $\mathbf{S}^2$ the orientation for which the mean curvature is negative, equal to -1. Using Proposition 4.4.1 we obtain

$$\left\langle \frac{\partial \mathbf{v}}{\partial u} \times N_v + N_u \times \frac{\partial \mathbf{v}}{\partial v}, N\right\rangle = |N_u \times N_v|\{\mathrm{Div}^*(\mathbf{v}^\top) + 2\langle \mathbf{v}, N\rangle\}$$

$$= \mathrm{Div}^*(\mathbf{v}^\top)|N_u \times N_v| + 2K\langle \mathbf{v}, N\rangle|\Phi_u \times \Phi_v|, \tag{5.12}$$

where $\mathrm{Div}^*(\mathbf{v}^\top)$ indicates the divergence of $\mathbf{v}^\top$ as the tangent vector field to $\mathbf{S}^2$ — which is fine since N is a diffeomorphism and the tangent spaces $T_p S$ and $T_{N(p)}\mathbf{S}^2$ are parallel. Now the total mean curvature of $\Phi^t(U) \subseteq S_t$ is $M_\Phi(t) = \int_U H^t |\Phi^t_u \times \Phi^t_v|\, du\, dv$, so that

$$M'_\Phi(0) = \int_U \frac{d}{dt}\{H^t|\Phi^t_u \times \Phi^t_v|\}\big|_{t=0}\, du\, dv. \qquad (5.13)$$

Combining formulas (5.9)-(5.13) and using Corollary 4.4.3, we finally obtain

$$M'(0) = -\frac{1}{2}\int_S \mathrm{Div}\,\mathbf{w}\,d\sigma - \frac{1}{2}\int_{\mathbf{S}^2}\mathrm{Div}^*(\mathbf{v}^\top)\,d\sigma - \int_S K\langle\mathbf{v},N\rangle\,d\sigma$$

$$= -\int_S K\langle\mathbf{v},N\rangle\,d\sigma. \qquad \square$$

Theorem 5.4.5 (Rigidity of the Sphere)

Let $S \subseteq \mathbb{R}^3$ be a compact surface with constant curvature K. Then S is a sphere.

Proof Being compact, S has some point of positive curvature (see Exercise 57 in Section 3.1), and therefore $K > 0$. S is then an oval, and we can fix the orientation $N: S \to \mathbf{S}^2$ such that $\langle N(p), q - p\rangle > 0$ for every pair of points $p \neq q$ on S. With this orientation we have $H(p) > 0$ at every point $p \in S$.

Let us put $k = \sqrt{K}$. By the inequality between the arithmetic and geometric means, we have $kH(p) - K \geq 0$, and the equality holds at p if and only if p is an umbilical point. Let $p_0 \in \mathbb{R}^3$ (whose existence is guaranteed by Proposition 5.4.2) be such that $\langle N(p), p_0 - p\rangle > 0$ for all $p \in S$, and let us put

$$\Delta_0 = \int_S (kH - K)\,d\sigma = kM - k^2 A,$$

$$\Delta_1 = \int_S (kH - K)\langle N, p_0 - p\rangle\,d\sigma$$

$$= k\int_S H\langle N, p_0 - p\rangle\,d\sigma - \int_S K\langle N, p_0 - p\rangle\,d\sigma$$

$$= kA - M \qquad \text{(by Minkowski's formulas).}$$

We thus have $\Delta_0 = -k\Delta_1$, but their definitions ensure that Δ_0 and Δ_1 are both non-negative. Hence, we have $\Delta_0 = \Delta_1 = 0$, and therefore the integrand function $kH - K$ is constantly zero. All points of S are therefore umbilical and, by Proposition 3.1.5, S is a sphere. $\qquad \square$

In particular, all surfaces in $\mathbb{R}^3$ that are isometric to the sphere are themselves spheres, and hence the theorem speaks of the rigidity of the sphere. The theorem has the following generalization (see [13]): *if $f: S_1 \to S_2$ is an isometry between two oval surfaces then f is the restriction of an isometry of $\mathbb{R}^3$* (which, as is known, is the composite of a linear isometry with a translation).

We now give another result of the same kind as Theorem 5.4.5.

Theorem 5.4.6 *Let $S \subseteq \mathbb{R}^3$ be an oval surface of constant mean curvature H. Then S is a sphere.*

We choose the orientation N and the point p_0 as above, and notice that $H^2 - K \geq 0$, with equality only at the umbilical points. Then

$$\int_S (H^2 - K)\langle N, p_0 - p \rangle\, d\sigma = H \int_S H\langle N, p_0 - p \rangle\, d\sigma - \int_S K\langle N, p_0 - p \rangle\, d\sigma$$

$$= HA - \int_S H\, d\sigma = 0$$

— and from this, since the integrand function is non-negative, it follows that $H^2 - K \equiv 0$, and therefore S is a sphere.

Let us point out that Theorem 5.4.6 remains valid without the assumption that S has positive curvature: *any compact surface $S \subseteq \mathbb{R}^3$ with constant mean curvature is a sphere*. An accessible proof of this result appears in Osserman's paper [20].

Exercise

130. Show that the open subset C bounded by the oval surface S (Proposition 5.4.2) is given by $\{(1-t)p + tq : p, q \in S,\ 0 < t < 1\}$.

5.5 Ovals: Areas and Volumes; Surfaces of Constant Width

In this section we prove a number of formulas involving the area, the total mean curvature, and the volume bounded by an oval surface. Some of these formulas concern convex bodies in $\mathbb{R}^3$ — which include not only solids bounded by oval surfaces but also by convex polyhedra. As we noted in Section 1.1, the length of a regular curve γ can be computed by considering polygonal lines inscribed in γ with increasing numbers of segments. The generalization to surfaces is not so obvious: there are approximations of the cylindrical surface $C = \{x^2 + y^2 = 1,\ 0 \leq z \leq 1\}$ by polyhedra whose vertices are all in C but whose areas do not converge to that of C (see Exercise 131).

The solution, for a compact convex surface S, is to approximate S by **convex** polyhedra: if $\mathcal{P}_1$ and $\mathcal{P}_2$ are convex polyhedra such that $\mathcal{P}_1 < S < \mathcal{P}_2$, where the sign < means "is in", then we have the expected inequality of areas

$$A(\mathcal{P}_1) < A(S) < A(\mathcal{P}_2). \tag{5.14}$$

Knowing that we can find $\mathcal{P}_1$ and $\mathcal{P}_2$ such that $\mathcal{P}_1 < S < \mathcal{P}_2$ and with $A(\mathcal{P}_2) - A(\mathcal{P}_1)$ as small as we want, it follows from (5.14) that

$$A(S) = \sup_{\mathcal{P}_1 < S} A(\mathcal{P}_1) = \inf_{S < \mathcal{P}_2} A(\mathcal{P}_2). \tag{5.15}$$

Formula (5.15) suggests that for certain formulas involving areas of convex surfaces, it is sufficient to prove them for polyhedra; moreover, it provides a definition of area that does not depend on whether the surface in question is regular or not.

The interested reader can find the details of this construction in several books on convexity (e.g., [9]). For now, we will make use of (5.15) to prove a Cauchy formula. Let S be a compact convex surface. Given $p \in \mathbf{S}^2$, let us denote by $A_S(p)$ the area of the orthogonal projection of S onto $T_p\mathbf{S}^2$.

Theorem 5.5.1 (Cauchy)

The area of S is given by

$$A = \frac{1}{\pi} \int_{\mathbf{S}^2} A_S(p)\, d\sigma. \tag{5.16}$$

Proof Let F be a polygon included in a plane Π, and let $\mathbf{v}$ be a unit vector orthogonal to Π. Let $\theta \in [0, \pi]$ be the angle between $\mathbf{v}$ and $\mathbf{Op}\,(p \in \mathbf{S}^2)$; the area of the orthogonal projection of F onto $T_p\mathbf{S}^2$ is $A_F(p) = A(F)|\cos\theta|$. Using spherical coordinates (φ, θ) relative to an orthonormal frame in which the third vector is $\mathbf{v}$, we then have

$$\int_{\mathbf{S}^2} A_F(p)\, d\sigma = \int_0^{2\pi} \left(\int_0^{\pi} A(F)|\cos\theta| \sin\theta\, d\theta \right) d\varphi$$

$$= 2\pi A(F) \int_0^{\pi} |\cos\theta| \sin\theta\, d\theta = 2\pi A(F).$$

Thus

$$A(F) = \frac{1}{2\pi} \int_{\mathbf{S}^2} A_F(p)\, d\sigma. \tag{5.17}$$

Now let $\mathcal{P}$ be a convex polyhedron and $F_1, \ldots, F_k$ its faces. Except for the points on the boundary (which are negligible), each point of the orthogonal projection of $\mathcal{P}$ in the plane $T_p\mathbf{S}^2$ is the image of exactly two points of $\mathcal{P}$, belonging to two distinct faces. We then have

$$A_{\mathcal{P}}(p) = \frac{1}{2} \sum_{i=1}^{k} A_{F_i}(p);$$

and, using (5.17), we obtain

$$A(\mathcal{P}) = \sum_{i=1}^{k} A(F_i) = \frac{1}{\pi} \int_{\mathbf{S}^2} \left(\frac{1}{2} \sum_{i=1}^{k} A_{F_i}(p) \right) d\sigma$$

$$= \frac{1}{\pi} \int_{\mathbf{S}^2} A_{\mathcal{P}}(p)\, d\sigma. \tag{5.18}$$

Noting that if $\mathcal{P}_1 < S < \mathcal{P}_2$ then $A_{\mathcal{P}_1}(p) \le A_S(p) \le A_{\mathcal{P}_2}(p)$ for every $p \in \mathbf{S}^2$, it follows from (5.18) that

$$A(\mathcal{P}_1) \le \frac{1}{\pi} \int_{\mathbf{S}^2} A_S(p)\, d\sigma \le A(\mathcal{P}_2),$$

which, together with (5.15), proves the theorem.   □

As in the case of curves (see Section 1.6), we say that an oval surface S has *constant curvature* $\mathfrak{L}$ if, for every pair of parallel planes tangent to S at two distinct points, the distance between them is equal to $\mathfrak{L}$.

Corollary 5.5.2 *If S has constant curvature $\mathfrak{L}$ and area A then*

$$A \leq \pi \mathfrak{L}^2,$$

with equality if and only if S is a sphere.

Sketch of the proof. The orthogonal projection of S onto the plane $T_p S^2$, which we denote by $S(p)$, is bounded by a curve of constant width $\mathfrak{L}$, having (by Theorem 1.6.3) perimeter $\pi \mathfrak{L}$. By the isoperimetric inequality (Theorem 1.8.2), the area of $S(p)$ satisfies the inequality

$$A_S(p) \leq \frac{\pi \mathfrak{L}^2}{4} \tag{5.19}$$

— with equality only in the case where $S(p)$ is a disk with radius $\mathfrak{L}/2$. Combining (5.19) and (5.16), we obtain

$$A \leq \frac{1}{\pi} \int_{S^2} \frac{\pi \mathfrak{L}^2}{4} \, d\sigma = \pi \mathfrak{L}^2,$$

with equality if and only if every orthogonal projection $S(p)$ of S is a disk with radius $\mathfrak{L}/2$ — and this last condition implies that S is a sphere (see Exercise 132).   □

Let us further consider an oval surface S, and on it the field of normal vectors N pointing into S. The variation of S induced by $-N$ is, as we have already defined, the family $S_t = \{p - tN(p): p \in S\}$. But in this case, the surfaces S_t are *parallel* to S, either surrounding it (for $t > 0$) or being surrounded by it (for $t < 0$) at a fixed distance equal to $|t|$. Furthermore S_t is a surface for all $t \geq 0$ (Exercise 135), though not for all $t < 0$.

Given a parameterization $\Phi(u, v)$ of S, let us put

$$\Phi^t(u, v) = \Phi(u, v) - tN(u, v).$$

Now we have

$$\begin{aligned}
\Phi_u^t \times \Phi_v^t &= \Phi_u \times \Phi_v - t\{\Phi_u \times N_v + N_u \times \Phi_v\} + t^2\{N_u \times N_v\} \\
&= (1 + 2tH + t^2 K)\{\Phi_u \times \Phi_v\} \quad \text{[per (4.18), Section 4.4].}
\end{aligned} \tag{5.20}$$

For $t > 0$ (and for negative t near 0), the expression $1 + 2tH + t^2 K$ is positive. As a consequence, and taking absolute values on both sides of (5.20), we conclude that the area of S_t is given by

$$A(t) = \int_S (1 + 2tH + t^2 K) \, d\sigma = A + 2Mt + 4\pi t^2, \tag{5.21}$$

where A and M are the area and the total mean curvature of S (where we recall that as S is diffeomorphic to the sphere its total curvature $\int_S K \, d\sigma$ is 4π). Formula (5.21) thus expresses the remarkable fact that *the area of a surface parallel to S is a polynomial function of its distance to S.*

We can apply (5.21) to deduce an analogous formula involving volumes. Let us denote by $V(t)$ the volume of the region bounded by S_t, where $V = V(0)$. Assuming that $t > 0$, the difference $V(t) - V$ is the volume of the region between S and S_t. This region is the union of the images of the functions $\Psi(u, v, s) = \Phi^s(u, v)$, with $(u, v, s) \in U \times [0, t]$, where (U, Φ) is a parameterization of S. Now

$$|\det J\Psi| = \left| \left\langle \frac{\partial \Psi}{\partial u} \times \frac{\partial \Psi}{\partial v}, \frac{\partial \Psi}{\partial s} \right\rangle \right| = |\langle \Phi_u^s \times \Phi_v^s, N \rangle| = |\Phi_u^s \times \Phi_v^s|,$$

and therefore the volume of the image of Ψ is

$$V(\Psi) = \int_0^t \left(\iint_U |\det J\Psi| \, du \, dv \right) ds$$
$$= \int_0^t \left(\iint_U |\Phi_u^s \times \Phi_v^s| \, du \, dv \right) ds = \int_0^t A(\Phi^s) \, ds, \tag{5.22}$$

where $A(\Phi^s)$ denotes the area of $\Phi^s(U)$. Using (5.22) and (5.21), we finally obtain

$$V(t) = V + \int_0^t A(s) \, ds = V + At + Mt^2 + \frac{4\pi}{3} t^3, \tag{5.23}$$

and here it is, the promised formula, which is also valid for negative t near 0. There is a formula analogous to (5.23) for the area of planar regions bounded by parallel curves as well, which we will give in Exercise 133.

To conclude the section, we again assume that S has constant width $\mathfrak{L}$. As in the case of curves, the antipode $\mathcal{A}(p)$ of $p \in S$ is given by

$$\mathcal{A}(p) = p + \mathfrak{L} N(p),$$

and $\mathcal{A} \colon S \to S$ is an involutive diffeomorphism (i.e., $\mathcal{A} \circ \mathcal{A} = \mathrm{id}$). Since S is inside the sphere with center $\mathcal{A}(p)$ and radius $\mathfrak{L}$, and is tangent to the sphere at the point p, the principal curvatures at p are both bounded by $1/\mathfrak{L}$ (see Exercise 57 in Section 3.1). If $\Phi(u, v)$ is a parameterization of S then, since $\mathcal{A}$ is a diffeomorphism, $\widetilde{\Phi} = \mathcal{A} \circ \Phi$ is another parameterization. But from the expression of $\mathcal{A}$, we see that with the above notation $\widetilde{\Phi} = \Phi^{-\mathfrak{L}}$, and from this, using (5.20), we take

$$\widetilde{\Phi}_u \times \widetilde{\Phi}_v = (1 - 2H\mathfrak{L} + K\mathfrak{L}^2)\{\Phi_u \times \Phi_v\} \tag{5.24}$$

— a formula that ensures that the expression $1 - 2H\mathfrak{L} + K\mathfrak{L}^2$ never vanishes. In terms of the principal curvatures k_1, k_2, we have

$$1 - 2H\mathfrak{L} + K\mathfrak{L}^2 = (k_1\mathfrak{L} - 1)(k_2\mathfrak{L} - 1) > 0,$$

since both factors are non-negative. It then follows from (5.24) that *for every continuous function $f : S \to \mathbb{R}$ we have*

$$\int_S f \, d\sigma = \int_S (f \circ \mathcal{A})(1 - 2H\mathfrak{L} + K\mathfrak{L}^2) \, d\sigma. \qquad (5.25)$$

The formula (5.25) has interesting consequences. For example, taking $f \equiv 1$, and using the fact that the total curvature of S is 4π, we obtain

$$A = A - 2M\mathfrak{L} + 4\pi\mathfrak{L}^2 \;\Rightarrow\; M = 2\pi\mathfrak{L}$$

— that is, *the total mean curvature of a surface of constant width $\mathfrak{L}$ is $M = 2\pi\mathfrak{L}$.*

For another application of (5.25), we will prove a Blaschke formula that relates the area A of a surface of constant width to the volume V of the region bounded by it.

Theorem 5.5.3 (Blaschke)

If S has constant width $\mathfrak{L}$ then $V = \frac{1}{2} A\mathfrak{L} - \frac{1}{3} \pi\mathfrak{L}^3$.

Proof Let p_0 be a point of the region Ω bounded by S. The volume of Ω is given by

$$V = \frac{1}{3} \int_S \langle N(p), p_0 - p \rangle \, d\sigma(p)$$

(this formula corresponds to regarding Ω as a union of "infinitesimal cones" of vertex p_0 and base in S, and is a particular case of the divergence theorem in $\mathbb{R}^3$ — see e.g. [16], p. 493). By (5.25), denoting by $\tilde{p}$ the antipode of p, we also have

$$V = \frac{1}{3} \int_S \langle N(\tilde{p}), p_0 - \tilde{p} \rangle (1 - 2H\mathfrak{L} + K\mathfrak{L}^2) \, d\sigma(p).$$

Since $N(\tilde{p}) = -N(p)$ and $\tilde{p} = p + \mathfrak{L}N(p)$, we obtain from this, using Minkowski's formulas (Theorem 5.4.3) and the fact that $M = 2\pi\mathfrak{L}$,

$$V = \frac{1}{3} \int_S (-\langle N(p), p_0 - p \rangle + \mathfrak{L})(1 - 2H\mathfrak{L} + K\mathfrak{L}^2) \, d\sigma(p)$$

$$= -V + \frac{1}{3} A\mathfrak{L} + \frac{2}{3} \left(\int_S H\langle p_0 - p, N \rangle \, d\sigma \right) \mathfrak{L} - \frac{1}{3} \left(\int_S K\langle p_0 - p, N \rangle \, d\sigma \right) \mathfrak{L}^2$$

$$= -V + \frac{1}{3} A\mathfrak{L} + \frac{2}{3} A\mathfrak{L} - \frac{1}{3} M\mathfrak{L}^2 = -V + A\mathfrak{L} - \frac{2}{3} \pi\mathfrak{L}^3,$$

which concludes the proof of the theorem. $\qquad\square$

Theorem 5.5.3 shows that among surfaces with a certain constant width $\mathfrak{L}$ those with the largest (or smallest) area are also those that enclose the largest (or smallest) volume. From Corollary 5.5.2 it then follows that *the maximal volume is that of the sphere.* The problem of finding the surface of a given constant width with minimal area (or minimal volume) is still open (see [7]).

Exercises

131. The segment C of the cylinder $x^2 + y^2 = 1$ bounded by the planes $z = 0$ and $z = 1$ has area 2π. Given $k \geq 1$ and $n \geq 3$, consider the $k + 1$ circles in C given by

$$z = 0, \ \frac{1}{k}, \frac{2}{k}, \dots, \frac{k-1}{k}, 1.$$

Divide each of these circles into n equal arcs, so that the ends of the arcs in each circle are vertically at the midpoints of the arcs of the preceding circle. The ends of these arcs define regular polygons of n sides inscribed in each of the circles. Joining each vertex to the two vertices closest to the neighboring polygons, we obtain a polyhedron $P(k,n)$ whose faces are triangles, all of which are congruent.

(a) Show that the area of $P(k,n)$ is

$$A(k,n) = 2n \sin\left(\frac{\pi}{n}\right)\sqrt{1 + 4k^2 \sin^4\left(\frac{\pi}{2n}\right)}.$$

(b) Compute $\lim\limits_{n \to +\infty} A(n^r, n)$ for $r = 1, 2, 3$. What conclusion can you draw?

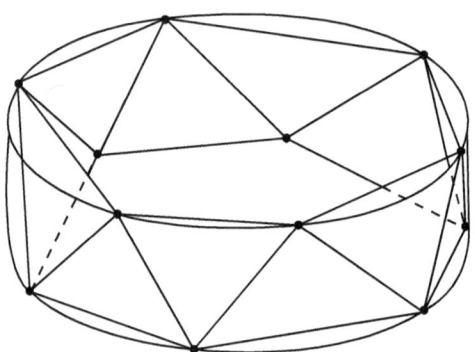

Figure 5.5

132. Let S be an oval surface and $r > 0$ such that the orthogonal projection of S onto each plane $P \subseteq \mathbb{R}^3$ is a disk with radius r. Show that:

(a) for every plane P, the surface S is inscribed in a straight circular cylinder C of height $2r$ whose base has radius r and is parallel to P;

(b) if γ is the equator of C then $\gamma \subseteq S$ and the normals to C and to S along γ coincide;

(c) each normal section of S is a circle with radius r, and therefore S is a sphere.

133. Let α be a convex, regular, closed planar curve. Denote by α_t the curve parallel to α at distance t from α, and by $\mathcal{U}(t)$ the area of the region bounded by α_t. Show that

$$\mathcal{U}(t) = \mathcal{U} + l(\alpha)t + \pi t^2 \quad [\text{where } \mathcal{U} = \mathcal{U}(0)].$$

Hint: verify that $l(\alpha_t) = l(\alpha) + 2\pi t$ and $\mathcal{U}(t) = \mathcal{U} + \int_0^t l(\alpha_s)\, ds$.

Note: since any convex curve can be approximated by a regular convex curve, the obtained formula is valid for any convex curve.

134. Let S be an oval surface, and denote by $l_S(p)$ the perimeter of the orthogonal projection of S onto $T_p S^2$. Show that the total mean curvature of S is given by

$$M = \frac{1}{2\pi} \int_{S^2} l_S(p)\, d\sigma.$$

Hint: use Exercise 133 and Theorem 5.5.1 to obtain an expression for the area $A(t)$ of the surface S_t parallel to S, and compare (5.21) with the formula obtained.

135. Let S be an oval surface and N be the normal field pointing into S. Show that, for all $t \geq 0$, the surface $S_t = \{p - tN(p): p \in S\}$ is diffeomorphic to S.

5.6 Abstract Surfaces. The Hyperbolic Plane

All measures intrinsic to a surface depend, as we know, on the inner product defined on the tangent space (i.e., the first fundamental form) — which, so far, has simply been the usual scalar product restriction on $\mathbb{R}^3$. But nothing prevents us from considering other inner products, obtaining in this way surfaces whose metric structure is not inherited from $\mathbb{R}^3$. The next step is to dispense with the ambient space, defining abstract surfaces that are not even diffeomorphic to surfaces of $\mathbb{R}^3$.

Let $U \subseteq \mathbb{R}^2$ be an open and connected region, and let $E, F, G: U \to \mathbb{R}$ be C^∞-functions such that

- E and G are strictly positive;
- $EG - F^2 > 0$ at all points of U.

For every point $(u, v) \in U$ we define an inner product $\langle \cdot, \cdot \rangle_{(u,v)}$ on $T_{(u,v)}U = \mathbb{R}^2$ as follows:

$$\langle (x_1, y_1), (x_2, y_2) \rangle_{(u,v)} = x_1 x_2\, E(u,v) + (x_1 y_2 + y_1 x_2) F(u,v) + y_1 y_2\, G(u,v).$$

If $\alpha: [a, b] \to U$ is a regular curve then, in this inner product, the norm of $\alpha'(t)$ is given by

$$\sqrt{I_{\alpha(t)}(\alpha'(t))} = \sqrt{u'(t)^2 E(\alpha(t)) + 2u'(t)v'(t)F(\alpha(t)) + v'(t)^2 G(\alpha(t))},$$

and the length of α is

$$l(\alpha) = \int_a^b \sqrt{I_{\alpha(t)}(\alpha'(t))}\, dt.$$

The area of a region $\Delta \subset U$ is computed, as usual, by

$$\iint_U \sqrt{EG - F^2}\, du\, dv.$$

The inner product thus imposed on U determines therefore all intrinsic measures: lengths of curves, angles between vectors, areas of regions. We say that U has been equipped with a *Riemannian metric*. We can define, for such a metric, the notions of Gaussian curvature, covariant derivative, geodesic — and, under the assumption that U is oriented, that of geodesic curvature. To this end, we make use of the formulas in Chapter 4 that express such notions using E, F, G, Christoffel's symbols, and their derivatives [such as (4.8), (4.9), (4.31)].

Examples 5.6.1 **A.** Let us take $\mathbb{R}^2$ with the Riemannian metric given by

$$ds^2 = du^2 + \{2 + \cos(u + v)\}^2 \, dv^2$$

(which is a shorthand for $E \equiv 1$, $F \equiv 0$, $G(u, v) = \{2 + \cos(u + v)\}^2$). Using formula (4.38) in Section 4.6, we find that the Gaussian curvature of this metric is

$$K(u, v) = \frac{\cos(u + v)}{\{2 + \cos(u + v)\}} .$$

B. Let us consider, also in $\mathbb{R}^2$, the metric

$$ds^2 = \frac{1}{1 + (u^2 + v^2)^2} \, (du^2 + dv^2).$$

This is a conformal metric, in the sense that angles are measured as usual in $\mathbb{R}^2$, since $F \equiv 0$ and $E = G$. Another particularity is that with this metric $\mathbb{R}^2$ has finite area and is not a complete surface (the proof of this statement is Exercise 136).   □

An *abstract surface* (of class C^∞) is a **connected** topological space S equipped with an *atlas* $\mathcal{A} = ((U_\alpha, \Phi_\alpha))_{\alpha \in \mathcal{I}}$ such that:

- every U_α is an open subset of $\mathbb{R}^2$, $\Phi_\alpha(U_\alpha)$ is an open subset of S, and
  $S = \bigcup_{\alpha \in \mathcal{I}} \Phi_\alpha(U_\alpha)$;
- $\Phi_\alpha : U_\alpha \to S$ is a homeomorphism onto its image;
- if $\Phi_\alpha(U_\alpha) \cap \Phi_\beta(U_\beta) = V \neq \emptyset$ then $\Phi_\beta^{-1} \circ \Phi_\alpha : \Phi_\alpha^{-1}(V) \to \Phi_\beta^{-1}(V)$ is C^∞.

To avoid pathologies (see the appendix to volume I of [25] for a catalogue of them) we further impose certain conditions on the topology of the surface S, namely: any two distinct points of S have disjoint open neighborhoods (S is *Hausdorff*) and there exists a subset of S which is dense and countable (S is *separable*).

By Proposition 2.2.1, and since the mentioned topological requirements are satisfied by any subset of $\mathbb{R}^n$, any regular connected surface of $\mathbb{R}^3$ is an abstract surface. What we have done was to require the coordinate changes on S to be C^∞-diffeomorphisms, which allows us to define all sorts of notions using local coordinates. Note that a surface does not determine an atlas uniquely: we can add to or take away from a given atlas a few mappings, and as long as the remaining ones still cover S and coordinate changes remain C^∞, we obtain several different atlases;

what matters is that they all define the same differentiable structure on S, and thus the same abstract surface.

Given an abstract surface S, it is not easy, now that we have no ambient space, to define a tangent space $T_p S$. Our approach, instead of defining it, is to explain how to work with it in local coordinates. So if we have a curve that in local coordinates is written $\alpha(t) = \Phi(u(t), v(t))$, we would still like it to be

$$\alpha'(t) = u'(t)\Phi_u + v'(t)\Phi_v \tag{5.26}$$

— whatever the meaning of the vectors Φ_u and Φ_v. If we use other coordinates $\Psi(\widetilde{u}, \widetilde{v})$, we should have

$$\Phi_u = \frac{\partial \widetilde{u}}{\partial u}\Psi_{\widetilde{u}} + \frac{\partial \widetilde{v}}{\partial u}\Psi_{\widetilde{v}},$$

$$\Phi_v = \frac{\partial \widetilde{u}}{\partial v}\Psi_{\widetilde{u}} + \frac{\partial \widetilde{v}}{\partial v}\Psi_{\widetilde{v}};$$

and, replacing in (5.26), we obtain

$$\alpha'(t) = \left(\frac{\partial \widetilde{u}}{\partial u}u'(t) + \frac{\partial \widetilde{u}}{\partial v}v'(t)\right)\Psi_{\widetilde{u}} + \left(\frac{\partial \widetilde{v}}{\partial u}u'(t) + \frac{\partial \widetilde{v}}{\partial v}v'(t)\right)\Psi_{\widetilde{v}}$$

$$= \widetilde{u}'(t)\Psi_{\widetilde{u}} + \widetilde{v}'(t)\Psi_{\widetilde{v}}$$

— which shows that (5.26) is compatible with the change of coordinates. Hence for us the tangent space to S at the point $\Phi(u, v)$ is simply the space generated by the two independent vectors Φ_u and Φ_v. The transition matrix from the basis $(\Psi_{\widetilde{u}}, \Psi_{\widetilde{v}})$ to (Φ_u, Φ_v) is the Jacobian of $\Psi^{-1} \circ \Phi$.

A *Riemannian metric* on an abstract surface S is given by an inner product $\langle \cdot, \cdot \rangle_p$ in the tangent space $T_p S$ for every $p \in S$. In local coordinates $\Phi(u, v)$, the matrix of this inner product with respect to the basis (Φ_u, Φ_v) is $\begin{bmatrix} E & F \\ F & G \end{bmatrix}$, and we usually require that E, F, G are C^∞ functions; the coefficients $\widetilde{E}, \widetilde{F}, \widetilde{G}$ of other coordinates $\Psi(\widetilde{u}, \widetilde{v})$ are obtained from these by the relation

$$\begin{bmatrix} \widetilde{E} & \widetilde{F} \\ \widetilde{F} & \widetilde{G} \end{bmatrix} = \{J(\Phi^{-1} \circ \Psi)\}^\top \begin{bmatrix} E & F \\ F & G \end{bmatrix} J(\Phi^{-1} \circ \Psi),$$

where $\{J(\Phi^{-1} \circ \Psi)\}^\top$ denotes the transpose of $J(\Phi^{-1} \circ \Psi)$.

We can define, using the Riemannian metric $(\langle \cdot, \cdot \rangle_p)_{p \in S}$, intrinsic notions such as those of Gaussian curvature, covariant derivative, etc., using the formulas that express such concepts via the coefficients E, F, G and the Christoffel symbols Γ_{ij}^k. Of course, we should now check that the definitions do not depend on the coordinates used (which was previously unnecessary since such concepts had been defined without any use of local coordinates), but we just assure the reader that such a check is possible; for details, see [13].

Examples 5.6.2 **A.** Let us consider the equivalence relation on $\mathbb{R}^2$ given by

$$(u, v) \sim (\tilde{u}, \tilde{v})$$

if and only if both differences $u - \tilde{u}$ and $v - \tilde{v}$ are integers, and let $[u, v]$ denote the equivalence class of the pair (u, v). Let $\mathbb{R}^2/\sim$ be the set of equivalence classes and $\Pi : \mathbb{R}^2 \rightarrow \mathbb{R}^2/\sim$ the *quotient mapping*, given by $\Pi(u, v) = [u, v]$. We define a topology on $\mathbb{R}^2/\sim$ by $U \subseteq \mathbb{R}^2/\sim$ being open if and only if $\Pi^{-1}(U)$ is an open subset of $\mathbb{R}^2$. Thus $\mathbb{R}^2/\sim$ is a surface, since a restriction of Π to all squares of the form $]u_0, u_0 + 1[\times]v_0, v_0 + 1[$ constitutes an atlas of $\mathbb{R}^2/\sim$.

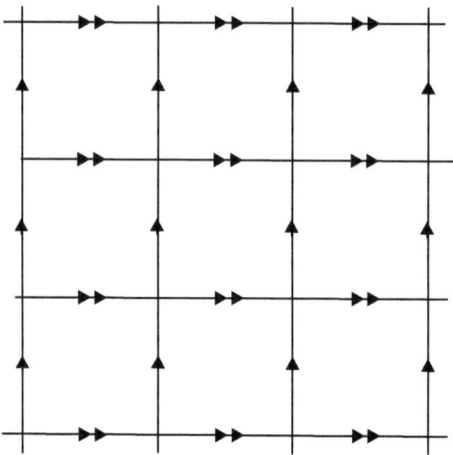

Figure 5.6

It is not difficult to verify that $\mathbb{R}^2/\sim$ is diffeomorphic to the torus $\mathbb{T}^2$. The mapping Π induces a Riemannian metric on $\mathbb{R}^2/\sim$, for which Π_u, Π_v constitute an orthonormal basis of $T_{[u,v]}(\mathbb{R}^2/\sim)$ ($E \equiv G \equiv 1$, $F \equiv 0$). This is the only metric such that $\Pi : \mathbb{R}^2 \rightarrow \mathbb{R}^2/\sim$ is a local isometry, and therefore $\mathbb{R}^2/\sim$ is a surface with zero constant curvature, commonly called a *flat torus*. In fact Π is an isometric covering.

We suggest as an exercise to show that the equivalence relation

$$(u, v) \simeq (\tilde{u}, \tilde{v}) \quad \Leftrightarrow \quad \exists n \in \mathbb{Z} : \tilde{u} = u + n \text{ and } \tilde{v} = (-1)^n v$$

defines a surface of zero curvature diffeomorphic to the Möbius strip.

B. Let us define a complete, simply connected surface of constant curvature equal to -1. This surface, which we denote by $\mathbb{D}$ (*hyperbolic plane*), is by Theorem 5.3.3 diffeomorphic to the plane, and it suffices therefore to find a Riemannian metric on $\mathbb{R}^2$ of curvature -1. But this is easy if we use polar coordinates and recall the formulas given at the end of Section 4.6. Then the coefficients of the parameterization $\Phi(\rho, \varphi) = (\rho \cos \varphi, \rho \sin \varphi)$ become

$$E \equiv 1, \qquad F \equiv 0, \qquad G \equiv \sinh^2 \rho \qquad\qquad (5.27)$$

— and we can take the coefficients of this metric in Cartesian coordinates. However, this is not the best model of $\mathbb{D}$, because the metric defined this way is not conformal. Let U be the open disk with radius λ $(0 < \lambda \leq +\infty)$ centered at the origin, and $f: [0, \lambda[\to [0, +\infty[$ a differentiable, strictly monotone function such that $f(0) = 0$, and consider the mapping $\Psi: U \to \mathbb{R}^2$ which transforms the polar coordinate point (ρ, φ) into the coordinate point $(f(\rho), \varphi)$. We want to find f so that the Riemannian metric induced by Ψ on U, from the metric defined by (5.27) on $\mathbb{R}^2$, is conformal. If p has coordinates (ρ, φ) then, letting $\mathbf{v}_\varphi = (\cos \varphi, \sin \varphi)$ and $\mathbf{w}_\varphi = (-\sin \varphi, \cos \varphi)$, we have

$$D\Psi_p(\mathbf{v}_\varphi) = f'(\rho)\mathbf{v}_\varphi, \quad D\Psi_p(\mathbf{w}_\varphi) = \frac{f(\rho)}{\rho}\mathbf{w}_\varphi \tag{5.28}$$

— by which we obtain

$$\langle \mathbf{v}_\varphi, \mathbf{v}_\varphi \rangle_p = [f'(\rho)]^2,$$

$$\langle \mathbf{v}_\varphi, \mathbf{w}_\varphi \rangle_p = 0, \tag{5.29}$$

$$\langle \mathbf{w}_\varphi, \mathbf{w}_\varphi \rangle_p = \frac{G(f(\rho), \varphi)}{\rho^2} = \frac{\sinh^2(f(\rho))}{\rho^2}.$$

For the metric (5.29) to be conformal, necessarily

$$f'(\rho) = \frac{\sinh(f(\rho))}{\rho}.$$

The general solution of this equation is $f(\rho) = 2\text{tgh}^{-1}(c\rho)$, where c is a real constant, and is defined for $\rho \in [0, \frac{1}{|c|}[$. We take $c = 1$, so that $\lambda = 1$ and U is the unit disk. In this case $f'(\rho) = \frac{2}{1-\rho^2}$, and therefore (5.29) defines in Cartesian coordinates the metric

$$ds^2 = \frac{4}{\{1 - (u^2 + v^2)\}^2}(du^2 + dv^2). \tag{5.30}$$

From now on, let $\mathbb{D}$ denote the disk $u^2 + v^2 < 1$ (or the disk $|z| < 1$ in the complex plane $\mathbb{C}$) equipped with the Riemannian metric (5.30). $\mathbb{D}$ is usually called *Poincaré's disk*. We next give some of its properties:

(1) $\mathbb{D}$ *has constant curvature equal to* -1. We verify this using formula (4.31) in Section 4.5. To obtain a surface of constant curvature $K < 0$, we would take, on the same disk, the metric

$$ds^2 = \frac{4}{|K|(1 - (u^2 + v^2))^2}(du^2 + dv^2).$$

(2) *The diameters of* $\mathbb{D}$ *are geodesic*. This can be seen by checking that its geodesic curvature is zero, but we prefer to show that the diameters are minimizing curves. Indeed, if $\alpha(t) = (u(t), v(t))$ is a curve from $\alpha(0) = (0, 0)$ to $\alpha(1) = (u_1, 0)$ $(u_1 > 0)$ then

$$l(\alpha) = \int_0^1 \sqrt{I_{\alpha(t)}(\alpha'(t))}\, dt = \int_0^1 \frac{2\sqrt{u'(t)^2 + v'(t)^2}}{1 - [u(t)^2 + v(t)^2]}\, dt \qquad (5.31)$$

$$\geq \int_0^1 \frac{2|u'(t)|}{1 - u(t)^2}\, dt \geq \int_0^1 \frac{2u'(t)}{1 - u(t)^2}\, dt = \log\left(\frac{1 + u_1}{1 - u_1}\right),$$

and equality holds if and only if $v(t) = 0$ and $u'(t) \geq 0$ for all $t \in [0, 1]$ — i.e., if and only if the trace of α is the line segment $[0, u_1] \times \{0\}$, which is therefore a minimizing curve. The diameter $]-1, 1[\times \{0\}$ is thus a geodesic of $\mathbb{D}$. Since rotations around the origin are isometries of $\mathbb{D}$, all other diameters are also geodesics.

It follows from (5.31) that geodesics starting from the origin have infinite length, and therefore (see Exercise 119) $\mathbb{D}$ is complete. Furthermore, the intrinsic distance between 0 and $z \in \mathbb{D}$ is

$$d_{\mathbb{D}}(0, z) = \log\left(\frac{1 + |z|}{1 - |z|}\right).$$

(3) Let $a, b \in \mathbb{C}$ be such that $|a| > |b|$, and consider the mapping

$$h_{a,b}(z) = \frac{az + \overline{b}}{bz + \overline{a}}.$$

The reader may check that $h_{a,b}$ sends $\mathbb{D}$ bijectively onto itself. More remarkable is that $h_{a,b}$ is an isometry of $\mathbb{D}$. Indeed, for $z \in \mathbb{D}$ and $w \in \mathbb{C}$, we have (abbreviating $h_{a,b}$ to h)

$$I_{h(z)}(Dh_z(w)) = I_z(w) \Leftrightarrow I_{h(z)}(h'(z)w) = I_z(w)$$

$$\Leftrightarrow \frac{4|h'(z)|^2}{(1 - |h(z)|^2)^2}|w|^2 = \frac{4}{(1 - |z|^2)^2}|w|^2 \qquad (5.32)$$

$$\Leftrightarrow |h'(z)| = \frac{1 - |h(z)|^2}{1 - |z|^2}.$$

Checking this last equality is a simple calculation.

Using Proposition 5.7.3 of the next section, we can show that all isometries of $\mathbb{D}$ that preserve orientation are of this form (one obtains the rotations by letting $b = 0$), and those that reverse it are the conjugates of these $\left(z \mapsto \dfrac{\overline{a}\,\overline{z} + b}{\overline{b}\,\overline{z} + a}\, , \text{ with } |a| > |b|\right)$.

Now given $z_0 \in \mathbb{D}$,

$$h(z) = \frac{z - z_0}{1 - \overline{z_0}z}$$

is an isometry that maps z_0 to 0, which allows us to deduce a formula for the distance between z_0 and another point $z_1 \in \mathbb{D}$:

$$d_{\mathbb{D}}(z_0, z_1) = d_{\mathbb{D}}(h(z_0), h(z_1)) = d_{\mathbb{D}}\left(0, \frac{z_1 - z_0}{1 - \overline{z_0}z_1}\right)$$

$$= \log\left(\frac{|1 - \overline{z_0}z_1| + |z_1 - z_0|}{|1 - \overline{z_0}z_1| - |z_1 - z_0|}\right). \tag{5.33}$$

(4) Mappings of the type

$$z \mapsto \frac{az + b}{cz + d},$$

where a, b, c, d are complex numbers such that $ad - bc \neq 0$, are called *Möbius transformations*, and are bijections of $\mathbb{C} \cup \{\infty\}$ (the Riemann sphere) onto itself. We can assume that $ad - bc = 1$, since if we multiply each of the numbers a, b, c, d by the same nonzero factor the transformation does not change.

Möbius transformations form a group $\mathfrak{M}$ with respect to the composition of functions; if to each matrix $M = \begin{bmatrix} a & b \\ c & d \end{bmatrix}$ with $ad - bc = 1$ we attach

$$f_M(z) = \frac{az + b}{cz + d},$$

we have $f_{M_1 M_2} = f_{M_1} \circ f_{M_2}$. We hence obtain a group homomorphism $\mathrm{Sl}(2, \mathbb{C}) \to \mathfrak{M}$ (where $\mathrm{Sl}(2, \mathbb{C})$ is the multiplicative group of the complex 2×2 matrices with determinant equal to 1).

We are now interested in the geometric properties of these transformations. Writing

$$\frac{az + b}{cz + d} = \frac{a}{c} + \frac{b - \frac{ad}{c}}{c\left(z + \frac{d}{c}\right)} \quad (\text{if } c \neq 0), \qquad \frac{az + b}{d} = \frac{a}{d}z + \frac{b}{d},$$

we recognize that any Möbius transformation is written as a composition of:

- translations $\quad z \mapsto z + \zeta \quad (\zeta \in \mathbb{C})$

- rotations $\quad z \mapsto e^{i\theta}z \quad (\theta \in [0, 2\pi])$

- homotheties $\quad z \mapsto \lambda z \quad (\lambda \in \,]0, +\infty[\,)$

- inversions $\quad z \mapsto \dfrac{1}{z}$

Transformations of the first three types have known properties: in particular, they transform straight lines into straight lines and circles into circles. Regarding the inversions, we have the following:

- *if r is a line passing through 0, its inverse is still a line. If r does not pass through 0, its inverse is a circle passing through 0;*
- *the inverse of a circle C is a straight line if $0 \in C$, otherwise it is also a circle.*

In fact, the inverse of $u + iv$ is the point $\tilde{u} + i\tilde{v}$ given by

$$\widetilde{u} = \frac{u}{u^2 + v^2}, \qquad \widetilde{v} = \frac{-v}{u^2 + v^2}.$$

If r is the line given by the equation $\alpha u + \beta v + \gamma = 0$ then, for $u + iv \in r$, we have

$$\alpha \widetilde{u} - \beta \widetilde{v} + \gamma(\widetilde{u}^2 + \widetilde{v}^2) = \frac{\alpha u + \beta v + \gamma}{u^2 + v^2} = 0$$

— which shows that $f(r)$ is a straight line if $\gamma = 0$, and is a circle otherwise. The second statement allows for an analogous verification.

We thus conclude that any Möbius transformation preserves the family of lines and circles in the plane. Moreover, every $f \in \mathfrak{M}$ is a conformal mapping and therefore keeps the orthogonality relation between two curves. Returning to the hyperbolic plane $\mathbb{D}$, the geodesics passing through a point $z_0 \neq 0$ are, in particular, images of the geodesics passing through 0 (which are line segments and intersect $\mathbf{S}^1$ orthogonally) by elements of $\mathfrak{M}$ which fix $\mathbf{S}^1$. Hence, *every geodesic of $\mathbb{D}$ is either a diameter of $\mathbf{S}^1$ or an arc of some circumference that intersects $\mathbf{S}^1$ orthogonally* (see Fig. 5.7).

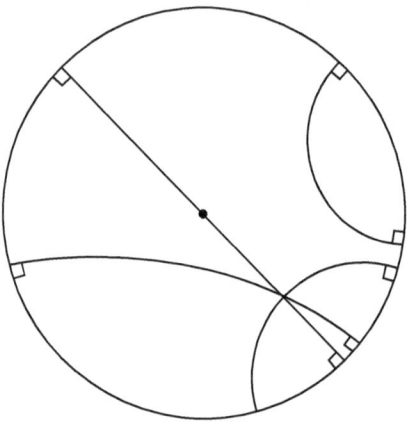

Figure 5.7

(5) If "lines" mean geodesics, Poincaré's disc provides a model of the non-Euclidean geometry of Lobachevski and Bolyai. In this geometry all the axioms of Euclidean geometry are valid, except the axiom of parallels: in $\mathbb{D}$, through a point outside a "line" r, pass infinitely many "lines" that do not intersect r — and not only one, as in the Euclidean case.

Exercises

136. Show that $\mathbb{R}^2$, with the metric of example 5.6.1.B, has finite area and is not complete.

In the remaining exercises in this section we work with the hyperbolic plane $\mathbb{D}$.

137. Consider two geodesics $\gamma_1(s)$ and $\gamma_2(s)$ which, at time $s = 0$, start from $z_0 \in \mathbb{D}$ in directions that make an angle θ with each other. Show that

$$\delta(\theta) = \lim_{s \to +\infty} \{d_{\mathbb{D}}(\gamma_1(s), \gamma_2(s)) - 2s\}$$

exists.

138. Check that for all $z_0, z_1 \in \mathbb{D}$, the set $\{z \in \mathbb{D}: d_{\mathbb{D}}(z, z_0) = d_{\mathbb{D}}(z, z_1)\}$ is a geodesic.

139. (a) Show that the hyperbolic circle $\mathbb{S}(z_0; r) = \{z \in \mathbb{D}: d_{\mathbb{D}}(z, z_0) = r\}$ is also a Euclidean circle.

(b) Check that any equilateral triangle in $\mathbb{D}$ (geodesic triangle with all sides equal) can be inscribed into a hyperbolic circle, but that this is no longer true for every geodesic triangle.

140. (a) Check that $g(z) = -\frac{i}{2} + \frac{1}{z-i}$ sends $\mathbb{D}$ into the half-plane $\{z \in \mathbb{C}: \Im m(z) > 0\}$.

(b) Let $\mathbb{H}$ be the half-plane $\{z \in \mathbb{C}: \Im m(z) > 0\}$ with the metric given by $E = G = 1/\Im m(z)^2$ and $F \equiv 0$. Show that g is an isometry of $\mathbb{D}$ on $\mathbb{H}$.

(c) Show that the geodesics of $\mathbb{H}$ are the vertical semicircles $\Re e(z) = $ constant and the half circumferences with center on the axis $\Im m(z) = 0$.

(d) Show that the isometries of $\mathbb{H}$ that preserve orientation are the functions

$$z \mapsto \frac{az + b}{cz + d},$$

where a, b, c, d are **real** numbers such that $ad - bc = 1$ (you can use Proposition 5.7.3 of the next section).

(e) Denote by $\Im(\mathbb{D})$ and $\Im(\mathbb{H})$ the groups of the isometries of $\mathbb{D}$ and $\mathbb{H}$ that preserve orientation. Note that $\Im(\mathbb{H}) = g \circ \Im(\mathbb{D}) \circ g^{-1}$, and therefore $\Im(\mathbb{D})$ and $\Im(\mathbb{H})$ are *conjugate* subgroups of the group $\mathfrak{M}$ of Möbius transformations.

141. Check that $M = \begin{bmatrix} a & b \\ c & d \end{bmatrix} \mapsto f_M(z) = \dfrac{az + b}{cz + d}$ is a homomorphism of $\mathrm{Sl}(2, \mathbb{C})$ on $\mathfrak{M}$, and that the kernel of this homomorphism is $\{I, -I\}$. Conclude that $f_M = f_N$ if and only if $M = \pm N$.

142. Two elements $f, g \in \mathfrak{M}$ are *conjugate* if there exists $h \in \mathfrak{M}$ such that $f = h \circ g \circ h^{-1}$.

(a) Given $f \in \mathfrak{M}$, define $\tau(f) = |\text{trace}(M)|$ if $f = f_M$ for $M \in \mathrm{Sl}(2, \mathbb{C})$. Show that if $f, g \neq \text{id}$ then f and g are conjugate if and only if $\tau(f) = \tau(g)$.

(b) Let $\Gamma = \Im(\mathbb{D})$ or $\Gamma = \Im(\mathbb{H})$. Show that if $f, g \in \Gamma$ are conjugate by an element of $\mathfrak{M}$, then they are conjugate by some element of Γ.

143. Denote by Γ the group $\Im(\mathbb{D})$ or $\Im(\mathbb{H})$, and let $f \in \Gamma$. Show that:

(a) if $\tau(f) > 2$ then f is conjugate to $z \mapsto \lambda z$ in $\mathbb{H}$, where $\lambda > 0$ satisfies $\tau(f) = \sqrt{\lambda} + \frac{1}{\sqrt{\lambda}}$;

(b) if $\tau(f) = 2$ and $f \neq \text{id}$ then h is conjugate to $z \mapsto z + 1$ in $\mathbb{H}$;

(c) if $\tau(f) < 2$ then f is conjugate to $z \mapsto e^{i\theta} z$ on $\mathbb{D}$, where $2\cos\left(\frac{\theta}{2}\right) = \tau(f)$.

Note: $f \neq \text{id}$ is called *hyperbolic, parabolic* or *elliptic* according to whether a), b) or c) of Ex. 143 holds.

144. Let $f \in \Im(\mathbb{D}) \setminus \mathrm{id}$. Show that:

(a) $\inf\limits_{z \in \mathbb{D}} d_{\mathbb{D}}(f(z), z) > 0$ if and only if f is hyperbolic.

(b) there exists z_0 such that $d_{\mathbb{D}}(f(z_0), z_0) = \inf\limits_{z \in \mathbb{D}} d_{\mathbb{D}}(f(z), z)$ if and only if f is elliptic or hyperbolic.

5.7 Complete Surfaces of Constant Curvature

In this section we will study the isometry groups of the complete and simply connected surfaces of constant curvature, and show that the other complete surfaces of equal curvature are obtained from these as quotients by a certain subgroup of the isometry group. This approach allows us to describe all complete surfaces of non-negative constant curvature.

We begin with a lemma that will be applied repeatedly:

Lemma 5.7.1 *Let* $f, g: S_1 \to S_2$ *be local isometries such that for a certain* $p \in S_1$ *we have* $f(p) = g(p)$ *and* $Df_p = Dg_p$. *Then* $f = g$.

Proof Given $\mathbf{v} \in T_p S_1$, let us consider the geodesic $\gamma(t) = \exp_p(t\mathbf{v})$. Then $f \circ \gamma$ and $g \circ \gamma$ are parametrized geodesics with the same initial conditions, since $f \circ \gamma(0) = g \circ \gamma(0) = f(p)$ and $(f \circ \gamma)'(0) = Df_p(\mathbf{v}) = Dg_p(\mathbf{v}) = (g \circ \gamma)'(0)$ — and therefore $f \circ \gamma(t) = g \circ \gamma(t)$ whenever $\gamma(t)$ is defined. We thus conclude that $f \circ \exp_p = g \circ \exp_p$, which implies that f and g coincide in a neighborhood of p. This shows that the set $U = \{q \in S_1 : f(q) = g(q), Df_q = Dg_q\}$ is non-empty and open. But its definition ensures that U is also closed, and therefore, S_1 being connected, $U = S_1$. □

We denote by S_K the complete, simply connected surface of constant curvature K. S_K is thus the sphere with radius $\frac{1}{\sqrt{K}}$ (if $K > 0$), the Euclidean plane (if $K = 0$), or the hyperbolic plane of curvature K (if $K < 0$). We can then rewrite Theorem 5.3.4 as follows:

Theorem 5.7.2 *Let* S *be a complete surface of constant curvature* K. *Then there exists an isometric covering* $f: S_K \to S$.

Proof The case $K \leq 0$ was treated in Theorem 5.3.4. Only the case $K > 0$ is left. Given $p \in S_K$, the mapping $\exp_p$ sends the disk $B_{\pi/\sqrt{K}}(p)$ diffeomorphically into $S_K \setminus \{-p\}$. Thus, if q is a point of S and $L: T_p S_K \to T_q S$ a linear isometry, the mapping $g: S_K \setminus \{-p\} \to S$ defined by $g = \exp_q \circ L \circ \exp_p^{-1}$ is a local isometry. Let us now take $\widetilde{p} \in S_K \setminus \{p, -p\}$, and let $\widetilde{q} = g(\widetilde{p})$, $\widetilde{L} = Dg_{\widetilde{p}}$ and $h: S_K \setminus \{-\widetilde{p}\} \to S$ be the mapping given by $h = \exp_{\widetilde{q}} \circ \widetilde{L} \circ \exp_{\widetilde{p}}^{-1}$. The mapping h is also a local isometry, and furthermore $g(\widetilde{p}) = h(\widetilde{p})$ and $Dg_{\widetilde{p}} = Dh_{\widetilde{p}}$. By Lemma 5.7.1, g and h coincide on the intersection of their domains, and we can thus define a local isometry $f: S_K \to S$ by $f(r) = g(r)$ if $r \neq -p$, and $f(r) = h(r)$ if $r \neq -\widetilde{p}$. Since S_K is compact, by Proposition 5.2.2 this local isometry is a covering. □

The following result is a consequence of Lemma 5.7.1 and the proofs of Theorems 5.3.4 and 5.7.2.

Proposition 5.7.3 *Given $p, q \in S_k$ and a linear isometry $L: T_p S_K \to T_q S_K$, there exists one and only one isometry $f: S_K \to S_K$ such that $f(p) = q$ and $D f_p = L$.*

Since the composite and inverse of isometries are still isometries, the set of isometries of a given surface forms a group. By the above proposition, the group of isometries of S_K, which we denote by $\mathfrak{I}_K$, is exceptionally large.

Let us now assume that $f: S_K \to S$ is an isometric covering. Given $q \in S$, let p_0 and p_1 be two of the preimages of q, and L_i $(i = 0, 1)$ the linear isometry $D f_{p_i}: T_{p_i} S_K \to T_q S$. By Proposition 5.7.3, there exists an isometry $g: S_K \to S_K$ such that $g(p_0) = p_1$ and $D g_{p_0} = L_1^{-1} \circ L_0$. Now $f \circ g: S_K \to S$ is a local isometry such that

$$f \circ g(p_0) = q = f(p_0),$$
$$D(f \circ g)_{p_0} = D f_{p_1} \circ D g_{p_0} = L_1 \circ (L_1^{-1} \circ L_0) = D f_{p_0}$$

— it follows, by Lemma 5.7.1, that $f \circ g = g$.

It is easily checked that the set $\mathfrak{I}_K(f) = \{g \in \mathfrak{I}_K : f \circ g = f\}$ is a subgroup of $\mathfrak{I}_K$; we call it the *covering group* of f.

Proposition 5.7.4 *For every $q \in S$, the group $\mathfrak{I}_K(f)$ acts transitively on $f^{-1}(\{q\})$ — that is, for every pair of points $p_0, p_1 \in f^{-1}(\{q\})$ there exists one and only one $g \in \mathfrak{I}_K(f)$ such that $g(p_0) = p_1$.*

The action of $\mathfrak{I}_K(f)$ on S_K is discontinuous. This means that every point p of S_K has an open neighborhood V such that $g(V) \cap V$ is empty for all $g \in \mathfrak{I}_K(f) \setminus \{\mathrm{id}\}$.

The first statement (apart from the uniqueness of g, which is easy) has already been proved. Regarding the second, let us take an evenly covered neighborhood U of $f(p)$ and let V be the component of $f^{-1}(U)$ that contains p. If $g \in \mathfrak{I}_K(f) \setminus \{\mathrm{id}\}$ and $q \in V$ then $q \neq g(q)$, since the identity is the only element of $\mathfrak{I}_K(f)$ with some fixed point. Since $f(q) = f(g(q))$, necessarily $g(q) \notin V$. Thus $g(V) \cap V = \varnothing$, which proves the statement.

It deserves mention that what we call *discontinuous action* is called *proper discontinuous action* by most authors, who reserve the former name for a weaker condition, of which we will make no use. We further say that a subgroup Γ of $\mathfrak{I}_K$ is *discrete* if its action on S_K is discontinuous (this terminology is also not the usual one).

The covering group completely determines the surface in the following sense: if we have two isometric coverings $f_i: S_K \to S_i$ $(i = 1, 2)$ such that $\mathfrak{I}_K(f_1) = \mathfrak{I}_K(f_2)$ then S_1 and S_2 are isometric. We can further ask which subgroups of $\mathfrak{I}_K$ are covering groups. The answer is simple:

Proposition 5.7.5 *A subgroup Γ of $\mathfrak{I}_K$ is a covering group if and only if it is discrete.*

Proof It remains to prove that such a subgroup is a covering group. We note that the action of Γ on S_K induces an equivalence relation whose classes are $[p] = \{g(p) : g \in \Gamma\}$. Let S_K/Γ be the set of equivalence classes and let $\Pi : S_K \to S_K/\Gamma$ be the quotient mapping. Given $p \in S$, let (U, Φ) be a parameterization in a neighborhood of p such that $g(\Phi(u)) \cap \Phi(U) = \varnothing$ for all $g \in \Gamma \setminus \{\text{id}\}$, and let us put $\Psi = \Pi \circ \Phi$: the set of mappings Ψ so defined constitutes an atlas of S_K/Γ, which is therefore a surface; moreover, $\Psi(U)$ is an evenly covered neighborhood of $[p]$, which shows that Π is a covering. With the Riemannian metric induced by Π on S_K/Γ the mapping Π is an isometric covering whose covering group is obviously Γ.
□

Consider, for example, the case of the sphere S_K given by the equation $x^2 + y^2 + z^2 = \frac{1}{K}$ $(K > 0)$. The isometries of S_K are the restrictions of the linear isometries of $\mathbb{R}^3$, and correspond to the orthogonal 3×3 matrices over $\mathbb{R}$ — the group of which is denoted by $O(3, \mathbb{R})$. An example of a discrete subgroup of $O(3, \mathbb{R})$ is $\{-I, I\}$, where I is the identity matrix. The surface $S_K/\{-I, I\}$ is called the *projective plane*, and is the surface obtained by identifying in S_K the pairs of diametrically opposed points. The projective plane is non-orientable, and in fact contains a Möbius strip (see Fig. 5.8)

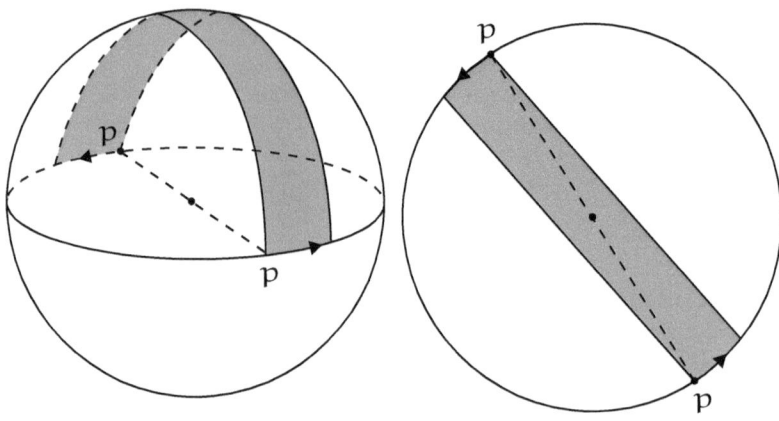

Figure 5.8

More generally, we have the following result (the proof of which is Exercise 145 of this section):

Proposition 5.7.6 *Let Γ be a discrete subgroup of $\Im_K$. Then S_K/Γ is orientable if and only if every isometry $g \in \Gamma$ preserves the orientation of S_K.*

We can now describe all complete surfaces of constant positive curvature.

Theorem 5.7.7 *The only complete surfaces of constant curvature $K > 0$ are, up to isometry, the sphere and the projective plane.*

Proof In view of Proposition 5.7.5, it suffices to show that the only discrete subgroups of $\mathfrak{I}_K \simeq O(3,\mathbb{R})$ are $\{I,-I\}$ and the trivial group $\{I\}$. Let Γ be such a subgroup: given $A \in \Gamma$, the isometry A has some real eigenvalue λ, which is necessarily 1 or -1. If $\lambda = 1$, then A has some fixed point in S_K, which implies that $A = I$. If $\lambda = -1$ then A^2 has the eigenvalue $\lambda^2 = 1$ and therefore $A^2 = I$. The eigenvalues of A are thus all equal to 1 or -1; but none of them can be 1, and therefore $A = -I$. We thus have $\Gamma = \{I\}$ or $\Gamma = \{I,-I\}$.   □

In example 5.6.2.A we described the torus as the quotient of $\mathbb{R}^2$ by the group Γ of the translations $T(\mathbf{v})$ associated with vectors $\mathbf{v}$ of integer coordinates. Γ is generated by the two independent translations $T(1,0)$ and $T(0,1)$; as we will see below, this is a typical situation. The square $]0,1[\times]0,1[$ is a fundamental region for Γ. In general, we say that an open subset U of S_K is a *fundamental region* for the action of a discrete subgroup Γ of $\mathfrak{I}_K$ if

- $g(U) \cap h(U) = \varnothing$ for all $g \neq h$ in Γ;
- S_K is the union of the closures of $g(U)$ for $g \in \Gamma$.

The most interesting fundamental regions are polygons, where the sides are geodesic segments. It is possible to reconstruct the surface S_K/Γ if one knows how to identify the sides of the polygon. In Fig. 5.9 we illustrate a fundamental region $\mathcal{P}$ for a certain discrete subset Γ of $\mathfrak{I}_K$ ($K < 0$): it is a regular polygon of eight sides whose sum of interior angles equals 2π; the pairs of sides to be identified are designated by the same letter.

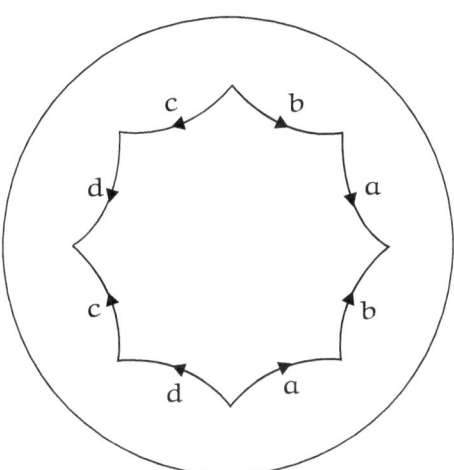

Figure 5.9

The surface S_K/Γ is, in this case, the double torus. We would obtain the n-torus, $n \geq 2$, from a regular polygon $\mathcal{P}_n$ of $4n$ sides and sum of angles equal to 2π ($n = 1$ is impossible because, by the Gauss-Bonnet theorem, the sum of the angles of any four-sided polygon in the hyperbolic plane is $< 2\pi$). A theorem of Poincaré ensures that the elements of Γ that identify the sides of $\mathcal{P}_n$ generate Γ. The interested reader can find details in [10], [2] and [3].

To conclude this section and the book, we will determine all discrete subgroups of the group $\mathfrak{I}_0$ of the isometries of $\mathbb{R}^2$ — which is equivalent, by Proposition 5.7.5, to determining all complete surfaces of constant zero curvature.

Lemma 5.7.8 *The isometries of* $\mathbb{R}^2$ *without fixed points are translations and glide reflections (reflection in an axis* r *followed by a translation in the direction of* r*). Translations preserve orientation, while glide reflections reverse it.*

Proof Every isometry of $\mathbb{R}^2$ is of the form $f(p) = L(p) + \mathbf{v}$, where L is a linear isometry and $\mathbf{v}$ a vector. If $I - L$ were an isomorphism then f would have some fixed point, and so for f to have no fixed points, L must have eigenvalue 1. Let $(\mathbf{e}_1, \mathbf{e}_2)$ be an orthonormal basis of $\mathbb{R}^2$ such that $L(\mathbf{e}_1) = \mathbf{e}_1$. Since L is an isometry, necessarily $L(\mathbf{e}_2) = \pm\mathbf{e}_2$. If $L(\mathbf{e}_2) = \mathbf{e}_2$ then L is the identity and f a translation. If $L(\mathbf{e}_2) = -\mathbf{e}_2$, then L is the reflection in the straight line generated by $\mathbf{e}_1$. Letting $\mathbf{v} = \alpha\mathbf{e}_1 + \beta\mathbf{e}_2$, we recognize that f is the composite of the reflection in the line $\lambda \mapsto \lambda\mathbf{e}_1 + \frac{\beta}{2}\mathbf{e}_2$ with the translation associated with the vector $\alpha\mathbf{e}_1$ (in particular, f has **no fixed points if and only if** $\alpha \neq 0$).

Regarding the orientation, just note that it is preserved by f if and only if it is by L.   □

Let $\Gamma \neq \{\mathrm{id}\}$ be a discrete subgroup of $\mathfrak{I}_0$. Assume first that $\mathbb{R}^2/\Gamma$ is orientable: by Proposition 5.7.6, this means that all elements of Γ preserve orientation — that is, that they are all translations. To simplify notation, we identify the translation associated with $\mathbf{v}$ with the vector $\mathbf{v}$ itself.

Since Γ is discrete, we can choose $\mathbf{v}_1 \neq 0$ in Γ such that $|\mathbf{v}_1|$ is as small as possible. Then any other $\mathbf{v} \in \Gamma$ that is collinear with $\mathbf{v}_1$ is an integer multiple of $\mathbf{v}_1$ (since, if $\mathbf{v} = \lambda\mathbf{v}_1$, then, denoting by $\lfloor \lambda \rfloor$ the integer part of λ, $\{\lambda - \lfloor \lambda \rfloor\}$ is an element of Γ with norm less than that of $\mathbf{v}_1$, and is therefore zero). If Γ contains only such vectors, it is therefore of the form

$$\Gamma = \{n\mathbf{v}_1 : n \in \mathbb{Z}\} \tag{5.34}$$

— *in which case* $\mathbb{R}^2/\Gamma$ *is a cylinder.*

If Γ contains elements that are non-collinear with $\mathbf{v}_1$, then let $\mathbf{v}_2$ be one such vector with minimal norm. Then

$$\Gamma = \{n\mathbf{v}_1 + m\mathbf{v}_2 : n, m \in \mathbb{Z}\}. \tag{5.35}$$

Indeed, given $\mathbf{v} \in \Gamma$, it belongs to some parallelogram $\mathcal{P} = \{\alpha\mathbf{v}_1 + \beta\mathbf{v}_2 : n_1 \leq \alpha \leq n_1 + 1, m_1 \leq \beta \leq m_1 + 1\}$. Denoting by $\mathbf{w}$ the vertex of $\mathcal{P}$ closest to $\mathbf{v}$ and by d the length of the longest diagonal of $\mathcal{P}$, we have

$$|\mathbf{v} - \mathbf{w}| \leq \frac{d}{2} < \frac{1}{2}\{|\mathbf{v}_1| + |\mathbf{v}_2|\} \leq |\mathbf{v}_2|$$

— which implies, by the choice of $\mathbf{v}_2$, that $\mathbf{v} - \mathbf{w}$ is collinear with $\mathbf{v}_1$, and therefore an integer multiple of $\mathbf{v}_1$. We have therefore proved equality (5.35). *If* Γ *is of this form,*

$\mathbb{R}^2/\Gamma$ *is a torus* — and a fundamental region for Γ is the parallelogram of sides $\mathbf{v}_1$ and $\mathbf{v}_2$.

Then $f \circ g(p) = L_1 \circ L_2(p) + \mathbf{w}$, where $\mathbf{w} = \mathbf{u} + L_1(\mathbf{v})$. Now $f \circ g$ **preserves** orientation and, by Lemma 5.7.8, it must be a translation. Therefore $L_1 \circ L_2$ is the identity, hence $L_2 = L_1^{-1} = L_1$. In conclusion:

there is a linear isometry L and a set $\Gamma_R \subseteq \mathbb{R}^2$ such that $\{p \mapsto L(p) + \mathbf{v} : \mathbf{v} \in \Gamma_R\}$ *is the set of the elements of Γ that reverse orientation.*

We further denote by Γ_T the set of vectors associated with the translations of Γ. Γ_T is a discrete subgroup and, from the discussion above, the only two possibilities are that Γ_T is either one-dimensional (of the form $\{n\mathbf{v}_1 : n \in \mathbb{Z}\}$) or two-dimensional (of the form $\{n\mathbf{v}_1 + m\mathbf{v}_2 : n, m \in \mathbb{Z}\}$).

Lemma 5.7.9 *If* $\mathbf{u}, \mathbf{v} \in \Gamma_R$ *and* $\mathbf{w} \in \Gamma_T$, *then:*

(i) $\mathbf{u} + L(\mathbf{v}) \in \Gamma_T$;
(ii) $-L(\mathbf{v}) \in \Gamma_R$;
(iii) $\mathbf{u} - \mathbf{v} \in \Gamma_T$;
(iv) $\mathbf{v} + \mathbf{w} \in \Gamma_R$;
(v) $L(\mathbf{w}) \in \Gamma_T$.

Proof The composite of $f(p) = L(p) + \mathbf{u}$ with $g(p) = L(p) + \mathbf{v}$ is given by $f \circ g(p) = p + \{\mathbf{u} + L(\mathbf{v})\}$, which proves (i). Regarding (ii), we observe that the inverse of $p \mapsto L(p) + \mathbf{v}$ is $p \mapsto L(p) - L(\mathbf{v})$. For (iii), we write $\mathbf{u} - \mathbf{v} = \mathbf{u} + L(-L(\mathbf{v}))$ and apply (i) and (ii). The composite of $h(p) = p + \mathbf{w}$ with $g(p) = L(p) + \mathbf{v}$ is $h \circ g(p) = L(p) + (\mathbf{v} + \mathbf{w})$, which proves (iv). Finally, we have $L(\mathbf{w}) = -L(\mathbf{v}) + L(\mathbf{v} + \mathbf{w})$ — and since, by (ii) and (iv), we have $-L(\mathbf{v}), \mathbf{v} + \mathbf{w} \in \Gamma_R$, it follows by (i) that $L(\mathbf{w}) \in \Gamma_T$, which proves (v).   □

Statement (v) says that $L(\Gamma_T) \subseteq \Gamma_T$. Applying L to both sides, we obtain the opposite inclusion $\Gamma_T \subseteq L(\Gamma_T)$; *we thus conclude that Γ_T is invariant under L.* Moreover, (iii) and (iv) say that Γ_R is the result of a translation on Γ_T: *for all* $\mathbf{v} \in \Gamma_R$ *we have* $\Gamma_R = \{\mathbf{v}\} + \Gamma_T$. This means that to obtain all the glide reflections of Γ, we just need to compose one of these transformations with each of the translations of Γ.

Let $(\mathbf{e}_1, \mathbf{v}_2)$ be an orthonormal basis of $\mathbb{R}^2$ such that $L(\mathbf{e}_1) = \mathbf{e}_1$, $L(\mathbf{e}_2) = -\mathbf{e}_2$. An important observation, contained in the proof of Lemma 5.7.8, is that if $\alpha \mathbf{e}_1 + \beta \mathbf{e}_2 \in \Gamma_R$ then $\alpha \neq 0$. With these remarks in mind, let us now look at the forms that the group Γ can take.

If Γ_T is of the form $\{n\mathbf{v}_1 : n \in \mathbb{Z}\}$, then $\mathbf{v}_1$ is an eigenvector of L, which is collinear with $\mathbf{e}_1$ or with $\mathbf{e}_2$. Take $\mathbf{v} = \alpha \mathbf{e}_1 + \beta \mathbf{e}_2 \in \Gamma_R$: then $\alpha \neq 0$ and, by (i), $2\alpha \mathbf{e}_1 = \mathbf{v} + L(\mathbf{v})$ belongs to Γ_T. We thus have $\mathbf{v}_1 = \lambda \mathbf{e}_1$, where we suppose $\lambda > 0$. Adding to $\mathbf{v}$, if necessary, an integer multiple of $\mathbf{v}_1$, we can assume that $0 < \alpha < \lambda$. Since $2\alpha \mathbf{e}_1$ is an integer multiple of $\mathbf{v}_1$, it follows that $\lambda = 2\alpha$ and $\mathbf{v}_1 = \mathbf{v} + L(\mathbf{v})$, which means that the translation associated with $\mathbf{v}_1$ is the composite of $f(p) = L(p) + \mathbf{v}$ with itself. Since $\Gamma_R = \{\mathbf{v}\} + \Gamma_T$, we conclude that Γ is the cyclic group generated by $f(p)$. Therefore:

If Γ contains elements that reverse orientation and Γ_T is one-dimensional, then Γ is generated by a single glide reflection. In this case $\mathbb{R}^2/\Gamma$ is a Möbius strip.

The case where Γ_T is two-dimensional is left. Since $L(\Gamma_T) = \Gamma_T$, there are two possibilities:

(a) $\Gamma_T = \{ n\mathbf{v}_1 + mL(\mathbf{v}_1) : n, m \in \mathbb{Z} \}$;

(b) $\Gamma_T = \{ n\lambda_1\mathbf{e}_1 + m\lambda_2\mathbf{e}_2 : n, m \in \mathbb{Z} \}$.

Suppose (a). Writing $\mathbf{v}_1 = \lambda\mathbf{e}_1 + \eta\mathbf{e}_2 (\lambda > 0, \eta \neq 0)$, we have $\Gamma_T \cap \langle\mathbf{e}_1\rangle = \{ 2n\lambda\mathbf{e}_1 : n \in \mathbb{Z} \}$. Take $\mathbf{v} = \alpha\mathbf{e}_1 + \beta\mathbf{e}_2 \in \Gamma_R$: we may suppose, by adding to $\mathbf{v}$ a multiple of $\mathbf{v}_1$, that $0 < \alpha < \lambda$. But $2\alpha\mathbf{e}_1 = \mathbf{v} + L(\mathbf{v})$ is in $\Gamma_T \cap \langle\mathbf{e}_1\rangle$, implying $\alpha = n\lambda$, for some $n \in \mathbb{Z}$, which is absurd.

Thus (b) must be true. Repeating the argument above, we see that there exists $\mathbf{v} = \alpha\mathbf{e}_1 + \beta\mathbf{e}_2 \in \Gamma_R$ such that $2\alpha = \lambda_1$, and therefore $\mathbf{v} + L(\mathbf{v}) = \lambda_1\mathbf{e}_1$. As $\Gamma_R = \{\mathbf{v}\} + \Gamma_T$, the group Γ is generated by $f(p) = L(p) + \mathbf{v}$ and the translation associated with the vector $\lambda_2\mathbf{e}_2$. To summarize:

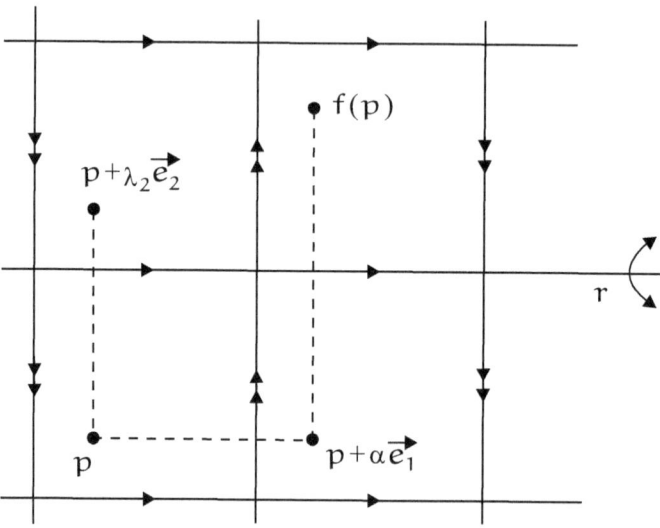

Figure 5.10

If Γ contains elements that reverse orientation and Γ_T is two-dimensional, then Γ is generated by a glide reflection, with axis on a line r say, and by a translation in the direction perpendicular to r. In this case $\mathbb{R}^2/\Gamma$ is a Klein bottle.

In Fig. 5.10 we show several copies of a fundamental region (a rectangle) for this group, marking the identifications to be made.

Let us summarize our findings:

Theorem 5.7.10 *Every complete surface of constant zero curvature is diffeomorphic to one of the following surfaces:*

- *the plane, the cylinder, or the torus, if it is orientable;*
- *the Möbius strip or the Klein bottle, if non-orientable.*

Exercises

145. Prove Proposition 5.7.6. **Hint:** if S_K/Γ is orientable and an orientation is fixed on it then the quotient mapping $S_k \to S_K/\Gamma$ induces an orientation on S_K.

146. (a) Let Γ_1 and Γ_2 be discrete subgroups of $\Im_K$. Show that S_K/Γ_1 and S_K/Γ_2 are isometric if and only if Γ_1 and Γ_2 are conjugate subgroups.

(b) Give an example of two tori of equal area and constant zero curvature that are not isometric.

147. Show that if Γ is a discrete subgroup of $\Im(\mathbb{D})$, then $\Gamma \smallsetminus \{id\}$ contains only hyperbolic isometries (see, in Section 5.6, exercises 140, 143 and 144).

148. (a) Consider on the torus of revolution $\mathbb{T}^2 \subseteq \mathbb{R}^3$, given by $\Phi(u,v) = ((2 + \cos v)\cos u, (2+\cos v)\sin u, \sin v)$, the equivalence relation $\sim$ that identifies (x,y,z) and $(-x,-y,-z)$. Show that $\mathbb{T}^2/\sim$ is a Klein bottle.

(b) If $\simeq$ is the equivalence relation that identifies (x,y,z) and $(-x,-y,z)$, what surface is $\mathbb{T}^2/\simeq$?

References

1. E. Barbier: *Note sur le problème de l'aiguille et le jeu du joint couvert*. J. Math. Pures Appl. (2) 5 (1860).
2. A.F. Beardon: *The Geometry of Discrete Groups*. Springer-Verlag 1983.
3. A.F. Beardon: *An introduction to Hyperbolic Geometry* [*in* Bedford, Keane, Series (eds.): *Ergodic Theory, Symbolic Dynamics, and Hyperbolic Spaces*]. Oxford U.P. 1991.
4. A.L. Besse: *Manifolds all of whose Geodesics are Closed*. Springer-Verlag 1978.
5. J.H. Cadwell: *Topics in Recreational Mathematics*. Cambridge University Press 1966.
6. M.P. do Carmo: *Differential Geometry of Curves and Surfaces*. Prentice-Hall 1976.
7. C.D. Charkerian, H. Groemer: *Convex bodies of constant width* [*in* P.M. Gruber, J.M. Wills (eds.): *Convexity and its applications*]. Birkhäuser 1983.
8. S.S. Chern: *Curves and Surfaces in Euclidean Space* [*in* S.S. Chern (ed.): *Global Differential Geometry*]. Math. Association of America 1988.
9. H.G. Eggleston: *Convexity*. Cambridge University Press 1958.
10. R. Fenn: *What is the Geometry of a Surface?* Am. Math. Monthly 90 (1983)
11. D.G. Figueiredo: *Análise de Fourier e equações diferenciais parciais*. Projeto Euclides, IMPA 1977.
12. A. Goetz: *Introduction to Differential Geometry*. Addison-Wesley 1970.
13. W. Klingenberg: *A course in Differential Geometry*. Springer-Verlag 1978.
14. E. Kreyszig: *Introduction to Differential Geometry and Riemannian Geometry*. University of Toronto Press 1968.
15. E.L. Lima: *Duas novas demonstrações do teorema de Jordan-Brouwer no caso diferenciável*. Matemática Universitária 4 (1986).
16. E.L. Lima: *Curso de Análise*, vol. 2 (3ª edição). Projeto Euclides, IMPA 1989.
17. E.E. Moise: *Geometric Topology in dimensions 2 and 3*. Springer-Verlag 1977.
18. I. Niven: *Maxima and minima without Calculus*. Math. Association of America 1981.
19. R. Osserman: *A survey of Minimal Surfaces*. Dover Publications 1986.
20. R. Osserman: *Curvature in the Eighties*. Am. Math. Monthly 97 (1990).
21. R. Osserman: *The four-or-more vertex theorem*. Am. Math. Monthly 92 (1985).
22. L.A. Santaló: *Integral Geometry* [*in* S.S. Chern (ed.): *Global Differential Geometry*]. Math. Association of America 1988.
23. J. Sotomayor: *Lições de equações diferenciais ordinárias*. Projeto Euclides, IMPA 1979.
24. M. Spivak: *Calculus*. Benjamin 1967.
25. M. Spivak: *A comprehensive introduction to Differential Geometry*, vol. I-IV. Publish or Perish 1970-75.

Index

© The Author(s), under exclusive license to Springer Nature Switzerland AG 2024
P. V. Araújo, *Differential Geometry*, https://doi.org/10.1007/978-3-031-62384-4